The Works Of Jacobus Arminius
Volume 1 - Orations Of Arminius
By Jacobus Arminius
Edited by Anthony Uyl

Devoted Publishing

Woodstock, Ontario, 2017

The Works Of Jacobus Arminius
Volume 1 - Orations Of Arminius
By Jacobus Arminius (1560-1609)
Edited by Anthony Uyl

Originally Published 1853

What kind of philosophies do you have?
Let us know!

Contact us at: devotedpub@hotmail.com
Visit our shop on Facebook: @DevotedPublishing

Published in Woodstock, Ontario, Canada 2017

For bulk educational rates, please contact us at the above email address.

ISBN: 978-1-77356-026-7

Table of Contents

ORATION I

THE OBJECT OF THEOLOGY

To Almighty God alone belong the inherent and absolute right, will, and power of determining concerning us. Since, therefore, it has pleased him to call me, his unworthy servant, from the ecclesiastical functions which I have for some years discharged in the Church of his Son in the populous city of Amsterdam, and to give me the appointment of the Theological Professorship in this most celebrated University, I accounted it my duty, not to manifest too much reluctance to this vocation, although I was well acquainted with my incapacity for such an office, which with the greatest willingness and sincerity I then confessed and must still acknowledge. Indeed, the consciousness of my own insufficiency operated as a persuasive to me not to listen to this vocation; of which fact I can cite as a witness that God who is both the Inspector and the Judge of my conscience. Of this consciousness of my own insufficiency, several persons of great probity and learning are also witnesses; for they were the cause of my engaging in this office, provided it were offered to me in a legitimate order and manner. But as they suggested, and as experience itself had frequently taught me, that it is a dangerous thing to adhere to one's own judgment with pertinacity and to pay too much regard to the opinion which we entertain of ourselves, because almost all of us have little discernment in those matters which concern ourselves, I suffered myself to be induced by the authority of their judgment to enter upon this difficult and burdensome province, which may God enable me to commence with tokens of his Divine approbation and under his propitious auspices.

Although I am beyond measure cast down and almost shudder with fear, solely at the anticipation of this office and its duties, yet I can scarcely indulge in a doubt of Divine approval and support when my mind attentively considers, what are the causes on account of which this vocation was appointed, the manner in which it is committed to execution, and the means and plans by which it is brought to a conclusion. From all these considerations, I feel a persuasion that it has been Divinely instituted and brought to perfection.

For this cause I entertain an assured hope of the perpetual presence of Divine assistance; and, with due humility of mind, I venture in God's holy name to take this charge upon me and to enter upon its duties. I most earnestly beseech all and each of you, and if the benevolence which to the present time you have expressed towards me by many and most signal tokens will allow such a liberty, I implore, nay, (so pressing is my present necessity,) I solemnly conjure you, to unite with me in ardent wishes and fervent intercessions before God, the Father of lights, that, ready as I am out of pure affection to contribute to your profit, he may be pleased graciously to supply his servant with the gifts which are necessary to the proper discharge of these functions, and to bestow upon me his benevolent favour, guidance and protection, through the whole course of this vocation.

But it appears to me, that I shall be acting to some good purpose, if, at the commencement of my office, I offer some general remarks on Sacred Theology, by way of preface, and enter into an explanation of its extent, dignity and excellence. This discourse will serve yet more and more to incite the mind, of students, who profess themselves dedicated to the service of this Divine wisdom, fearlessly to proceed in the career upon which they have entered, diligently to urge on their progress and to keep up an unceasing contest till they arrive at its termination. Thus may they hereafter become the instruments of God unto salvation in the Church of his Saints, qualified and fitted for the sanctification of his divine name, and formed "for the edifying of the body of Christ," in the Spirit. When I have effected this design, I shall think, with Socrates, that in such an entrance on my duties I have discharged no inconsiderable part of them to some good effect. For that wisest of the Gentiles was accustomed to say, that he had properly accomplished his duty of teaching, when he had once communicated an impulse to the minds of his hearers and had inspired them with an ardent desire of learning. Nor did he make this remark without reason. For, to a willing man, nothing is difficult, especially when God has promised the clearest revelation of his secrets to those "who shall meditate on his law day and night." (Psalm i. 2.) In such a manner does this promise of God act, that, on those matters which far surpass the capacity of the human mind, we may adopt the expression of Isocrates, If thou be desirous of receiving instruction, thou shalt learn many things."

This explanation will be of no small service to myself. For in the very earnest recommendation of this study which I give to others, I prescribe to myself a law and rule by which I ought to walk in its profession; and an additional necessity is thus imposed on me of conducting myself in my new office with holiness and modesty, and in all good conscience; that, in case I should afterwards turn aside from the right path, (which may our gracious God prevent,) such a solemn recommendation of this study may be cast in my face to my shame.

In the discussion of this subject, I do not think it necessary to utter any protestation before professors most learned in Jurisprudence, most skillful in Medicine, most subtle in Philosophy, and most erudite in the languages. Before such learned persons I have no need to enter into any protestation, for the purpose of removing from myself a suspicion of wishing to bring into neglect or contempt that particular study which each of them cultivates. For to every kind of study in the most noble theater of the sciences, I assign, as it becomes me, its due place, and that an honourable one; and each being content with its subordinate station, all of them with the greatest willingness concede the president's throne to that science of which I am now treating.

I shall adopt that plain and simple species of oratory which, according to Euripides, belongs peculiarly to truth. I am not ignorant that some resemblance and relation ought to exist between an oration and the subjects that are discussed in it; and therefore, that a certain divine method of speech is required when we attempt to speak on divine things according to their dignity. But I choose plainness and simplicity, because Theology needs no ornament, but is content to be taught, and because it is out of my power to make an effort towards acquiring a style that may be in any degree worthy of such a subject.

In discussing the dignity and excellence of sacred Theology, I shall briefly confine it within four titles. In imitation of the method which obtains in human sciences, that are estimated according to the excellence of their OBJECT, their AUTHOR, and their END, and of the IMPORTANCE of the reasons by which each of them is supported--I shall follow the same plan, speaking, first, of The OBJECT of Theology, then of its AUTHOR, afterwards of its END, and lastly, of its CERTAINTY.

I pray God, that the grace of his Holy Spirit may be present with me while I am speaking; and that he would be pleased to direct my mind, mouth and tongue, in such a manner as to enable me to advance those truths which are holy, worthy of our God, and salutary to you his creatures, to the glory of his name and for the edification of his Church.

I intreat you also, my most illustrious and polite hearers, kindly to grant me your attention for a short time while I endeavour to explain matters of the greatest importance; and while your observation is directed to the subject in which I shall exercise myself, you will have the goodness to regard IT, rather than any presumed SKILL in my manner of treating it. The nature of his great subject requires us, at this hour especially, to direct our attention, in the first instance, to the Object of Theology. For the objects of sciences are so intimately related, and so essential to them, as to give them their appellations.

But God is himself the Object of Theology. The very term indicates as much: for Theology signifies a discourse or reasoning concerning God. This is likewise indicated by the definition which the Apostle gives of this science, when he describes it as "the truth which is after godliness." (Tit. i. 1.) The Greek word here used for godliness, is eusebeia signifying a worship due to God alone, which the Apostle shews in a manner of greater clearness, when he calls this piety by the more exact term qeosebeia. All other sciences have their objects, noble indeed, and worthy to engage the notice of the human mind, and in the contemplation of which much time, leisure and diligence may be profitably occupied.

In General Metaphysics, the object of study is, "BEING"

But let us consider the conditions that are generally employed to commend the object of any science. That OBJECT is most excellent (1.) which is in itself the best, and the greatest, and immutable; (2.) which, in relation to the mind, is most lucid and clear, and most easily proposed and unfolded to the view of the mental powers; and (3.) which is likewise able, by its action on the mind, completely to fill it, and to satisfy its infinite desires. These three conditions are in the highest degree discovered in God, and in him alone, who is the subject of theological study.

1. He is the best being; he is the first and chief good, and goodness itself; he alone is good, as good as goodness itself; as ready to communicate, as it is possible for him to be communicated: his liberality is only equaled by the boundless treasures which he possesses, both of which are infinite and restricted only by the capacity of the recipient, which he appoints as a limit and measure to the goodness of his nature and to the communication of himself. He is the greatest Being, and the only great One; for he is able to subdue to his sway even nothing itself, that it may become capable of divine good by the communication of himself. "He calleth those things which are not, as though they were," (Rom. iv. 17) and in that manner, by his word, he places them in the number of beings, although it is out of darkness that they have received his commands to emerge and to come into existence. "All nations before him are as nothing, the inhabitants thereof are as grasshoppers, and the princes nothing." (Isa. xl. 17, 22, 23.) The whole of this system of heaven and earth appears scarcely equal to a point "before him, whose

center is every where, but whose circumference is no where." He is immutable, always the same, and endureth forever; "his years have no end." (Psalm 102)

Nothing can be added to him, and nothing can be taken from him; with him "is no variableness, neither shadow of turning." (James i. 17.) Whatsoever obtains stability for a single moment, borrows it from him, and receives it of mere grace. Pleasant, therefore, and most delightful is it to contemplate him, on account of his goodness; it is glorious in consideration of his greatness; and it is sure, in reference to his immutability.

2. He is most resplendent and bright; he is light itself, and becomes an object of most obvious perception to the mind, according to this expression of the apostle, That they should seek the Lord, if haply they might feel after him, and find Him, though he be not far from every one of us; for in him we live, and move, and have our being; for we are also his offspring:" (Acts xvii. 27, 28.) And according to another passage, "God left not himself without witness, in that he did good, and gave us rain from heaven, and fruitful seasons, filling our hearts with food and gladness." (Acts xiv. 17.) Being supported by these true sayings, I venture to assert, that nothing can be seen or truly known in any object, except in it we have previously seen and known God himself.

In the first place he is called "Being itself," because he offers himself to the understanding as an object of knowledge. But all beings, both visible and invisible, corporeal and incorporeal, proclaim aloud that they have derived the beginning of their essence and condition from some other than themselves, and that they have not their own proper existence till they have it from another. All of them utter speech, according to the saying of the Royal Prophet:

"The heavens declare the glory of God, and the firmament showeth his handy-work." (Psalm xix. 1.) That is, the firmament sounds aloud as with a trumpet, and proclaims, that it is "the work of the right hand of the Most High." Among created objects, you may discover many tokens indicating "that they derive from some other source whatever they themselves possess," mere strongly than "that they have an existence in the number and scale of beings." Nor is this matter of wonder, since they are always nearer to nothing than to their Creator, from whom they are removed to a distance that is infinite, and separated by infinite space: while, by properties that are only finite, they are distinguished from nothing, the primeval womb from whence they sprung, and into which they may fall back again; but they can never be raised to a divine equality with God their maker. Therefore, it was rightly spoken by the ancient heathens,

"Of Jove all things are full."

3. He alone can completely fill the mind, and satisfy its (otherwise) insatiable desires. For he is infinite in his essence, his wisdom, power, and goodness. He is the first and chief verity, and truth itself in the abstract. But the human mind is finite in nature, the substance of which it is formed; and only in this view is it a partaker of infinity--because it apprehends Infinite Being and the Chief Truth, although it is incapable of comprehending them. David, therefore, in an exclamation of joyful self-gratulation, openly confesses, that he was content with the possession of God alone, who by means of knowledge and love is possessed by his creatures. These are his words: "Whom have I in heaven but thee? and there is none upon earth that I desire beside thee." (Psalm lxxiii. 25.)

If thou be acquainted with all other things, and yet remain in a state of ignorance with regard to him alone, thou art always wandering beyond the proper point, and thy restless love of knowledge increases in the proportion in which knowledge itself is increased. The man who knows only God, and who is ignorant of all things else, remains in peace and tranquillity, and, (like one that has found "a pearl of great price," although in the purchase of it he may have expended the whole of his substance,) he congratulates himself and greatly triumphs. This luster or brightness of the object is the cause why an investigation into it, or an inquiry after it, is never instituted without obtaining it; and, (such is its fullness,) when it has once been found, the discovery of it is always attended with abundant profit.

But we must consider this object more strictly; for we treat of it in reference to its being the object of our theology, according to which we have a knowledge of God in this life. We must therefore clothe it in a certain mode, and invest it in a formal manner, as the logical phrase is; and thus place it as a foundation to our knowledge.

Three Considerations of this matter offer themselves to our notice: The First is, that we cannot receive this object in the infinity of its nature; our necessity, therefore, requires it to be proposed in a manner that is accommodated to our capacity. The Second is, that it is not proper, in the first moment of revelation, for such a large measure to be disclosed and manifested by the light of grace, as may be received into the human mind when it is illuminated by the light of glory, and, (by that process,) enlarged to a greater capacity: for by a right use of the knowledge of grace, we must proceed upwards, (by the rule of divine righteousness,) to the more sublime knowledge of glory, according to that saying, "To him that hath shall be given." The Third is, that this object is not laid before our theology merely to be known, but, when known, to be worshipped. For the Theology which belongs to this world, is Practical and through Faith:

Theoretical Theology belongs to the other world, and consists of pure and unclouded vision, according to the expression of the apostle, "We walk by faith, and not by sight;" (2 Cor. v. 7,) and that of another apostle, "Then shall we be like him, for we shall see him as he is." (1 John iii. 2.) For this reason, we must clothe the object of our theology in such a manner as may enable it to incline us to worship God, and fully to persuade and win us over to that practice.

This last design is the line and rule of this formal relation according to which God becomes the subject of our Theology.

But that man may be induced, by a willing obedience and humble submission of the mind, to worship God, it is necessary for him to believe, from a certain persuasion of the heart: (1.) That it is the will of God to be worshipped, and that worship is due to him. (2.) That the worship of him will not be in vain, but will be recompensed with an exceedingly great reward. (3.) That a mode of worship must be instituted according to his command. To these three particulars ought to be added, a knowledge of the mode prescribed.

Our Theology, then, delivers three things concerning this object, as necessary and sufficient to be known in relation to the preceding subjects of belief. The First is concerning the nature of God. The Second concerning his actions. And the Third concerning his will.

(1.) Concerning his nature; that it is worthy to receive adoration, on account of its justice; that it is qualified to form a right judgment of that worship, on account of its wisdom; and that it is prompt and able to bestow rewards, on account of its goodness and the perfection of its own blessedness.

(2.) Two actions have been ascribed to God for the same purpose; they are Creation and Providence. (i.) The Creation of all things, and especially of man after God's own image; upon which is founded his sovereign authority over man, and from which is deduced the right of requiring worship from man and enjoining obedience upon him, according to that very just complaint of God by Malachi, "If then I be a father, where is mine honour? and if I be a master, were is my fear," (i, 6.) (ii.) That Providence is to be ascribed to God by which he governs all things, and according to which he exercises a holy, just, and wise care and oversight over man himself and those things which relate to him, but chiefly over the worship and obedience which he is bound to render to his God.

(3.) Lastly, it treats of the will of God expressed in a certain covenant into which he has entered with man, and which consists of two parts: (i.) The one, by which he declares it to be his pleasure to receive adoration from man, and at the same time prescribes the mode of performing that worship; for it is his will to be worshipped from obedience, and not at the option or discretion of man. (ii.) The other, by which God promises that he will abundantly compensate man for the worship which he performs; requiring not only adoration for the benefits already conferred upon man, as a trial of his gratitude; but likewise that He may communicate to man infinitely greater things to the consummation of his felicity. For as he occupied the first place in conferring blessings and doing good, because that high station was his due, since man was about to be called into existence among the number of creatures; so likewise it is his desire that the last place in doing good be reserved for him, according to the infinite perfection of his goodness and blessedness, who is the fountain of good and the extreme boundary of happiness, the Creator and at the same time the Glorifier of his worshippers. It is according to this last action of his, that he is called by some persons "the Object of Theology," and that not improperly, because in this last are included all the preceding.

In the way which has been thus compendiously pointed out, the infinite disputes of the schoolmen, concerning the formal relation by which God is the Object of Theology, may, in my opinion, be adjusted and decided. But as I think it a culpable deed to abuse your patience, I shall decline to say any more on this part of the subject.

Our sacred Theology, therefore, is chiefly occupied in ascribing to the One True God, to whom alone they really belong, those attributes of which we have already spoken, his nature, actions, and will. For it is not sufficient to know, that there is some kind of a NATURE, simple, infinite, wise, good, just, omnipotent, happy in itself, the Maker and Governor of all things, that is worthy to receive adoration, whose will it is to be worshipped, and that is able to make its worshippers happy. To this general kind of knowledge there ought to be added, a sure and settled conception, fixed on that Deity, and strictly bound to the single object of religious worship to which alone those qualities appertain. The necessity of entertaining fixed and determinate ideas on this subject, is very frequently inculcated in the sacred page: "I am the Lord thy God." (Exod. xx. 2.) "I am the Lord and there is none else." (Isa. xlv. 5.) Elijah also says, "If the Lord be God, follow him; but if Baal, then follow him." (1 Kings xviii. 21.) This duty is the more sedulously inculcated in scripture, as man is more inclined to depart from the true idea of Deity. For whatever clear and proper conception of the Divine Being the minds the Heathens had formed, the first stumbling-block over which they fell appears to have been this, they did not attribute that just conception to him to whom it ought to have been given; but they ascribed it either, (1.) to some vague and uncertain individual, as in the expression of the Roman poet, "O Jupiter, whether thou be heaven, or air, or earth!" Or, (2) some imaginary and fabulous Deity, whether it be among created things, or a mere idol of the brain, neither partaking of the Divine nature nor any other, which the Apostle Paul, in his

Epistle to the Romans and to the Corinthians, produces as a matter of reproach to the Gentiles. (Rom. 1, and 1 Corinthians 8.) Or (3,) lastly, they ascribed it to the unknown God; the title of Unknown being given to their Deity by the very persons who were his worshippers. The Apostle relates this crime as one of which the Athenians were guilty: But it is equally true when applied to all those who err and wander from the true object of adoration, and yet worship a Deity of some description. To such persons that sentence justly belongs which Christ uttered in conversation with the woman of Samaria: "Ye worship YE KNOW NOT WHAT." (John iv. 22.)

Although those persons are guilty of a grievous error who transgress in this point, so as to be deservedly termed Atheists, in Scripture aqeoi "men without God;" yet they are by far more intolerably insane, who, having passed the extreme line of impiety, are not restrained by the consciousness of any Deity. The ancient heathens considered such men as peculiarly worthy of being called Atheists. On the other hand, those who have a consciousness of their own ignorance occupy the step that is nearest to sanity. For it is necessary to be careful only about one thing; and that is, when we communicate information to them, we must teach them to discard the falsehood which they had imbibed, and must instruct them in the truth alone. When this truth is pointed out to them, they will seize it with the greater avidity, in proportion to the deeper sorrow which they feel at the thought that they have been surrounded for a long series of years by a most pernicious error.

But Theology, as it appears to me, principally effects four things in fixing our conceptions, which we have just mentioned, on that Deity who is true, and in drawing them away from the invention and formation of false Deities. First. It explains, in an elegant and copious manner, the relation in which the Deity stands, lest we should ascribe to his nature any thing that is foreign to it, or should take away from it any one of its properties. In reference to this, it is said, "Ye. heard the voice, but saw no similitude; take ye therefore good heed unto yourselves, lest you make you a graven image." (Deut. iv. 15, 16.) - Secondly. It describes both the universal and the particular actions of the only true God, that by them it may distinguish the true Deity from those which are fabulous. On this account it is said, "The gods that have not made the heavens and the earth, shall perish from the earth, and under these heavens." (Jer. x. 11.) Jonah also said, "I fear the Lord, the God of heaven, who hath made the sea and the dry land." (i, 9.) And the Apostle declares, "Forasmuch then as we are the offspring of God, we ought not to think that the Godhead is like unto gold, or silver, or stone, graven by art and by man's device:" (Acts xvii. 29.) In another passage it is recorded, "I am the Lord thy God which brought thee out of the land of Egypt;" (Deut. v. 6.) "I am the God that appeared to thee in Bethel." (Gen. xxvi. 13.) And, "Behold the days come, saith the Lord, that they shall no more say, The Lord liveth, which brought up the children of Israel out of the land of Egypt, but, The Lord liveth which brought up and which led the seed of the house of Israel out of the North Country," &c. (Jer. xxiii. 7, 8.) Thirdly. It makes frequent mention of the covenant into which the true Deity has entered with his worshippers, that by the recollection of it the mind of man may be stayed upon that God with whom the covenant was concluded. In reference to this it is said, "Thus shalt thou say unto the Children of Israel, the Lord God of your fathers, the God of Abraham, the God of Isaac, and the God of Jacob, hath sent me unto you: this is my name for ever, and this is. my memorial unto all generations", (Exod. iii. 15.) Thus Jacob, when about to conclude a compact with Laban his father-in-law, swears "by the fear of his father Isaac." (Gen. xxxi. 53.) And when Abraham's servant was seeking a wife for his master's son, he thus invoked God, "O Lord God of my master Abraham!" (Gen. xxiv. 12.) Fourthly. It distinguishes and points out the true Deity, even by a most appropriate, particular, and individual mark, when it introduces the mention of the persons who are partakers of the same Divinity; thus it gives a right direction to the mind of the worshipper, and fixes it upon that God who is THE FATHER OF OUR LORD JESUS CHRIST. This was manifested with some degree of obscurity in the Old Testament, but with the utmost clearness in the New. Hence the Apostle says, "I bow my knee unto the Father of our Lord Jesus Christ." (Ephes. iii. 14.) All these remarks are comprehended and summed up by Divines, in this brief sentence, "That God must be invoked who has manifested himself in his own word." But the preceding observations concerning the Object of Theology, properly respect Legal Theology, which was accommodated to man's primeval state. For when man in his original integrity acted under the protecting favour and benevolence of a good and just God, he was able to render to God that worship which had been prescribed according to the law of legal righteousness, that says, "This do, and thou shalt live" he was able to "love with all his heart and soul" that Good and Just Being; he was able, from a consciousness of his integrity, to repose confidence in that Good and Just One; and he was able to evince towards him, as such, a filial fear, and to pay him the honour which was pleasing and due to him, as from a servant to his Lord. God also, on his part, without the least injury to his justice, was able to act towards man, while in that state, according to the proscript of legal righteousness, to reward his worship according to justice, and, through the terms of the legal covenant, and consequently "of debt," to confer life upon him. This God could do, consistency with his goodness, which required the fulfillment of the promise. There was no call for any other property of his nature, which might contribute by its agency to accomplish this purpose: No further progress of Divine goodness was necessary than that which might repay good for good, the good of perfect felicity, for the good of entire obedience: No other action was required, except that of creation, (which had then been performed,) and that of a preserving and governing providence, in conformity with the condition with which man was placed: No other volition of God was needed, than that by which he might both require the perfect obedience of the law and might repay that obedience with life eternal. In that state of human affairs, therefore, the knowledge of the nature described in those properties, the knowledge of those actions, and of that will, to which may be added the knowledge of the Deity to whom they really pertained, was necessary for the performance of worship to God, and was of itself amply sufficient.

But when man had fallen from his primeval integrity through disobedience to the law, and had rendered himself "a child of wrath" and had become devoted to condemnations, this goodness mingled with legal justice could not be sufficient for the salvation of man. Neither could this act of creation and providence, nor this will suffice; and therefore this legal Theology was itself insufficient. For sin was to be condemned if men were absolved; and, as the Apostle says, (in the eighth chapter of his Epistle to the Romans,) "it could not be condemned by the law." Man was to be justified: but he could not be justified by the law, which, while it is the strength of sin, makes discovery of it to us, and is the procurer of wrath.

This Theology, therefore, could serve for no salutary purpose, at that time: such was its dreadful efficacy in convincing man of sin and consigning him to certain death. This unhappy change, this unfavourable vicissitude of affairs was introduced by the fault and the infection of sin; which was likewise the cause why "the law which was ordained to life and honour," (Rom. vii. 10,) became fatal and destructive to our race, and the procurer of eternal ignominy. (1.) Other properties, therefore, of the Divine Nature were to be called into action; every one of God's benefits was to be unfolded and explained; mercy, long suffering, gentleness, patience, and clemency were to be brought forth out of the repository of his primitive goodness, and their services were to be engaged, if it was proper for offending man to be reconciled to God and reinstated in his favour. (2.) Other actions were to be exhibited: "A new creation" was to be effected; "a new providence," accommodated in every respect to this new creation, was to be instituted and put in force; "the work of redemption" was to be performed; "remission of sins" was to be obtained; "the loss of righteousness" was to be repaired; "the Spirit of grace" was to be asked and obtained; and a "lost salvation" restored. (3.) Another decree was likewise to be framed concerning the salvation of man; and another covenant, a new one," was to be made with him, "not according to that former one, because those" who were parties on one side "had not continued in that covenant:" (Heb. viii. 11,) but, by another and a gracious will, they "were to be sanctified" who might be "consecrated to enter into the Holiest by a new and living way." (Heb. x. 20.) All these things were to be prepared and laid down as foundations to the new manifestation.

Another revelation, therefore, and a different species of Theology, were necessary to make known those properties of the Divine Nature, which we have described, and which were most wisely employed in repairing our salvation; to proclaim the actions which were exhibited; and to occupy themselves in explaining that decree and new covenant which we have mentioned.

But since God, the punisher and most righteous avenger of sinners, was either unwilling, or, (through the opposition made by the justice and truth which had been originally manifested in the law,) was unable to unfold those properties of his nature, to produce those actions, or to make that decree, except by the intervention of a Mediator, in whom, without the least injury to his justice and truth, he might unfold those properties, perform those actions, might through them produce those necessary benefits, and might conclude that most gracious decree; on this account a Mediator was to be ordained, who, by his blood, might atone for sinners, by his death might expiate the sin of mankind, might reconcile the wicked to God, and might save them from his impending anger; who might set forth and display the mercy, long suffering and patience of God, might provide eternal redemption, obtain remission of sin, bring in an everlasting righteousness, procure the Spirit of grace, confirm the decree of gracious mercy, ratify the new covenant by his blood, recover eternal salvation, and who might bring to God those that were to be ultimately saved.

A just and merciful God, therefore, did appoint as Mediator, his beloved Son, Jesus Christ. He obediently undertook that office which was imposed on him by the Father, and courageously executed it; nay, he is even now engaged in executing it. He was, therefore, ordained by God as the Redeemer, the saviour, the King, and, (under God,) the Head of the heirs of salvation. It would have been neither just nor reasonable, that he who had undergone such vast labours, and endured such great sorrows, who had performed so many miracles, and who had obtained through his merits so many benefits for us, should ingloriously remain among us in meanness and obscurity, and should be dismissed by us without honour. It was most equitable, that he should in return be acknowledged, worshipped, and invoked, and that he should receive those grateful thanks which are due to him for his benefits.

But how shall we be able to adore, worship and invoke him, unless "we believe on him? How can we believe in him, unless we hear of him? And how can we hear concerning him," except he be revealed to us by the word? (Rom. x. 14.) From this cause, then, arose the necessity of making a revelation concerning Jesus Christ; and on this account two objects, (that is, God and his Christ,) are to be placed as a foundation to that Theology which will sufficiently contribute towards the salvation of sinners, according to the saying of our saviour Christ: "And this is life eternal, that they might know thee, the only true God, and Jesus Christ, whom thou hast sent." (John xvii. 3.) Indeed, these two objects are not of such a nature as that the one may be separated from the other, or that the one may be collaterally joined to the other; but the-latter of them is, in a proper and suitable manner, subordinate to the former. Here then we have a Theology, which, from Christ, its object, is most rightfully and deservedly termed Christian, which is manifested not by the Law, but in the earliest ages by promise, and in these latter days by the Gospel, which is called that "of Jesus Christ," although the words (Christian and Legal) are sometimes confounded. But let us consider the union and the subordination of both these objects.

I. Since we have God and his Christ for the object of our Christian Theology, the manner in which Legal Theology explains God unto us, is undoubtedly much amplified by this addition, and our Theology is thus infinitely ennobled above that which is legal.

For God has unfolded in Christ all his own goodness. "For it pleased the Father, that in him should all fullness dwell;" (Col. i. 19,) and that the "fullness of the Godhead should dwell in him," not by adumbration or according to the shadow, but "bodily:" For this reason he is called "the image of the invisible God;" (Col. i. 15,) "the brightness of his Father's glory, and the express image of his person," (Heb. i. 3,) in whom the Father condescends to afford to us his infinite majesty, his immeasurable goodness, mercy and philanthropy, to be contemplated, beheld, and to be touched and felt; even as Christ himself says to Philip, "He that hath seen me, hath seen the Father." (John xiv. 9.) For those things which lay hidden and indiscernible within the Father, like the fine and deep traces in an engraved seal, stand out, become prominent, and may be most clearly and distinctly seen in Christ, as in an exact and protuberant impression, formed by the application of a deeply engraved seal on the substance to be impressed.

1. In this Theology God truly appears, in the highest degree, the best and the greatest of Beings: (1.) The Best, cause he is not only willing, as in the former Theology, to communicate himself (for the happiness of men,) to those who correctly discharge their duty, but to receive into his favour and to reconcile to himself those who are sinners, wicked, unfruitful, and declared enemies, and to bestow eternal life on them when they repent. (2.) The Greatest, because he has not only produced all things from nothing, through the annihilation of the latter, and the creation of the former, but because he has also effected a triumph over sin, (which is far more noxious than nothing, and conquered with greater difficulty,) by graciously pardoning it, and powerfully putting it away;" and because he has "brought in everlasting righteousness," by means of a second creation, and a regeneration which far exceeded the capacity of "the law that acted as schoolmaster." (Gal. iii. 24.) For this cause Christ is called "the wisdom and the power of God," (1 Cor. i. 24,) far more illustrious than the wisdom and the power which were originally displayed in the creation of the universe. (3.) In this Theology, God is described to us as in every respect immutable, not only in regard to his nature but also to his will, which, as it has been manifested in the gospel, is peremptory and conclusive, and, being the last of all, is not to be corrected by another will. For "Jesus Christ is the same, yesterday, today, and forever"; (Heb. xiii. 8,) by whom God hath in these last days spoken unto us." (Heb. i. 2.) Under the law, the state of this matter was very different, and that greatly to our ultimate advantage. For if the will of God unfolded in the law had been fatal to us, as well as the last expression of it, we, of all men most miserable, should have been banished forever from God himself on account of that declaration of his will; and our doom would have been in a state of exile from our salvation. I would not seem in this argument to ascribe any mutability to the will of God. I only place such a termination and boundary to his will, or rather to something willed by him, as was by himself before affixed to it and predetermined by an eternal and peremptory decree, that thus a vacancy might be made for a "better covenant established on better promises" (Heb. vii. 22; viii, 6.)

2. This Theology offers God in Christ as an object of our sight and knowledge, with such clearness, splendour and plainness, that we with open face, beholding as in a glass the glory of the Lord, are changed into the same image from glory to glory even as by the Spirit of the Lord." (1 Cor. iii. 18.) In comparison with this brightness and glory, which was so pre-eminent and surpassing, the law itself is said not to have been either bright or glorious: For it "had no glory in this respect, by reason of the glory that excelleth." (2 Cor. iii. 8.) This was indeed "the wisdom of God which was kept secret since the world began :" (1 Cor. ii. 7; Rom. xvi. 25.) Great and inscrutable is this mystery; yet it is exhibited in Christ Jesus, and "made manifest" with such luminous clearness, that God is said to have been "manifest in the flesh" (1 Tim. iii. 16,) in no other sense than as though it would never have been possible for him to be manifested without the flesh; for the express purpose "that the eternal life which was with the Father, and the Word of life which was from the beginning with God, might be heard with our ears, seen with our eyes, and handled with our hands." (1 John i. 1, 2.)

3. The Object of our Theology being clothed in this manner, so abundantly fills the mind and satisfies the desire, that the apostle openly declares, he was determined "to know nothing among the

Corinthians save Jesus Christ, and him crucified." (1 Cor. ii. 2.) To the Phillipians he says, that he "counted all things but lost for the excellency of the knowledge of Christ Jesus; for whom he had suffered the loss of all things, and he counted them but dung that he might know Christ, and the power of his resurrection, and the fellowship of his sufferings." (Phil. iii. 8, 10.) Nay, in the knowledge of the object of our theology, modified in this manner, all true glorying and just boasting consist, as the passage which we before quoted from Jeremiah, and the purpose to which St. Paul has accommodated it, most plainly evince. This is the manner in which it is expressed: "Let him. that glorieth glory in this, that he understandeth and knoweth me, that I am the Lord which exercise lovingkindness, judgment and righteousness in the earth." (Jer. ix. 24.) When you hear any mention of mercy, your thoughts ought necessarily to revert to Christ, out of whom "God is a consuming fire" to destroy the sinners of the earth. (Deut. iv. 24; Heb. xii. 29) The way in which St. Paul has accommodated it, is this:

"Christ Jesus is made unto us by God, wisdom, righteousness, and sanctification, and redemption; that, according as it is written, He that glorieth, let him glory in the Lord!"(1 Cor. i. 30, 31.) Nor is it wonderful, that the mind should desire to "know nothing save Jesus Christ," or that its otherwise insatiable desire of knowledge should repose itself in him, since in him and in his gospel "are hidden all the treasures of wisdom, and knowledge." (Col. ii. 3, 9.)

II. Having finished that part of our subject which related to this Union, let us now proceed to the Subordination which subsists between these two objects. We will first inspect the nature of this subordination, and then its necessity.

First. Its nature consists in this, that every saving communication which God has with us, or which we have with God, is performed by means of the intervention of Christ.

1. The communication which God holds with us is (i.) either in his benevolent affection towards us, or, (ii.) in his gracious decree concerning us, or, (iii.) in his saving efficacy in us. In all these particulars, Christ comes in as a middle man between the parties. For (i.) when God is willing to communicate to us the affection of his goodness and mercy, he looks upon his Anointed One, in whom, as "his beloved, he makes us accepted, to the praise of the glory of his grace." (Ephes. i. 6.) (ii.) When he is pleased to make some gracious decree of his goodness and mercy, he interposes Christ between the purpose and the accomplishment, to announce his pleasure; for "by Jesus Christ he predestinates us to the adoption of children." (Ephes. i. 5.) (iii.) When he is willing out of this abundant affection to impart to us some blessing, according to his gracious decree, it is through the intervention of the same Divine person. For in Christ as our Head, the Father has laid up all these treasures and blessings; and they do not descend to us, except through him, or rather by him, as the Father's substitute, who administers them with authority, and distributes them according to his own pleasure.

2. But the communication which we have with God, is also made by the intervention of Christ. It consists of three degrees -access to God, cleaving to him, and the enjoyment of him.

These three particulars become the objects of our present consideration, as it is possible for them to be brought into action in this state of human existence, and as they may execute their functions by means of faith, hope, and that charity which is the offspring of faith.

(1.) Three things are necessary to this access; (i.) that God be in a place to which we may approach; (ii.) that the path by which we may come to him be a high-way and a safe one; and (iii.) that liberty be granted to us and boldness of access. All these facilities have been procured for us by the mediation of Christ. (i.) For the Father dwelleth in light inaccessible, and sits at a distance beyond Christ on a throne of rigid justice, which is an object much too formidable in appearance for the gaze of sinners; yet he hath appointed Christ to be "apropitiation. through faith in his blood ;" (Rom. iii. 25,) by whom the covering of the ark, and the accusing, convincing, and condemning power of the law which was contained in that ark, are taken away and removed as a kind of veil from before the eyes of the Divine Majesty; and a throne of grace has been established, on which God is seated, "with whom in Christ we have to do." Thus has the Father in the Son been made euwrositov "easy of access to us." (ii.) It is the same Lord Jesus Christ who "hath not only through his flesh consecrated for us a new and living way," by which we may go to the Father, (Heb. x. 20,) but who is likewise "himself the way" which leads in a direct and unerring manner to the Father. (John xiv. 6.) (iii.) "By the blood of Jesus" we have liberty of access, nay we are permitted "to enter into the holiest," and even "within the veil whither Christ, as a High Priest presiding over the house of God and our fore runner, is entered for us,." (Heb. v. 20,) that "we may draw near with a true heart, in the sacred and full assurance of faith, (x, 22,) and may with great confidence of mind "come boldly unto the throne of grace." (iv, 16.) Have we therefore prayers to offer to God? Christ is the High Priest who displays them before the Father. He is also the altar from which, after being placed on it, they will ascend as incense of a grateful odour to God our Father. Are sacrifices of thanksgiving to be offered to God? They must be offered through Christ, otherwise "God will not accept them at our hands." (Mal. i. 10.) Are good works to be performed? We must do them through the Spirit of Christ, that they may obtain the recommendation of him as their author; and they must be sprinkled with his blood, that they may not be rejected by the Father on account of their deficiency.

(2.) But it is not sufficient for us only to approach to God; it is likewise good for us to cleave to him. To confirm this act of cleaving and to give it perpetuity, it ought to depend upon a communion of nature. But with God we have no such communion. Christ, however, possesses it, and we are made possessors of it with Christ, "who partook of our flesh and blood." (Heb. ii. 14.) Being constituted our head, he imparts unto us of his Spirit, that we, (being constituted his members, and cleaving to him as "flesh of his flesh and bone of his bone,") may be one with him, and through him with the Father, and with both may become "one Spirit."

(3.) The enjoyment remains to be considered. It is a true, solid and durable taste of the Divine goodness and sweetness in this life, not only perceived by the mind and understanding, but likewise by the heart, which is the seat of all the affections. Neither does this become ours, except in Christ, by whose Spirit dwelling in us that most divine testimony is pronounced in our hearts, that "we are the children of God, and heirs of eternal life." (Rom. viii. 16.) On hearing this internal testimony, we conceive joy ineffable, "possess our souls in hope and patience," and in all our straits and difficulties we call upon God and cry, Abba Father, with an earnest expectation of our final access to God, of the consummation of our abiding in him and our cleaving to him, (by which we shall have "all in all,") and of the most blessed fruition, which will consist of the clear and unclouded vision of God himself. But the third division of our present subject, will be the proper place to treat more fully on these topics.

Secondly. Having seen the subordination of both the objects of Christian Theology, let us in a few words advert to its Necessity. This derives its origin from the comparison of our contagion and vicious depravity, with the sanctity of God that is incapable of defilement, and with the inflexible rigor of his justice, which completely separates us from him by a gulf so great as to render it impossible for us to be united together while at such a vast distance, or for a passage to be made from us to him--unless Christ had trodden the wine press of the wrath of God, and by the streams of his most precious blood, plentifully flowing from the pressed, broken, and disparted veins of his body, had filled up that otherwise impassable gulf, "and had purged our consciences, sprinkled with his own blood, from all dead works ;" (Heb. ix. 14, 22,) that, being thus sanctified, we might approach to "the living God and might serve him without fear, in holiness and righteousness before him, all the days of our life." (Luke i. 75.)

But such is the great Necessity of this subordination, that, unless our faith be in Christ, it cannot be in God: The Apostle Peter says, "By him we believe in God, that raised him from the dead, and gave him glory; that your faith and hope might be in God." (1 Pet., i, 21.) On this account the faith also which we have in God, was prescribed, not by the law, but by the gospel of the grace of our Lord Jesus Christ, which is properly "the word of faith" and "the word of promise."

The consideration of this necessity is of infinite utility, (i.) both in producing confidence in the consciences of believers, trembling at the sight of their sins, as appears most evidently from our preceding observations; (ii.) and in establishing the necessity of the Christian Religion. I account it necessary to make a few remarks on this latter topic, because they are required by the nature of our present purpose and of the Christian Religion itself.

I observe, therefore, that not only is the intervention of Christ necessary to obtain salvation from God, and to impart it unto men, but the faith of Christ is also necessary to qualify men for receiving this salvation at his hands; not that faith in Christ by which he may be apprehended under the general notion of the wisdom, power, goodness and mercy of God, but that faith which was announced by the Apostles and recorded in their writings, and in such a saviour as was preached by those primitive heralds of salvation.

I am not in the least influenced by the argument by which some persons profess themselves induced to adopt the opinion, "that a faith in Christ thus particular and restricted, which is required from all that become the subjects of salvation, agrees neither with the amplitude of God's mercy, nor with the conditions of his justice, since many thousands of men depart out of this life, before even the sound of the Gospel of Christ has reached their ears." For the reasons and terms of Divine Justice and Mercy are not to be determined by the limited and shallow measure of our capacities or feelings; but we must leave with God the free administration and just defense of these his own attributes. The result, however, will invariably prove to be the same, in what manner soever he may be pleased to administer those divine properties--for, "he will always overcome when he is judged." (Rom. iii. 4.) Out of his word we must acquire our wisdom and information. In primary, and certain secondary matters this word describes--the Necessity of faith in Christ, according to the appointment of the just mercy and the merciful justice of God. "He that believeth on the Son, hath everlasting life; and he that believeth not the Son, shall not see life; but the wrath of God abideth on him." (John iii. 36.) This is not an account of the first kindling of the wrath of God against this willful unbeliever; for he had then deserved the most severe expressions of that wrath by the sins which he had previously committed against the law; and this wrath "abides upon him," on account of his continued unbelief, because he had been favoured with the opportunity as well as the power of being delivered from it, through faith in the Son of God. Again: If ye believe not that I am he, ye shall die in your sins." (John viii. 24.) And, in another passage, Christ declares, "This is life eternal, that they might know thee the only true God, and Jesus Christ whom thou hast sent." (John xvii. 3.) The Apostle says, "It pleased God by the foolishness of preaching to save them that believe." That preaching thus described is the doctrine of the cross, "to the Jews a stumbling block and unto the Greeks foolishness:

But unto them which are called both Jews and Greeks, Christ the power of God and the wisdom of God:" (1 Cor. i. 21, 23, 24.) This wisdom and this power are not those attributes which God employed when he formed the world, for Christ is here plainly distinguished from them; but they are the wisdom and the power revealed in that gospel which is eminently "the power of God unto salvation to every one that believeth." (Rom. i. 16.) Not only, therefore, is the cross of Christ necessary to solicit and procure redemption, but the faith of the cross is also necessary in order to obtain possession of it.

The necessity of faith in the cross does not arise from the circumstance of the doctrine of the cross being preached and propounded to men; but, since faith in Christ is necessary according to the decree of God, the doctrine of the cross is preached, that those who believe in it may be saved. Not only on account of the decree of God is faith in Christ necessary, but it is also necessary on account of the promise made unto Christ by the Father, and according to the Covenant which was ratified between both of them. This is the word of that promise: "Ask of me, and I will give thee the Heathen for thine inheritance." (Psalm ii. 8.) But the inheritance of Christ is the multitude of the faithful; "the people, who, in the days of his power shall willingly come to him, in the beauties of holiness." (Psalm cx. 3.) "in thee shall all nations be blessed; so then they which be of faith are blessed with faithful Abraham." (Gal. iii. 8, 9 In Isaiah it is likewise declared, "When thou shalt make his soul an offering for sin, he shall see his seed. He shall prolong his days, and the pleasure of the Lord shall prosper in his hands. He shall see of the travail of his soul, and shall be satisfied: by the knowledge of himself [which is faith in him] shall my righteous servant justify many; for he shall bear their iniquities." (Isa. liii. 10, 11.) Christ adduces the covenant which has been concluded with the Father, and founds a plea upon it when he says, "Father glorify thy Son; that thy Son also may glorify thee: as thou hast given him power over all flesh, that he should give eternal life to as many as thou hast given him. And this is life eternal," &c., &c. (John xvii. 1, 2, 3, 4.) Christ therefore by the decree, the promise and the covenant of the Father, has been constituted the saviour of all that believe on him, according to the declaration of the Apostle: "And being made perfect he became the author of eternal salvation, to all them that obey him." (Heb. v. 9.) This is the reason why the Gentiles without Christ are said to be "alien from the commonwealth of Israel, and strangers from the covenants of promise, having no hope, and without God in the world." Yet through faith "those who some time were thus afar off and in darkness" are said to be made nigh, and "are now light in the Lord." (Ephes. ii. 12, 13, and v, 8.) It is requisite, therefore, earnestly to contend for the Necessity of the Christian religion, as for the altar and the anchor of our salvation, lest, after we have suffered the Son to be taken away from us and from our Faith, we should also be deprived of the Father:

"For whosoever denieth the Son, the same hath not the Father." (1 John ii. 23.) But if we in the slightest degree connive at the diminution or limitation of this Necessity, Christ himself will be brought into contempt among Christians, his own professing people; and will at length be totally denied and universally renounced. For it is not an affair of difficulty to take away the merit of salvation, and the power to save from Him to whom we are not compelled by any necessity to offer our oaths of allegiance. Who believes, that it is not necessary to return thanks to him who has conferred a benefit? Nay, who will not openly and confidently profess, that he is not the Author of salvation whom it is not necessary to acknowledge in that capacity. The union, therefore, of both the objects, God and Christ, must be strongly urged and enforced in our Christian Theology; nor is it to be endured that under any pretext they be totally detached and removed from each other, unless we wish Christ himself to be separated and withdrawn from us, and for us to be deprived at once of him and of our own salvation.

The present subject would require us briefly to present to your sight all and each of those parts of which the consideration of this object ought to consist, and the order in which they should be placed before our eyes; but I am unwilling to detain this most famous and crowded auditory by a more prolix oration.

Since, therefore, thus wonderfully great are the dignity, majesty, splendour and plenitude of Theology, and especially of our Christian Theology, by reason of its double object which is God and Christ, it is just and proper that all those who glory in the title of "men formed in the image of God," or in the far more august title of "Christians" and "men regenerated after the image of God and Christ, should most seriously and with ardent desire apply themselves to the knowledge of this Theology; and that they should think no object more worthy, pleasant, or useful than this, to engage their labourious attention or to awaken their energies. For what is more worthy of man, who is the image of God, than to be perpetually reflecting itself on its great archetype? What can be more pleasant, than to be continually irradiated and enlightened by the salutary beams of his Divine Pattern? What is more useful than, by such illumination, to be assimilated yet more and more to the heavenly Original? Indeed there is not any thing the knowledge of which can be more useful than this is, in the very search for it; or, when discovered, can be more profitable to the possessor. What employment is more becoming and honourable in a creature, a servant, and a son than to spend whole days and nights in obtaining a knowledge of God his Creator, his Lord, and his Father? What can be more decorous and comely in those who are redeemed by the blood of Christ, and who are sanctified by his Spirit, than diligently and constantly to meditate upon Christ, and always to carry him about in their minds, and hearts, and also on their tongues?

I am fully aware that this animal life requires the discharge of various functions; that the superintendence of them must be entrusted to those persons who will execute each of them to the common advantage of the republic; and that the knowledge necessary for the right management of all such duties, can only be acquired by continued study and much labour. But if the very persons to whom the management of these concerns has been officially committed, will acknowledge the important principle--that in preference to all others, those things should be sought which appertain to the kingdom of God and his righteousness, (Matt. vi. 33,) they will confess that their ease and leisure, their meditations and cares, should yield the precedence to this momentous study. Though David himself was the king of a numerous people, and entangled in various wars, yet he never ceased to cultivate and pursue this study in preference to all others. To the benefit which he had derived from such a judicious practice, he attributes the portion of wisdom which he had obtained, and which was "greater than that of his enemies." (Psalm cxix. 98,) and by it also "he had more understanding than all his teachers." (99.) The three most noble treatises which Solomon composed, are to the present day read by the Church with admiration and thanksgiving; and they testify the great advantage which the royal author obtained from a knowledge of Divine things, while he was the chief magistrate of the same people on the throne of his Father. But since, according to the opinion of a Roman Emperor, "nothing is more difficult than to govern well" what just cause will any one be able to offer for the neglect of a study, to which even kings could devote their time and attention. Nor is it wonderful that they acted thus; for they addicted themselves to this profitable and pleasant study by the command of God; and the same Divine command has been imposed upon all and each of us, and is equally binding. It is one of Plato's observations, that "commonwealths would at length enjoy happiness and prosperity, either when their princes and ministers of state become philosophers, or when philosophers were chosen as ministers of state and conducted the affairs of government." We may transfer this sentiment with far greater justice to Theology, which is the true and only wisdom in relation to things Divine.

But these our admonitions more particularly concern you, most excellent and learned youths, who, by the wish of your parents or patrons, and at your own express desire, have been devoted, set apart, and consecrated to this study; not to cultivate it merely with diligence, for the sake of promoting your own salvation, but that you may at some future period be qualified to engage in the eligible occupation, (which is most pleasing to God,) of teaching, instructing, and edifying the Church of the saints--"which is the body of Christ, and the fullness of him that filleth all in all." (Ephes. i. 23.) Let the extent and the majesty of the object, which by a deserved right engages all our powers, be constantly placed before your eyes; and suffer nothing to be accounted more glorious than to spend whole days and nights in acquiring a knowledge of God and his Christ, since true and allowable glories consists in this Divine knowledge. Reflect what great concerns those must be into which angels desire to look. Consider, likewise, that you are now forming an entrance for yourselves into a communion, at least of name, with these heavenly beings, and that God will in a little time call you to the employment for which you are preparing, which is one great object of my hopes and wishes concerning you.

Propose to yourselves for imitation that chosen instrument of Christ, the Apostle Paul, whom you with the greater willingness acknowledge as your teacher, and who professes himself to be inflamed with such an intense desire of knowing Christ, that he not only held every worldly thing in small estimation when put in competition with this knowledge, but also "suffered the loss of all things, that he might win the knowledge of Christ." (Phil. iii. 8.) Look at Timothy, his disciple, whom he felicitates on this account--"that from a child he had known the holy scriptures." (2 Tim. iii. 15.) You have already attained to a share of the same blessedness; and you will make further advances in it, if you determine to receive the admonitions, and to execute the charge, which that great teacher of the Gentiles addresses to his Timothy.

But this study requires not only diligence, but holiness, and a sincere desire to please God. For the object which you handle, into which you are looking, and which you wish to know, is sacred--nay, it is the holy of holies. To pollute sacred things, is highly indecent; it is desirable that the persons by whom such things are administered, should communicate to them no taint of defilement. The ancient Gentiles when about to offer sacrifice were accustomed to exclaim,

"Far, far from hence, let the profane depart!"

This caution should be re-iterated by you, for a more solid and lawful reason when you proceed to offer sacrifices to God Most High, and to his Christ, before whom also the holy choir of angels repeat aloud that thrice-hallowed song, "Holy, holy, holy, Lord God Almighty!" While you are engaged in this study, do not suffer your minds to be enticed away by other pursuits and to different objects. Exercise yourselves, continue to exercise yourselves in this, with a mind intent upon what has been proposed to you according to the design of this discourse. If you do this, in the course of a short time you will not repent of your labour; but you will make such progress in the way of the knowledge of the Lord, as will render you useful to others. For "the secret of the Lord, is with them that fear him." (Psalm xxv. 14) Nay, from the very circumstance of this unremitting attention, you will be enabled to declare, that you "have chosen the good part which alone shall not be taken away from you," (Luke x. 42) but which will daily receive fresh increase. Your minds will be so expanded by the knowledge of God and of his Christ, that they will hereafter become a most ample habitation for God and Christ through the Spirit. I have finished.

ORATION II

THE AUTHOR AND THE END OF THEOLOGY

They who are conversant with the demonstrative species of oratory, and choose for themselves any subject of praise or blame, must generally be engaged in removing from themselves, what very readily assails the minds of their auditors, a suspicion that they are impelled to speak by some immoderate feeling of love or hatred; and in showing that they are influenced rather by an approved judgment of the mind; and that they have not followed the ardent flame of their will, but the clear light of their understanding, which accords with the nature of the subject which they are discussing. But to me such a course is not necessary. For that which I have chosen for the subject of my commendation, easily removes from me all ground for such a suspicion.

I do not deny, that here indeed I yield to the feeling of love; but it is on a matter which if any one does not love, he hates himself, and perfidiously prostitutes the life of his soul. Sacred Theology is the subject whose excellence and dignity I now celebrate in this brief and unadorned Oration; and which, I am convinced, is to all of you an object of the greatest regard. Nevertheless, I wish to raise it, if possible, still higher in your esteem. This, indeed, its own merit demands; this the nature of my office requires. Nor is it any part of my study to amplify its dignity by ornaments borrowed from other objects; for to the perfection of its beauty can be added nothing extraneous that would not tend to its degradation and loss of its comeliness. I only display such ornaments as are, of themselves, its best recommendation. These are, its Object, its Author, its End and its Certainty. Concerning the Object, we have already declared whatever the Lord had imparted; and we will now speak of its Author and its End. God grant that I may follow the guidance of this Theology in all respects, and may advance nothing except what agrees with its nature, is worthy of God and useful to you, to the glory of his name, and to the uniting of all of us together in the Lord. I pray and beseech you also, my most excellent and courteous hearers, that you will listen to me, now when I am beginning to speak on the Author, and the End of Theology, with the same degree of kindness and attention as that which you evinced when you heard my preceding discourse on its Object.

Being about to treat of the Author, I will not collect together the lengthened reports of his well merited praises, for with you this is unnecessary. I will only declare (1.) Who the Author is; (2.) In what respect he is to be considered; (3.) Which of his properties were employed by him in the revelation of Theology; and (4.) In what manner he has made it known.

I. We have considered the Object of Theology in regard to two particulars. And that each part of our subject may properly and exactly answer to the other, we may also consider its Author in a two-fold respect--that of Legal and of Evangelical Theology. In both cases, the same person is the Author and the Object, and the person who reveals the doctrine is likewise its matter and argument. This is a peculiarity that belongs to no other of the numerous sciences. For although all of them may boast of God, as their Author, because he a God of knowledge; yet, as we have seen, they have some other object than God, which something is indeed derived from him and of his production. But they do not partake of God as their efficient cause, in an equal manner with this doctrine, which, for a particular reason, and one entirely distinct from that of the other sciences, lays claim to God , its Author. God, therefore, is the author of Legal Theology; God and his Christ, or God in and through Christ, is the Author of that which is evangelical. For to this the scripture bears witness, and thus the very nature of the object requires, both of which we will separately demonstrate.

1. Scripture describes to us the Author of legal theology before the fall in these words: "And the Lord God commanded the man, saying, Of every tree of the garden thou mayest freely eat; but of the tree of the knowledge of good and evil, thou shalt not eat of it:" (Gen. ii. 16, 17.) A threat was added in express words, in case the man should transgress, and a promise, in the type of the tree of life, if he complied with the command. But there are two things, which, as they preceded this act of legislation, should have been previously known by man: (1.) The nature of God, which is wise, good, just, and powerful; (2.) The authority by which he issues his commands, the right of which rests on the act of creation. Of both these, man had a previous knowledge, from the manifestation of God, who familiarly conversed with him, and held communication with his own image through that Spirit by whose inspiration he said, "This is now bone of my bones, and flesh of my flesh." (Gen. ii. 23.) The apostle has

attributed the knowledge of both these things to faith, and, therefore, to the manifestation of God. He speaks of the former in these words: "For he that cometh to God must have believed [so I read it,] that he is, and that he is a rewarder of them that diligently seek him." (Heb. xi. 6.) If a rewarder, therefore, he is a wise, good, just, powerful, and provident guardian of human affairs. Of the latter, he speaks thus: "Through faith we understand that the world was framed by the word of God, so that things which are seen were not made of things which do appear." (Heb. xi. 3.) And although that is not expressly and particularly stated of the moral law, in the primeval state of man; yet when it is affirmed of the typical and ceremonial law, it must be also understood in reference to the moral law. For the typical and ceremonial law was an experiment of obedience to the moral law, that was to be tried on man, and the acknowledgement of his obligation to obey the moral law. This appears still more evidently in the repetition of the moral law by Moses after the fall, which was specially made known to the people of Israel in these words: "And God spake all these words :" (Exod. xx. 1,) and "What nation is there so great that hath statutes and judgments so righteous as all this law, which I set before you this day," (Deut. iv. 8.) But Moses set it before them according to the manifestation of God to him, and in obedience to his command, as he says: "The secret things belong unto the Lord our God; but those things which are revealed belong unto us and to our children forever, that we may do all the words of this law." (Deut. xxix. 29.) And according to Paul, "That which may be known of God, is manifest in them; for God hath shewed it unto them." (Rom. i. 19.)

2. The same thing is evinced by the nature of the object. For since God is the Author of the universe, (and that, not by a natural and internal operation, but by one that is voluntary and external, and that imparts to the work as much as he chooses of his own, and as much as the nothing, from which it is produced, will permit,) his excellence and dignity must necessarily far exceed the capacity of the universe, and, for the same reason, that of man. On this account, he is said in scripture, "to dwell in the light unto which no man can approach," (1 Tim. vi. 16,) which strains even the most acute sight of any creature, by a brightness so great and dazzling, that the eye is blunted and overpowered, and would soon be blinded unless God, by some admirable process of attempering that blaze of light, should offer himself to the view of his creatures: This is the very manifestation before which darkness is said to have fixed its habitation.

Nor is he himself alone inaccessible, but, as the heavens are higher than the earth, so are his ways higher than our ways, and his thoughts than our thoughts." (Isa. lv. 9.) The actions of God are called "the ways of God," and the creation especially is called "the beginning of the way of God," (Prov. 8,) by which God began, as it were, to arise and to go forth from the throne of his majesty. Those actions, therefore, could not have been made known and understood, in the manner in which it is allowable to know and understand them, except by the revelation of God. This was also indicated before, in the term "faith" which the apostle employed. But the thoughts of God, and his will, (both that will which he wishes to be done by us, and that which he has resolved to do concerning us,) are of free disposition, which is determined by the divine power and liberty inherent in himself; and since he has, in all this, called in the aid of no counselor, those thoughts and that will are of necessity "unsearchable and past finding out." (Rom. xi. 33.) Of these, Legal Theology consists; and as they could not be known before the revelation of them proceeded from God, it is evidently proved that God is its Author.

To this truth all nations and people assent. What compelled Radamanthus and Minos, those most equitable kings of Crete, to enter the dark cave of Jupiter, and pretend that the laws which they had promulgated among their subjects, were brought from that cave, at the inspiration of Deity? It was because they knew those laws would not meet with general reception, unless they were believed to have been divinely communicated. Before Lycurgus began the work of legislation for his Lacedaemonians, imitating the example of those two kings, he went to Apollo at Delphos, that he might, on his return, confer on his laws the highest recommendation by means of the authority of the Delphic Oracle. To induce the ferocious minds of the Roman people to submit to religion, Numa Pompilius feigned that he had nocturnal conferences with the goddess Aegeria. These were positive and evident testimonies of a notion which had preoccupied the minds of men, "that no religion except one of divine origin, and deriving its principles from heaven, deserved to be received." Such a truth they considered this, "that no one could know God, or any thing concerning God, except through God himself."

2. Let us now look at Evangelical Theology. We have made the Author of it to be Christ and God, at the command of the same scriptures as those which establish the divine claims of Legal Theology, and because the nature of the object requires it with the greater justice, in proportion as that object is the more deeply hidden in the abyss of the divine wisdom, and as the human mind is the more closely surrounded and enveloped with the shades of ignorance.

(1.) Exceedingly numerous are the passages of scripture which serve to aid and strengthen us in this opinion. We will enumerate a few of them: First, those which ascribe the manifestation of this doctrine to God the Father; Then, those which ascribe it to Christ. "But we" says the apostle, "speak the wisdom of God in a mystery, even the hidden wisdom, which God ordained before the world unto our glory. But God hath revealed it unto us by his Spirit." (1 Cor. ii. 7,10.) The same apostle says, "The gospel and the preaching of Jesus Christ, according to the revelation of the mystery, which was kept secret since the world began, but now is made manifest by the scriptures of the prophets, according to the commandment of the everlasting God." (Rom. xvi. 25, 26.) When Peter made a correct and just confession of Christ, it was said to him by the saviour, "Flesh and blood hath not revealed it unto thee, but my Father which is in heaven." (Matt. xvi. 17.) John the Baptist attributed the same to Christ, saying, "The only begotten Son, which is in the bosom of the Father, he hath declared God to us." (John i. 18.) Christ also ascribed this manifestation to himself in these words: "No man knoweth the Son but the Father; neither knoweth any man the Father save the Son, and he to whomsoever the Son will reveal him." (Matt. xi. 27.) And, in another place, "I have manifested thy name unto the men whom thou gavest me out of the world, and they have believed that thou didst send me." (John xvii. 6, 8.)

(2.) Let us consider the necessity of this manifestation from the nature of its Object.

This is indicated by Christ when speaking of Evangelical Theology, in these words: "No man knoweth the Son but the Father; neither knoweth any man the Father save the Son." (Matt. xi. 27.) Therefore no man can reveal the Father or the Son, and yet in the knowledge of them are comprised the glad tidings of the gospel. The Baptist is an assertor of the necessity of this manifestation when he declares, that "No man hath seen God at any time." (John i. 18.) It is the wisdom belonging to this Theology, which is said by the Apostle to be "hidden in a mystery, which none of the princes of this world knew, and which eye hath not seen, nor ear heard, neither hath it entered into the heart of man." (1 Cor. ii. 7, 8, 9.) It does not come within the cognizance of the understanding, and is not mixed up, as it were, with the first notions or ideas impressed on the mind at the period of its creation; it is not acquired in conversation or reasoning; but it is made known "in the words which the Holy Ghost teacheth." To this Theology belongs "that manifold wisdom of God which must be made known by the Church unto the principalities and powers in heavenly places," (Ephes. iii. 10,) otherwise it would remain unknown even to the angels themselves. What! Are the deep things of God "which no man knoweth but the Spirit of God which is in himself," explained by this doctrine? Does it also unfold "the length and breadth, and depth and height" of the wisdom of God? As the Apostle speaks in another passage, in a tone of the most impassioned admiration, and almost at a loss what words to employ in expressing the fullness of this Theology, in which are proposed, as objects of discovery, "the love of Christ which passeth knowledge, and the peace of God which passeth all understanding." (Ephes. iii. 18.) From these passages it most evidently appears, that the Object of Evangelical Theology must have been revealed by God and Christ, or it must otherwise have remained hidden and surrounded by perpetual darkness; or, (which is the same thing,) that Evangelical Theology would not have come within the range of our knowledge, and, on that account, as a necessary consequence, there could have been none at all.

If it be an agreeable occupation to any person, (and such it must always prove,) to look more methodically and distinctly through each part, let him cast the eyes of his mind on those properties of the Divine Nature which this Theology displays, clothed in their own appropriate mode; let him consider those actions of God which this doctrine brings to light, and that will of God which he has revealed in his gospel: When he has done this, (and of much more than this the subject is worthy,) he will more distinctly understand the necessity of the Divine manifestation.

If any one would adopt a compendious method, let him only contemplate Christ; and when he has diligently observed that admirable union of the Word and Flesh, his investiture into office and the manner in which its duties were executed; when he has at the same time reflected, that the whole of these arrangements and proceedings are in consequence of the voluntary economy, regulation, and free dispensation of God; he cannot avoid professing openly, that the knowledge of all these things could not have been obtained except by means of the revelation of God and Christ.

But lest any one should take occasion, from the remarks which we have now made, to entertain an unjust suspicion or error, as though God the Father alone, to the exclusion of the Son, were the Author of the legal doctrine, and the Father through the Son were the Author of the Evangelical doctrine--a few observations shall be added, that may serve to solve this difficulty, and further to illustrate the matter of our discourse. As God by his Word, (which is his own Son,) and by his Spirit, created all things, and man according to the image of himself, so it is likewise certain, that no intercourse can take place between him and man, without the agency of the Son and of the Holy Spirit. How is this possible, since the ad extra works of the Deity are indivisible, and when the order of operation ad extra is the same as the order of procession ad intra? We do not, therefore, by any means exclude the Son as the Word of the Father, and the Holy Ghost who is "the Spirit of Prophecy," from efficiency in this revelation.

But there is another consideration in the manifestation of the gospel, not indeed with respect to the persons testifying, but in regard to the manner in which they come to be considered. For the Father, the Son, and the Holy Spirit, have not only a natural relation among themselves, but another likewise which derives its origin from the will; yet the latter entirely agrees with the natural relation that subsists among them. There is an internal procession in the persons; and there is an external one, which is called in the scriptures and in the writings of the Father, by the name of "Mission" or "sending." To the latter mode of procession, special regard must be had in this revelation. For the Father manifests the Gospel through his Son and Spirit. (i.) He manifests it through the Son, as to his being, sent for the purpose of performing the office of Mediator between God and sinful men; as to his being the Word made flesh, and God manifest in the flesh; and as to his having died, and to his being raised again to life, whether that was done in reality, or only in the decree and foreknowledge of God. (ii.) He also manifests it through his Spirit, as to his being the Spirit of Christ, whom he asked of his Father by his passion and his death, and whom he obtained when he was raised from the dead, and placed at the right hand of the Father.

I think you will understand the distinction which I imagine to be here employed: I will afford you an opportunity to examine and prove it, by adducing the clearest passages of scripture to aid us in confirming it. (I.) "All things," said Christ, "are delivered to me of my Father; and no man knoweth the Son, but the Father; neither knoweth any man the Father, save the Son." (Matt. xi. 27.) They were delivered by the Father, to him as the Mediator, "in whom it was his pleasure that all fullness should dwell." (Col. i. 19. See also ii, 9.) In the same sense must be understood what Christ says in John: "I have given unto them the words which thou gavest me;" for it is subjoined, "and they have known surely that I came out from thee, and they have believed that thou didst send me." (xvii, 8.) From hence it appears, that the Father had given those words to him as the Mediator: on which account he says, in another place, "He whom God hath sent, speaketh the words of God." (John iii. 34.) With this the saying of the Baptist agrees, "The law was given by Moses, but grace and truth came by Jesus Christ." (John i. 17.) But in reference to his being opposed to Moses, who accuses and condemns sinners, Christ is considered as the Mediator between God and sinners. The following passage tends to the same point: "No man hath seen God at any time: the only begotten Son which is in the bosom of the Father," [that is, "admitted," in his capacity of Mediator, to the intimate and confidential view and knowledge of his Father's secrets,] "he hath declared him:" (John i. 18.) "For the Father loveth the Son, and hath given all things into his hand;" (John iii. 35,) and among the things thus given, was the doctrine of the gospel, which he was to expound and declare to others, by the command of God the Father. And in every revelation which has been made to us through Christ, that expression which occurs in the beginning of the Apocalypse of St. John holds good and is of the greatest validity: "The revelation of Jesus Christ, which God gave unto him, to shew unto his servants." God has therefore manifested Evangelical Theology through his Son, in reference to his being sent forth by the Father, to execute among men, and in his name, the office of Mediator.

(ii.) Of the Holy Spirit the same scripture testifies, that, as the Spirit of Christ the Mediator, who is the head of his church, he has revealed the Gospel. "Christ, by the Spirit," says Peter, "went and preached to the spirits in prison." (1 Pet. iii. 19.) And what did he preach? Repentance. This therefore, was done through his Spirit, in his capacity of Mediator, For, in this respect alone, the Spirit of God exhorts to repentance. This appears more clearly from the Same Apostle: "Of which salvation the prophets have inquired and searched diligently, who prophesied of the grace that should come unto you: searching what, or what manner of time, the Spirit of Christ which was in them did signify, when it testified beforehand the sufferings of Christ, and the glory that should follow." And this was the Spirit of Christ in his character of Mediator and head of the Church, which the very object of the testimony foretold by him sufficiently evinces. A succeeding passage excludes all doubt; for the gospel is said in it, to be preached by the Holy Ghost sent down from heaven." (1 Pet. i. 12.) For he was sent down by Christ when he was elevated at the right hand of God, as it is mentioned in the second chapter of the Acts of the Apostles; which passage also makes for our purpose, and on that account deserves to have its just meaning here appreciated. This is its phraseology, "Therefore, being by the right hand of God exalted, and having received of the Father the promise of the Holy Ghost, he hath shed forth this, which ye now see and hear." (Acts ii. 33.) For it was by the Spirit that the Apostles prophesied and spoke in divers languages. These passages might suffice; but I cannot omit that most noble sentence spoken by Christ to console the minds of his disciples, who were grieving on account of his departure, "If I go not away the Comforter [or rather, the Advocate, who shall, in my place, discharge the vicarious office,' as Tertullian expresses himself,] If I go not away, the Comforter will not come unto you; but if I depart, I will send him unto you. And when he is come he will reprove the world, &c. (John xvi. 7, 8.) He shall glorify me: For he shall receive of mine, and shall shew it unto you." Christ, therefore, as Mediator, "will send him," and he "will receive of that which belongs to Christ the Mediator. He shall glorify Christ," as constituted by God the Mediator and the Head of the Church; and he shall glorify him with that glory, which, according to the seventeenth chapter of St. John's Gospel , Christ thought it necessary to ask of his Father. That passage brings another to my recollection, which may be called its parallel in merit: John says, "The Holy Ghost was not yet given; because that Jesus was not yet glorified." (vii, 39.) This remark was not to be understood of the person of the Spirit, but of his gifts, and especially that of prophecy. But Christ was glorified in quality of Mediator: and in that glorified capacity he sends the Holy Ghost; therefore, the Holy Spirit was sent by Christ as the Mediator. On this account also, the Spirit of Christ the Mediator is the Author of Evangelical Prophecy. But the Holy Ghost was sent, even before the glorification of Christ, to reveal the Gospel. The existing state of the Church required it at that period, and the Holy Spirit was sent to meet that necessity. "Christ is likewise the same yesterday, today and forever." (Heb. xiii. 8.) He was also "slain from the foundation of the world;" (Rev. xiii. 8,) and was, therefore, at that same time raised again and glorified; but this was all in the decree and fore-knowledge of God. To make it evident, however, that God has never sent the Holy Spirit to the Church, except through the agency of Christ the Mediator, and in regard to him, God deferred that plentiful and exuberant effusion of his most copious gifts, until Christ, after his exaltation to heaven, should send them down in a communication of the greatest abundance. Thus he testified by a clear and evident proof, that he had formerly poured out the gifts of the Spirit upon the Church, by the same person, as he by whom, (when through his ascension the dense and overcharged cloud of water above the heavens had been disparted,) he poured down the most plentiful showers of his graces, inundating and over spreading the whole body of the Church.

III. But the revelation of Evangelical Theology is attributed to Christ in regard to his Mediatorship, and to the Holy Ghost in regard to his being the appointed substitute and Advocate of Christ the Mediator. This is done most consistently and for a very just reason, both because Christ, as Mediator, is placed for the ground-work of this doctrine, and because in the duty of mediation those actions were to be performed, those sufferings endured, and those blessings asked and obtained, which complete a goodly portion of the matters that are disclosed in the gospel of Christ. No wonder, therefore, that Christ in this respect, (in which he is himself the object of the gospel,) should likewise be the revealer of it, and the person who asks and procures all evangelical graces, and who is at once the Lord of them and the communicator. And since the Spirit of Christ, our Mediator and our head, is the bond of our union with Christ, from which we also obtain communion with Christ, and a participation in all his blessings--it is just and reasonable, that, in the respect which we have just mentioned, Christ should reveal to our minds, and seal upon our hearts, the evangelical charter and evidence of that faith by which he dwelleth in our hearts. The consideration of this matter exhibits to us (1.) the cause why it is possible for God to restrain himself with such great forbearance, patience, and long suffering, until the gospel is obeyed by those to whom it is preached; and (2.) it affords great consolation to our ignorance and infirmities.

I think, my hearers, you perceive that this single view adds no small degree of dignity to our Evangelical Theology, beside that which it possesses from the common consideration of its Author. If we may be allowed further to consider what wisdom, goodness and power God expended when he instituted and revealed this Theology, it will give great importance to our proposition. Indeed, all kinds of sciences have their origin in the wisdom of God, and are communicated to men by his goodness and power. But, if it be his right, (as it undoubtedly is,) to appoint gradations in the external exercise of his divine properties, we shall say, that all other sciences except this, have arisen from an inferior wisdom of God, and have been revealed by a less degree of goodness and power. It is proper to estimate this matter according to the excellence of its object. As the wisdom of God, by which he knows himself, is greater than that by which he knows other things; so the wisdom employed by him in the manifestation of himself is greater than that employed in the manifestation of other things. The goodness by which he permits himself to be known and acknowledged by man as his Chief Good, is greater than that by which he imparts the knowledge of other things. The power also, by which nature is raised to the knowledge of supernatural things, is greater than that by which it is brought to investigate things that are of the same species and origin with itself. Therefore, although all the sciences may boast of God as their author, yet in these particulars, Theology, soaring above the whole, leaves them at an immense distance.

But as this consideration raises the dignity of Theology, on the whole far above all other sciences, so it likewise demonstrates that Evangelical far surpasses Legal Theology; on which point we may be allowed, with your good leave, to dwell a little. The wisdom, goodness and power, by which God made man, after his own image, to consist of a rational soul and a body, are great, and constitute the claims to precedence on the part of Legal Theology. But the wisdom, goodness and power, by which "the Word was made flesh," (John i. 14,) and God was manifest in the flesh," (1 Tim. iii. 16,) and by which he "who was in the form of God took upon himself the form of a servant," (Phil. ii. 7,) are still greater, and they are the claims by which Evangelical Theology asserts its right to precedence. The wisdom and goodness, by the operation of which the power of God has been revealed to salvation, are great; but that by which is revealed "the power of God to salvation to every one that believeth," (Rom. ii. 16,) far exceeds it. Great indeed are the wisdom and goodness by which the righteousness of God by the law is made manifest," and by which the justification of the law was ascribed of debt to perfect obedience; but they are infinitely surpassed by the wisdom and goodness through which the righteousness of God by faith is manifested, and through which it is determined that the man is justified "that worketh not, and [being a sinner,] believeth on him who justifieth the ungodly," according to the most glorious riches of his grace. Conspicuous and excellent were the wisdom and goodness which appointed the manner of union with God in legal righteousness, performed out of conformity to the image of God, after which man was created. But a solemn and substantial triumph is achieved through faith in Christ's blood by the wisdom and goodness, which, having devised and executed the wonderful method of qualifying justice and mercy, appoint the manner of union in Christ., and in his righteousness, "who is the brightness of his Father's glory and the express image of his person." (Heb. i. 3.) Lastly, it is the wisdom, goodness and power, which, out of the thickest darkness of ignorance brought forth the marvelous light of the gospel; which, from an infinite multitude of sins, brought in everlasting righteousness; and which, from death and the depths of hell, "brought life and immortality to light." The wisdom, goodness and power which have produced these effects, exceed those in which the light that is added to light, the righteousness that is rewarded by a due recompense, and the animal life that is regulated according to godliness by the command of the law, are each of them swallowed up and consummated in that which is spiritual and eternal.

A deeper consideration of this matter almost compels me to adopt a more confident daring, and to give to the wisdom, goodness and power of God, which are unfolded in Legal Theology, the title of Natural," and as in some sense the beginning of the going forth of God towards his image, which is man, and a commencement of Divine intercourse with him. The others, which are manifested in the gospel, I fearlessly call "Supernatural wisdom, power and goodness," and "the extreme point and the perfect completion of all revelation;" because in the manifestation of the latter, God appears to have excelled himself, and to have unfolded every one of his blessings. Admirable was the kindness of God, and most stupendous his condescension in admitting man to the most intimate communion with himself--a privilege full of grace and mercy, after his sins had rendered him unworthy of having the establishment of such an intercourse. But this was required by the unhappy and miserable condition of man, who through his greater unworthiness had become the more indigent, through his deeper blindness required illumination by a stronger light, through his more grievous wickedness demanded reformation by means of a more extensive goodness, and who, the weaker he had become, needed a stronger exertion of power for his restoration and establishment. It is also a happy circumstance, that no aberration of ours can be so great, as to prevent God from recalling us into the good way; no fall so deep, as to disable him from raising us up and causing us to stand erect; and no evil of ours can be of such magnitude, as to prove a difficult conquest to his goodness, provided it be his pleasure to put the whole of it in motion; and this he will actually do, provided we suffer our ignorance and infirmities to be corrected by his light and power, and our wickedness to be subdued by his goodness.

IV. We have seen that, (1.) God is the Author of Legal Theology; and God and his Christ, that of Evangelical Theology. We have seen at the same time (2.) in what respect God and Christ are to be viewed in making known this revelation, and (3.) according to what properties of the Divine Nature of both of them it has been perfected.

We will now just glance at the Manner. The manner of the Divine manifestation appears to be threefold, according , the three instruments or organs of our capacity. (1.) The External Senses, (2.) The Inward Fancy or Imagination, and (3.) The Mind or Understanding. God sometimes reveals himself and his will by an image or representation offered to the external sight, or through an audible speech or discourse addressed to the ear. Sometimes he introduces himself by the same method to the imagination; and sometimes he addresses the mind in a manner ineffable, which is called Inspiration. Of all these modes scripture most clearly supplies us with luminous examples. But time will not permit me to be detained in enumerating them, lest I should appear to be yet more tedious to this most accomplished assembly.

THE END OF THEOLOGY

We have been engaged in viewing the Author,: let us now advert to the End. This is the more eminent and divine according to the greater excellence of that matter of which it is the end. In that light, therefore, this science is far more illustrious and transcendent than all others; because it alone has a relation to the life that is spiritual and supernatural, and has an End beyond the boundaries of the present life: while all other sciences have respect to this animal life, and each has an End proposed to itself, extending from the center of this earthly life and included within its circumference. Of this science, then, that may be truly said which the poet declared concerning his wise friend, "For those things alone he feels any relish, the rest like shadows fly." I repeat it, "they fly away," unless they be referred to this science, and firmly fix their foot upon it and be at rest. But the same person who is the Author and Object, is also the End of Theology. The very proportion and analogy of these things make such a connection requisite. For since the Author is the First and the Chief Being, it is of necessity that he be the First and Chief Good. He is, therefore, the extreme End of all things. And since He, the Chief Being and the Chief Good, subjects, lowers and spreads himself out, as an object to some power or faculty of a rational creature, that by its action or motion it may be employed and occupied concerning him, nay, that it may in a sense be united with him; it cannot possibly be, that the creature, after having performed its part respecting that object, should fly beyond it and extend itself further for the sake of acquiring a greater good. It is, therefore, of necessity that it restrain itself within him, not only as within a boundary beyond which it is impossible for it to pass on account of the infinitude of the object and on account of its own importance, but also as within its End and its Good, beyond which, because they are both the Chief in degree, it neither wishes nor is capable of desiring anything; provided this object be united with it as far as the capacity of the creature will admit. God is, therefore, the End of our Theology, proposed by God himself, in the acts prescribed in it; intended by man in the performance of those actions, and to be bestowed by God, after man shall have piously and religiously performed his duty. But because the chief good was not placed in the promise of it, nor in the desire of obtaining it, but in actually receiving it, the end of Theology may with the utmost propriety be called THE UNION OF GOD WITH MAN.

But it is not an Essential union, as if two essences, (for instance that of God and man,) were compacted together or joined into one, or as that by which man might himself be absorbed into God. The former of these modes of union is prohibited by the very nature of the things so united, and the latter is rejected by the nature of the union. Neither is it a formal union, as if God by that union might be made in the form of man, like a Spirit united to a body imparting to it life and motion, and acting upon it at pleasure, although, by dwelling in the body, it should confer on man the gift of life eternal. But it is an objective union by which God, through the agency of his pre-eminent and most faithful faculties and actions, (all of which he wholly occupies and completely fills,) gives such convincing proofs of himself to man, that God may then be said to be "all in all." (1 Cor. xv. 21.) This union is immediate, and without any bond that is different to the limits themselves. For God unites himself to the understanding and to the will of his creature, by means of himself alone, and without the intervention of image, species or appearance. This is what the nature of this last and supreme union requires, as being that in which consists the Chief Good of a rational creature, which cannot find rest except in the greatest union of itself with God. But by this union, the understanding beholds in the clearest vision, and as if "face to face," God himself, and all his goodness and incomparable beauty. And because a good of such magnitude and known by the clearest vision cannot fail of being loved on its own account; from this very consideration the will embraces it with a more intense love, in proportion to the greater degree of knowledge of it which the mind has obtained.

But here a double difficulty presents itself, which must first be removed, in order that our feet may afterwards without stumbling run along a path that will then appear smooth and to have been for some time well trodden. (1.) The one is, "How can it be that the eye of the human understanding does not become dim and beclouded when an object of such transcendent light is presented to it?" (2.)

The other is, "How can the understanding, although its eye may not be dim and blinded, receive and contain that object in such great measure and proportion?" The cause of the first is, that the light exhibits itself to the understanding not in the infinity of its own nature, but in a form that is qualified and attempered. And to what is it thus accommodated? Is it not to the understanding? Undoubtedly, to the understanding; but not according to the capacity which it possessed before the union: otherwise it could not receive and contain as much as would suffice to fill it and make it happy. But it is attempered according to the measure of its extension and enlargement, to admit of which the understanding is exquisitely formed, if it be enlightened and irradiated by the gracious and glorious shining of the light accommodated to that expansion. If it be thus enlightened, the eye of the understanding will not be overpowered and become dim, and it will receive that object in such a vast proportion as will most abundantly suffice to make man completely happy. This is a solution for both these difficulties. But an extension of the understanding will be followed by an enlargement of the will, either from a proper and adequate object offered to it, and accommodated to the same rule; or, (which I prefer,) from the native agreement of the will and understanding, and the analogy implanted in both of them, according to which the understanding extends itself to acts of volition, in the very proportion of its understanding and knowledge. In this act of the mind and will in seeing a present God, in loving him, and therefore in the enjoyment of him, the salvation of man and his perfect happiness consist. To which is added , conformation of our body itself to this glorious state of soul, which, whether it be effected by the immediate action of God on the body, or by means of an agency resulting from the action of the soul on the body, it is neither necessary for us here to inquire, nor at this time to discover. From hence also arises and shines forth illustriously the chief and infinite glory of God, far surpassing all other glory, that he has displayed in every preceding function which he administered. For since that action is truly great and glorious which is good, and since goodness alone obtains the title of "greatness," according to that elegant saying, to eu mega then indeed the best action of God is the greatest and the most glorious. But that is the best action by which he unites himself immediately to the creature and affords himself to be seen, loved and enjoyed in such an abundant measure as agrees with the creature dilated and expanded to that degree which we have mentioned. This is, therefore, the most glorious of God's actions. Wherefore the end of Theology is the union , God with man, to the salvation of the one and the glory of the other; and to the glory which he declares by his act, not that glory which man ascribes to God when he is united to him. Yet it cannot be otherwise, than that man should be incited to sing forever the high praises of God, when he beholds and enjoys such large and overpowering goodness.

But the observations we have hitherto made on the End of Theology, were accommodated to the manner of that which is legal. We must now consider the End as it is proposed to Evangelical Theology. The End of this is (1.) God and Christ, (2.) the union of man with both of them, and (3.) the sight and fruition of both, to the glory of both Christ and God. On each of these particulars we have some remarks to make from the scriptures, and which most appropriately agree with, and are peculiar to, the Evangelical doctrine.

But before we enter upon these remarks, we must shew that the salvation of man, to the glory of Christ himself, consists also in the love, the sight, and the fruition of Christ. There is a passage in the fifteenth chapter of the first Epistle of the Apostle Paul to the Corinthians, which imposes this necessity upon us, because it appears to exclude Christ from this consideration. For in that place the apostle says, "When Christ shall have delivered up the kingdom to God, even the Father, then the Son also himself shall be subject unto him, that God may be all in all." (1 Cor. xv. 24.) From this passage three difficulties are raised, which must be removed by an appropriate explanation. They are these: (1.) "If Christ shall deliver up the kingdom to God, even the Father,' he will no longer reign himself in person." (2.) "If he shall be subject to the Father,' he will no more preside over his Church:" and (3.) "If God shall be all in all,' then our salvation is not placed in the union, sight and fruition of him." I will proceed to give a separate answer to each of these objections. The kingdom of Christ embraces two objects: The Mediatorial function of the regal office, and the Regal glory: The royal function, will be laid aside, because there will then be no necessity or use for it, but the royal glory will remain because it was obtained by the acts of the Mediator, and was conferred on him by the Father according to covenant. The same thing is declared by the expression "shall be subject," which here signifies nothing more than the laying aside of the super-eminent power which Christ had received from the Father, and which he had, as the Father's Vicegerent, administered at the pleasure of his own will: And yet, when he has laid down this power, he will remain, as we shall see, the head and the husband of his Church. That sentence has a similar tendency in which it is said, "God shall be ALL IN ALL." For it takes away even the intermediate and deputed administration of the creatures which God is accustomed to use in the communication of his benefits; and it indicates that God will likewise immediately from himself communicate his own good, even himself to his creatures. Therefore, on the authority of this passage, nothing is taken away from Christ which we have been wishful to attribute to him in this discourse according to the scriptures.

This we will now shew by some plain and apposite passages. Christ promises an union with himself in these words, "If a man love me, he will keep my words; and my Father will love him, and we will come unto him, and make our abode with him." (John xiv. 23.) Here is a promise of good: therefore the good of the Church is likewise placed in union with Christ; and an abode is promised, not admitting of termination by the bounds of this life, but which will continue for ever, and shall at length, when this short life is ended, be consummated in heaven. In reference to this, the Apostle says, "I desire to depart and to be with Christ;" and Christ himself says, "I will that they also whom thou hast given me, be with me where I am." (John xvii. 24.) John says, that the end of his gospel is, "that our fellowship may be with the Father and the Son;" (1 John i. 3,) in which fellowship eternal life must necessarily consist, since in another place he explains the same end in these words, "But these are written, that ye might believe that Jesus is the Christ: and that, believing, ye might have life through his name." (John xx. 31.) But from the meaning of the same Apostle, it appears, that this fellowship has an union antecedent to itself. These are his words, "If that which ye have heard from the beginning shall remain in you ye also shall continue in the Son, and in the Father." (1 John ii. 24.) What! Shall the union between Christ and his Church cease at a period when he shall place before his glorious sight his spouse sanctified to himself by his own blood? Far be the idea from us! For the union, which had commenced here on earth, will then at length be consummated and perfected.

If any one entertain doubts concerning the vision of Christ, let him listen to Christ in this declaration: "He that loveth me shall be loved of my Father; and I will love him, and will manifest myself to him." (John xiv. 21.) Will he thus disclose himself in this world only? Let us again hear Christ when he intercedes with the Father for the faithful: "Father, I will that they also, whom thou hast given me, be with me where I am; that they may behold my glory, which thou hast given me: for thou lovedst me before the foundation of the world." (John xvii. 34) Christ, therefore, promises to his followers the sight of his glory, as something salutary to them; and his Father is intreated to grant this favour. The same truth is confirmed by John when he says, "Then we shall see him as he is." (1 John iii. 2.) This passage may without any impropriety be understood of Christ, and yet not to the exclusion of God the Father. But what do we more distinctly desire than that Christ may become, what it is said he will be, "the light" that shall enlighten the celestial city, and in whose light "the nations shall walk?" (Rev. xxi. 23, 24.)

Although the fruition of Christ is sufficiently established by the same passages as those by which the sight of him is confirmed, yet we will ratify it by two or three others. Since eternal felicity is called by the name of "the supper of the lamb," and is emphatically described by this term, "the marriage of the Lamb," I think it is taught with adequate clearness in these expressions, that happiness consists in the fruition or enjoyment of the Lamb. But the apostle, in his apocalypse, has ascribed both these epithets to Christ, by saying, "Let us be glad and rejoice, and give honour to him, for the marriage of the Lamb is come, and his wife hath made herself ready :" (Rev. xix. 7,) and a little afterwards, he says, "Blessed are they which are called to the marriage-supper of the Lamb." (verse 9.) It remains for us to treat on the glory of Christ, which is inculcated in these numerous passages of Scripture in which it is stated that "he sits with the Father on his throne," and is adored and glorified both by angels and by men in heaven.

Having finished the proof of those expressions, the truth of which we engaged to demonstrate, we will now proceed to fulfill our promise of explanation, and to show that all and each of these benefits descend to us in a peculiar and more excellent manner, from Evangelical Theology, than they could have done from that which is Legal, if by it we could really have been made alive.

2. And, that we may, in the first place, dispatch the subject of Union, let the brief remarks respecting marriage which we have just made, be brought again to our remembrance. For that word more appropriately honours this union, and adorns it with a double and remarkable privilege; one part of which consists of a deeper combination, the other of a more glorious title. The Scripture speaks thus of the deeper combination; "And the two shall be one flesh. This is a great mystery: but I speak concerning Christ and the church!" (Ephes. v. 31, 32.) It will therefore be a connubial tie that will unite Christ with the church. The espousals of the church on earth are contracted by the agency of the brides-men of Christ, who are the prophets, the apostles, and their successors, and particularly the Holy Ghost, who is in this affair a mediator and arbitrator. The consummation will then follow, when Christ will introduce his spouse into his bride-chamber. From such an union as this, there arises, not only a communion of blessings, but a previous communion of the persons themselves; from which the possession of blessings is likewise assigned, by a more glorious title, to her who is united in the bonds of marriage. The church comes into a participation not only of the blessings of Christ, but also of his title. For, being the wife of the King, she enjoys it as a right due to her to be called QUEEN; which dignified appellation the scripture does not withhold from her. "Upon thy right hand stands the Queen in gold of Ophir:" (Psalm xlv. 9.) "There are three-score queens, and four-score concubines, and virgins without number. "My dove, my undefiled, is but one; she is the only one of her mother, she is the choice one of her that bare her. The daughter saw her, and blessed her; yea, the queens and the concubines; and they praised her." (Song of Sol. vi. 8, 9.) The church could not have been eligible to the high honour of such an union, unless Christ has been made her beloved, her brother, sucking the breasts of the same mother." (Cant. 8.) But there would have been no necessity for this union, "if righteousness and salvation had come to us by the law." That was, therefore, a happy necessity, which, out of compassion to the emergency of our wretched condition, the divine condescension improved to our benefit, and filled with such a plenitude of dignity! But the manner of this our union with Christ is no small addition to that union

which is about to take place between us and God the Father. This will be evident to any one who considers what and how great is the bond of mutual union between Christ and the Father.

3. If we turn our attention to sight or vision, we shall meet with two remarkable characters which are peculiar to Evangelical Theology.

(1.) In the first place, the glory of God, as if accumulated and concentrated together into one body, will be presented to our view in Christ Jesus; which glory would otherwise have been dispersed throughout the most spacious courts of a "heaven immense;" much in the same manner as the light, which had been created on the first day, and equally spread through the whole hemisphere, was on the fourth day collected, united and compacted together into one body, and offered to the eyes as a most conspicuous and shining object. In reference to this, it is said in the Apocalypse, that the heavenly Jerusalem "had no need of the sun, neither of the moon; for the glory of God did lighten it, and the Lamb will be the future light thereof," (Rev. xxi. 23,) as a vehicle by which this most delightful glory may diffuse itself into immensity.

(2.) We shall then not only contemplate, in God himself, the most excellent properties of his nature, but shall also perceive that all of them have been employed in and devoted to the procuring of this good for us, which we now possess in hope, but which we shall in reality then possess by means of this union and open vision.

The excellence, therefore, of this vision far exceeds that which could have been by the law; and from this source arises a fruition of greater abundance and more delicious sweetness. For, as the light in the sun is brighter than that in the stars, so is the sight of the sun, when the human eye is capable of bearing it, more grateful and acceptable, and the enjoyment of it is far more pleasant. From such a view of the Divine attributes, the most delicious sweetness of fruition will seem to be doubled. For the first delight will arise from the contemplation of properties so excellent; the other from the consideration of that immeasurable condescension by which it has pleased God to unfold all those his properties, and the whole of those blessings which he possesses in the exhaustless and immeasurable treasury of his riches, and to give this explanation, that he may procure salvation for man and may impart it to his most miserable creature. This will then be seen in as strong a light, as if the whole of that which is essentially God appeared to exist for the sake of man alone, and for his solo benefit. There is also the addition of this peculiarity concerning it: "Jesus Christ shall change our vile body, [the body of our humiliation,] that it may be fashioned like unto his glorious body: (Phil. iii. 21,) and as we have borne the image of the earthy [Adam], we shall also bear the image of the heavenly." (1 Cor. xv. 49.) Hence it is, that all things are said to be made new in Christ Jesus; (2 Cor. v. 17,) and we are described in the scriptures as "looking, according to his promise, for new heavens and a new earth, (2 Pet. iii. 13,) and a new name written on a white stone, (Rev. ii. 17,) the new name of my God, and the name of the city of my God, which is the new Jerusalem, (Rev. iii. 12.) and they shall sing a new song to God and his Christ forever." (Rev. v. 9.)

Who does not now see, how greatly the felicity prepared for us by Christ, and offered to us through Evangelical Theology excels that which would have come to us by "the righteousness of the law," if indeed it had been possible for us to fulfill it? We should in that case have been similar to the elect angels; but now we shall be their superiors, if I be permitted to make such a declaration, to the praise of Christ and our God, in this celebrated Hall, and before an assembly among whom we have some of those most blessed spirits themselves as spectators. They now enjoy union with God and Christ, and will probably be more closely united to both of them at the time of the "restitution of all things." But there will be nothing between the two parties similar to that Conjugal Bond which unites us, and in which we may be permitted to glory.

They will behold God himself "face to face," and will contemplate the most eminent properties of his nature; but they will see some among those properties devoted to the purpose of man's salvation, which God has not unfolded for their benefit, because that was not necessary; and which he would not have unfolded, even if it had been necessary. These things they will see, but they will not be moved by envy; it will rather be a subject of admiration and wonder to them, that God, the Creator of both orders, conferred on man, (who was inferior to them in nature,) that dignity which he had of old denied to the spirits that partook with themselves of the same nature. They will behold Christ, that most brilliant and shining light of the city of the living God, of which they also are inhabitants: and, from this very circumstance their happiness will be rendered more illustrious through Christ. Christ "took not on him the nature of angels, but the seed of Abraham;" (Heb. ii, 16,) to whom also, in that assumed nature, they will present adoration and honour, at the command of God, when he introduces his First begotten into the world to come. Of that future world, and of its blessings, they also will be partakers: but "it is not put in subjection to them," (Heb. ii. 5,) but to Christ and his Brethren, who are partakers of the same nature, and are sanctified by himself. A malignant spirit, yet of the same order as the angels, had hurled against God the crimes of falsehood and envy. But we see how signally God in Christ and in the salvation procured by him, has repelled both these accusations from himself. The falsehood intimated an unwillingness on the part of God that man should be reconciled to him, except by the intervention of the death of his Son. His envy was excited, because God had raised man, not only to the angelical happiness, (to which even that impure one would have attained had "he kept his first estate,) but to a state of blessedness far superior to that of angels.

That I may not be yet more prolix, I leave it as a subject of reflection to the devoted piety of your private meditations, most accomplished auditors, to estimate the vast and amazing greatness of the glory of God which has here manifested itself, and to calculate the glory due from us to him for such transcendent goodness.

In the mean time, let all of us, however great our number, consider with a devout and attentive mind, what duty is required of us by this doctrine, which having received its manifestation from God and Christ, plainly and fully announces to us such a great salvation, and to the participation of which we are most graciously invited. It requires to be received, understood, believed, and fulfilled, in deed and in reality. It is worthy of all acceptation, on account of its Author; and necessary to be received on account of its End.

1. Being delivered by so great an Author, it is worthy to be received with a humble and submissive mind; to have much diligence and care bestowed on a knowledge and perception of it; and not to be laid aside from the hand, the mind, or the heart, until we shall have "obtained the End of it--THE SALVATION OF OUR SOULS." Why should this be done? Shall the Holy God open his mouth, and our ears remain stopped? Shall our Heavenly Master be willing to communicate instruction, and we refuse to learn? Shall he desire to inspire our hearts with the knowledge of his Divine truth, and we, by closing the entrance to our hearts, exclude the most evident and mild breathings of his Spirit? Does Christ, who is the Father's Wisdom, announce to us that gospel which he has brought from the bosom of the Father, and shall we disdain to hide it in the inmost recesses of our heart? And shall we act thus, especially when we have received this binding command of the Father, which says, "Hear ye him!" (Matt. xvii. 5,) to which he has added a threat, that "if we hear him not, our souls shall be destroyed from among the people; (Acts iii. 23,) that is, from the commonwealth of Israel? Let none of us fall into the commission of such a heinous offense! "For if the word spoken by angels was steadfast, and every transgression and disobedience received a just recompense of reward; how shall we escape if we neglect so great salvation, which at the first began to be spoken by the Lord, and was confirmed unto us by them that heard him ," (Heb. ii. 2, 3.)

2. To all the preceding considerations, let the End of this doctrine be added, and it will be of the greatest utility in enforcing this the work of persuasion on minds that are not prodigal of their own proper and Chief Good--an employment in which its potency and excellence are most apparent. Let us reflect, for what cause God has brought us out of darkness into this marvelous light; has furnished us with a mind, understanding, and reason; and has adorned us with his image. Let this question be revolved in our minds, "For what purpose or End has God restored the fallen to their pristine state of integrity, reconciled sinners to himself, and received enemies into favour," and we shall plainly discover all this to have been done, that we might be made partakers of eternal salvation, and might sing praises to him forever. But we shall not be able to aspire after this End, much less to attain it, except in the way which is pointed out by that Theological Doctrine which has been the topic of our discourse. If we wander from this End, our wanderings from it extend, not only beyond the whole earth and sea, but beyond heaven itself--that city of which nevertheless it is essentially necessary for us to be made free men, and to have our names enrolled among the living. This doctrine is "the gate of heaven," and the door of paradise; the ladder of Jacob, by which Christ descends to us, and we shall in turn ascend to him; and the golden chain, which connects heaven with earth. Let us enter into this gate; let us ascend this ladder; and let us cling to this chain. Ample and wide is the opening of the gate, and it will easily admit believers; the position of the ladder is movable, and will not suffer those who ascend it to be shaken or moved; the joining which unites one link of the chain with another is indissoluble, and will not permit those to fall down who cling to it, until we come to "him that liveth forever and ever," and are raised to the throne of the Most High; till we be united to the living God, and Jesus Christ our Lord, "the Son of the Highest."

But on you, O chosen youths, this care is a duty peculiarly incumbent; for God has destined you to become "workers together with him," in the manifestation of the gospel, and instruments to administer to the salvation of others. Let the Majesty of the Holy Author of your studies, and the necessity of the End, be always placed before your eyes. (1.) On attentively viewing the Author, let the words of the Prophet Amos recur to your remembrance and rest on your mind: "The lion hath roared, who will not fear? The Lord God hath spoken, who can but prophesy?" (Amos ii. 8.) But you cannot prophesy, unless you be instructed by the Spirit of Prophesy. In our days he addresses no one in that manner, except in the Scriptures; he inspires no one, except by means of the Scriptures, which are divinely inspired. (2.) In contemplating the End, you will discover, that it is not possible to confer on any one, in his intercourse with mankind, an office of greater dignity and utility, or an office that is more salutary in its consequences, than this, by which he may conduct them from error into the way of truth, from wickedness to righteousness, from the deepest misery to the highest felicity; and by which he may contribute much towards their everlasting salvation. But this truth is taught by Theology alone; there is nothing except this heavenly science that prescribes the true righteousness; and by it alone is this felicity disclosed, and our salvation made known and revealed. Let the sacred Scriptures therefore be your models:

"Night and day read them, read them day and night. Colman.

If you thus peruse them, "they will make you that you shall not be barren nor unfruitful in the knowledge of our Lord Jesus Christ; (2 Pet. i. 8,) but you will become good ministers of Jesus Christ, nourished up in the words of faith and of good doctrine; (1 Tim. iv. 6,) and ready to every good work; (Tit. iii. 1,) workmen who need not to be ashamed;" (2 Tim. ii. 15,) sowing the gospel with diligence and patience; and returning to your Lord with rejoicing, bringing with you an ample harvest, through the blessing of God and the grace of our Lord Jesus Christ: to whom be praise and glory from this time, even forever more! Amen !

ORATION III

THE CERTAINTY OF SACRED THEOLOGY

Although the observations which I have already offered in explanation of the Object, the Author and the End of sacred Theology, and other remarks which might have been made, if they had fallen into the hands of a competent interpreter, although all of them contain admirable commendations of this Theology, and convince us that it is altogether divine, since it is occupied concerning God, is derived from God, and leads to God; yet they will not be able to excite within the mind of any person a sincere desire of entering upon such a study, unless he be at the same time encouraged by the bright rays of an assured hope of arriving at a knowledge of the desirable Object, and of obtaining the blessed End. For since the perfection of motion is rest, vain and useless will that motion be which is not able to attain rest, the limit of its perfection. But no prudent person will desire to subject himself to vain and useless labour. All our hope, then, of attaining to this knowledge is placed in Divine revelation. For the anticipation of this very just conception has engaged the minds of men, "that God cannot be known except through himself, to whom also there can be no approach but through himself." On this account it becomes necessary to make it evident to man, that a revelation has been made by God; that the revelation which has been given is fortified and defended by such sure and approved arguments, as will cause it to be considered and acknowledged as divine; and that there is a method, by which a man may understand the meanings declared in the word, and may apprehend them by a firm and assured faith. To the elucidation of the last proposition, this third part of our labour must be devoted. God grant that I may in this discourse again follow the guidance of his word as it is revealed in the scriptures, and may bring forth and offer to your notice such things as may contribute to establish our faith, and to promote the glory of God, to the uniting together of all of us in the Lord. I pray and beseech you also, my very famous and most accomplished hearers, not to disdain to favour me with a benevolent and patient hearing, while I deliver this feeble oration in your presence.

As we are now entering upon a consideration of the Certainty of Sacred Theology, it is not necessary that we should contemplate it under the aspect of Legal and Evangelical; for in both of them there is the same measure of the truth, and therefore, the same measure of knowledge, and that is certainty. We will treat on this subject, then, in a general manner, without any particular reference or application.

But that our oration may proceed in an orderly course, it will be requisite in the first place briefly to describe Certainty in general; and then to treat at greater length on the Certainty Of Theology.

I. Certainty, then, is a property of the mind or understanding, and a mode of knowledge according to which the mind knows an object as it is, and is certain that it knows that object as it is. It is distinct from Opinion; because it is possible for opinion to know a matter as it is, but its knowledge is accompanied by a suspicion of the opposite falsity. Two things, therefore, are required, to constitute certainty. (1.) The truth of the thing itself, and (2.) such an apprehension of it in our minds as we have just described. This very apprehension, considered as being formed from the truth of the thing itself, and fashioned according to such truth, is also called Truth on account of the similitude; even as the thing itself is certain, on account of the action of the mind which apprehends it in that manner. Thus do those two things, (certainty and truth,) because of their admirable union, make a mutual transfer of their one to the other names, the one to the other.

But truth may in reality be viewed in two aspects--one simple, and the other compound. (1.) The former, in relation to a thing as being in the number of entities; (2.) the latter, in reference to something inherng in a thing, being present with it or one of its circumstantials--or in reference to a thing as producing something else, or as being
produced by some other--and if there be any other affections and relations of things among themselves. The process of truth in the mind is after the same manner. Its action is of two kinds. (1.) On a simple being or entity which is called "a simple apprehension;" and (2.) on a complex being, which is termed composition." The mode of truth is likewise, in reality, two-fold--necessary and contingent; according to which, a thing, whether it be simple or complex, is called "necessary" or "contingent." The necessity of a simple thing is the necessary existence of the thing itself, whether it obtain the place of a subject or that of an attribute. The necessity of a complex thing is the unavoidable and essential

disposition and habitude that subsists between the subject and the attribute.

That necessity which, as we have just stated, is to be considered in simple things, exists in nothing except in God and in those things which, although they agree with him in their nature, are yet distinguished from him by our mode of considering them. All other things, whatever may be their qualities, are contingent, from the circumstance of their being brought into action by power; neither are they contingent only by reason of their beginning, but also of their continued duration. Thus the existence of God, is a matter of necessity; his life, wisdom, goodness, justice, mercy, will and power, likewise have a necessary existence. But the existence and preservation of the creatures are not of necessity. Thus also creation, preservation, government, and whatever other acts are attributed to God in respect of his creatures, are not of necessity. The foundation of necessity is the nature of God; the principle of contingency is the free will of the Deity. The more durable it has pleased God to create anything, the nearer is its approach to necessity, and the farther it recedes from contingency; although it never pass beyond the boundaries of contingency, and never reach the inaccessible abode of necessity.

Complex necessity exists not only in God, but also in the things of his creation. It exists in God, partly on account of the foundation of his nature, and partly on account of the principle of his free-will. But its existence in the creatures is only from the free will of God, who at once resolved that this should be the relation and habitude between two created objects. Thus "God lives, understands, and loves," is a necessary truth from his very nature as God. "God is the Creator," "Jesus Christ is the saviour," "An angel is a created spirit endowed with intelligence and will," and "A man is a rational creature," are all necessary truths from the free will of God.

From this statement it appears, that degrees may be constituted in the necessity of a complex truth; that the highest may be attributed to that truth which rests upon the nature of God as its foundation; that the rest, which proceed from the will of God, may be excelled by that which (by means of a greater affection of his will,) God has willed to invest with such right of precedence; and that it may be followed by that which God has willed by a less affection of his will. The motion of the sun is necessary from the very nature of that luminary; but it is more necessary that the children of Israel be preserved and avenged on their enemies; the sun is therefore commanded to stand still in the midst of the heavens. (Josh. x. 13.) It is necessary that the sun be borne along from the east to the west, by the diurnal motion of the heavens. But it is more necessary that Hezekiah receive, by a sure sign, a confirmation of the prolongation of his life; the sun, therefore, when commanded, returns ten degrees backward; (Isa. xxxviii. 8,) and thus it is proper, that the less necessity should yield to the greater, and that from the free will of God, which has imposed a law on both of them. As this kind of necessity actually exists in things, the mind, by observing the same gradations, apprehends and knows it, if such a mode of cognition can truly deserve the name of "knowledge."

But the causes of this Certainty are three. For it is produced on the mind, either by the senses, by reasoning and discourse, or by revelation. The first is called the certainty of experience; the second, that of knowledge; and the last, that of faith. The first is the certainty of particular objects which come within the range and under the observation of the senses; the second is that of general conclusions deduced from known principles; and the last is that of things remote from the cognizance both of the senses and reason.

II. Let these observations now be applied to our present purpose. The Object of our Theology is God, and Christ in reference to his being God and Man. God is a true Being, and the only necessary one, on account of the necessity of his and he is also a necessary Being, because he will endure to all eternity. The things which are attributed to God in our Theology: partly belong to his nature, and partly agree with it by his own free will. By his nature, life, wisdom, goodness, justice, mercy, will and power belong to him, by a natural and absolute necessity. By his free will, all his volitions and actions concerning the creatures agree with his nature, and that immutably; because he willed at the same time, that they should not be retracted or repealed. All those things which are attributed to Christ, belong to him by the free will of God, but on this condition, that "Christ be the same yesterday, and to-day, and forever," (Heb. xiii. 8,) entirely exempt from any future change, whether it be that of a subject or its attributes, or of the affection which exists between the two. All other things, which are found in the whole superior and inferior nature of things, (whether they be considered simply in themselves, or as they are mutually affected among themselves,) do not extend to any degree of this necessity. The truth and necessity of our Theology, therefore, far exceed the necessity of all other sciences, in as much as both these [the truth and necessity,] are situated in the things themselves. The certainty of the mind, while it is engaged in the act of apprehending and knowing things, cannot exceed the Truth and Necessity of the thing's themselves; on the contrary, it very often may not reach them, [the truth and necessity,] through some defect in its capacity. For the eyes of our mind are in the same condition with respect to the pure truth of things, as are the eyes of owls with respect to the light of the sun. On this account, therefore, it is of necessity, that the object of no science can be known with greater certainty than that of Theology; but it follows rather, that a knowledge of this object may be obtained with the greatest degree of certainty, if it be presented in a qualified and proper manner to the inspection of the understanding according to its capacity. For this object is not of such a nature and condition as to be presented to the external senses; nor can its attributes, properties, affections, actions and passions be known by means of the observation and experience of the external senses. It is too sublime for them; and the attributes, properties, affections, actions and passions, which agree with it, are so high that the mind, even when assisted by reason and discourse, can neither know it, investigate its attributes, nor demonstrate that they agree with the subject, whatever the principles may be which it has applied, and to whatever causes it may have had recourse, whether they be such as arise from the object itself, from its attributes, or from the agreement which subsists between them. The Object is known to itself alone; and the whole truth and necessity are properly and immediately known to Him to whom they belong; to God in the first place and in an adequate degree; to Christ, in the second place, through the communication of God. To itself, in an adequate manner, in reference to the knowledge which it has of itself; in an inferior degree to God, in reference to his knowledge of him, [Christ.] Revelation is therefore necessary by which God may exhibit himself and his Christ as an object of sight and knowledge to our understanding; and this exhibition to be made in such a manner as to unfold at once all their attributes, properties, affections, actions and passions, as far as it is permitted for them to be known, concerning God and his Christ, to our salvation and to their glory; and that God may thus disclose all and every portion of those theorems in which both the subjects themselves and all their attending attributes are comprehended. Revelation is necessary, if it be true that God and his Christ ought to be known, and both of them be worthy to receive Divine honours and worship. But both of them ought to be known and worshipped; the revelation, therefore, of both of them is necessary; and because it is thus necessary, it has been made by God. For if nature, as a partaker and communicator of a good that is only partial, is not deficient in the things that are necessary; how much less ought we even to suspect such a deficiency in God, the Author and Artificer of nature, who is also the Chief Good?

But to inspect this subject a little more deeply and particularly, will amply repay our trouble; for it is similar to the foundation on which must rest the weight of the structure--the other doctrines which follow. For unless it should appear certain and evident, that a revelation has been made, it will be in vain to inquire and dispute about the word in which that revelation has been made and is contained. In the first place, then, the very nature of God most clearly evinces that a revelation has been made of himself and Christ. His nature is good, beneficent, and communicative of his blessedness, whether it be that which proceeds from it by creation, or that which is God himself. But there is no communication made of Divine good, unless God be made known to the understanding, and be desired by the affections and the will. But he cannot become an object of knowledge except by revelation. A revelation, therefore, is made, as a necessary instrument of communication.

2. The necessity of this revelation may in various ways be inferred and taught from the nature and condition of man. First. By nature, man possesses a mind and understanding. But it is just that the mind and understanding should be turned towards their Creator; this, however, cannot be done without a knowledge of the Creator, and such knowledge cannot be obtained except by revelation; a revelation has, therefore, been made. Secondly. God himself formed the nature of man capable of Divine Good. But in vain would it have had such a capacity, if it might not at some time partake of this Divine Good; but of this the nature of man cannot be made a partaker except by the knowledge of it; the knowledge of this Divine Good has therefore been manifested. Thirdly. It is not possible, that the desire which God has implanted within man should be vain and fruitless. That desire is for the enjoyment of an Infinite Good, which is God; but that Infinite Good cannot be enjoyed, except it be known; a revelation, therefore, has been made, by which it may be known.

3. Let that relation be brought forward which subsists between God and man, and the revelation that has been made will immediately become manifest. God, the Creator of man, has deserved it as his due, to receive worship and honour from the workmanship of his hands, on account of the benefit which he conferred by the act of creation. Religion and piety are due to God, from man his creature; and this obligation is coeval with the very birth of man, as the bond which contains this requisition was given on the very day in which he was created. But religion could not be a human invention. For it is the will of God to receive worship according to the rule and appointment of his own will. A revelation was therefore made, which exacts from man the religion due to God, and prescribes that worship which is in accordance with his pleasure and his honour.

4. If we turn our attention towards Christ, it is amazing how great the necessity of a manifestation appears, and how many arguments immediately present themselves in behalf of a revelation being communicated. Wisdom wishes to be acknowledged as the deviser of the wonderful attempering and qualifying of justice and mercy. Goodness and gracious mercy, as the administrators of such an immense benefit sought to be worshipped and honoured. And power, as the hand-maid of such stupendous wisdom and goodness, and as the executrix of the decree made by both of them, deserved to receive adoration. But the different acts of service which were due to each of them, could not be rendered to them without revelation. The wisdom, mercy and power of God, have, therefore, been revealed and displayed most copiously in Christ Jesus. He performed a multitude of most wonderful

works, by which we might obtain the salvation that we had lost; he endured most horrid torments and inexpressible distress, which, when pleaded in our favour, served to obtain this salvation for us; and by the gift of the Father he was possessed of an abundance of graces, and, at the Divine command, he became the distributor of them. Having, therefore, sustained all these offices for us, it is his pleasure to receive those acknowledgments, and those acts of Divine honour and worship, which are due to him on account of his extraordinary merits. But in vain will he expect the performance of these acts from man, unless he be himself revealed. A revelation of Christ has, therefore, been made. Consult actual experience, and that will supply you with numberless instances of this manifestation. The devil himself, who is the rival of Christ, has imitated these instances of gracious manifestation, has held converse with men under the name and semblance of the true God, has demanded acts of devotion from them, and prescribed to them a mode of religious worship. We have, therefore, the truth and the necessity of our Theology agreeing together in the highest degree; we have an adequate notion of it in the mind of God and Christ, according to the word which is called emfutov "engrafted." (James i. 21.) We have a revelation of this Theology made to men by the word preached; which revelation agrees both with the things themselves and with the notion which we have mentioned, but in a way that is attempered and suited to the human capacity. And as all these are preliminaries to the certainty which we entertain concerning this Theology, it was necessary to notice them in these introductory remarks.

Let us now consider this Certainty itself. But since a revelation has been made in the word which has been published, and since the whole of it is contained in that word, (so that This Word is itself our Theology,) we can determine nothing concerning the certainty of Theology in any other way than by offering some explanation concerning our certain apprehension of that word. We will assume it as a fact which is allowed and confirmed, that this word is to be found in no other place than in the sacred books of the Old and New Testament; and we shall on this account confine this certain apprehension of our mind to that word. But in fulfilling this design, three things demand our attentive consideration: First. The Certainty, and the kind of certainty which God requires from us, and by which it is his pleasure that this word should be received and apprehended by us as the Chief Certainty. Secondly. The reasons and arguments by which the truth of that word, which is its divinity, may be proved. Thirdly. How a persuasion of that divinity may be wrought in our minds, and this Certainty may be impressed on our hearts.

I. The Certainty "with which God wishes this word to be received, is that of faith; and it therefore depends on the veracity of him who utters it." By this Certainty "it is received," not only as true, but as divine; and it is not of that involved and mixed kind "of faith" by which any one, without understanding the meanings expressed by the word as by a sign, believes that those books which are contained in the Bible, are divine: for not only is a doubtful opinion opposed to faith, but an obscure and perplexed conception is equally inimical. Neither is it that species "of historical faith" which believes the word to be divine that it comprehends only by a theoretical understanding. But God demands that faith to be given to his word, by which the meanings expressed in this word may be understood, as far as it is necessary for the salvation of men and the glory of God; and may be so assuredly known to be divine, that they may be believed to embrace not only the Chief Truth, but also the Chief Good of man. This faith not only believes that God and Christ exist, it not only gives credence to them when they make declarations of any kind, but it believes in God and Christ when they affirm such things concerning themselves, as, being apprehended by faith, create a belief in God as our Father, and in Christ as our saviour. This we consider to be the office of an understanding that is not merely theoretical, but of one that is practical. For this cause not only is asfaleia (certainty,) attributed in the Scriptures to true and living faith, but to it are likewise ascribed both wlhroforia (a full assurance, Heb. vi. 2,) and wewoiqhsiv (trust or confidence,2 Cor. iii. 4,) and it is God who requires and demands such a species of certainty and of faith.

II. We may now be permitted to proceed by degrees from this point, to a consideration of those arguments which prove to us the divinity of the word; and to the manner in which the required certainty and faith are produced in our minds. To constitute natural vision we know that, (beside an object capable of being seen,) not only is an external light necessary to shine upon it and to render it visible, but an internal strength of eye is also required, which may receive within itself the form and appearance of the object which has been illuminated by the external light, and may thus be enabled actually to behold it. The same accompaniments are necessary to constitute spiritual vision; for, beside this external light of arguments and reasoning, an internal light of the mind and soul is necessary to perfect this vision of faith. But infinite is the number of arguments on which this world builds and establishes its divinity. We will select and briefly notice a few of those which are more usual, lest by too great a prolixity we become too troublesome and disagreeable to our auditory.

1. THE DIVINITY OF SCRIPTURE

Let scripture itself come forward, and perform the chief part in asserting its own Divinity. Let us inspect its substance and its matter. It is all concerning God and his Christ, and is occupied in declaring the nature of both of them, in further explaining the love, the benevolence, and the benefits which have been conferred by both of them on the human race, or which have yet to be conferred; and prescribing, in return, the duties of men towards their Divine Benefactors. The scripture, therefore, is divine in its object.

(2.) But how is it occupied in treating on these subjects? It explains the nature of God in such a way as to attribute nothing extraneous to it, and nothing that does not perfectly agree with it. It describes the person of Christ in such a manner, that the human mind, on beholding the description, ought to acknowledge, that "such a person could not have been invented or devised by any created intellect," and that it is described with such aptitude, suitableness and sublimnity, as far to exceed the largest capacity of a created understanding. In the same manner the scripture is employed in relating the love of God and Christ towards us, and in giving an account of the benefits which we receive. Thus the Apostle Paul, when he wrote to the Ephesians on these subjects, says, that from his former writings, the extent of "his knowledge of the mystery of Christ" might be manifest to them; (Ephes. iii. 4.) that is, it was divine, and derived solely from the revelation of God. Let us contemplate the law in which is comprehended the duty of men towards God. What shall we find, in all the laws of every nation, that is at all similar to this, or (omitting all mention of "equality,") that may be placed in comparison with those ten short sentences? Yet even those commandments, most brief and comprehensive as they are, have been still further reduced to two chief heads--the love of God, and the love of our neighbour. This law appears in reality to have been sketched and written by the right hand of God. That this was actually the case, Moses shews in these words, What nation is there so great, that hath statutes and judgments so righteous as all this law, which I set before you this day?" (Deut. iv. 8.) Moses likewise says, that so great and manifest is the divinity which is inherent in this law, that it compelled the heathen nations, after they had heard it, to declare in ecstatic admiration of it. "Surely this great nation is a wise and understanding people?" (Deut. iv. 6.) The scripture, therefore, is completely divine, from the manner in which it treats on those matters which are its subjects.

(3.) If we consider the End, it will as clearly point out to us the divinity of this doctrine. That End is entirely divine, being nothing less than the glory of God and man's eternal salvation. What can be more equitable than that all things should be referred to him from whom they have derived their origin? What can be more consonant to the wisdom, goodness, and power of God, than that he should restore, to his original integrity, man who had been created by him, but who had by his own fault destroyed himself; and that he should make him a partaker of his own Divine blessedness? If by means of any word God had wished to manifest himself to man, what end of manifestation ought he to have proposed that would have been more honourable to himself and more salutary to man? That the word, therefore, was divinely revealed, could not be discerned by any mark which was better or more legible, than that of its showing to man the way of salvation, taking him as by the hand and leading him into that way, and not ceasing to accompany him until it introduced him to the full enjoyment of salvation: In such a consummation as this, the glory of God most abundantly shines forth and displays itself. He who may wish to contemplate what we are declaring concerning this End, in a small but noble part of this word, should place "the Lord's Prayer" before the eyes of his mind; he should look most intently upon it; and, as far as that is possible for human eyes, he should thoroughly investigate all its parts and beauties. After he has done this, unless he confess, that in it this double end is proposed in a manner that is at once so nervous, brief, and accurate, as to be above the strength and capacity of every created intelligence, and unless he acknowledge, that this form of prayer is purely divine, he must of necessity have a mind surrounded and enclosed by more than Egyptian darkness.

2. THE AGREEMENT OF THIS DOCTRINE IN ITS PARTS

Let us compare the parts of this doctrine together, and we shall discover in all of them an agreement and harmony, even in points the most minute, that it is so great and evident as to cause us to believe that it could not be manifested by men, but ought to have implicit credence placed in it as having certainly proceeded from God.

Let the Predictions alone, that have been promulgated concerning Christ in different ages, be compared together. For the consolation of the first parents of our race, God said to the serpent, "The seed of the woman shall bruise thy head." (Gen. iii. 15.) The same promise was repeated by God, and was specially made to Abraham: "In thy seed shall all the nations be blessed." (Gen. xxii. 18.) The patriarch Jacob, when at the point of death, foretold that this seed should come forth from the lineage and family of Judah, in these words: "The scepter shall not depart from Judah, nor a lawgiver from between his feet, until Shiloh come; and unto him shall the gathering of the people be." (Gen. xlix. 10.)

Let the alien prophet also be brought forward, and to these predictions he will add that oracular declaration which he pronounced by the inspiration and at the command of the God of Israel, in these words: Balaam said, "There shall come a star out of Jacob, and a scepter shall rise out of Israel, and shall smite the corners of Moab, and destroy all the children of Sheth." (Num. xxiv. 17.) This blessed seed was afterwards promised to David, by Nathan, in these words: "I will set up thy seed after thee, which shall proceed out of thy bowels, and I will establish his kingdom." (2 Sam. vii. 12.) On this account Isaiah says, "There shall come forth a rod out of the stem of Jesse, and a branch shall grow out of his roots." (xi, 1.) And, by way of intimating that a virgin would be his mother, the same prophet says, "Behold a virgin shall conceive, and bear a son, and shall call his name Immanuel!" (Isa. vii. 14.) It would be tedious to repeat every declaration that occurs in the psalms and in the other Prophets, and that agrees most appropriately with this subject. When these prophecies are compared with those occurrences that have been described in the New Testament concerning their fulfillment, it will be evident from the complete harmony of the whole, that they were all spoken and written by the impulse of one Divine Spirit. If some things in those sacred books seem to be contradictions, they are easily reconciled by means of a right interpretation. I add, that not only do all the parts of this doctrine agree among themselves, but they also harmonize with that Universal Truth which has been spread through the whole of Philosophy; so that nothing can be discovered in Philosophy, which does not correspond with this doctrine. If any thing appear not to possess such an exact correspondence, it may be clearly confuted by means of true Philosophy and right reason.

Let the Style and Character of the scriptures be produced, and, in that instant, a most brilliant and refulgent mirror of the majesty which is luminously reflected in it, will display itself to our view in a manner the most divine. It relates things that are placed at a great distance beyond the range of the human imagination--things which far surpass the capacities of men. And it simply relates these things without employing any mode of argumentation, or the usual apparatus of persuasion: yet its obvious wish is to be understood and believed. But what confidence or reason has it for expecting to obtain the realization of this its desire? It possesses none at all, except that it depends purely upon its own unmixed authority, which is divine. It publishes its commands and its interdicts, its enactments and its prohibitions to all persons alike; to kings and subjects, to nobles and plebians, to the learned and the ignorant, to those that "require a sign" and those that "seek after wisdom," to the old and the young; over all these, the rule which it bears, and the power which it exercises, are equal. It places its sole reliance, therefore, on its own potency, which is able in a manner the most efficacious to restrain and compel all those who are refractory, and to reward those who are obedient.

Let the Rewards and Punishments be examined, by which the precepts are sanctioned, and there are seen both a promise of life eternal and a denunciation of eternal punishments. He who makes such a commencement as this, may calculate upon his becoming an object of ridicule, except he possess an inward consciousness both of his own right and power; and except he know, that, to subdue the wills of mortals, is a matter equally easy of accomplishment with him, as to execute his menaces and to fulfill his premises. To the scriptures themselves let him have recourse who may be desirous to prove with the greatest certainty its majesty, from the kind of diction which it adopts: Let him read the charming swan-like Song of Moses described in the concluding chapters of the Book of Deuteronomy: Let him with his mental eyes diligently survey the beginning of Isaiah's prophecy: Let him in a devout spirit consider the hundred and fourth Psalm. Then, with these, let him compare whatever choice specimens of poetry and eloquence the Greeks and the Romans can produce in the most eminent manner from their archives; and he will be convinced by the most demonstrative evidence, that the latter are productions of the human spirit, and that the former could proceed from none other than the Divine Spirit. Let a man of the greatest genius, and, in erudition, experience, and eloquence, the most accomplished of his race--let such a well instructed mortal enter the lists and attempt to finish a composition at all similar to these writings, and he will find himself at a loss and utterly disconcerted, and his attempt will terminate in discomfiture. That man will then confess, that what St. Paul declared concerning his own manner of speech, and that of his fellow-labourers, may be truly applied to the whole scripture: "Which things also we speak, not in the words which man's wisdom teacheth, but which the Holy Ghost teacheth; comparing spiritual things with spiritual." (1 Cor. ii. 13.)

3. THE PROPHECIES

Let us next inspect the prophecies scattered through the whole body of the doctrine; some of which belong to the substance of the doctrine, and others contribute towards procuring authority to the doctrine and to its instruments. It should be particularly observed, with what eloquence and distinctness they foretell the greatest and most important matters, which are far removed from the scrutinizing research of every human and angelical mind, and which could not possibly be performed except by power Divine: Let it be noticed at the same time with what precision the predictions are answered by the periods that intervene between them, and by all their concomitant circumstances; and the whole world will be compelled to confess, that such things could not have been foreseen and foretold, except by an omniscient Deity. I need not here adduce examples; for they are obvious to any one that opens the Divine volume. I will produce one or two passages, only, in which this precise agreement of the prediction and its fulfillment is described. When speaking of the children of Israel under the Egyptian bondage, and their deliverance from it according to the prediction which God had communicated to Abraham in a dream, Moses says, "And it came to pass at the end of the four hundred and thirty years, even the self-same day it came to pass, that all the hosts of the Lord went out from the land of Egypt:" (Exod. xii. 41.) Ezra speaks thus concerning the liberation from the Babylonish captivity, which event, Jeremiah foretold, should occur within seventy years: "Now in the first year of Cyrus, king of Persia, that the word of the Lord by the mouth of Jeremiah might be fulfilled, the Lord stirred up the spirit of Cyrus, king of Persia," &c. (Ezra i. 1.) But God himself declares by Isaiah, that the divinity of the scripture may be proved, and ought to be concluded, from this kind of prophecies. These are his words: "Shew the things that are to come hereafter, that we may know that ye are Gods." (Isa. xli. 23.)

4. MIRACLES

An illustrious evidence of the same divinity is afforded in the miracles, which God has performed by the stewards of his word, his prophets and apostles, and by Christ himself, for the confirmation of his doctrine and for the establishment of their authority. For these miracles are of such a description as infinitely to exceed the united powers of all the creatures and all the powers of nature itself, when their energies are combined. But the God of truth, burning with zeal for his own glory, could never have afforded such strong testimonies as these to false prophets and their false doctrine: nor could he have borne such witness to any doctrine even when it was true, provided it was not his, that is, provided it was not divine. Christ, therefore, said, "If I do not the works of my Father, believe me not; but if I do, though you believe not me, believe the works." (John x. 37, 38.) It was the same cause also, which induced the widow of Sarepta to say, on receiving from the hands of Elijah her son, who, after his death, had been raised to life by the prophet: "Now by this I know that thou art a man of God, and that the word of the Lord in thy mouth is truth." (1 Kings xvii. 24.) That expression of Nicodemus has the same bearing: "Rabbi, we know that thou art a teacher come from God; for no man can do these miracles that thou doest, except God be with him." (John iii. 2.) And it was for a similar reason that the apostle said, "The signs of an apostle were wrought among you in all patience, in signs, and wonders, and mighty deeds." (2 Cor. xii. 12.) There are indeed miracles on record that were wrought among the gentiles, and under the auspices of the gods whom they invoked: It is also predicted, concerning False Prophets, and Antichrist himself, that they will exhibit many signs and wonders: (Rev. xix. 20.) But neither in number, nor in magnitude, are they equal to those which the true God has wrought before all Israel, and in the view of the whole world. Neither were those feats of their real miracles, but only astonishing operations performed by the agency and power of Satan and his instruments, by means of natural causes, which are concealed from the human understanding, and escape the cognizance of men. But to deny the existence of those great and admirable miracles which are related to have really happened, when they have also the testimony of both Jews and gentiles, who were the enemies of the true doctrine--is an evident token of bare-faced impudence and execrable stupidity.

5. THE ANTIQUITY OF THE DOCTRINE

Let the antiquity, the propagation, the preservation, and the truly admirable defense of this doctrine be added--and they will afford a bright and perspicuous testimony of its divinity. If that which is of the highest antiquity possesses the greatest portion of truth," as Tertullian most wisely and justly observes, then this doctrine is one of the greatest truth, because it can trace its origin to the highest antiquity. It is likewise Divine, because it was manifested at a time when it could not have been devised by any other mind; for it had its commencement at the very period when man was brought into existence. An apostate angel would not then have proposed any of his doctrines to man, unless God had previously revealed himself to the intelligent creature whom he had recently formed: That is, God hindered the fallen angel, and there was then no cause in existence by which he might be impelled to engage in such an enterprise. For God would not suffer man, who had been created after his own image, to be tempted by his enemy by means of false doctrine, until, after being abundantly instructed in that which was true, he was enabled to know that which was false and to reject it. Neither could any odious feeling of envy against man have tormented Satan, except God had considered him worthy of the communication of his word, and had deigned, through that communication, to make him a partaker of eternal. felicity, from which Satan had at that period unhappily fallen.

The Propagation, Preservation, and Defense of this doctrine, most admirable when separately considered, will all be found divine, if, in the first place, we attentively fix our eyes upon those men among whom it is propagated; then on the foes and adversaries of this doctrine; and, lastly, on the manner in which its propagation, preservation and defense have hitherto been and still are conducted. (1.) If we consider those men among whom this sacred doctrine flourishes, we shall discover that their nature, on account of its corruption, rejects this doctrine for a two-fold reason; (i.) The first is, because in one of its parts it is so entirely contrary to human and worldly wisdom, as to subject itself to the accusation of Folly from men of corrupt minds. (ii.) The second reason is, because in another of its parts it is decidedly hostile and inimical to worldly lusts and carnal desires. It is, therefore, rejected by the human understanding and refused by the will, which are the two chief faculties in man; for it is according to their orders and commands that the other faculties are either put in motion or remain at rest. Yet, notwithstanding all this natural repugnance, it has been received and believed. The human mind, therefore, has been conquered, and the subdued will has been gained, by Him who is the author of both. (2.)

This doctrine has some most powerful and bitter enemies: Satan, the prince of this world, with all his angels, and the world his ally: These are foes with whom there can be no reconciliation. If the subtlety, the power, the malice, the audacity, the impudence, the perseverance, and the diligence of these enemies, be placed in opposition to the simplicity, the inexperience, the weakness, the fear, the inconstancy, and the slothfulness of the greater part of those who give their assent to this heavenly doctrine; then will the greatest wonder be excited, how this doctrine, when attacked by so many enemies, and defended by such sorry champions, can stand and remain safe and unmoved. If this wonder and admiration be succeeded by a supernatural and divine investigation of its cause, then will God himself be discovered as the propagator, preserver, and defender of this doctrine. (3.) The manner also in which its propagation, preservation and defense are conducted, indicates divinity by many irrefragible tokens. This doctrine is carried into effect, without bow or sword--without horses chariots, or horsemen; yet it proceeds prosperously along, stands in an erect posture, and remains unconquered, in the name of the Lord of Hosts: While its adversaries, though supported by such apparently able auxiliaries and relying on such powerful aid, are overthrown, fall down together, and perish. It is accomplished, not by holding out alluring promises of riches, glory, and earthly pleasures, but by a previous statement of the dreaded cross, and by the prescription of such patience and forbearance as far exceed all human strength and ability. "He is a chosen vessel unto me, to bear my name before the gentiles, and kings, and the children of Israel; for I will shew him How Great Things he must suffer for my name's sake." (Acts ix. 15, 16.) "Behold, I send you forth as sheep in the midst of wolves." (Matt. x. 16)

Its completion is not effected by the counsels of men, but in opposition to all human counsels-- whether they be those of the professors of this doctrine, or those of its adversaries. For it often happens, that the counsels and machinations which have been devised for the destruction of this doctrine, contribute greatly towards its propagation, while the princes of darkness fret and vex themselves in vain, and are astonished and confounded, at an issue so contrary to the expectations which they had formed from their most crafty and subtle counsels.

St. Luke says, "Saul made havoc of the church, entering into every house, and, haling men and women, committed them to prison. Therefore they that were scattered abroad, went every where preaching the word." (Acts vii. 3, 4.) And by this means Samaria received the word of God. In reference to this subject St. Paul also says, "But I would ye should understand, brethren, that the things which happened unto me have fallen out rather unto the furtherance of the gospel; so that my bonds are manifest in all the palace, and in all other places." (Phil. i. 12, 13.) For the same cause that common observation has acquired all its just celebrity: "The blood of the martyrs is the seed of the church." What shall we say to these things? "The stone which the builders refused, is become the head stone of the corner: This is the Lord's doing; it is marvelous in our eyes." (Psalm cxviii. 22, 23.)

Subjoin to these the tremendous judgments of God on the persecutors of this doctrine, and the miserable death of the tyrants. One of these, at the very moment when he was breathing out his polluted and unhappy spirit, was inwardly constrained publicly to proclaim, though in a frantic and outrageous tone, the divinity of this doctrine in these remarkable words: "Thou Hast Conquered, O Galilean!"

Who is there, now, that, with eyes freed from all prejudice, will look upon such clear proofs of the divinity of Scripture, and that will not instantly confess: the Apostle Paul had the best reasons for exclaiming, "If our gospel be hid, it is hid to them that are lost; in whom the God of this world hath blinded the minds of them which believe not; lest the light of the glorious gospel of Christ, who is the image of God, should shine unto them." (2 Cor. iv. 3, 4) As if he had said, "This is not human darkness; neither is it drawn as a thick veil over the mind by man himself; but it is diabolical darkness, and spread by the devil, the prince of darkness, upon the mind of man, over whom, by the just judgment of God, he exercises at his pleasure the most absolute tyranny. If this were not the case, it would be impossible for this darkness to remain; but, how great soever its density might be, it would be dispersed by this light which shines with such overpowering brilliancy."

6. THE SANCTITY OF THOSE BY WHOM IT HAS BEEN ADMINISTERED

The sanctity of those by whom the word was first announced to men and by whom it was committed to writing, conduces to the same purpose--to prove its Divinity. For since it appears that those who were entrusted with the discharge of this duty, had divested themselves of the wisdom of the world, and of the feelings and affections of the flesh, entirely putting off the old man--and that they were completely eaten up and consumed by their zeal for the glory of God and the salvation of men--it is manifest that such great sanctity as this had been inspired and infused into them, by Him alone who is the Holiest of the holy.

Let Moses be the first that is introduced: He was treated in a very injurious manner by a most ungrateful people, and was frequently marked out for destruction; yet was he prepared to purchase their salvation by his own banishment. He said, when pleading with God, "Yet now, if thou wilt, forgive their sin; and if not, blot me, I pray thee, out of thy book which thou hast written." (Exod. xxxii. 32.) Behold his zeal for the salvation of the people entrusted to his charge--a zeal for the glory of God! Would you see another reason for this wish to be devoted to destruction? Read what he had previously said: "Wherefore should the Egyptians speak and say? For mischief did the Lord bring them out to slay them in the mountains," (Exod. xxxii. 12,) "because he was not able to bring them out unto the land which he swear unto their Fathers." (Num. xiv. 16.) We observe the same zeal in Paul, when he wishes that himself "were accursed from Christ for his brethren the Jews, his kinsmen according to the flesh," (Rom. 9) from whom he had suffered many and great indignities.

David was not ashamed publicly to confess his heavy and enormous crimes, and to commit them to writing as an eternal memorial to posterity. Samuel did not shrink from marking in the records of perpetuity the detestable conduct of his sons; and Moses did not hesitate to bear a public testimony against the iniquity and the madness of his ancestors. If even the least desire of a little glory had possessed their minds, they might certainly have been able to indulge in taciturnity, and to conceal in silence these circumstances of disgrace. Those of them who were engaged in describing the deeds and achievements of other people, were unacquainted with the art of offering adulation to great men and nobles, and of wrongfully attributing to their enemies any unworthy deed or motive. With a regard to truth alone, in promoting the glory of God, they placed all persons on an equality; and made no other distinction between them than that which God himself has commanded to be made between piety and wickedness. On receiving from the hand of God their appointment to this office, they at once and altogether bade farewell to all the world, and to all the desires which are in it. "Each of them said unto his father and to his mother, I have not seen him; neither did he acknowledge his brethren; for they observed the word of God, and kept his covenant." (Deut. xxxiii. 9.)

7. THE CONSTANCY OF ITS PROFESSORS AND MARTYRS

But what shall we say respecting the constancy of the professors and martyrs, which they displayed in the torments that they endured for the truth of this doctrine? Indeed, if we subject this constancy to the view of the most inflexible enemies of the doctrine, we shall extort from unwilling judges a confession of its Divinity. But, that the strength of this argument may be placed in a clearer light, the mind must be directed to four particulars: the multitude of the martyrs, and their condition; the torments which their enemies inflicted on them, and the patience which they evinced in enduring them.

(1.) If we direct our inquiries to the multitude of them, it is innumerable, far exceeding thousands of thousands; on this account it is out of the power of any one to say, that, because it was the choice of but a few persons, it ought to be imputed to frenzy or to weariness of a life that was full of trouble.

(2.) If we inquire into their condition, we shall find nobles and peasants, those in authority and their subjects, the learned and the unlearned, the rich and the poor, the old and the young; persons of both sexes, men and women, the married and the unmarried, men of a hardy constitution and inured to dangers, and girls of tender habits who had been delicately educated, and whose feet had scarcely ever before stumbled against the smallest pebble that arose above the surface of their smooth and level path. Many of the early martyrs were honourable persons of this description, that no one might think them to be inflamed by a desire of glory, or endeavouring to gain applause by the perseverance and magnanimity that they had evinced in the maintenance of the sentiments which they had embraced.

(3.) Some of the torments inflicted on such a multitude of persons and of such various circumstances in life, were of a common sort, and others unusual, some of them quick in their operation and others of them slow. Part of the unoffending victims were nailed to crosses and part of them were decapitated; some were drowned in rivers, whilst others were roasted before a slow fire. Several were ground to powder by the teeth of wild beasts, or were torn in pieces by their fangs; many were sawn asunder, while others were stoned; and not a few of them were subjected to punishments which cannot be expressed, but which are accounted most disgraceful and infamous, on account of their extreme turpitude and indelicacy. No species of savage cruelty was omitted which either the ingenuity of human malignity could invent, which rage the most conspicuous and furious could excite, or which even the infernal labouratory of the court of hell could supply.

(4.) And yet, that we may come at once to the patience of these holy confessors, they bore all these tortures with constancy and equanimity; nay, they endured them with such a glad heart and cheerful countenance, as to fatigue even the restless fury of their persecutors, which has often been compelled, when wearied out, to yield to the unconquerable strength of their patience, and to confess itself completely vanquished. And what was the cause of all this endurance? It consisted in their unwillingness to recede in the least point from that religion, the denial of which was the only circumstance that might enable them to escape danger, and, in many instances, to acquire glory. What then was the reason of the great patience which they shewed under their acute sufferings? It was because they believed, that when this short life was ended, and after the pains and distresses which they were called to endure on earth, they would obtain a blessed immortality. In this particular the combat which God has maintained with Satan, appears to have resembled a duel; and the result of it has been, that the Divinity of God's word has been raised as a superstructure out of the infamy and ruin of Satan.

8. THE TESTIMONY OF THE CHURCH

The divine Omnipotence and Wisdom have principally employed these arguments, to prove the Divinity of this blessed word. But, that the Church might not defile herself by that basest vice, ingratitude of heart, and that she might perform a supplementary service in aid of God her Author and of Christ her Head, she also by her testimony adds to the Divinity of this word. But it is only an addition; she does not impart Divinity to it; her province is merely an indication of the Divine nature of this word, but she does not communicate to it the impress of Divinity. For unless this word had been Divine when there was no Church in existence, it would not have been possible for her members "to be born of this word, as of incorruptible seed," (1 Pet. i. 23,) to become the sons of God, and, through faith in this word, "to be made partakers of the Divine Nature." (2 Pet. i. 4.) The very name of "authority" takes away from the Church the power of conferring Divinity on this doctrine. For Authority is derived from an Author: But the Church is not the Author, she is only the nursling of this word, being posterior to it in cause, origin, and time. We do not listen to those who raise this objection: "The Church is of greater antiquity than the scripture, because at the time when that word had not been consigned to writing, the Church had even then an existence." To trifle in a serious matter with such cavils as this, is highly unbecoming in Christians, unless they have changed their former godly manners and are transformed into Jesuits. The Church is not more ancient than this saying: "The seed of the woman shall bruise the serpent's head ;" (Gen. iii. 15,) although she had an existence before this sentence was recorded by Moses in Scripture. For it was by the faith which they exercised on this saying, that Adam and Eve became the Church of God; since, prior to that, they were traitors, deserters and the kingdom of Satan-- that grand deserter and apostate. The Church is indeed the pillar of the truth, (1 Tim. iii. 15,) but it is built upon that truth as upon a foundation, and thus directs to the truth, and brings it forward into the sight of men. In this way the Church performs the part of a director and a witness to this truth, and its guardian, herald, and interpreter. But in her acts of interpretation, the Church is confined to the sense of the word itself, and is tied down to the expressions of Scripture: for, according to the prohibition of St. Paul, it neither becomes her to be wise above that which is written;" (1 Cor. iv. 6,) nor is it possible for her to be so, since she is hindered both by her own imbecility, and the depth of things divine.

But it will reward our labour, if in a few words we examine the efficacy of this testimony, since such is the pleasure of the Papists, who constitute "the authority of the Church" the commencement and the termination of our certainty, when she bears witness to the scripture that it is the word of God. In the first place, the efficacy of the testimony does not exceed the veracity of the witness. The veracity of the Church is the veracity of men. But the veracity of men is imperfect and inconstant, and is always such as to give occasion to this the remark of truth, "All men are liars." Neither is the veracity of him that speaks, sufficient to obtain credit to his testimony, unless the veracity of him who bears witness concerning the truth appear plain and evident to him to whom he makes the declaration. But in what manner will it be possible to make the veracity of the Church plain and evident? This must be done, either by a notion conceived , long time before, or by an impression recently made on the minds of the hearers. But men possess no such innate notion of the veracity of the Church as is tantamount to that which declares, "God is true and cannot lie." (Tit. i. 2.) It is necessary, therefore, that it be impressed by some recent action; such impression being made either from within or from without. But the Church is not able to make any inward impression, for she bears her testimony by external instruments alone, and does not extend to the inmost parts of the soul. The impression, therefore, will be external; which can be no other than a display and indication of her knowledge and probity, as well as testimony, often truly so called. But all these things can produce nothing more than an opinion in the minds of those to whom they are offered. Opinion, therefore, and not knowledge, is the supreme effect of this efficacy.

But the Papists retort, "that Christ himself established the authority of his Church by this saying,

"He that heareth you, heareth me." (Luke x. 16.) When these unhappy reasoners speak thus, they seem not to be aware that they are establishing the authority of Scripture before that of the Church. For it is necessary that credence should be given to that expression as it was pronounced by Christ, before any authority can, on its account, be conceded to the Church. But the same reason will be as tenable in respect to the whole Scripture as to this expression. Let the Church then be content with that honour which Christ conferred on her when he made her the guardian of his word, and appointed her to be the director and witness to it, the herald and the interpreter.

III. Yet since the arguments arising from all those observations which we have hitherto adduced, and from any others which are calculated to prove the Divinity of the scriptures, can neither disclose to us a right understanding of the scriptures, nor seal on our minds those meanings which we have understood, (although the certainty of faith which God demands from us, and requires us to exercise in his word, consists of these meanings,) it is a necessary consequence, that to all these things ought to be added something else, by the efficacy of which that certainty may be produced in our minds. And this is the very subject on which we are not prepared to treat in this the third part of our discourse

9. THE INTERNAL WITNESS OF THE HOLY SPIRIT

We declare, therefore, and we continue to repeat the declaration, till the gates of hell re-echo the sound, "that the Holy Spirit, by whose inspiration holy men of God have spoken this word, and by whose impulse and guidance they have, as his amanuenses, consigned it to writing; that this Holy Spirit is the author of that light by the aid of which we obtain a perception and an understanding of the divine meanings of the word, and is the Effector of that Certainty by which we believe those meaning to be truly divine; and that He is the necessary Author, the all sufficient Effector." (1.) Scripture demonstrates that He is the necessary Author, when it says, "The things of God knoweth no man but the Spirit of God. (1 Cor. ii. 11.) No man can say that Jesus is the Lord, but by the Holy Ghost." (1 Cor. xii. 3.) (2.) But the Scripture introduced him as the sufficient and the more than sufficient Effector, when it declares, "The wisdom which God ordained before the world unto our glory, he hath revealed unto us by his Spirit; for the Spirit searcheth all things, yea, the deep things of God." (1 Cor. ii. 7, 10.) The sufficiency, therefore, of the Spirit proceeds from the plenitude of his knowledge of the secrets of God, and from the very efficacious revelation which he makes of them. This sufficiency of the Spirit cannot be more highly extolled than it is in a subsequent passage, in which the same apostle most amply commends it, by declaring, "he that is spiritual [a partaker of this revelation,] judgeth all things," (verse 15,) as having the mind of Christ through his Spirit, which he has received. Of the same sufficiency the Apostle St. John is the most illustrious herald. In his general Epistle he writes these words: "But the anointing which ye have received of Him, abideth in you; and ye need not that any man teach you; but as the same anointing teacheth you of all things, and is truth, and is no lie, and even as it hath taught you, ye shall abide in Him." (1 John ii. 27.) "He that believeth on the Son of God, hath the witness in himself." (1 John v. 10.) To the Thessalonians another apostle writes thus: "Our Gospel came not unto you in word only, but also in power, and in the Holy Ghost, and in much assurance. (1 Thess. i. 3.) In this passage he openly attributes to the power of the Holy Ghost the Certainty by which the faithful receive the word of the gospel. The Papists reply, "Many persons boast of the revelation of the Spirit, who, nevertheless, are destitute of such a revelation. It is impossible, therefore, for the faithful safely to rest in it." Are these fair words? Away with such blasphemy! If the Jews glory in their Talmud and their Cabala, and the Mahometans in their Alcoran, and if both of these boast themselves that they are Churches, cannot credence therefore be given with sufficient safety to the scriptures of the Old and New Testaments, when they affirm their Divine Origin? Will the true Church be any less a Church because the sons of the stranger arrogate that title to themselves? This is the distinction between opinion and knowledge. It is their opinion, that they know that of which they are really ignorant. But they who do know it, have an assured perception of their knowledge. "It is the Spirit that beareth witness that the Spirit is truth" (1 John v. 8,) that is, the doctrine and the meanings comprehended in that doctrine, are truth."

"But that attesting witness of the Spirit which is revealed in us, cannot convince others of the truth of the Divine word." What then? It will convince them when it has also breathed on them: it will breathe its Divine afflatus on them, if they be the sons of the church, all of whom shall be taught of God: every man of them will hear and learn of the Father, and will come unto Christ." (John vi. 45.) Neither can the testimony of any Church convince all men of the truth and divinity of the sacred writings. The Papists, who arrogate to themselves exclusively the title of "the Church," experience the small degree of credit which is given to their testimonies, by those who have not received an afflatus from the spirit of the Roman See.

"But it is necessary that there should be a testimony in the Church of such a high character as to render it imperative on all men to pay it due deference." True. It was the incumbent duty of the Jews to pay deference to the testimony of Christ when he was speaking to them; the Pharisees ought not to have contradicted Stephen in the midst of his discourse; and Jews and Gentiles, without any exception, were bound to yield credence to the preaching of the apostles, confirmed as it was by so many and such astonishing miracles. But the duties here recited, were disregarded by all these parties. What was the reason of this their neglect? The voluntary hardening of their hearts, and that blindness of their minds, which was introduced by the Devil.

If the Papists still contend, that "such a testimony as this ought to exist in the Church, against which no one shall actually offer any contradiction," we deny the assertion. And experience testifies, that a testimony of this kind never yet had an existence, that it does not now exist, and (if we may form our judgment from the scriptures,) we certainly think that it never will exist.

"But perhaps the Holy Ghost, who is the Author and Effector of this testimony, has entered into an engagement with the Church, not to inspire and seal on the minds of men this certainty, except through her, and by the intervention of her authority." The Holy Ghost does, undoubtedly, according to the good pleasure of his own will, make use of some organ or instrument in performing these his offices. But this instrument is the word of God, which is comprehended in the sacred books of scripture; an instrument produced and brought forward by Himself, and instructed in his truth. The Apostle to the Hebrews in a most excellent manner describes the efficacy which is impressed on this instrument by the Holy Spirit, in these words: "For the word of God is quick and powerful, and sharper than any two edged sword, piercing even to the dividing asunder of soul and spirit, and of the joints and marrow, and is a discerner of the thoughts and intents of the heart." (Heb. iv, 10.) Its effect is called "Faith," by the Apostle. "Faith cometh by hearing, and hearing by the word of God." (Rom. x. 7.) If any act of the Church occurs in this place, it is that by which she is occupied in the sincere preaching of this word, and by which she sedulously exercises herself in promoting its publication. But even this is not so properly the occupation of the Church, as of "the Apostles, Prophets, Evangelists, Pastors and Teachers," whom Christ has constituted his labourers "for the edifying of his body, which is the Church.'" (Ephes. iv. 11.) But we must in this place deduce an observation from the very nature of things in genera], as well as of this thing in particular; it is, that the First Cause can extend much farther by its own action, than it is possible for an instrumental cause to do; and that the Holy Ghost gives to the word all that force which he afterwards employs, such being the great efficacy with which it is endued and applied, that whomsoever he only counsels by his word he himself persuades by imparting Divine meanings to the word, by enlightening the mind as with a lamp, and by inspiring and sealing it by his own immediate action. The Papists pretend, that certain acts are necessary to the production of true faith; and they say that those acts cannot be performed except by the judgment and testimony of the Church--such as to believe that any book is the production of Matthew or Luke--to discern between a Canonical and an Apocryphal verse, and to distinguish between this or that reading, according to the variation in different copies. But, since there is a controversy concerning the weight and necessity of those acts, and since the dispute is no less than how far they may be performed by the Church-- lest I should fatigue my most illustrious auditory by two great prolixity, I will omit at present any further mention of these topics; and will by Divine assistance explain them at some future opportunity.

My most illustrious and accomplished hearers, we have already perceived, that both the pages of our sacred Theology are full of God and Christ, and of the Spirit of both of them. If any inquiry be made for the Object, God and Christ by the Spirit are pointed out to us. If we search for the Author, God and Christ by the operation of the Spirit spontaneously occur. If we consider the End proposed, our union with God and Christ offers itself--an end not to be obtained except through the communication of the Spirit. If we inquire concerning the Truth and Certainty of the doctrine; God in Christ, by means of the efficacy of the Holy Ghost, most clearly convinces our minds of the Truth, and in a very powerful manner seals the Certainty on our hearts.

All the glory, therefore, of this revelation is deservedly due to God and Christ in the Holy Spirit: and most deservedly are thanks due from us to them, and must be given to them, through the Holy Ghost, for such an august and necessary benefit as this which they have conferred on us. But we can present to our God and Christ in the Holy Spirit no gratitude more grateful, and can ascribe no glory more glorious, than this, the application of our minds to an assiduous contemplation and a devout meditation on the knowledge of such a noble object. But in our meditations upon it, (to prevent us from straying into the paths of error,) let us betake ourselves to the revelation which has been made of this doctrine. From the word of this revelation alone, let us learn the wisdom of endeavouring, by an ardent desire and in an unwearied course, to attain unto that ultimate design which ought to be our constant aim--that most blessed end of our union with God and Christ. Let us never indulge in any doubts concerning the truth of this revelation; but, "the full assurance of faith being impressed upon our minds and hearts by the inspiration and sealing of the Holy Spirit, let us adhere to this word, "till[at length] we all come in the unity of the faith and of the knowledge of the Son of God, unto a perfect man, unto the measure of the stature of the fullness of Christ." (Ephes. iv. 13.) I most humbly supplicate and intreat God our merciful Father, that he would be pleased to grant this great blessing to us, through the Son of his love, and by the communication of his Holy Spirit. And to him be ascribed all praise, and honour, and glory, forever and ever. Amen.

ORATION IV

THE PRIESTHOOD OF CHRIST

The Noble the Lord Rector--the Very Famous, Reverend, Skillful, Intelligent, and Learned Men, who are the Fathers of this Most Celebrated University--the Rest of You, Most Worthy Strangers of Every Degree--and You, Most Noble and Studious Young Men, who are the Nursery of the Republic and the Church, and who are Increasing Every Day in Bloom and vigour:

If there be any order of men in whom it is utterly unbecoming to aspire after the honours of this world, especially after those honours which are accompanied by pomp and applause, that, without doubt, is the order ecclesiastical--a body of men who ought to be entirely occupied with a zeal for God, and for the attainment of that glory which is at his disposal. Yet, since, according to the laudable institutions of our ancestors, the usage has obtained in all well regulated Universities, to admit no man to the office of instructor in them, who has not previously signalized himself by some public and solemn testimony of probity and scientific ability--this sacred order of men have not refused a compliance with such public modes of decision, provided they be conducted in a way that is holy, decorous, and according to godliness. So far, indeed, are those who have been set apart to the pastoral office from being averse to public proceedings of this kind, that they exceedingly covet and desire them alone, because they conceive them to be of the first necessity to the Church of Christ. For they are mindful of this apostolical charge, "Lay hands suddenly on no man ;" (1 Tim. v. 29,) and of the other, which directs that a Bishop and a Teacher of the Church be "apt to teach, holding fast the faithful word as he hath been taught, that he may be able, by sound doctrine, both to exhort and to convince the gainsayers." (Tit. i. 9.) I do not, therefore, suppose one person, in this numerous assembly, can be so ignorant of the public ceremonies of this University, or can hold them in such little estimation, as either to evince surprise at the undertaking in which we are now engaged, or wish to give it an unfavourable interpretation. But since it has always been a part of the custom of our ancestors, in academic festivities of this description, to choose some subject of discourse, the investigation of which in the fear of the Lord might promote the Divine glory and the profit of the hearers, and might excite them to pious and importunate supplication, I also can perceive no cause why I ought not conscientiously to comply with this custom. And although at the sight of this very respectable, numerous and learned assembly, I feel strongly affected with a sense of my defective eloquence and tremble not a little, yet I have selected a certain theme for my discourse which agrees well with my profession, and is full of grandeur, sublimnity and adorable majesty. In making choice of it, I have not been overawed by the edict of Horace, which says,

"Select, all ye who write, a subject fit, A subject not too mighty for your wit! And ere you lay your shoulders to the wheel, Weigh well their strength, and all their wetness feel!"

For this declaration is not applicable in the least to theological subjects, all of which by their dignity and importance exceed the capacity and mental energy of every human being, and of angels themselves. A view of them so affected the Apostle Paul, (who, rapt up into the third heaven, had heard words ineffable,) that they compelled him to break forth into this exclamation: "Who is sufficient for these things," (2 Cor. ii. 16.) If, therefore, I be not permitted to disregard the provisions of this Horatian statute, I must either transgress the boundaries of my profession, or be content to remain silent. But I am permitted to disregard the terms of this statute; and to do so, is perfectly lawful.

For whatever things tend to the glory of God and to the salvation of men, ought to be celebrated in a devout spirit in the congregations of the saints, and to be proclaimed with a grateful voice. I therefore propose to speak on THE PRIESTHOOD OF CHRIST: Not because I have persuaded myself of my capability to declare anything concerning it, which is demanded either by the dignity of my subject, or by the respectability of this numerous assembly; for it will be quite sufficient, and I shall consider that I have abundantly discharged my duty, if according to the necessity of the case I shall utter something that will contribute to the general edification: But I choose this theme that I may obtain, in behalf of my oration, such grace and favour from the excellence of its subject, as I cannot possibly confer on it by any eloquence in the mode of my address. Since, however, it is impossible for us either to form in our minds just and holy conceptions about such a sublime mystery, or to give utterance to them with our lips, unless the power of God influence our mental faculties and our tongues, let us by prayer and supplication implore his present aid, in the name of Jesus Christ our great High Priest. "Do thou, therefore, O holy and merciful God, the Father of our Lord Jesus Christ, the Fountain of all grace and truth, vouchsafe to grant thy favourable presence to us who are a great congregation assembled together in thy holy name. Sprinkle thou our spirits, souls, and bodies, with the most gracious dew of thy immeasurable holiness, that the converse of thy saints with each other may be pleasing to thee. Assist us by the grace of thy Holy Spirit, who may yet more and more illuminate our minds--imbued with the true knowledge of Thyself and thy Son; may He also inflame our hearts with a sincere zeal for thy glory; may He open my mouth and guide my tongue, that I may be enabled to declare concerning the Priesthood of thy Son those things which are true and just and holy, to the glory of thy name and to the gathering of all of us together in the Lord. Amen."

Having now in an appropriate manner offered up those vows which well become the commencement of our undertaking, we will, by the help of God, proceed to the subject posed, after I have intreated all of you, who have been pleased to grace this solemn act of ours with your noble, learned and most gratifying presence, to give me that undivided attention which the subject deserves, while I speak on a matter of the most serious importance, and, according to your accustomed kindness, to shew me that favour and benevolence which are to me of the greatest necessity. That I may not abuse your patience, I engage to consult brevity as much as our theme will allow. But we must begin with the very first principles of Priesthood, that from thence the discourse may appropriately be brought down to the Priesthood of Christ, on which we profess to treat.

First. The first of those relations which subsist between God and men, has respect to something given and something received. The latter requires another relation supplementary to itself--a relation which taking its commencement from men, may terminate in God; and that is, an acknowledgment of a benefit received, to the honour of the munificent Donor. It is also a debt, due on account of a benefit already conferred, but which is not to be paid except on the demand and according to the regulation of the Giver; whose intention it has always been, that the will of a creature should not be the measure of his honour. His benignity likewise is so immense, that he never requires from those who are under obligations to him, the grateful acknowledgment of the benefit communicated in the first instance, except when he has bound them to himself by the larger, and far superior benefit, of a mutual covenant. But the extreme trait in that goodness, is, that he has bound himself to bestow on the same persons favours of yet greater excellence by infinite degrees. This is the order which he adopts; he wishes himself first to be engaged to them, before they are considered to be engaged to Him. For every covenant; that is concluded between God and men, consists of two parts: (1.) The preceding promise of God, by which he obliges himself to some duty and to acts correspondent with that duty: and (2.) The subsequent definition and appointment of the duty, which, it is stipulated, shall in return be required of men, and according to which a mutual correspondence subsists between men and God. He promises, that he will be to them a king and a God, and that he will discharge towards them all the offices of a good King; while he stipulates, as a counter obligation, that they become his people, that in this relation they live according to his commands and that they ask and expect all blessings from his goodness. These two acts--a life according to his commands, and an expectation of all blessings from his goodness--comprise the duty of men towards God, according to the covenant into which he first entered with them.

On the whole, therefore, the duties of two functions are to be performed between God and men who have entered into covenant with him: First, a regal one, which is of supreme authority: Secondly, a religious one, of devoted submission.

(1.) The use of the former is in the communication of every needful good, and in the imposing of laws or the act of legislation. Under it we likewise comprehend the gift of prophecy, which is nothing more than the annunciation of the royal pleasure, whether it be communicated by God himself, or by some one of his deputies or ambassadors as a kind of internuncio to the covenant. That no one may think the prophetic office, of which the scriptures make such frequent mention, is a matter of little solicitude to us, we assign it the place of a substitute under the Chief Architect.

(2.) But the further consideration of the regal duty being at present omitted, we shall proceed to a nearer inspection of that which is religious.. We have already deduced its origin from the act of covenanting; we have propounded it, in the exercise of the regal office, as something that is due; and we place its proper action in thanksgiving and intreaty. This action is required to be religiously performed, according to their common vocation, by every one of the great body of those who are in covenant; and to this end they have been sanctified by the word of the covenant, and have all been constituted priests to God, that they might offer gifts and prayers to The Most High. But since God loves order, he who is himself the only instance of order in its perfection, willed that, out of the number of those who were sanctified, some one should in a peculiar manner be separated to him; that he who was thus set apart should, by a special and extraordinary vocation, be qualified for the office of the priesthood; and that, approaching more intimately and with greater freedom to the throne of God, he should, in the place of his associates in the same covenant and religion, take the charge and management of whatever affairs

43

were to be transacted before God on their account.

From this circumstance is to be traced the existence of the office of the priesthood, the duties of which were to be discharged before God in behalf of others--an office undoubtedly of vast dignity and of special honour among mankind. Although the priest must be taken from among men, and must be appointed in their behalf, yet it does not appertain to men themselves, to designate whom they will to sustain that office; neither does it belong to any one to arrogate that honour to himself. But as the office itself is an act of the divine pleasure, so likewise the choice of the person who must discharge its duties, rests with God himself: and it was his will, that the office should be fulfilled by him who for some just reason held precedence among his kindred by consanguinity. This was the father and master of the family, and his successor was the first born. We have examples of this in the holy patriarchs, both before and after the deluge. We behold this expressly in Noah, Abraham, and Job. There are also those, (not occupying the lowest seats in judgment,) who say that Cain and Abel brought their sacrifices to Adam their father, that he might offer them to the Lord; and they derive this opinion from the word aykh used in the same passage. Though these examples are selected from the description of that period when sin had made its entrance into the world, yet a confirmation of their truth is obtained in this primitive institution of the human race, of which we are now treating. For it is peculiar to that period, that all the duties of the priesthood were confined within the act of offering only an eucharistic sacrifice and supplications. Having therefore in due form executed these functions, the priest, in the name of his compeers, was by the appeased Deity admitted to a familiar intercourse with Him, and obtained from Him a charge to execute among his kindred, in the name of God himself, and as "the messenger, or angel, of the Lord of Hosts." For the Lord revealed to him the Divine will and pleasure; that, on returning from his intercourse with God, he might declare it to the people. This will of God consisted of two parts: (1.) That which he required to be performed by his covenant people; and (2.) That which it was his wish to perform for their benefit. In this charge, which was committed to the priest, to be executed by him, the administration of prophecy was also included; on which account it is said, "They should seek the LAW at the mouth of the priest, for he is the messenger of the Lord of Hosts." (Mal. ii. 7.) And since that second part of the Divine will was to be proclaimed from an assured trust and confidence in the truth of the Divine promises, and with a holy and affectionate feeling toward his own species--in that view, he was invested with a commission to dispense benedictions. In this manner, discharging the duties of a double embassy, (that of men to God, and that of God to men,) he acted, on both sides, the part of a Mediator of the covenant into which the parties had mutually entered. Nevertheless, not content with having conferred this honour on him whom he had sanctified, our God, all-bountiful, elevated him likewise to the delegated or vicarious dignity of the regal office, that he, bearing the image of God among his brethren, might then be able to administer justice to them in His Name, and might manage, for their common benefit, those affairs with which he was entrusted. From this source arose what may be considered the native union of the Priestly and the Kingly offices, which also obtained among the holy patriarchs after the entrance of sin, and of which express mention is made in the person of Melchizedec. This was signified in a general manner by the patriarch Jacob, when he declared Reuben, his first born son, to be "the excellency of dignity and the excellency of power," which were his due on account of the right of primogeniture. For certain reasons, however, the kingly functions were afterwards separated from the priestly, by the will of God, who, dividing them into two parts among his people the children of Israel, transferred the kingly office to Judah and the priestly to Levi.

But it was proper, that this approach to God, through the oblation of an eucharistic sacrifice and prayers, should be made with a pure mind, holy affections, and with hands, as well as the other members of the body, free from defilement. This was required, even before the first transgression. "Sanctify yourselves, and be ye holy; for I the Lord your God am holy." (Lev. xix. 2, &c.) "God heareth not sinners." (John ix. 31.) "Bring no more vain oblations, for your hands are full of blood." (Isa. i. 15). The will of God respecting this is constant and perpetual. But Adam, who was the first man and the first priest, did not long administer his office in a becoming manner; for, refusing to obey God, he tasted the fruit of the forbidden tree; and, by that foul crime of disobedience and revolt, he at once defiled his soul which had been sanctified to God, and his body. By this wicked deed he both lost all right to the priesthood, and was in reality deprived of it by the Divine sentence, which was clearly signified by his expulsion from Paradise, where he had appeared before God in that which was a type of His own dwelling-place. This was in accordance with the invariable rule of Divine Justice: "Be it far from me, [that thou shouldst any longer discharge before me the duties of the priesthood:] for them that honour me, I will honour; and they that despise me, shall be lightly esteemed." (1 Sam. ii. 30.) But he did not fall alone: All whose persons he at that time represented and whose cause he pleaded, (although they had not then come into existence,) were with him cast down from the elevated summit of such a high dignity. Neither did they fall from the priesthood only, but likewise from the covenant, of which the priest was both the Mediator and the Internuncio; and God ceased to be the King and God of men, and men were no longer recognized as his people. The existence of the priesthood itself was at an end; for there was no one capable of fulfilling its duties according to the design of that covenant. The eucharistic sacrifice, the invocation of the name of God, and the gracious communication between God and men, all ceased together.

Most miserable, and deserving of the deepest commiseration, was the condition of mankind in that state of their affairs, if this declaration be a true one, "Happy is the people whose God is the Lord !" (Psalm cxliv. 15.) And this inevitable misery would have rested upon Adam and his race for ever, had not Jehovah, full of mercy and commiseration, deigned to receive them into favour, and resolved to enter into another covenant with the same parties; not according to that which they had transgressed, and which was then become obsolete and had been abolished; but into a new covenant of grace. But the Divine justice and truth could not permit this to be done, except through the agency of an umpire and surety, who might undertake the part of a Mediator between the offended God and sinners. Such a Mediator could not then approach to God with an eucharistic sacrifice for benefits conferred upon the human race, or with prayers which might intreat only for a continuance and an increase of them: But he had to approach into the Divine presence to offer sacrifice for the act of hostility which they had committed against God by transgressing his commandment, and to offer prayers for obtaining the remission of their transgressions. Hence arose the necessity of an Expiatory Sacrifice; and, on that account, a new priesthood was to be instituted, by the operation of which the sin that had been committed might be expiated, and access to the throne of God's grace might be granted to man through a sinner: this is the priesthood which belongs to our Christ, the Anointed One, alone.

But God, who is the Supremely Wise Disposer of times and seasons, would not permit the discharge of the functions appertaining to this priesthood to commence immediately after the formation of the world, and the introduction of sin. It was his pleasure, that the necessity of it should be first correctly understood and appreciated, by a conviction on men's consciences of the multitude, heinousness and aggravated nature of their sins. It was also his will, that the minds of men should be affected with a serious and earnest desire for it, yet so that they might in the mean time be supported against despair, arising from a consciousness of their sins, which could not be removed except by means of that Divine priesthood, the future commencement of which inspired them with hope and confidence. All these purposes God effected by the temporary institution of that typical priesthood, the duties of which infirm and sinful men "after the law of a carnal commandment" could perform, by the immolation of beasts sanctified for that service; which priesthood was at first established in different parts of the world, and afterwards among the Israelites, who were specially elected to be a sacerdotal nation. When the blood of beasts was shed, in which was their life, (Lev. xvii. 14) the people contemplated, in the death of the animals, their own demerits, for the beasts had not sinned that they by death should be punished as victims for transgression. After investigating this subject with greater diligence, and deliberately weighing it in the equal balances of their judgment, they plainly perceived and understood that their sins could not possibly be expiated by those sacrifices, which were of a species different from their own, and more despicable and mean than human beings. From these premises they must of necessity have concluded, that, notwithstanding they offered those animals, they in such an act delivered to God nothing less than their own bond, sealing it in his presence with an acknowledgment of their personal sins, and confessing the debt which they had incurred. Yet, because these sacrifices were of Divine Institution, and because God received them at the hands of men as incense whose odour was fragrant and agreeable, from these circumstances the offenders conceived the hope of obtaining favour and pardon, reasoning thus within themselves, as did Sampson's mother: "If the Lord were pleased to kill us, he would not have received burnt-offering and a meat-offering at our hands." (Judges xiii. 23.) With such a hope they strengthened their spirits that were ready to faint, and, confiding in the Divine promise, they expected in all the ardour of desire the dispensation of a priesthood which was prefigured under the typical one; "searching what, or what manner of time, the Spirit of Christ which was in them did signify, when it testified beforehand the Sufferings of Christ, and the Glory that should follow." (1 Pet. i. 11.) But, since the mind pants after the very delightful consideration of this priesthood, our oration hastens towards it; and, having some regard to the lateness of the hour, and wishing not to encroach on your comfort, we shall omit any further allusion to that branch of the priesthood which has hitherto occupied our attention.

Secondly. In discoursing on the Priesthood of Christ, we will confine our observations to three points; and, on condition that you receive the succeeding part of my oration with that kindness and attention which you have hitherto manifested, and which I still hope and desire to receive, we will describe: First. The Imposing of the Office. Secondly. Its Execution and Administration. And Thirdly. The Fruits of the Office thus Administered, and the Utility Which We Derive From It.

I. In respect to the Imposing of the Office, the subject itself presents us with three topics to be discussed in order. (1.) The person who imposes it. (2.) The person on whom it is imposed, or to whom it is entrusted. And (3.) The manner of his appointment, and of his undertaking this charge.

1. The person imposing it is God, the Father of our Lord Jesus Christ. Since this act of imposing belongs to the economy and dispensation of our salvation, the persons who are comprised under this one

Divine Monarchy are to be distinctly considered according to the rule of the scriptures, which ought to have the precedence in this inquiry, and according to the rules and guidance of the orthodox Fathers that agree with those scriptures. It is J EHOVAH who imposes this office, and who, while the princes of darkness fret themselves and rage in vain, says to his Messiah, "Thou art my Son; this day have I begotten thee. Ask of me, and I shall give thee the Heathen for thine inheritance, and the uttermost parts of the earth for thy possession." (Psalm ii. 8.) He it is who, when he commanded Messiah to sit at his right hand, repeated his holy and revered word with an oath, saying, "Thou art a Priest forever after the order of Melchizedec." (Psalm cx. 4.) This is He who imposes the office, and that by a right the most just and deserved. For "with him we have to do, who, dwelling in the light unto which no man can approach," remains continually in the seat of his Majesty. He preserves his own authority safe and unimpaired to himself, "without any abasement or lessening of his person," as the voice of antiquity expresses it; and retains entire, within himself, the right of demanding satisfaction from the sinner for the injuries which He has sustained. From this right he has not thought fit to recede, or to resign any part of it, on account of the rigid inflexibility of his justice, according to which he hates iniquity and does not permit a wicked person to dwell in his presence. This, therefore, is the Divine Person in whose hands rest both the right and the power of imposition; the fact of his having also the will, is decided by the very act of imposition.

But an inquiry must be made into the Cause of this imposition which we shall not find, except, first, in the conflict between justice and gracious mercy; and, afterwards, in their amicable agreement, or rather their junction by means of wisdom's conciliating assistance.

(1.) Justice demanded, on her part, the punishment due to her from a sinful creature; and this demand she the more rigidly enforced, by the greater equity with which she had threatened it, and the greater truth with which it had been openly foretold and declared.

Gracious Mercy, like a pious mother, moving with bowels of commiseration, desired to avert that punishment in which was placed the extreme misery of the creature. For she thought that, though the remission of that punishment was not due to the cause of it, yet such a favour ought to be granted to her by a right of the greatest equity; because it is one of her chief properties to "rejoice against judgment." (James ii. 13.)

Justice, tenacious of her purpose, rejoined, that the throne of grace, she must confess, was sublimely elevated above the tribunal of justice: but she could not bear with patient indifference that no regard should be paid to her, and her suit not to be admitted, while the authority of managing the whole affair was to be transferred to mercy. Since, however, it was a part of the oath administered to justice when she entered into office, "that she should render to every one his own," she would yield entirely to mercy, provided a method could be devised by which her own inflexibility could be declared, as well as the excess of her hatred to sin.

(2.) But to find out that method, was not the province of Mercy. It was necessary, therefore, to call in the aid of Wisdom to adjust the mighty difference, and to reconcile by an amicable union those two combatants that were, in God, the supreme protectresses of all equity and goodness. Being called upon, she came, and at once discovered a method, and affirmed that it was possible to render to each of them that which belonged to her; for if the punishment due to sin appeared desirable to Justice and odious to Mercy, it might be transmuted into an expiatory sacrifice, the oblation of which, on account of the voluntary suffering of death, (which is the punishment adjudged to sin,) might appease Justice, and open such a way for Mercy as she had desired. Both of them instantly assented to this proposal, and made a decree according to the terms of agreement settled by Wisdom, their common arbitrator.

2. But, that we may come to the Second Point, a priest was next to be sought, to offer the sacrifice: For that was a function of the priesthood. A sacrifice was likewise to be sought; and with this condition annexed to it, that the same person should be both priest and sacrifice. This was required by the plan of the true priesthood and sacrifice, from which the typical and symbolical greatly differs. But in the different orders of creatures neither sacrifice nor priest could be found.

It was not possible for an angel to become a priest; because "he was to be taken from among men and to be ordained from men in things pertaining to God." (Heb. v. 1.) Neither could an angel be a sacrifice; because it was not just that the death of an angel should be an expiation for a crime which a man had perpetrated: And if this had even been most proper, yet man could never have been induced to believe that an angelical sacrifice had been offered by an angel for him, or, if it had been so offered, that it was of the least avail. Application was then to be made to men themselves. But, among them, not one could be found in whom it would have been a becoming act to execute the office of the priesthood, and who had either ability or inclination for the undertaking. For all men were sinners; all were terrified with a consciousness of their delinquency; and all were detained captive under the tyranny of sin and Satan. It was not lawful for a sinner to approach to God, who is pure Light, for the purpose of offering sacrifice; because, being affrighted by his own internal perception of his crime, he could not support a sight of the countenance of an incensed God, before whom it was still necessary that he should appear. Being placed under the dominion of sin and Satan, he was neither willing, nor had he the power to will, to execute an office, the duties of which were to be discharged for the benefit of others, out of love to them. The same consideration likewise tends to the rejection of every human sacrifice. Yet the priest was to be taken from among men, and the oblation to God was to consist of a human victim.

In this state of affairs, the assistance of Wisdom was again required in the Divine Council. She declared that a man must be born from among men, who might have a nature in common with the rest of his brethren, that, being in all things tempted as they were, he might be able to sympathize with others in their sufferings; and yet, that he should neither be reckoned in the order of the rest, nor should be made man according to the law of the primitive creation and benediction; that he should not be under dominion of sin; that he should be one in whom Satan could find nothing worthy of condemnation, who should not be tormented by a consciousness of sin, and who should not even know sin, that is, one who should be "born in the likeness of sinful flesh, and yet without sin. For such a high priest became us, who is holy, harmless, undefiled and separate from sinners." (Heb. vii. 26.) But, that he might have a community of nature with men, he ought to be born of a human being; and, that he might have no participation in crime with them, but might be holy, he ought to be conceived by the Holy Ghost, because sanctification is his proper work. By the Holy Spirit, the nativity which was above and yet according to nature, might through the virtue of the mystery, restore nature, as it surpassed her in the transcendent excellence of the miracle. But the dignity of this priesthood was greater, and its functions more weighty and important, than man even in his pure state was competent to sustain or discharge. The benefits also to be obtained by it, infinitely exceeded the value of man when in his greatest state of purity. Therefore, the Word of God, who from the beginning was with God, and by whom the worlds, and all things visible and invisible, were created, ought himself to be made flesh, to undertake the office of the priesthood, and to offer his own flesh to God as a sacrifice for the life of the world. We now have the person who was entrusted with the priesthood, and to whom the province was assigned of atoning for the common offense: It is Jesus Christ, the Son of God and of man, a high priest of such great excellence, that the transgression whose demerits have obtained this mighty Redeemer, might almost seem to have been a happy circumstance.

3. Let us proceed to the mode of its being imposed or undertaken. This mode is according to covenant, which, on God's part, received an oath for its confirmation. As it is according to covenant, it becomes a solemnity appointed by God, with whom rests the appointment to the priesthood. For the Levitical priesthood was conferred on Levi according to covenant, as the Lord declares by the prophet Malachi: "My covenant was with him of life and peace." (ii, 5.) It is, however, peculiar to this priesthood of Christ, that the covenant on which it is founded, was confirmed by an oath. Let us briefly consider each of them.

The covenant into which God entered with our High Priest, Jesus Christ, consisted, on the part of God, of the demand of an action to be performed, and of the promise of an immense remuneration. On the part of Christ, our High Priest, it consisted of an accepting of the Promise, and a voluntary engagement to Perform the Action. First, God required of him, that he should lay down his soul as a victim in sacrifice for sin, (Isa. liii. 11,) that he should give his flesh for the light of the world, (John vi. 51,) and that he should pay the price of redemption for the sins and the captivity of the human race. God "promised" that, if he performed all this, "he should see a seed whose days should be prolonged," (Isa. liii. 11,) and that he should be himself "an everlasting Priest after the order of Melchizedec," (cx, 4,) that is, he should, by the discharge of his priestly functions, be elevated to the regal dignity. Secondly, Christ, our High Priest, accepted of these conditions, and permitted the province to be assigned to him of atoning for our transgressions, exclaiming "Lo, I come that I may do thy will, O my God." (Psalm xl. 8.) But he accepted them under a stipulation, that, on completing his great undertaking, he should forever enjoy the honour of a priesthood similar to that of Melchizedec, and that, being placed on his royal throne, he might, as King of Righteousness and Prince of Peace, rule in righteousness the people subject to his sway, and might dispense peace to his people. He, therefore, "for the joy that was set before him, endured the cross, despising the shame," (Heb. xii. 2,) that, "being anointed with the oil of gladness above his fellows," (Psalm xlv. 7,) he might sit forever in the throne of equity at the right hand of the throne of God.

Great, indeed, was the condescension of the all-powerful God in being willing to treat with our High Priest rather in the way of covenant, than by a display of his authority. And strong were the pious affections of our High Priest, who did not refuse to take upon himself, on our account, the discharge of those difficult and arduous duties which were full of pain, trouble, and misery. Most glorious act, performed by thee, O Christ, who art infinite in goodness! Thou great High Priest, accept of the honours due to thy pious affection, and continue in that way to proceed to glory, to the complete consecration of our salvation! For it was the will of God, that the duties of the office should be administered from a voluntary and disinterested zeal and affection for his glory and the salvation of sinners; and it was a deed worthy of his abundant benignity, to recompense with a large reward the voluntary promptitude which Christ exhibited.

God added an oath to the covenant, both for the purpose of confirming it, and as a demonstration of the dignity and unchangeable nature of that priesthood. Though the constant and unvarying veracity of God's nature might very properly set aside the necessity of an oath, yet as he had conformed to the customs of men in their method of solemnizing agreements, it was his pleasure by an oath to confirm his covenant; that our High Priest, relying in assured hope on the two-fold and immovable anchor of the promise and of the oath, "might despise the shame and endure the cross." The immutability and perpetuity of this priesthood have been pointed out by the oath which was added to the covenant. For whatever that be which God confirms by an oath, it is something eternal and immutable.

But it may be asked, "Are not all the words which God speaks, all the promises which he makes, and all the covenants into which he enters, of the same nature, even when they are unaccompanied by the sanctity of an oath ," Let me be permitted to describe the difference between the two cases here stated, and to prove it by an important example. There are two methods or plans by which it might be possible for man to arrive at a state of righteousness before God, and to obtain life from him. The one is according to righteousness through the law, by works and "of debt;" the other is according to mercy through the gospel, "by grace, and through faith:" These two methods are so constituted as not to allow both of them to be in a course of operation at the same time; but they proceed on the principle, that when the first of them is made void, a vacancy may be created for the second. In the beginning, therefore, it was the will of God to prescribe to man the first of these methods; which arrangement was required by his righteousness and the primitive institution of mankind. But it was not his pleasure to deal strictly with man according to the process of that legal covenant, and peremptorily to pronounce a destructive sentence against him in conformity with the rigor of the law. Wherefore, he did not subjoin an oath to that covenant, lest such an addition should have served to point out its immutability, a quality which God would not permit it to possess. The necessary consequence of this was, that when the first covenant was made void through sin, a vacancy was created by the good pleasure of God for another and a better covenant, in the manifestation of which he employed an oath, because it was to be the last and peremptory one respecting the method of obtaining righteousness and life. "By myself have I sworn, saith the Lord, that in thy seed shall all the nations of the earth be blessed." (Gen. xxii. 18.) "As I live, saith the Lord, have I any pleasure at all that the wicked should die, and not that he should return from his ways and live" (Ezek. xviii. 23.) "So I swear in my wrath, They shall not enter into my rest. And to whom swear he that they should not enter into his rest, but to them that believed not? So we see that they could not enter in because of unbelief." (Heb. iii. 11, 18.) For the same reason, it is said, "The wrath of God, [from which it is possible for sinners to be liberated by faith in Christ,] abides on those who are unbelievers." (John iii. 36.) A similar process is observed in relation to the priesthood. For he did not confirm with an oath the Levitical priesthood, which had been imposed until the time of reformation." (Heb. ix. 10.) But because it was his will that the priesthood of Christ should be everlasting, he ratified it by an oath. The apostle to the Hebrews demonstrates the whole of this subject in the most nervous style, by quotations from the 110th Psalm. Blessed are we in whose behalf God was willing to swear! but most miserable shall we be, if we do not believe on him who swears. The greatest dignity is likewise obtained to this priesthood, and imparted to it, by the addition of an oath, which elevates it far above the honour to which that of Levi attained. "For the law of a carnal commandment maketh men priests who have infirmities, and are sinners, to offer both gifts and sacrifices, that could not make him perfect who did the service, as pertaining to the conscience;" (Heb. ix. 9) neither could they abolish sin, or procure heavenly blessings. "But the words of the oath, which was since the law, constituteth the Son a High Priest consecrated forevermore, who, after the power of an endless life and through the Eternal Spirit, offers himself without spot to God, and by that one offering, he perfects forever them that are sanctified, their consciences being purified to serve the living God: by how much also it was a more excellent covenant, by so much the more ought it to be confirmed, since it was established upon better promises: (Heb. 7-10,) and that which God hath deigned to honour with the sanctity of an oath, should be viewed as an object of the most momentous importance.

II. We have spoken of the act of Imposing the priesthood, as long as our circumscribed time will allow us. Let us contemplate its Execution, in which we have to consider the duties to be performed, and in them the feeling and condition of who performs them. The functions to be executed were two:

(1.) The Oblation of an expiatory sacrifice, and (2.) Prayer.

1. The Oblation was preceded by a preparation through the deepest privation and abasement, the most devoted obedience, vehement supplications, and the most exquisitely painful experience of human infirmities, on each of which it is not now necessary to speak. The oblation consists of two parts succeeding each other: The First is the immolation or sacrifice of the body of Christ, by the shedding of his blood on the altar of the cross, which was succeeded by death--thus paying the price of redemption for sins by suffering the punishment due to them. The Other Part consists of the offering of his body re-animated and sprinkled with the blood which he shed--a symbol of the price which he has paid, and of the redemption which he has obtained. The First Part of this oblation was to be performed without the Holy of Holies, that is, on earth, because no effusion of blood can take place in heaven, since it is necessarily succeeded by death For death has no more sway in heaven, in the presence and sight of the

majesty of the true God, than sin itself has, which contains within it the deserts of death, and as death contains within itself the punishment of sin. For thus says the scriptures, "The Son of man came, not to be ministered unto, but to minister, and to give his life a ransom for many." (Matt. xx. 28.) "For this is my blood of the New Testament, which is shed for many for the remission of sins." (Matt. xxvi. 28.) "Christ Jesus gave himself a ransom for all, to be testified in due time." (1 Tim. ii. 6). But the Second Part of this offering was to be accomplished in heaven, in the Holy of Holies. For that body which had suffered the punishment of death and had been recalled to life, was entitled to appear before the Divine Majesty besprinkled with its own blood, that, remaining thus before God as a continual memorial, it might also be a perpetual expiation for transgressions. On this subject, the Apostle says: "Into the second tabernacle went the High Priest alone once every year, not without blood, which he offered for himself, and for the errors of the people. But Christ being come a High Priest of good things to come, not by the blood of goat, and calves, but by his own blood he entered in once into the Holy Place, having obtained eternal redemption for us;" (Heb. ix. 11) that is, by his own blood already poured out and sprinkled upon him, that he might appear with it in the presence of God. That act, being once performed, was never repeated; "for in that he died, he died unto sin once." But this is a perpetual act; "for in that he liveth, he liveth unto God." (Rom. vi. 10.) "This man, because he continueth ever, hath an unchangeable priesthood." (Heb. vii. 24) The former was the act of the Lamb to be slain, the latter, that of the Lamb already slain and raised again from death to life. The one was completed in a state of the deepest humiliation, the other in a state of glory; and both of them out of a consummate affection for the glory of God and the salvation of sinners. Sanctified by the anointing of the Spirit, he completed the former act; and the latter was likewise his work, when he had been further consecrated by his sufferings and sprinkled with his own blood. By the former, therefore, he sanctified himself, and made a kind of preparation on earth that he might be qualified to discharge the functions of the latter in heaven.

2. The Second of the two functions to be discharged, was the act of prayer and intercession, the latter of which depends upon the former. Prayer is that which Christ offers for himself, and intercession is what he offers for believers; each of which is most luminously described to us by John, in the seventeenth chapter of his Gospel, which contains a perpetual rule and exact canon of the prayers and intercessions which Christ offers in heaven to his Father. For although that prayer was recited by Christ while he remained upon earth, yet it properly belongs to his sublime state of exaltation in heaven: and it was his will that it should be described in his word, that we on earth, might derive from it perpetual consolation. Christ offers up a prayer to the Father for himself, according to the Father's command and promise combined, "Ask of me, and I shall give thee the heathen for thine inheritance." (Psalm ii. 8.) Christ had regard to this promise, when he said, "Father, glorify thy Son, that thy Son also may glorify thee, as thou hast given him power over all flesh, that he should give eternal life to as many as thou hast given him." This sort of intreaty must be distinguished from those "supplications which Christ, in the days of his flesh, offered up to the Father, with strong cries and tears;" (Heb. v. 7,) for by them he intreated to be delivered from anguish, while by the other he asks, "to see his seed whose days should be prolonged, and to behold the pleasure of the Lord which should prosper in his hands." (Isa. liii. 10.) But, for the faithful, intercession is made, of which the apostle thus speaks, "Who is he that condemneth, It is Christ that died, yea, rather, that is risen again, who is even at the right hand of God, who also maketh intercession for us." (Rom. viii. 34) And, in the Epistle to the Hebrews, he says, "Wherefore he is able also to save them to the uttermost that come unto God by him, seeing He ever liveth to make intercession for them" (vii, 25.) But Christ is said to intercede for believers, to the exclusion of the world, because, after he had offered a sacrifice sufficient to take away the sins of all mankind, he was consecrated a great "High Priest to preside over the house of God," (Heb. x. 21,) "which house those are who hold fast the confidence and the rejoicing of the hope firm unto the end." (iii, 6.) Christ discharges the whole of this part of his function in heaven, before the face of the Divine Majesty; for there, also, is the royal seat and the throne of God, to which, when we are about to pray, we are commanded to lift up our eyes and our minds. But he executes this part of his office, not in anguish of spirit, or in a posture of humble genuflection, as though fallen down before the knees of the Father, but in the confidence of the shedding of his own blood, which, sprinkled as it is on his sacred body, he continually presents, as an object of sight before his Father, always turning it towards his sacred countenance. The entire efficacy of this function depends on the dignity and value of the blood effused and sprinkled over the body; for, by his blood-shedding, he opened a passage for himself "into the holiest, within the veil." From which circumstance we may with the greatest certainty conclude, that his prayers will never be rejected, and that whatever we shall ask in his name, will, in virtue of that intercession, be both heard and answered.

The sacerdotal functions being thus executed, God, the Father, mindful of his covenant and sacred oath, not only continued the priesthood with Christ forever, but elevated him likewise to the regal dignity, "all power being given unto him in heaven and in earth, (Matt. xxviii. 18,) also power over all flesh: (John xvii. 2,) a name being conferred on him which is far above all principality, and might, and dominion, and every name that is named, not only in this world, but also in that which is to come, (Ephes. i. 21,) angels, and authorities, and powers being made subject unto him," (1 Pet. iii. 22,) that he might be the Christ and the Lord of his whole Israel, King of Kings and Lord of Lords. By this admirable covenant, therefore, God hath united those two supreme functions in one, even in Christ Jesus, and has thus performed his promise, by which he had sworn that this Priest should be forever after the order of Melchizedec, "who was at once a King and a Priest; and is to the present time without beginning of days or end of life," because his genealogy is not described in the Scriptures, which in this case are subservient to the figure. This conjunction of the sacerdotal and regal functions is the highest point and the extreme limit of all the divine work, a never ending token of the justice and the mercy of God attempered together for the economy of our salvation, a very luminous and clear evidence of the most excellent glory of God, and an immovable foundation for the certainty of obtaining salvation through this royal Priest. If man is properly styled "the extreme Colophon of the creation," "a microcosm," on account of the union of his body and soul, "an epitome of the whole world," and "the marriage of the Universe," what judgment shall we form of this conjunction, which consists of a most intimate and inseparable union of the whole church of believers and of God himself, "who dwells in the light unto which no man can approach," and by what amplitude of title shall we point out its divinity. This union hath a name above every name that can be named. It is ineffable, inconceivable, and incomprehensible. If, chiefly in respect to this I shall say, that Christ is styled "the brightness of the Father's glory," "the express image of his person" and "the image of the invisible God," I shall have expressed its excellency as fully as it is possible to do.

What can be a more illustrious instance of the admixture of justice with mercy than that even the Son of God, when he had "made himself of no reputation and assumed the form of a servant," could not be constituted a King except through a discharge of the sacerdotal functions; and that all those blessings which he had to bestow as a King on his subjects, could not be asked except through the priesthood, and which, when obtained from God, could not, (except through the intervention of this royal Mediator,) be communicated by his vicarious distribution under God? What can be a stronger and a better proof of the certainty of obtaining salvation through Christ, than that he has, by the discharge of his sacerdotal functions in behalf of men, asked and procured it for men, and that, being constituted a King through the priesthood, he has received salvation from the Father to be dispensed to them? In these particulars consists the perfection of the divine glory.

III. But this consideration, I perceive, introduces us, almost imperceptibly, to the third and last portion of our subject, in which we have engaged to treat on THE FRUITS OF THE SACERDOTAL OFFICE in its administration by Christ. We will reduce all these fruits, though they are innumerable, to four chief particulars; and, since we hasten to the end of this discourse, we bind ourselves down to extreme brevity. These benefits are, (1.) The concluding and the confirmation of a New Covenant; (2.) The asking, obtaining, and application of all the blessings necessary for the salvation of the human race; (3.) The institution of a new priesthood, both eucharistic and royal; and (4.) lastly, The extreme and final bringing to God of all his covenant people.

1. The FIRST UTILITY is the contracting and the confirmation of a New Covenant, in which is the direct way to solid felicity.

We rejoice and glory, that this has been obtained by the priesthood of Christ. For since the first covenant had been made weak through sin and the flesh, and was not capable of bringing righteousness and life, it was necessary, either to enter into another, or that we should be forever expelled from God's presence. Such a covenant could not be contracted between a just God and sinful men, except in consequence of a reconciliation, which it pleased God, the offended party, should be perfected by the blood of our High Priest, to be poured out on the altar of the cross. He who was at once the officiating priest and the Lamb for sacrifice, poured out his sacred blood, and thus asked and obtained for us a reconciliation with God. When this great offering was completed, it was possible for the reconciled parties to enter into an agreement. Hence, it pleased God, that the same High Priest who had acted as Mediator and Umpire in this reconciliation, should, with the very blood by which he had effected their union, go between the two parties, as a middle-man, or, in the capacity of an ambassador, and as a herald to bear tidings of war or peace, with the same blood as that by which the consciences of those who were included in the provisions of the covenant, being sprinkled, might be purged from dead works and sanctified; with the very blood, which, sprinkled upon himself, might always appear in the sight of God; and with the same blood as that by which all things in the heavens might be sprinkled and purified. Through the intervention, therefore, of this blood, another covenant was contracted, not one of works, but of faith, not of the law, but of grace, not an old, but a new one--and new, not because it was later than the first, but because it was never to be abrogated or repealed; and because its force and vigour should perpetually endure. "For that which decayeth and waxeth old, is ready to vanish away." (Heb. viii. 13). If such a covenant as is described in this quotation should be again contracted, in the several ages which succeed each other, changes ought frequently to occur in it; and, all former covenants being rendered obsolete, others more recent ought to succeed. But it was necessary, at length, that a pause should occur in one of them, and that such a covenant should at once be made as might endure forever. It was also to be ratified with blood. But how was it possible to be confirmed with blood of greater value than that of the High Priest, who was the Son, both of God and man. But the covenant of which we are now treating, was ratified with that blood; it was, therefore, a new one, and never to be annulled. For the perpetual presence and sight of such a great High Priest, sprinkled with his own blood, will not suffer the mind of his Father to be regardless of the covenant ratified by it, or his sacred breast to be moved with repentance. With what other blood will it be possible for the consciences of those in covenant to be cleansed and sanctified to God, if, after having become parties to the covenant of grace, they pollute themselves with any crime, "There remaineth no more sacrifice for sins, if any man have trodden under foot this High Priest, and counted the blood of the covenant wherewith he was sanctified, an unholy thing." (Heb. x. 29). The covenant, therefore, which has been concluded by the intervention of this blood and this. High Priest, is a new one, and will endure forever.

2. The SECOND FRUIT is the asking, obtaining, and application, of all the blessings necessary to those who are in covenant for the salvation both of soul and body. For, since every covenant must be confirmed by certain promises, it was necessary that this also should have its blessings, by which it might be sanctioned, and those in covenant rendered happy.

(1.) Among those blessings, the remission of sins first offers itself; according to the tenor of the New Covenant, "I will be merciful to their unrighteousness, and their sins and their iniquities will I remember no more." (Heb. viii. 12). But the scripture testifies, that Christ has asked this blessing by his blood, when it says, "This is my blood of the New Testament, which is shed for many, for the remission of sins." (Matt. xxvi. 28). The scripture also proves his having obtained such a blessing by the discharge of the same office, in these words: "By his own blood Christ entered in once into the holy place, HAVING OBTAINED eternal redemption for us." (Heb. ix. 12.) It adds its testimony to the application, saying, "In Christ WE HAVE REDEMPTION through his blood, the forgiveness of sins, according to the riches of his grace." (Ephes. i. 7.)

(2.) This necessary blessing is succeeded by adoption into sons and by a right to the heavenly inheritance: And we owe it to the Priesthood of Christ, that this blessing was asked and obtained for us, as well as communicated to us. For he being the proper and only begotten Son of the Father, and the sole heir of all his Father's blessings, was unwilling to enjoy such transcendent benefits alone, and desired to have co-heirs and partners, whom he might anoint with the oil of his gladness, and might receive into a participation of that inheritance. He made an offering, therefore, of his soul for sin, that, the travail of his soul being finished, he might see his seed prolonged in their days--the seed of God which might come into a participation with him both of name and inheritance. "He was made under the law, to redeem them that were under the law, that we might receive THE ADOPTION OF SONS." (Gal. iv. 5). According to the command of the Father, he asked, that the Heathen might be given to him for an inheritance. By these acts, therefore, which are peculiar to his priesthood, he asked for this right of adoption in behalf of his believing people, and obtained it for the purpose of its being communicated to them, nay, in fact, he himself became the donor. "For to as many as believed on his name Christ gave power to become the sons of God." (John i. 12). Through him and in regard to him, God has adopted us for sons, who are beloved in him the Son of his love. He, therefore, is the sole heir, by whose death the inheritance comes to others; which circumstance was predicted by the perfidious husbandmen, (Mark xii. 7,) who, being Scribes and Pharisees, uttered at that time a remarkable truth, although they were ignorant of such a great mystery.

(3.) But because it is impossible to obtain benefits of this magnitude except in union with the High Priest himself, it was expected of him that he should ask and obtain the gift of the HOLY SPIRIT, the bond of that union, and should pour it out on his own people. But since the spirit of grace is the token as well as the testimony of the love of God towards us, and the earnest of our inheritance, Christ could not ask this great gift till a reconciliation had taken place, and to effect this was the duty of the priest. When, therefore, this reconciliation was effected, he asked of his Father another Comforter for his people, and his request was granted. Being elevated to the right hand of God, he obtained this Paraclete promised in the terms of the sacerdotal covenant; and, when he had procured this Spirit, he poured it out in a most copious manner on his followers, as the scripture says, "Therefore being by the right hand of God exalted, and having received of the Father the promise of the Holy Ghost, he hath shed forth this which ye now see and hear." (Acts ii. 33.)

That the asking, the obtaining, and the communication of all these blessings, have flowed from the functions of the priesthood, God has testified by a certain seal of the greatest sanctity, when he constituted Christ the Testator of these very blessings, which office embraces conjointly both the full possession of the good things devised as legacies in the Will, and absolute authority over their distribution.

3. The THIRD FRUIT of Christ's administration is the institution of a new priesthood both eucharistic and regal, and our sanctification for the purpose of performing its duties; for when a New Covenant was concluded, it was needful to institute a new eucharistic priesthood, (because the old one had fallen into disuse,) and to sanctify priests to fulfill its duties.

(1.) Christ, by his own priesthood, completed such an institution; and he sanctified us by a discharge of its functions. This was the order in which he instituted it:

First, he constituted us his debtors, and as bound to thanksgiving on account of the immense benefits procured for us and bestowed upon us by his priesthood. Then he instructed us how to offer sacrifices to God, our souls and bodies being sanctified and consecrated by the sprinkling of his blood and by the unction of the Holy Spirit, that, if they were offered as sacrifices to God, they might meet with acceptance. It was also his care to have an altar erected in heaven before the throne of grace, which being sprinkled with his own blood he consecrated to God, that the sacrifices of his faithful people, being placed upon it, might continually appear before the face of the Majesty of heaven and in presence of his throne. Lastly, he placed on that altar an eternal and never-ceasing fire--the immeasurable favour of God, with which the sacrifices on that altar might be kindled and reduced to ashes.

(2.) But it was also necessary that priests should be consecrated: the act of consecration, therefore, was performed by Christ, as the Great High Priest, by his own blood. St. John says, in the Apocalypse, "He hath loved us, and washed us from our sins in his own blood, and hath made us kings and priests unto God and his Father." (i, 6.) "Thou hast redeemed us to God by thy blood, out of every kindred, and tongue, and people, and nation; and hast made us unto our God kings and priests." (v, 10.) Not content to have us joint-heirs in the participation of his inheritance, he willed that we should likewise partake of the same dignity as that which he enjoyed. But he made us partners with him of that dignity in such a manner, as in the mean time always to retain within himself the first place, "as Head of his body the Church, the first-born among many brethren and the Great High Priest who presides over the whole of the House of God." To Him, we, who are "born again," ought to deliver our sacrifices, that by him they may be further offered to God, sprinkled and perfumed with the grateful odour of his own expiatory sacrifice, and may thus through him be rendered acceptable to the Father. For this cause, the Apostle says, "By him, therefore, let us offer the sacrifice of praise to God continually, that is, the fruit of our lips, giving thanks to his name." (Heb. xiii. 15). We are indeed, by his favour "a holy priesthood," to offer up spiritual sacrifices; but those sacrifices are rendered "acceptable to God, only by Jesus Christ." (1 Pet. ii. 5.) Not only was it his pleasure that we should be partakers of this sacerdotal dignity, but likewise of the eternity attached to it, that we also might execute the office of the priesthood after the order of Melchizedec, which by a sacred oath was consecrated to immortality. For though, at the close of these ages of time, Christ will not any longer perform the expiatory part of the priesthood, yet he will forever discharge its eucharistic duties in our favour. These eucharistic duties we shall also execute in him and through him, unless, in the midst of the enjoyment of the benefits received by us from him, we should desire our memories no longer to retain the recollection, that through him we obtained those blessings, and through him we have been created priests to render due thanksgiving to God the chief Donor of all. But, since we are not able to offer to God, so long as we remain in this mortal body, the sacrifices due to him, except by the strenuous resistance which we offer to Satan, the world, sin, and our own flesh, and through the victory which we obtain over them, (both of which are royal acts,) and since, after this life, we shall execute the sacerdotal office, being elevated with him on the throne of his Father, and having all our enemies subdued under us, he hath therefore made us both kings and priests, yea "a royal priesthood" to our God, that nothing might be found in the typical priesthood of Melchizedec, in the enjoyment of which we should not equally participate.

4. The FOURTH, and last FRUIT of the Priesthood of Christ, proposed to be noticed by us, is the act of bringing to God all the church of the faithful; which is the end and completion of the three preceding effects. For with this intent the covenant was contracted between God and men; with this intent the remission of sins, the adoption of sons, and the Spirit of grace were conferred on the church; for this purpose the new eucharistic and royal priesthood was instituted; that, being made priests and kings, all the covenant people might be brought to their God. In most expressive language the Apostle Peter ascribes this effect to the priesthood of Christ, in these words: "For Christ also hath once suffered for sins, the just for the unjust, THAT HE MIGHT BRING US TO GOD." (1 Pet. iii. 18.) The following are also the words of an Apostle concerning the same act of bringing them to God: "Then cometh the end, when he shall have delivered up the kingdom to God, even the Father." (1 Cor. xv. 24). In Isaiah's prophecy it is said, "Behold I and the children whom the Lord hath given me!" Let these words be considered as proceeding out of the mouth of Christ, when he is bringing his children and addressing the Father; not that they may be for signs and for wonders" to the people, but "a peculiar treasure to the Lord."

Christ will therefore bring all his church, whom he hath redeemed to himself by his own blood, that they may receive, from the hands of the Father of infinite benignity, the heavenly inheritance which has been procured by his death, promised in his word, and sealed by the Holy Spirit, and may enjoy it forever. He will bring his priests, whom sprinkled with his blood, he hath sanctified unto God, that they may serve him forever. He will bring his kings, that they may with God possess the kingdom forever and ever: for in them, by the virtue of his Holy Spirit, he has subdued and overcome Satan the Chief, and his auxiliaries, the world, sin, and their own flesh, yea, and "death itself, the last enemy that shall be destroyed."

Christ will bring, and God even the Father will receive. He will receive the church of Christ, and will command her as "the bride, the Lamb's wife," on her introduction into the celestial bride-chamber, to celebrate a perpetual feast with the Lamb, that she may enjoy the most complete fruition of pleasure, in the presence of the throne of his glory. He will receive the priests, and will clothe them with the comely and beautiful garments of perfect holiness, that they may forever and ever sing to God a new song of thanksgiving. And then he will receive the kings, and place them on the throne of his Majesty, that they may with God and the Lamb obtain the kingdom and may rule and reign forever.

These are the fruits and benefits which Christ, by the administration of his priesthood, hath asked and obtained for us, and communicated to us. Their dignity is undoubtedly great, and their utility immense. For what could occur of a more agreeable nature to those who are "alienated from the life of God, and strangers to the covenants of promise," (Ephes. ii. 12,) than to be received by God into the covenant of grace, and to be reckoned among his people? What could afford greater pleasure to the consciences which were oppressed with the intolerable burden of their sins, and fainting under the weight of the wrath of God, than the remission and pardon of all their transgressions? What could prove more acceptable to men, sons of the accursed earth, and to those who are devoted to hell, than to receive from God the adoption of sons, and to be written in heaven? What greater pleasure could those enjoy who he under the dominion of Satan and the tyranny of sin, than a freedom from such a state of most horrid and miserable servitude, and a restoration to true liberty? What more glorious than to be admitted into a participation of the Priesthood and of the Monarchy, to be consecrated priests and kings to God, even royal priests and priestly kings? And, lastly, what could be more desirable than to be brought to God, the Chief Good and the Fountain of all happiness, that, in a beautiful and glorious state, we may spend with him a whole eternity?

This priesthood was imposed by God himself, "with whom we have to do," on Christ Jesus--the Son of God and the Son of man, our first-born brother, formerly encompassed about with infirmities, tempted in all things, merciful, holy, faithful, undefiled, and separate from sinners; and its imposition was accompanied by a sacred oath, which it is not lawful to revoke. Let us, therefore, rely with assured faith on this priesthood of Christ, entertaining no doubt that God hath ratified and confirmed, is now ratifying and confirming, and will forever ratify and confirm all those things which have been accomplished, are now accomplishing, and will continue even to the consummation of this dispensation to be accomplished, on our account, by a High Priest taken from among ourselves and placed in the Divine presence, having received in our behalf an appointment from God, who himself chose him to that office.

Since the same Christ hath by the administration of his own priesthood obtained a perpetual expiation and purgation of our sins, and eternal redemption, and hath erected a throne of grace for us in heaven, "let us draw near [to this throne of grace] with a true heart and in full assurance of faith, having our hearts sprinkled from an evil conscience," (Heb. x. 22,) "and our conscience purged from dead works," (ix, 14,) assuredly concluding "that we shall obtain mercy, and find grace to help in time of need." (iv, 16.)

LASTLY. Since, by the administration of this priesthood, so many and such excellent benefits have been obtained and prepared for us of which we have already received a part as "the first-fruits," and since we expect to reap in heaven the choicest part of these benefits, and the whole of them in the mass, and that most complete--what shall we render to our God for such a transcendent dignity? What thanks shall we offer to Christ who is both our High Priest and the Lamb? "We will take the cup of salvation, and call upon the name of the Lord." We will offer to God "the calves of our lips," and will "present to him our bodies, souls, and spirits, a living sacrifice, holy and acceptable." (Rom. xii. 1.) Even while remaining in these lower regions, we will sing, with the four and twenty elders that stand around the throne, this heavenly song to the God and Father of all: "Thou art worthy, O Lord, to receive glory, and honour, and power. For thou hast created all things, and for thy pleasure they are and were created." (Rev. iv. 11.) To Christ our High Priest and the Lamb, we will, with the same elders, chant the new song, saying, "Thou art worthy to take the book, and to open the seals thereof: for thou wast slain, and hast redeemed us to God by thy blood out of every kindred, and tongue, and people, and nation; and hast made us unto our God kings and priests: and we shall reign on the earth." (v, 10.) Unto both of them together we will unite with every creature in singing, "BLESSING, AND honour, AND GLORY, AND MIGHT BE TO HIM WHO SITTETH UPON THE THRONE, AND UNTO THE LAMB FOREVER AND EVER."-I have finished.

After the Academic Act of his promotion to a Doctor's degree was completed, Arminius, according to the custom at Leyden, which still obtains in many Universities, briefly addressed the same audience in the following manner:

Since the countenance necessary for the commencement of every prosperous action proceeds from God, it is proper that in him also every one of our actions should terminate. Since, therefore, his Divine clemency and benignity have hitherto regarded us in a favourable light, and have granted to this our act the desired success, let us render thanks to Him for such a great display of His benevolence, and utter praise to His holy name.

"O thou Omnipotent and Merciful God, the Father of our Lord Jesus Christ, we give thanks to thee for thine infinite benefits conferred upon us miserable sinners. But we would first praise thee for having willed that thy Son Jesus Christ should be the victim and the price of redemption for our sins; that thou hast out of the whole human race collected for thyself a church by thy word and Holy Spirit; that thou hast snatched us also from the kingdom of darkness and of Satan, and hast translated us into the kingdom of light and of thy Son; that thou hast called Holland, our pleasant and delightful country, to know and confess thy Son and to enjoy communion with him; that thou hast hitherto preserved this our native land in safety against the machinations and assaults of a very powerful adversary; that thou hast instituted, in our renowned city, this university as a seminary of true wisdom, piety and righteousness; and that thou hast to this hour accompanied these scholastic exercises with thy favour. We intreat thee, O holy and indulgent God, that thou wouldst forever continue to us these benefits; and do not suffer us, by our ingratitude, to deserve at thy bands, to be deprived of them. But be pleased rather to increase them, and to confirm the work which thou hast begun. Cause us always to reflect with retentive minds on these things, and to utter eternal praises to thy most holy name on account of them, through our Lord Jesus Christ. Amen."

I thank you, Doctor Francis Gomarus, and am grateful to you, most illustrious man and very learned promoter, for this great privilege with which you have invested one who is undeserving of it. I promise at all times to acknowledge with a grateful mind this favour, and to strive that you may never have just cause to repent of having conferred this honour upon me.

To you also, most noble Lord Rector, and to the very honourable the Senate of the University, (unless I should desire to defile myself with the crime of an ungrateful spirit,) I owe greater thanks than I am able to express, for the honourable judgment which you have formed concerning me, and for your liberal testimony, which by no deed of mine have I ever deserved. But I promise and bind myself to exert my powers to the utmost, that I may not at any time be found to be entirely unworthy of it. If I thus exert myself, I know that you will accept it as a payment in full of all the debt of gratitude which you have a right to demand.

I now address you, most noble, honourable and famous men, to all and to each of whom I confess myself to be greatly indebted for your continued and liberal benevolence towards me, which you have abundantly demonstrated by your wish to honour this our act with your most noble, honourable, famous and worthy presence. I would promise to make you a requital at some future period, did not the feebleness of my powers shrink from the magnitude of the undertaking implied in that expression, and did not the eminence of your stations repress the attempt.

In the duty of returning thanks which I am now discharging, I must not omit you, most noble and studious youths: For I owe this acknowledgment to your partial and kind inclination to me, of which you have given a sufficiently exuberant declaration in your honourable appearance and modest demeanor while you have been present at this our act. I give my promise and solemn undertaking, that if an occasion hereafter offer itself in which I can render myself serviceable to you, I will endeavour in every capacity to compensate you for this your kind partiality. The occurrence of such an opportunity is at once the object of my hopes and my wishes.

ORATION V

ON RECONCILING RELIGIOUS DISSENSIONS AMONG CHRISTIANS

Never since the first entrance of sin into the world, have there been any ages so happy as not to be disturbed by the occurrence of some evil or other; and, on the contrary, there has been no age so embittered with calamities, as not to have had a sweet admixture of some good, by the presence of the divine benevolence renewed towards mankind. The experience of all ages bears witness to the truth of this observation; and it is taught by the individual history of every nation. If, from a diligent consideration of these different histories and a comparison between them, any person should think fit to draw a parallel of the blessings and of the calamities which have either occurred at one and the same period, or which have succeeded each other, he would in reality be enabled to contemplate, as in a mirror of the greatest clearness and brilliancy, how the Benignity of God has at all times contended with his Just Severity, and what a conflict the Goodness of The Deity has always maintained with the Perversity of men. Of this a fair specimen is afforded to us in the passing events of our own age, within that part of Christendom with which we are more immediately acquainted. To demonstrate this, I do not deem it necessary to recount all the Evils which have rushed, like an overwhelming inundation, upon the century which has been just completed: for their infinity would render such an attempt difficult and almost impossible. Neither do I think it necessary, to enumerate, in a particular manner, the Blessings which those evils have been somewhat mitigated.

To confirm this truth, it will be abundantly sufficient to mention one very remarkable Blessing, and one Evil of great magnitude and directly opposed to that blessing. This Blessing is, that the Divine clemency irradiates our part of the world by the illustrious light of his sacred truth, and enlightens it with the knowledge of true religion, or Christianity. The Evil opposed to it is, that either human ignorance or human perversity deteriorates and corrupts the clear light of this Divine truth, by aspersing and beclouding it with the blackest errors; creates separation and division among those who have devoted themselves exclusively to the service of religion; and severs them into parties, and even into shreds of parties, in direct contradiction to the nature and genius of Christianity, whose Author is called the "Prince of peace," its doctrine "the Gospel of peace," and its professors "the Sons of peace." The very foundation of it is an act of pacification concluded between God and men, and ratified by the blood of the Prince of peace. The precepts inculcated in each of its pages, are concerning peace and concord; its fruits are "righteousness, peace, and joy in the Holy Ghost;" and its end is peace and eternal tranquillity. But although the light from this torch of truth, which is diffused through the Christian world, affords no small refreshment to my mind; and although a view of that clearer light which shines among the Churches that profess to have been Reformed from Popery, is most exhilarating; yet I cannot dissemble the intense grief which I feel at my heart on account of that religious discord which has been festering like a gangrene, and pervading the whole of Christianity:

Unhappily, its devastations have not terminated. In this unfeigned feeling of deep regret, I think, all those who love Christ and his Church, will partake with me; unless they possess hearts of greater hardness than Parian marble, and bowels secured from compassionate attacks by a rigidity stronger than that of the oak, and by defenses more impregnable than those of triple brass.

This is the cause which has incited me to offer a few remarks on religious dissensions in the Christian world; for, according to that common proverb, "Whenever a man feels any pain, his hand is almost spontaneously moved to the part affected." This, therefore, is the subject which I propose to introduce to the notice of the present celebrated assembly, in which the province has been awarded to me, of delivering an oration at this Academic Festival, according to an established and laudable custom. I shall confine myself to three particulars: In the first place, I will give a dissertation on This Discord Itself and The Evils Which Spring From It. I will then show its Causes; and, lastly, its Remedies.

The first particular includes within itself the Necessity of removing such a great evil; and the last prescribes the Manner in which it may be removed, to which the middle particular materially contributes. The union of the whole together explains and justifies the nature of the design which I have now undertaken.

I humbly pray and intreat the God of peace, that he will, by his Spirit of truth and peace, be present with me while engaged in speaking; and that he will govern my mind and direct my tongue, that

I may utter such things as may be pleasing to him and salutary to the Church of Christ, for the glory of his name and our mutual instruction.

I likewise prefer a request to you, my very famous and accomplished hearers, that you will deign to grant me your favourable attention, while I glance at each of these particular, with much brevity, and discharge the office of a director to you rather than that of an orator, lest I trespass on your patience.

I. Union is a great good: it is indeed the chief good and therefore the only one, whether we separately consider each thing of which it is composed, or more of them contained together by a certain social tie or relation between themselves. For all things together, and each thing separately, are what they are by that very thing by which they are one; and, by this union, they are preserved in what they really are. And, if they have need and are capable of further perfection, they are, by the same union, still more strengthened, increased, and perfected, until they attain to the utmost boundary prescribed to them by nature or by grace, or by God the Author of both grace and nature. Of such certainty is this truth, that even the blessedness of God consists in that union by which he is ONE and always present with himself, and having all things belonging to him present together with him. Nothing, therefore, can be more agreeable or desirable than Union, whether viewed in reference to single things or to the whole together; nothing can be more noxious and detestable than Dissension, by which all things begin at first to decline from their own condition, are afterwards diminished by degrees, and, at length, perish. But as there are differences of Good, so are there likewise of Union. More excellent than another is that good which in its own nature obtains the pre-eminence above the other, on account of its being more general and durable, and on account of its approaching more nearly to the Chief Good. In like manner that union is also more excellent which consists of a thing of greater excellence, belongs to many, is more durable and unites itself most intimately with the Deity. The union of true religion is, therefore, one of the greatest excellence.

But as those evil things which are opposed to the good things of greatest excellence, are the very worst of their kind, so no discord is more shocking and hideous than that about religion. The truth of this remark is confirmed by the inward nature of this discord; and it is further manifested most clearly by the effects which proceed from it.

1. We shall see its Nature (1.) in the object of discord, (2.) in the ready inclination for this object, which is evinced by the discordant partizans, (3.) in its extensive range, and (4.) its long continuance.

(1.) The Christian Religion is the Object of this discord or dissension. When viewed with respect to its form, this religion contains the true knowledge of the true God and of Christ; and the right mode in which both of them may be worshipped. And when viewed with regard to its end, it is the only medium by which we can be bound and united to God and Christ, and by which on the other hand God and Christ can be bound and united to us. From this idea of connecting the parties together, the name of religion is derived, in the opinion of Lactantius. In the term "Religion," therefore, are contained true wisdom and true virtue, and the union of both with God as the Chief Good, in all of which is comprehended the supreme and the only happiness of this world and of that which is to come. And not only in reality, but in the estimation also of every one on whose mind a notion of religion has been impressed, (that is, on the whole of mankind,) men are distinguished from other animals, not by reason, but by a genuine character much more appropriate and indeed peculiar to them, and that is Religion, according to the authority of the same Lactantius.

(2.) But if bounds be imposed on the desire towards any thing by such an opinion of its value as is preconceived in the mind, an inclination or propensity towards religion is deservedly entitled to the highest consideration, and holds the preeminence in the mind of a religious person. Nay, more than this, if, according to St. Bernard and to truth itself, "the measure to be observed in loving God, is to love him without measure," a propensity or inclination towards religion, (of which the chief and choicest part consists of love to God and Christ,) is itself without bounds: For it is at once illimitable and immeasurable. This is tantamount to the declaration of Christ, the Author of our religion, who said, "If any man come to me, and hate not his father and mother, and wife and children, and brethren and sisters, yea, and his own life also, he cannot be my disciple." (Luke xiv. 26.) This strong affection for religion answers equally to that immeasurable love by which any one desires the union of himself with God, that is, desires the greatest happiness, because he knows that Religion is the strongest bond and the most adhesive cement of this union. Most serious, therefore, is religious discord when it is engaged in disputes about the altar itself.

(3.) Besides, it spreads and diffuses itself most extensively; for it involves within its vortex all the persons that have been initiated in the sacred rites of the Christian religion. No one is permitted to profess neutrality; nay, it is impossible for any man to remain neutral in the midst of religious dissension. For he who makes no advances towards the opposite sentiments of each of the dissidents, is induced thus to act from one of these four causes: (i.) He either cherishes a third opinion in the Christian Religion, far removed from both the others: (ii.) He thinks some other religion better than Christianity. (iii.) He places Christianity and other systems of religion on an equality: Or, (iv.) He entertains an equal disregard for the Christian system and all other modes of religion. The first of these characters is not neutral, but becomes a third party among the disputants. The second and the third dissent entirely from the Christian Religion, the axioms of which are, "that it is true, and that it alone is true:" for it is not so accommodating as Paganism, it admits of no other system to be its associate. Besides, the second of these characters is an Atheist according to the Christian Religion, one of the statutes of which, is, that "whosoever denieth Christ the Son, the same hath not God the Father." (1 John ii. 23.) Against the third party this sentence is pronounced:

"He that gathereth not with me, scattereth abroad." (Matt. xii. 30.) The fourth is considered an Atheist by all mankind, and is deemed a second and adverse party in that most general kind of dissension which exists between true religion and its adversaries.

(4.) Lastly. This discord is very long in its continuance and almost incapable of reconciliation. For these traits in it, two causes may, I think, be assigned, and both of them deducible from the very nature of religion.

The first is, that since religion is both in reality a matter that belongs to the Deity, and is so accounted by every one, being subject to his sole pleasure and management, and exempt from the jurisdiction of men; and since it has been bestowed, that it may exercise authority as a rule for the direction of life, and for prescribing some limits to liberty, and not that it may be slavishly subservient to the wills of men, like a Lesbian rule, which may be accommodated to every condition; since these are some of the properties of religion, man is not permitted to stipulate concerning it, and scarcely any one has had the audacity to arrogate to himself such an assumption of authority.

The other cause is, that the parties individually think, if they concede even the smallest particle of the matter of discord, such a concession is nearly connected with the peril of their own salvation. But this is the genius of all separatists, not to enter into any treaties of concord with their adversaries, unless they be permitted to have life at least, and liberty, secured to them inviolate. But every one thinks, that his life, (that is, his spiritual life,) and the liberty which is proper for that life, are included in religion and its exercise.

To these a third cause may be added, which consists of the opinion, that each party supposes life and eternal salvation to be denied to them by their opponents, from this circumstance, because those opponents disapprove of their religion, and when it is compared with their own, they treat it with the utmost contempt. This injury appears to be the most grievous and aggravating. But every act of pacification has its commencement in the oblivion of all injuries, and its foundation in the omission of those injuries which (to an eye that is jaundiced with such a prejudice as that which we have just stated,) seem to be continued and perpetual grievances.

When the nature and tendency of this species of discord have become quite apparent to worldly-minded Rulers, they have often employed it, or at least the semblance of it, for the purpose of involving their subjects in enmities, dissensions and wars, in which they had themselves engaged for other reasons. Having in this manner frequently implicated the people committed to his charge, a prince has become at pleasure prodigal of their property and their persons. These were readily sacrificed by the people to the defense of the ancient religion; but they were perverted by their rulers, to obtain the fulfillment of their desires, which they would never have procured, had they been deprived of such popular assistance. The magnitude of the dissension induces the willing parties cheerfully to make contributions of their property to their prince; the multitude of the Dissidents ensures their ability to contribute as much as may be sufficient; and the obstinate spirit which is indigenous to dissension, causes the parties never to grow weary of giving, while they retain the ability.

We have now in some sort delineated the nature of this discord or dissension, and have shewn that it is most important in its bearings, most extensive in its range, and most durable in its continuance.

2. Let us further see what have been, and what still are, the Effects of an evil of such a magnitude, in this part of the Christian world. We may, I think, refer the infinitude of these effects to two chief kinds. The first kind is derived from the force of the dissension on the Minds of men; and the second kind has its commencement in the operation of the same dissension on their Hearts and affections.

First. From the force of this dissension on the Minds of men, arises, (1.) a degree of doubtful uncertainty respecting religion. When the people perceive that there is scarcely any article of Christian doctrine concerning which there are not different and even contradictory opinions; that one party calls that "horrid blasphemy" which another party has laid down as a "complete summary of the truth;" that those points which some professors consider the perfection of piety, receive from others the contumelious appellation of "cursed idolatry;" and that controversies of this description are objects of warm discussion between men of learning, respectability, experience and great renown. When all these things are perceived by the people, and when they do not observe any discrepancy in the life and manners of the opposite disputants, sufficiently great to induce them to believe that God vouchsafes assistance by "the spirit of his truth," to one of these parties, in preference to the other, on account of any superior sanctity, they begin then to indulge in the imagination, that they may esteem the principles of religion alike obscure and uncertain.

(2.) If an intense desire to institute an inquiry into some subject shall succeed this dubious uncertainty about religion, its warmth will abate and become cool, as soon as serious difficulties arise in the search, and an utter despair of being able to discern the truth will be the consequence. For what simple person can hope to discover the truth, when he understands that a dispute exists about its very principles--whether they be contained in the scriptures alone, or in traditions not committed to writing? What hope can he entertain when he sees that, question often arises concerning the translation of some passage of scripture, which can be solved only by a knowledge of the Hebrew and Greek languages? How can he hope to find out the truth, when he remarks, that the opinions of learned men, who have written on religious subjects, are not unfrequently quoted in the place of evidence--while he is ignorant of all languages except that of the country in which he was born, is destitute of all other books, and possesses only a copy of the scriptures translated into the vernacular language? How can such a person be prevented from forming an opinion, that nothing like certainty respecting the chief doctrines of religion can be evident to any one, except that man who is well skilled in the two sacred languages, has a perfect knowledge of all traditions, has perused with the closest attention the writings of all the great Doctors of the Church, and has thoroughly instructed himself in the sentiments which they held respecting each single principle of religion?

(3.) But what follows this despair? Either a most perverse opinion concerning all religion, an entire rejection of every species of it, or Atheism. These produce Epicurism, a still more pestilent fruit of that ill-fated tree. For when the mind of man is in despair about discovering the truth, and yet is unable to throw aside at the first impulse all care concerning religion and personal salvation, it is compelled to devise a cunning charm for appeasing conscience: (i.) The human mind in such a state will either conclude, that it is not only unnecessary for common people to understand the axioms of religion , and to be well assured of what they believe; but that the attainment of these objects is a duty incumbent on the clergy alone, to the faith of whom, as of "them that must give account" to God for the salvation of souls, (Heb. xiii. 17,) it is quite sufficient for the people to signify their assent by a blind concurrence in it. The clergy also themselves, with a view to their own advantage, not unfrequently discourage all attempts, on the part of the people, to gain such a knowledge of religion and such an assured belief. (ii.) Or the mind in such circumstances will persuade itself, that all worship paid to God, with the good intention of a devout mind, is pleasing to him; and therefore under every form of religion, (provided such good intention be conscientiously observed,) a man may be saved, and all sects are to be considered as placed in a condition of equality. The men who have imbibed such notions as these, which point out an easy mode of pacifying the conscience, and one that in their opinion is neither troublesome nor dangerous--these men not only desert all study of divine things themselves, but lay folly to the charge of that person who institutes a labourious inquiry and search for that which they imagine can never be discovered, as though he purposely sought something on which his insanity might riot.

But not less steep and precipitous is the descent from this state of despair to absolute Atheism. For since these persons despair of offering to the Deity the adoration of true religion, they think they may abstain from all acts of worship to him without incurring any greater harm or punishment; because God considers no worship agreeable to him except that which he has prescribed, and he bestows a reward on no other. The efficacy of this despair is increased by their religion which seems to be interwoven with the natural dispositions of some men, and which, eagerly seizing on every excuse for sin, deceives itself, and veils its native profaneness and want of reverence for the Deity under the cloak of the grievous dissensions which have been introduced about religion. But other two reasons may be adduced why Religious differences are, in the Christian world, the fruitful causes of Atheism. (i.) The first is, that by this battering-ram of dissensions, the foundations of Divine Providence, which constitute the basis of all Religion, experience a violent concussion. When this thought enters the mind, that "it appears to be the first duty of providence, (if it actually have an existence,) to place her dearest daughter, Religion, in such a luminous light, that she may stand manifest and apparent to the view of all who do not willingly drag their eyes out of their sockets." (ii.) The other is, that when men are not favoured with Christian prophecy, which comprises religious instruction, and are destitute of the exercise of Divine worship, they first almost imperceptibly slide into ignorance and into the complete disuse of all worship, and afterwards prolapse into open impiety. But it has not unfrequently been the case, that men have suffered themselves to be deprived of these blessings, sometimes by the prohibition of their own consciences, and sometimes by those of others. (i.) By the prohibition of their own consciences, when they do not think it lawful for them to be present at the public sermons and other religious ordinances of a party that is adverse to them. (ii.) By that of the consciences of others, when the prevailing party forbid their weaker opponents to assemble together as a congregation, to hear what they account most excellent truths, and to perform their devotions with such rites and ceremonies as are agreeable to themselves. In this manner, therefore, even conscience, when resting on the foundation of religion, becomes the agent of impiety, where discord reigns in a religious community. From Atheism, as a root, Epicurism buds forth, which dissolves all the ties of morality, is ruinous to it, and causes it to degenerate into licentiousness. All this, Epicurism effects, by previously breaking down the barriers of the fear of God, which alone restrain men within the bounds of their duty.

Secondly. All these evils proceed from religious dissension when its operation is efficacious on the Mind. Most sincerely do I wish that it would remain there, content itself with displaying its insolence in the hall of the mind where discord has its proper abode, and would not attack the Affections of the Heart. But, vain is my wish! For so extensively does it pervade the heart and subdue all its affections, that it abuses at pleasure the slaves that act as assistants.

1. For since all similarity in manners, studies and opinions, possesses very great power in conciliating love and regard; and since any want of resemblance in these particulars is of great potency in engendering hatred, it often happens that from religious dissension arise Enmities more deadly than that hatred which Vatinius conceived against Cicero, and such exasperations of heart as are utterly irreconcilable. When religious discord makes its appearance, even amongst men the most illustrious in name and of the greatest celebrity, who had been previously bound together and united among themselves by a thousand tender ties of nature and affection, they instantly renounce, one against another, all tokens of friendship, and burst asunder the strictest bands of amity. This is signified by Christ, when he says, "I came not to send peace on earth, but a sword. For I am come to set a man at variance against his father, and the daughter against her mother, and the daughter-in-law against her mother-in-law. And a man's foes shall be they of his own household." (Matt. x. 31-36.) These words do not indicate the end and purpose of the coming of Christ, but an event which would succeed his coming; because he was then about to introduce into the world a religion which differed greatly from that which was publicly established, and concerning which many dissensions would afterwards arise, through the vicious corruption of mankind.

This dissimilarity was the origin of the rancor of the Jews against the Samaritans, which displayed itself in not allowing themselves to derive any benefit from the services of the Samaritans, even in matters that were necessary for their own convenience. It was the existence of this feeling which caused the woman of Samaria to wonder, concerning Jesus, "how he, who was a Jew, could ask drink of her, a Samaritan woman." (John iv. 9.) Indeed, it is the utmost stretch of hatred, to be unwilling to derive any advantage from another person that is an enemy.

2. Enmities and dissensions of the heart and affections branch out and become Schisms, factions and secessions into different parties. For as love is an affection of union, so is hatred an affection of separation. Thus synagogues are erected, consecrated and thronged with people, in opposition to other synagogues, churches against churches, and alters against altars, when neither party wishes to have intercourse with the other. This also is the reason why we frequently hear expressions, entirely similar to those which were clamorously echoed through the assembled multitude of the Children of Israel when they were separating into parties, "To your tents, O Israel! for our adversaries have no portion in God, nor any inheritance in his Son Christ Jesus." (1 Kings xii. 16.) For both factions equally appropriate to themselves the renowned name of "the true Israel," which they severally deny to their adversaries, in such a peremptory manner as might induce one to imagine each of them exclusively endowed with a plenary power of passing judgment upon the other, and as though it had been previously concluded, that the name of ISRAEL, by which God accosts in a most gracious manner the whole of his Church, cannot encircle within its embrace those who differ in any point from the rest of their brethren.

3. But the irritation of inflamed hearts does not prescribe a boundary to itself in schism alone. For if it happen, that one party considers itself the more powerful, it will not be afraid of instituting Persecutions against the party opposed to it, and of attempting its entire extermination. In effecting this, it spares no injury, which either human ingenuity can devise, the most notable fury can dictate, or even the office of the infernal regions can supply. Rage is excited and cruelty exercised against the reputation, the property, and the persons of the living; against the ashes, the sepulchers, and the memory of the dead; and against the souls both of the living and the dead. Those who differ from the stronger party are attacked with all kinds of weapons; with cruel mockings, calumnies, execrations, curses, excommunications, anathemas, degrading and scandalous libels, prisons and instruments of torture. They are banished to distant or uninhabited islands, condemned to the mines, prohibited from having any communication with their fellow-creatures by land or sea, and excluded from a sight of either heaven or earth. They are tormented by water, fire and the sword, on crosses and stakes, on wheels of torture and gibbets, and by the claws of wild beasts, without any measure, bounds or end, until the party thus oppressed have been destroyed, or have submitted themselves to the pleasure of the more powerful, by rejecting with abjurations the sentiments which they formerly held, and by embracing with apparent devotion those of which they had previously disapproved; that is, by destroying themselves through the hypocritical profession which had been extolled from them by violence. Call to mind how the Heathens persecuted the Christians; and the persecuting conduct of the Aryans against the orthodox, of the worshippers of images against the destroyers of images, and vice versa. That we may wander to no great distance let us look at what has occurred within the period of our recollection and that of our fathers, in Spain, Portugal, France, England, and the Low Countries; and we shall confess with tears, that these

remarks are lamentably too true.

4. But if it happen that the contending parties are nearly equal in power, or that one of them has been long oppressed, wearied out by persecutions, and inflamed with a desire for liberty, after having had their patience converted into fury, (as it is called,) or rather into just indignation, and if the pressed party assume courage, summon all its strength, and collect its forces, then most mighty wars arise, grievances are repeated, after a flourish of trumpets the herald's hostile spear is sent forth in defiance, war is proclaimed, the opposing armies charge each other, and the struggle is conducted in a most bloody and barbarous manner. Both the belligerents observe a profound silence about entering into negotiations for peace, lest that party which first suggests such a course, should, from that very circumstance, create a prejudice against its own cause and make it appear the weaker of the two and the more unjust. Nay, the strife is carried on with such willful obstinacy, that he can scarcely be endured who for a moment suspends their mutual animosities by a mention of peace, unless he have placed a halter around his neck, and be prepared to be suspended by it on a gibbet, in case his discourse on this topic happens to displease. For such a lover of peace would be stigmatized as a deserter from the common cause, and considered guilty of heresy, a favourer of heretics, an apostate and a traitor.

Indeed, all these Enmities, Schisms, Persecutions and Wars, are commenced, carried on, and conducted with the greater animosity, on account of every one considering his adversary as the most infectious and pestilent fellow in the whole Christian world, a public incendiary, a murderer of souls, an enemy of God, and a servant of the devil--as a person who deserves to be suddenly smitten and consumed by fire descending from heaven--and as one, whom it is not only lawful to hate, to curse and to murder without incurring any guilt, but whom it is also highly proper to treat in that manner, and to be entitled to no slight commendation for such a service, because no other work appears in his eyes to be more acceptable to God, of greater utility in the salvation of man, more odious to Satan, or more pernicious to his kingdom. Such a sanguinary zealot professes to be invited, instigated and constrained to deeds like these, by a zeal for the house of God, for the salvation of men, and for the divine glory. This conduct of violent partizans is what was predicted by the Judge and the Master of our religion: "When they shall persecute you and kill you for my sake, they will think that they do God service." (John xvi. 2.) When the very conscience, therefore, arouses, assists and defends the affections, no obstacle can offer a successful resistance to their impetuosity. Thus we see, that religion itself, through the vicious corruption of men, has been made a cause of dissension, and has become the field in which they may perpetually exercise themselves in cruel and bloody contests.

If, in addition to these things, some individual arrogate to himself, and, with the consent of a great multitude, usurp authority to prescribe laws with respect to religion, to strike with the thunderbolt of excommunication whomsoever he pleases, to dethrone kings, to absolve subjects from their oaths of allegiance and fidelity, to arm them against their lawful rulers, to transfer the right over the dominions of one prince to others who are his sworn confederates, or to such as are prepared to seize upon them in the first instance, to pardon crimes however great their enormity may be, and whether already perpetrated or to be hereafter committed, and to canonize ruffians and assassins--the mere nod of such a man as is here described, must be instantly obeyed with blind submission, as if it were the command of God. Blessed God! what a quantity of most inflammable matter is thus thrown upon the fire of enmities, persecutions and wars. What an Iliad of disasters is thus introduced into the Christian world! It is, therefore, not without just reason that a man may exclaim, "Is it possible, that Religion can have persuaded men to introduce this great mass of evils?"

But all the ills which we have enumerated do not only proceed from real dissensions, in which some fundamental truth is the subject of discussion, but also from those which are imaginary, when things affect the mind not as they are in reality, but according to their appearances. I call these imaginary dissensions. (i.) Either, because they exist among parties that have only a fabulous religion, which is at as great a distance from the true one, as the heaven is distant from the earth, or as the followers of such a phantom are from God himself. Differences of this description are found among the Mahomedans, some parties of whom, (as the Turks,) follow the interpretation of Omar; while others, (as the Persians,) are proselytes to the commentaries of Ali. (ii.) Or, because the discordant parties believe these imaginary differences to be in the substance of the true doctrine, when they have it in no existence whatever. Of such a difference Victor, the Bishop of Rome, afforded an instance, when he wished to excommunicate all the Eastern Churches, because they dissented from him in the proper time of celebrating the Christian festival of Easter.

But, to close this part of my discourse, the very summit and conclusion of all the evils which arise from religious discord, is, the destruction of that very religion about which all the controversy has been raised. Indeed, religion experiences almost the same fate, as the young lady mentioned by Plutarch, who was addressed by a number of suitors; and when each of them found that she could not become entirely his own, they divided her body into parts, and thus not one of them obtained possession of her whole person. This is the nature of discord, to disperse and destroy matters of the greatest consequence. Of this a very mournful example is exhibited to us in certain extensive dominions and large kingdoms, the inhabitants of which were formerly among the most flourishing professors of the Christian Religion; but the present inhabitants of those countries have unchristianized themselves by embracing Mahomedanism--a system which derived its origin, and had its chief means of increase, from the dissensions which arose between the Jews and the Christians, and from the disputes into which the Orthodox entered with the Sabellians, the Aryans, the Nestorians, the Eutychians, and with the Monothelites.

II. Let us proceed to contemplate the Causes of this Dissention. Philosophers generally divide causes, into those which directly and of themselves produce an effect, and into those which indirectly and by accident contribute to the same purpose. The consideration of each of these classes will facilitate our present inquiries.

1. The accidental cause of this dissension is (1.) the very nature of the Christian religion, which not only transcends the human mind and its affections or passions, but appears to be altogether contrary to both it and to them. (i.) For the Christian Religion has its foundation in the Cross of Christ; and it holds forth this humbling truth, "JESUS THE CRUCIFIED, IS THE saviour OF THE WORLD," as an axiom most worthy of all acceptation. For this reason also, the word of which this religion is composed, is termed "the doctrine of the cross." (1 Cor. i. 18.) But what can appear to the mind more absurd or foolish, than for a crucified and dead person to be accounted the saviour of the world, and for men to believe that salvation centers in the cross? On this account the Apostle declares in the same passage, that the doctrine of the cross, [or, the preaching of Christ Crucified,] is unto the Jews a stumbling-block and unto the Greeks foolishness. (ii.) What is more opposed to the human affections than "for a man to hate and deny himself, to despise the world and the things that are in the world, and to mortify the flesh with the affections and lusts?" Yet this is another axiom of the Christian Religion, to which he who does not give a cheerful assent in mind, in will and in deed, is excluded from the discipleship of Christ Jesus. This indispensable requisite is the cause why he who is alienated in mind from the Christian Religion, does not yield a ready compliance with these its demands; and why he who has enrolled his name with Christ, and who is too weak and pusillanimous to inflict every species of violence on his nature, invents certain fictions, by which he attempts to soften and mitigate a sentence, the exact fulfillment of which fills him with horror. From these circumstances, after men have turned aside from purity of doctrine, dissensions are excited against religion and its firm and constant professors.

(2.) In the scriptures, as in the only authentic document, the Christian Religion is at present registered and sealed; yet even they are seized upon as an occasion of error and dissension, when, as the Apostle Peter says, "the unlearned and unstable wrest them unto their own destruction," because they contain "some things hard to be understood." (2 Pet. iii. 16.) The figurative expressions and ambiguous sentences, which occur in certain parts of the scriptures, are undesignedly forced to conduce to the adulteration of the truth among those persons, "who have not their senses exercised" in them.

2. But omitting any further notice of these matters, let us take into our consideration the proper causes of this dissension: (1.) In the front of these, Satan appears, that most bitter enemy of truth and peace, and the most wily disseminator of falsehood and dissension, who acts as leader of the hostile band. Envying the glory of God and the salvation of man, and attentively looking out on all occasions, he marks every movement; and whenever an opportunity occurs, during the Lord's seed time, he sows the tares of heresies and schisms among the wheat. From such a malignant and surreptitious mode of sowing while men are sleeping, (Matt. xiii. 23,) he often obtains a most abundant harvest. (2.) Man himself follows next in this destructive train, and is easily induced to perform any service for Satan, however pernicious its operation may prove to his own destruction; and that most subtle enemy, the serpent, finds in man several instruments most appropriately fitted for the completion of his purposes.

First. The mind of man is the first in subserviency to Satan, both with regard to its blindness and its vanity. First. The Blindness of the mind is of two kinds, the one a native blindness, the other accidental. The former of these grows up with us even from the birth: our very origin is tainted with the infection of the primitive offense of the Old Adam, who turned away from God the Great Source of all his light. This blindness has so fascinated our eyes, as to make us appear like owls that become dim-sighted when the light of truth is seen. Yet this truth is not hidden in a deep well; but though it is placed in the heavens, we cannot perceive it, even when its beams are clearly shining upon us from above. The latter is an accidental and acquired blindness, which man has chosen for himself to obscure the few beams of light which remain him. "The God of this world hath blinded the minds of them which believe not; lest the light of the glorious gospel of Christ should shine unto them." (2 Cor. iv. 4.) God himself, the just punisher of those who hate the truth, has inflicted on them this blindness, by giving efficacy to error. This is the cause why the veil that remains upon the mind, operates as a preventive and obstructs the view of the gospel; (2 Cor. 3,) and why he on whom the truth has shone in vain, "believes a lie." (2 Thess. ii. 11.) But assent to a falsehood is a dissent and separation from those who are the assertors of truth. Secondly. The vanity of the mind succeeds its blindness, and is prone to turn aside from the path of true religion, in which no one can continue to walk except by a firm and invariable purpose of heart. This vanity is also inclined to invent to itself such a Deity as may be most agreeable to its own vain nature, and to fabricate a mode of worship that may be thought to please that fictitious Deity. Each of these ways constitutes a departure from the unity of true religion, on deserting which men rush heedlessly into dissensions.

Secondly. But the affections of the mind are, of all others, the most faithful and trusty in the assistance which they afford to Satan, and conduct themselves like abject slaves devoted to his service; although it must be acknowledged that they are frequently brought thus to act, under a false conception that they are by such deeds promoting their own welfare and rendering good service to God himself. Love and Hatred, the two chief affections, and the fruitful parents and instigators of all the rest, occupy the first, second, third, and indeed all the places, in this slavish employment. Each of them is of a three-fold character, that nothing might be wanting which could contribute to the perfection of their number.

The Former of them consists of the love of glory, of riches, and of pleasures, which the disciple whom Jesus loved, thus designates, "the lust of the flesh, and the lust of the eyes, and the pride of life." (1 John ii. 16.) The Latter consists of hatred to the truth, to peace, and to the professors of the truth.

(i.) Pride, then, that most prolific mother of dissensions in religion, produces its fetid offspring in three different ways: For, First, either it "exalteth itself against the knowledge of God," (2 Cor. x. 5,) and does not suffer itself to be brought into captivity by the truth to obey God, being impatient of the yoke which is imposed by Christ, though it is both easy and light. Pride says in reality, "Let us break their bands asunder, and cast away their cords from us." (Psalm ii. 3.) From this baneful source arose the sedition of Korah, Dathan, and Abiram, who arrogantly claimed for themselves a share in the priesthood, which God had given exclusively to Aaron. (Num. 16.) Or, Secondly, it loveth to have the pre-eminence in the Church of God, and "to have dominion over another's faith;" the very crime of which St. John accuses Diotrephes, when he complains that "neither doth he himself receive the brethren, and forbiddeth them that would, and casteth them out of the Church." (3 John 9, 10.) Or, Lastly, having usurped an impotent sovereignty over the souls of men by appointing and altering at its pleasure the laws concerning Religion, and over the bodies of men by employing menaces and force to bring into subjection to it the consciences of men, it compels those churches which cannot with a safe conscience bear this most iniquitous tyranny, to depart from the rest and to assume to themselves the management of their own affairs. The Greek Church declared itself to be influenced by this cause, in refusing to hold communion with the Latin Church, because the Roman Pontiff had, in opposition to all right and law, and in defiance of the rule of Christ and of the decrees of the Fathers, "arrogated to himself a plenitude of power." From the same fountain has flowed that immense schism which in this age distracts and divides all Europe. This has been ably manifested to the whole world by the just complaints and allegations of Protestant States and Protestant Princes.

But envy, anger, and an eager desire to know all things, are other three darts, which Pride hurls against concord in religion. For, first, if any one excels his fellows in the knowledge of divine things, and in holiness of life, and if by these means he advances in favour and authority with the people, pride immediately injects envy into the minds of some persons, which contaminates all that is fair and lovely; asperses and defiles whatever is pure; obscures, by vile calumnies, either his course of life or the doctrines which he professes; puts a wrong construction, by means of a malevolent interpretation, on what was well intended and correctly expressed by him; commences disputes with him who is thus high in public estimation; and endeavours to lay the foundations of its own praise on the mass of ignominy which it heaps upon his name and reputation. If by such actions as these it cannot obtain for itself a situation equal to its desires, it then invents new dogmas and draws away the people after it; that it may enjoy such a dignity, among some individuals who have separated from the rest of the body, which it was impossible for it to obtain from the whole while they lived together in concord and harmony. Secondly. Pride is also the parent of anger, which may stimulate any one to revenge, if he think himself injured even in the slightest degree by a professor of the truth. Such a person reckons scarcely any injury better suited to his purpose or more pernicious to the affairs of his adversary, than to speak contumeliously and in disparagement of his sentiments, and publicly to proclaim him a Heretic--than which no term can be more opprobrious or an object of greater hatred among mortals. Because, as this crime does not consist of deeds, but of sentiments, the aspersions cast upon them cannot be so completely washed away as to leave no stains adhering to them, or as to create a possibility at least for the calumniator to remove from himself by some evasive subterfuge the infamy which attaches itself to him who is an utterer of slanders. The third weapon which pride employs in this warfare, is a passionate desire to explore and know all things. This passion leaves no subject untouched, that its learning may be displayed to advantage; and, (not to lose the reward of its labour,) it obtrusively palms upon others as things necessary to be known, those matters which, by means of great exertion, it seems to have drawn out from behind the darkness of ignorance, and accompanies all its remarks by great boldness of assertion. From such a disposition and conduct as this, offenses. and schisms must arise in the Church.

(ii.) Avarice, likewise, or, the love of money, which is termed by the Apostle, "the root of all evil," (1 Tim. vi. 10,) brings its hostile standard into this embattled field. For, since the doctrine of truth is not a source of profit, when those who have faithfully taught it are succeeded by unbelieving teachers, "who are ravening wolves, and suppose gain to be godliness," the latter effect a great change in it, (1.) either by "binding heavy burdens, and grievous to be borne, and laying them on the shoulders of the disciples," (Matt. xxiii. 4,) for whose redemption votive offerings may be daily made; (2.) by inventing profitable plans for expiating sins; or, lastly, by preaching, in soft and complimentary language, such things as are agreeable to the ears of the people, for the purpose of gaining their favour, which, according to the expression of the Apostle, is a "corrupting of the word of God," or making a gain of it. (2 Cor. ii. 17.) From these causes dissensions have often arisen; (1.) either when the faithful teachers that are in the church, or those whom God raises up for the salvation of his people, marshal themselves in opposition to the doctrine which is prepared for the sake of profit; or, (2.) when the people themselves, growing weary of impositions and rapine, become seceders from these pastors, by uniting themselves with such as are really better, or by receiving those as their substitutes who are in their estimation better. This was the torch of dissension between the Pharisees and Christ, who opposed their avarice and came to loose all those grievous burdens. This was also the primary consideration by which Luther was excited to obstruct the sale of Popish indulgencies; and from that small beginning, he gradually proceeded to reforms of greater importance.

(iii.) Nor only that Pleasure or "lust of the flesh," which specially comes under this denomination, and which denotes a feeling or disposition for carnal things, takes its part in the performance of this tragedy, but that also which in a general sense contains a desire to commit sin without any remorse of conscience: and both these kinds of pleasure most assiduously employ themselves in collecting inflammable materials for augmenting the flame of discord in religion.

For this passion or affection, having had some experience in the important "doctrine of the cross," desires as the very summit of all its wishes, both to riot, while here, in the pleasures of voluptuousness, and yet to cherish some hopes of obtaining the happiness of heaven. With two such incompatible objects in view this passion chooses teachers for itself, who may in an easy manner "place under the arm-holes of their disciples, pillows sewed and filled with soft feathers," (Ezek. xiii. 18,) on which they may recline themselves and take sweet repose, although their sins, like sharply pointed thorns, continue to sting and molest them in every direction. They flatter them with the idea of easily obtaining pardon, provided they purchase the favour of the Deity, by means of certain exercises apparently of some importance, but possessing in reality no consequence whatever, and by means of great donations with which they may fill his sanctuary. This is the complaint of the Apostle, who, when writing to Timothy, says, "For the time will come when they will not endure sound doctrine; but after their own lusts shall they heap to themselves teachers, having itching ears; and they shall turn away their ears from the truth, and shall be turned unto fables." To this is subjoined an admonition, that Timothy should watch and discharge with fidelity the duties of his ministry. (2 Tim. iv. 3-5). According to this quotation, a difference must of necessity exist between Timothy and those teachers.

But these three capital vices are serviceable to Satan, their author, in another way, and contribute under his direction to introduce changes in religion, and, consequently, to excite discord among Christians. In both sacred and profane history, egregious examples are recorded of princes and private men, who, being instigated by such a desire of power as partook at once of ambition and avarice, have invented new modes of religion, and accommodated them to the capacities, the wishes, and the opinions of their people; by means of which they might either restrain their own subjects within the bounds of their duty, or might subdue to their way the people that were under the rule of other princes. Ambition and avarice suggest to such aspiring persons the desire of inventing those modes of religious worship; while an itching for novelty, a wish to enjoy their pleasures, and the obvious agreement of the new doctrine with their preconceived opinions, influence the people to embrace the modish religion. With these intentions, and under the impulse of these views, Jeroboam was the first author of a change of religion in the Israelitish Church. He built altars in Dan and Bethel, and made golden calves, that he might prevent the people from proceeding at stated periods to Jerusalem, for the purpose of offering sacrifice, according to the command of God, and from returning to the house of David, from which they had rent themselves. The same reasons also induced Mahomet to invent a new religion. By his frequent intercourse with Jews and Christian, he had learned from both parties those things which were most agreeable to them; he therefore adopted the very crafty counsel of Sergius, the monk, and devised a new mode of religion, which was gratifying to the human senses, and which, as it was digested in his Alcoran, he persuaded many people to embrace. The few individuals with whom he was able to prevail, were the foundation from which arose the immense Ottoman empire, and those extensive dominions which are to the present time in possession of the Turks.

2. We have now seen in what manner the love of glory, of riches, and pleasure, performs its several parts in this theater of religious dissensions. Let Hatred next appear and exhibit to us its actions, which, from the very nature of the cause, have a proper and direct tendency to excite discord.

(1.) The first of its actors that appears upon the stage, is a hatred of the truth, and of true doctrine. This species of hatred is conceived, partly from an anticipated notion of the mind, which, since it cannot be reconciled to the doctrine of truth, and yet is with difficulty drawn away from it, excites hatred against a sentiment that is opposed to itself. It is also partly conceived, because the true doctrine becomes the accuser of man, forbidding those things which are the objects of his desires, and commanding those things which he is most reluctant to perform. While it urges its precepts so rigidly, that every one who does not seriously regulate and conform his life to the conditions which they contain, is excluded from all hope of salvation.

(2.) The next in order, is the hatred of peace and concord. For there are men of a certain description who cannot exist without having an enemy, which Trogus Pompeius declares to have been a trait in the character of the ancient Spaniards. To such persons concord or amity is so offensive, that, out of pure hatred to it, they willingly expose themselves to the enmity of others. If such characters happen to obtain a station of some honour in the Church, it is amazing what scruples and difficulties they will not raise, what intricate sophisms they will not frame and contrive, and what accusations they will not institute, that they may have an opportunity of raising a contest about the articles of religion, from which proceed private enmity and rancor that can never be appeased, and dissensions of a more deadly kind than the greatest of those which relate to the present life.

(3.) The last which comes forward, is a hatred against the professors of the true doctrine, from which the descent is very rapid downwards to a dissent from that doctrine which those good men profess; because it is the anxious study of every one that hates another, not to have anything in common with his adversary. Of this the Arabians afford an example. Out of hatred to Heraclius Cæsar, and to the stipendiary Greek and Latin troops who served under him, they, who had long before departed from them in will and affection, effected a still more serious separation from them in religion; for, although they had previously been professors of Christianity, from that period they embraced the doctrines of the Alcoran and became followers of Mahomet.

But the professors of the true doctrine incur this species of hatred, either through some fault of their own, or through the pure malice of men. (i.) They incur this hatred by their own fault, if they do not administer the doctrine of the truth, with that prudence and gentleness which are appropriate to it; if they appear to have a greater regard for their own advantage, than for the advancement of religion, and, lastly, if their manner of life is in opposition to the doctrine. From all these circumstances a bad opinion is entertained of them, as though they scarcely believed the principles which they inculcate. (ii.) This hatred is also incurred by the fault of another, because the delicate and lascivious hearts of men cannot bear to have their ulcers sprinkled and purified by the sharp salt of truth, and because they with difficulty admit any censors on their life and manners. With a knowledge of this trait of the human heart, the Apostle inquires, "Am I therefore become your enemy, because I tell you the truth ," (Gal. iv. 16.) For truth is almost invariably productive of hatred, while an obsequious complaisance obtains friends as its reward.

3. The preceding appear to be the procuring causes of dissensions in religion; and as long as their efficacy endures, they tend to perpetuate these dissensions. There are other causes that we may justly class among those which perpetuate discord when once it has arisen, and which prevent the restoration of peace and unity.

(1.) Among these perpetuating and preventing causes, the first place is claimed for the various prejudices by which the minds of the Dissidents are occupied, concerning our adversaries and their opinions, concerning our parents and ancestors, and the Church to which we belong, and, lastly, concerning ourselves and our teachers.

(i.) The prejudice against our adversaries is, not that we think them under the influence of Error, but under that of pure malice, and because their minds have indulged their humour in thus dissenting. This cuts off all hope of leading them to adopt correct sentiments, and despair refuses to make the attempt. (ii.) The prejudice against the opinions of our adversary is, that we condemn them ourselves not only for being false, but for having been already condemned by the public judgment of the Church; we therefore consider them unworthy of being again brought into controversy, and subjected anew to examination. (iii.) But the preconceived opinion which we have formed concerning our parents and ancestors, is also a preventive of reconciliation, both because we account them to have been possessed of such a great share of wisdom and piety, as rendered it improbable that they could ever have been guilty of error; and because we conceive favourable hopes of their salvation, which is very properly an object of our most earnest wishes in their behalf. But these hopes we seem to call in question, if, in an opinion opposed to theirs, we acknowledge any portion of the truth appertaining to salvation, of which they have either been ignorant or have disapproved. It is on this principle that parents leave their posterity heirs as of their property so also of their opinions and dissensions. (iv.) Besides, the splendour of the Church, to which we have bound ourselves by an oath, dazzles our eyes in such a manner that we cannot suffer any persuasion whatever to induce us to believe the possibility, in former times or at present, of that church having deviated in any point from the right way. (v.) Lastly. Our thoughts and sentiments concerning ourselves and our teachers are so exalted, that our minds can scarcely conceive it possible either for them to have been ignorant, or not to have had a sufficiently clear perception of things, or for us to err in judgment when we approve of their opinions. So prone is the human understanding to exempt from all suspicion of error itself and those whom it loves and esteems!

(2.) It is no wonder if these prejudices produce a pertinacity in eagerly defending a proposition once laid down, which is a most powerful impediment to reconciliation.

Two kinds of fear render this pertinacity the more obstinate:

(i.) One is a fear of that disgrace which, we foolishly think, will be incurred if we acknowledge ourselves to have been at all in error. (ii.) The other is a fear which causes us to think, that the whole doctrine is exposed to the utmost peril, if we discover it even in one point to be erroneous.

(3.) In addition to these, the mode of action commonly adopted both towards an adversary and his opinion, is no small obstacle to reconciliation, although that mode may seem to have been chosen for conciliatory purposes.

(i.) An adversary is treated in a perverse manner, when he is overwhelmed by curses and reproaches, assailed with detractions and calumnies, and when he is menaced with threats of violence. If he despises all these things, which is not an uncommon occurrence when "the testimony of his conscience" is in opposition to them, (2 Cor. i. 19,) they produce no effect whatever. But if his spirit broods over them, his mind becomes disturbed, and, like one stricken by the Furies, he is driven to madness, and is thus much worse qualified than before to acknowledge his error. In both these ways he is confirmed rather the more in his own opinion; either because he perceives, that those who use arms of this kind openly betray the weakness as well as the injustice of their cause; or, because he draws this conclusion in his own mind, that it is not very probable that those persons are instructed by the Spirit of truth, who adopt such a course of conduct.

(ii.) But contention is rashly instituted against the opinion of an adversary, first, when it is not proposed according to the mind and intention of him who is the assertor; Secondly, when it is discussed beyond all due bounds, and its deformity is unseasonably exaggerated; and, lastly, when its refutation is attempted by arguments ill calculated to produce that effect.

The first occurs when we do not attend to the words of an adversary, with a becoming tranquillity of mind and suitable patience; but immediately and at the mention of the first word, we are accustomed to guess at his meaning. The second arises from the circumstance of no one wishing it to appear as if he had begun to contend about a thing of trifling importance. The last proceeds from ignorance or from too great impetuosity, which, on being precipitously impelled into fury, augments its mischievous capabilities. It then seizes upon anything for a weapon, and hurls it against the adversary. When the first mode is adopted, the person whose meaning is misrepresented, thinks that an opinion, not his own, has been calumniously attributed to him. The second course, according to his judgment, has been pursued for the purpose of affixing an envious mark upon his opinion, and upon the dignity which it has acquired. When the last is put in practice, be considers his opinion to be incapable of refutation, because he observes that it remains uninjured amidst all the arguments which have been directed against it. All and each of these add fuel to the flame of dissensions, and render the blazing fire inextinguishable.

III. We have now considered the Nature, the Effects and the Causes of religious dissension. It remains for us to inquire into the Remedies for such a great evil. While I attempt this in a brief manner, I beg that you will favour me with that degree of attention which you have already manifested. The professors of medicine describe the nature of all remedies thus, "they are never used without some effect." For if they be true remedies, they must prove beneficial; and, if they do not profit, they prove hurtful. This latter circumstance reminds me, that I ought first to remove certain corrupt remedies which have been devised by some persons and occasionally employed.

1. The first of these false remedies which obtrudes itself, is the fable of the sufficiency of implicit faith, by which people are called upon, without any knowledge of the matter, to believe that which is an object of belief with the Church and the Prelates. But the Scripture places righteousness "in the faith of the heart," and salvation "in the confession of the mouth;" (Rom. x. 10,) and says, "The just shall live by his faith," (Heb. ii. 4,) and "I believe and therefore have spoken." (2 Cor. iv. 13.) This monstrous absurdity is, therefore, exploded by the scripture. Not only does this fable take away all cause of religious dissension, but it also destroys religion itself, which, when it is destitute of Knowledge and Faith, can have no existence.

2. The next figment is nearly allied to this; it concludes, that every one may be saved in his own religion. But while this remedy professes to cure one evil, it produces another much more hurtful and of greater magnitude; and that is, the certain destruction of those who are held in bondage by this error. Because this opinion renders the error incurable; since no one will give himself any trouble to lay it aside or to correct it. This was Mahomet's devise, for the purpose of establishing his Alcoran free from all liability of its becoming an object of dispute. The same doctrine obtained in Paganism, where the worship of demons flourished, as is evident from the title on a certain altar among the Athenians, the high stewards of Pagan wisdom. That altar bore the following inscription, "To The Gods of Asia, Europe, and Africa; To The Unknown and Foreign Gods:" which was after the manner of the Romans, at that period, "the masters of the world," who were accustomed to invoke the tutelary deities of an enemy's city before they commenced hostilities against it. In this manner has Satan exerted himself, lest

his "kingdom, being divided against itself should fall."

3. The third false remedy is a prohibition of all controversies respecting religion, which lays down the most stupid ignorance for a foundation, and raises upon it the superstructure of religious concord: In Russia, where such an ordinance is in operation, this is obvious to every one that contemplates its effects. Yet it is hurtful, whether it be true religion that flourishes, or it be false. In the first case, on account of the inconstancy of the human mind; and in the second case, because it stamps perpetuity on error, unless the preceding fiction concerning the equality of all religions meet with approval, for on that foundation, Mahomet raised this prohibition against religious controversies.

4. Next to this in absurdity is the advice, not to explain the sacred Scriptures, but only to read them: which is not only pernicious, on account of the omission of their particular application, and repugnant to the usage both of the ancient Jewish Church and of the primitive Church of Christ; but it is also of no avail in the cure of the evil, since any one might, by reading, discover the meaning for himself, according to his own fancy; and that reading which is instituted at the will of the reader, would act the part of an explanation, on account of the parallelism of similar and dissimilar passages.

But the Popish Church exhibits to us Three Remedies.

First, that, for the sake of certainty, we mall have recourse to the Church Universal. However, since the whole of this church cannot meet together, the court of Rome has appointed in its place a representative assembly, consisting of the Pope, the Cardinals, the Bishops, and the rest of the prelates who are devoted to the Roman See, and subject to the Pontiff. But, in addition to this, because it believes that it is possible for all the Cardinals, Bishops and Prelates to err, even when united together in one body, and because it considers the Pope alone to be placed beyond the possibility of error, it declares that we must apply to him for the sake of obtaining a decisive judgment concerning Religion. This remedy is not only vain and inefficient, but it is far more difficult to induce the rest of the Christian world to adopt it than any controverted article in the whole circle of religion: And since the Papists endeavour to prove this point from the scriptures, by that very circumstance they declare that the scriptures are the only sanctuary to which we can repair for religious information.

Secondly. Their next remedy is proposed, if I may, be allowed the expression, merely for the sake of form, and lies in the writings and agreement of the ancient Fathers. But, since the Christian Fathers have not all been authors, and few of those who have written, have concerned themselves with controversies, (which takes away from us the universal consent of all of them together,) this remedy is also useless, because it is a fact to the truth of which the Papists themselves assent, that it was possible for each of these Fathers to err. From this circumstance, therefore, we conclude, that the consent of all of them is not free from the risk of error, even if each had separately declared his own individual opinion in his writings. Besides, this general agreement is no easy matter; nay, it is to be obtained with the greatest difficulty; because it is in the power of very few persons, (if of any man whatever,) to make themselves acquainted with such universal consent, both on account of the bulky and almost innumerable volumes in which the writings of the Fathers are contained, and because the dispute among different parties is no less concerning the meaning of those Fathers than concerning that of the Scriptures, the contents of which are comprised in a book of small size when compared with the dimensions of their massy tomes. We are thus sent forth on an endless excursion, that we may at length be compelled to return to the Sovereign Pontiff.

Thirdly. The other remedy of the papists is not much dissimilar to the preceding one. It is thus stated: The decrees of former councils may be consulted; from which, if it should appear that the controversy has been decided, the judgment then passed upon it must stand in the place of a definitive sentence: nor must any matter, the merits of which have been once decided, be brought again into judgment. But of what avail would this be, if a good cause had been badly defended, and had been overpowered and borne down, not by any defect in itself, but through the fault of those who were its defenders, and who were either awed into silence through fear, or betrayed their trust by an incompetent, foolish and injudicious defense? And of what consequence does such a remedy appear, if one and the same spirit of error have conducted on such an occasion both the attack and the defense. But grant that it has been fairly defended: Yet, I declare that The Cause Of Religion, Which Is The Cause Of God, Is Not An Affair To Be Submitted To Human Decision, or to be judged of man's judgment."

The Papists add a Fourth remedy, which, on account of its fierce and most violent efficacy, will not easily be forgotten by us as a people who have been called to endure some of its cruelties. It acts like the fulcrum of a lever for confirming all the preceding suggestions, and is the foundation of the whole composition. It is this: "Whosoever refuses to listen to the councils and writings of the fathers, and to receive them as explained by the Church of Rome--whosoever refuses to listen to the Church, and especially to her husband, that High Priest and Prophet, the vicar of Christ and the successor of St. Peter, let that soul be cut off from among his people: And he who is unwilling to yield to an authority so sacred, must be compelled, under the sword of the executioner, to express his consent, or he must be avoided," which, in their language, signifies that he must be deprived of life. To murder and utterly to destroy the adverse and gainsaying parties is indeed, a most compendious method of removing all dissensions!

In the midst of these difficulties, some persons have invented other remedies, which, since they are not within the power of man, ought, according to their views, to be asked of God in prayer.

1. One is, that God would be pleased to raise some one from the dead, and send him to men: From such a messenger, they might then hope to know what is God's decisive judgment concerning the clashing opinions of the various dissidents. But this remedy is discountenanced by Christ when he says, "If they hear not Moses and the Prophets, neither will they be persuaded, though one rose from the dead." (Luke xvi. 31.)

2. Another of these remedies is, that God would by a miracle distinguish that party of whose sentiments he approves; which appears to have been a practice in the times of Elijah. But if no sect be entirely free from every particle of error, can it be expected that God will set the seal of his approval on any portion of falsity? But this wish is unnecessary, since the things which Christ did and spoke "are written that we might believe that Jesus is the Christ, the Son of God, and that, believing, we might have life through his name." (John xx. 31.) But the remedy itself, if applied, would prove to be inefficacious. For even in the days of Christ and his apostles, dissensions existed; and many of them were excited against the primitive heralds of the gospel, although they had acquired great renown by the benevolent exercise of the miraculous powers with which they were endued. To this remark I must add that the approaching advent of Antichrist is predicted to be "with all power, and signs, and lying wonders." (2 Thess. ii. 9.)

3. A third remedy, of a horrid description, remains to be noticed, which, nevertheless, is resorted to by some persons. It is an adjuration of the devil, to induce him by means of incantations and exorcisms to deliver an answer, from the bodies of deceased persons, concerning the truth of such doctrines as are at any period the existing subjects of controversy. This method is both a mark of the utmost desperation, and an execrable and insane love of demons.

But, dismissing all these violent medicines, that are of a bad character and import, I proceed to notice such as are holy, true and saving; these I distribute into preparatives and aphæretics or removers, of this dissension.

1. To the class of preparatives belong, (1.) in the first place, Prayers and Supplications to God, that we may obtain a knowledge of the truth, and that the peace of the Church may be preserved: and these religious acts are to be performed, at the special command of the magistrates, with fasting, and in dust and ashes, with seriousness, in faith, and with assiduity. These services, when thus performed, cannot fail of being efficacious; because they are done according to the ordinance of God, whose command it is, that "we pray for the peace of Jerusalem," (Psalm cxxii. 6,) and according to the promise of Christ, who has graciously engaged that "the Spirit of truth shall be given to those who ask him." (Luke xi. 13.)

(2.) Let a serious amendment of life and a conscientious course of conduct be added: For, without these, all our prayers are rendered ineffectual, because they are displeasing to God, on the ground, that "he who misemploys that portion of knowledge which he possesses, becomes, by his own act, unworthy of all further communications and increase of knowledge." This is in accordance with that saying of Christ: "Unto every one that hath, shall be given; and from him that hath not, even that which he hath shall be taken away from him." (Luke xix. 26.) But to all those who employ and improve the knowledge which is given to them, Christ promises the spirit of discernment. in these words: "If any man will do the will of my Father, he shall know of the doctrine, whether it be of God, or whether I speak of myself." (John viii. 17.)

2. But amongst the very first removals, let those causes be put away which, as we have previously stated, have their origin in the affections, and which are not only the instigators of this dissension, but tend to perpetuate and keep it alive. Let humility overcome pride; let a mind contented with its condition become the successor of avarice; let the love of celestial delights expel all carnal pleasures; let good will and benevolence occupy the place of envy; let patient forbearance subdue anger; let sobriety in acquiring wisdom prescribe bounds to the desire of knowledge, and let studious application take the place of learned ignorance. Let all hatred and bitterness be laid aside; and, on the contrary, "let us put on bowels of mercies" towards those who differ from us, and who appear either to wander about in the paths of error, or to scatter its noxious seeds among others.

These necessary concessions we shall obtain from our minds without much difficulty, if the following four considerations become the objects of our sedulous attention:

First. How extremely difficult it is to discover the truth an all subjects, and to avoid error. On this topic, St. Augustine most beautifully descants, when he thus addresses those worst of heretics, the Manichees: "Let those persons be enraged against you, who are ignorant of the immense labour that is required for the discovery of truth, and how difficult it is to guard against error. Let those be enraged against you who know not how uncommon a circumstance and how arduous a toil it is to overcome carnal fantasies, when such a conquest is put in comparison with serenity of mind. Let those be enraged against you who are not aware of the great difficulty with which the eye of "the inner man" is healed, so as to be able to look up to God as the sun of the system. Let those be enraged against you, who are personally unconscious of the many sighs and groans which must be uttered before we are capable of understanding God in the slightest degree. And, lastly, let them be enraged against you, who have never been deceived by an error of such a description as that under which they see you labouring. But how angry soever all these persons may be, I cannot be in the least enraged against you, whose weaknesses it is my duty to bear, as those who were near me at that period bore with mine; and I ought now to treat you with as much patience as that which was exercised towards me when, frantic and blind, I went astray in the errors of your doctrine."

Secondly. That those who hold erroneous opinions have been induced through ignorance to adopt them, is far more probable, than that malice has influenced them to contrive a method of consigning themselves and other people to eternal destruction.

Thirdly. It is possible that they who entertain these mistaken sentiments, are of the number of the elect, whom God, it is true, may have permitted to fall, but only with this design, that he may raise them up with the greater glory. How then can we indulge ourselves in any harsh or unmerciful resolutions against these persons, who have been destined to possess the heavenly inheritance, who are our brethren, the members of Christ, and not only the servants but the sons of the Lord Most High?

Lastly. Let us place ourselves in the circumstances of an adversary, and let him in return assume the character which we sustain; since it is as possible for us, as it is for him, to hold wrong principles. When we have made this experiment, we may be brought to think, that the very person whom we had previously thought to be in error, and whose mistakes in our eyes had a destructive tendency, may perhaps have been given to us by God, that out of his mouth we may learn the truth which has hitherto been unknown to us.

To these four reflections, let there be added, a consideration of all those articles of religion respecting which there exists on both sides a perfect agreement. These will perhaps be found to be so numerous and of such great importance, that when a comparison is instituted between them, and the others which may properly be made the subjects of controversy, the latter will be found to be few in number and of small consequence. This is the very method which a certain famous prince in France is reported to have adopted, when Cardinal Lorraine attempted to embroil the Lutherans, or those who adhered to the Augustan Confession, with the French Protestants, that he might interrupt and neutralize the salutary provisions of the Conference at Poissy, which had been instituted between the Protestants and the Papists.

But since it is customary after long and grievous wars, to enter into a truce, or a cessation from hostilities, prior to the conclusion of a treaty of peace and its final ratification; and, since, during the continuance of a truce, while every hostile attempt is laid aside, peaceful thoughts are naturally suggested, till at length a general solicitude is expressed with regard to the method in which a firm peace and lasting reconciliation may best be effected; it is my special wish, that there may now be among us a similar cessation from the asperities of religious warfare, and that both parties would abstain from writings full of bitterness, from sermons remarkable only for the invectives which they contain, and from the unchristian practice of mutual anathematizing and execration. Instead of these, let the controversialists substitute writings full of moderation, in which the matters of controversy may, without respect of persons, be clearly explained and proved by cogent arguments:

Let such sermons be preached as are calculated to excite the minds of the people to the love and study of truth, charity, mercy, long-suffering, and concord; which may inflame the minds both of Governors and people with a desire of concluding a pacification, and may make them willing to carry into effect such a remedy as is, of all others, the best accommodated to remove dissensions.

That remedy is, an orderly and free convention of the parties that differ from each other: In such an assembly, (called by the Greeks a Synod and by the Latins a Council,) after the different sentiments have been compared together, and the various reasons of each have been weighed, in the fear of the Lord, and with calmness and accuracy, let the members deliberate, consult and determine what the word of God declares concerning the matters in controversy, and afterwards let them by common consent promulge and declare the result to the Churches.

The Chief Magistrates, who profess the Christian religion, will summon and convene this Synod, in virtue of the Supreme official authority with which they are divinely invested, and according to the practice that formerly prevailed in the Jewish Church, and that was afterwards adopted by the Christian Church and continued nearly to the nine hundredth year after the birth of Christ, until the Roman Pontiff began through tyranny to arrogate this authority to himself. Such an arrangement is required by the public weal, which is never committed with greater safety to the custody of any one than to his whose private advantage is entirely unconnected, with the issue.

But men endued with wisdom will be summoned to this Synod, and will be admitted into it--men who are well qualified for a seat in it by the sanctity of their lives, and their general experience--men burning with zeal for God and for the salvation of their mankind, and inflamed with the love of truth and peace. Into such a choice assembly all those persons will be admitted who are acknowledged for any probable reason to possess the Spirit of Christ, the Spirit of discernment between truth and falsehood, between good and evil, and those who promise to abide by the Scriptures, that have been inspired by the same Holy Spirit. Not only will ecclesiastics be admitted, but also laymen, whether they be entitled to any superiority on account of the dignity of the office which they sustain, or whether they be persons in private stations. Not only will the representatives of one party, or of some parties, be admitted, but deputies from all the parties that disagree, whether they have been defenders of the conflicting opinions that are at issue, or whether they have never publicly explained their own sentiments either in discourse or by writing. But it is of the utmost consequence, that this sentence should, after the manner of Plato, be inscribed in letters of gold on the porch of the building in which this sacred meeting holds its sittings:

"Let no one that is not desirous of promoting the interests of truth and peace, enter this hallowed dome" It is my sincere and earnest wish, that God would "place his angel with a flaming two-edged sword at the entrance of this paradise," in which Divine Truth and the lovely Concord of the Church will be the subjects of discussion; and that he would by his Angel drive away all those who might be animated with a spirit averse to truth and concord, while the sacred guardian repeats, in tones terrific and a voice of thunder, the warning words used by the followers of Pythagoras and Orpheus preparatory to the commencement of their sacred rites:

Far, far from hence, ye multitude profane!

The situation and other circumstances of the town or city appointed for holding such a Council, must not be neglected. It should be so accommodated to the convenience of those who have to assemble in it, that neither the difficulty of approaching it, nor the length of the journey to it, should operate as a hindrance on any of the members deputed. It should be a place free from danger and violence, and secured against all surprise and ambuscades, in order that those who are summoned may come to it, remain in it, and return to their homes, in perfect safety. To secure these benefits, it will be necessary for a public pledge to be given to all the members and solemnly observed.

In this council the subjects of discussion will not be, the jurisdiction, honours, and rights of precedence on the part of princes, the wealth, power and privileges of Bishops, the commencement of war against the Turks, or any other political matters. But its discussions will relate solely to those things which pertain to Religion: Of this description are the doctrines which concern faith and manners, and ecclesiastical order. (1.) In these doctrines, there are two objects worthy of consideration, which are indeed of the greatest consequence: (i.) Their truth, and (ii.) The degree of necessity which exists for knowing, believing and practicing ecclesiastical order, because a good part of it is positive and only requires to be accommodated to persons, places and seasons, it will be easily dispatched.

The end of such a holy convention will be the illustration, preservation, and propagation of the truth; the extirpation of existing errors, and the concord of the Church. The consequence of all which, will be the glory of God and the eternal salvation of men.

The presidency of that assembly belongs to HIM ALONE who is the Head and the Husband of the Church, to Christ by his Holy Spirit. For he has promised to be present in a company that may consist only of two or three individuals gathered together in his name: His assistance, therefore, will be earnestly implored at the beginning and end of each of their sessions. But for the sake of order, moderation, and good government, and to avoid confusion, it will be necessary to have presidents subordinate to Christ Jesus. It is my sincere wish that the magistrates would themselves undertake that office in the Council; and this might be obtained from them as a favour. But in case of their reluctance, either some members deputed from their body, or some persons chosen by the whole Synod, ought to act in that capacity. The duties of these Presidents will consist in convening the assembly, proposing the subjects of deliberation, putting questions to the vote, collecting the suffrages of each member by means of accredited secretaries, and in directing the whole of the proceedings. The course of action to be adopted in the Synod itself, is this; (1.) a regular and accurate debate on the matters in controversy, (2.) mature consultation concerning them, and (3.) complete liberty for every one to declare his opinion. The rule to be observed in all these transactions is the Word of God, recorded in the books of the Old and New Testament. The power and influence which the most ancient Councils ascribed to this sacred rule, were pointed out by the significant action of placing a copy of the Gospels in the first and most honourable seat in the assembly. On this point the parties between whom the difference subsists, should be mutually agreed. (1.) The debates will not be conducted according to the rules of Rhetoric, but according to Dialectics. But a logical and concise mode of reasoning will be employed; and all precipitancy of speech and extempore effusions will be avoided. To each of the parties such an equal space of time will be allowed as may appear necessary for due meditation: and, to avoid many inconveniences and absurdities, every speech intended for delivery will be comprised in writing, and will be recited from the manuscript. No one shall be permitted to interrupt or to close a disputation, unless, in the opinion of the whole assembly, it appear that sufficient reasons have been advanced to satisfy the subject under discussion. (2.) When a disputation is finished, a grave and mature deliberation will be instituted both concerning the controversies themselves and the arguments employed by both sides; that, the limits of the matter under dispute being laid down with great strictness, and the amplitude of debate being contracted into a very narrow compass, the question on which the assembly has to decide and pronounce may be perceived as at one glance with complete distinctness. (3.) To these will succeed, in the proper course, a free declaration of opinion--a right, the benefit of which will belong equally to all that are convened of each party, without excluding from it any of those who though not invited, may have voluntarily come to the town or city in which the Synod is convened, and who may have been admitted into it by the consent of the members.

And since nothing to the present period has proved to be a greater hindrance to the investigation of truth or to the conclusion of an agreement, than this circumstance--that those who have been convened were so restricted and confined to received opinions as to bring from home with them the declaration which they were to make on every subject in the Synod: it is, therefore, necessary that all the members assembled, should, prior to the commencement of any proceedings, take a solemn oath, not to indulge in prevarication or calumny. By this oath they ought to promise that every thing shall be transacted in the fear of the Lord, and according to a good conscience; the latter of which consists, in not asserting that which they consider to be false, in not concealing that which they think to be the truth, (how much soever such truth may be opposed to them and their party,) and in not pressing upon others for absolute certainties those points which seem, even to themselves, to be doubtful. By this oath they should also promise that every thing shall be conducted according to the rule of the word of God, without favour or affection, and without any partiality or respect of persons; that the whole of their attention in that assembly shall be solely directed to promote an inquiry after truth and to consolidate Christian concord; and that they will acquiesce in the sentence of the Synod on all those things of which they shall be convinced by the word of God. On which account let them be absolved from all other oaths, either immediately or indirectly contrary to this by which they have been bound either to Churches and their confessions, or to schools and their masters, or even to princes themselves, with an exception in favour of the right and jurisdiction which the latter have over their subjects. Constituted after this manner, such a Synod will truly be a free assembly, most suitable and appropriate for the investigation of truth and the establishment of concord. This is an opinion which is countenanced by St. Augustine, who, expostulating with the Manichees, in continuation of the passage which we have just quoted, proceeds thus: "But that you may become milder and may be the more easily pacified, O Manicheans, and that you may no longer place yourselves in opposition to me, with a mind full of hostility which is most pernicious to yourselves, it is my duty to request of you (whoever he may be that shall judge betwixt us,) that all arrogance be laid aside by both parties; and that none of us say, that he has discovered the truth. But rather let us seek it, as though it were unknown to each of us. For thus it will be possible for each of us to be engaged in a diligent and amicable search for it, if we have not by a premature and rash presumption believed that it is an object which we had previously discovered, and with which we are well acquainted."

From a Synod thus constructed and managed, those who rely on the promise of God may expect most abundant profit and the greatest advantages. For, though Christ be provoked to anger by our manifold trespasses and offenses, yet the thought must not be once indulged, that his church will be neglected by him; or, when his faithful servants and teachable disciples are, with simplicity of heart, engaged in a search after truth and peace, and are devoutly imploring the grace of his Holy Spirit, that He will on any account suffer them to fall into such errors as are opposed to truths accounted fundamental, and to persevere in them when their tendency is thus injurious. From the decisions of a Synod that is influenced by such expectations, unanimity and agreement will be obtained on all the doctrines, or at least on the principal part of them, and especially on those which are supported by clear testimonies from the Scriptures.

But if it should happen, that a mutual consent and agreement cannot be obtained on some articles, then, it appears to me, one of these two courses must be pursued. First. It must become a matter of deep consideration, whether a fraternal concord in Christ, cannot exist between the two parties, and whether one cannot acknowledge the other for partakers of the same faith and fellow-heirs of the same salvation, although they may both hold different sentiments concerning the nature of faith and the manner of salvation. If either party refuse to extend to the other the right hand of fellowship, the party so offending shall, by the unanimous declaration of all the members, be commanded to prove from plain and obvious passages of scripture, that the importance attached to the controverted articles is so great as not to permit those who dissent from them to be one in Christ Jesus. Secondly. After having made every effort toward producing a Christian and fraternal union, if they find that this cannot be effected, in such a state of affairs the second plan must be adopted, which indeed the conscience of no man can under any pretext refuse. The right hand of friendship should be extended by both parties, and all of them should enter into a solemn engagement, by which they should bind themselves, as by oath, and under the most sacred obligations, to abstain in future from all bitterness, evil speaking, and railing; to preach with gentleness and moderation, to the people entrusted to their care, that truth which they deem necessary; and to confute those falsities which they consider to be inimical to salvation and injurious to the glory of God; and, while engaged in such a confutation of error, (however great their earnestness may be,) to let their zeal be under the direction of knowledge and attempered with kindness. On him who shall resolve to adopt a course of conduct different to this, let the imprecations of an incensed God and his Christ be invoked, and let the magistrates not only threaten him with deserved punishment, but let it be actually inflicted.

But the Synod will not assume to itself the authority of obtruding upon others, by force, those resolutions which may have been passed by unanimous consent. For this reflection should always suggest itself, "Though this Synod appears to have done all things conscientiously, it is possible, that, after all, it has committed an error in judgment. Such a diffidence and moderation of mind will possess greater power, and will have more influence, than any immoderate or excessive rigor can have, on the consciences both of the contumacious dissidents, and of the whole body of the faithful; because, according to Lactantius, "To recommend faith to others, we must make it the subject of persuasion, and not of compulsion." Tertullian also says, "Nothing is less a religious business than to employ coercion about religion." For these disturbers will either then (1.) desist from creating further trouble to the Church by the frequent, unreasonable and outrageous inculcation of their opinions, which, with all their powers of persuasion, they were not able to prevail with such a numerous assembly of impartial and moderate men to adopt. Or, (2.) being exposed to the just indignation of all these individuals, they will scarcely find a person willing to lend an ear to teachers of such a refractory and obstinate disposition. If this should not prove to be the result, then it must be concluded that there are no remedies calculated to remove all evils; but those must be employed which have in them the least peril. The mild and affectionate expostulation of Christ our saviour, must also live in our recollections. He addressed his disciples and said, "Will ye also go away ," (John vi. 67.) We must use the same interrogation; and must rest at that point and cease from all ulterior measures.

My very famous, most polite and courteous hearers, these are the remarks which have been impressed on my mind, and which I have accounted it my duty at this time to declare concerning the reconciliation of religious differences. The short time usually allotted to the delivery of an address on this occasion, and the defects of my own genius, have prevented me from treating this subject according to its dignity and amplitude.

May the God of truth and peace inspire the hearts of the magistrates, the people and the ministers of religion, with an ardent desire for truth and peace. May He exhibit before their eyes, in all its naked deformity, the execrable and polluting nature of dissension concerning religion; and may He affect their hearts with a serious sense of these evils which flow so copiously from it; that they may unite all their prayers, counsels, endeavours, and desires, and may direct them to one point, the removal of the causes of such a great evil, the adoption of a mild and sanatory process, and the application of gentle remedies for healing this dissension, which are the only description of medicines of which the very weak and sickly condition of the body of the Church, and the nature of the malady, will admit. "The God of peace," who dignifies "the peace makers" alone with the ample title of "children,"(Matt. v. 9,) has called us to the practice of peace. Christ, "the Prince of peace," who by his precious blood, procured peace for us, has bequeathed and recommended it to us with a fraternal affection. (John xiv. 27.) It has also been sealed to us by the Holy Spirit, who is the bond of peace, and who has united all of us in one body by the closest ties of the new covenant. (Ephes. iv. 3.)

Let us be ashamed of contaminating such a splendid title as this by our petty contentions; let it rather be to us an object of pursuit, since God has called us to such a course. Let us not suffer that which has been purchased at such a great price to be consumed, and wasted away in the midst of our disputes and dissensions; but let us embrace it, because our Lord Christ has given it the sanction of his recommendation. Let us not permit a covenant of such great sanctity to be made void by our factious divisions; but, since it is sealed to us by the Holy Spirit, let us attend to all its requisitions and preserve the terms inviolate. Fabius, the Roman ambassador, told the Carthaginians, "that he carried to them in his bosom both War and Peace, that they might choose either of them that was the object of their preference." Depending not on my own strength, but on the goodness of God, the promises of Christ, and on the gentle attestations of the Holy Spirit, I venture to imitate his expressions, (full of confidence although they be,) and to say, "Only let us choose peace and God will perfect it for us." Then will the happy period arrive when with gladness we shall hear the voices of brethren mutually exhorting each other, and saying, "Let us go into the house of the Lord," that he may explain to us his will; that "our feet may joyfully stand within the gates of Jerusalem;" that in an ecstasy of delight we may contemplate the Church of Christ," as a city that is compact together, whither the tribes go up, the tribes of the Lord, unto the testimony of Israel to give thanks unto the name of the Lord:" that with thanksgiving we may admire "the thrones of judgment which are set there, the thrones of the house of David," the thrones of men of veracity, of princes who in imitation of David's example are peace makers, and of magistrates who conform themselves to the similitude of the man after God's own heart. Thus shall we enjoy the felicity to accost each other in cheerful converse, and by way of encouragement sweetly to whisper in the ears of each other, "pray for the peace of the Church Universal," and in our mutual prayers let us invoke "prosperity on them that love her;" that with unanimous voice, from the inmost recesses of our hearts, we may consecrate to her these votive intercessions and promises. "Peace be within thy walls, and prosperity within thy palaces: for our brethren and companions' sakes, we will now say, peace be within thee! Because of the house of the Lord our God we will seek thy good." (Psalm 122.) Thus at length shall it come to pass, that, being anointed with spiritual delights we shall sing together in jubilant strains, that most pleasant Song of Degrees, "Behold how good and how pleasant it is for brethren to dwell together in unity," &c. And, from a sight of the orderly walk and peaceable conduct of the faithful in the house of God, filled with the hopes of consummating these acts of pacification in heaven, we may conclude in these words of the Apostle, "And as many as walk according to this rule, peace be on them, and mercy upon the Israel of God." (Gal. vi. 16.) Mercy, therefore, and Peace, be upon the Israel of God. I have concluded.

A Declaration Of The Sentiments Of Arminius On

On Predestination
Divine Providence
The Freedom Of The Will
The Grace Of God
The Perseverance Of The Saints
The Assurance Of Salvation
The Perfection Of Believers In This Life
The Divinity Of The Son Of God
The Justification Of Man Before God

REVISION OF THE DUTCH CONFESSION & HEIDELBERG CATECHISM

To the noble and most potent the states of Holland and West Friezland, my Supreme Governor, my most noble, potent, wise and prudent Lords:

After the conference which, by the command of your mightinesses, was convened here at the Hague, between Gomarus and myself, had been held in the presence of four ministers and under the superintendence of their Lordships the Counselors of the Supreme Court, the result of that meeting was reported to your highnesses. Some allusion having been made in that report to the nature and importance of the controversy between us, it soon afterward, seemed good to your highnesses to cite each of us, with those four ministers, to appear openly before you in your honourable assembly, and in that public manner to intimate to all of us whatever you then judged to be expedient. After we had appeared before Your mightinesses, Gomarus affirmed, "that the controversy between him and me, was of such immense importance, that, with the opinions which I professed, he durst not appear in the presence of his maker." He likewise asserted, "that, unless some mode of prevention were promptly devised, the consequence would be, that the various provinces, churches, and cities of our native land, and even the citizens themselves, would be placed in a state of mutual enmity and variance, and would rise up in arms against each other." To all those allegations I then made no reply, except "that I certainly was not conscious of entertaining any such atrocious sentiments in religion, as those of which he had spoken; and I confidently expressed a hope, that I should never afford either cause or occasion for schism and separation, in the Church of God or in our common country." In confirmation of which, I added, "that I was prepared to make an open and bona fide declaration of all my sentiments, views, and designs on every subject connected with religion, whenever I might receive a summons to appear before this august assembly, and even prior to my retiring at that time from your presence." Your highnesses having since deliberated upon the proposal and offer which I then made, deem it proper now to summon me before you, for the purpose of redeeming, in this hall, the pledge which I had previously given. To fulfill that promise, I now appear in this place, and will with all due fidelity discharge my duty, whatever it be that is demanded of me in relation to this affair.

Yet since a sinister report, has for a long time been industriously and extensively circulated about me, not only among my own countrymen but also among foreigners, in which report, I am represented to have hitherto refused, after frequent solicitations, to make an open profession of my sentiments on the matter of religion and my designs concerning it; and since this unfounded rumor has already operated most injuriously against me, I importunately intreat to be favoured with your gracious permission to make an ingenuous and open declaration of all the circumstances which relate to this business, before I proceed to the discussion of other topics.

1. Account of a Conference proposed to me, but which I refused.

On the 30th of June, in the year 1605, three Deputies of the Synod of South Holland came to me at Leyden; they were Francis Lansbergius, Libertus Fraxinus, and Daniel Dolegius of pious memory, each of them the minister of their respective churches at Rotterdam, the Hague, and Delft. Two members of the Synod of North Holland accompanied them-John Bogardus, minister of the Church at Haerlem, and James Rolandus of the Church at Amsterdam. They told me, "they had heard, that at the regular meetings of certain of their classes, in the examination to which candidates for holy orders must submit prior to their admission into the Christian ministry, some of the students of the University of Leyden had returned such answers to the questions propounded to them as were of a novel description and contrary to the common and received doctrine of the Churches. Those novelties," it was said, "the young men affirmed to have been instilled into them while under my tuition." In such a situation of affairs, they desired me "to engage in a friendly conference with them, by which they might have it in their power to perceive if there were any truth in this charge, and that they might afterwards be the better qualified to consult the interests of the Church." To these suggestions I replied, "that I could by no means approve of the mode of proceeding which they recommended: For such a course would inevitably subject me to frequent and almost incessant applications for a friendly interview and conversation, if any one thought it needful to pester me in that manner whenever a student made use of a new or uncommon answer, and in excuse pretended to have learned it from me. The following therefore appeared to me a plan of greater wisdom and prudence: As often as a student during his examination returned any answer, which, according to his affirmation, had been derived from my instructions, provided the brethren considered such answer to stand in opposition to the confession and catechism of the Belgic Churches, they should immediately confront that student with me; and, for the sake of investigating such an affair, I was ready to proceed at my own expense to any town, however distant, which it might please the brethren to appoint for that purpose. The obvious consequence of this method would be, that, after it had been resorted to a few times, it would cause it clearly and evidently to appear whether the student's assertion were the truth or only a calumny.

But when Francis Lansbergius, in the name of the rest of his brethren, continued to urge and solicit a conference I gave it as a further reason why I could not see the propriety of entering into a conference with them, that they appeared before me in the character of deputies, who had afterwards to render to the Synod an account of all their proceedings; and that I was not therefore at liberty to accede to their wishes, unless, not only with the knowledge and consent, but at the express command of others who were my superiors, and whom I was equally with them bound to obey. Besides, it would be connected with no small risk and danger to me, if, in the relation of the event of our conference which they might hereafter give to the Synod, I should leave that relation entirely to their faithfulness and discretion. They had likewise no cause for demanding any thing of this kind from me, who was quite unconscious of having propounded a single doctrine, either at Leyden or Amsterdam, that was contrary to the word of God or to the Confession and Catechism of the Churches in the Low Countries. For no such accusation had ever yet been brought against me by any person; and, I was confident, no attempt would be made to substantiate against me a charge of this description, if he who preferred such a charge were bound at the same time either to establish it by proofs, or, in failure of his proofs, to confess his uncharitable offense."

2. An offer on my part, of a conference with these Deputies, which they refused.

I then told these five gentlemen, "that, notwithstanding all this, if they would consent to relinquish the title Deputies, and would each in his own private capacity enter into a conference with me, I was ready at that very moment to engage in it." The conditions which I proposed to be mutually observed by us, were these: (i.) That they should explain their opinions on every single article and then I would explain mine; (ii.) They should adduce their proofs, and I would adduce mine; and (iii.) That they should at last attempt a refutation of my sentiments and reasons, and I would in return try to refute theirs. (iv.) If in this manner either party could afford complete satisfaction to the other, the result would be agreeable: but, if neither party could satisfy the other, then no mention of the subjects discussed in our private conference, or of its unfavourable termination, should be made in any place or company whatever, until the whole affair should be referred to a national Synod."

But when to this proposition they had given a direct refusal, we should have separated from each other without further discourse, had I not requested "that they would offer a conference in the same manner to Gomarus, as well as to Trelcatius of pious memory, because it did not appear to me, that I had given them any cause for making such a demand upon me, rather than upon either of my two colleagues." At the same time I enforced my concluding expressions with several arguments, which it would be too tedious now to repeat in the presence of your mightinesses. When I had finished, the deputies replied, "that they would comply with my request, and would wait on the two other professors of divinity and make them a similar offer:" and prior to their departure from Leyden, they called and assured me, that they had in this particular fulfilled their promise.

This, then, is the first of the many requests that have been preferred to me. It was the cause of much conversation at the time when it occurred: For many persons spoke about it. Some of them related it imperfectly, and in a manner very different from what were the real circumstances of the whole transaction; while others suppressed many essential particulars, and studiously concealed the counter-proposal which I had tendered to the deputies and the strong reasons which I produced in its support.

3. Another application is made to me.

A few days afterwards, that is, on the 28th of July in the same year, 1605, a request of a similar character was likewise presented to me, in the name of the Presbytery of the Church of Leyden: but on this condition, that if I approved of it, other persons, whom such a request equally concerned, should also be summoned before the same ecclesiastical tribunal: but if this offer did not receive my approbation, nothing further should be attempted. But when I had intimated, that I did not clearly perceive, how this request could possibly obtain approval from me, and when I had subjoined my reasons which were of the same description as those which I had employed on the preceding occasion, my answer was perfectly satisfactory to Bronchovius the Burgomaster [of Leyden] and Merula of pious memory, both of whom had come to me in the name of that Church of which they were the elders, and they determined to abandon all ulterior proceedings in that business.

4. The request of the Deputies of the Synod of South Holland to their Lordships, the visitors of the University, and the answer which they received.

On the ninth of November, in the same year, 1605, the deputies of the Synod of South Holland, Francis Lansbergius, Festus Hommius, and their associates, presented nine questions to their Lordships, the curators of the University of Leyden; these were accompanied with a petition, "that the Professors of Divinity might be commanded to answer them." But the curators replied, "that they could on no account sanction by their consent the propounding of any questions to the Professors of Divinity; and if any one supposed that something was taught in the University contrary to truth and rectitude, that person had it in his power to refer the matter of his complaint to a national Synod, which, it was hoped, would, at the earliest opportunity be convened, when it would come regularly under the cognizance of that assembly, and receive the most ample discussion." When this answer had been delivered, the deputies of the Synod did not hesitate earnestly to ask it as a particular favour, "that, by the kind permission of their Lordships, they might themselves propose those nine questions to the Professors of Divinity, and might, without troubling their Lordships, personally inform themselves what answer of his own accord, and without reluctance, each of those three Divines would return." But, after all their pleading, they were unable to obtain the permission which they so strenuously desired. The whole of this unsuccessful negotiation was conducted in such a clandestine manner, and so carefully concealed from me, that I was totally ignorant even of the arrival of those reverend deputies in our city; yet soon after their departure, I became acquainted with their mission and its failure.

5. A fourth request of the same kind.

After this, a whole year elapsed before I was again called to an account about such matters. But I must not omit to mention, that in the year 1607, a short time before the meeting of the Synod of South Holland at Delft, John Bernards, minister of the Church at Delft, Festus Hommius, minister of Leyden, and Dibbetius of Dort, were deputed by the Synod to come to me and inquire what progress I had made in the refutation of the Anabaptists. When I had given them a suitable reply concerning that affair, which was the cause of much conversation among us on both sides, and when they were just on the point of taking their leave, they begged "that I would not hesitate to reveal to them whatever views and designs I had formed on the subject of religion, for the purpose of their being communicated to the Synod, by the Deputies, for the satisfaction of the brethren." But I refused to comply with their intreaties, "because the desired explanation could not be given either conveniently or to advantage; and I did not know any place in which it was possible to explain these matters with greater propriety, than in the national Synod; which, according to the resolution of their most noble and high mightinesses, the States General, was expected very shortly to assemble." I promised "that I would use every exertion that I might be enabled in that assembly openly to profess the whole of my sentiments; and that I would employ none of that alleged concealment or dissimulation about any thing of which they might then complain." I concluded by saying, "that if I were to make my profession before them as deputies of the Synod of South Holland, I could not commit to their fidelity the relation of what might transpire, because, in matters of this description, every one was the most competent interpreter of his own meaning." After these mutual explanations, we parted from each other.

6. The same request is privately repeated to me, and my answer to it.

In addition to these different applications, I was privately desired, by certain ministers, "not to view it as a hardship to communicate my views and intentions to their colleagues, the brethren assembled in Synod:" while others intreated me "to disclose my views to them, that they might have an opportunity of pondering and examining them by themselves, in the fear of the Lord," and they gave me an assurance "that they would not divulge any portion of the desired communication" To the first of these two classes, I gave in common my usual answer, "that they had no reason for demanding such an account from me, rather than from others, but to one of these ministers, who was not among the last of the two kinds of applicants, I proposed a conference at three different times, concerning all the articles of our religion; in which we might consider and devise the best means that could possibly be adopted for establishing the truth on the most solid foundation, and for completely refuting every species of falsehood. It was also a part of my offer that such conference should be held in the presence of certain of the principal men of our country; but he did not accept of this condition. To the rest of the inquirers, I returned various answers; in some of which I plainly denied what they requested of me, and in others, I made some disclosures to the inquirers. My sole rule in making such a distinction, was, the more intimate or distant degree of acquaintance which I had with the parties. In the mean time it frequently happened, that, a short time after I had thus revealed any thing in confidence to an individual, it was slanderously related to others--how seriously soever he might have asserted in my presence, that what I had then imparted to him was, according to his judgment, agreeable to the truth, and although he had solemnly pledged his honour that he would on no account divulge it.

7. What occurred relative to the same subject in the Preparatory Convention.

To these it is also necessary to add a report which has been spread abroad by means of letters, not only within these provinces, but far beyond their confines: it is, "that, in the preparatory convention which was held at the Hague, in the month of June, 1607, by a company of the brethren who were convened by a summons from their high mightinesses, the States General, after I had been asked in a manner the most friendly to consent to a disclosure, before the brethren then present, of my views on the subject of the Christian faith, I refused; and although they promised to endeavour, as far as it was possible, to give me satisfaction, I still declined to comply with their wishes." But since I find by experience that this distorted version of the matter has procured for me not a few proofs of hatred and ill will from many persons who think that far more honourable deference ought to have been evinced by me towards that assembly, which was a convention of Divines from each of the United Provinces. I perceive a necessity is thus imposed upon me to commence at the very origin of this transaction, when I am about to relate the manner in which it occurred:

Before my departure from Leyden for the convention at the Hague which has just been mentioned, five articles were put into my hands, said to have been transmitted to some of the provinces, to have been perused by certain ministers and ecclesiastical assemblies, and considered by them as documents which embraced my sentiments on several points of religion. Those points of which they pretended to exhibit a correct delineation, were Predestination, the Fall of Adam, Free-will, Original Sin, and the Eternal Salvation of Infants. When I had read the whole of them, I thought that I plainly perceived, from the style in which they were written, who was the author of them; and as he was then present, (being one of the number summoned on that occasion,) I accosted him on this subject, and embraced that opportunity freely to intimate to him that I had good reasons for believing those articles to have been of his composition. He did not make any attempt to deny the correctness of this supposition, and replied, that they had not been distributed precisely as my articles, but as those on which the students at Leyden had held disputations." In answer to this remark, I told him, "of one thing he must be very conscious, that, by the mere act of giving circulation to such a document, he could not avoid creating a grievous and immediate prejudice against my innocence, and that the same articles would soon be ascribed to me, as if they had been my composition: when, in reality," as I then openly affirmed, "they had neither proceeded from me, nor accorded with my sentiments, and, as well as I could form a judgment they appeared to me to be at variance with the word of God."

After he and I had thus discoursed together in the presence of only two other persons, I deemed it advisable to make some mention of this affair in the convention itself, at which certain persons attended who had read those very articles, and who had, according to their own confession, accounted them as mine. This plan I accordingly pursued; and just as the convention was on the point of being dissolved, and after the account of our proceedings had been signed, and some individuals had received instructions to give their high mightinesses the States General a statement of our transactions, I requested the brethren "not to consider it an inconvenience to remain a short time together, for I had something which I was desirous to communicate." They assented to this proposal, and I told them "that I had received the five articles which I held in my hand and the tenor of which I briefly read to them; that I discovered they had been transmitted by a member of that convention, into different provinces; that I was positive concerning their distribution in Zealand and the diocese of Utrecht; and that they had been read by some ministers in their public meetings, and were considered to be documents which comprehended my sentiments." Yet, notwithstanding, I protested to the whole of that assembly, with a good conscience, and as in the presence of God, "that those articles were not mine, and did not contain my sentiments." Twice I repeated this solemn asseveration, and besought the brethren "not so readily to attach credit to reports that were circulated concerning me, nor so easily to listen to any thing that was represented as proceeding from me or that had been rumored abroad to my manifest injury."

To these observations, a member of that convention answered, "that it would be well for me, on this account, to signify to the brethren what portion of those articles obtained my approbation, and what portion I disavowed, that they might thus have an opportunity of becoming acquainted in some degree with my sentiments." Another member urged the same reasons; to which I replied, "that the convention had not been appointed to meet for such a purpose, that we had already been long enough detained together, and that their high mightinesses, the States General were now waiting for our determination," in that manner, we separated from each other, no one attempting any longer to continue the conversation, neither did all the members of the convention express a joint concurrence in that request, nor employ any kind of persuasion with me to prove that such an explanation was in their judgment quite equitable. Besides, according to the most correct intelligence which I have since gained, some of those who were then present, declared afterwards, "that it was a part of the instructions which had been previously given to them, not to enter into any conference concerning doctrine; and that, if a discussion of that kind had arisen, they must have instantly retired from the convention." These several circumstances therefore prove that I was very far from being "solicited by the whole assembly" to engage in the desired explanation.

8. *My reasons for refusing a Conference.*

Most noble and potent Lords, this is a true narration of those interviews and conferences which the brethren have solicited, and of my continued refusal: from the whole of which, every person may, in my opinion, clearly perceive that there is no cause whatever for preferring an accusation against me on account of my behaviour throughout these transactions; especially when he considers their request, with the manner in which it was delivered, and at the same time my refusal with the reasons for it; but this is still more obvious from my counter-proposal.

1. Their request, which amounted to a demand upon me for a declaration on matters of faith, was not supported by any reasons, as far as I am enabled to form a judgment. For I never furnished a cause to any man why he should require such a declaration from me rather than from other people, by my having taught any thing contrary to the word of God, or to the Confession and Catechism of the Belgic Churches. At no period have I ceased to make this avowal, and I repeat it on this occasion. I am likewise prepared to consent to an inquiry being instituted into this my profession, either by a Provincial or a National Synod, that the truth of it may by that means, be made yet more apparent--if from such an examination it may be thought possible to derive any advantage.

2. The manner in which their request was delivered, proved of itself to be a sufficient obstacle, because it was openly made by a deputation. I was also much injured by the way in which the Synod prejudged my cause; for we may presume that it would not through its deputies invite any man to a conference, unless he had given strong grounds for such an interview. For this reason I did not consider myself at liberty to consent to a conference of this description, lest I should, by that very act, and apparently through a consciousness of guilt, have confessed that I had taught something that was wrong or unlawful.

3. The reasons of my refusal were these:

First. Because as I am not subject to the jurisdiction either of the North Holland Synod or that of South Holland, but have other superiors to whom I am bound to render an account of all my concerns, I could not consent to a conference with deputies, except by the advice of those superiors and at their express command: especially since a conference of this kind was not incumbent on me in consequence of the ordinary discharge of my duty. It was also not obscurely hinted by the deputies, that the conference, [in 1605,] would by no means be a private one; but this they discovered in a manner sufficiently intelligible, when they refused to enter into a conference with me, divested of their title of "deputies." I should, therefore, have failed in obedience to my superiors, if I had not rejected a conference which was in this manner proposed. I wish the brethren would remember this fact, that although every one of our ministers is subject as a member to the jurisdiction of the particular Synod to which he belongs, yet not one of them has hitherto dared to engage in a conference, without the advice and permission of the magistrates under whom he is placed; that no particular magistrates have ever allowed any minister within their jurisdiction to undertake a conference with the deputies of the Churches, unless they had themselves previously granted their consent; and that it was frequently their wish, to be present at such conference, in the persons of their own deputies. Let it be recollected what transpired at Leyden, in the case of Coolhasius [Koolhaes,] at Gouda with Herman Herberts, at Horn in the case of Cornelius Wiggeri, [Wiggerston,] and at Medenblick in the case of Tako, [Sybrants.]

The second reason by which I was dissuaded from a conference, is this: I perceived that there would be a great inequality in the conference which was proposed, when, on the contrary, it is necessary that the greatest equality should exist between the parties who are about to confer together on any subject. For (1.) they came to me armed with public authority; while, with respect to myself, everything partook of a private character. And I am not so ignorant in these matters as not to perceive the powerful support which that man enjoys who transacts any business under the sanction of the public authority. (2.) They were themselves three in number, and had with them two deputies of the Synod of North Holland. On the other hand, I was alone, and destitute not only of all assistance, but also of persons who might act as witnesses of the proceedings that were then to have commenced, and to whom they as well as myself might have safely entrusted our several causes. (3.) They were not persons at their own disposal, but compelled to depend on the judgment of their superiors; and they were bound most pertinaciously to contend for those religious sentiments, which their superiors had within their own minds determined to maintain. To such a length was this principle extended, that they were not even left to their own discretion--to admit the validity of the argument which I might have adduced, however cogent and forcible they might have found them to be, and even if they had been altogether unanswerable. From these considerations I could not see by what means both parties could obtain that mutual advantage, which ought properly to accrue from such a conference. I might have gained some beneficial result from it; because I was completely at liberty, and, by employing my own conscience alone in forming a decision, I could, without prejudice to any one, have made those admissions which my conviction of the truth might have dictated to me as correct. Of what great importance this last circumstance might be, your Lordships would have most fully discovered by experience, had any of you been present in the Preparatory Convention, as the representatives of your own august body.

My third reason is, that the account which they would have rendered to their superiors after the conference, could not but have operated in many ways to my injury, whether I had been absent or present at the time when they delivered their report. (1.) Had I been absent, it might easily have happened either through the omission or the addition of certain words, or through the alteration of others, in regard to their sense or order, that some fact or argument would be repeated in a manner very different from that in which it really occurred. Such an erroneous statement might also have been made, either through the inconsiderateness which arises from a defect in the intellect, through the weakness of an imperfect memory, or through a prejudice of the affections. (2.) And indeed by my presence, I could with difficulty have avoided or corrected this inconvenience; because a greater degree of credit would have been given to their own deputies, than to me who was only a private individual.

Lastly. By this means I should have conveyed to that assembly, [the Provincial Synod,] a right and some kind of prerogative over me; which, in reference to me, it does not actually possess; and which, consistently with that office whose duties I discharge, it would not be possible for me to transfer to the Synod without manifest injustice towards those persons under whose jurisdiction it has been the pleasure of the general magistracy of the land to place me. Imperious necessity, therefore, as well as equity, demanded of me to reject the terms on which this conference was offered.

4. But however strong my sentiments might be on this subject, I gave these deputies an opportunity of gaining the information which they desired. If it had been their wish to accept the private conference which I proposed, they would have become possessed of my sentiments on every article of the Christian Faith. Besides, this conference would have been much better adapted to promote our mutual edification and instruction, than a public one could be; because it is customary in private conferences, for each person to speak everything with greater familiarity and freedom, than when all the formalities of deputations are observed, if I may so express myself. Neither had they the least reason to manifest any reluctance on this point; because every one of them was at liberty, (if he chose,) to enter into a private conference between him and me alone. But when I made this offer to all and to each of them, I added as one of my most particular stipulations, that, whatever the discussions might be which arose between us, they should remain within our bosoms, and no particle of them should be divulged to any person living. If on these terms they had consented to hold a conference with me, I entertain not the smallest doubt that we should either have given each other complete satisfaction: or we should at least have made it apparent, that, from our mutual controversy, no imminent danger could easily arise, to injure either that truth which is necessary to salvation, piety, or Christian peace and amity.

9. The complaint concerning my refusal to make a declaration of my sentiments, does not agree with the rumors concerning me which are in general circulation.

But omitting all further mention of those transactions, I am not able entirely to satisfy myself by what contrivance these two complaints appear consistent with each other. (1.) That I refuse to make a profession of my sentiments; and yet (2.) Invectives are poured forth against me, both in foreign countries and at home, as though I am attempting to introduce into the Church and into the Christian religion, novel, impure and false doctrines. If I do not openly profess my sentiments, from what can their injurious tendency be made evident? If I do not explain myself, by what method can I be introducing false doctrines? If they be mere groundless suspicions that are advanced against me, it is uncharitable to grant them entertainment, or at least to ascribe to them such great importance.

But it is cast upon me as a reproach, "that I do certainly disclose a few of my opinions, but not all of them; and that, from the few which I thus make known, the object at which I aim is no longer obscure, but becomes very evident."

In reference to this censure, the great consideration ought to be, "can any of those sentiments which I am said to have disclosed, be proved to stand in contradiction either to the word of God, or the Confession of the Belgic Churches" (1.) If it be decided, that they are contrary to the Confession, then I have been engaged in teaching something in opposition to a document, "against which never to propound any doctrine," was the faithful promise which I made, when I signed it with my own hand. If, therefore, I be found thus criminal, I ought to be visited with merited punishment. (2.) But if it can be proved, that any of those opinions are contrary to the word of God, then I ought to experience a greater degree of blame, and to suffer a severer punishment, and compelled either to utter a recantation or to resign my office, especially if those heads of doctrine which I have uttered, are of such a description as to be notoriously prejudicial to the honour of God and the salvation of mankind. (3.) But if those few sentiments which I am accused of having advanced, are found neither to be at variance with the word of God nor with the Confession, which I have just mentioned, then those consequences which are elicited from them, or seem dependent on them, cannot possibly be contradictory either to the word of God or to the Belgic Confession. For, according to the rule of the schoolmen, "if the consectaries or consequences of any doctrine be false, it necessarily follows that the doctrine itself is also false, and vice versa." The one of these two courses, therefore, ought to have been pursued towards me, either to have instituted an action against me, or to have given no credit to those rumors. If I might have my own choice, the latter course is that which I should have desired; but of the former I am not at all afraid. For, how extensively soever and in all directions those Thirty-One Articles which concern me have been dispersed to my great injury and disparagement, and though they have been placed in the hands of several men of great eminence, they afford sufficient internal testimony, from the want of sense and of other requisites visible in their very composition, that they are charged upon me through a total disregard to justice, honour and conscience.

10. The principal reasons why I durst not disclose to the deputies my opinions on the subject of Religion.

But some person will perhaps say: "for the sake of avoiding these disturbances, and partly in order by such a measure to give some satisfaction to a great number of ministers, you might undoubtedly have made to your brethren an open and simple declaration of your sentiments on the whole subject of religion, either for the purpose of being yourself maturely instructed in more correct principles, or that they might have been able in an opportune manner to prepare themselves for a mutual conference."

But I was deterred from adopting that method, on account of three inconveniences, of which I was afraid:

First,. I was afraid that if I had made a profession of my sentiments, the consequence would have been, that an inquiry would be instituted on the part of others, with regard to the manner in which an action might be framed against me from those premises. Secondly. Another cause of my fear, was, that such a statement of my opinions would have furnished matter for discussion and refutation, in the pulpits of the Churches and the scholastic exercises of the Universities. Thirdly. I was also afraid, that my opinions would have been transmitted to foreign Universities and Churches, in hopes of obtaining from them a sentence of condemnation, and the means of oppressing me." That I had very weighty reasons to fear every one of these consequences together, it would not be difficult for me clearly to demonstrate from the Thirty-One Articles, and from the writings of certain individuals.

With respect to "the personal instruction and edification," which I might have hoped to derive from such a disclosure, it is necessary to consider, that not only I but many others, and even they themselves, have peculiar views which they have formed on religious topics; and, therefore, that such instruction cannot be applied to any useful purpose, except in some place or other where we may all hereafter appear together, and where a definitive sentence, as it is called, both may and must be pronounced. With respect to "the opportune and benefiting preparation which my brethren ought in the mean time to be making for a conference," I declare that it will at that time be most seasonable and proper when all shall have produced their views, and disclosed them before a whole assembly, that thus an account may be taken of them all at once, and they may be considered together.

Since none of these objections have any existence in this august assembly, I proceed to the declaration of my sentiments.

Having in this manner refuted all those objections which have been made against me, I will now endeavour to fulfill my promise, and to execute those commands which your Lordships have been pleased to lay upon me. I entertain a confident persuasion, that no prejudice will be created against me or my sentiments from this act, however imperfectly I may perform it, because it has its origin in that obedience which is due from me to this noble assembly, next to God, and according to the Divine pleasure.

I. ON PREDESTINATION

The first and most important article in religion on which I have to offer my views, and which for many years past has engaged my attention, is the Predestination of God, that is, the Election of men to salvation, and the Reprobation of them to destruction. Commencing with this article, I will first explain what is taught concerning it, both in discourses and writings, by certain persons in our Churches, and in the University of Leyden. I will afterwards declare my own views and thoughts on the same subject, while I shew my opinion on what they advance.

On this article there is no uniform and simple opinion among the teachers of our Churches; but there is some variation in certain parts of it in which they differ from each other.

1. The first opinion, which I reject, but which is espoused by those [Supralapsarians] who assume the very highest ground of this Predestination.

The opinion of those who take the highest ground on this point, as it is generally contained in their writings, is to this effect:

"I. God by an eternal and immutable decree has predestinated, from among men, (whom he did not consider as being then created, much less as being fallen,) certain individuals to everlasting life, and others to eternal destruction, without any regard whatever to righteousness or sin, to obedience or disobedience, but purely of his own good pleasure, to demonstrate the glory of his justice and mercy; or, (as others assert,) to demonstrate his saving grace, wisdom and free uncontrollable power.

"II. In addition to this decree, God has pre-ordained certain determinate means which pertain to its execution, and this by an eternal and immutable decree. These means necessarily follow by virtue of the preceding decree, and necessarily bring him who has been predestinated, to the end which has been fore-ordained for him. Some of these means belong in common both to the decree of election and that of rejection, and others of them are specially restricted to the one decree or to the other.

"III. The means common to both the decrees, are three: the first is, the creation of man in the upright [or erect] state of original righteousness, or after the image and likeness of God in righteousness and true holiness. The second is, the permission of the fall of Adam, or the ordination of God that man should sin, and become corrupt or vitiated. The third is, the loss or the removal of original righteousness and of the image of God, and a being concluded under sin and condemnation.

"IV. For unless God had created some men, he would not have had any upon whom he might either bestow eternal life, or superinduce everlasting death. Unless he had created them in righteousness and true holiness, he would himself have been the author of sin, and would by this means have possessed no right either to punish them to the praise of his justice, or to save them to the praise of his mercy. Unless they had themselves sinned, and by the demerit of sin had rendered themselves guilty of death, there would have been no room for the demonstration either of justice or of mercy.

"V. The means pre-ordained for the execution of the decree of election, are also these three. The first is, the pre-ordination, or the giving of Jesus Christ as a Mediator and a saviour, who might by his meet deserve, [or purchase,] for all the elect and for them only, the lost righteousness and life, and might communicate them by his own power [Or virtue]. The second is, the call [or vocation] to faith outwardly by the word, but inwardly by his Spirit, in the mind, affections and will; by an operation of such efficacy that the elect person of necessity yields assent and obedience to the vocation, in so much that it is not possible for him to do otherwise than believe and be obedient to this vocation. From hence arise justification and sanctification through the blood of Christ and his Spirit, and from them the existence of all good works. And all that, manifestly by means of the same force and necessity. The third is, that which keeps and preserves the elect in faith, holiness, and a zeal for good works; or, it is the gift of perseverance; the virtue of which is such, that believing and elect persons not only do not sin with a full and entire will, or do not fall away totally from faith and grace, but it likewise is neither possible for them to sin with a full and perfect will, nor to fall away totally or finally from faith and grace.

"VI. The two last of these means [vocation and perseverance,] belong only to the elect who are of adult age. But God employs a shorter way to salvation, by which he conducts those children of believers and saints who depart out of this life before they arrive at years of maturity; that is, provided they belong to the number of the elect, (who are known to God alone,) for God bestows on them Christ as their saviour, and gives them to Christ, to save them by his blood and Holy Spirit, without actual faith and perseverance in it [faith]; and this he does according to the promise of the covenant of grace, I will be a God unto you, and unto your seed after you.

"VII. The means pertaining to the execution of the decree of reprobation to eternal death, are partly such as peculiarly belong to all those who are rejected and reprobate, whether they ever arrive at years of maturity or die before that period; and they are partly such as are proper only to some of them. The mean that is common to all the reprobate, is desertion in sin, by denying to them that saving grace which is sufficient and necessary to the salvation of any one. This negation [or denial,] consists of two parts. For, in the first place, God did not will that Christ should die for them [the reprobate,] or become their saviour, and this neither in reference to the antecedent will of God, (as some persons call it,) nor in reference to his sufficient will, or the value of the price of reconciliation; because this price was not offered for reprobates, either with respect to the decree of God, or its virtue and efficacy. (1.) But the other part of this negation [or denial] is, that God is unwilling to communicate the Spirit of Christ to reprobates, yet without such communication they can neither be made partakers of Christ nor of his benefits.

"VIII. The mean which belongs properly only to some of the reprobates, is obduration, [or the act of hardening,] which befalls those of them who have attained to years of maturity, either because they have very frequently and enormously sinned against the law of God, or because they have rejected the grace of the gospel. (1.) To the execution of the first species of induration, or hardening, belong the illumination of their conscience by means of knowledge, and its conviction of the righteousness of the law. For it is impossible that this law should not necessarily detain them in unrighteousness, to render them inexcusable. (2.) For the execution of the second species of induration, God employs a call by the preaching of his gospel, which call is inefficacious and insufficient both in respect to the decree of God, and to its issue or event. This calling is either only an external one, which it is neither in their desire nor in their power to obey. Or it is likewise an internal one, by which some of them may be excited in their understandings to accept and believe the things which they hear; but yet it is only with such a faith as that with which the devils are endowed when they believe and tremble. Others of them are excited and conducted still further, so as to desire in a certain measure to taste the heavenly gift. But the latter are, of all others, the most unhappy, because they are raised up on high, that they may be brought down with a heavier fall. And this fate it is impossible for them to escape, for they must of necessity return to their vomit, and depart or fall away from the faith. "9.

"IX. From this decree of Divine election and reprobation, and from this administration of the means which pertain to the execution of both of them, it follows, that the elect are necessarily saved, it being impossible for them to perish--and that the reprobate are necessarily damned, it being impossible for them to be saved; and all this from the absolute purpose [or determination] of God, which is altogether antecedent to all things, and to all those causes which are either in things themselves or can possibly result from them."

These opinions concerning predestination are considered, by some of those who advocate them, to be the foundation of Christianity, salvation and of its certainty. On these sentiments they suppose, "is founded the sure and undoubted consolation of all believers, which is capable of rendering their consciences tranquil; and on them also depends the praise of the grace of God, so that if any contradiction be offered to this doctrine, God is necessarily deprived of the glory of his grace, and then the merit of salvation is attributed to the free will of man and to his own powers and strength, which ascription savours of Pelagianism."

These then are the causes which are offered why the advocates of these sentiments labour with a common anxiety to retain the purity of such a doctrine in their churches and why they oppose themselves to all those innovations which are at variance with them.

2. MY SENTIMENTS ON THE PRECEDING SCHEME OF PREDESTINATION.

But, for my own part, to speak my sentiments with freedom, and yet with a salvo in favour of a better judgment, I am of opinion, that this doctrine of theirs contains many things that are both false and impertinent, and at an utter disagreement with each other; all the instances of which, the present time will not permit me to recount, but I will subject it to an examination only in those parts which are most prominent and extensive. I shall, therefore, propose to myself four principal heads, which are of the greatest importance in this doctrine; and when I have in the first place explained of what kind they are, I will afterwards declare more fully the judgment and sentiments which I have formed concerning them. They are the following:

"I. That God has absolutely and precisely decreed to save certain particular men by his mercy or grace, but to condemn others by his justice: and to do all this without having any regard in such decree to righteousness or sin, obedience or disobedience, which could possibly exist on the part of one class of men or of the other.

"II. That, for the execution of the preceding decree, God determined to create Adam, and all men in him, in an upright state of original righteousness; besides which he also ordained them to commit sin, that they might thus become guilty of eternal condemnation and be deprived of original righteousness.

"III. That those persons whom God has thus positively willed to save, he has decreed not only to salvation but also to the means which pertain to it; (that is, to conduct and bring them to faith in Christ Jesus, and to perseverance in that faith ;) and that He also in reality leads them to these results by a grace and power that are irresistible, so that it is not possible for them to do otherwise than believe, persevere in faith, and be saved.

"IV. That to those whom, by his absolute will, God has fore-ordained to perdition, he has also decreed to deny that grace which is necessary and sufficient for salvation, and does not in reality confer it upon them; so that they are neither placed in a possible condition nor in any capacity of believing or of being saved."

After a diligent contemplation and examination of these four heads, in the fear of the Lord, I make the following declaration respecting this doctrine of predestination.

3. I REJECT THIS PREDESTINATION FOR THE FOLLOWING REASONS:

I. Because it is not the foundation of Christianity, of Salvation, or of its certainty.

1. It is not the foundation of Christianity: (1.) For this Predestination is not that decree of God by which Christ is appointed by God to be the saviour, the Head, and the Foundation of those who will be made heirs of salvation. Yet that decree is the only foundation of Christianity. (2.) For the doctrine of this Predestination is not that doctrine by which, through faith, we as lively stones are built up into Christ, the only corner stone, and are inserted into him as the members of the body are joined to their head.

2. It is not the foundation of Salvation: (1.) For this Predestination is not that decree of the good pleasure of God in Christ Jesus on which alone our salvation rests and depends. (2.) The doctrine of this Predestination is not the foundation of Salvation: for it is not "the power of God to salvation to every one that believeth :" because through it "the righteousness of God" is not "revealed from faith to faith."

3. Nor is it the foundation of the certainty of salvation:

For that is dependent upon this decree, "they who believe, shall be saved :" I believe, therefore, I shall be saved. But the doctrine of this Predestination embraces within itself neither the first nor the second member of the syllogism.

This is likewise confessed by some persons in these words:

"we do not wish to state that the knowledge of this [Predestination] is the foundation of Christianity or of salvation, or that it is necessary to salvation in the same manner as the doctrine of the Gospel," &c.

II. This doctrine of Predestination comprises within it neither the whole nor any part of the Gospel. For, according to the tenor of the discourses delivered by John and Christ, as they are described to us by the Evangelist, and according to the doctrine of the Apostles and Christ after his ascension, the Gospel consists partly of an injunction to repent and believe, and partly of a promise to bestow forgiveness of sins, the grace of the Spirit, and life eternal. But this Predestination belongs neither to the injunction to repent and believe, nor to the annexed promise. Nay, this doctrine does not even teach what kind of men in general God has predestinated, which is properly the doctrine of the Gospel; but it embraces within itself a certain mystery, which is known only to God, who is the Predestinater, and in which mystery are comprehended what particular persons and how many he has decreed to save and to condemn. From these premises I draw a further conclusion, that this doctrine of Predestination is not necessary to salvation, either as an object of knowledge, belief, hope, or performance. A Confession to this effect has been made by a certain learned man, in the theses which he has proposed for discussion on this subject, in the following words:

"Wherefore the gospel cannot be simply termed the book or the revelation of Predestination, but only in a relative sense. Because it does not absolutely denote either the matter of the number or the form; that is, it neither declares how many persons in particular, nor (with a few exceptions,) who they are, but only the description of them in general, whom God has predestinated."

III. This doctrine was never admitted, decreed, or approved in any Council, either general or particular, for the first six hundred years after Christ.

1. Not in the General Council of Nice, in which sentence was given against Arius and in favour of the Deity and Consubstantiality of the Son of God. Not in the first Council of Constantinople, in which a decree was passed against Macedonius, respecting the Deity of the Holy Spirit. Not in the Council of Ephesus, which determined against Nestorius, and in favour of the Unity of the Person of the Son of God. Not in that of Chalcedon, which condemned Eutyches, and determined, "that in one and the same person of our Lord Jesus Christ, there were two distinct natures, which differ from each other in their essence." Not in the second Council of Constantinople, in which Peter, Bishop of Antioch, and Anthymus, Bishop of Constantinople, with certain other persons, were condemned for having asserted "that the Father had likewise suffered," as well as the Son. Nor in the third Council of Constantinople, in which the Monothelites were condemned for having asserted "that there was only one will and operation in Jesus Christ."

2. But this doctrine was not discussed or confirmed in particular Councils, such as that of Jerusalem, Orange, or even that of Mela in Africa, which was held against Pelagius and his errors, as is apparent from the articles of doctrine which were then decreed both against his person and his false opinions.

But so far was Augustine's doctrine of Predestination from being received in those councils, that when Celestinus, the Bishop of Rome, who was his contemporary, wrote to the Bishops of France, and condemned the doctrines of the Pelagians, he concluded his epistle in these words: "but as we dare not despise, so neither do we deem it necessary to defend the more profound and difficult parts of the questions which occur in this controversy, and which have been treated to a very great extent by those who opposed the heretics. Because we believe, that whatever the writings according to the forementioned rules of the Apostolic See have taught us, is amply sufficient for confessing the grace of God, from whose work, credit and authority not a little must be subtracted or withdrawn," &c. In reference to the rules which were laid down by Celestinus in that epistle, and which had been decreed in the three preceding particular Councils, we shall experience no difficulty in agreeing together about them, especially in regard to those matters which are necessary to the establishment of grace in opposition to Pelagius and his errors.

IV. None of those Doctors or Divines of the Church who held correct and orthodox sentiments for the first six hundred years after the birth of Christ, ever brought this doctrine forward or gave it their approval. Neither was it professed and approved by a single individual of those who shewed themselves the principal and keenest defenders of grace against Pelagius. Of this description, it is evident, were St. Jerome, Augustine, the author of the treatise entitled, De Vocatione Gentium, ["The calling of the Gentiles,"] Prosper of Aquitaine, Hilary, Fulgentius, and Orosius. This is very apparent from their writings.

V. It neither agrees nor corresponds with the Harmony of those confessions which were printed and published together in one volume at Geneva, in the name of the Reformed and Protestant Churches. If that harmony of Confessions be faithfully consulted, it will appear that many of them do not speak in the same manner concerning Predestination; that some of them only incidentally mention it; and that they evidently never once touch upon those heads of the doctrine, which are now in great repute and particularly urged in the preceding scheme of Predestination, and which I have already adduced. Nor does any single Confession deliver this doctrine in the same manner as it has just now been propounded by me. The Confessions of Bohemia, England and Wirtemburgh, and the first Helvetian [Swiss] Confession, and that of the four cities of Strasburgh, Constance, Memmingen, and Lindau, make no mention of this Predestination. Those of Basle and Saxony, only take a very cursory notice of it in three words. The Augustan Confession speaks of it in such a manner as to induce the Genevan editors to think, that some annotation was necessary on their part, to give us a previous warning. The last of the Helvetian [Swiss] Confessions, to which a great portion of the Reformed Churches have expressed their assent and which they have subscribed, likewise speaks of it in such a strain as makes me very desirous to see what method can possibly be adopted to give it any accordance with that doctrine of Predestination which I have just now advanced. Yet this [Swiss] Confession is that which has obtained the approbation of the Churches of Geneva and Savoy.

VI. Without the least contention or caviling, it may very properly be made a question of doubt, whether this doctrine agrees with the Belgic Confession and the Heidelberg Catechism; as I shall briefly demonstrate.

1. In the 14th Article of the Dutch Confession, these expressions occur: "Man knowingly and willingly subjected himself to sin, and, consequently, to death and cursing, while he lent an ear to the deceiving words and impostures of the devil," &c. From this sentence I conclude, that man did not sin on account of any necessity through a preceding decree of Predestination: which inference is diametrically opposed to that doctrine of Predestination against which I now contend. Then, in the 16th Article, which treats of the eternal election of God, these words are contained: "God shewed himself Merciful, by delivering from damnation, and by saving, those persons whom, in his eternal and immutable counsel and cording to his gratuitous goodness, he chose in Christ Jesus our Lord, without any regard to their works. And he shewed himself just, in leaving others in that their fall and perdition into which they had precipitated themselves." It is not obvious to me, how these words are consistent with this doctrine of Predestination.

2. In the 20th question of the Heidelberg Catechism, we read:

"salvation through Christ is not given [restored] to all them who had perished in Adam, but to those only who are engrafted into Christ by the faith, and who embrace his benefits." From this sentence I infer, that God has not absolutely Predestinated any men to salvation; but that he has in his decree considered [or looked upon] them as believers. This deduction is at open conflict with the first and third points of this Predestination. In the 54th question of the same Catechism, it is said: "I believe that, from the beginning to the end of the world, the Son of God out of the entire race of mankind doth by his word and Spirit gather or collect unto himself a company chosen unto eternal life and agreeing together in the true faith." In this sentence "election to eternal life," and "agreement in the faith," stand in mutual juxtaposition; and in such a manner, that the latter is not rendered subordinate to the former, which, according to these sentiments on Predestination ought to have been done. In that case the words should have been placed in the following order: "the son of God calls and gathers to himself, by his word and Spirit, a company chosen to eternal life, that they may believe and agree together in the true faith."

Since such are the statements of our Confession and Catechism, no reason whatever exists, why those who embrace and defend these sentiments on Predestination, should either violently endeavour to obtrude them on their colleagues and on the Church of Christ; or why they should take it amiss, and put the worst construction upon it, when any thing is taught in the Church or University that is not exactly accordant with their doctrine, or that is opposed to it.

VII. I affirm, that this doctrine is repugnant to the Nature of God, but particularly to those Attributes of his nature by which he performs and manages all things, his wisdom, justice, and goodness.

1. It is repugnant to his wisdom in three ways. (1.) Because it represents God as decreeing something for a particular end [or purpose] which neither is nor can be good: which is, that God created something for eternal perdition to the praise of his justice. (2.) Because it states, that the object which God proposed to himself by this Predestination, was, to demonstrate the glory of his mercy and justice: But this glory he cannot demonstrate, except by an act that is contrary at once to his mercy and his justice, of which description is that decree of God in which he determined that man should sin and be rendered miserable. (3.) Because it changes and inverts the order of the two-fold wisdom of God, as it is displayed to us in the Scriptures. For it asserts, that God has absolutely predetermined to save men by the mercy and wisdom that are comprehended in the doctrine of the cross of Christ, without having foreseen this circumstance, that it was impossible for man (and that, truly, through his own fault,) to be saved by the wisdom which was revealed in the law and which was infused into him at the period of his creation: When the scripture asserts, on the contrary, that "it pleased God by the foolishness of preaching to save them that believe;" that is, "by the doctrine of the cross, after that in the wisdom of God the world by wisdom knew not God." (1 Cor. i. 21.)

2. It is repugnant to the justice of God, not only in reference to that attribute denoting in God a love of righteousness and a hatred of iniquity, but also in reference to its being a perpetual and constant desire in him to render to every one that which is his due. (1.) It is at variance with the first of these ideas of justice in the following manner: Because it affirms, that God has absolutely willed to save certain individual men, and has decreed their salvation without having the least regard to righteousness or obedience: The proper inference from which, is, that God loves such men far more than his own justice [or righteousness.] (2.) It is opposed to the second idea of his justice: Because it affirms, that God wishes to subject his creature to misery, (which cannot possibly have any existence except as the punishment of sin,) although, at the same time, he does not look upon [or consider] the creature as a sinner, and therefore as not obnoxious either to wrath or to punishment. This is the manner in which it lays down the position, that God has willed to give to the creature not only something which does not belong to it, but which is connected with its greatest injury. Which is another act directly opposed to his justice. In accordance, therefore, with this doctrine, God, in the first place, detracts from himself that which is his own, [or his right,] and then imparts to the creature what does not belong to it, to its great misery and unhappiness.

3. It is also repugnant to the Goodness of God. Goodness is an affection [or disposition] in God to communicate his own good so far as his justice considers and admits to be fitting and proper. But in this doctrine the following act is attributed to God, that, of himself, and induced to it by nothing external, he wills the greatest evil to his creatures; and that from all eternity he has pre-ordained that evil for them, or pre-determined to impart it to them, even before he resolved to bestow upon them any portion of good. For this doctrine states, that God willed to damn; and, that he might be able to do this, be willed to create; although creation is the first egress [or going forth] of God's goodness towards his creatures. How vastly different are such statements as these from that expansive goodness of God by which he confers benefits not only on the unworthy, but also on the evil, the unjust and on those who are deserving of punishment, which trait of Divine beneficence in our Father who is in heaven, we are commanded to imitate. (Matt. v. 45.)

VIII. Such a doctrine of Predestination is contrary to the nature of man, in regard to his having been created after the Divine image in the knowledge of God and in righteousness, in regard to his having been created with freedom of will, and in regard to his having been created with a disposition and aptitude for the enjoyment of life eternal. These three circumstance, respecting him, may be deduced from the following brief expressions: "Do this, and live :" (Rom. x, 5) "In the day that thou eatest thereof, thou shalt surely die." (Gen. ii. 17.) If man be deprived of any of these qualifications, such admonitions as these cannot possibly be effective in exciting him to obedience.

1. This doctrine is inconsistent with the Divine image, which consists of the knowledge of God and holiness. For according to this knowledge and righteousness man was qualified and empowered, he was also laid under an obligation to know God, to love, worship, and serve him. But by the intervention, or rather by the prevention, of this Predestination, it was pre-ordained that man should be formed vicious and should commit sin, that is, that he should neither know God, love, worship, nor serve him; and that he should not perform that which by the image of God, he was well qualified and empowered to do, and which he was bound to perform. This is tantamount to such a declaration as the following, which any one might make:

"God did undoubtedly create man after his own image, in righteousness and true holiness; but, notwithstanding this, he fore-ordained and decreed, that man should become impure and unrighteous, that is, should be made conformable to the image of Satan."

2. This doctrine is inconsistent with the freedom of the will, in which and with which man was created by God. For it prevents the exercise of this liberty, by binding or determining the will absolutely to one object, that is, to do this thing precisely, or to do that. God, therefore, according to this statement,

may be blamed for the one or the other of these two things, (with which let no man charge his Maker!) either for creating man with freedom of will, or for hindering him in the use of his own liberty after he had formed him a free agent. In the former of these two cases, God is chargeable with a want of consideration, in the latter with mutability. And in both, with being injurious to man as well as to himself.

3. This Predestination is prejudicial to man in regard to the inclination and capacity for the eternal fruition of salvation, with which he was endowed at the period of his creation. For, since by this Predestination it has been pre-determined, that the greater part of mankind shall not be made partakers of salvation, but shall fall into everlasting condemnation, and since this predetermination took place even before the decree had passed for creating man, such persons are deprived of something, for the desire of which they have been endowed by God with a natural inclination. This great privation they suffer, not in consequence of any preceding sin or demerit of their own, but simply and solely through this sort of Predestination.

IX. This Predestination is diametrically opposed to the Act of Creation.

1. For creation is a communication of good according to the intrinsic property of its nature. But, creation of this description, whose intent or design is, to make a way through itself by which the reprobation that had been previously determined may obtain its object, is not a communication of good. For we ought to form our estimate and judgment of every good, from the mind and intention of Him who is the Donor, and from the end to which or on account of which it is bestowed. In the present instance, the intention of the Donor would have been, to condemn, which is an act that could not possibly affect any one except a creature; and the end or event of creation would have been the eternal perdition of the creature. In that case creation would not have been a communication of any good, but a preparation for the greatest evil both according to the very intention of the Creator and the actual issue of the matter; and according to the words of Christ, "it had seen good for that man, if he had never been born!" (Matt. xxvi. 24.)

2. Reprobation is an act of hatred, and from hatred derives its origin. But creation does not proceed from hatred; it is not therefore a way or means, which belongs to the execution of the decree of reprobation.

3. Creation is a perfect act of God, by which he has manifested his wisdom, goodness and omnipotence: It is not therefore subordinate to the end of any other preceding work or action of God. But it is rather to be viewed as that act of God, which necessarily precedes and is antecedent to all other acts that he can possibly either decree or undertake. Unless God had formed a previous conception of the work of creation, he could not have decreed actually to undertake any other act; and until he had executed the work of creation, he could by no means have completed any other operation.

4. All the actions of God which tend to the condemnation of his creatures, are strange work or foreign to him; because God consents to them, for some other cause that is quite extraneous. But creation is not an action that is foreign to God, but it is proper to him. It is eminently an action most appropriate to Him, and to which he could be moved by no other external cause, because it is the very first of the Divine acts, and, till it was done, nothing could have any actual existence, except God himself; for every thing else that has a being, came into existence through this action.

5. If creation be the way and means through which God willed the execution of the decree of his reprobation, he was more inclined to will the act of reprobation than that of creation; and he consequently derived greater satisfaction from the act of condemning certain of his innocent creatures, than in the act of their creation.

6. Lastly. Creation cannot be a way or means of reprobation according to the absolute purpose of God: because, after the creation was completed, it was in the power of man still to have remained obedient to the divine commands, and not to commit sin; to render this possible, while God had on one part bestowed on him sufficient strength and power, he had also on the other placed sufficient impediments; a circumstance most diametrically opposed to a Predestination of this description.

X. This doctrine is at open hostility with the Nature of Eternal Life, and the titles by which it is signally distinguished in the Scriptures. For it is called "the inheritance of the sons of God ;" (Tit. iii. 7,) but those alone are the sons of God, according to the doctrine of the Gospel, "who believe in the name of Jesus Christ." (John i. 12.) It is also called, "the reward of obedience," (Matt. v. 12,) and of "the labour of love;" (Heb. vi. 10,) "the recompense of those who fight the good fight and who run well, a crown of righteousness," &c. (Rev. ii. 10; 2 Tim. iv. 7, 8.) God therefore has not, from his own absolute decree, without any consideration or regard whatever to faith and obedience, appointed to any man, or determined to appoint to him, life eternal.

XI This Predestination is also opposed to the Nature of Eternal Death, and to those appellations by which it is described in Scripture. For it is called "the wages of sin; (Rom. vi. 23,) the punishment of everlasting destruction, which shall be recompensed to them that know not God, and that obey not the gospel of our Lord Jesus Christ; (2 Thess. i. 8, 9,) the everlasting fire prepared for the devil and his angels, (Matt. xxv. 41,) a fire which shall devour the enemies and adversaries of God." (Heb. x. 27.)

God, therefore, has not, by any absolute decree without respect to sin and disobedience, prepared eternal death for any person.

XII This Predestination is inconsistent with the Nature and Properties of Sin in two ways: (1.) Because sin is called "disobedience" and "rebellion," neither of which terms can possibly apply to any person who by a preceding divine decree is placed under an unavoidable necessity of sinning. (2.) Because sin is the meritorious cause of damnation. But the meritorious cause which moves the Divine will to reprobate, is according to justice; and it induces God, who holds sin in abhorrence, to will reprobation. Sin, therefore, which is a cause, cannot be placed among the means, by which God executes the decree or will of reprobation.

XIII. This doctrine is likewise repugnant to the Nature of Divine Grace, and as far as its powers permit, it effects its destruction. Under whatever specious pretenses it may be asserted, that "this kind of Predestination is most admirably adapted and quite necessary for the establishment of grace," yet it destroys it in three ways:

1. Because grace is so attempered and commingled with the nature of man, as not to destroy within him the liberty of his will, but to give it a right direction, to correct its depravity, and to allow man to possess his own proper notions. While, on the contrary, this Predestination introduces such a species of grace, as takes away free will and hinders its exercise.

2. Because the representations of grace which the scriptures contain, are such as describe it capable of "being resisted, (Acts vii. 51,) and received in vain;" (2 Cor. vi. 1,) and that it is possible for man to avoid yielding his assent to it; and to refuse all co-operation with it. (Heb. xii. 15; Matt. xxiii. 37; Luke vii. 30.) While, on the contrary, this Predestination affirms, that grace is a certain irresistible force and operation.

3. Because, according to the primary intention and chief design of God, grace conduces to the good of those persons to whom it is offered and by whom it is received: while, on the contrary, this doctrine drags along with it the assertion, that grace is offered even to certain reprobates, and is so far communicated to them as to illuminate their understandings and to excite within them a taste for the heavenly gifts, only for this end and purpose, that, in proportion to the height to which they are elevated, the abyss into which they are precipitated may be the deeper, and their fall the heavier; and that they may both merit and receive the greater perdition.

XIV. The doctrine of this Predestination is Injurious to the Glory of God, which does not consist of a declaration of liberty or authority, nor of a demonstration of anger and power, except to such an extent as that declaration and demonstration may be consistent with justice, and with a perpetual reservation in behalf of the honour of God's goodness. But, according to this doctrine, it follows that God is the author of sin, which may be proved by four arguments:

1. One of its positions is, that God has absolutely decreed to demonstrate his glory by punitive justice and mercy, in the salvation of some men, and in the damnation of others, which neither was done, nor could have possibly been done, unless sin had entered into the world.

2. This doctrine affirms, that, in order to obtain his object, God ordained that man should commit sin, and be rendered vitiated; and, from this Divine ordination or appointment, the fall of man necessarily followed.

3. It asserts that God has denied to man, or has withdrawn from him, such a portion of grace as is sufficient and necessary to enable him to avoid sin, and that this was done before man had sinned: which is an act that amounts to the same as if God had prescribed a law to man, which it would be utterly impossible for him to fulfill, when the nature in which he had been created was taken into consideration.

4. It ascribes to God certain operations with regard to man, both external and internal, both mediate (by means of the intervention of other creatures) and immediate--which Divine operations being once admitted, man must necessarily commit sin, by that necessity which the schoolmen call "a consequential necessity antecedent to the thing itself," and which totally destroys the freedom of the will. Such an act does this doctrine attribute to God, and represents it to proceed from his primary and chief intention, without any foreknowledge of an inclination, will, or action on the part of man.

From these premises, we deduce, as a further conclusion, that God really sins. Because, according to this doctrine, he moves to sin by an act that is unavoidable, and according to his own purpose and primary intention, without having received any previous inducement to such an act from any preceding sin or demerit in man.

From the same position we might also infer, that God is the only sinner. For man, who is impelled by an irresistible force to commit sin, (that is, to perpetrate some deed that has been prohibited,) cannot be said to sin himself.

As a legitimate consequence it also follows, that sin is not sin, since whatever that be which God does, it neither can be sin, nor ought any of his acts to receive that appellation.

Besides the instances which I have already recounted, there is another method by which this doctrine inflicts a deep wound on the honour of God--but these, it is probable, will be considered at present to be amply sufficient.

XV. This doctrine is highly dishonourable to Jesus Christ our saviour. For, 1. It entirely excludes him from that decree of Predestination which predestinates the end: and it affirms, that men were predestinated to be saved, before Christ was predestinated to save them; and thus it argues, that he is not the foundation of election. 2. It denies, that Christ is the meritorious cause, that again obtained for us the salvation which we had lost, by placing him as only a subordinate cause of that salvation which had been already foreordained, and thus only a minister and instrument to apply that salvation unto us. This indeed is in evident congruity with the opinion which states "that God has absolutely willed the salvation of certain men, by the first and supreme decree which he passed, and on which all his other decrees depend and are consequent." If this be true, it was therefore impossible for the salvation of such men to have been lost, and therefore unnecessary for it to be repaired and in some sort regained afresh, and discovered, by the merit of Christ, who was fore-ordained a saviour for them alone.

XVI. This doctrine is also hurtful to the salvation of men.

1. Because it prevents that saving and godly sorrow for sins that have been committed, which cannot exist in those who have no consciousness of sin. But it is obvious, that the man who has committed sin through the unavoidable necessity of the decree of God, cannot possibly have this kind of consciousness of sin. (2 Cor. vii. 10.)

2. Because it removes all pious solicitude about being converted from sin unto God. For he can feel no such concern who is entirely passive and conducts himself like a dead man, with respect not only to his discernment and perception of the grace of God that is exciting and assisting, but also to his assent and obedience to it; and who is converted by such an irresistible impulse, that he not only cannot avoid being sensible of the grace of God which knocks within him, but he must likewise of necessity yield his assent to it, and thus convert himself, or rather be converted. Such a person it is evident, cannot produce within his heart or conceive in his mind this solicitude, except he have previously felt the same irresistible motion. And if he should produce within his heart any such concern, it would be in vain and without the least advantage. For that cannot be a true solicitude, which is not produced in the heart by any other means except by an irresistible force according to the absolute purpose and intention of God to effect his salvation. (Rev. ii. 3; iii, 2.)

3. Because it restrains, in persons that are converted, all zeal and studious regard for good works, since it declares "that the regenerate cannot perform either more or less good than they do." For he that is actuated or impelled by saving grace, must work, and cannot discontinue his labour; but he that is not actuated by the same grace, can do nothing, and finds it necessary to cease from all attempts. (Tit. iii. 14.)

4. Because it extinguishes the zeal for prayer, which yet is an efficacious means instituted by God for asking and obtaining all kinds of blessings from him, but principally the great one of salvation. (Luke xi. 1-13.) But from the circumstance of it having been before determined by an immutable and inevitable decree, that this description of men [the elect] should obtain salvation, prayer cannot on any account be a means for asking and obtaining that salvation. It can only be a mode of worshipping God; because according to the absolute decree of his Predestination he has determined that such men shall be saved.

5. It takes away all that most salutary fear and trembling with which we are commanded to work out our own salvation. (Phil. ii. 12) for it states "that he who is elected and believes, cannot sin with that full and entire willingness with which sin is committed by the ungodly; and that they cannot either totally or finally fall away from faith or grace."

6. Because it produces within men a despair both of performing that which their duty requires and of obtaining that towards which their desires are directed. For when they are taught that the grace of God (which is really necessary to the performance of the least portion of good) is denied to the majority of mankind, according to an absolute and peremptory decree of God -- - and that such grace is denied because, by a preceding decree equally absolute, God has determined not to confer salvation on them but damnation; when they are thus taught, it is scarcely possible for any other result to ensue, than that the individual who cannot even with great difficulty work a persuasion within himself of his being elected, should soon consider himself included in the number of the reprobate. From such an apprehension as this, must arise a certain despair of performing righteousness and obtaining salvation.

XVII. This doctrine inverts the order of the Gospel of Jesus

Christ. For in the Gospel God requires repentance and faith on the part of man, by promising to him life everlasting, if he consent to become a convert and a believer. (Mark i. 15; xvi, 16.) But it is stated in this [Supralapsarian] decree of Predestination, that it is God's absolute will, to bestow salvation on certain particular men, and that he willed at the same time absolutely to give those very individuals repentance and faith, by means of an irresistible force, because it was his will and pleasure to save them. In the Gospel, God denounces eternal death on the impenitent and unbelieving. (John iii. 36.) And those threats contribute to the purpose which he has in view, that he may by such means deter them from unbelief and thus may save them. But by this decree of Predestination it is taught, that God wills not to confer on certain individual men that grace which is necessary for conversion and faith because he has absolutely decreed their condemnation.

The Gospel says, "God so loved the world that he gave his only-begotten son, that whosoever believeth in him should have everlasting life." (John iii. 16.)

But this doctrine declares; "that God so loved those whom he had absolutely elected to eternal life, as to give his son to them alone, and by an irresistible force to produce within them faith on him." To embrace the whole in few words, the Gospel says, "fulfill the command, and thou shalt obtain the promise; believe, and thou shalt live." But this [supralapsarian] doctrine says, "since it is my will to give thee life, it is therefore my will to give thee faith:" which is a real and most manifest inversion of the Gospel.

XVIII. This Predestination is in open hostility to the ministry of the Gospel.

1. For if God by an irresistible power quicken him who is dead in trespasses and sins, no man can be a minister and "a labourer together with God," (1 Cor. iii. 9,) nor can the word preached by man be the instrument of grace and of the Spirit, any more than a creature could have been an instrument of grace in the first creation, or a dispenser of that grace in the resurrection of the body from the dead.

2. Because by this Predestination the ministry of the gospel is made "the savour of death unto death" in the case of the majority of those who hear it, (2 Cor. ii. 14-16,) as well as an instrument of condemnation, according to the primary design and absolute intention of God, without any consideration of previous rebellion.

3. Because, according to this doctrine, baptism, when administered to many reprobate children, (who yet are the offspring of parents that believe and are God's covenant people,) is evidently a seal [or ratification] of nothing, and thus becomes entirely useless, in accordance with the primary and absolute intention of God, without any fault [or culpability] on the part of the infants themselves, to whom it is administered in obedience to the Divine command.

4. Because it hinders public prayers from being offered to God in a becoming and suitable manner, that is, with faith, and in confidence that they will be profitable to all the hearers of the word; when there are many among them, whom God is not only unwilling to save, but whom by his absolute, eternal, and immutable will, (which is antecedent to all things and causes whatever,) it is his will and pleasure to damn: In the mean time, when the apostle commands prayers and supplications to be made for all men, he adds this reason, "for this is good and acceptable in the sight of God our saviour; who will have all men to be saved, and to come unto the knowledge of the truth." (1 Tim. ii. 1-4.)

5. The constitution of this doctrine is such, as very easily to render pastors and teachers slothful and negligent in the exercise of their ministry: Because, from this doctrine it appears to them as though it were impossible for all their diligence to be useful to any persons, except to those only whom God absolutely and precisely wills to save, and who cannot possibly perish; and as though all their negligence could be hurtful to none, except to those alone whom God absolutely wills to destroy, who must of necessity perish, and to whom a contrary fate is impossible.

XIX. This doctrine completely subverts the foundation of religion in general, and of the Christian Religion in particular.

1. The foundation of religion considered in general, is a two-fold love of God; without which there neither is nor can be any religion: The first of them is a love for righteousness [or justice] which gives existence to his hatred of sin. The second is a love for the creature who is endowed with reason, and (in the matter now before us,) it is a love for man, according to the expression of the Apostle to the Hebrews. "for he that cometh to God must believe that he is, and that he is a rewarder of them that diligently seek Him." (xi, 6.) God's love of righteousness is manifested by this circumstance, that it is not his will and pleasure to bestow eternal life on any except on "those who seek him." God's love of man consists in his being willing to give him eternal life, if he seek Him.

A mutual relation subsists between these two kinds of love, which is this. The latter species of love, which extends itself to the creatures, cannot come into exercise, except so far as it is permitted by the former, [the love of righteousness]: The former love, therefore, is by far the most excellent species; but in every direction there is abundant scope for the emanations of the latter, [the love of the creature,] except where the former [the love of righteousness] has placed some impediment in the range of its exercise. The first of these consequences is most evidently proved from the circumstance of God's condemning man on account of sin, although he loves him in the relation in which he stands as his creature; which would by no means have been done, had he loved man more than righteousness, [or justice,] and had he evinced a stronger aversion to the eternal misery of man than to his disobedience. But the second consequence is proved by this argument, that God condemns no person, except on account of sin; and that he saves such a multitude of men who turn themselves away [or are converted] from sin; which he could not do, unless it was his will to allow as abundant scope to his love for the creatures, as is permitted by righteousness [or justice] under the regulation of the Divine judgment.

But this [Supralapsarian] doctrine inverts this order and mutual relation in two ways: (1.) The one is when it states, that God wills absolutely to save certain particular men, without having had in that his intention the least reference or regard to their obedience. This is the manner in which it places the love of God to man before his love of righteousness, and lays down the position--that God loves men (as such) more than righteousness, and evinces a stronger aversion to their misery than to their sin and disobedience. (2.) The other is when it asserts, on the contrary, that God wills absolutely to damn certain particular men without manifesting in his decree any consideration of their disobedience. In this manner it detracts from his love to the creature that which belongs to it; while it teaches, that God hates the creature, without any cause or necessity derived from his love of righteousness and his hatred of iniquity. In which case, it is not true, "that sin is the primary object of God's hatred, and its only meritorious cause."

The great influence and potency which this consideration possesses in subverting the foundation of religion, may be appropriately described by the following simile: Suppose a son to say, "My father is such a great lover of righteousness and equity, that, notwithstanding I am his beloved son, he would disinherit me if I were found disobedient to him. Obedience, therefore, is a duty which I must sedulously cultivate, and which is highly incumbent upon me, if I wish to be his heir." Suppose another son to say: "My father's love for me is so great, that he is absolutely resolved to make me his heir. There is, therefore, no necessity for my earnestly striving to yield him obedience; for, according to his unchangeable will, I shall become his heir. Nay, he will by an irresistible force draw me to obey him, rather than not suffer me to be made his heir." But such reasoning as the latter is diametrically opposed to the doctrine contained in the following words of John the Baptist: "And think not to say within yourselves, we have Abraham to our father: For I say unto you, that God is able of these stones to raise up children unto Abraham." (Matt. iii. 9.)

2. But the Christian religion also has its superstructure built upon this two-fold love as a foundation. This love, however, is to be considered in a manner somewhat different, in consequence of the change in the condition of man, who, when he had been created after the image of God and in his favour, became by his own fault a sinner and an enemy to God. (1.) God's love of righteousness [or justice] on which the Christian religion rests, is, first, that righteousness which he declared only once, which was in Christ; because it was his will that sin should not be expiated in any other way than by the blood and death of his Son, and that Christ should not be admitted before him as an Advocate, Deprecator and Intercessor, except when sprinkled by his own blood. But this love of righteousness is, secondly, that which he daily manifests in the preaching of the gospel, in which he declares it to be his will to grant a communication of Christ and his benefits to no man, except to him who becomes converted and believes in Christ. (2.) God's love of miserable sinners, on which likewise the Christian religion is founded, is, first, that love by which he gave his Son for them, and constituted him a saviour of those who obey him. But this love of sinners is, secondly, that by which he hath required obedience, not according to the rigor and severity to which he was entitled by his own supreme right, but according to his grace and clemency, and with the addition of a promise of the remission of sins, provided fallen man repent.

The [supralapsarian] doctrine of Predestination is, in two ways, opposed to this two-fold foundation: first, by stating, "that God has such a great love for certain sinners, that it was his will absolutely to save them before he had given satisfaction, through Christ Jesus, to his love of righteousness, [or justice,] and that he thus willed their salvation even in his own fore-knowledge and according to his determinate purpose." Besides, it totally and most completely overturns this foundation, by teaching it to be "God's pleasure, that satisfaction should be paid to his justice, [or righteousness,] because he willed absolutely to save such persons:" which is nothing less, than to make his love for justice, manifested in Christ, subordinate to his love for sinful man whom it is his will absolutely to save. Secondly. It opposes itself to this foundation, by teaching, "that it is the will of God absolutely to damn certain sinners without any consideration of their impenitency;" when at the same time a most plenary and complete satisfaction had been rendered, in Christ Jesus, to God's love of righteousness [or justice] and to his hatred of sin. So that nothing now can hinder the possibility of his extending mercy to the sinner, whosoever he may be, except the condition of repentance. Unless some person should choose to assert, what is stated in this doctrine, "that it has been God's will to act towards the greater part of mankind with the same severity as he exercised towards the devil and his angels, or even with greater, since it was his pleasure that neither Christ nor his gospel should be productive of greater blessings to them than to the devils, and since, according to the first offense, the door of grace is as much closed against them as it is against the evil angels." Yet each of those angels sinned, by himself in his own proper person, through his individual maliciousness, and by his voluntary act; while men sinned, only in Adam their parent, before they had been brought into existence.

But, that we may more clearly understand the fact of this two-fold love being the foundation of all religion and the manner in which it is so, with the mutual correspondence that subsists between each other, as we have already described them, it will be profitable for us to contemplate with greater attention the following words of the Apostle to the Hebrews: "He that cometh to God, must believe that He is and that He is a rewarder of them that diligently seek Him." In these words two things are laid down as foundations to religion, in opposition to two fiery darts of Satan, which are the most pernicious pests to it, and each of which is able by itself to overturn and extirpate all religion. One of them is security, the other despair. Security operates, when a man permits himself, that, how inattentive soever he may be to the worship of God, he will not be damned, but will obtain salvation. Despair is in operation, when a person entertains a persuasion, that, whatever degree of reverence he may evince towards God, he will not receive any remuneration. In what human mind soever either of these pests is fostered, it is impossible that any true and proper worship of God can there reside. Now both of them are overturned by the words of the Apostle: For if a man firmly believes, "that God will bestow eternal life on those alone who seek Him, but that He will inflict on the rest death eternal," he can on no account indulge himself in security. And if he likewise believes, that "God is truly a rewarder of those who diligently seek Him," by applying himself to the search he will not be in danger of falling into despair. The foundation of the former kind of faith by which a man firmly believes, "that God will bestow eternal life on none except on those who seek Him," is that love which God bears to his own righteousness, [or justice,] and which is greater than that which he entertains for man. And, by this alone, all cause of security is removed. But the foundation of the latter kind of faith, "that God will undoubtedly be a rewarder of those who diligently seek Him," is that great love for man which neither will nor can prevent God from effecting salvation for him, except he be hindered by his still greater love for righteousness or justice. Yet the latter kind of love is so far from operating as a hindrance to God from becoming a rewarder of those who diligently seek Him, that on the contrary, it promotes in every possible way the bestowment of that reward. Those persons, therefore, who seek God, can by no means indulge in a single doubt concerning his readiness to remunerate. And it is this which acts as a preservative against despair or distrust. Since this is the actual state of the case, this two-fold love, and the mutual relation which each part of it bears to the other and which we have just unfolded, are the foundations of religion, without which no religion can possibly exist. That doctrine, therefore, which is in open hostility to this mutual love and to the relation that mutually subsists between them, is, at the same time, subversive of the foundation of all religion.

XX. Lastly. This doctrine of Predestination has been rejected both in former times and in our own days, by the greater part of the professors of Christianity.

1. But, omitting all mention of the periods that occurred in former ages, facts themselves declare, that the Lutheran and Anabaptist Churches, as well as that of Rome, account this to be an erroneous doctrine.

2. However highly Luther and Melancthon might at the very commencement of the reformation, have approved of this doctrine, they afterwards deserted it. This change in Melancthon is quite apparent from his latter writings: And those who style themselves "Luther's disciples," make the same statement respecting their master, while they contend that on this subject he made a more distinct and copious declaration of his sentiments, instead of entirely abandoning those which he formerly entertained. But Philip Melancthon believed that this doctrine did not differ greatly from the fate of the Stoics: This appears from many of his writings, but more particularly in a certain letter which he addressed to Gasper Peucer, and in which, among other things, he states: "Lælius writes to me and says, that the controversy respecting the Stoical Fate is agitated with such uncommon fervour at Geneva, that one individual is cast into prison because he happened to differ from Zeno. O unhappy times! When the doctrine of salvation is thus obscured by certain strange disputes!"

3. All the Danish Churches embrace a doctrine quite opposed to this, as is obvious from the writings of Nicholas Hemmingius in his treatise on Universal Grace, in which he declares that the contest between him and his adversaries consisted in the determination of these two points: "do the Elect believe ," or, "are believers the true elect?" He considers "those persons who maintain the former position, to hold sentiments agreeable to the doctrine of the Manichees and Stoics; and those who maintain the latter point, are in obvious agreement with Moses and the Prophets, with Christ and his Apostles."

4. Besides, by many of the inhabitants of these our own provinces, this doctrine is accounted a grievance of such a nature, as to cause several of them to affirm, that on account of it, they neither can nor will have any communion with our Church. Others of them have united themselves with our Churches, but not without entering a protest, "that they cannot possibly give their consent to this doctrine." But, on account of this kind of Predestination, our Churches have been deserted by not a few individuals, who formerly held the same opinions as ourselves: Others, also, have threatened to depart from us, unless they be fully assured that the Church holds no opinion of this description.

5. There is likewise no point of doctrine which the Papists, Anabaptists, and Lutherans oppose with greater vehemence than this, and through whose sides they create a worse opinion of our Churches or procure for them a greater portion of hatred, and thus bring into disrepute all the doctrines which we profess. They likewise affirm "that of all the blasphemies against God which the mind of man can conceive or his tongue can express, there is none so foul as not to be deduced by fair consequence from this opinion of our doctors."

6. Lastly. Of all the difficulties and controversies which have arisen in these our Churches since the time of the Reformation, there is none that has not had its origin in this doctrine, or that has not, at least, been mixed with it. What I have here said will be found true, if we bring to our recollection the controversies which existed at Leyden in the affair of Koolhaes, at Gouda in that of Herman Herberts, at Horn with respect to Cornelius Wiggerston, and at Mendenblich in the affair of Tako Sybrants. This consideration was not among the last of those motives which induced me to give my most diligent attention to this head of doctrine, and endeavour to prevent our Churches from suffering any detriment from it; because, from it, the Papists have derived much of their increase. While all pious teachers ought most heartily to desire the destruction of Popery, as they would that of the kingdom of Antichrist, they ought with the greatest zeal, to engage in the attempt, and as far as it is within their power, to make the most efficient preparations for its overthrow.

The preceding views are, in brief, those which I hold respecting this novel doctrine of Predestination. I have propounded it with all good faith from the very expressions of the authors themselves, that I might not seem to invent and attribute to them any thing which I was not able clearly to prove from their writings.

2. A SECOND KIND OF PREDESTINATION.

But some other of our doctors state the subject of God's Predestination in a manner somewhat different. We will cursorily touch upon the two modes which they employ. Among some of them the following opinion is prevalent:

1. God determined within himself, by an eternal and immutable decree, to make (according to his own good pleasure,) the smaller portion out of the general mass of mankind partakers of his grace and glory, to the praise of his own glorious grace. But according to his pleasure he also passed by the greater portion of men, and left them in their own nature, which is incapable of every thing supernatural, [or beyond itself,] and did not communicate to them that saving and supernatural grace by which their nature, (if it still retained its integrity,) might be strengthened, or by which, if it were corrupted, it might be restored--for a demonstration of his own liberty. Yet after God had made these men sinners and guilty of death, he punished them with death eternal--for a demonstration of his own justice.

2. Predestination is to be considered in respect to its end and to the means which tend to it. But these persons employ the word "Predestination" in its special acceptation for election and oppose it to reprobation. (1.) In respect to its end, (which is salvation, and an illustration of the glorious grace of God,) man is considered in common and absolutely, such as he is in his own nature. (2.) But in respect to the means, man is considered as perishing from himself and in himself, and as guilty in Adam.

3. In the decree concerning the end, the following gradations are to be regarded. (1.) The prescience of God, by which he foreknew those whom he had predestinated. Then (2.) The Divine prefinition, [or predetermination,] by which he foreordained the salvation of those persons by whom he had foreknown. First, by electing them from all eternity: and secondly, by preparing for them grace in this life, and glory in the world to come.

4. The means which belong to the execution of this Predestination, are (1.) Christ himself: (2.) An efficacious call to faith in Christ, from which justification takes its origin: (3.) The gift of perseverance unto the end.

5. As far as we are capable of comprehending their scheme of reprobation it consists of two acts, that of preterition and that of predamnatian. It is antecedent to all things, and to all causes which are either in the things themselves or which arise out of them; that is, it has no regard whatever to any sin, and only views man in an absolute and general aspect.

6. Two means are fore-ordained for the execution of the act of preterition: (1.) Dereliction [or abandoning] in a state of nature, which by itself is incapable of every thing supernatural: and (2.) Non-communication [or a negation] of supernatural grace, by which their nature (if in a state of integrity,) might be strengthened, and (if in a state of corruption,) might be restored.

7. Predamnation is antecedent to all things, yet it does by no means exist without a fore-knowledge of the causes of damnation. It views man as a sinner, obnoxious to damnation in Adam, and as on this account perishing through the necessity of Divine justice.

8. The means ordained for the execution of this predamnation, are (1.) Just desertion, which is either that of exploration, [or examination,] in which God does not confer his grace, or that of punishment when God takes away from a man all his saving gifts, and delivers him over to the power of Satan. (2.) The second means are induration or hardening, and those consequences which usually follow even to the real damnation of the person reprobated.

3. A THIRD KIND OF PREDESTINATION.

But others among our doctors state their sentiments on this subject in the following manner:

1. Because God willed within himself from all eternity to make a decree by which he might elect certain men and reprobate the rest, he viewed and considered the human race not only as created but

likewise as fallen or corrupt, and on that account obnoxious to cursing and malediction. Out of this lapsed and accursed state God determined to liberate certain individuals and freely to save them by his grace, for a declaration of his mercy; but he resolved in his own just judgment to leave the rest under the curse [or malediction] for a declaration of his justice. In both these cases God acts without the least consideration of repentance and faith in those whom he elects, or of impenitence and unbelief in those whom he reprobates.

2. The special means which relate particularly to the execution both of election and reprobation, are the very same as those which we have already expounded in the first of these kinds of Predestination, with the exception of those means which are common both to election and reprobation; because this [third] opinion places the fall of man, not as a means fore-ordained for the execution of the preceding decree of Predestination, but as something that might furnish a fixed purpose or occasion for making this decree of Predestination.

4. MY JUDGMENT RESPECTING THE TWO LAST DESCRIBED SCHEMES OF PREDESTINATION.

Both these opinions, as they outwardly pretend, differ from the first in this point--that neither of them lays down the creation or the fall as a mediate cause fore-ordained by God for the execution of the preceding decree of Predestination. Yet, with regard to the fall, some diversity may be perceived in the two latter opinions. For the second kind of Predestination places election, with regard to the end, before the fall; it also places before that event preterition, [or passing by,] which is the first part of reprobation. While the third kind does not allow any part of election and reprobation to commence till after the fall of man. But, among the causes which seem to have induced the inventors of the two latter schemes to deliver the doctrine of Predestination in this manner, and not to ascend to such a great height as the inventors of the first scheme have done, this is not the least--that they have been desirous of using the greatest precaution, lest it might be concluded from their doctrine that God is the author of sin, with as much show of probability as, (according to the intimation of some of those who yield their assent to both the latter kinds,) it is deducible from the first description of Predestination.

Yet if we be willing to inspect these two latter opinions a little more closely, and in particular if we accurately examine the second and third kind and compare them with other sentiments of the same author concerning some subjects of our religion, we shall discover, that the fall of Adam cannot possibly, according to their views, be considered in any other manner than as a necessary means for the execution of the preceding decree of Predestination.

1. In reference to the second of the three, this is apparent from two reasons comprised in it:

The first of these reasons is that which states God to have determined by the decree of reprobation to deny to man that grace which was necessary for the confirmation and strengthening of his nature, that it might not be corrupted by sin; which amounts to this, that God decreed not to bestow that grace which was necessary to avoid sin; and from this must necessarily follow the transgression of man, as proceeding from a law imposed on him. The fall of man is therefore a means ordained for the execution of the decree of reprobation.

The second of these reasons is that which states the two parts of reprobation to be preterition and predamnation. These two parts, according to that decree, are connected together by a necessary and mutual bond, and are equally extensive. For, all those whom God passed by in conferring Divine grace, are likewise damned. Indeed no others are damned, except those who are the subjects of this act of preterition. From this therefore it may be concluded, that "sin must necessarily follow from the decree of reprobation or preterition, because, if it were otherwise, it might possibly happen, that a person who had been passed by, might not commit sin, and from that circumstance might not become liable to damnation; since sin is the sole meritorious cause of damnation: and thus certain of those individuals who had been passed by, might neither be saved nor damned--which is great absurdity.

This second opinion on Predestination, therefore, falls into the same inconvenience as the first. For it not only does not avoid that [conclusion of making God the author of sin,] but while those who profess it make the attempt, they fall into a palpable and absurd self-contradiction--while, in reference to this point, the first of these opinions is alike throughout and consistent with itself.

2. The third of these schemes of Predestination would escape this rock to much better effect, did not the patrons of it, while declaring their sentiments on Predestination and providence, employ certain expressions, from which the necessity of the fall might be deduced. Yet this necessity cannot possibly have any other origin than some degree of Predestination.

(1.) One of these explanatory expressions is their description of the Divine permission, by which God permits sin. Some of them describe it thus: "permission is the withdrawing of that Divine grace, by which, when God executes the decrees of his will through rational creatures, he either does not reveal to the creature that divine will of his own by which he wills that action to be performed, or does not bend the will of the creature to yield obedience in that act to the Divine will." To these expressions, the following are immediately subjoined: "if this be a correct statement, the creature commits sin through necessity, yet voluntarily and without restraint." If it be objected that "this description does not comport with that permission by which God permitted the sin of Adam:" We also entertain the same opinion about it. Yet it follows, as a consequence, from this very description, that "other sins are committed through necessity."

(2.) Of a similar tendency are the expressions which some of them use, when they contend, that the declaration of the glory of God, which must necessarily be illustrated, is placed in "the demonstration of mercy and of punitive justice." But such a demonstration could not have been made, unless sin, and misery through sin, had entered into the world, to form at least some degree of misery for the least sin. And in this manner is sin also necessarily introduced, through the necessity of such a demonstration of the Divine glory. Since the fall of Adam is already laid down to be necessary, and, on that account, to be a means for executing the preceding decree of Predestination; creation itself is likewise at the same time laid down as a means subservient to the execution of the same decree. For the fall cannot be necessarily consequent upon the creation, except through the decree of Predestination, which cannot be placed between the creation and the fall, but is prefixed to both of them, as having the precedence, and ordaining creation for the fall, and both of them for executing one and the same decree--to demonstrate the justice of God in the punishment of sin, and his mercy in its remission. Because, if this were not the case, that which must necessarily ensue from the act of creation had not seen intended by God when he created, which is to suppose an impossibility.

But let it be granted, that the necessity of the fall of Adam cannot be deduced from either of the two latter opinions, yet all the preceding arguments which have been produced against the first opinion, are, after a trifling modification to suit the varied purpose, equally valid against the two latter. This would be very apparent, if, to demonstrate it, a conference were to be instituted.

5. MY OWN SENTIMENTS ON PREDESTINATION.

I have hitherto been stating those opinions concerning the article of Predestination which are inculcated in our Churches and in the University of Leyden, and of which I disapprove. I have at the same time produced my own reasons, why I form such an unfavourable judgment concerning them; and I will now declare my own opinions on this subject, which are of such a description as, according to my views, appear most conformable to the word of God.

I. The first absolute decree of God concerning the salvation of sinful man, is that by which he decreed to appoint his Son, Jesus Christ, for a Mediator, Redeemer, saviour, Priest and King, who might destroy sin by his own death, might by his obedience obtain the salvation which had been lost, and might communicate it by his own virtue.

II. The second precise and absolute decree of God, is that in which he decreed to receive into favour those who repent and believe, and, in Christ, for his sake and through Him, to effect the salvation of such penitents and believers as persevered to the end; but to leave in sin, and under wrath, all impenitent persons and unbelievers, and to damn them as aliens from Christ.

III. The third Divine decree is that by which God decreed to administer in a sufficient and efficacious manner the means which were necessary for repentance and faith; and to have such administration instituted (1.) according to the Divine Wisdom, by which God knows what is proper and becoming both to his mercy and his severity, and (2.) according to Divine Justice, by which He is prepared to adopt whatever his wisdom may prescribe and put it in execution.

IV. To these succeeds the fourth decree, by which God decreed to save and damn certain particular persons. This decree has its foundation in the foreknowledge of God, by which he knew from all eternity those individuals who would, through his preventing grace, believe, and, through his subsequent grace would persevere, according to the before described administration of those means which are suitable and proper for conversion and faith; and, by which foreknowledge, he likewise knew those who would not believe and persevere.

Predestination, when thus explained, is

1. The foundation of Christianity, and of salvation and its certainty.

2. It is the sum and the matter of the gospel; nay, it is the gospel itself, and on that account necessary to be believed in order to salvation, as far as the two first articles are concerned.

3. It has had no need of being examined or determined by any council, either general or particular, since it is contained in the scriptures clearly and expressly in so many words; and no contradiction has ever yet been offered to it by any orthodox Divine.

4. It has constantly been acknowledged and taught by all Christian teachers who held correct and orthodox sentiments.

5. It agrees with that harmony of all confessions, which has been published by the protestant Churches.

6. It likewise agrees most excellently with the Dutch Confession and Catechism. This concord is such, that if in the Sixteenth article these two expressions "those persons whom" and "others," be explained by the words "believers" and "unbelievers" these opinions of mine on Predestination will be comprehended in that article with the greatest clearness. This is the reason why I directed the thesis to

be composed in the very words of the Confession, when, on one occasion, I had to hold a public disputation before my private class in the University. This kind of Predestination also agrees with the reasoning contained in the twentieth and the fifty-fourth question of the Catechism.

7. It is also in excellent accordance with the nature of God with his wisdom, goodness, and righteousness; because it contains the principal matter of all of them, and is the clearest demonstration of the Divine wisdom, goodness, and righteousness [or justice]

8. It is agreeable in every point with the nature of man--in what form soever that nature may be contemplated, whether in the primitive state of creation, in that of the fall, or in that of restoration.

9. It is in complete concert with the act of creation, by affirming that the creation itself is a real communication of good, both from the intention of God, and with regard to the very end or event; that it had its origin in the goodness of God; that whatever has a reference to its continuance and preservation, proceeds from Divine love; and that this act of creation is a perfect and appropriate work of God, in which he is at complaisance with himself, and by which he obtained all things necessary for an unsinning state.

10. It agrees with the nature of life eternal, and with the honourable titles by which that life is designated in the scriptures.

11. It also agrees with the nature of death eternal, and with the names by which that death is distinguished in scripture.

12. It states sin to be a real disobedience, and the meritorious cause of condemnation; and on this account, it is in the most perfect agreement with the fall and with sin.

13. In every particular, it harmonizes with the nature of grace, by ascribing to it all those things which agree with it, [or adapted to it,] and by reconciling it most completely to the righteousness of God and to the nature and liberty of the human will.

14. It conduces most conspicuously to declare the glory of God, his justice and his mercy. It also represents God as the cause of all good and of our salvation, and man as the cause of sin and of his own damnation.

15. It contributes to the honour of Jesus Christ, by placing him for the foundation of Predestination and the meritorious as well as communicative cause of salvation.

16. It greatly promotes the salvation of men: It is also the power, and the very means which lead to salvation--by exciting and creating within the mind of man sorrow on account of sin, a solicitude about his conversion, faith in Jesus Christ, a studious desire to perform good works, and zeal in prayer--and by causing men to work out their salvation with fear and trembling. It likewise prevents despair, as far as such prevention is necessary.

17. It confirms and establishes that order according to which the gospel ought to be preached, (1.) By requiring repentance and faith -- (2.) And then by promising remission of sins, the grace of the spirit, and life eternal.

18. It strengthens the ministry of the gospel, and renders it profitable with respect to preaching, the administration of the sacraments and public prayers.

19. It is the foundation of the Christian religion; because in it, the two-fold love of God may be united together--

God's love of righteousness [or justice], and his love of men, may, with the greatest consistency, be reconciled to each other.

20. Lastly. This doctrine of Predestination, has always been approved by the great majority of professing Christians, and even now, in these days, it enjoys the same extensive patronage. It cannot afford any person just cause for expressing his aversion to it; nor can it give any pretext for contention in the Christian Church.

It is therefore much to be desired, that men would proceed no further in this matter, and would not attempt to investigate the unsearchable judgments of God--at least that they would not proceed beyond the point at which those judgments have been clearly revealed in the scriptures.

This, my most potent Lords, is all that I intend now to declare to your mightinesses, respecting the doctrine of Predestination, about which there exists such a great controversy in the Church of Christ. If it would not prove too tedious to your Lordships, I have some other propositions which I could wish to state, because they contribute to a full declaration of my sentiments, and tend to the same purpose as that for which I have been ordered to attend in this place by your mightinesses.

There are certain other articles of the Christian religion, which possess a close affinity to the doctrine of Predestination, and which are in a great measure dependent on it: Of this description are the providence of God, the free-will of man, the perseverance of saints, and the certainty of salvation. On these topics, if not disagreeable to your mightinesses, I will in a brief manner relate my opinion.

II. THE PROVIDENCE OF GOD

I consider Divine Providence to be "that solicitous, continued, and universally present inspection and oversight of God, according to which he exercises a general care over the whole world, but evinces a particular concern for all his [intelligent] creatures without any exception, with the design of preserving and governing them in their own essence, qualities, actions, and passions, in a manner that is at once worthy of himself and suitable to them, to the praise of his name and the salvation of believers. In this definition of Divine Providence, I by no means deprive it of any particle of those properties which agree with it or belong to it; but I declare that it preserves, regulates, governs and directs all things and that nothing in the world happens fortuitously or by chance. Beside this, I place in subjection to Divine Providence both the free-will and even the actions of a rational creature, so that nothing can be done without the will of God, not even any of those things which are done in opposition to it; only we must observe a distinction between good actions and evil ones, by saying, that "God both wills and performs good acts," but that "He only freely permits those which are evil." Still farther than this, I very readily grant, that even all actions whatever, concerning evil, that can possibly be devised or invented, may be attributed to Divine Providence Employing solely one caution, "not to conclude from this concession that God is the cause of sin." This I have testified with sufficient clearness, in a certain disputation concerning the Righteousness and Efficacy of Divine Providence concerning things that are evil, which was discussed at Leyden on two different occasions, as a divinity-act, at which I presided. In that disputation, I endeavoured to ascribe to God whatever actions concerning sin I could possibly conclude from the scriptures to belong to him; and I proceeded to such a length in my attempt, that some persons thought proper on that account to charge me with having made God the author of sin. The same serious allegation has likewise been often produced against me, from the pulpit, in the city of Amsterdam, on account of those very theses; but with what show of justice such a charge was made, may be evident to any one, from the contents of my written answer to those Thirty-one Articles formerly mentioned, which have been falsely imputed to me, and of which this was one.

III. THE FREE-WILL OF MAN

This is my opinion concerning the free-will of man: In his primitive condition as he came out of the hands of his creator, man was endowed with such a portion of knowledge, holiness and power, as enabled him to understand, esteem, consider, will, and to perform the true good, according to the commandment delivered to him. Yet none of these acts could he do, except through the assistance of Divine Grace. But in his lapsed and sinful state, man is not capable, of and by himself, either to think, to will, or to do that which is really good; but it is necessary for him to be regenerated and renewed in his intellect, affections or will, and in all his powers, by God in Christ through the Holy Spirit, that he may be qualified rightly to understand, esteem, consider, will, and perform whatever is truly good. When he is made a partaker of this regeneration or renovation, I consider that, since he is delivered from sin, he is capable of thinking, willing and doing that which is good, but yet not without the continued aids of Divine Grace.

IV. THE GRACE OF GOD

In reference to Divine Grace, I believe, 1. It is a gratuitous affection by which God is kindly affected towards a miserable sinner, and according to which he, in the first place, gives his Son, "that whosoever believes in him might have eternal life," and, afterwards, he justifies him in Christ Jesus and for his sake, and adopts him into the right of sons, unto salvation. 2. It is an infusion (both into the human understanding and into the will and affections,) of all those gifts of the Holy Spirit which appertain to the regeneration and renewing of man--such as faith, hope, charity, &c.; for, without these gracious gifts, man is not sufficient to think, will, or do any thing that is good. 3. It is that perpetual assistance and continued aid of the Holy Spirit, according to which He acts upon and excites to good the man who has been already renewed, by infusing into him salutary cogitations, and by inspiring him with good desires, that he may thus actually will whatever is good; and according to which God may then will and work together with man, that man may perform whatever he wills.

In this manner, I ascribe to grace the commencement, the continuance and the consummation of all good, and to such an extent do I carry its influence, that a man, though already regenerate, can neither conceive, will, nor do any good at all, nor resist any evil temptation, without this preventing and exciting, this following and co-operating grace. From this statement it will clearly appear, that I by no means do injustice to grace, by attributing, as it is reported of me, too much to man's free-will. For the whole controversy reduces itself to the solution of this question, "is the grace of God a certain irresistible force?" That is, the controversy does not relate to those actions or operations which may be ascribed to grace, (for I acknowledge and inculcate as many of these actions or operations as any man ever did,) but it relates solely to the mode of operation, whether it be irresistible or not. With respect to which, I believe, according to the scriptures, that many persons resist the Holy Spirit and reject the grace that is offered.

V. THE PERSEVERANCE OF THE SAINTS

My sentiments respecting the perseverance of the saints are, that those persons who have been grafted into Christ by true faith, and have thus been made partakers of his life-giving Spirit, possess sufficient powers [or strength] to fight against Satan, sin, the world and their own flesh, and to gain the victory over these enemies--yet not without the assistance of the grace of the same Holy Spirit. Jesus Christ also by his Spirit assists them in all their temptations, and affords them the ready aid of his hand; and, provided they stand prepared for the battle, implore his help, and be not wanting to themselves, Christ preserves them from falling. So that it is not possible for them, by any of the cunning craftiness or power of Satan, to be either seduced or dragged out of the hands of Christ. But I think it is useful and will be quite necessary in our first convention, [or Synod] to institute a diligent inquiry from the Scriptures, whether it is not possible for some individuals through negligence to desert the commencement of their existence in Christ, to cleave again to the present evil world, to decline from the sound doctrine which was once delivered to them, to lose a good conscience, and to cause Divine grace to be ineffectual.

Though I here openly and ingenuously affirm, I never taught that a true believer can, either totally or finally fall away from the faith, and perish; yet I will not conceal, that there are passages of scripture which seem to me to wear this aspect; and those answers to them which I have been permitted to see, are not of such a kind as to approve themselves on all points to my understanding. On the other hand, certain passages are produced for the contrary doctrine [of unconditional perseverance] which are worthy of much consideration.

VI. THE ASSURANCE OF SALVATION

With regard to the certainty [or assurance] of salvation, my opinion is, that it is possible for him who believes in Jesus Christ to be certain and persuaded, and, if his heart condemn him not, he is now in reality assured, that he is a son of God, and stands in the grace of Jesus Christ. Such a certainty is wrought in the mind, as well by the action of the Holy Spirit inwardly actuating the believer and by the fruits of faith, as from his own conscience, and the testimony of God's Spirit witnessing together with his conscience. I also believe, that it is possible for such a person, with an assured confidence in the grace of God and his mercy in Christ, to depart out of this life, and to appear before the throne of grace, without any anxious fear or terrific dread: and yet this person should constantly pray, "O lord, enter not into judgment with thy servant!"

But, since "God is greater than our hearts, and knoweth all things," and since a man judges not his own self--yea, though a man know nothing by himself, yet is he not thereby justified, but he who judgeth him is the Lord, (1 John iii. 19; 1 Cor. iv. 3,) I dare not [on this account] place this assurance [or certainty] on an equality with that by which we know there is a God, and that Christ is the saviour of the world. Yet it will be proper to make the extent of the boundaries of this assurance, a subject of inquiry in our convention.

VII. THE PERFECTION OF BELIEVERS IN THIS LIFE

Beside those doctrines on which I have treated, there is now much discussion among us respecting the perfection of believers, or regenerated persons, in this life; and it is reported, that I entertain sentiments on this subject, which are very improper, and nearly allied to those of the Pelagians, viz: "that it is possible for the regenerate in this life perfectly to keep God's precepts." To this I reply, though these might have been my sentiments yet I ought not on this account to be considered a Pelagian, either partly or entirely, provided I had only added that "they could do this by the grace of Christ, and by no means without it." But while I never asserted, that a believer could perfectly keep the precepts of Christ in this life, I never denied it, but always left it as a matter which has still to be decided. For I have contented myself with those sentiments which St. Augustine has expressed on this subject, whose words have frequently quoted in the University, and have usually subjoined, that I had no addition to make to them.

Augustine says, "four questions may claim our attention on this topic. The first is, was there ever yet a man without sin, one who from the beginning of life to its termination never committed sin? The second, has there ever been, is there now, or can there possibly be, an individual who does not sin, that is, who has attained to such a state of perfection in this life as not to commit sin, but perfectly to fulfill the law of God? The third, is it possible for a man in this life to exist without sin? The fourth, if it be possible for a man to be without sin, why has such an individual never yet been found?" St. Augustine says, that such a person as is described in the first question never yet lived, or will hereafter be brought into existence, with the exception of Jesus Christ. He does not think, that any man has attained to such perfection in this life as is portrayed in the second question. With regard to the third, he thinks it possible for a man to be without sin, by means of the grace of Christ and free-will. In answer to the fourth, man does not do what it is possible for him by the grace of Christ to perform, either because that which is good escapes his observation, or because in it he places no part of his delight." From this quotation it is apparent, that St. Augustine, one of the most strenuous adversaries of the Pelagian doctrine, retained this sentiment, that "it is possible for a man to live in this world without sin."

Beside this, the same Christian father says, "let Pelagius confess, that it is possible for man to be without sin, in no other way than by the grace of Christ, and we will be at peace with each other." The opinion of Pelagius appeared to St. Augustine to be this--"that man could fulfill the law of God by his own proffer strength and ability; but with still "greater facility by means of the grace of Christ." I have already most abundantly stated the great distance at which I stand from such a sentiment; in addition to which I now declare, that I account this sentiment of Pelagius to be heretical, and diametrically opposed to these words of Christ, "Without me ye can do nothing:" (John xv. 5.) It is likewise very destructive, and inflicts a most grievous wound on the glory of Christ.

I cannot see that anything is contained in all I have hitherto produced respecting my sentiments, on account of which any person ought to be "afraid of appearing in the presence of God," and from which it might be feared that any mischievous consequences can possibly arise. Yet because every day brings me fresh information about reports concerning me, "that I carry in my breast destructive sentiments and heresies," I cannot possibly conceive to what points those charges can relate, except perhaps they draw some such pretext from my opinion concerning the Divinity of the Son of God, and the justification of man before God. Indeed, I have lately learnt, that there has been much public conversation, and many rumors have been circulated, respecting my opinion on both these points of doctrine, particularly since the last conference [between Gomarus and myself] before the Counselors of the Supreme Court. This is one reason why I think, that I shall not be acting unadvisedly if I disclose to your mightinesses the real state of the whole matter.

VIII. THE DIVINITY OF THE SON OF GOD

With regard to the Divinity of the Son of God and the word autoqeov both of which have been discussed in our University in the regular form of scholastic disputations, I cannot sufficiently wonder what the motive can be, which has created a wish in some persons to render me suspected to other men, or to make me an object of suspicion to themselves. This is still more wonderful, since this suspicion has not the least ground of probability on which to rest, and is at such an immense distance from all reason and truth, that, whatever reports have been spread abroad respecting this affair to the prejudice of my character, they can be called nothing better than "notorious calumnies." At a disputation held one afternoon in the University, when the thesis that had been proposed for disputation was the Divinity of the Son of God, one of the students happened to object, "that the Son of God was autotheos, and that he therefore had his essence from himself and not from the Father." In reply to this I observed, "that the word autotheos was capable of two different acceptations, since it might signify either "one who is truly God," or "one who is God of himself;" and that it was with great propriety and correctness attributed to the Son of God according to the former signification, but not according to the latter." The student, in prosecution of his argument, violently contended, that the word was justly applicable to the Son of God, principally according to the second of these significations: and that the essence of the Father could not be said to be communicated to the Son and to the Holy Spirit, in any other than in an improper sense; but that it was in perfect correctness and strict propriety common alike to the Father, the Son, and the Holy Ghost." He added "that he asserted this with the greater confidence because he had the younger Trelcatius of pious memory, [but who was then living,] as an authority in his favour on this point; for that learned Professor had written to the same purport in his Common Places." To these observations I answered, "that this opinion was at variance with the word of God, and with the whole of the ancient

Church, both Greek and Latin, which had always taught, that the Son had His Deity from the Father by eternal generation." To these remarks I subjoined, "that from such an opinion as this, necessarily followed the two mutually conflicting errors, Tri-theism and Sabellianism; that is, (1.) It would ensue as a necessary consequence, from these premises, that there are three Gods, who have together and collaterally the Divine essence, independently of this circumstance--that one of them (being only personally distinguished from the rest) has that essence from another of the persons. Yet the proceeding of the origin of one person from another, (that is, of the Son from the Father,) is the only foundation that has ever been used for defending the Unity of the Divine Essence in the Trinity of Persons. (2.) It would likewise follow as another consequence, that the Son would himself be the Father, because he would differ from the Father in nothing but in regard to name, which was the opinion of Sabellius. For, since it is peculiar to the Father to derive his Deity from himself, or (to speak more correctly,) to derive it from no one, if, in the sense of being "God of himself," the Son be called autotheos, it follows that he is the Father." Some account of this disputation was dispersed abroad in all directions, and it reached Amsterdam. A minister of that city, who now rests in the Lord, having interrogated me respecting the real state of this affair, I related the whole of it to him plainly, as I have now done: and I requested him to make Trelcatius of blessed memory acquainted with it as it had actually occurred, and to advise him in a friendly manner to amend his opinion, and to correct those inappropriate words in his Common Places: this request the minister from Amsterdam engaged to fulfill in his own way.

In all this proceeding I am far from being liable to any blame; for I have defended the truth and the sentiments of the Catholic and Orthodox Church. Trelcatius undoubtedly was the person most open to animadversion; for he adopted a mode of speaking which detracted somewhat from the truth of the matter. But such has always been either my own infelicity or the zeal of certain individuals that, as soon as any disagreement arises, all the blame is instantly cast upon me, as if it was impossible for me to display as much veracity [or orthodoxy] as any other person. Yet on this subject I have Gomarus himself consenting with me; for, soon after Trelcatius had published his common places, a disputation on the Trinity having been proposed in the University, Gomarus did in three several parts of his theses express himself in such terms as were diametrically opposed to those of Trelcatius. The very obvious difference in opinion between those two Professors I pointed out to the Amsterdam minister, who acknowledged its existence. Yet, notwithstanding all these things, no one endeavoured to vindicate me from this calumny; while great exertion was employed to frame excuses for Trelcatius, by means of a qualified interpretation of his words, though it was utterly impossible to reconcile their palliative explanations with the plain signification of his unperverted expressions. Such are the effects which the partiality of favour and the fervour of zeal can produce!

The milder and qualified interpretation put upon the words of Trelcatius, was the following: "the Son of God may be styled autotheos, or may be said to have his Deity from himself, in reference to his being God, although he has his Deity from the Father, in reference to his being the Son." For the sake of a larger explanation, it is said, "God, or the Divine Essence, may be considered both absolutely and relatively. When regarded absolutely, the Son has his Divine essence from himself; but, when viewed relatively, he derives it from the Father." But these are new modes of speaking and novel opinions, and such as can by no means consist together. For the Son, both in regard to his being the Son, and to his being God, derives his Deity from the Father. When he is called God, it is then only not expressed that he is from the Father; which derivation is particularly noted when the word Son is employed. Indeed, the essence of God can in no manner come under our consideration, except it be said, "that the Divine Essence is communicated to the Son by the Father." Nor can it possibly in any different respect whatever be said, that this essence is both "communicated to him" and "not communicated;" because these expressions are contradictory, and can in no diverse respect be reconciled to each other. If the Son have the Divine Essence from himself in reference to its being absolutely considered, it cannot be communicated to him. If it be communicated to him in reference to its being relatively considered, he cannot have it from himself in reference to its being absolutely considered.

I shall probably be asked, "do you not acknowledge that, to be the Son of God, and to be God, are two things entirely distinct from each other?" I reply, undoubtedly I subscribe to such distinction. But when those who make it proceed still further, and say, "since to be the Son of God signifies that he derives his essence from the Father, to be God in like manner signifies nothing less than that he has his essence from himself or from no one;" I deny this assertion, and declare, at the same time, that it is a great and manifest error, not only in sacred theology, but likewise in natural philosophy. For, these two things, to be the Son and to be God, are at perfect agreement with each other; but to derive his essence from the Father, and, at the same time, to derive it from no one, are evidently contradictor, and mutually destructive the one of the other.

But, to make this fallacy still more apparent, it must be observed, how equal in force and import are certain double ternary and parallel propositions, when standing in the following juxta-position:

God is from eternity, possessing the Divine Essence from eternity. The Father is from no one, having the Divine Essence from no one. The Son is from the Father, having the Divine Essence from the

Father.

The word "God" therefore signifies, that He has the true Divine Essence; but the word "Son" signifies, that he has the Divine Essence from the Father. On this account, he is correctly denominated both God and the Son of God. But since he cannot be styled the Father, he cannot possibly be said to have the Divine Essence from himself or from no one. Yet much labour is devoted to the purpose of excusing these expressions, by saying, "that when the son of God in reference to his being God is said to have his essence from that form of speech signifies nothing more, than that the Divine essence is not derived from any one." But if this be thought to be the most proper mode of action which should be adopted, there will be no depraved or erroneous sentiment which can be uttered that may not thus find a ready excuse. For though God and the divine Essence do not differ substantially, yet whatever may be predicated of the Divine Essence can by no means be equally predicated of God; because they are distinguished from each other in our mode of framing conceptions, according to which mode all forms of speech ought to be examined, since they are employed only with a design that through them we should receive correct impressions. This is very obvious from the following examples, in which we speak with perfect correctness when we say, "Deum mortuum esse," and "the Essence of God is communicated;" but very incorrectly when we say, "God is communicated." That man who understands the difference existing between concrete and abstract, about which there were such frequent disputes between us and the Lutherans will easily perceive what a number of absurdities will ensue, if explanations of this description be once tolerated in the Church of God. Therefore, in no way whatever can this phrase, "the Son of God is autotheos," ["God of himself," or "in his own right,"] be excused as a correct one, or as having been happily expressed. Nor can that be called a proper form of speech which says, "the Essence of God is common to three persons;" but it is improper, since the Divine Essence is declared to be communicated by one of them to another.

The observations which I now make, I wish to be particularly regarded, because it may appear from them how much we are capable of tolerating in a man whom we do not suspect of heresy; and, on the contrary, with what avidity we seize upon any trivial circumstance by which we may inculpate another man whom we hold under the ban of suspicion. Of such partiality, this incident affords two manifest examples.

IX. THE JUSTIFICATION OF MAN BEFORE GOD

I am not conscious to myself, of having taught or entertained any other sentiments concerning the justification of man before God, than those which are held unanimously by the Reformed and Protestant Churches, and which are in complete agreement with their expressed opinions.

There was lately a short controversy in relation to this subject, between John Piscator, Professor of Divinity in the University of Herborn in Nassau, and the French Churches. It consisted in the determination of these two questions: (1.) "is the obedience or righteousness of Christ, which is imputed to believers and in which consists their righteousness before God, is this only the passive obedience of Christ?" which was Piscator's opinion. Or (2.) "is it not, in addition to this, that active righteousness of Christ which he exhibited to the law of God in the whole course of his life, and that holiness in which he was conceived?" Which was the opinion of the French Churches. But I never durst mingle myself with the dispute, or undertake to decide it; for I thought it possible for the Professors of the same religion to hold different opinions on this point from others of their brethren, without any breach of Christian peace or the unity of faith. Similar peaceful thoughts appear to have been indulged by both the adverse parties in this dispute; for they exercised a friendly toleration towards each other, and did not make that a reason for mutually renouncing their fraternal concord. But concerning such an amicable plan of adjusting differences, certain individuals in our own country are of a different judgment.

A question has been raised from these words of the Apostle Paul: "Faith is imputed for righteousness." (Rom. 4) The inquiry was, (1.) Whether those expressions ought to be properly understood, "so that faith itself, as an act performed according to the command of the gospel, is imputed before God for or unto righteousness--and that of grace; since it is not the righteousness of the law." (2.) Whether they ought to be figuratively and improperly understood, "that the righteousness of Christ, being apprehended by faith, is imputed to us for righteousness." Or (3.) Whether it is to be understood "that the righteousness, for which, or unto which, faith is imputed, is the instrumental operation of faith;" which is asserted by some persons. In the theses on justification, which were disputed under me when I was moderator, I have adopted the former of these opinions not in a rigid manner, but simply, as I have likewise done in another passage which I wrote in a particular letter. It is on this ground that I am accounted to hold and to teach unsound opinions concerning the justification of man before God. But how unfounded such a supposition is, will be very evident at a proper season, and in a mutual conference. For the present, I will only briefly say, "I believe that sinners are accounted righteous solely by the obedience of Christ; and that the righteousness of Christ is the only meritorious cause on account of which God pardons the sins of believers and reckons them as righteous as if they had perfectly fulfilled the law. But since God imputes the righteousness of Christ to none except believers, I conclude that, in this sense, it may be well and properly said, to a man who believes, faith is imputed for righteousness through grace, because God hath set forth his Son, Jesus Christ, to be a propitiation, a throne of grace, [or mercy seat] through faith in his blood." Whatever interpretation may be put upon these expressions, none of our Divines blames Calvin or considers him to be heterodox on this point; yet my opinion is not so widely different from his as to prevent me from employing the signature of my own hand in subscribing to those things which he has delivered on this subject, in the third book of his Institutes; this I am prepared to do at any time, and to give them my full approval. Most noble and potent Lords, these are the principal articles, respecting which I have judged it necessary to declare my opinion before this august meeting, in obedience to your commands.

X. THE REVISION OF THE DUTCH CONFESSION, AND THE HEIDELBERG CATECHISM

But, besides these things, I had some annotations to make on the Confession of the Dutch Churches and on the Heidelberg Catechism; but they will be discussed most appropriately in our Synod, which at the first opportunity we hope to obtain through your consent, or rather by means of your summons. This is the sole request which I prefer to your mightinesses, that I may be permitted to offer a few brief remarks on a certain clause, subject to which their high mightinesses, the States General, gave their consent to the convening of a National Synod in this province, (Holland,) and the substance of which was, that in such Synod the Confession and Catechism of the Dutch Churches should be subjected to examination.

This clause has given great umbrage to many persons, not only because they account it unnecessary, but likewise unjust, to subject the Confession and Catechism to examination. They also suppose, that I and a certain individual of great reputation, are the persons who prevailed with the States General to have such a clause inserted. But it is by no means true that the revision of the Confession and Catechism is unnecessary and unjust, or that we were the instigators of their high mightinesses in this affair. With regard to the last of these two suppositions, so far were we from having any concern with the origin of that clause, that, eleven or twelve years ago, at the pressing importunity of the Churches that prayed for a National Synod, the States of South Holland and West Friezland at last judged it proper to consent to it by their decree, on no other condition than that in such Synod the Confession of the Dutch Churches should be subjected to examination. Yet we, at that time, neither endeavoured by our advice, nor by our influence, to promote any such measure. But if we had with all our might made the attempt, we should have been doing nothing but what was compatible with our official duties; because it is obviously agreeable to reason as well as to equity, and quite necessary in the present posture of affairs, that such a measure should be adopted.

First. That it may openly appear to all the world that we render to the word of God alone such due and suitable honour, as to determine it to be beyond (or rather above) all disputes, too great to be the subject of any exception, and worthy of all acceptation.

Secondly. Because these pamphlets are writings that proceed from men, and may, on that account, contain within them some portion of error, it is, therefore, proper to institute a lawful inquiry, that is, in a National Synod, whether or not there be any thing in those productions which requires amendment.

1. The first inquiry may be, whether these human writings are accordant, in every part, with the word of God, with regard to the words themselves, the construction of the sentences and the correct meaning.

2. Whether they contain whatever is necessary to be believed unto salvation, so that salvation is, according to this rule, not denied to those things to which it appertains.

3. Whether it [the rule of these formularies] does not contain far too many particulars, and embrace several that are not necessary to be believed unto salvation, so that salvation is consequently attributed to those things to which it does not belong.

4. Whether certain words and forms of speech are not employed in them, which are capable of being understood in different ways and furnishing occasion for disputes. Thus, for example, in the Fourteenth article of the Confession, we read the following words, "nothing is done without God's ordination," [or appointment]: if by the word "ordination" is signified, "that God appoints things of any kind to be done," this mode of enunciation is erroneous, and it follows as a a consequence from it, that God is the author of sin. But if it signify, that "whatever it be that is done, God ordains it to a good end," the terms in which it is conceived are in that case correct.

5. Whether things utterly repugnant to each other may not be discovered in them. For instance, a certain individual who is highly honoured in the Church, addressed a letter to John Piscator, Professor

of Divinity in the University of Herborn in Nassau, and in it he exhorted him to confine himself within the opinion of the Heidelberg Catechism on the doctrine of Justification. For this purpose he cited three passage, which he considered to be at variance with Piscator's sentiments. But the learned Professor replied, that he confined himself completely within the doctrinal boundaries of the Catechism; and then quoted out of that formulary ten or eleven passages as proofs of his sentiments. But I solemnly declare, I do not perceive by what method these several passages can possibly be reconciled with each other.

6. Whether every thing in these writings is digested in that due order in which the Scripture requires them to be placed.

7. Whether all things are disposed in a manner the most suitable and convenient for preserving peace and unity with the rest of the reformed Churches.

Thirdly. The third reason is, because a National Synod is held for the purpose of discovering whether all things in the Church are in a proper state or right condition. One of the chief duties which appertains to such an assembly, is, the examination of doctrine, whether it be that which is admitted by unanimous consent, or that for which particular Divines contend.

Fourthly. The fourth reason is, because an examination of this description will obtain for these writings a greater degree of authority, when after a mature and rigid examination they shall be found to agree with the word of God, or shall be made conformable to it in a still greater measure. Such an examination will also excite within the minds of men a greater value for Christian ministers, when they perceive that these sacred functionaries hold in the highest estimation that truth which is revealed in Scripture, and that their attachment to it is so great as to induce them to spare no labour in order to render their own doctrine more and more conformable to that revealed truth.

Fifthly. The fifth reason why at this, if at any period, it is necessary to adopt the suggestion which we have mentioned, is, (1.) Because there are several individuals in the ministry who have certain views and considerations respecting some points contained in these writings, which they reserve in secret and reveal to no one, because they hope that such points will become subjects of discussion in a National Synod. Because such a convention has been promised, some of them have suffered themselves to be persuaded not to give the least publicity to any of the views or considerations which they have formed on these subjects.

(2.) Besides, this will be the design of a National Synod--

That their high mightinesses the States General may be pleased to establish and arm with public authority certain ecclesiastical sanctions, according to which every one may be bound to conduct himself in the Church of God. That this favour may be obtained from their high mightinesses and that they may execute such a measure with a good conscience, it is necessary that they be convinced in their own understandings, that the doctrine contained in the formulary of union is agreeable to the word of God. This is a reason which ought to induce us spontaneously to propose an examination of our Confession before their high mightinesses, and to offer either to shew that it is in accordance with the word of God, or to render it conformable to that Divine standard.

Sixthly. The sixth reason is drawn from the example of those who are associated together under the Augustan Confession, and from the conduct of the Swiss and the French Churches, that have within two or three years enriched their Confessions with one entirely new article. And the Dutch Confession has itself been subjected to examination since it was first published: some things having been taken away from it and others added, while some of the rest have undergone various alterations.

Numerous other reasons might be produced, but I omit them; because I consider those already mentioned to be quite sufficient for proving, that the clause concerning examination and revision, as it is termed, was with the greatest justice and propriety inserted in the instrument of consent of which we have made previous mention.

I am not ignorant, that other reasons are adduced, in opposition to these; and one in particular, which is made a principal subject of public conversation, and is accounted of all others the most solid. To it, therefore I consider it necessary to offer a brief reply. It is thus stated: "by such an examination as this, the doctrine of the Church will be called in question; which is neither an act of propriety nor of duty.

"I. Because this doctrine has obtained the approbation and suffrages of many respectable and learned men; and has been strenuously defended against all those who have offered it any opposition.

"II. Because it has been sealed with the blood of many thousand martyrs.

"III. Because from such an examination will arise, within the Church, confusion, scandal, offenses, and the destruction of consciences; and, out of the Church, ridicule, calumnies and accusations."

To all these I answer:

1. It would be much better, not to employ such odious forms of speech, as to call in question, and others of that class, when the conversation is only respecting some human composition, which is liable to have error intermixed with its contents. For with what right can any writing be said to be called in question or in doubt, which was never of itself unquestionable, or ought to be considered as indubitable?

2. The approbation of Divines, the defense of a composition against its adversaries, and the sealing

of it with the blood of martyrs, do not render any doctrine authentic or place it beyond the limits of doubt: because it is possible both for Divines and martyrs to err--a circumstance which can admit of no denial in this argument.

3. A distinction ought to be made between the different matters contained in the Confession. For while some of them make a near approach to the foundation of salvation and are fundamental articles of the Christian religion, others of them are built up as a superstructure on the foundation, and of themselves are not absolutely necessary to salvation. The doctrines of this former class are approved by the unanimous consent of all the Reformed, and are effectually defended against all gainsaying adversaries. But those of the latter class become subjects of controversy between different parties: and some of these are attacked by enemies not without some semblance of truth and justice.

The blood of martyrs has sealed those of the former class but by no means those of the latter. In reference to this affair, it ought to be diligently observed, what was proposed by the martyrs of our days, and on what account they shed their blood. If this be done, it will be found, that no man among them was even interrogated on that subject which I consider it equitable to make a prominent part in the deliberations of a Synod, and, therefore, that no martyr ever sealed it with his blood. I will produce an example: when a question was raised about the meaning of the seventh chapter of the epistle to the Romans, one individual said, "that the passage was quoted in the margin of the Confession exactly in the same sense as he had embraced it, and that the martyrs had with their own blood sealed this Confession." But, in reply to this, it was stated, "that if the strictest search be instituted throughout the entire large history of the martyrs, as it is published by the French, it will be discovered, that no martyr has at any period been examined on that passage, or has shed his blood on that account."

To sum up the whole: the blood of the martyrs tends to confirm this truth, that they have made profession of their faith "in simplicity and sincerity of conscience." But it is by no means conclusive, that the Confession which they produced is free from every degree of reprehension or superior to all exception; unless they had been led by Christ into all truth and therefore rendered incapable of erring.

4. If the Church be properly instructed in that difference which really does and always ought to exist between the word of God and all human writings, and if the Church be also rightly informed concerning that liberty which she and all Christians possess, and which they will always enjoy, to measure all human compositions by the standard rule of God's word, she will neither distress herself on that account, nor will she be offended on perceiving all human writings brought to be proved at the touch-stone of God's word. On the contrary, she will rather feel far more abundant delight, when she sees, that God has bestowed on her in this country such pastors and teachers, as try at the chief touch-stone their own doctrine, in a manner at once suitable, proper, just, and worthy of perpetual observance; and that they do this, to be able exactly and by every possible means to express their agreement with the word of God, and their consent to it even in the most minute particulars.

5. But it is no less proper, that the doctrine once received in the Church should be subjected to examination, however great the fear may be "lest disturbances should ensue, and lest evil disposed persons should make such revision an object of ridicule, calumny or accusation," or should even turn it to their own great advantage, [by representing the matter so as to induce a persuasion,] "that those who propose this examination are not sufficiently confirmed in their own religion ;" when, on the contrary, this is one of God's commands, "search and try the spirits whether they be of God." (1 John iv. 1.) If cogitations of that description had operated as hindrances on the minds of Luther, Zuinglius, and others, they would never have pried into the doctrine of the Papists, or have subjected it to a scrutinizing examination. Nor would those who adhere to the Augustan Confession have considered it proper to submit that formulary again to a new and complete revision, and to alter it in some particulars. This deed of theirs is an object of our praise and approval. And we conclude, that, when Luther towards the close of his life was advised by Philip Melancthon to bring the eucharistic controversy on the sacrament of the Lord's Supper to some better state of concord, (as it is related in the writings of our own countrymen,) he acted very improperly in rejecting that counsel, and in casting it back as a reproach on Philip, for this reason, as they state his declaration, "lest by such an attempt to effect an amicable conclusion, the whole doctrine should be called in question." Besides, if reasons of this kind ought to be admitted, the Papists with the best right and the greatest propriety formerly endeavoured to prevent the doctrine, which had for many preceding centuries been received in the Church, from being called in question or subjected again to examination.

But it has been suggested, in opposition to these reasons, "that if the doctrine of the Churches be submitted to an entirely new revision as often as a National Synod shall be held, the Church would never have any thing to which it might adhere or on which it might fully depend, and it will be possible to declare with great justice, concerning Churches thus circumstanced, that, they have an anniversary faith: are tossed to and fro, and carried about with every wind of doctrine. (Ephes. iv. 14.)

1. My first answer to these remarks, is, the Church always has Moses and the Prophets, the Evangelists and the Apostles, that is, the Scriptures of the Old and of the New Testament; and these Scriptures fully and clearly comprehend whatever is necessary to salvation. Upon them the Church will

lay the foundation of her faith, and will rest upon them as on an immovable basis, principally because, how highly soever we may esteem Confessions and Catechisms every decision on matters of faith and religion must obtain its final resolution in the Scriptures.

2. Some points in the Confession are certain and do not admit of a doubt: these will never be called in question by any one, except by heretics. Yet there are other parts of its contents which are of such a kind, as may with the most obvious utility become frequent subjects of conference and discussion between men of learning who fear God, for the purpose of reconciling them with those indubitable articles as nearly as is practicable.

3. Let it be attempted to make the Confession contain as few articles as possible; and let it propose them in a very brief form, conceived entirely in the expressions of Scripture. Let all the more ample explanations, proofs, digressions, redundancies, amplifications and exclamations, be omitted; and let nothing be delivered in it, except those truths which are necessary to salvation. The consequences of this brevity will be, that the Confession will be less liable to be filled with errors, not so obnoxious to obloquy, and less subject to examination. Let the practice of the ancient Church be produced as an example, that comprehended, in as brief a form of words as was practicable, those articles which she judged necessary to be believed.

Some individuals form a distinction between the Confession and the Catechism with respect to revision; and, since the Confession is the peculiar property of the Dutch Churches, and is on that account found in the hands of comparatively few people, they conclude, "that it is possible without any difficulty to revise it in a Synod and subject it to examination., But since the Catechism belongs not only to us, but likewise and principally to the Churches of the Palatinate, and is therefore to be found in the hands of all men, the same persons consider the examination of it "to be connected with great peril." But to this I reply, if we be desirous of constituting the Heidelberg Catechism a formulary of concord among the teachers of the Churches, and if they be obliged to subscribe it, it is still necessary to subject it to examination. For no Churches whatever ought to hold such a high station in our esteem, as to induce us to receive any writing of their composition without, at the same time, reserving to ourselves the liberty of submitting it to a nice scrutiny. And I account this to be the principal cause, why the Churches of different provinces, although at perfect agreement with each other on the fundamental points of Christian doctrine, have each composed for themselves their own Confessions. But if the Heidelberg Catechism be not allowed, to become a formulary of this kind, and if a suitable liberty be conceded in the explanation of it, it will not then be necessary either to revise it or subject it to examination; provided, I repeat, that the obligatory burden of subscription be removed, and a moderate liberty be conceded in its explanation.

This is all that I had to propose to your mightinesses, as to my most noble, potent, wise and prudent masters. While I own myself bound to render an account of all my actions, to the members of this most noble and potent assembly, (next after God,) I at the same time present to them my humble and grateful acknowledgments, because they have not disdained to grant me a courteous and patient audience. I embrace this opportunity solemnly to declare, that I am sincerely prepared to institute an amicable and fraternal conference with my reverend brethren, (at whatever time or place and on whatever occasion this honourable assembly may judge proper to appoint,) on all the topics which I have now mentioned, and on any other concerning which it will be possible for a controversy to exist, or at some future period to arise. I also make this additional promise, that I will in every conference conduct myself with equanimity, moderation and docility, and will shew myself not less actuated by the desire of being taught, than by that of communicating to others some portion of instruction. And, since in the discussion of every topic on which it will be possible to institute a conference, two points will become objects of attention. First. "Whether that be true which is the subject of the controversy," and, secondly, "Whether it be necessary to be believed unto salvation," and since both these points ought to be discussed and proved out of the Scriptures, I here tender my sacred affirmation, and solemnly bind myself hereafter to observe it, that, however cogently I may have proved by the most solid [human] arguments any article to be agreeable to the word of God, I will not obtrude it for an article of belief on those of my brethren who may entertain a different opinion respecting it, unless I have plainly proved it from the word of God and have with equal clearness established its truth, and the necessity unto salvation that every Christian should entertain the same belief.

If my brethren will be prepared to act in this manner, as far as I know the complexion of my own opinions, there will not easily arise among us any schism or controversy. But, that I may on my part remove every cause of fear that can possibly invade this most noble assembly, occupied and engaged as its honourable members now are with important concerns on which in a great measure depends the safety of our native country and of the Reformed Churches, I subjoin this remark, "that to hinder my toleration of any matters in my brethren, they must be very numerous and very important. For I am not of the congregation of those who wish to have dominion over the faith of another man, but am only a minister to believers, with the design of promoting in them an increase of knowledge, truth, piety, peace and joy in Jesus Christ our Lord."

But if my brethren cannot perceive how they can possibly tolerate me, or allow me a place among them, in reference to myself I indulge in no hope that a schism will on this account be formed. May God avert any such catastrophe, since far too many schisms have already arisen and spread themselves abroad among Christians. It ought rather to be the earnest endeavour of every one, to diminish their number and destroy their influence. Yet, even under such circumstances, [when I shall be rejected from the communion of my brethren,] in patience will I possess my soul; and though in that case I shall resign my office, yet I will continue to live for the benefit of our common Christianity as long as it may please God to lengthen out my days and prolong my existence. Never forgetting this sentiment, Sat Ecclesæ, sat Patriæ daturm, Enough has been done to satisfy the Church of Christ and my country!

Section 3

CERTAIN articles relating to the Christian Religion are now in a course of circulation. In a paper which was not long since delivered into my hands, the number of them is distinguished into two series, one consisting of twenty and the other of eleven articles. Some of them are attributed to me, others to Adrian Borrius, and several both to him and me. Those persons by whom they were first disseminated, attempt in them to render us suspected of having introduced into the church and the University of Leyden, novelties and heretical instructions, and to accuse us of error and heresy, that both the students of Divinity and the common people may stand on their guard against us, who have this black mark imprinted on us, lest they become infected with the same envenomed disorder, and that those persons who enjoy the supremacy both in Church and State, may seasonably interpose their authority, to prevent the evil from extending any further, or rather to extinguish it in its very commencement; which, if "they neglect to do, they will be instrumental in producing the greatest detriment to Divine Truth, and to the Political and Ecclesiastical concord of these Provinces."

The dispersion of some of these articles is not a very recent circumstance; for, above two years ago, seventeen out of these thirty-one came into my hands, expressed exactly in the same words as those that occur in the writing which is the subject of my present remarks. But I was silent, and concealed my regret; for I thought that those articles would, in their very infancy, die a natural death, since part of them were destitute of the truth of historical narration, by not being attributed to those who had been the authors of them; and part of them were void of all real theological sense, by the strange intermixture of truth and falsehood. But the issue did not answer my expectation. For they not only remained without diminution, but gained an increase, by the addition of other fourteen to the former seventeen articles, and by a far wider dispersion of the whole than had at first been made. This unexpected result had the effect of inducing me to think that I ought to oppose their progress by a moderate answer, lest my continued silence should be interpreted as tantamount to a confession. If this be the interpretation which, on many occasions is given to silence, it is an easy matter thus to construe it respecting any doctrine that is aspersed as. a heresy, "under which imputation," it is said in a vaunting tone, "St. Jerome would have no man to remain patient."

In this reply I will use candour and conscience. Whatever I know to be true, I will confess and defend. On whatever subjects I may feel hesitation, I will not conceal my ignorance; and whatever my mind dictates to be false, I will deny and refute. May the God of truth and peace direct my mind and my hand by his Holy Spirit! Amen.

ARTICLES I & II

I. Faith, that is, justifying faith, is not peculiar to the elect.
II. It is possible for believers finally to decline and fall away from faith and salvation.

ANSWER
The connection between these two articles is so intimate, that when the first of them is granted, the second is necessarily inferred; and, in return, when the latter is granted, the former is to be inferred, according to the intention of those persons who framed these articles. For if "faith be not peculiar to the elect," and if perseverance in faith and salvation belong to the elect alone, it follows that believers not only can, but that some of them actually do, "fall away from faith and salvation." And, on the contrary, if it be "possible for believers finally to fall away from faith and salvation," it follows that "faith is not peculiar to the elect," they being the individuals concerning whom the framers of these articles assert, that it is impossible for them not to be saved. The reason of the consequence is, because the words

FAITH and BELIEVERS, according to this hypothesis, have a wider signification than the words ELECTION and THE ELECT. The former comprehend some persons that are not elect, that is, "some who finally fall away from faith and salvation." No necessity, therefore, existed for composing both these articles; it was quite sufficient to have proposed one. And if the authors of them had sought for such amplification, as had no real existence, but consisted of mere words, it was possible to deduce the Second from the First in the form of a consectary. Thus it is evident that the multitude of the articles, was the great object to be attempted for the purpose of making it appear as if those persons ERRED IN VERY MANY POINTS, whom the too sedulous curiosity of the brethren is desirous without cause, of rendering suspected of heresy.

I. But, to treat of each article singly, I declare, respecting THE FIRST, that I never said, either in public or in private, "Faith is not peculiar to the elect." This article, therefore, is not attributed to its proper author; and thus is committed a historical error.

I add, even if I had made such a declaration as this, a defense of it would have been ready. For I omit the scriptures, from which a more prolix discussion of this subject might be formed; and since the Christian Fathers have with great semblance of truth defended their sentiments from that divine source, I might employ the consent of those Fathers as a shield to ward off from myself the charge of NOVELTY; and the Harmony of Confessions, which are severally the composition of those Churches that have seceded from Popery, and that come under the denomination of" Protestants" and "the Reformed," I might adopt for a polished breast-plate, to intercept or turn aside the dart of HERESY which is hurled against me. Neither should I be much afraid of this subject being placed for adjudication in the balances of the Belgic Confession and the Heidelberg Catechism.

1. Let St. Augustine, Prosper, and the author of the book entitled The Vocation of the Gentiles, be brought forward to bear testimony respecting "the consent of the Fathers."

(1.) AUGUSTINE says, "It is wonderful, and indeed most wonderful, that God does not bestow perseverance on certain of his sons, whom he hath regenerated in Christ, and to whom he has given faith, hope and love; while he pardons such great acts of wickedness in sons that are alienated from him, and, by imparting his grace, makes them his children." (De Corrept. et Gratia, cap. 8.)

(2.) PROSPER says, "It is a lamentable circumstance which is proved by many examples, that some of those persons who were regenerated in Christ Jesus, have relinquished the faith, and, ceasing to preserve their former sanctity of manners, have apostatized from God, and their ungodly course has been terminated under his displeasure and aversion." (Ad Capita Galatians resp. 7.) (3.) The author of The Vocation of the Gentiles says, "God bestows the power of willing to obey him, in such a manner as not to take away, even from those who will persevere, that mutability by which it is possible for them to be unwilling [to obey God]. If this were not the case, none of the believers would have departed from the faith." (Lib. ii, c. 9.)

2. The HARMONY OF CONFESSIONS might in the following manner, contribute to my defense: This dogma states that "faith is the peculiar property of the elect," and that "it is impossible for believers finally to decline from faith and salvation." Now, if this be a dogma necessary to salvation, then that Confession which does not contain it, or which asserts some thing contradictory to it, cannot be considered as harmonizing with the rest on the subject of religion. For wherever there is harmony, it is proper that there should be neither defect nor contradiction in things pertaining to salvation. But the Augustan or Lutheran Confession says that "it condemns the Anabaptists, who deny that those persons who have once been justified, can lose the Holy Spirit." Besides, Philip Melancthon with his followers, and the greater portion of the Lutheran Churches, are of opinion, that faith is bestowed even on the non-elect." Yet we are not afraid of acknowledging these Lutherans for brethren.

3. The BELGIC Confession does not contain this dogma, that "faith is peculiar to the elect ;" and without controversy it cannot be deduced from our CATECHISM. For when it is said, in the article on the Church, "I believe that I shall perpetually remain a member of the Church;" and, in the first question, "God keeps and preserves me in such a manner, as to make all things necessarily subservient to my salvation;" those expressions are to be understood of a believer, in reference to his actual believing. For he who is truly such a one, answers to the character of a Christian. But no man is such except through faith. Faith is therefore presupposed in both the expressions.

II. With regard to the SECOND Article, I say, that a distinction ought to be made between power and action. For it is one thing to declare, that "it is possible for the faithful to fall away from faith and salvation," and it is another to say, that "they do actually fall away." This distinction is of such extensive observance, that even antiquity itself was not afraid of affirming, concerning the elect and those who were to be saved, "that it was possible for them not to be saved;" and that "the mutability by which it was possible for them not to be willing to obey God, was not taken away from them," although it was the opinion of the ancients, "that such persons never would in reality be damned." On this very subject, too, the greater part of our own doctors lay down a difference. For they say, "that it is possible for such persons to fall away, if their nature, which is inclined to lapses and defection, and if the temptations of the world and Satan, be the only circumstances taken into consideration: but that they will not finally fall away, because God will bring back to himself his own elect before the end of life." If any one asserts, "that it is not possible for believers, in consideration of their being elect persons, finally to fall away from salvation, because God has decreed to save them," I answer, the decree concerning saving does not take away the possibility of damning, but it removes damnation itself. For "to be actually saved," and "a possibility of not being saved," are two things not contrary to each other, but in perfect agreement.

I therefore add, that in this way I have hitherto discriminated these two cases. And at one time I certainly did say, with an explanation subjoined to it, "that it was possible for believers finally to decline or fall away from faith and salvation." But at no period have I asserted, "that believers do finally decline or fall away from faith or salvation." This article, therefore, is ascribed to one who is not its author; and it is another offense against historical veracity.

I subjoin, that there is a vast difference between the enunciation of these two sentences. (1.) "It is possible for believers to decline from the FAITH ;" and (2.) "It is possible for believers to decline from SALVATION." For the latter, when rigidly and accurately examined, can scarcely be admitted; it being impossible for believers, as long as they remain believers, to decline from salvation. Because, were this possible, that power of God would be conquered which he has determined to employ in saving believers. On the other hand, if believers fall away from the faith and become unbelievers, it is impossible for them to do otherwise than decline from salvation, that is, provided they still continue unbelievers. Therefore, whether this hypothesis be granted or not, the enunciation cannot be accurately expressed. For if this hypothesis (their perseverance in faith) be granted, they cannot decline; but if it be not granted, they cannot do otherwise than decline. (2.) But that first enunciation includes no hypothesis; and therefore an answer may be given to it simply, either that it is possible, or that it is impossible. For this cause, the second article ought to be corrected in the following manner: "It is possible for believers finally to fall away or decline from the faith;" or rather, "Some believers finally fall away and decline from the faith." This being granted, the other can be necessarily inferred, "therefore they also actually decline from salvation." Respecting the truth of this [Second] article, I repeat the same observations which I made about the First. For the following expressions are reciprocal to each other, and regular consequences: "Faith is peculiar to the elect," and "believers do not finally fall away from the faith." In like manner, "Faith is not peculiar to the elect," and "Some believers finally decline from the faith."

ARTICLE III

It is a matter of doubt, whether the faith by which Abraham is said to be justified, was a faith in Jesus Christ who was still to come. No proof can be adduced of his having understood the promises of God in any other manner, than that he should be the heir of the world.

ANSWER

There are two members in this article, or rather, those members are two distinct articles, each of which presents itself to be separately considered by us, after I have observed, that in this passage no affirmation or negation, each of which properly constitutes a heretic, is attributed to us, but a mere doubt alone, that betokens a consciousness of ignorance and infirmity, which those who arrogate to themselves the knowledge of all these things, ought to endeavour to remove by a mild course of instruction, and not to make it a subject of reviling or provocation.

I. To the FIRST MEMBER I reply:

First. I never uttered this expression; but have, on more occasions than one, taught both in public and private a contrary doctrine. Yet I remember, when a certain minister at Leyden had boasted of the clearness of this article, and was astonished how any persons could be found who entertained a different opinion about it, I told him, that the proof of it would not be a very easy occupation to him if he had to encounter a powerful adversary, and I challenged him to make a trial, which challenge I now repeat. I wish him to prove this assertion by such plain arguments, as will not leave a man just reasons for doubting any longer about the matter. This is a point on which the labours of a divine will be more profitably expended, than on publishing and magnifying the doubts of the infirm, whose confidence in themselves is not equal to that which he manifests.

Secondly. "Faith in Christ" may be received in two acceptations. Either according to promise, which was involved in the types, figures and shadows of words and things, and proposed in that manner: Or, it is according to the gospel, that is clearly manifested. The difference between these two is so great, that with regard to it the Jews are said "to have been detained or kept under the law before faith came, concluded or shut up unto that faith which should afterwards be revealed." (Gal. iii. 23.) And the

Apostle says, "the children of Israel were prevented, by the veil placed over the countenance of Moses, from steadfastly looking to the end of that which is abolished," (2 Cor. iii. 13,) that is, to the end of the law, as is evident from the whole chapter, and from Romans x. 4, where Christ is said to be "the end of the law for righteousness to every one that believeth." Let the whole description of the faith of Abraham, which the Apostle gives at great length in Romans 4, be attentively considered, and it will appear, that no express mention of Jesus Christ is made in it, but it is implied in such a way as it is not easy for any one to explain.

Let it be added that faith in Jesus Christ seems to some persons to be used by metonymy, for "that faith which is concerning the types and figures which adumbrate and prefigure Jesus Christ," although it has not united with it an understanding of those types, unless it be a very obscure one, and such as appears suitable to the infant Church, according to the economy of the times and ages which God in his wisdom employs. Let a comparison be instituted between that servitude under which the heir, so long as he is a child, is said by the Apostle to be held, (Gal. iv. 1-3,) and that bondage from which the Spirit of the Lord is declared to liberate the man whose heart is converted to Him; (2 Cor. iii. 16-18,) and this doubting will then be considered ascribable to the proper fear of a trembling [scrupulous] conscience, rather than to a disposition that has a powerful propensity towards heresy.

II. TO THE SECOND MEMBER OF THIS ARTICLE, I ANSWER:

First. I never made such an assertion.

Secondly. If even I had, it would not have called for any deserved reprehension, except from a man that was desirous by that very act to betray at once the weakness of his judgment and his want of experience. (1.) It is a sign of a judgment not the most accurate, to blame any man for saying that which, it is possible to prove, has been written by the Apostle himself in so many words. For if the heir-ship of the world was promised to Abraham in these words, "Thou shalt be the father of many nations," what wonder is there if Abraham understood the promises in no other manner than as they had been divinely pronounced? (2.) It is a mark of great inexperience in the men who framed these articles, to suppose that the heir-ship of the world which was promised to Abraham, appertained to this animal life and to carnal benefits; because the world of which mention is made in that passage, is that future world to which belongs the calling of the Gentiles, by which vocation Abraham was made the father of many nations. This is apparent from the consideration, that he is said to have been made the heir of the world by the righteousness of faith, of which St. Paul (Rom. iv. 13,) proves the Gentiles likewise to be partakers; and in Ephes. iii. 1-11, the Apostle treats on the vocation of the Gentiles, and says, it belongs to "the grace of the gospel, and to the fellowship of the mystery which from the beginning of the world hath been hidden in God and is now brought to light by Christ, by whom God created all things." I repeat it, that vocation does not belong to the wisdom by which God formed the world, but to that by which he constituted Christ his wisdom and power to salvation to them that believe; and by which he founded the Church, which will endure forever. See 1 Corinthians i. 21-23; ii, 6-8; Ephes. iii. 1-11. If the forgers of this article say, "that they have likewise perceived this, but had supposed that my opinion was different;" I reply, it is not the part of a prudent man to frame a foolish adversary for himself.

ARTICLE IV

Faith is not an effect of election, but is a necessary requisite foreseen by God in those who are to be elected. And the decree concerning the bestowing of faith precedes the decree of election.

ANSWER

Of this article also there are two entire members:

I. In the FIRST of them, three assertions are included. (1.)

"Faith is not an effect of election." (2.) "Faith is a necessary requisite in those who are to be elected or saved." (3.) "This requisite is foreseen by God in the persons to be elected." I confess, all these, when rightly understood and correctly explained, agree entirely with my opinion, on the subject. But the last of the members is proposed in terms too odious, since it makes no mention of God, whose benefit and gift I acknowledge faith to be.

I will now proceed to explain myself on each of these assertions:

1. With regard to the FIRST, the word "Election" is ambiguous. For it either signifies "the election by which God determines to justify believers, while those who are unbelievers or workers are rejected from righteousness and salvation: "Or it signifies "the election by which he determines to save certain particular persons, as such, and to bestow faith on them in order to their salvation, other particular persons being also rejected, merely in reference to their being such particular individuals." Election is received according to this latter signification, by those who charge me with these articles. I take it in the former acceptation, according to Romans ix. 11: "For the children being not yet born, neither having

done any good or evil, that the purpose of God according to election might stand, not of works, but of Him that calleth, it was said unto her, the elder shall serve the younger."

I will not now enter into a prolix disputation, whether or not the sense in which I receive it, be the correct one. It is evident, at least, that there is some decree of God by which he determines to justify believers; and which, since it excludes unbelievers from righteousness and salvation, is appropriately called "the decree according to election" or "with election," as being that which does not include all men within its embrace. This decree I consider as the foundation of Christianity, of man's salvation, and of his assurance of salvation; and it is this of which the Apostle treats in the ninth, tenth and eleventh chapters of his Epistle to the Romans, and in the first chapter to the Ephesians.

But I have not yet declared what my sentiments in general are about that decree by which God is said "to have determined absolutely to save certain particular persons, and to bestow faith upon them in order to their salvation, while others are reprobated from salvation and faith;" although I have confessed, that there is a certain decree of God, according to which he determines to administer the means to faith and salvation, as he knows them to be suitable and proper to his righteousness, mercy and severity. From these premises it is deduced as a most manifest consequence, that faith is not an effect of that election by which God determines to justify those who believe.

2. With regard to the SECOND assertion, from the particulars thus explained it is concluded, that "faith is a necessary requisite in those who shall be partakers of salvation according to the election of God ;" or, that "it is a condition prescribed and required by God, to be performed by those who shall obtain his salvation." "This is the will of God, that whosoever believeth in the Son hath eternal life; he that believeth not, shall be condemned." The propositions contained in this passage cannot be resolved into any other than this brief one, which is likewise used in the Scripture, "Believe, and thou shalt be saved." In which the word "believe" has the force of a demand or requirement; and the phrase "thou shalt be saved" has that of a suasion, by means of a good that is promised. This truth is so clear and perspicuous, that the denial of it would be a proof of great perversity or of extreme unskilfullness. If any one say, "It is a condition, but yet an evangelical one, which God may himself perform in us, or, (as it is better expressed,) which he may by his grace cause us to perform; "the man who speaks thus, does not contradict this truth, but confirms it when he adds this explanation, "of what description soever that condition may be."

3. With regard to the THIRD, I say that we must distinguish between the condition by which it is required, that by which it is performed, and that by which it is seen or foreseen as performed. This third member, therefore, is proposed in a manner much too confused. Yet, when this confusion is corrected by the distinction which we have stated, nothing of absurdity will be apparent even in that member. Because foreseeing or seeing, in the very nature and order of things follows the performance itself; the performance has its own causes into which it is to be resolved; and the efficiency of those causes is not necessary, unless faith be prescribed and required by the law of faith and the gospel. Since therefore faith is said "to be foreseen by God in those who are to be saved," those causes, without the intervention of which there could be no faith, are not removed, but are rather appointed. Among those causes, I consider the preventing, accompanying and succeeding [subsequent] grace of God, as the principal. And I say, with Fulgentius, "Those persons will be saved, or they have been predestinated and elected, who, God foreknew, would believe by the assistance of his preventing grace, (I add and of his accompanying grace,) and would persevere by the aid of his subsequent grace." In this first member, then, there is nothing except truth of the greatest purity.

II. The second member is, "The decree concerning the gift of faith, precedes the decree of election;" in the explanation of which I employ the same distinction as in the former, and say, "The decree of election, by which God determines to justify and save believers, precedes the decree concerning the bestowment of faith." For faith is unnecessary, nay it is useless, without this previous decree. And the decree of election, by which God resolves to justify and save this or that particular person, is subsequent to that decree according to which he determines to administer the means necessary and efficacious to faith, that is, the decree concerning the gift of faith.

If any one says, "God wills first absolutely to save some particular person; and, since he wills that, he also wills to bestow faith on him, because without faith, it is not possible for him to be saved." I tell him, that he lays down contradictory propositions--that "God wills absolutely to save some one without regard to faith," and yet that, "according to the will of God, he cannot be saved without faith." Through the will of God it has been revealed to us, without faith it is impossible for any man to please God, or to be saved. There is, therefore, in God no other will, by which he wills any one to be absolutely saved without consideration of faith. For contradictory wills cannot be attributed to God. If any person replies, "God wills the end before he wills the means leading to the end; but salvation is the end, and faith the means leading to the end," I answer, first, Salvation is not the end of God; but salvation and faith are the gifts of God, bound and connected together in this order between themselves through the will of God, that faith should precede salvation, both with regard to God, the donor of it; and in reality. Secondly, Faith is a CONDITION required by God to be performed by him who shall be saved, before it is

MEANS of obtaining that salvation. Since God will not bestow salvation on any one, except on him who believes, man is on this account incited to be willing to believe, because he knows that his chief good is placed in salvation. Man, therefore, tried by faith, as the means, to attain to salvation as the end; because he knows that he cannot possibly obtain salvation except through that means. And this knowledge he does not acquire except through the declaration of the divine Will, by which God requires faith from those who wish to be saved, that is, by which he places faith as a condition in the object, that is, in the person to be saved.

ARTICLE V

Naught among things contingent can be said to be NECESSARILY done in respect to the Divine decree.

ANSWER
My opinion concerning Necessity and Contingency is "that they can never be applicable at once to one and the same event." But I speak of the necessity and contingency that are both of the same kind, not those which are different in their genus. The schoolmen state, that there is one necessitas consequentis--an absolute necessity -- , and another, necessitas consequentiæ--a hypothetical necessity. The former is, when the necessity arises from a cause antecedent to the thing itself. But necessitas consequentiæ--a hypothetical necessity--arises from certain premises, or principles, antecedent to the conclusion. A consequent, or absolute contingency cannot consist with a consequent, or absolute necessity; nor can they meet together in one event. In the same manner, one conclusion cannot be both necessary and contingent in regard to its consequence; that is, it cannot have, at the same time, a necessity and a contingency that are hypothetical. But the cause why one thing cannot be necessary and contingent at the same time, is this "that what is necessary, and what is contingent, divide the whole amplitude of being. For every being is either necessary or contingent. But those things which divide the whole of being, cannot coincide or meet together in any single being. Otherwise they would not divide the whole range of being. What is contingent, and what is necessary, likewise, differ in their entire essences and in the whole of their definition. For that is necessary which cannot possibly not be or not be done. And that is contingent which is possible not to be or to be done. Thus contradictorily are they opposed to each other; and this opposition is infinite, and, therefore, always dividing truth from falsehood: as, "this thing is either a man or it is not a man;" it is not possible for any thing to be both of these at once--that is, it is impossible for any thing of one essence. Otherwise, in another sense," Christ is a man," as proceeding from his mother, Mary; "he is not a man," in reference to his having been begotten of the Father from all eternity; but these are two things and two natures.

But they say: "It is possible for one and the same event to be necessary and contingent in different respects--necessary with regard to the first cause, which is God--and contingent in respect to second causes." I answer, FIRST. Those things which differ in their entire essences, do not coincide in respects. SECONDLY. The necessity or contingency of an event is to be estimated, not from one cause, but from all the causes united together. For after ten causes have been fixed, from which a thing is produced, not necessarily but contingently, if one be added from which the thing may be necessarily completed, the whole of that thing is said to have been done not contingently but necessarily. Because, when all these causes were together appointed, it was impossible for that thing to hinder itself from being produced, and from being brought into existence. That thing, I confess indeed, when distinctly compared by our mind with each of its causes, has a different relation to them respectively. But since none of those causes is the total cause of that event, and since all of them united together form the total cause, the thing ought itself to be accounted and declared to have been done from that total cause, either necessarily or contingently.

It is not only a rash saying, but a false and an ignorant one, "that a thing which, in regard to second causes, is done contingently is said to be done necessarily in regard to the divine decree." For the divine decree itself, being an internal action of God, is not immediately the cause of the thing; but, whatever effects it may produce, it performs them by power, according to the mode of which a thing will be said to be either necessarily or contingently. For if God resolve to use an irresistible power in the execution of his decree, or if he determine to employ such a quantum of power as nothing can resist or can hinder it from completing his purpose, it will follow that the thing will necessarily be brought into existence. Thus, "wicked men who persevere in their sins, will necessarily perish," for God will by an irresistible force, cast them down into the depths of hell. But if he resolve to use a force that is not irresistible, but that can be resisted by the creature, then that thing is said to be done, not necessarily but contingently, although its actual occurrence was certainly foreknown by God, according to the infinity of his understanding, by which he knows all results whatever, that will arise from certain causes which are laid down, and whether those causes produce a thing necessarily or contingently. From whence the schoolmen say that "all things are done by a necessity of infallibility," which phrase is used in a determinate sense, although the words in which its enunciation is expressed are ill-chosen. For infallibility is not an affection of a being, which exists from causes; but it is an affection of a Mind that sees or that foresees what will be the effect of certain causes. But I readily endure a catachrestic metalepsis, when it is evident concerning a thing, although it is my wish that our enunciations were always the best accommodated to the natures of the things themselves.

But the inventors of these articles try to prove by the examples which they produce, that "one and the same thing, which, with respect to second causes, is done contingently, is, in respect to the Divine Decree, done necessarily." They say "It was possible for the bones of Christ to be broken, or not to be broken. It was possible for them to be broken, if any person considers the nature of bones; for they were undoubtedly fragile. But they could not be broken, if the decree of God be taken into the account." In answer to this, I deny that in respect of the DIVINE DECREE, they could not be broken. For God did not decree that it was impossible for them to be broken, but that they should not be broken. This is apparent from the manner in which the transaction was actually conducted. For God did not employ an irresistible power by which he might prevent the bones of Christ from being broken by those who approached to break them; but by a mild kind of suasion, he caused that they should not will to break the bones of Christ, by an argument drawn from its inutility. For, since Christ had already given up the ghost, before those who broke the legs had arrived at the cross, they were not at all inclined to undertake a vain and fruitless labour in breaking the legs of our saviour. Because the breaking of legs, with the design to hasten death, was only done lest the bodies should remain suspended on the cross on a festival or sacred day, contrary to the divine law. Indeed, if the divine Wisdom knows how to effect that which it has decreed, by employing causes according to their nature and motion--whether their nature and motion be contingent or free, the praise due to such Wisdom is far greater than if it employ a power which no creature can possibly resist. Although God can employ such a power whensoever it may seem expedient to his Wisdom. I am therefore, of opinion that I committed no offense when I said, "No contingent thing--that is, nothing which is done or has been done CONTINGENTLY--can be said to be or have been done NECESSARILY, with regard to the divine decree."

ARTICLE VI

All things are done contingently.

ANSWER

This Article is expressed in such a stupid and senseless manner, that they who attribute it to me, declare by this very circumstance, that they do not perceive under how many falsities this expression labours; nay, they do not understand what is the meaning of the words which they employ. For if that is said to be done contingently which it is possible not to do, or which may not be done, after all the causes required for its being done have been fixed; and, on the other hand, if that is said to be done necessarily which cannot be left undone which cannot but be done-after all the causes required for its performance have been fixed; and if I grant, that, after some causes have been fixed, it is impossible for any other event to ensue than that the thing should be done and exist, how then can I be of opinion that" all things are done, or happen, contingently?." But they have deceived themselves by their own ignorance; from which it would be possible for them to be liberated, if they would bestow a becoming and proper attention on sentiments that are more correct, and would in a friendly manner obtain from the author a knowledge of his views and opinions.

I have both declared and taught that "necessity, in reference to its being said to be or to happen necessarily, is either absolute or relative." It is an absolute necessity, in relation to a thing being said simply "to be or to happen necessarily," without any regard being had to the supposition, or laying down, of any cause whatever. It is a relative necessity, when a thing is said "to be or to happen necessarily," after some cause had been laid down or fixed. Thus, God exists by an absolute necessity; and by the same absolute necessity, he both understands and loves himself. But the world, and all things produced from it, are, according to an absolute consideration, contingent, and are produced contingently by God, freely operating. But it being granted that God wills to form the world by his infinite power, to which NOTHING ITSELF must be equal to matter in the most perfect state of preparation--and it being likewise granted that God actually employs this power--it will then be said, "It was impossible for the world to do otherwise than exist from this cause;" or, "from this cause, the world could not but exist." And this is a relative necessity, which is so called from the hypothesis of an antecedent cause being laid down or fixed.

I will explain my meaning in a different manner. Two things in this place come under our consideration, the CAUSE and the EFFECT. If both of them be necessarily fixed, that is, if not only the effect be fixed necessarily when the cause fixed, but if the cause also necessarily exist and be necessarily supposed to operate, the necessity of the effect is in that case simple and absolute. In this manner arises the absolute necessity of the Divine effect, by which God is said to know and love himself; for the Divine understanding and the Divine will cannot be inoperative, [cannot but operate]. This operation of God is not only an internal one, but it is also ad intra, [inwards,] tending towards an object, which is himself. But whatever God may do ad extra, [externally,] that is, when acting on an object which is something beside himself, [or something different from himself,] whether this object be united to him in understanding and he tend towards it by an internal act, or whether it be in reality separated from him and towards which he tends by an external act, the whole of this he does freely, and the whole of it is, therefore, said to be absolutely contingent. Thus God freely decreed to form the world, and did freely form it. And, in this sense, all things are done contingently in respect to the]Divine decree; because no necessity exists why the decree of God should be appointed, since it proceeds from his own pure and free [or unconstrained] will.

Or, to express it in another form: That is called the simple and absolute necessity of any effect, "when the cause necessarily exists, necessarily operates, and employs that power through which it is impossible for the thing not to exist," [or through which it cannot but exist]. In the nature of things, such an effect as this cannot be contemplated. For the intellect of the Deity, by which he understands himself, proceeds from a cause that necessarily exists and that necessarily understands itself; but it does not proceed from a cause which employs a power of action for such an understanding.

Under this consideration, the relative necessity of any event is two-fold. FIRST. When a cause that necessarily exists, but does not necessarily operate, uses a power of action that cannot be resisted. Thus it being fixed, that "God, who is a necessary being, wills to create a world by his omnipotence," a world must in that case necessarily come into existence. SECONDLY. When a cause that does not necessarily exist and yet necessarily operates, acts with such efficacy as is impossible to be resisted by the matter or subject on which it operates. Thus, straw is said to be necessarily burnt [or consumed] by the fire, if it be cast into the flame. Because it is impossible either for the fire to restrain its power of burning so as not actually to burn, or for the straw to resist the fire. But because God can prevent the fire from burning any combustible matter that is brought near it or put into it, this kind of necessity is called partial in respect to the cause, and only according to the nature of the things themselves and the mutual affection [or relation] between them.

When these matters have been thus explained, I could wish to see what can possibly be said in opposition.Iam desirous, that we should in preference contend FOR THE NECESSITY OF GOD ALONE, that is, for his necessary existence and for the necessary production of his ad intra [internal] acts, and that we should contend for the CONTINGENCY OF ALL OTHER THINGS AND EFFECTS. Such a procedure on our part would conduce far more to the glory of God; to whom by this method would be attributed both the GLORY of his necessary existence, that is, of his eternity, according to which it is a pure act without [the exercise of] power, and the GLORY of his free creation of all other things, by which also his goodness becomes a supreme object of our commendation.

ARTICLE VII

God has not by his eternal decree determined future and contingent things to the one part or the other.

ANSWER

A calumny which lies concealed under ambiguous terms, is capable of inflicting a deep injury with the greatest security; but after such equivocal expressions are explained, the slander is exposed, and loses all its force among men of skill and experience.

The word "DETERMINED" is of this ambiguous description. For it signifies (1.) either "the determination of God by which he resolves that something shall be done; and when such a determination is fixed, (by an action, motion and impulse of God, of whatever kind it may be,) the second cause, both with regard to its power and the use of that power, remains free either to act or not to act, so that, if it be the pleasure of this second cause, it can suspend [or defer] its own action." Or it signifies (2.) "such a determination, as, when once it is fixed, the second cause (at least in regard to the use of its power,) remains no longer free so as to be able to suspend its own action, when God's action, motion and impulse have been fixed; but by this determination, it [the second cause] is necessarily bent or inclined to the one course or the other, all indifference to either part being completely removed before this determined act be produced by a free and unconstrained creature."

1. If the word "DETERMINED," in the article here proposed, be interpreted according to this first method, far be it from me to deny such a sort of Divine determination. For I am aware that it is said, in the fourth chapter of the. Acts of the Apostles, "Both Herod and Pontius Pilate, with the Gentiles and the people of Israel, were gathered together against Jesus, to do whatsoever God's hand and counsel

determined before (or previously appointed) to be done." But I also know, that Herod, Pontius Pilate, and the Jews, freely performed those very actions; and (notwithstanding this "fore-determination of God," and though by his power every Divine action, motion and impulse which was necessary for the execution of this "fore-determination," were all fixed,) yet it was possible for this act (the crucifixion of Christ,) which had been "previously appointed" by God, not to be produced by those persons, and they might have remained free and indifferent to the performance of this action, up to the moment of time in which they perpetrated the deed. Let the narrative of the passion of our Lord be perused, and let it be observed how the whole matter was conducted, by what arguments Herod, Pontius Pilate and the Jews were moved and induced, and the kind of administration [or management] that was employed in the use of those arguments, and it will then be evident, that it is the truth which I here assert.

2. But if the word "DETERMINED" be received according to the second acceptation, I confess, that I abominate and detest that axiom (as one that is FALSE, ABSURD, and preparing the way for MANY BLASPHEMIES,) which, declares that "God by his eternal decree has determined to the one part or to the other future contingent things." By this last phrase understand "those things which are performed by the free will of the creature."

(1.) I execrate it as a FALSEHOOD: Because God in the administration of his Providence conducts all things in such a manner that when he is pleased to employ his creatures in the execution of his decrees, he does not take away from them their nature, natural properties or the use of them, but allows them to perform and complete their own proper motions. Were it otherwise, Divine Providence, which ought to be accommodated to the creation, would be in direct opposition.

(2.) I detest it as AN ABSURDITY: Because it is contradictory in the adjunct, that "something is done contingently," that is, it is done in such a manner as makes it POSSIBLE not to be done; and yet this same thing is determined to the one part or the other in such a manner, as makes it IMPOSSIBLE to leave undone that which has been determined to be done. What the patrons of such a doctrine advance about "that liberty not being taken away which belongs to the nature of the creature," is not sufficient to destroy this contradiction:

Because it is not sufficient for the establishment of contingency and liberty to have the presence of a power which can freely act according to nature; but it is requisite that the use and employment of that power and liberty should on no account be impeded. What insanity therefore is it, [according to the scheme of these men,] to confer at the creation a power on the creature of acting freely or of suspending its action, and yet to take away the use of such a power when the liberty comes at length to be employed. That is, to grant it when there is no use for it, but when it becomes both useful and necessary, then in the very act to prevent the exercise of its liberty. Let Tertullian against Marcion be examined, (lib. ii. c. 5, 6, 7,) where he discusses this matter in a most erudite and nervous manner. I yield my full assent to all that he advances.

(3.) I abhor it as CONDUCING TO MULTIPLIED BLASPHEMIES. For I consider it impossible for any art or sophistry to prevent this dogma concerning "such a previous determination" from producing the following consequences: FIRST. It makes God to be the author of sin, and man to be exempt from blame. SECONDLY. It constitutes God as the real, proper and only sinner: Because when there is a fixed law which forbids this act, and when there is such "a fore-determination" as makes it "impossible for this act not to be committed," it follows as a natural consequence, that it is God himself who transgresses the law, since he is the person who performs this deed against the law. For though this be immediately perpetrated by the creature, yet, with regard to it, the creature cannot have any consideration of sin; because this act was unavoidable on the part of man, after such "fore-determination" had been fixed. THIRDLY. Because, according to this dogma, God needed sinful man and his sin, for the illustration of his justice and mercy. FOURTHLY. And, from its terms, sin is no longer sin.

I never yet saw a refutation of those consequences which have been deduced from this dogma by some other persons. I wish such a refutation was prepared, at least that it would be seriously attempted. When it is completed, if I am not able to demonstrate, even then, that these objections of mine are not removed, I will own myself to be vanquished, and will ask pardon for my offense. Although I am not accustomed to charge and oppress this sentiment [of theirs] with such consequences before other people, yet I usually confess this single circumstance, (and this, only when urged by necessity,) that "I cannot possibly free their opinion from those objections."

ARTICLE VIII

Sufficient grace of the Holy Spirit is bestowed on those to whom the gospel is preached, whosoever they may be; so that, if they will, they may believe: otherwise, God would only be mocking mankind.

ANSWER

At no time, either in public or in private, have I delivered this proposition in these words, or in any expressions that were of equivalent force, or that conveyed a similar meaning. This assertion I confidently make, even though a great number of persons might bear a contrary testimony. Because, unless this Article received a modified explanation, I neither approve of it at present, nor has it at any time obtained any portion of my approval. Of this fact it is in my power to afford evidence, from written conferences which I have had with other people on the same subject.

In this Article there are three topics concerning which I am desirous of giving a suitable explanation.

FIRST. Concerning the difference which subsists among the persons to whom the gospel is preached. Frequent mention of this difference is made in the scriptures, and particularly in the following passages. "I thank thee, O Father, Lord of heaven and earth, because thou hast hid these things from the wise and prudent, and hast revealed them unto babes." (Matt. xi. 25.) The explanation of these words may be discovered in 1 Corinthians 1 and 2. "Into whatsoever city or town ye shall enter, inquire who in it is worthy; and there abide till ye go thence. And when ye come into a house, salute it. And if the house be worthy, let your peace come upon it; but. if it be not worthy, let your peace return to you." (Matt. x. 11-13.) The Jews of Berea "were more noble than those in Thessalonica, in that they received the word with all readiness of mind," &c. (Acts xvii. 11.) "Pray for us, that the word of the Lord may have free course, and be glorified, even as it is with you; and that we may be delivered from unreasonable and wicked men. For all men have not faith. But the Lord is faithful," &c. (2 Thess. iii. 1, 2.)

SECONDLY. Concerning the bestowing of sufficient grace what is to be understood by such a gift? It is well known, that there is habitual grace, and [the grace of] assistance. Now the phraseology of the article might be understood according to this acceptation, as though some kind of habitual grace were infused into all those to whom the gospel is preached, which would render them apt or inclined to give it credence, or believe the gospel. But this interpretation of the. phrase is one of which I do not approve. But this SUFFICIENCY, after all that is said about it, must, in my opinion, be ascribed to the assistance of the Holy Spirit, by which he assists the preaching of the gospel, as the organ, or instrument, by which He, the Holy Spirit, is accustomed to be efficacious in the hearts of the hearers. But it is possible to explain this operation of the assistance of the Holy Spirit, in a manner so modified and appropriate, and such sufficiency may be ascribed to it, as to keep at the greatest possible distance from Pelagianism.

THIRDLY. Concerning the expression, "By this grace they may believe, if they will." These words, when delivered in such a crude and undigested form, are capable of being brought to bear a very bad interpretation, and a meaning not at all agreeable to the scriptures, as though, after that power had been bestowed, the Holy Spirit and Divine Grace remain entirely quiescent, waiting to see whether the man will properly use the power which he has received, and will believe the gospel. When, on the contrary, he who wishes to entertain and to utter correct sentiments on this subject, will account it necessary to ascribe to Grace its own province, which, indeed, is the principal one, in persuading the human will that it may be inclined to yield assent to those truths which are preached.

This exposition completely frees me from the slightest suspicion of heresy on the point here mentioned; and proves it to be a report not entitled to the least credit, that I have employed such expressions, as I am unwilling to admit, except with the addition of a sound and proper explanation.

In reference to the REASON which is appended to this proposition, that, otherwise, God would only be mocking mankind, I confess it to be a remark which several adversaries employ against the opinion entertained by many of our divines, to convict it of absurdity. And it is not used without just cause, which might easily have been demonstrated, had it pleased the inventors of these Articles, (instead of ascribing them to me,) to occupy themselves in openly declaring on this subject their own sentiments, which they keep carefully concealed within their own bosoms.

ARTICLE IX

The temporal afflictions of believers are not correctly termed "CHASTISEMENTS," but are PUNISHMENTS for sins. For Christ has rendered satisfaction only for eternal punishments.

ANSWER

This Article is attributed to me by a double and most flagrant falsehood: the first of which will be found in the Article itself, and the second in the reason appended.

1. Concerning the FIRST. Those who are mere novices in Divinity know that the afflictions and calamities of this animal life, are either punishments, chastisements, or trials. That is, in sending them, God either intends punishment for sins, in regard to their having been already committed, and without any other consideration; or, He intends chastisement, that those who are the subjects of it may not afterwards fall into the commission of other or similar offenses; or, in sending afflictions and calamities, God purposes to try the faith, hope, charity, patience, and the like conspicuous virtues and graces of his people. What man would be so silly as to say, when the Apostles were called before the Jewish Council, and were beaten with rods, that "it was a PUNISHMENT!" although "they departed from the presence of the Council, that they were counted worthy to suffer shame for his name." (Acts v. 41.) Is not the following expression of the Apostle familiar to every one? "For this cause many are weak and sickly among you, and many sleep. For if we would judge ourselves, we should not be judged. But when we are judged, we are CHASTENED, (reproved and instructed,) OF THE LORD, that we should not be condemned with the world." (1 Cor. xi. 30-32.) By not reflecting on these and similar passages of scripture, the persons who attributed these articles to me betrayed their ignorance, as well as their audacity. If they had bestowed the least reflection upon such texts, by what strange infatuation of mind has it happened, that they ascribe to me a sentiment which is thus confuted by plain and obvious quotations from the word of God?

On one occasion, when the subject of discussion was the calamities inflicted on the house of David on account of criminal conduct towards Uriah; and when the passages of scripture which were adduced tended with great semblance of truth to prove, that those calamities bore some relation to PUNISHMENT, I stated, that "no necessity whatever existed for as to allow ourselves to be brought into such straits by our adversaries the Papists, from which we could with difficulty escape; since the words appear to make against the opinion which asserts that they have by no means any reference to punishment. And because sin merits both an eternal punishment corresponding with its grievous enormity, and a temporal punishment, (if indeed God be pleased to inflict the latter, which is not always his practice even with respect to those who persevere in their transgressions, as may be seen in Psalm 73, and Job 21,) it might, not unseasonably, be said, that, after God has pardoned the guilt so far as it is meritorious of eternal punishment, he reserves or retains it in reference to temporal punishment." And I shewed, that, "from these premises, no patronage could be obtained for the Popish dogma of a Purgatory," which was the subject of that discussion.

2. With regard to the REASON appended, it is supported by the same criminal falsehood as the preceding part of the Article, and with no less absurdity of object, as I will demonstrate. For I affirm, in the first place, that this expression at no time escaped from my lips, and that such a thought never entered my imagination. My opinion on this subject is, "Christ is our Redeemer and saviour from sins, which merit both temporal and eternal death; and He delivers us not only from death eternal, but from death temporal, which is the separation of the soul from the body." But it is amazing, that this opinion "Christ has rendered satisfaction for temporal punishments alone," could possibly have been attributed to me by men of discretion, when the scriptures expressly declare, "Christ was also a partaker of flesh and blood, that, through death, he might destroy him that had the power of death, that is, the devil." (Heb. ii. 14.) By the term DEATH in this place must be understood either "the death of the body alone," or "that in conjunction with eternal death. "The Son of God was manifested, that he might destroy the works of the devil." (1 John iii. 8.) And among those works to be destroyed, we must reckon death temporal. For "by the envy of the devil, death entered into the world." In another passage it is said, "For since by man came death, by MAN came also the resurrection of the dead;" this man is Christ. (1 Cor. xv. 21.) "Christ shall change our vile body, that it may be fashioned like unto his glorious body, according to the working whereby he is able even to subdue all things unto himself." (Phil. iii. 21.) The greatest necessity exists for that man to become conversant with the scriptures, who denies, that "by the death, of Christ we are redeemed from temporal death, and obtain a right and title to a happy resurrection."

The following is an affirmation which I have made: "We are not actually delivered from temporal death, except by the resurrection from the dead, through which our last enemy, death, will be destroyed. These two truths, therefore, are, in my judgment, to be considered and taught, (1.) Christ, by his death, immediately took away from death the authority or right which he had over us, that of detaining us under his power, even as it was not possible that Christ himself should be holden by t]he bonds [pains] of death. (Acts ii. 24.) But (2.) Christ will in his own time deliver us from its actual dominion, according to the administration or appointment of God, whose pleasure it is to concede to the soul an early period of liberation, and to the body one that is later." But, I confess, that I cannot with an unwavering conscience assert, and therefore, dare not do it as if it were an object of certain knowledge, that temporal death, which is imposed or inflicted on the saints, is not a punishment, or has no regard to punishment," when it is styled "an ENEMY that is to be destroyed" by the Omnipotence of Christ.

The contrary opinion to this is not proved by the argument, that "our corporeal death is a passage into eternal life:" because it is a passage of the soul, and not of the body; the latter of which, while it remains buried in the earth, is held under the dominion of death. Nor is it established by the remark that "the saints long for the death of the body." (Phil. i. 21, 23.) For when they "have a desire to be dissolved [to depart] and be with Christ," that desire is according to the soul; the body in the mean time remaining under the dominion of death its enemy, until it likewise, (after being again united to its own soul,) be glorified with it. The address of Christ to Peter may also be stated in opposition: "When thou shalt be old, thou shalt stretch forth thy hands, and another shall gird thee, and carry thee whither thou wildest not. This spake he, signifying by what death he should glorify God." (John xxi. 19.)

The framers of these articles, therefore, have imputed this opinion to me, not only without truth, but without a sufficient sanction from their own discretion. Of this weakness of their judgment I observe, in this Article, other two tokens:

FIRST. They do not distinguish between the magnitude of each error in a proper manner. For he falls into a far greater error who DENIES, that "Christ has rendered satisfaction for corporeal punishments," that is, for the punishment of death temporal, than is his who ASSENTS, that "the death of the body has regard to punishment, since it is inflicted even on holy persons." But they have placed the latter error as the proposition; and the former one is brought, as a reason, for its confirmation. When they ought to have adopted an opposite mode of stating them, according to the relative estimate of each of these errors thus, "Christ has rendered satisfaction for eternal punishment alone. Therefore, the temporal afflictions of believers are not correctly called chastisements, but are punishments for sins."

SECONDLY. Because they make me employ an argument, which I cannot discover to be possessed of any force towards proving the proposition. For I grant, that Christ has rendered satisfaction even for temporal punishments; and yet I say, "It may likewise be true that temporal death has a reference to PUNISHMENT, even when it is inflicted on believers."

THIRDLY. From these considerations, a third mark of an inconstant and wavering judgment discovers itself. For when they employ this mode of argumentation, "Christ has liberated us from temporal punishments. Therefore our death cannot have any respect to punishment," they do not perceive that I might with equal facility draw from the same premises the following conclusion, "Therefore, it is not equitable that the saints should die a temporal death." My method of reasoning is [direct] a re ad rem, from subject to subject, "Because Christ has borne the death of the body, it is not to be borne by us." Their method is [relative] a re ad respectum rei, from the subject to its relation, thus, "Because Christ has borne the death of the body, it is indeed inflicted on us, but not so as to have any reference to punishment."

God will himself approve and verify this argument a re ad rem, from subject to subject, by the effect which He will give to it at some future period. But the argument will be prepared and stated in a legitimate form, thus, "Christ has borne the death of the body; and, (secondly,) has taken it away, which fact is apparent from his resurrection. Therefore, God will take away death from us in his own good time."

ARTICLE X

It cannot be proved from Scripture, that believers under the Old Testament, before the ascension of Christ, were in Heaven.

ANSWER

I never taught such a doctrine as this in public, and I never asserted it affirmatively in private. I recollect, however, that I said, on one occasion, to a minister of God's word, in reference to a sermon which he had then delivered, "there are many passages of Scripture which seem to prove, that believers under the Old Testament, before the ascension of Christ, were not in Heaven." I produced some of those passages, against which he had little to object. But I added, that I thought it could not now be propounded with much usefulness to any church that held a contrary opinion; but that, after it has been diligently examined and found to be true, it may be taught with profit to the church and to the glory of Christ, when the minds of men have been duly prepared. I am still of the same opinion. But, about the matter itself, I affirm nothing on either side. I perceive that each of these views of the subject has arguments in its favour, not only in passages of scripture and in conclusions deduced from them, but likewise in the sentiments of divines. Having investigated all of them to the best of my ability, I confess that I hesitate, and declare that neither view seems to me to be very evident [or to have the preponderance.] In this opinion I have the assent of a vast majority of divines, especially those of our own age. Most of the Christian Fathers place the souls of the Patriarchs under the Old Testament beyond or out of Heaven, either in the lower regions, in Purgatory, or in some other place, which yet is situated out of the verge of what is properly called Heaven. With St. Augustine, therefore, "I prefer doubting about secret things, to litigation about those which are uncertain." Nor is there the least necessity. For why should I, in these our days, when Christ, by his ascension into Heaven, having become our Forerunner, hath opened for us a way and entrance into that holy place, why should I now contend about the place in which the souls of the Fathers rested in the times of the Old Testament?

But lest, as is usual in my case, a calumnious report should be raised on the consequences to be deduced from this opinion, as though I was favourable to the Popish dogma of a Purgatory, or as though I approach nearly to those who think that the souls of the dead sleep or have slept, or, which is the worst of all, as though I seem to identify myself with those who say, "the Fathers were like swine that were fed and fattened without any hope of a better life," lest such reports as these should be fabricated, I will openly declare what my opinion is about the state of the Fathers prior to Christ's ascension into Heaven. (1.) I believe that human souls are immortal, that is, they will never die. (2.) From this I deduce, that souls do not sleep. (3.) That, after this life, a state of felicity or of misery is opened for all men, into the one or the other of which they enter immediately on their departure out of this world. (4.) That the souls of the Fathers, who passed their days of sojourning on earth in faith and in waiting for the Redeemer, departed into a place of quiet, joy, and blessedness, and began to enjoy the blissful presence of God, as soon as they escaped out of the body. (5.) I dare not venture to determine where that place of quiet is situated, whether in Heaven, properly so called, into which Christ ascended, or somewhere out of it. If any other person be more adventurous on this subject, I think he ought to be required to produce reasons for his opinion, or be enjoined to keep silence. (6.) I add, that, in my opinion, the felicity of those souls was much increased by the ascension of Christ into Heaven, and that it will be fully consummated after the resurrection of the body, and when all the members of the Church universal are introduced into Heaven.

I know certain passages of Scripture which are produced, as proofs that the souls of the Old Testament Saints have been in Heaven. (1.) "The spirit shall return unto God who gave it." (Eccl. xii. 7.) But this expression must either be understood in reference to all the spirits of men of every description, and thus will afford no assistance to this argument; or, if it be understood as relating to the souls of good men alone, it does not even then follow, that, because "the spirit returns unto God," it ascends into Heaven property so called. I prefer, however, the former mode of interpretation, a return to God the Creator and the Preserver of spirits, and the Judge of the deeds done in the body. (2.) Enoch is said to have been taken to God, (Gen. v. 24) and Elijah to have ascended by a whirlwind into Heaven. (2 Kings ii. 11.) But, beside the fact of these examples being out of the common order, it does not follow of course that because Enoch was taken to God, he was translated into the highest heaven. For the word "Heaven" is very wide in its signification. The same observation applies to Elijah. See Peter Martyr and Vatablus on 2 Kings ii. 13. (3.) "Christ is now become the first fruits of them that slept." (1 Cor. xv. 20.) This would not appear to be correct, if Enoch and Elijah ascended into the highest Heaven, clothed in bodies endued with immortality. (4.) "Lazarus was carried by the angels into Abraham's bosom," where he enjoyed consolation. (Luke xvi. 22.) But it is not proved, that Heaven itself is described by the term, "Abraham's bosom." It is intimated, that Lazarus was gathered into the bosom of his father Abraham, in which he might rest in hope of a full beatification in Heaven itself, which was to be procured by Christ. For this reason the Apostle, after the ascension of Christ into Heaven, "had a desire to be with Christ." (Phil. i. 23.) (5.) "Many shall come from the East and the West, and shall sit down with Abraham, Isaac, and Jacob, in the kingdom of Heaven." (Matt. viii. 11.) But it does not thence follow, that the Fathers have been in Heaven, properly so called, before they, who are to be called from among the Gentiles, sit down with them. (6.) It appears from Matthew 25, that there are only two places, one destined for the pious, the other for the wicked. But it does not hence necessarily follow, that the place destined for the pious has always been Heaven supreme. There have never been more places, because there have never been more states. But it is not necessary, that they should always be the same places without any change. The authority of this declaration is preserved inviolate, provided a third place be never added to the former two. (7.) "The reward" which awaits the pious "in heaven," is said to be "great." (Matt. v. 12.) Let this be granted. Therefore, [will some reasoner say,] they must instantly after death be translated into the supreme heaven." This does not necessarily follow. For it is well known, that the Scriptures have in these promises a reference to the period which immediately succeeds the last judgment, according to the following expression: "Behold I come quickly, and my reward is with me." The spouse replies, "Even so come, Lord Jesus!" (Rev. xxii. 12, 20) In the same manner must be understood that passage in Luke, "They may receive you into everlasting habitations;" (Luke xvi. 9;)

that is, after the last judgment, at least after [the ascension of] Christ, whose office it was to prepare those mansions for his people. (John xiv. 2.) (8.) "The Fathers are said to have been justified by the same faith as we are." (Acts xiii. 33.) I acknowledge this. "Therefore they have always been in Heaven even before [the ascension of] Christ, and we shall be after Him." This is not a necessary consequence. For there are degrees in glorification. Nor is it at all wonderful, if they be said to be rendered more blessed and glorious after the ascension of Christ into Heaven. (9.) "But Jesus said to the malefactor, to-day shalt thou be with me in Paradise." (.Luke xxiii. 43.) I reply, FIRST, It is not necessary that by "Paradise" should here be understood the third heaven, or the eternal abode of the blessed. For it denotes in general a place of felicity. SECONDLY, St. Chrysostom says, the crucified thief was the first person whose spirit entered into heaven. Yet he did not ascend there before Christ, nor before the vail of the temple had been rent in twain."

But to these passages is opposed that admirable dispensation or economy of God, which is distinguished according to the times preceding Christ, and those which followed. Of this dispensation the temple at Jerusalem was an illustrious [exemplar] pattern. For its external part, by means of an interposing vail, was separated and divided from that in which the priests daily appeared, and which was called "The Holy of Holies," in contradistinction to that which is called "The Sanctuary," (Heb. ix. 2, 3.) Heaven itself is designated by "The Holy of Holies" in Heb. ix. 24. It was shut as long as the former tabernacle stood, and until Christ entered into it by his own blood. (Heb. ix. 8-12.) It was his province as "our Forerunner" to precede us, that we also might be able to enter into those things which are within the vail. (Heb. vi. 19.) For this purpose it was necessary that liberty should be granted to us of "entering into the Holiest by the blood of Jesus, by that new and living way which he hath consecrated for us through the vail, that is to say, his flesh." (Heb. x. 19, 20.) On this account the ancient worthies, who, "through faith have" most evidently "gained this testimony that they pleased God," are said, "not to have received or obtained the promise; God having provided some better thing for us," who follow Christ, "that they without us should not be made perfect." (Heb. xi. 40.) These passages of scripture, and a view of the dispensation which they describe, are among the principal reasons why I cannot give my assent to the opinion which affirms, that the Fathers have been in Heaven properly so called.

But, that our brethren may not so highly blame me, I will oppose to them one or two of the approved divines of our church. CALVIN, in his INSTITUTES," (lib. iv, c. 1, s. 12,) says: "For what churches would dissent from each other on this account alone--that one of them, without any of the licentiousness of contention or the obstinacy of assertion, holds the opinion that souls, when they leave their bodies, soar up to Heaven; while another church does not venture to define anything about the place, but only maintains with certainty that they still live in the Lord." Peruse also the following passage in his "Institutes," (lib. iii, c. 25, s. 6.) "Many persons torment themselves by disputing about the place which departed souls occupy, and whether they be now in the enjoyment of heavenly glory or not. But it is foolish and rash to inquire about things unknown, more deeply than God permits us to know them." Behold, Calvin here says, that it is frivolous to contend whether the souls of the dead already enjoy celestial glory or not; and, in his judgment, it ought not to be made a subject of contention. Yet I am condemned, or at least am accused, because I dare not positively affirm "that the souls of the Fathers before Christ, were in Heaven, properly so called." PETER MARTYR proceeds still further, and is bold enough to assert, in his observations on 2 Kings ii. 13, "that the souls of the Fathers before Christ, were not in Heaven properly so called." He says, "Now if I be asked, to what place were Enoch and Elijah translated? I will say simply that I do not know, because that circumstance is not delivered in the divine volume. Yet if we might follow a very probable analogy, I would say, they were conducted to the place of the Fathers, or into Abraham's bosom, that they might there pass their time with the blessed Patriarchs in expectation of the resurrection of Christ, and that they might afterwards be elevated above the Heavens with Him when he was raised up again." Where it is to be noted, that Martyr entertains doubts concerning Enoch and Elijah, but speaks decisively about those who are in Abraham's bosom, that is, about the Fathers, "that they were raised up above the heavens with Christ at his resurrection." This likewise appears from what he mentions a little afterwards. With regard to that sublime ascension, we grant that no one enjoyed it before Christ. Enoch, therefore, and Elijah went to the Fathers, and there with them waited for Christ, upon whom, in company with the rest, they were attendants when he entered into heaven." See also BULLINGER on Luke xvi. 23;

Heb. ix. 8; 1 Pet. iii. 19.

From the preceding explanation and extracts, I have, I think, rendered it evident, that not only had I just causes for being doubtful concerning this matter, but that I likewise ought not therefore to be blamed, even though I had uttered what they here charge upon me as an error; nay, what is still more, that I ought to be tolerated had I simply asserted, "that the souls of the Fathers were not in Heaven prior to the ascension of Christ to that blissful abode."

ARTICLE XI

It is a matter of doubt, whether believers under the Old Testament understood that the legal ceremonies were types of Christ and of his benefits.

ANSWER

I do not remember to have said this at any time: nay, I am conscious that I have never said it, because I never yet durst utter any such expression. But I have said, that an inquiry not altogether unprofitable might be instituted, "how far the ancient Jews understood the legal ceremonies to be types of Christ?" At least I feel myself well assured, that they did not understand those ceremonies, as we do to whom the mystery of the Gospel is revealed. Nor do I suppose that any one will venture to deny this. But I wish our brethren would take upon themselves the task of proving, that believers under the Old Testament understood the legal ceremonies to be types of Christ and his benefits. For they not only know that this opinion of theirs is called in question by some persons, but that it is likewise confidently denied. Let them make the experiment, and they will perceive how difficult an enterprise they have undertaken. For the passages which seem to prove their proposition, are taken away from them in such a specious manner by their adversaries, that a man who is accustomed to yield assent to those things alone which are well supported by proofs, may be easily induced to doubt whether the believers under the Old Testament had any knowledge of this matter; especially if he consider, that, according to Gal. iv. 3, the whole of the ancient [Jewish] Church was in a state of infancy or childhood, and therefore possessed only the understanding of a child. Whether an infant be competent to perceive in these corporal things the spiritual things which are signified by them, let those decide who are acquainted with that passage, "When I was a child, I understood as a child." (1 Cor. xiii. 11.) Let those passages also be inspected which, we will venture to say, have a typical signification, because we have been taught so to view them by Christ and his Apostles; and it will be seen whether they be made so plain and obvious, as, without the previous interpretation of the Messiah, to have enabled us to understand them according to their spiritual meaning. It is said, (John viii. 56,) "Abraham saw the day of Christ, and was glad." Those who are of a contrary sentiment, interpret this passage as if it was to be understood by a metonymy, because, Abraham saw the day of Isaac, who was a type of Christ, and therefore his day was "the day of Christ." It is an undoubted fact, that no mention is made in the scriptures of any other rejoicing than of this. The faith of Abraham and its object occupy nearly the whole of the fourth chapter of the Epistle to the Romans. Let what is there said be compared together; and let it be demonstrated from this comparison, that Abraham saw Christ in those promises which he apprehended by faith. Who would understand "the sign of Jonah," to have been instituted to typify the three days in which Christ remained in the bowels of the earth, unless Christ had himself given that explanation? What injury does this opinion produce, since those who hold it do not deny, that the Fathers were saved by the infantile faith which they possessed? For an infant is as much the heir of his father's property, as an adult son.

Should any one say, it follows as a necessary consequence, that "the Fathers were saved without faith in Christ." I reply, the faith which has respect to the salvation of God that has been promised by him, and "waits for the redemption of Israel," understood under a general notion, is "faith in Christ," according to the dispensation of that age. This is easily perceived from the following passages: "I have waited for thy salvation, or thy saving mercy, O Lord! (Gen. xlix, 18.) "And the same man, (Simeon,) was just and devout, waiting for the consolation of Israel." (Luke ii. 25.) In the same chapter it is said, "Anna, a prophetess, spake of him to all them that looked for redemption in Jerusalem."

But if we consider the "faith in Christ," which is that of the New Testament, and which has regard to Him as a Spiritual and Heavenly King, who bestows upon his followers those celestial benefits which he has procured for them by his passion and death; then a greater difficulty will hence arise. What man ever received more promises concerning the Messiah than David, or who has prophesied more largely about Him? Yet any one may with some show of reason, entertain doubts, whether David really understood that the Messiah would be a Spiritual and Heavenly Monarch; for when he seemed to be pouring out his whole soul before the Lord, (2 Sam. 7,) he did not suffer a single word to escape that might indicate the bent of his understanding to this point, which, nevertheless, would have been of great potency in magnifying Jehovah and in confirming his own confidence.

The knowledge which all Israel had of the Messiah and of his kingdom, in the days when Christ was himself on earth, appears not only from the Pharisees and the whole of the populace, but also from his own disciples after they had for three years and more enjoyed constant opportunities of communication with him, and had heard from his own lips frequent and open mention of the kingdom of Heaven. Nay, what is still more wonderful, immediately after the resurrection of Christ from the dead, they did not even then comprehend his meaning. (Luke xxiv. 21-25.) From this, it seems, we must say, either "that the knowledge which they formerly possessed had gradually died away," or "that the Pharisees, through their hatred against Jesus, had corrupted that knowledge." But neither of these assertions appears to be at all probable. (1.) The former is not; because the nearer those times were to the Messiah, the clearer were the prophecies concerning him, and the more manifest the apprehension of them. And this for a good reason, because it then began to be still more necessary for men to believe that person to be the Messiah, or at least the time was fast approaching in which such a faith would become necessary. (2.) The latter is not probable; because the Pharisees conceived that hatred against him on account of his preaching and miracles. But it was at the very commencement of his office that he called into his service those twelve disciples. There are persons, I am aware, who produce many things from the Rabbinical writers of that age, concerning the spiritual kingdom of Christ; but I leave those passages to the authors of them, because it is out of my power to pronounce a decision on the subject.

While I have been engaged in the contemplation of this topic, and desirous to prove from the preceding prophecies, that the kingdom of Christ the Messiah, was to be spiritual, no small difficulty has arisen, especially after consulting most of those who have written upon it. Let those who on this point do not allow any one to indulge in a single doubt, try an experiment. Let them exhibit a specimen of the arguments by which they suppose their doctrine can be proved, even in this age, which is illuminated with the light of the New Testament. I will engage, that, after this experiment, they will not pass such a sinister judgment on those who confess to feel some hesitation about this point.

These observations have been adduced by me, not with the design of denying that the opinion of the brethren on this matter is true, much less for the purpose of confuting it. But I adduce them, to teach others to bear with the weakness of that man who dares not act the part of a dogmatist on this subject.

ARTICLE XII

Christ has died for all men and for every individual.

ANSWER

This assertion was never made by me, either in public or private, except when it was accompanied by such an explanation as the controversies which are excited on this subject have rendered necessary. For the phrase here used possesses much ambiguity. Thus it may mean either that "the price of the death of Christ was given for all and for every one," or that "the redemption, which was obtained by means of that price, is applied and communicated to all men and to every one." (1.) Of this latter sentiment I entirely disapprove, because God has by a peremptory decree resolved, that believers alone should be made partakers of this redemption. (2.) Let those who reject the former of these opinions consider how they can answer the following scriptures, which declare, that Christ died for all men; that He is the propitiation for the sins of the whole world; (1 John ii. 2;) that He took away the sin of the world; (John i. 29;) that He gave his flesh for the life of the world; (John vi. 51;) that Christ died even for that man who might be destroyed with the meat of another person; (Rom. xiv. 15;) and that false teachers make merchandise even of those who deny the Lord that bought them, and bring upon themselves swift destruction; (2 Pet. ii. 1, 3.) He therefore who speaks thus, speaks with the Scriptures; while he who rejects such phraseology, is a daring man, one who sits in judgment on the Scriptures and is not an interpreter of them. But he who explains those passages agreeably to the analogy of faith, performs the duty of a good interpreter and prophesier [or preacher] in the Church of God.

All the controversy, therefore, lies in the interpretation. The words themselves ought to be simply approved, because they are the words of Scripture. I will now produce a passage or two from Prosper of Aquitain, to prove that this distinction was even in his time employed: "He who says that the saviour was not crucified for the redemption of the whole world, has regard, not to the virtue of the sacrament, but to the case of unbelievers, since the blood of Jesus Christ is the price paid for the whole world. To that precious ransom they are strangers, who, either being delighted with their captivity, have no wish to be redeemed, or, after they have been redeemed, return to the same servitude." (Sent. 4, super cap. Gallorum.) In another passage he says, "With respect both to the magnitude and potency of the price, and with respect to the one general cause of mankind, the blood of Christ is the redemption of the whole world. But those who pass through this life without the faith of Christ, and without the sacrament of regeneration, are utter strangers to redemption." Such is likewise the concurrent opinion of all antiquity. This is a consideration to which I wish to obtain a little more careful attention from many persons, that they may not so easily fasten the crime of novelty on him who says anything which they had never before heard, or which was previously unknown to them.

ARTICLES XIII AND XIV

Original Sin will condemn no man.

In every nation, all infants who die without [having committed] actual sins, are saved.

ANSWER

These articles are ascribed to Borrius. To augment their number, they have made them two, when one would have been sufficient, from which the other necessarily follows, even according to their own opinion. For if "original sin condemns no one," it is a necessary consequence that "all those will be saved who have not themselves committed actual transgressions." Of this class are all infants without distinction; unless some one will invent a state between salvation and damnation, by a folly similar to that by which, according to St. Augustine, Pelagius made a distinction between salvation and the kingdom of heaven.

But Borrius denies having ever publicly taught either the one or the other. He conferred indeed in private on this subject, with some candidates for Holy Orders: and he considers that it was not unlawful for him so to do, or to hold such an opinion, under the influence of reasons which he willingly submits to the examination of his brethren; who, when they have confuted them, may teach him more correct doctrine, and induce him to change his opinion. His reasons are the following:

1. Because God has taken the whole human race into the grace of reconciliation, and has entered into a covenant of grace with Adam, and with the whole of his posterity in him. In which he promises the remission of all sins to as many as stand steadfastly, and deal not treacherously, in that covenant. But God not only entered into it with Adam, but also afterwards renewed it with Noah, and at length confirmed and perfected it through Christ Jesus. And since infants have not transgressed this covenant, they do not seem to be obnoxious to condemnation; unless we maintain, that God is unwilling to treat with infants, who depart out of this life before they arrive at adult age, on that gracious condition under which, notwithstanding, they are also comprehended as parties to the covenant; and therefore that their condition is much worse than that of adults, to whom is tendered the remission of all sins, not only of that which they perpetrated in Adam, but likewise, of those which they have themselves personally committed. The condition of infants, however is, in this case, much worse, by no fault or demerit of their own, but because it was God's pleasure thus to act towards them. From these premises it would follow, that it was the will of God to condemn them for the commission of sin, before He either promised or entered into a covenant of grace; as though they had been excluded and rejected from that covenant by a previous decree of God, and as though the promise concerning the saviour did not at all belong to them.

2. When Adam sinned in his own person and with his free will, God pardoned that transgression. There is no reason then why it was the will of God to impute this sin to infants, who are said to have sinned in Adam, before they had any personal existence, and therefore, before they could possibly sin at their own will and pleasure.

3. Because, in this instance, God would appear to act towards infants with far more severity than towards the very devils. For the rigor of God against the apostate angels was extreme, because he would not pardon the crime which they had perpetrated. There is the same extreme rigor displayed against infants, who are condemned for the sin of Adam. But it is much greater; for all the [evil] angels sinned in their own persons, while infants sinned in the person of their first father Adam. On this account, the angels themselves were in fault, because they committed an offense which it was possible for them to avoid; while infants were not in fault, only so far as they existed in Adam, and were by his will involved in sin and guilt.

These reasons are undoubtedly of such great importance, that I am of opinion those who maintain the contrary are bound to confute them, before they can affix to any other person a mark of heresy. I am aware, that they place antiquity in opposition, because [they say] its judgment was in their favour. Antiquity, however, cannot be set up in opposition by those who, on this subject, when the salvation of infants is discussed, are themselves unwilling to abide by the judgment of the ancients. But our brethren depart from antiquity, on this very topic, in two ways:

(1.) Antiquity maintains, that all infants who depart out of this life without having been baptized, would be damned; but that such as were baptized and died before they attained to adult age, would be saved. St. Augustine asserts this to be the Catholic doctrine in these words: "If you wish to be a Catholic, be unwilling to believe, declare, or teach, that infants who are prevented by death from being baptized, can attain to the remission of original sins." (De anima et ejus Orig., lib. 3, cap. 9.) To this doctrine our brethren will by no means accede; but they contradict both parts of it.

(2.) Antiquity maintains that the grace of baptism takes away original sin, even from those who have not been predestinated; according to this passage from Prosper of Aquitain: "That man is not a Catholic who says, that the grace of baptism, when received, does not take away original sin from those who have not been predestinated to life." (Ad Cap. Gallorum, Sent. 2.) To this opinion also our brethren strongly object. But it does not appear equitable, that, whenever it is agreeable to themselves, they should be displeased with those who dissent from them, because they dissent from the Fathers; and again, that, whenever it is their good pleasure, the same parties do themselves dissent from the Fathers on this very subject.

But with respect to the sentiments of the ancient Christian Fathers, about the damnation of the unbaptized solely on account of original sin, they and their successors seem to have mitigated, or at least, to have attempted to soften down such a harsh opinion. For some of them have declared, "that the unbaptized would be in the mildest damnation of all;" and others, "that they would be afflicted, not with the punishment of feeling, but only with that of loss." To this last opinion some of them have added, "that this punishment would be inflicted on them without any stings from their own consciences." Though it is a consequence of not being baptized, that the parties are said to endure only the punishment of loss, and not that of feeling; yet this feeling exists wherever the stings or gnawings of conscience exists, that is, where the gnawing worm never dies. But let our brethren consider what species of damnation that is which is inflicted on account of sin, and from which no gnawing remorse proceeds.

From these observations, thus produced, it is apparent what opinion ought to be formed of the Fourteenth Article. It is at least so dependent on the Thirteenth, that it ought not to have been composed as a separate article, by those who maintain that there is no cause why infants should perish, except original sin which they committed in Adam, or which they received by propagation from Adam. But it is worth the trouble to see, on this subject, what were the sentiments of Dr. Francis Junius, who a few years ago was Professor of Divinity in this our University. He affirms, that "all infants who are of the covenant and of election, are saved;" but he presumes, in charity, that "those infants whom God calls to himself, and timely removes out of this miserable vale of sins, are rather saved." (De Natura et Gratia, R. 28.) Now, that which this divine either "affirms according to the doctrine of faith," or "presumes through charity," may not another man be allowed, without the charge of heresy, to hold within his own breast as a matter of opinion, which he is not in the least solicitous to obtrude on others or persuade them to believe? Indeed, "this accepting of men's persons" is far too prevalent, and is utterly unworthy of wise men. And what inconvenience, I pray, results from this doctrine? Is it supposed to follow as a necessary consequence from it, that, if the infants of unbelievers are saved, they are saved without Christ and his intervention?. Borrius, however, denies any such consequence, and has Junius assenting with him on this subject. If the brethren dissent from this opinion, and think that the consequences which they themselves deduce are agreeable to the premises, then all the children of unbelievers must be subject to condemnation, the children of unbelievers, I repeat, who are "strangers from the covenant." For this conclusion no other reason can be rendered, than their being the children of those who are "strangers from the covenant." From which it seems, on the contrary, to be inferred, that all the children of those who are in the covenant are saved, provided they die in the age of infancy. But since our brethren deny this inference, behold the kind of dogma which is believed by them. "All the infants of those who are strangers from the covenant are damned; and of the offspring of those parents who are in the covenant, some infants that die are damned, while others are saved." I leave it to those who are deeply versed in these matters, to decide, whether such a dogma as this ever obtained in any church of Christ.

ARTICLE XV

If the Heathen, and those who are strangers to the true knowledge of God, do those things which by the powers of nature they are enabled to do, God will not condemn them, but will reward these their works by a more enlarged knowledge, by which they may be bought to salvation.

ANSWER

This was never uttered by me, nor indeed by Borrius, under such a form, and in these expressions. Nay, it is not very probable, that any man, how small soever his skill might be in sacred things, would deliver the apprehensions of his mind in a manner so utterly confused and indigested, as to beget the suspicion of a falsehood in the very words in which he enunciates his opinion. For what man is there, who, as a stranger to the true knowledge of God, will do a thing that can in any way be acceptable to God? It is necessary that the thing which will please God, be itself good, at least, in a certain respect. It is further necessary, that he who performs it knows it to be good and agreeable to God. "For whatsoever is not of faith, is sin," that is, whatsoever is done without an assured knowledge that it is good and agreeable to God. Thus far, therefore, it is needful for him to have a true knowledge of God, which the Apostle attributes even to the Gentiles. (Rom. i, 18-21, 25, 28; ii, 14, 15.) Without this explanation there will be a contradiction in this enunciation. "He who is entirely destitute of the true knowledge of God, can perform something which God considers to be so grateful to Himself as to remunerate it with some reward." These, our good brethren, either do not perceive this contradiction; or they suppose, that the persons to whom they ascribe this opinion are such egregious simpletons as they would thus make them appear.

Then, what is the nature of this expression, "if they do those things which the powers of nature enable them to perform?" Is "nature," when entirely destitute of grace and of the Spirit of God, furnished with the knowledge of that truth which is said to be "held in unrighteousness," by the knowledge of "that which may be known of God, even his eternal power and Godhead," which may instigate man to glorify God, and which deprives him of all excuse, if he does not glorify God as he knows Him? I do not think, that such properties as these can, without falsehood and injury to Divine Grace, be ascribed to "nature," which, when destitute of grace and of the Spirit of God, tends directly downward to those things which are earthly.

If our brethren suppose, that these matters exhibit themselves in this foolish manner, what reason have they for so readily ascribing such an undigested paragraph to men, who, they ought to have known, are not entirely destitute of the knowledge of sacred subjects? But if our brethren really think that man can do some portion of good by the powers of nature, they are themselves not far from Pelagianism, which yet they are solicitous to fasten on others. This Article, enunciated thus in their own style, seems to indicate that they think man capable of doing something good "by the powers of nature;" but that, by such good performance, he will "neither escape condemnation nor obtain a reward." For these attributes are ascribed to the subject in this enunciation; and because these attributes do not in their opinion, agree with this subject, they accuse of heresy the thing thus enunciated. If they believe that "a man, who is a stranger to the true knowledge of God," is capable of doing nothing good, this ought in the first place, to have been charged with heresy. If they think that no one "by the powers of nature," can perform any thing that is pleasing to God, then this ought to be reckoned as an error, if any man durst affirm it. From these remarks, it obviously follows, either that they are themselves very near the Pelagian heresy, or that they are ignorant of what is worthy, in the first instance or in the second, of reprehension, and what ought to be condemned as heretical.

It is apparent, therefore, that it has been their wish to aggravate the error by this addition. But their labour has been in vain; because, by this addition, they have enabled us to deny that we ever employed any such expression or conceived such a thought; they have, at the same time, afforded just grounds for charging them with the heresy of Pelagius. Thus the incautious hunter is caught in the very snare which he had made for another. They would, therefore, have acted with far more caution and with greater safety, if they had omitted their exaggeration, and had charged us with this opinion, which they know to have been employed by the scholastic divines, and which they afterwards inserted in the succeeding Seventeenth Article, but enunciated in a manner somewhat different, "God will do that which is in Him, for the man who does what is in himself." But, even then, the explanation of the schoolmen ought to have been added, "that God will do this, not from (the merit of) condignity, but from (that of) congruity; and not because the act of man merits any such thing, but because it is befitting the great mercy and beneficence of God." Yet this saying of the schoolmen I should myself refuse to employ, except with the addition of these words: "God will bestow more grace upon that man who does what is in him by the power of divine grace which is already granted to him, according to the declaration of Christ, To him that hath shall be given," in which he comprises the cause why it was "given to the apostles to know the mysteries of the kingdom of heaven," and why "to others it was not given." (Matt. xiii. 11, 12.) In addition to this passage, and the first and second chapters of the Epistle to the Romans, which have already been quoted, peruse what is related in the Acts of the Apostles, (10, 16, 17,) about Cornelius the Centurion, Lydia, the seller of purple, and the Bereans.

ARTICLE XVI

The works of the unregenerate can be pleasing to God, and are (according to Borrius) the occasion, and (according to Arminius) the impulsive cause, by which God will be moved to communicate to them his saving grace.

ANSWER

About two years ago, were circulated Seventeen Articles, which were attributed to me, and of which the fifteenth is thus expressed: "Though the works of the unregenerate cannot possibly be pleasing to God, yet they are the occasion by which God is moved to communicate to them his saving grace." This difference induces me to suspect that the negative, cannot, has been omitted in this sixteenth article, unless, perhaps, since that time, having proceeded from bad to worse, I now positively affirm this, which, as I was a less audacious and more modest heretic, I then denied. However this may be, I assert that these good men neither comprehend our sentiments, know the phrases which we employ, nor, in order to know them, do they understand the meaning of those phrases. In consequence of this, it is no matter of surprise that they err greatly from the truth when they enunciate our sentiments in their words, or when they affix other (that is, their own) significations to our words. Of this transformation, they afford a manifest specimen in this article.

1. For the word "the unregenerate," may be understood in two senses, (i.) Either as it denotes those who have felt no motion of the regenerating Spirit, or of its tendency or preparation for regeneration, and who are therefore, destitute of the first principle of regeneration. (ii.) Or it may signify those who are in the process of the new birth, and who feel those motions of the Holy Spirit which belong either to preparation or to the very essence of regeneration, but who are not yet regenerate; that is, they are brought by it to confess their sins, to mourn on account of them, to desire deliverance, and to seek out the Deliverer, who has been pointed out to them; but they are not yet furnished with that power of the Spirit by which the flesh, or the old man, is mortified, and by which a man, being transformed to newness of life, is rendered capable of performing works of righteousness.

2. A thing is pleasing to God, either as an initial act, belonging to the commencement of conversion, or as a work perfect in its own essence, and as performed by a man who is converted and born again. Thus the confession, by which any one acknowledges himself to be "a cold, blind and poor creature," is pleasing to God; and the man, therefore, flies to Christ to "buy of him eye-salve, white raiment, and gold." (Rev. iii. 15-18.) Works which proceed from fervent love are also pleasing to God. See the distinction which Calvin draws between "initial and filial fear;" and that of Beza, who is of opinion that "sorrow and contrition for sin do not belong to the essential parts of regeneration, but only to those which are preparatory;" but he places "the very essence of regeneration in mortification, and in vivification or quickening."

3. "The occasion," and the impulsive cause, by which God is moved," are understood not always in the same sense, but variously. It will answer our purpose if I produce two passages, from a comparison of which a distinction may be collected, at once convenient and sufficient for our design. The king says, (Matt. xviii. 32) "I forgave thee all that debt because thou desiredest me." And God says to Abraham, (Gen. xxii. 16, 17,) "Because thou hast done this thing, and hast not withheld thy son, thine only son, in blessing, I will bless thee." He who does not perceive, in these passages, a difference in the impelling motives, as well as in the pleasure derived, must be very blind with respect to the Scriptures.

4. "The saving grace of God" may be understood either as primary or secondary, as preceding or subsequent, as operating or cooperating, and as that which knocks or opens or enters in. Unless a man properly distinguishes each of these, and uses such words as correspond with these distinctions, he must of necessity stumble, and make others appear to stumble, whose opinions he does not accurately understand. But if a man will diligently consider these remarks, he will perceive that this article is agreeable to the Scriptures, according to one sense in which it may be taken, but that, according to another, it is very different.

Let the word "unregenerate" be taken for a man who is now in the act of the new birth, though he be not yet actually born again; let "the pleasure" which God feels be taken for an initial act; let the impulsive cause be understood to refer to the final reception of the sinner into favour; and let secondary, subsequent, cooperating and entering grace be substituted for "saving grace;" and it will instantly be manifest, that we speak what is right when we say: "Serious sorrow on account of sin is so far pleasing to God, that by it, according to the multitude of his mercies, he is moved to bestow grace on a man who is a sinner."

From these observations, I think, it is evident with what caution persons ought to speak on subjects on which the descent into heresy, or into the suspicion of heresy, is so smooth and easy. And our brethren ought in their prudence to have reflected that we are not altogether negligent of this cautiousness, since they cannot be ignorant that we are filly aware how much our words are exposed and obnoxious to injurious interpretations, and even to calumny. But unless they had earnestly searched for a multitude of Articles, they might have embraced this and the preceding, as well as that which succeeds, in the same chapter.

ARTICLE XVII

God will not deny his grace to any one who does what is in him.

ANSWER

This Article is so naturally connected with those which precede it, that he who grants one of the three, may, by the same effort, affirm the remainder; and he who denies one may reject all the others. They might, therefore, have spared some portion of this needless labour, and might, with much greater convenience, have proposed one article of the following description, instead of three: "It is possible for a man to do some good thing without the aid of grace; and if he does it, God will recompense or remunerate that act by more abundant grace." But we could always have fastened the charge of falsehood upon an article of this kind. It was, therefore, a much safer course for them to play with equivocations, that the fraud contained in the calumny might not with equal facility he made known to all persons.

But with respect to this article, I declare that it never came into our minds to employ such confused expressions as these, which, at the very first sight of them, exclude grace from the commencement of conversion; though we always, and on all occasions, make this grace to precede, to accompany, and to follow; and without which, we constantly assert, no good action whatever, can be produced by man. Nay, we carry this principal so far as not to dare to attribute the power here described, even to the nature of Adam himself, without the help of Divine grace, both infused and assisting. It thus becomes evident, that the fabricated opinion is imposed on us through calumny. If our brethren entertain the same sentiments, we are perfectly at agreement. But if they are of opinion that Adam was able by nature, without supernatural aid, to fulfill the law imposed on him, they seem not to recede far from Pelagians, since this saying of Augustine is received by these our brethren: "Supernatural things were lost, natural things were corrupted." Whence it follows, what remnant soever there was of natural things, just so much power remained to fulfill the law--what is premised being granted, that Adam was capable by his own nature to obey God without grace, as the latter is usually distinguished in opposition to nature. When they charge us with this doctrine, they undoubtedly declare, that in their judgment, it is such as may fall in with our meaning; and, therefore, that they do not perceive so much absurdity in this article as there is in reality; unless they think that nothing can be devised so absurd that we are not inclined and prepared to believe and publish.

We esteem this article as one of such great absurdity that we would not be soon induced to attribute it to any person of the least skill in sacred matters. For how can a man, without the assistance of Divine Grace, perform any thing which is acceptable to God, and which he will remunerate with the saving reward either of further grace or of life eternal? But this article excludes primary grace with sufficient explicitness when it says, "To him who does what is in himself." For if this expression be understood in the following sense: "To him who does what he can by the primary grace already conferred upon him," then there is no absurdity in this sentence: "God will bestow further grace upon him who profitably uses that which is primary;" and, by the malevolent suppression of what ought to have been added, the brethren openly declare that it was their wish for this calumny to gain credence.

ARTICLE XVIII

God undoubtedly converts, without the external preaching of the Gospel, great numbers of persons to the saving knowledge of Christ, among those who have no outward preaching; and he effects such conversions either by the inward revelation of the Holy Spirit, or by the ministry of angels. (BORRIUS & ARMINIUS.)

ANSWER

I never uttered such a sentiment as this. Borrius has said something like it, though not exactly the same, in the following words: "It is possible that God, by the inward revelation of the Holy Spirit, or by the ministry of angels, instructed the wise men, who came from the east, concerning Jesus, whom they came to adore." But the words "undoubtedly," and "great numbers of persons," are the additions of calumny, and is of a most audacious character, charging us with that which, it is very probable, we never spoke, and of which we never thought; and we have learned that this audacity of boldly affirming any thing whatsoever, under which the junior pastors generally labour, and those who are ignorant of the small stock of knowledge that they possess, is an evil exceedingly dangerous in the church of Christ.

1. Is it probable, that any prudent man will affirm that "something is undoubtedly done in great numbers of persons," of which he is not able, when required, to produce a single example? We confess, that we cannot bring an instance of what is here imputed to us. For, if it were produced by us, it would become a subject of controversy; as has been the fate of the sentiments of Zwinglius concerning the salvation of Socrates, Aristides, and of others in similar circumstances, who must have been instructed concerning their salvation by the Holy Ghost or by angels. For it is scarcely within the bounds of probability, that they had seen the Sacred Scriptures and had been instructed out of them.

2. Besides, if this saying of Christ had occurred to the recollection of our brethren, "Speak, Paul! and hold not thy peace: For I have much people in this city," (Acts xix. 9, 10,) they would not so readily have burdened us with this article, who have learned from this saying of Christ, that God sends the external preaching of his word to nations, when it is his good pleasure for great numbers of them to be converted.

3. The following is a saying in very common and frequent use.

"The ordinary means and instrument of conversation is the preaching of the Divine word by mortal men, to which therefore all persons are bound; but the Holy Spirit has not so bound himself to this method, as to be unable to operate in an extraordinary way, without the intervention of human aid, when it seemeth good to Himself." Now if our brethren had reflected, that this very common sentence obtains our high approval, they would not have thought of charging this article upon us, at least they would not have accounted it erroneous. For, with regard to the FIRST, what is extraordinary does not obtain among "great numbers of persons;" for if it did, it would immediately begin to be ordinary. With regard to the SECOND, if "the preaching of the word by mortal men," be "the ordinary means," by which it is also intimated that some means are extraordinary, and since the whole of our church, nay, in my opinion, since the whole Christian world bears its testimony to this, then indeed it is neither a heresy nor an error to say, "Even without this means [without the preaching of the word] God can convert some persons." To this might likewise be added the word "undoubtedly." For if it be doubtful whether any one be saved by any other means, (that is, by "means extraordinary,") than by human preaching; then it becomes a matter of doubt, whether it be necessary for "the preaching of the Divine word by mortal men," to be called "the ordinary means."

4. What peril or error can there be in any man saying, "God converts great numbers of persons, (that is, very many,) by the internal revelation of the Holy Spirit or by the ministry of angels; "provided it be at the same time stated, that no one is converted except by this very word, and by the meaning of this word, which God sends by men to those communities or nations whom He hath purposed to unite to himself. The objectors will perhaps reply, "It is to be feared, that, if a nation of those who have been outwardly called should believe this, rejecting external preaching, they would expect such an internal revelation or the address of an angel." Truly, this would be as unnatural a subject of fear, as that a man would be unwilling to taste of the bread which was laid before him, because he understands, "Man shall not live by bread alone, but by every word that proceedeth out of the mouth of God." But I desist; lest, while instituting an examination into the causes of this fear, I should proceed much further, and arrive at a point to which our brethren might be unwilling for me on this occasion to advance. A word is sufficient for the wise.

ARTICLE XIX

Before his fall, Adam had not the power to believe, because there was no necessity for faith; God, therefore, could not require faith from him after the fall.

ANSWER

Unless I was well acquainted with the disposition of certain persons, I could have taken a solemn oath, that the ascription of this article to me, as the words now stand, is an act which is attributed to them through calumny. Can I be of opinion that "before his fall Adam had not the power to believe; "and, forsooth, on this account, "because there was no necessity for faith." Who is unacquainted with that expression of the apostle? "He who approaches to God must believe that He exists and that He is a rewarder of those who diligently seek him." I do not think, that there is a single Mahometan or Jew who dare make any such assertion as this article contains. The man who will affirm it, must be ignorant of the nature of faith in its universal acceptation. But who is able to love, fear, worship, honour and obey God, without faith, that is the principle and foundation of all those acts which can be performed to God according to his will?

This calumny against me is audacious and foolish. But I think, it was the wish of its inventors to have added the words, "the power to believe in Christ;" and indeed they ought to have made this addition. Yet perhaps some one is insane enough to say, that "all faith in God is faith in Christ." being inclined to such persuasion by the argument "that there is now no true faith in God, which is not faith in Christ." I say therefore, I affirm and assert, I profess and teach, "that, before his fall, Adam had not the power to believe in Christ, because faith in Christ was not then necessary; and that God therefore could not require this faith from him after the fall:" That is to say, God could not require it on this account, "because Adam had lost that power of believing by his own fault," which is the opinion of those who charge me with the doctrine of this article. But God could have required it, because he was prepared, to bestow those gracious aids which were necessary and sufficient for believing in Christ, and therefore to bestow faith itself in Christ.

But since I here confine myself to a simple denial, the proof of these three things is incumbent upon the brethren who affirm them. (1.) The Proposition, (2.) The Reason added, and (3.) The Conclusion deduced from it. The PROPOSITION is this:

"Before his fall, Adam had the power to believe in Christ."

The REASON is, "because this faith was necessary for him." The CONCLUSION is, "Therefore God could of right demand this faith from him after the fall."

1. A certain learned man endeavours to prove the PROPOSITION, which he thus enunciates. "Before his fall, Adam had an implanted power to believe the Gospel," that is "on the hypothesis of the

Gospel;" or, as I interpret it, "If the Gospel had been announced to him." The argument which this learned man employs in proof is, "Because Adam did not labour under blindness of mind, hardness of heart, or perturbation of the passions; (which are the internal causes of an incapacity to believe;) but he possessed a lucid mind, and an upright will and affections, and, if the Gospel of God had been announced to him, he was able clearly to perceive and approve its truth, and with his heart to embrace its benefits."

2. I do not suppose any one will disapprove of the REASON which they assign, and therefore I do not require a proof of it from them; yet I wish the following suggestions to be well considered, if faith, in Christ was not necessary for Adam, to what purpose was the power of believing in Christ conferred upon him?

3. But the necessity of proving the CONCLUSION is incumbent on our brethren, because they express it themselves in those terms, and indeed with a reason added to it, "Because Adam by his own fault through sin lost that power." Out of respect to the person, I will abstain from a confutation of this argument; not because I account it incapable of a satisfactory refutation, which, I hope, will in due time make its appearance.

I will now produce a few arguments in proof of my opinion.

FIRST. With regard to the Proposition, I prove, "that, before his fall, Adam did not possess the power to believe in Christ." (1.) Because such a belief would have been futile. For there was no necessity, no utility in believing in Christ. But nature makes nothing in vain; much less does God. (2.) Because, prior to his sin, God could not require of him faith in Christ. For Faith in Christ is faith in Him as a saviour from sins; he therefore, who will believe in Christ ought to believe that he is a sinner. But, before Adam had committed any offense, this would have been a false belief. Therefore, in commanding Adam to believe in Christ, God would have commanded him to believe a falsehood. That power, then, was not capable of being produced into an act, and is on the same account useless. (3.) Faith in Christ belongs to a new creation, which is effected by Christ, in his capacity of a Mediator between sinners and God. This is the reason why He is called "the Second Adam," and "the New Man." It is not, therefore, matter of wonder, that the capability of believing in Christ was not bestowed on man by virtue of the first creation. (4.) Faith in Christ is prescribed in the Gospel. But the Law and the Gospel are so far opposed to each other in the Scriptures, that a man cannot be saved by both of them at the same time; but if he be saved by the Law, he will not require to be saved by the Gospel; if he must be saved by the Gospel, then it would not be possible for him to be saved by the Law. God willed to treat with Adam, and actually did treat with him, in his primeval state, before he had sinned, according to the tenor of the legal covenant. What cause, therefore, can be devised, why God, in addition to the power of believing in Himself according to the Law, should likewise have bestowed on Adam the power of believing the Gospel and in Christ? If our brethren say, "that this power was one and the same," I will grant it, when the word "power" is taken in its most general notion, and according to its most remote application--that of the power of understanding and volition, and also the knowledge of common things and of all notions impressed on the mind. But I shall deny the correctness of their observation, if the word "power" is received as signifying any other thing than what is here specified. For that wisdom of God which is revealed in the Gospel excels, by many degrees, the wisdom which was manifested by the creation of the world and in the law.

SECONDLY. With regard to the reason, "Because there was no necessity for Adam in his primitive condition to believe in Christ." No one will refute this argument, unless by asserting, that God infused a power into man, which was of no service, and which could be of none whatever, except when man is reduced to that state into which God himself forbids him to fall, and into which he cannot fall but through the transgression of the Divine command. But I must here be understood as always speaking about a power to believe the Gospel and in Christ, as distinct from a power of believing in God according to the legal prescript.

THIRDLY. With regard to what belongs to the Conclusion which is to be deduced from the preceding, I will burden it only with one absurdity. If matters be as they have stated them, "that man in his primeval state possessed a power to believe in Christ," when no necessity existed for the exercise of such faith in Christ; and if this power was withdrawn from him after the fall, when it began to be really necessary for him; such a dispensation of God has been very marvelous, and completely opposed to the Divine wisdom and goodness, the province of which consists in making provision about things necessary for those who live under the government and care of these attributes.

I desist from adding any more; because the absurdity of this dogma will not easily obtain credit with such persons as have learned to form a judgment from the Scriptures, and not from prejudices previously imbibed. I will only subjoin, that this dogma never obtained in the church of Christ, nor has it ever been accounted an article relating to faith.

ARTICLE XX

It cannot possibly be proved from the Sacred Writings, that the angels are now confirmed in their estate.

ANSWER

This article also has been besprinkled with calumny; though I am of opinion, that it was done in ignorance by him from whose narration it is attributed to me. For I did not deny that this fact was incapable of proof from the Scriptures; but I inquired of him, "if it be denied, with what arguments from Scripture will you prove it?" I am not so rash as to say, that no proof can be given from Scripture for a matter, whose contrary I am not able satisfactorily to establish by Scripture, at least if such proof has not produced certainty in my own mind. For I ought to believe, that there are other persons who can prove this, though I am myself incapable; as those persons, in like manner, with whom I occasionally enter into conversation, ought to believe thus concerning themselves because I cannot instantly deny that they are unable to do what, I am sure, they will experience much difficulty in performing. For they must themselves be aware, that from their frequent conversations, and from the sermons which they address to the people, some judgment may be formed of their own progress in the knowledge of the truth and in understanding the Scriptures. I wish them, therefore to undertake the labour of proving that, about which they will not allow me to hesitate.

I know what has been written by St. Augustine, and others of the Fathers, about the estate of the angels, about their blessedness, their confirmation in good, and the certainty by which they know that they will never fall from this condition. I also know, that the schoolmen incline towards this opinion. But when I examine the arguments which they advance in its support, they do not appear to me to possess such strength as may justly entitle it to be prescribed for belief to other persons as an approved article of faith.

The passage generally quoted from St. Matthew, (xxii, 30,) "But they are as angels of God in heaven," treats only on the similitude [between young children and angels,] in neither marrying nor being given in marriage; he does not say, that the angels of God are now happy in heaven.

That in Matt. xviii. 10, "In heaven their angels do always behold the face of my Father who is in heaven," does not speak of the beatific vision, but of that vision with which those who stand around the throne of God wait for his commands. This is apparent from the design of Christ, who wished thus to persuade them "not to offend one of these little ones;" their beholding God, helps to confirm this persuasion, not the beatific sight, but such a sight of God as is suited for the reception of the [Divine] commands to keep these little ones.

"But ye are come to the heavenly Jerusalem, and to an innumerable company of angels." (Heb. xii. 22. This does not necessarily prove, that angels are now blessed and confirmed in good; because, even now, those who are neither beatified nor confirmed in good do themselves belong to that celestial city, that is, those who are said to have "come to this heavenly city," who still "walk by faith," and "see through a glass darkly." (1 Cor. xiii. 12.) "Then the angels will be in a more unhappy condition than the souls of pious men, who are now enjoying blessedness with Christ and in his presence." This reason which they adduce is not conclusive. For "the angels are ministering spirits, sent forth to minister for them who shall be heirs of eternal salvation" This service of theirs will endure to the end of the world. In the mean time, "those who have died in the Lord, rest from their labours." (Rev. xiv. 13.)

Neither is that a stronger argument, which says, "It is possible for the angels to fall, if they are not confirmed in good; and therefore they must always of necessity be tormented by a fear of their fall, which may happen; and by a fear which is the greater, on account of the clearer knowledge that they have of the evil into which the apostate angels are fallen." For it is possible for the angels to be assured of their stability, that is, that they shall never fall away, although they be neither blessed, nor so far confirmed in that which is good as not to be capable of falling. They may be assumed, either with such a certainty as excludes all anxious "fear that hath torment," but is consistent with that "fear and trembling," with which we are commanded to "work out our salvation," who are said to have "the full assurance of faith" concerning our salvation.

But what necessity is there to enter into this disputation, which cannot without great difficulty be decided from the Scriptures; and which, when it is decided, will be of small service to us. Let us rather devote our attention to this study. Doing now the will of God as the angels do in heaven, let us endeavour to be enabled hereafter to become partakers with them of eternal blessedness. This is especially our duty, since the things which have been written for us respecting the state of angels, and which are commanded to be received by faith, are exceedingly few in number.

This, therefore, is my reply to the former twenty of these articles, which have been ascribed partly to me alone, and partly also to Borrius. There is not one of them whose contrary has been believed by the Church Universal and held as an article of faith. Some of them, however, are so artfully constructed, that those which are their opposites savour of novelty and send forth an odour of falsehood. Beside the fact, that the greatest part of them are attributed to us through calumny. I now proceed to the consideration of the eleven which follow that I may see whether the fabricators have acted in a more happy and judicious manner, either in imputing them to me, or in reckoning them as errors or heresies. May God direct my mind and my hand, that I may with a good conscience declare those things which are in unison with the truth, and which may conduce to the peace and tranquillity of our brethren.

ARTICLE XXI (I.)

It is a new, heretical and Sabellian mode of speaking, nay, it is blasphemous, to say "that the Son of God is autoqeon (very God,)" for the Father alone is very God, but not the Son of the Holy Spirit.

ANSWER

Most of those persons who are acquainted with me at all, know with what deep fear, and with what conscientious solicitude, I treat that sublime doctrine of a Trinity of Persons. The whole manner of my teaching demonstrates, that when I am explaining this article I take no delight either in inventing new phrases, that are unknown to Scripture and to orthodox antiquity, or in employing such as have been fabricated by others. All my auditors too will testify, how willingly I bear with those who adopt a different mode of speaking from my own, provided they intend to convey a sound meaning. These things I premise, lest any one should suppose, that I had sought to stir up a controversy about this word, with other persons who had employed it.

But when, in the course of a particular disputation, a certain young man with much pertinacity and assurance defended not only the word itself, but likewise that meaning which I believe and know to be contrary to all antiquity, as well as to the truth of the Scriptures, and was not backward in expressing his serious disapproval of the more orthodox opinions; I was compelled to explain what were my sentiments about the word and its meaning.

I said that the word is not contained in the Scriptures; yet, because it had been used by the orthodox, both by Epiphanius, (Heres. 69,) and by some divines in our days, I do not reject it, provided it be correctly received.

But it may be received in a two fold signification, according to the etymon of the word; and may mean, either one who is truly and in himself God, or one who is God from himself. In the former signification, I said, the word might be tolerated; but in the latter, it was in opposition to the Scriptures and to orthodox antiquity.

When the opponent still urged, that he received the word in this last sense, and that Christ was indeed autoqeon that is,. God from himself, who has in reality an essence in common with the Father, but not communicated by the Father; and when he asserted this with the greater boldness, because he knew that in this opinion he had Trelactrius of pious memory agreeing with him, from whose instructions he appeared to have derived his ideas on the subject; I said that this opinion was a novel one, which was never heard of by the ancients, and unknown both to the Greek and Latin Fathers; and that, when rigidly examined, it would be found to be heretical, and nearly allied to the opinion of Sabellius, which was, that the Father and the Son are not distinct persons, but one person called by different names. I added, that, from this opinion, the entirely opposite heresy might likewise be deduced, which is, that the Son and the Father are two different persons, and two collateral gods; this is blasphemous. I proved my remarks by the following brief arguments: FIRST. It is the property of the person of the Father, to have his being from himself, or, which is a better phrase, to have his being from no one. But the Son is now said to have his being from himself, or rather, from no one: therefore, the Son is the Father; which is Sabellianism. SECONDLY. If the Son have an essence in common with the Father, but not communicated by the Father, he is collateral with the Father, and, therefore, they are two gods. Whereas, all antiquity defended the unity, the Divine essence in three distinct persons, and placed a salvo on it by this single explanation, "that the Son has the same essence directly, which is communicated to him by the Father; but that the Holy Spirit has the very same essence from the Father and the Son."

This is the explanation which I adduced at that time, and in the maintenance of which I still persist: and I affirm, that in this opinion I have the Scriptures agreeing with me, as well as the whole of antiquity, both of the Greek and the Latin churches. It is therefore most wonderful, that our brethren have dared to charge this upon me as an erroneous sentiment. Yet, in doing this, they do not act with sincerity, since they do not explain the word autoqeon by removing its ambiguity; which they undoubtedly ought to have done, lest any person should suppose that I denied the Son to be in every sense, and therefore that he is not very and true God. This they ought the more particularly to have done, because they know that I have always made a distinction between these significations, and have admitted one of them, but rejected the other.

Since the matter really stands thus, I might simply accuse this article of making a false charge; because in a certain sense I confess the son to be autoqeon also the Holy Spirit, and not the Father alone. But, for the sake of justifying this phrase and opinion, the framers of it declare, "When it is said, the Son is God from himself, then the phrase must be received in this sense, the essence which the Son has, is from himself, that is, from no one. For the Son is to be considered as he is God, and as he is the Son. As God, he has his being from himself. As the Son, he has it from the Father. Or two things are to be subjects of consideration in the Son, his essence and his relation. According to his essence, the Son is from no one or from himself. According to his relation, he is from the Father."

But I answer, FIRST. This mode of explanation cannot, except by an impropriety of speech, excuse him who says, "the Son has indeed an essence in common with the Father, but not communicated."

SECONDLY. "The essence, which the Son has, is from no one," is not tantamount to the phrase, "the Son, who has an essence, is from no one." For, "Son" is the name of a person that has relation to a Father, and therefore without that relation it cannot become a subject either of definition or of consideration. But "Essence" is something absolute: and these two are so circumstanced between themselves, that "essence" does not enter into the definition of "Son," except indirectly, thus, "he is the Son, who has the Divine essence communicated to him by the Father;" which amounts to this, "he is the Son, who is begotten of the Father." For, to beget, is to communicate his essence.

THIRDLY. These two respects in which He is God and in which He is the Son, have not the same affection or relation between each other, as these two have, "to exist from himself or from no one," and "to exist from the Father," or "to have his essence from himself," or "from no one," and "to have it from the Father:" which I demonstrate thus by two most evident arguments. (1.) "God" and "the Son" are consentaneous and subordinate: for the Son is God. But "to derive his being from no one" and "to derive it from another," "to have his essence from no one," and "to have it from another," are opposites, and cannot be spoken about the same person. In the comparison which they institute, those things which ought to be collated together are not properly compared, nor are they opposed to each of their parallels and classes or affinities. For a double ternary must here come under consideration, which is this:

HE IS GOD: -- HE IS THE FATHER: -- HE IS THE SON:

He has the Divine essence,: He has it from no one,: He has it from the Father:

These are affinities and parallels. (1.) "He is God," and "has the Divine essence." (2.) "He is the Father," and, "has the Divine essence from no one." (3.) "He is the Son," and, "has the Divine essence from the Father."

But, by the comparison which our objectors institute in their explanation, these things will be laid down as parallels. "He is God," and "has his essence from no one." If this comparison be correctly formed, then either the Father alone is God, or there are three collateral Gods. But far be it from me to charge with such a sentiment as this those who say, "the Son is autoqeon that is, God from himself." For I know that they occasionally explain themselves in a modified manner. But their explanation does not agree with the phraseology which they employ. For this reason Beza excuses Calvin, and openly confesses "that he had not with sufficient strictness observed the difference between these particles a se and per se."

I have stated only what follow as consequences from these phrases, and from the opinion which agrees with them; and I have therefore said, that people must refrain from the use of such phraseology. I abstain from proofs, multitudes of which I could bring from the Scriptures and the Fathers; and if necessity require, I will immediately produce them: for I have had them many years in readiness.

GOD is from eternity, having the Divine Essence.

THE FATHER is from no one, having the Divine Essence from no one, which others say is "from himself."

THE SON is from the Father, having the Divine Essence from the Father.

This is a true parallelism, and one which, if in any manner it be inverted or transposed, will be converted into a heresy. So that I wonder much, how our brethren could consider it proper to make any mention of this matter; from which they would with far more correctness and prudence have abstained, if, while meditating upon it, they had weighed it in equal balances.

ARTICLE XXII (II.)

It is the summit of blasphemy to say, that God is freely good.

ANSWER

In this article likewise, our brethren disclose their own disgraceful proceedings, which I would gladly allow to remain buried in oblivion. But, because they recall this affair to my recollection, I will now relate how it occurred.

In a disputation, it was asked, "can necessity and liberty be so far reconciled to each other, that a person may be said necessarily or freely to produce one and the same effect?" These words being used properly according to their respective strict definitions, which are here subjoined. "An agent acts necessarily, who, when all the requisites for action are laid down, cannot do otherwise than act, or cannot suspend his acting. An agent acts freely, who, when all the requisites for action are laid down, can refrain from beginning to act, or can suspend his acting," I declared, "that the two terms could not meet in one subject." Other persons said, "that they could," evidently for the purpose of confirming the dogma which asserts, "Adam sinned freely indeed, and yet necessarily. FREELY, with respect to himself and according to his nature: NECESSARILY, with respect to the decree of God."

Of this their explanation I did not admit, but said necessarily and freely differ not in respects, but in their entire essences, as do necessity and contingency, or what is necessary and what is contingent, which, because they divide the whole amplitude of being, cannot possibly coincide together, more than can finite and infinite. But Liberty appertains to Contingency.

To disprove this my opinion, they brought forward an instance, or example, in which Necessity and Liberty met together; and that was God, who is both necessarily and freely good. This assertion of theirs displeased me so exceedingly, as to cause me to say, that it was not far removed from blasphemy. At this time, I entertain a similar opinion about it; and in a few words I thus prove its falsity, absurdity, and the blasphemy [contained] in the falsity.

(1.) Its falsity. He who by natural necessity, and according to his very essence and the whole of his nature, is good, nay, who is Goodness itself, the Supreme Good, the First Good from whom all good proceeds, through whom every good comes, in whom every good exists, and by a participation of whom what things soever have any portion of good in them are good, and more or less good as they are nearer or more remote from it. He is not FREELY good. For it is a contradiction in an adjunct, or an opposition in an apposition. But God is good by natural necessity, according to his entire nature and essence, and is Goodness itself, the supreme and primary Good, from whom, through whom: and in whom is all good, &c. Therefore, God is not freely good.

(2.) Its absurdity. Liberty is an affection of the Divine Will; not of the Divine Essence, Understanding, or Power; and therefore it is not an affection of the Divine Nature, considered in its totality. It is indeed an effect of the will, according to which it is borne towards an object that is neither primary nor adequate, and that is different from God himself; and this effect of the will, therefore, is posterior in order to that affection of the will according to which God is borne towards a proper, primary and adequate object, which is himself. But Goodness is an affection of the whole of the Divine Nature, Essence, Life, Understanding, Will, Power, &c. Therefore, God is not freely good; that is, he is not good by the mode of liberty, but by that of natural necessity. I add, that it cannot be affirmed of anything in the nature of things, that it is freely, or that it is this or that freely, not even then when man was made what he is, by actions proceeding from free will: as no man is said to be "freely learned," although he has obtained erudition for himself by study which proceeded from free will.

(3.) I prove that blasphemy is contained in this assertion: because, if God be freely good, (that is, not by nature and natural necessity,) he can be or can be made not good. As whatever any one wills freely, he has it in his power not to will; and whatever any one does freely, he can refrain from doing. Consider the dispute between the ancient Fathers and Eunomius and his followers, who endeavoured to prove that the Son was not eternally begotten of the Father, because the Father had neither willingly nor unwillingly begotten the Son. But the answer given to them by Cyril, Basil, and others, was this: "The Father was neither willing nor unwilling; that is, He begat the Son not by will, but by nature. The act of generation is not from the Divine Will, but from the Divine nature." If they say, "God may also be said to be freely good, because He is not good by co-action or force:" I reply, not only is co-action repugnant to liberty, but nature is likewise; and each of them, nature and co-action, constitutes an entire, total and sufficient cause for the exclusion of liberty. Nor does it follow, "co-action does not exclude liberty from this thing; therefore, it is freely that which it actually is. A stone does not fall downwards by co-action; it, therefore, falls by liberty. Man wills not his own salvation by force, therefore, he wills it freely." Such objections as these are unworthy to be produced by MEN; and in the refutation of them shall I expend my time and leisure, Thus, therefore, the Christian Fathers justly attached blasphemy to those who said, "the Father begat the Son willingly, or by his own will;" because from this it would follow, that the Son had an origin similar to that of the creatures. But with how much greater equity does blasphemy fasten itself upon those who declare, "that God is freely good? For if he be freely good, he likewise freely knows and loves himself, and besides does all things freely, even when He begets the Son and breathes forth the Holy Spirit.

ARTICLE XXIII (III.)

It frequently happens that a creature who is not entirely hardened in evil, is unwilling to perform an action because it is joined with sin; unless when certain arguments and occasions are presented to him, which act as incitements to its commission. The management of this presentation, also, is in the hand of the providence of God, who presents these incitements, that he may accomplish his own work by the act of the creature.

ANSWER

Unless certain persons were under the excitement of a licentious appetite for carping at those things which proceed from me, they would undoubtedly never have persuaded themselves to create any trouble about this matter. Yet, I would pardon them this act of officiousness, as the rigid and severe examiners of truth, provided they would sincerely and without calumny relate those things which I have actually spoken or written; that is, that they would not corrupt or falsify my sayings, either by adding to or diminishing from them, by changing them or giving them a perverted interpretation. But some men seem to have been so long accustomed to slander, that, even when they can be openly convicted of it, still they are not afraid of hurling it against an innocent person. Of this fact, they afford a luminous example in the present article. For those things which I advanced in the Theses, On the Efficacy and Righteousness of the Providence of God concerning evil, and which were disputed in the month of May, 1605, are here quoted, but in a mutilated manner, and with the omission of those things which are capable of powerfully vindicating the whole from the attacks of slander. The following are the words which I employed in the fifteenth thesis of that disputation.

"But since an act, though it be permitted to the ability and the will of the creature, may yet be taken away from his actual power or legislation; and since, therefore, it will very frequently happen, that a creature, who is not entirely hardened in evil, is unwilling to perform an act because it is connected with sin, unless when some arguments and occasions are presented to him, which resemble incitements to its commission. The management of this presenting (of arguments and occasions) is also in the hand of the Providence of God, who presents these incitements, both that He may fully try whether the creature be willing to refrain from sinning, even when urged on, or provoked, by incitements; because the praise of abstaining from sin is very slight, in the absence of such provocatives; and that, if the creature wills to yield to these incitements, God may effect his own work by the act of the creature."

These are my words from which the brethren have extracted what seemed suitable for establishing the slander, but have omitted and quite taken away those things which, in the most manifest manner, betray and confute the calumny. For I laid down two ends of that administration by which God manages the arguments, occasions, incitements, and irritatives to commit that act which is joined with sin. And these two ends were neither collateral, that is, not equally intended; nor were they connected together by a close conjunction. The FIRST of them, which is the exploration or trial of his creature, God primarily, properly, and of himself intends. But the LATTER, which is, that God may effect his own work by the act of the creature, is not intended by God, except after he has foreseen that his Creature will not resist these incitements, but will yield to them, and that of his own free will, in opposition to the command of God, which it was his duty and within his power to follow, after having rejected and refused those allurements and incitements of arguments and occasions. But this article of theirs propounds my words in such a way, as if I had made God to intend this last end only and of itself, omitting entirely the first; and thus omitting the previous condition under which God intends this second end through the act of his creature, that is, when it is the will of the creature to yield to these incitements.

This calumny, therefore, is two-fold, and evidently invented for the purpose of drawing a conclusion from these, my words -- that I have in them represented God as the author of sin. A certain person, having lately quoted my expressions in a public discourse, was not afraid of drawing from them this conclusion. But this was purely through calumny, as I will now prove with the utmost brevity.

The reason by which it can be concluded, from the words that have been quoted in this article from my Thesis, "that God is the author of the sin which is committed by the creature," when God incites him by arguments and occasions, is universally, three-fold:

The FIRST is, that God absolutely intends to effect his own work by the act of the creature, which act cannot be performed by the creature without sin. This is resolvable into two absolute intentions of God, of which the first is that by which he absolutely intends to effect this, his work; and the second, that by which he absolutely intends to effect this work in no other way, than by such an act of a creature as cannot be done by that creature without sin.

The SECOND REASON IS, that the creature being invited by the presenting of these allurements and provocatives to commit that act, cannot do otherwise than commit it; that is, such an excitation being laid down, the creature cannot suspend that act by which God intends to erect his work, otherwise God might be frustrated of his intention: Hence arises

The THIRD REASON which has its origin in these two--that God intends by these incentives to move the creature to perform an act which is joined to sin, that is, to move him to the commission of sin.

All these things seem, with some semblance of probability, to be drawn as conclusions from the words thus placed, as they are quoted in this their article, because it is represented as the sole and absolute end of this administration and presenting-that God effects his work by the act of the creature. But those words which I have inserted, and which they have omitted, meet these three reasons, and in the most solid manner, confute the whole objection which rests upon them.

1. My own words meet the FIRST of these reasons thus: For they deny that God absolutely intends to effect his own work by the act of the creature; because they say that God did not intend to employ the act of the creature to complete his work, before he foresaw that the creature would yield to those incitements, that is, would not resist them.

2. They meet the SECOND by denying that, after assigning this presentation of incitements, the creature is unable to suspend his act; since they say, likewise, that, if it be the will of the creature to yield to these incitements, then God effects his own work by the act of the creature. What does this mean if it be his will to yield? Is not the freedom of the will openly denoted, by which, when this presenting of arguments and occasions is laid down, the will can yet refuse to yield,

3. They also meet the THIRD: For they deny that God intends by those incitements to move the creature to the commission of an act which is joined to sin, that is, to commit sin, because they say, that God intends the trial of his creature, whether he will obey God even after having been irritated by these incitements. And when God saw that the creature preferred to yield to these incitements, rather than to obey him, then he intended, not the act of the creature, for that is unnecessary; because, his intention being now to try, he obtains the issue of the act performed by the will of the creature. But God intended to effect his own work by an act founded on the will and the culpability of the creature.

It is apparent, therefore, that these words which my brethren have omitted, most manifestly refute the calumny, and in the strongest manner solve the objection. This I will likewise point out in another method, that the whole iniquity of this objection may be rendered quite obvious.

That man who says, "God tries his creature by arguments and occasions of sinning, whether he will obey him even after he has been stirred up by incitements," openly declares that it is in the power of the creature to resist these incitements, and not to sin: otherwise, this [act of God] would be, not a trial of obedience, but a casting down, and an impelling to necessary disobedience. Then, the man who says--"God, by these provocatives and incitements, tries the obedience of his creature," intimates by these expressions, that those occasions and arguments which are presented by God when he intends to try, are not incitements and irritations to sin, through the end and aim of God. But they are incitements, first, by capability according to the inclination of the creature who can be incited by them to commit an act connected with sin. They are also incitements, secondly, in their issue, because the creature has been induced by them to sin, but by his own fault; for it was his duty, and in his power, to resist this inclination, and to neglect and despise these incitements.

It is wonderful, therefore, and most wonderful indeed, that any man, at all expert in theological matters, should have ventured to fabricate from my words this calumny against me. Against me, I say, who dare not accede to some of the sentiments and dogmas of my brethren, as they well know, for this sole reason--because I consider it flows from them that God is the author of sin. And I cannot accede to them on this account--because I think my brethren teach those things from which I can conclude by good and certain consequence, that God absolutely intends the sin of his creature, and thence, that he so administers all things, as, when this administration is laid down, man necessarily sins, and cannot, in the act itself, and in reality, omit the act of sin. If they shew that the things which I say, do not follow from their sentiments, on this account at least, I shall not suffer myself to be moved by their consent in them. Let the entire theses be read, and it will be evident how solicitously I have guarded against saying any thing, from which by the most distant probability, this blasphemy might be deduced; and yet, at the same time, I have been careful to subtract from the providence of God nothing, which, according to the Scriptures, ought to be ascribed to it. But I scarcely think it necessary, for me now to prove at great length, that the fact of God's providential efficacy respecting evil is exactly as I have taught in those words; especially after I have premised this explanation. I will, however, do this in a very brief manner.

Eve was not only "a creature not entirely hardened in evil," but she was not at all evil; and she willed to abstain from eating the forbidden fruit because "it was connected with sin," as is apparent from the answer which she gave to the serpent: "God hath, said, Ye shall not eat of it." Her compliance with this command was easy, in the midst of such an abundance of fruit; and the trial of her obedience would have been very small, if she had been solicited with no other argument by the tempter. It happened, therefore, that, in addition to this, the serpent presented to Eve an argument of persuasion, by which he might stimulate her to eat, saying, "Ye shall not surely die, but ye shall be as gods." This argument, according to the intention of the serpent, was an incitement to commit sin: Without it, the serpent perceived, she would not be moved to eat, because he had heard her expressing her will to abstain from the act because it was "connected with sin."

I ask now, Is the whole management of this temptation to be ascribed to God, or not? If they say, "It must not be attributed to him," they offend against Providence, the Scriptures, and the opinion of all our divines. If they confess that it should be ascribed to him, they grant what I have said. But what was the end of this management? An experiment, or trial, whether Eve, when solicited by arguments, and stimulated by Satan, would resolve to refrain from an act, that she might obtain from her Lord and Creator, the praise of obedience. The instance of Joseph's brethren, which is quoted in the fifteenth thesis of my ninth public disputation, proves this in the plainest manner, as I have shown in that thesis.

Let the case of Absalom be inspected, who committed incest with his father's concubines. Was not this the occasion of perpetrating that act--God gave his father's concubines into his hands, that is, he permitted them to his power. Was not the argument inducing him to commit that act, from which nature is abhorrent, furnished by the advice of Ahithophel, whose counsels were considered as oracles? (2 Sam. xvi. 20-23.) Without doubt, these are the real facts of the case. But that God himself managed the whole of this affair, appears from the Scripture, which says that God did it. (2 Sam. xii. 11-12.)

Examine what God says in Deut. xiii. 1-3, "Thou shalt not obey the words of that prophet, who persuades thee to worship other gods, although he may have given thee a sign or a wonder which may have actually come to pass? Is not the diction of "the sign," [by this false prophet,] when confirmed by the event itself, an argument which may gain credit for him? And is not the credit, thus obtained, an incitement, or an argument to effect a full persuasion of that which this prophet persuaded? And what necessity is there for arguments, incitements and incentives, if a rational creature has such a propensity to the act, which cannot be committed without sin, that he wills to commit it without any argument whatsoever, Under such circumstances, the grand tempter will cease from his useless labour. But because the tempter knows, that the creature is unwilling to commit this act, unless he be incited by arguments, and opportunities be offered, he brings forward all that he can of incentives to allure the creature to sin. God, however, presides over all these things, and by his Providence administers the whole of them, but to an end far different from that to which the temptor directs them. For God manages them, in the first place, for the trial of his creatures, and, afterwards, (if it be the will of the creature to yield,) for Himself to effect something by that act.

If any think, that there is something reprehensible in this view, let them so circumscribe the right and the capability of God, as to suppose Him unable to try the obedience of his creature by any other method, than by creating that in which sin can be committed, and from which He commanded him by a law to abstain. But if He can try the obedience of his creature by some other method than this, let these persons shew us what that method is beside the presenting of arguments and occasions, and why God uses the former method more than the preceding one which I have mentioned. Is it not because he perceives, that the creature will not, by the former, be equally strongly solicited to evil, and that therefore it is a trivial matter to abstain from sin, to the commission of which he is not instigated by any other incentives?

Let the history of Job be well considered, whose patience God tried in such a variety of ways, and to whom were presented so many incitements to sin against God by impatience; and the whole of this matter will very evidently appear. God said to Satan; "Hast thou considered my servant Job, a perfect and an upright man, one that feareth God and departeth from evil,." Satan answered the Lord and said: "What wonder is there in this, since thou hast so abundantly blessed him. But try him now by afflictions." And the Lord said unto Satan: "Behold, all that he hath is in thy power. Only upon himself put not forth thine hand." What other meaning have these words than, "Behold, incite him to curse me! I grant thee permission, since thou thinkest small praise is due to that man who abounds with blessings, and yet fears me. Satan did what he was permitted, and produced none of the effects; [which he had prognosticated]; so that God said, "Job still holdeth fast his integrity, although thou movedst me against him." (ii, 3.) This trial being finished, when Satan asked permission to employ against him greater incentives to sin, he obtained his request; and, after all, effected nothing. Therefore God was glorified in the patience of Job, to the confusion of Satan.

I suppose these remarks will be sufficient to free the words of my Theses from all calumny and from sinister and unjust interpretations. When I have ascertained the arguments which our brethren employ to convict these words of error, I will endeavour to confute them; or if I cannot do this, I will field to what may then be deemed the truth.

ARTICLE XXIV (IV.)

The Righteousness of Christ is not imputed to us for Righteousness; but to believe [or the act of believing] justifies us.

ANSWER

I do not know what I can most admire in this article--the unskillfulness, the malice, or the supine negligence of those who have been its fabricators! (1.) Their NEGLIGENCE is apparent in this, that they do not care how and in what words they enunciate the sentiments which they attribute to me; neither do they give themselves any trouble to know what my sentiments are, which yet they are desirous to reprehend. (2.) Their UNSKILLFULNESS. Because they do not distinguish the things which ought to be distinguished, and they oppose those things which ought not to be opposed. (3.) The MALICE is evident, because they attribute to me those things which I have neither thought nor spoken; or because they involve matters in such a way as to give that which was correctly spoken the appearance of having been uttered in perverseness, that they may discover some grounds for calumny. But, to come to the affair itself.

Though in this article there seem to be only two distinct enunciations, yet in potency they are three, which must also be separated from each other to render the matter intelligible. The FIRST is, "the righteousness of Christ is imputed to us." SECOND, "the righteousness of Christ is imputed for righteousness." THIRD, "the act of believing is imputed for righteousness." For thus ought they to have spoken, if their purpose was correctly to retain my words; because the expression, "justifies us," is of wider acceptation than, "is imputed for righteousness." For God justifies, and it is not imputed for righteousness. Christ, "the righteous servant of God, justifies many by his knowledge." But that by which He thus does this, is not "imputed for righteousness."

1. With regard to the FIRST. I never said, "the righteousness of Christ is not imputed to us." Nay, I asserted the contrary in my Nineteenth Public Disputation on Justification, Thesis 10. "The righteousness by which we are justified before God may in an accommodated sense be called imputative, as being righteousness either in the gracious estimation of God, since it does not according to the rigor of right or of law merit that appellation, or as being the righteousness of another, that is, of Christ, it is made ours by the gracious imputation of God." I have, it is true, placed these two in alternation. By this very thing I declare, that I do not disapprove of that phrase. "The righteousness of Christ is imputed to us, because it is made ours by the gracious estimation of God," is tantamount to, "it is imputed to us;" for "imputation" is "a gracious estimation." But lest any one should seize on these expressions as an occasion for calumny, I say, that I acknowledge, "the righteousness of Christ is imputed to us" because I think the same thing is contained in the following words of the Apostle, "God hath made Christ to be sin for us, that we might be made the righteousness of God in Him." (2 Cor. v. 21.)

2. I have said, that I disapprove of the SECOND enunciation, "the righteousness of Christ is imputed to us for righteousness." And why may not I reject a phrase which does not occur in the Scriptures, provided I do not deny any true signification which can be proved from the Scriptures? But this is the reason of my rejection of that phrase. "Whatever is imputed for righteousness, or to righteousness, or instead of righteousness, it is not righteousness itself strictly and rigidly taken. But the righteousness of Christ, which He hath performed in obeying the Father, is righteousness itself strictly and rigidly taken. THEREFORE, it is not imputed for righteousness." For that is the signification of the word "to impute," as Piscator against Bellarmine, when treating on justification, (from Romans iv. 4,) has well observed and safisfactorily proved.

The matter may be rendered clearer by an example. If a man who owes another a hundred florins, pays this his creditor the hundred which he owes, the creditor will not speak with correctness if he says, "I impute this to you for payment." For the debtor will instantly reply, "I do not care any thing about your imputation;" because he has truly paid the hundred florins, whether the creditor thus esteems it or not. But if the man owe a hundred florins and pay only ten, then the creditor, forgiving him the remainder, may justly say, "I impute this to you for full payment; I will require nothing more from you." This is the gracious reckoning of the creditor, which the debtor ought also to acknowledge with a grateful mind. It is such an estimation as I understand as often as I speak about the imputation of the righteousness which is revealed in the Gospel, whether the obedience of Christ be said to be imputed to us, and to be our righteousness before God, or whether faith be said to be imputed for righteousness. There is, therefore, a crafty design latent in this confusion. For if I deny this, their enunciation, they will say I deny that the righteousness of Christ is imputed to us. If I assent to it, I fall into the absurdity of thinking that the righteousness of Christ is not righteousness itself. If they say, that the word "impute" is received in a different acceptation, let them prove their assertion by an example; and when they have given proof of this, (which will be a work of great difficulty to them,) they will have effected nothing.

For "the righteousness of Christ is imputed to us by the gracious estimation of God." It is imputed, therefore, either by the gracious estimation of God for righteousness; or it is imputed by his non-gracious estimation. If it be imputed by His gracious estimation for righteousness, (which must be asserted,) and if it be imputed by His nongracious estimation; then it is apparent, in this confusion of these two axioms, that the word "impute" must be understood ambiguously, and that it has two meanings.

3. The THIRD is thus enunciated: "Faith, or the act of believing, is imputed for righteousness" which are my own words. But omitting my expressions, they have substituted for them the phrase, "The act of believing justifies us." I should say, "They have done this in their simplicity," if I thought they had not read the fourth chapter of the Epistle to the Romans, in which this phrase is used eleven times,

"Faith, or the act of believing, is imputed for righteousness." Thus it is said in the third verse, "Abraham believed God, and it was imputed unto him for righteousness; that is, his believing was thus imputed. Our brethren, therefore, do not reprehend ME, but the APOSTLE, who has employed this phrase so many times in one chapter, and who does not refrain from the use of the other phrase, "to be justified by faith, and through faith," in the third and fifth chapters of the same epistle. They ought, therefore, to have reprehended, not the phrase itself, but the signification which I attach to it, if I explain it in a perverted manner. Thus incorrectly should I seem to have explained the Apostle's phrase if I had said, "the righteousness of Christ is not imputed to us or does not justify us, but faith, or the act of believing, does." But I have already replied, that this assertion concerning me is untrue, and I have declared that I believe both these expressions to be true, "the righteousness of Christ is imputed to us," and "faith is imputed for righteousness." When they place these phrases in opposition to each other, they do this, not from the meaning which I affix to them, but from their own; and, therefore, according to the signification which they give to them severally, they fabricate this calumny, which is an act of iniquity. But they will say, that I understand this phrase, "Faith is imputed for righteousness," in its proper acceptation, when it must be figuratively understood. This they ought, therefore, to have said, because this alone is what they were able to say with truth. Such in fact are my real sentiments on this subject; and the words make for the proper acceptation of the phrase. If a figure lies concealed under it, this ought to be proved by those who make the assertion.

ARTICLE XXV (V.)

The whole of that in which we appear before God, justifies us. But we appear before God, not only by Faith, but also by Works. Therefore, we are justified before God, not only by Faith, but likewise by Works.

ANSWER

A man who is ignorant of those things which are here the order of the day, and who reads this article, will undoubtedly think, that, in the point of justification, I favour the party of the Papists, and am their professed defender. Nay, he will suppose, that I have proceeded to such a pitch of impudence, as to have the audacity to maintain a conclusion directly contrary to the words of the Apostle, who says, "We conclude, therefore, that a man is justified by faith, without the works of the law." But when he shall understand the origin of this article, and why it is charged on me, then it will be evident to him that it arises from calumny and from a corruption of my words. I deny, therefore, that I made that syllogism, or ever intended to draw that conclusion, or to propound those things from which such a conclusion might be deduced.

This brief defense would suffice for all upright minds, to give a favourable interpretation, if perchance anything had been spoken which could give occasion to unjust suspicion. But it will be labour well bestowed, for me to transcribe my own words from a certain disputation on JUSTIFICATION, from which this article has been taken; that it may appear with what kind of fidelity they have made their extract. The Ninth Thesis in it is thus expressed:

"From these things, thus laid down according to the Scriptures, we conclude, that JUSTIFICATION, when used for the act of a judge, is either purely the imputation of righteousness, bestowed, through mercy from the throne of grace in Christ the Propitiation, on a sinner, but on one who believes; or that man is justified before God, of debt, according to the rigor of justice, without any forgiveness. Because the Papists deny the latter, they ought to concede the former. And this is so far true, that, how highly soever any one of the saints may be endowed with faith, hope, and charity, and how numerous soever and excellent may be the works of faith, hope, and charity, which he has performed, yet he will not obtain from God, the judge, a sentence of justification, unless He quit the tribunal of His severe justice, and place Himself in the throne of Grace, and out of it pronounce a sentence of absolution in his favour, and unless the Lord of his mercy and pity, graciously account for righteousness the whole of that good with which the saint appears before Him. For woe to a life of the greatest innocence, if it be judged without mercy! This truth even the Papists seem to acknowledge, who assert, that the works of the saints cannot stand before the judgment of God, unless they be sprinkled with the blood of Christ."' (Public Disput. XIX.)

Thus far my Thesis. Could any person imagine that the major in this article can, according to my sentiments and design, be deduced from it, "The whole of that in which we appear before God, justifies us;" how can this be deduced, when I say, "that not even this good, which the Papists are able or know how to attribute to the most holy men, can obtain from God a sentence of justification, unless He, through mercy from the throne of grace, reckon this graciously for righteousness." Who does not perceive, that I grant this through sufferance and concession?" "God considers and esteems for righteousness all this good in which, the Papists say, the saints appear before God." I yield this, that I may the more firmly confute them; and I thus obtain, "that not even that total can be accounted for righteousness, except graciously and through mercy." This conduct is real malignity, and a violent distortion of my words; on account of which I have indeed no small occasion given to me of complaining before God of this injury. But I contain myself, lest my complaint to God should be detrimental to their souls; I would rather beseech God to be pleased to grant them a better mind.

The matter, with regard to me, stands thus; as if any one should say to a Monk or a Pharisee, who was boasting of his virtues and works of his faith, hope, love, obedience, voluntary chastity and similar excellences: "O man! unless God were to omit the severity of his justice, and unless from the throne of Grace, He were to pronounce a sentence of absolution concerning thee, unless He were graciously to reckon all that good of thine, however great it may be, and thus to account it for righteousness, thou wouldst not be able to stand before Him, or to be justified." I declare, and before Christ I make the declaration, that this was my meaning. And every man is the best interpreter of his own expressions. But let it be allowed, that I have said these things from my own sentiments; was this proposition [of their fabrication] to be deduced from my words? If it was, they ought to have proceeded thus according to scientific method. They ought to have briefly laid down the enunciation which I employed, and which might be in this form: "Unless God graciously account for righteousness the whole of this good in which a saint appears before Him, that saint cannot be justified before God." From which will be deduced this affirmative proposition, "If God graciously accounts for righteousness this good in which a holy man appears, then this holy man can be justified before God," or "he will then be justified before God" The word "the whole," has a place in the negative proposition; because it conduces to the exaggeration. But it ought not to have a place in that which is affirmative. Let this question, however, have a place here: Why have my brethren omitted these words? "The Lord graciously of his mercy, from the throne of his Grace, having omitted the severity of judgment, accounts that good for righteousness." And why have they proposed only these? "The whole of that in which we appear before God, justifies us." This is, indeed, not to deny the fact; but a pretext is thus sought for calumny, under the equivocation of the word "justifies," as justification may be either of grace, or of debt or severe judgment. But I have excluded that which is of debt or severe judgment from my expressions, and have included only the justification which is of grace. Let these remarks suffice for the major proposition.

I now proceed to the assumption that they have subjoined to this proposition, which is theirs and not mine. It reads thus: "But we appear before God, not only by Faith, but also by Works" Then is it your pleasure, my brethren, to appear thus before God? David was not of this opinion, when he said: "Enter not into judgment with thy servant. For in thy sight shall no man living be justified," or "shall justify himself." (Psalm cxliii. 2.) Which is thus rendered by the Apostle Paul, "For by the works of the law shall no flesh be justified." (Gal. ii. 16.) But perhaps you will say, that you do not appear before God "by the works of the law, but by works produced from faith and love." I wish you to explain to me, what it is to appear by faith, and what to appear by works; and whether it can possibly happen, that a man may appear both by faith and works. I know, the saints who will be placed before the tribunal of the Divine Justice, have had Faith, and through Faith have performed good Works. But, I think, they appear and stand before God with this confidence or trust, "that God has set forth his Son Jesus Christ as a propitiation through Faith in his blood, that they may thus be justified by the Faith of Jesus Christ, through the remission of sins." I do not read, that Christ is constituted a propitiation through Works in his blood, that we may also be justified by Works.

My desire indeed is, to appear before the tribunal of God thus, [with this confidence or trust in Christ, as a propitiation through Faith in his blood] and "to be graciously judged through mercy from the throne of grace". If I be otherwise judged, I know I shall be condemned; which sore judgment may the Lord, who is full of clemency and pity, avert according to his great mercy, even from you, my brethren, though you thus speak, whether the words which you use convey your own meaning, or whether you attribute this meaning to me. I also might thus draw wonderful conclusions from this assumption, which is laid down, if an accusation were to be set aside by retaliation or a recriminating charge, and not by innocence. But I will not resort to such a course, lest I seem to return evil for evil; though I might do this with a somewhat greater show of reason.

ARTICLE XXVI (VI.)

Faith is not the instrument of Justification.

ANSWER

IN THE enunciation of this article is given another proof of desperate and finished negligence. What man is so utterly senseless as universally to deny, that Faith can be called "an instrument," since it receives and apprehends the promises which God has given, and does also in this way concur to justification, But who, on the other hand, will venture to say, that, in the business of justification, faith has no other relation than that of an instrument? It should therefore be explained, how faith is an instrument, and how, as an instrument, it concurs to justification.

It is, at least, not the instrument of God; not that which He uses to justify us. Yet this is the meaning first intended to be conveyed by these words, when rigidly taken. For God is the primary cause of justification. But since justification is an estimate of the mind, although made at the command of the will, it is not performed by an instrument. For it is when God wills and acts by his power, that He employs instruments. Then, in these words, "Believe in Christ, and thy sins shall be forgiven thee," or, which is the same thing, "and thou shalt be justified;" I say, that faith is the requirement of God, and the act of the believer when he answers the requirement. But they will say, "that it is the act of apprehending and accepting, and that therefore, this faith bears relation to an instrument?' I reply, faith as a quality has in that passage relation to the mode of an instrument; but the acceptance or apprehension itself is an act, and indeed one of obedience, yielded to the gospel. Let that phrase likewise which is so often used by the Apostle in Romans 6, be seriously considered, "Faith is imputed for righteousness." Is this faith as an instrument, or as an act? St. Paul resolves the question, by a quotation from the book of Genesis, when he says, "Abraham believed God, and it was imputed to him for righteousness." The thing itself, as it is explained by our brethren, also solves the question. "Faith is imputed for righteousness on account of Christ, the object which it apprehends." Let this be granted. Yet the apprehending of Christ is nearer than the instrument which apprehends, or by which He is apprehended. But apprehending is an act; therefore, faith, not as it is an instrument, but as it is an act, is imputed for righteousness, although such imputation be made on account of Him whom it apprehends. In brief, the capability or the quality by which any thing is apprehended, and the apprehension itself, have each relation to the object which is to be apprehended, the former a mediate relation, the latter an immediate. The latter, therefore, is a more modest metonymy, as being derived from that which is nearer; even when it is granted that this phrase, "it is imputed for righteousness"--must be explained by a metonymy. The man, then, who says, "the act of faith is imputed for righteousness, does not deny that faith as an instrument concurs to justification. It is evident, therefore, from this answer, that our brethren fabricate and "get up" articles of this kind without the least care or solicitude, and charge me with them. This, I think, will be acknowledged even by themselves, if they examine how they manufactured those nine questions which, two years ago, by the consent of their Lordships the Curators of our University, they endeavoured to offer to the Professors of Divinity, that they might obtain their reply to them. Gravity and sobriety are highly becoming in Divines, and serious solicitude is required to the completion of such great matters as these.

ARTICLE XXVII (VII.)

Faith is not the pure gift of God, but depends partly on the grace of God, and partly on the powers of Free Will; that, if a man will, he may believe or not believe.

ANSWER

I never said this, I never thought of saying it, and, relying on God's grace, I never will enunciate my sentiments on matters of this description in a manner thus desperate and confused. I simply affirm, that this enunciation is false, "faith is not the pure gift of God;" that this is likewise false, if taken according to the rigor of the words, "faith depends partly on the grace of God, and partly on the powers of free will" and that this is also false when thus enunciated, "If a man will, he can believe or not believe." If they suppose, that I hold some opinions from which these assertions may by good consequence be deduced, why do they not quote my words? It is a species of injustice to attach to any person those consequences, which one may frame out of his words as if they were his sentiments. But the injustice is still more flagrant, if these conclusions cannot by good consequence be deduced from what he has said. Let my brethren, therefore, make the experiment, whether they can deduce such consectaries as these, from the things which I teach; but let the experiment be made in my company, and not by themselves in their own circle. For that sport will be vain, equally void of profit or of victory; as boys sometimes feel, when they play alone with dice for what already belongs to them.

For the proper explanation of this matter, a discussion on the concurrence and agreement of Divine grace and of free will, or of the human will, would be required; but because this would be a labour much too prolix, I shall not now make the attempt. To explain the matter I will employ a simile, which yet, I confess, is very dissimilar; but its dissimilitude is greatly in favour of my sentiments. A rich man bestows, on a poor and famishing beggar, alms by which he may be able to maintain himself and his family. Does it cease to be a pure gift, because the beggar extends his hand to receive it? Can it be said with propriety, that "the alms depended partly on the liberality of the Donor, and partly on the liberty of the Receiver," though the latter would not have possessed the alms unless he had received it by stretching out his hand? Can it be correctly said, because the beggar is always prepared to receive, that "he can have the alms, or not have it, just as he pleases?" If these assertions cannot be truly made about a beggar who receives alms, how much less can they be made about the gift of faith, for the receiving of which far more acts of Divine grace are required! This is the question which it will be requisite to discuss, "what acts of Divine grace are required to produce faith in man?" If I omit any act which is necessary, or which concurs, [in the production of faith,] let it be demonstrated from the Scriptures, and I will add it to the rest.

It is not our wish to do the least injury to Divine grace, by taking from it any thing that belongs to it. But let my brethren take care, that they themselves neither inflict an injury on Divine justice, by attributing that to it which it refuses; nor on Divine grace, by transforming it into something else, which cannot be called GRACE. That I may in one word intimate what they must prove, such a transformation they effect when they represent "the sufficient and efficacious grace, which is necessary to salvation, to be irresistible," or as acting with such potency that it cannot be resisted by any free creature.

ARTICLE XXVIII (VIII.)

The grace sufficient for salvation is conferred on the Elect, and on the Non-elect; that, if they will, they may believe or not believe, may be saved or not saved.

ANSWER

OUR brethren here also manifest the same negligence. They take no pains to know what my sentiments are; they are not careful in examining what truth there is in my opinions; and they exercise no discretion about the words in which they enunciate my sentiments and their own. They know that I use the word "Election" in two senses. (i.) For the decree by which God resolves to justify believers and to condemn unbelievers, and which is called by the Apostle, "the purpose of God according to election." (Rom. ix. 11.) (ii.) And for the decree by which He resolves to elect these or those nations and men with the design of communicating to them the means of faith, but to pass by other nations and men. Yet, without this distinction, they fasten these sentiments on me; when, by its aid, I am enabled to affirm, not only, sufficient grace is conferred on, or rather is offered to, the Elect and the Nonelect;" but also, "sufficient grace is not offered to any except the Elect." (i.) "It is offered to the Elect and the Non-elect," because it is offered to unbelievers, whether they will afterwards believe or not believe. (ii.) "It is offered to none except the Elect," because, by that very thing which is offered to them, they cease to be of the number of those of whom it is said, "He suffered them to walk in their own ways;" (Acts xiv. 16;) and, "He hath not dealt so with any nation." (Psalm cxlvii. 20.) And who shall compel me to use words of their prescribing, unless proof be brought from scripture that the words are to be thus and in no other way received?

I now proceed to the other words of the article. "That, if they will, they may believe or not believe, be saved or not saved." I say, in two different senses may these words be received, "if they will, they may believe," that is, either by their own powers, or as they are excited and assisted by this grace. "Or they may not believe," while rejecting this grace by their own free will, and resisting it. "They may be saved or not saved," that is, saved by the admission and right use of grace, not saved by their own wickedness, rejecting that without which they cannot be saved.

To the whole together I reply, that nothing is declared in these words, in whatever manner they may be understood, which St. Augustine himself and his followers would not willingly have acknowledged as true. I say, in these words are enunciated the very sentiments of St. Augustine; yet he was the chief champion against the Pelagian heresy, being accounted in that age its most successful combatant. For in his treatise on nature and grace, (c. 67.) St. Augustine speaks thus:, Since He is every where present, who, by many methods through the creature that is subservient to Him as his Lord, can call him who is averse, can teach a believer, can comfort him who hopes, can exhort the diligent man, can aid him who strives, and can lend an attentive ear to him who deprecates; it is not imputed to thee as a fault, that thou art unwillingly ignorant, but that thou neglectest to inquire after that of which thou art ignorant; not that thou dost not collect and bind together the shattered and wounded members, but that thou despisest Him who is willing to heal thee." The book entitled "The Vocation of the Gentiles," which is attributed with a greater semblance of probability to Prosper, than to St. Ambrose, has the following passage: "On all men has always been bestowed some measure of heavenly doctrine, which, though it was of more sparing and hidden grace, was yet sufficient, as the Lord has judged, to serve some men for a remedy, and all men for a testimony." (Lib. 2. c. 5.) In the commencement of the ninth chapter of the same book, he explains the whole matter by saying: "The Grace of God has indeed the decided pre-eminence in our justifications, persuading us by exhortations, admonishing us by examples, affrighting us by dangers, exciting us by miracles, by giving understanding, by inspiring counsel, and by illuminating the heart itself and imbuing it with the affections of faith. But the will of man is likewise subjoined to it and is united with it, which has been excited to this by the before mentioned succours, that it may co-operate in the Divine work within itself, and may begin to follow after the reward which, by the heavenly seed, it has conceived for the object of its desire, ascribing the failure to its own mutability, and the success (if the issue be prosperous) to the aid of grace. This aid is afforded to all men, by innumerable methods both secret and manifest; and the rejection of this assistance by many persons, is to be ascribed to their negligence; but its reception by many persons, is both of Divine grace and of the human will."

I do not produce these passages, as if I thought that either my brethren or I must abide by the sentiments of the Fathers, but only for the purpose of removing from myself the crime of Pelagianism in this matter.

ARTICLE XXIX (IX.)

Believers can perfectly fulfill the Law, and live in the world without sin.

ANSWER

This is what I never said. But when a certain person once, in a public disputation on the Baptism of Infants, was endeavouring, by a long digression, to bring me to the point either to declare that believers could perfectly fulfill the law of God, or that they could not--I declined an answer, but quoted the opinion of St. Augustine, from the second book of his Treatise On the demerits and remission of sins, against the Pelagians. That passage, I will here transcribe, that I may defend myself against the charge of Pelagianism; because, I perceive that the men with whom I have to do, consider even these sentiments to be Pelagian, though they can on no count whatever, be reckoned such.

St. Augustine says: "We must not instantly with an incautious rashness, oppose those who assert that it is possible for man to be in this life without sin. For if we deny the possibility of this, we shall derogate both from the free will of man, which desires to be in such a perfect state by willing it; and from the power or mercy of God, who effects it by the assistance which He affords. But it is one question whether it be possible, and another whether such a man actually exists. It is one question, if such a perfect man is not in existence when it is possible, why is he not? And it is another, not only whether there is any one who has never had any sin at all, but likewise, whether there could at any time have been such a man, or that it is now possible? In this fourfold proposal of questions, if I be asked "is it possible for a man to exist in the present life without sin;" I shall confess, that it is possible by the grace of God, and by man's free will." (Cap. 6.)

In another of his works, St. Augustine says: "Pelagius disputes correctly, that they confess it not to be impossible, by the very circumstance of either many or all persons wishing to do it; [perfectly to fulfill the law of God;] but let him confess whence it is possible, and peace is instantly established. For the possibility arises from the grace of God through Christ Jesus," &c. (On Nature and Grace, against the Pelagians, cap. 59, 60.) And in a subsequent passage: "For it may be made a question among true and pious Christians, has there ever been, is there now, or can there be, in this life, any man who lives so justly as to have no sin at all? Whosoever doubts about the possibility of the existence of such a person after this life, he is destitute of understanding. But I am unwilling to enter into a contest, about this possibility even in the present life." See the paragraphs which immediately succeed in the same chapter. And in the 69th chapter of that work, he says: "By the very thing, by which we most firmly believe that a just and good God could not command impossibilities, we are admonished both of what we may do in things easy of accomplishment, and of what we may ask in matters of difficulty; because all things are easy to charity," &c.

I do not oppose this opinion of St. Augustine; but I do not enter into a contest about any part of the whole matter. For I think the time may be far more happily and usefully employed in prayers to obtain what is lacking in each of us, and in serious admonitions that every one endeavour to proceed and to press forward towards the mark of perfection, than when spent in such disputations.

But my brethren will say, that in the 114th question of our Catechism this very subject is treated, and that it is there asked, "Can those persons who are converted to God, perfectly observe the Divine

Commands," The answer subjoined is, "By no means." To this observation I reply, that I do not say anything against it; but that the reason of the negative answer [or scriptural proof added] is about the act, when the question itself is about the possibility; and that, therefore, from this, nothing is proved. It is also well known that this answer had been rejected by some persons; and that it was only by the intervention of the brethren, who added an explanation to it, that it afterwards obtained the approbation of the same individuals. But I shall be perfectly willing to enter into a conference with my brethren about this matter, whenever it shall be convenient; and I hope we shall easily agree in opinion.

ARTICLE XXX (X.)

It may admit of discussion, whether Semi-Pelagianism is not real Christianity.

ANSWER

In a certain lecture I said, that it would be easy, under the pretext of Pelagianism, to condemn all those things of which we do not approve, if we may invent half, quarter, three-fourths, four-fifths Pelagianism, and so upwards. And I added, that it might admit of discussion whether Semi-Pelagian is not real Christianity. By these remarks it was not my wish to patronize Pelagian doctrine; but I was desirous to intimate, that something might be accounted as Semi-Pelagianism which does not depart from the truth of Christian doctrine. For as, when a departure is once made from the truth, the descent towards falsehood becomes more and more rapid; so, by receding from falsehood, it is possible for men to arrive at truth, which is often accustomed to stand as the mean between two extremes of falsehood. Such indeed is the state of the matter in Pelagianism and Manicheism. If any man can enter on a middle way between these two heresies, he will be a true Catholic, neither inflicting an injury on Grace, as the Pelagians do, nor on Free Will as do the Manichees. Let the Refutation be perused which St. Augustine wrote against both these heresies, and it will appear that he makes this very acknowledgement. For this reason it has happened, that, for the sake of confirming their different opinions, St. Augustine's words, when writing against the Manichees, have been frequently quoted by the Pelagians; and those which he wrote against the Pelagians, have been quoted by the Manichees.

This, therefore, is what I intended to convey; and that my brethren may understand my meaning, I declare openly, "that it will be quite as easy a task for me to convict the sentiments of some among them of Manicheism, and even of Stoicism, as they will be really capable of convicting others of Pelagianism, whom they suspect of holding that error." But I wish us all to abstain from odious names of this description, as they are employed without producing any benefit. For he who is accused will either deny that his sentiments are the same as those of Pelagius; or, if he acknowledges the existence of a similarity, he will say that Pelagius was wrongly condemned by the Church. It would be better then to omit these epithets, and to confer solely about the matter itself; unless, approaching to the opinion of the Papists, we hold that what has once been determined by the Church, cannot be drawn into controversy.

ARTICLE XXXI (XI.)

It is not correctly said in the Catechism, that "God is angry with us for birth-sins;" because original sin is a punishment. But whatever is a punishment is not properly a sin.

ANSWER

Nearly two months ago, a certain minister of God's word, came to me, desirous, as he declared, to confer with me about the opinion which I held concerning the Catechism and Dutch Confession being subjected to examination in our National Synod. On this subject we had some conversation together, and I concluded the expression of my opinion with this syllogism:

"Every human writing which is not in itself entitled to implicit credit, not authentic, and not divine, may be examined, and indeed ought to be; when it can be done in order, and after a legitimate manner, that is, in a Synod, to which [the consideration of] these writings belongs. But such productions are the Catechism and our Confession. Therefore, they may and ought to be subjected to examination." When he had wearied himself in opposing a few things to this syllogism, which I soon dispersed by the clearest light of truth, he began to inquire what [objections] they were which I had against the Confession and Catechism; I replied, that I had nothing against those formularies, for that would be an act of prejudging, which I would not take upon myself; but that there were matters in those two productions, about which it was my wish to confer in a legitimate and orderly manner, with my brethren at their own time, in a Synod, whether on every point they be agreeable to the scriptures, or whether they dissent in any respect from them. For this purpose, that if, after a serious and strict examination, they be found to agree with the scriptures, they may be approved and confirmed by recent and fresh sanctions; or that, if found to dissent from them, they may be corrected as commodiously as possible.

He became urgent with me, therefore, and requested that I would disclose to him those points about which I was desirous to confer; and he declared, that he asked this favour for no other reason than that he might be able himself to think seriously about them. Unwilling positively to deny this his request, I began to produce some parts of the Confession, and especially the fourteenth Article. But he said, "that he made small account of this, because he thought something might easily be discovered in the Confession, which did not perfectly and in every respect correspond with the scriptures, at least with regard to its phraseology, for it was the composition of only a few persons, and in fact was written in the earliest times of the Reformation from Popery; and that he perceived very little danger in the Confession being corrected in some passages, since it was not much in use among the people."

But when he began to be still more urgent concerning the Catechism, desirous in that particular likewise to gratify him, I adduced some passages, and, among others, the answer to the tenth question, in which God is said "by horrid methods to be angry both on account of birth-sins, and on account of those also which we ourselves commit," &c. I said two things, in these words, might admit of discussion. (1.) Whether we could correctly call this universal taint in our nature "birth-sins" in the plural number. I had scarcely made this remark, when he, without waiting for any further explanation, said, "that on one occasion, while he was explaining the Catechism to some students, he had himself begun to think whether it was a good and proper phrase; but that he had defended it by this argument-- The Catechism employs the plural number on account of original sin itself, and on account of the sin committed by Adam which was the cause of that original sin." But as I considered that kind of defense to be unworthy of any confutation, I said, it was better for him at once to own that these words required emendation, than to give such an explanation of them. After this conversation, I added another remark. (2.) It may admit of discussion, whether God could be angry on account of original sin which was born with us, since it seemed to be inflicted on us by God as a punishment of the actual sin which had been committed by Adam and by us in Him. For, in that case, the progress would be infinite, if God, angry on account of the actual sin of Adam, were to punish us with this original sin; were He again to be angry with us for this original sin, and inflict on us another punishment; and, for a similar cause were He a third time to be angry on account of that second punishment which had been inflicted, guilt and punishment thus mutually and frequently succeeding each other, without the intervention of any actual sin. When to this observation he replied, "that still it was sin." I said, I did not deny that it was sin, but it was not actual sin. And I quoted the seventh chapter of the Epistle to the. Romans, in which the Apostle treats on the sin, and says that "it produces in the unregenerate all manner of concupiscence," thus intimating that we must distinguish between actual sin, and that which was the cause of other sins, and which, on this very account might be denominated "sin."

Matters were at that interview discussed between us in this placid manner, and for the purpose which I have just stated; and I know that I never spoke upon this subject in any other place. Yet this our conversation was related to a certain learned man, the very same day on which it occurred, either by the minister himself, or by some one who had heard it from him. I had it from the lips of this learned man himself; who urged it against me as an objection, within a few days after the minister and I had held this discourse: for the minister had resided at this learned man's house, during his stay in Leyden.

Is it equitable that things which are thus discussed among brethren for the sake of conference, should be instantly disseminated, and publicly proclaimed as heretical? I confess that I am devoid of all discernment, if such conduct as this is not the very violation of the law of all familiarity and friendship. Yet these are the persons who complain, that I decline to confer with them; that, when I am calmly asked, I refuse to declare my sentiments; and that I hold their minds in suspense.

To this article, therefore, I briefly reply: It is false that I said, "that this is not correctly expressed in the Catechism." For I told that minister openly, that I would not prejudge the matter; that I was desirous to wait for the judgment of my brethren on matters of this kind, and on others which were comprised in the Catechism and Confession; and that, after things had been thus maturely and accurately weighed, something determinate might be concluded.

But a previous conference of this description seems to be attended with some utility on this account, it prevents any man from offering to the Synod itself for examination and abjudication those matters which, by such a private conversation as this, he might understand to have no difficulties in them. Let the brethren recall to mind what was asked of the Professors of Divinity in our University, by the Synod of South Holland, held at Gorchum, and let them compare it among themselves. We are asked diligently to read through the Confession and Catechism, and, if we find anything in them which merits animadversion, to announce the same seasonably and in order. And this, on my own part, I promised to do. For this purpose, is not a private conference with brethren highly useful, that what can be removed by it may not be proposed to the Synod for discussion, But that minister and I had known each other for many years; I had also long held epistolary correspondence with him, and had conversed with him on the articles of faith. On this account therefore, I thought that I ought to comply with his request, as an experiment whether he could expedite the affair.

CONCLUSION

THIS then is the answer which I have thought proper to make, at present, to the THIRTY-ONE ARTICLES that have been objected against me. If I have not given satisfaction by it to some men, I am prepared to confer in order with any of them upon these subjects and others which pertain to the Christian Religion, for this purpose, that we may either agree in our sentiments; or, if this result cannot be obtained by a conference, that we bear with each other, when it has become evident how far we severally proceed together in the matter of religion, and what things they are of which we approve or disapprove, and that these points of difference are not of such a description as to forbid professors of the same religion to hold different sentiments about them.

Some persons perhaps will reproach me with "appearing sometimes to answer with doubt and desitation, when it is the duty of a Divine and a Professor of Theology to be fully persuaded about those things which he will teach to others, and not to fluctuate in his opinions." To these persons I wish to reply.

1. The most learned man, and he who is most conversant with the Scriptures, is ignorant of many things, and is always but a scholar in the school of Christ and of the Scriptures. But one, who is thus ignorant of many things, cannot, without hesitation, give answer in reference to all things about which an opportunity or necessity for speaking is presented either by adversaries or by those who wish to ask and ascertain his sentiments by private or public conference and disputation. For it is better for him to speak somewhat doubtfully, than dogmatically, about those things of which he has no certain knowledge; and to intimate that he himself requires daily progress, and seeks for instruction as well as they. For I think no one has proceeded to such a pitch of audacity, as to style himself a master that is ignorant of nothing, and that indulges no doubts about any matter whatever.

2. It is not everything which becomes a subject of controversy that is of equal importance. Some things are of such a nature as to render it unlawful for any man to feel a doubt concerning them, if he have any wish to be called by the name of Christian. But there are other things which are not of the same dignity, and about which those who treat on catholic sentiments [such orthodox doctrines as are held by all real Christians,] have dissented from each other, without any breach of truth and Christian peace. Of what description those subjects may be which are discussed in these Articles, and about which I have appeared to answer with hesitation, and whether they be of absolute necessity, may likewise become in due time a topic of discussion.

3. My reply [to these thirty-one articles] is not peremptory:

Not that I have in them said anything against conscience, but because I did not consider it requisite to bring forward, in the first instance, all those things which I might be able to say. I accounted my answer sufficient, and more than sufficient, for all those objections, which have not the slightest foundation on any reasons whatsoever; not only because they were untruly charged against me, but because they did not impinge against the truth of the Scriptures. In the greater number of these Articles, I might have discharged the whole of my duty, in simply denying them, and in demanding proof. But I have gone further than this, that I might in some degree give satisfaction, and that I might besides challenge my brethren to a conference, if they should think it necessary. This I will never decline, provided it be lawfully instituted, and in such a manner as to inspire hopes of any benefits to be derived from it. If after that conference it be discovered that, either because I am ignorant of necessary things which ought to be taught in the Church and in the University; or because I hold unsound opinions about articles on which some importance is placed for obtaining salvation and for the illustration of divine glory; or because I doubt concerning such things as ought to be delivered dogmatically and inculcated with seriousness and rigor, if for these reasons it be discovered that, according to this our unhappy [natural] condition, I am unworthy to hold any office in the Church or University, (for who is sufficient for these things,) I will, without reluctance, resign my situation, and give place to a man possessed of greater merit.

But I wish to advise my brethren, particularly those of them who are my juniors, and who have not "their senses so much exercised" in the Scriptures as to be enabled to deliver out of those Scriptures determinate opinions about all things, that they be not too bold in asserting anything, of which when required to give their reasons, they will be able with great difficulty to produce them; and, besides, that they be sedulously on their guard lest, after they have strenuously affirmed anything which I call in doubt without employing the contrary affirmation, and it be discovered that the arguments which I employ in justification of my doubts are stronger than those on which they rely in that their affirmation, they incur the charge of immodesty and arrogance among men of prudence, and from this very circumstance be accounted unworthy of the place which they hold with so much presumption. For it becomes a Bishop and a Teacher of the Church, not only to hold fast the faithful word as he hath been taught, that he may be able by his sound doctrine, both to exhort and to convince the gainsayers, (Tit. i. 9,7,) but likewise not to be given to self-will, arrogance, and boldness. Into which faults novices easily fall, (1 Tim. iii. 6,)who, "by their inexperience, are unacquainted with the vast difficulty with which the eye of the inward man is healed, that it may be enabled to look upon its sun; with the sighs and groans by which we are able in any small degree to attain to an understanding of God; with the labour necessary for the discovery of truth; and with the difficulty of avoiding errors." Let them consider, that nothing is more easy for them, than not only to assert, but also to think, that they have discovered the truth. But they will themselves at length acknowledge the real difficulties with which the discovery is attended, when with seriousness and earnestness they enter into a conference about the matters in controversy, and have after a rigid examination discussed all those things which may have been alleged on both sides.

NINE QUESTIONS

Exhibited, by the Deputies of the Synod, to Their Lordships the Curators of the University of Leyden, for the Purpose of Obtaining an Answer to each of them from the Professors of Divinity; and the Replies which James Arminius Gave to them, in November, 1605. With Other Nine Opposite Questions

THE NINE QUESTIONS...AND NINE OPPOSITE QUESTIONS

I. Which is first, Election, or Faith Truly Foreseen, so that God elected his people according to faith foreseen?

I. Is the decree "for bestowing Faith on any one," previous to that by which is appointed "the Necessity of Faith to salvation?"

ANSWER TO THIS QUESTION

The equivocation in the word "Election," makes it impossible to answer this question in any other manner, than by distinction. If therefore "Election" denotes "the decree which is according to election concerning the justification and salvation of believers." I say Election is prior to Faith, as being that by which Faith is appointed as the means of obtaining salvation. But if it signifies "the decree by which God determines to bestow salvation on some one," then Faith foreseen is prior to Election. For as believers alone are saved, so only believers are predestinated to salvation. But the Scriptures know no Election, by which God precisely and absolutely has determined to save anyone without having first considered him as a believer. For such an Election would be at variance with the decree by which he hath determined to save none but believers.

QUESTION AND..... QUESTION REVERSED

II. If it be said, "that God, by his eternal decree, has determined and governs all things and every thing, even the depraved wills of men, to appointed good ends," does it follow from this, that God is the author of sin?

II. Is "to determine or direct all things and every thing, even the depraved wills of men, to appointed good ends," the same thing as "to determine that man be made corrupt, by which a way may be opened for executing God's absolute decree concerning damning some men through wrath, and saving others through mercy?"

ANSWER TO THIS QUESTION

Sin is the transgression of the law; therefore, God will be the author of sin, if He cause any man to transgress the law. This is done by denying or taking away what is necessary for fulfilling the law, or by impelling men to sin. But if this "determination" be that of a will which is already depraved, since it does not signify the denying or the removing of grace nor a corrupt impelling to sin, it follows, that the consequence of this cannot be that God is the author of sin. But if this "determination" denote the decree of God by which He resolved that the will should become depraved, and that man should commit sin, then it follows from this that God is the author of sin.

QUESTION AND.....QUESTION REVERSED

III. Does original sin, of itself, render man obnoxious to eternal death, even without the addition of any actual sin? Or is the guilt of original sin taken away from all and every one by the benefits of Christ the Mediator?

III. If some men are condemned solely on account of the sin committed by Adam, and others on account of their rejection of the Gospel, are there not two peremptory decrees concerning the damnation of men, and two judgments, one Legal, the other Evangelical?

ANSWER TO THIS QUESTION

Those things which in this question are placed in opposition to each other, easily agree together. For original sin can render man obnoxious to eternal death, and its guilt can be taken away from all men by Christ. Indeed, in order that guilt may be removed, it is necessary that men be previously rendered guilty. But to reply to each part separately: It is perversely said, that "original sin renders a man obnoxious to death," since that sin is the punishment of Adam's actual sin, which punishment is preceded by guilt, that is, an obligation to the punishment denounced by the law. With regard to the second member of the question, it is very easily answered by the distinction of the soliciting, obtaining, and the application of the benefits of Christ. For as a participation of Christ's benefits consists in faith alone, it follows that, if among these benefits "deliverance from this guilt" be one, believers only are delivered from it, since they are those upon whom the wrath of God does not abide.

QUESTION AND.....QUESTION REVERSED

IV. Are the works of the unregenerate, which proceed from the powers of nature, so pleasing to God, as to induce Him on account of them to confer supernatural and saving grace on those who perform them?

IV. Are a serious consciousness of sin, and an initial fear so pleasing to God, that by them He is induced to forgive sins, and to create a filial fear?

ANSWER TO THIS QUESTION

Christ says, "To him that hath shall be given, and from him that hath not shall be taken away even that which he hath." Not, indeed, because such is the worthiness and the excellence of the use of any blessing conferred by God, either according to nature or to grace, that God should be moved by its merits to confer greater benefits; but, because such are the benignity and liberality of God, that, though these works are unworthy, yet He rewards them with a larger blessing. Therefore, as the word "pleasing" admits of two meanings, we can reply to the question proposed in two ways - - either affirmatively, if that word be viewed as signifying "to please," "to find favour in his eyes," and "to obtain complacency for itself;" or negatively if "placeo" be received for that which it also signifies, "to please by its own excellence." Yet it might be said, that good works are rewarded, in a moral view, not so much through the powers of nature, as by some operation in them of the Holy Spirit.

QUESTION AND.....QUESTION REVERSED

V. Can God now, in his own right, require faith from fallen man in Christ, which he cannot have of himself? But does God bestow on all and every one, to whom the Gospel is preached, sufficient grace by which they may believe, if they will?

V. Can God require that man to believe in Jesus Christ, for whom He has determined by an absolute decree that Christ should not die, and to whom by the same decree He has determined to refuse the grace necessary for believing?

ANSWER TO THIS QUESTION

The parts of this question are not opposed to each other; on the contrary, they are at the most perfect agreement. So that the latter clause may be considered the rendering of a reason, why God may require from fallen man faith in Christ, which he cannot have of himself. For God may require this, since he has determined to bestow on man sufficient grace by which he may believe. Perhaps, therefore, the question may be thus corrected: "Can God, now, in his own right, demand from fallen man faith in Christ, which he cannot have of himself, though God neither bestows on him, nor is ready to bestow, sufficient grace by which he may believe?" This question will be answered by a direct negative. God cannot by any right demand from fallen man faith in Christ, which he cannot have of himself, except God has either bestowed, or is ready to bestow, sufficient grace by which he may believe if he will. Nor do I perceive what is false in that reply, or to what heresy it has affinity. It has no alliance with the Pelagian heresy: for Pelagius maintained, that with the exception of the preaching of the Gospel, no internal grace is required to produce faith in the minds of men. But what is of more consequence, this reply is not opposed to St. Augustine's doctrine of Predestination; "yet this doctrine of his, we do not account it necessary to establish," as Innocent, the Roman Pontiff, has observed.

VI. Is justifying faith the effect and the mere gift of God alone, who calls, illuminates, and reforms the will? and is it peculiar to the elect alone from all eternity?

VI. Can that be called a mere gift which, though offered by the pure liberality of Him who makes the offer, is still capable of being rejected by him to whom it is offered? But does a voluntary acceptance render it unworthy of the name of a gift? It may likewise be asked, "Is faith bestowed on these who are to be saved? Or is salvation bestowed on those who have faith?" Or can both these questions be answered affirmatively in a different respect? If they can, how is it then that there is not in those decrees a circle, in which nothing is first and nothing last?

ANSWER TO THIS QUESTION

A double question requires a double answer. (1.) To the first I reply, Faith is the effect of God illuminating the mind and sealing the heart, and it is his mere gift. (2.) To the second I answer, by making a distinction in the word Election. If it be understood as signifying Election to salvation; since this, according to the scriptures, is the election of believers, it cannot be said, "Faith is bestowed on the elect, or on those who are to be saved," but that "believers are elected and saved." But if it be received for the decree by which God determines variously to administer the means necessary to salvation; in this sense I say that Faith is the gift of God, which is conferred on those only whom He hath chosen to this, that they may hear the word of God, and be made partakers of the Holy Spirit.

QUESTION AND.....QUESTION REVERSED

VII. May every one who is a true believer be assured in this life of his individual salvation; and is it his duty to have this assurance?

VII. Does justifying faith precede, in the order of nature, remission of sins, or does it not? And can any man be bound to any other faith than that which justifies?

ANSWER TO THIS QUESTION

Since God promises eternal life to all who believe in Christ, it is impossible for him who believes, and who knows that he believes, to doubt of his own salvation, unless he doubts of this willingness of God [to perform his promise.] But God does not require him to be better assured of his individual salvation as a duty which must be performed to himself or to Christ; but it is a consequence of that promise, by which God engages to bestow eternal life on him who believes.

QUESTION AND.....QUESTION REVERSED

VIII. May true believers and elect persons entirely lose faith for a season?

VIII. May any man who has faith and retains it, arrive at such a moment, as, if he were then to die, he would be damned?

ANSWER TO THIS QUESTION

Since Election to salvation comprehends within its limits not only Faith, but likewise perseverance in Faith; and since St. Augustine says, "God has chosen to salvation those who he sees will afterwards believe by the aid of his preventing or preceding grace, and who will persevere by the aid of his subsequent or following grace; "believers and the elect are not correctly taken for the same persons. Omitting, therefore, all notice of the word "Election," I reply, believers are sometimes so circumstanced, as not to produce, for a season, any effect of true faith, not even the actual apprehension of grace and the promises of God, nor confidence or trust in God and Christ; yet this is the very thing which is necessary to obtain salvation. But the apostle says, concerning faith, in reference to its being a quality and a capability of believing, "some, having cast away a good conscience concerning faith, have made shipwreck."

QUESTION AND.....QUESTION REVERSED

IX. Can believers under the grace of the New Covenant, perfectly observe the law of God in this life?

IX. May God, or may He not, require of those who are partakers of the New Covenant, that the flesh do not lust against the Spirit, as a duty corresponding with the grace of that covenant?

ANSWER TO THIS QUESTION

The performance of the law is to be estimated according to the mind of Him who requires it to be observed. The answer will be two-fold, since He either wills it to be rigidly observed in the highest degree of perfection, or only according to epieikeian clemency; that is, if he require this according to clemency, and if the strength or powers which he confers be proportionate to the demand. (1.) Man cannot perfectly perform such a law of God, if it be considered as to be performed according to rigor. (2.) But if he require it according to clemency, and if the powers conferred be proportionate, (which must be acknowledged, since He requires it according to the evangelical covenant,) the answer is, it can be perfectly observed. But the question about capability is not of such great importance, "provided a man confesses that it is possible to be done by the grace of Christ," as St. Augustine justly observes.

REMARKS ON THE PRECEDING QUESTIONS, AND ON THOSE OPPOSED TO THEM

In reply to some queries which Uytenbogard had addressed to Arminius, concerning these nine questions and their opposites, the latter gave his friend the following explanation, in a letter dated the 31st of January, 160vi,

"I. In answer to the First Question, this is the order of the decrees. (1.) It is my will to save believers. (2.) On this man I will bestow faith and preserve him in it. (3.) I will save this man. For thus does the first of these decrees prescribe, which must necessarily be placed foremost; because, without this, faith is not necessary to salvation, and therefore no necessity exists to administer the means for faith. But to this is directly opposed the opinion which asserts, that faith is bestowed on him on whom God had previously willed to bestow salvation. For, in this case, it would be his will to save one who did not believe. All that has been said about the difference of the decree and its execution, is futile; as if, in fact, God willed salvation to any one prior to faith, and yet not to bestow salvation on any others than believers. For, beside the consistent agreement of these, [the decree and its execution,] it is certain that God cannot will to bestow that which, on account of his previous decree, He cannot bestow. As therefore faith is, in a general manner, placed before salvation by the first decree; so it must, specially and particularly, be placed before the salvation of this and that man, even in the special decree which has the subsequent execution.

"III. To the Third Question I shall in preference oppose the following: Has God determined peremptorily to act with some men according to the strict rigor of the law, as He did with the fallen angels, and to act with others according to the grace of the Gospel? If they deny this, I have what I wish. But if they affirm it, such a sentiment must be overwhelmed with absurdities; because in such a case God would have acted towards many men with greater severity, than towards the fallen angels, who, as being creatures purely spiritual, each sinned of himself, through his own wickedness without persuasion from any one.

"IV. They will not be able to deny my Fourth opposite Question. For remission is promised to those who confess their sins; and the fear is called initial in reference to the filial fear which follows. If they acknowledge it, but say, Yet God is not induced by them;' I will then command them to erase the same word out of their interrogatory, and in a better form to enunciate their own opinion.

"V. They will not consider it their duty entirely to deny my Fifth opposing Question. If they affirm it, they will declare a falsehood, and will incur the ill opinion of all prudent persons, even of those who are weak. Let them therefore search out what they may place as an intermediate postulate between theirs and mine, and I will then show that it co-incides either with their postulate or with mine.

"VI. I have placed two questions in opposition to the Sixth, because their question is also a double one. On the First of them you require no observation. About the Second I have said, for the sake of explanation, that it is a circle, in which nothing is first and nothing last,' but in every part of it a beginning and an end are found--which cannot, without absurdity, have place in the decrees of God. I ask, has God determined to bestow salvation on those who believe, or to bestow faith on those who are to be saved? If both of these be asserted, I ask, which of them is the first, and which the last? They will reply, neither; and it is then a circle. If they affirm the latter, that God has determined to bestow faith on those who are to be saved; I will prove, that He has determined to bestow salvation on those who believe, and shall then have formed a circle, notwithstanding their unwillingness. If they adduce the different respect, I will endeavour to confute it; which cannot be a work of much difficulty in so very plain a matter.

"VII. In the Seventh opposite Question, I had regard to the expression, is it his duty? for about its possibility there is no contention. But justifying faith is not that by which I believe that my sins are remitted; for thus the same thing will be the object and the effect of justifying faith. By this [justifying faith] I obtain remission of sins, therefore it precedes the other object; [the remission of sins;] and no one can believe that his sins are remitted, unless he knows that he believes by a justifying faith. For this reason, also, no one can believe that his future sins will likewise be remitted, unless he knows that he will believe to the end. For sins are forgiven to him who believes, and only after they have been committed; wherefore the promise of forgiveness, which is that of the New Testament, must be considered as depending on a condition stipulated by God, that is FAITH, without which there is no covenant.

"VIII. With respect to the Eighth Question, let a distinction be made between Faith as it is a quality or habit, and between the same as it is an art. Actual believing justifies, or the act of believing is imputed for righteousness. Because God requires actual faith; for our capability to perform which, He infuses that which is habitual. Therefore, as actual faith does not consist with moral sin, he who falls into mortal sin may be damned. But it is possible for a believer to fall into mortal sin, of which David is seen as an instance Therefore, he may fall at such a moment as, if he were then to die, he would be damned. If our heart condemn us not, then have we confidence toward God.' Therefore, if it does condemn us, we have no confidence, we cannot have any; because God is greater than our heart, and knoweth all things.' What is said about the impossibility of this event, because, God has determined not to take such persons out of the world at that moment, conduces nothing in favour of their hypothesis. For this is opposed to final destruction, not to temporary, and to their total destruction for a season, which is the subject of their Eighth Question.

"IX. If it be replied to my Ninth opposing Question, that, in the covenant of grace, God requires a duty which is impossible to man; they will be forced to confess, that, in addition to this covenant, another is necessary, according to which God pardons a duty not performed according to that covenant of grace; as it was necessary that there should be another covenant, by which God might pardon a duty not performed according to the legal covenant. And thus shall we proceed on ad infinitum. At length we must arrive at the point from which we can say, God save sinners, of his infinite mercy, which is limited by no conditions prescribed by his equity. This seems to be an expression which will be entirely conformable to the whole doctrine of those who urge absolute predestination, For, since wrath and mercy are opposed to each other, as wrath is infinite, may not mercy too, be infinite? According to their doctrine, whatever they oppose to the contrary, wrath makes men sinners, that it may have those whom it can punish. But they expressly say, mercy makes men believers by an omnipotent force, and preserves them from the possibility of falling, that it may have those whom it can save. But, as Nicasius Van der Schuer says, if God could make a sinner, that He might have one whom He could punish; He could also punish without sin; therefore He could likewise mercifully save without faith. And as Wrath willed to have a just title for damnation, through the intervention of sin, so it became Mercy to save, without the intervention of any duty, that it might be manifest that the whole is of mercy without the semblance of justice. I say, without the semblance of justice; because it begets faith by an irresistible force, and by an irresistible force it causes man to continue in faith to the end, and thus necessarily to be saved, according to the decree, he that believes and perseveres, shall be saved This being laid down, all equity is excluded, as well from the decree of predestination to salvation, as from that of predestination to death. These objections, I am conscientiously of opinion, may, without calumny, be made to their sentiments; and I am prepared to maintain this very thing against any patron whatsoever of those sentiments. For they do not extricate themselves when they say, that man spontaneously sins, and believes by a spontaneous motion. For that which is spontaneous, and that which is natural, are not in opposition. And that which is spontaneous coincides with that which is absolutely necessary; as, a stone is moved downwards; a beast eats, and propagates its species; man loves that which is good for himself. But all excuses terminate in this spontaneous matter."

The passage immediately subsequent to this, is the one which I have quoted in pages 179, 180 of the First Volume of these Works, respecting the two sick persons who were desirous of obtaining an assurance of the Divine Favour, and respecting the very important distinction to be observed between a faith which is merely historical, and that by which a sinner is justified, a distinction, the neglect of which has, in every age of the Church, been a prolific source of error among the professors of our common Christianity.

Public Disputations James Arminius, D.D.

TWENTY-FIVE PUBLIC DISPUTATIONS

The Authority & Certainty Of The Sacred Scriptures
Sufficiency & Perfection Of Scripture Vs. Tradition
Sufficiency & Perfection Of Scriptures Vs. Human Traditions
On The Nature Of God
The Person Of The Father & The Son
The Holy Spirit
The First Sin Of The First Man
On Actual Sins
The Righteousness Of God's Providence Concerning Evil
The Righteousness Of God's Providence Concerning Evil
The Free Will Of Man And Its Powers
The Law Of God
The Comparison Of The Law & The Gospel
The Offices Of Our Lord Jesus Christ
Divine Predestination
The Vocation Of Men To Salvation
On Repentance
The Church And Its Head
The Justification Of Man Before God
Christian Liberty
The Roman Pontiff, & His Principal Titles
Alleged Secession Of All Protestant Churches
On Idolatry
The Invocation Of Saints
On Magistracy

DEDICATION

To those most honourable and Prudent Gentlemen, the Burgomaster, Aldermen, and Sheriffs, who are the very Worthy Magistrates of the Famous City of Leyden, and our most Revered Lords and Patrons.

Most Prudent and honourable Gentlemen,

It is now eight years since our reverend father, who lately died in the Lord, was, by your authority and command, and by that of the most noble the Curators, summoned to this illustrious University, from the very flourishing Church of Amsterdam, to which he had devoted his pastoral labours for fifteen years, and was called to fill the vacant situation of Doctor Francis Junius, of pious memory, who was then recently deceased. We, his nine orphan children, the three youngest of whom have been born in this city, removed here at the same time with our mother, who is at present plunged in the deepest affliction. From that period our ever-to-be honoured father had no higher object than that of bestowing the whole of his time, industry and endeavours, in promoting the interests of your University, and in strictly discharging his functions with as much fidelity as accorded with his abilities and his duty. We call upon your honours as competent witnesses to this, our testimony, respecting his fidelity and diligence, because he exercised these virtues under your immediate inspection, for the space of six years; and the truth of our declaration can be no secret to those persons who, while he was in the act of performing his duty to the University, were themselves either not far from the scene of action, or openly beheld and admired his daily and unwearied labours in public and private. With regard to his uncommon industry and accurate skill in communicating instruction, which gifts had been bestowed on him by Almighty God, in his ineffable liberality, independently of any merits either on his part or on ours, you always approved of these qualities by your honourable suffrages, and, on all occasions when you considered it either necessary or expedient, you extolled his genius. You also exhibited to him the most indubitable and lucid expressions not only of your very laudable opinion of his talents, but likewise of your consequent intimate affections for him, during the whole period in which he devoted his labours to your honourable service. So that he scarcely ever felt a desire for any thing which he did not obtain.

But the best testimony to this character of our father is that given to him, by those persons who either assiduously attended his daily lectures in immense numbers, and several of whom are now performing most important services to the Churches; or by those who resorted, often from places at a great distance, to hear his disputations, and all of whom admired and abundantly eulogized his acute and penetrating genius, but especially his incredible acquaintance with the Holy Scriptures, on which alone he was almost constantly meditating, and to the study of which he had devoted the choicest years of his life. These persons were also continually and pertinaciously importunate that the Theses which had been proposed for disputation under him, and which had been written out and placed in order by himself, should be published without the least delay, and brought forth to the light of men, for the benefit of the public, and especially of those who were far removed from Leyden. To their pressing solicitations, after much reluctance on the part of our father, he was at length induced to yield; and he put to press and published those Theses which were extant in his class of Public Disputations, and which, after being written out by himself in so many words, had been appointed, and soon afterwards disputed and discussed under him [as Moderator.] That collection is now republished, with the sole addition of one Thesis on Repentance.

But, that we may make the studies and labours of our most excellent father still better known to you than they are, most honourable and prudent gentlemen, and to foreigners, as well to those whose residence is nearer to us, we now publish those Theses likewise which he proposed for disputation in his own house, at moments of leisure and on extraordinary occasions; for he had devoted himself entirely to the promotion of the welfare of the students. They were proposed as subjects in the last class of his Private Disputations, and were also written out and composed by himself, at the very earnest intreaty of those youthful scholars. Indeed, we publish these Theses in preference to any others; for having already served the purposes of his private disputations, they may now afford abundant testimony to the fidelity and diligence of our father in instructing and adorning the candidates for holy orders. Beside the matter or subject on which he treated with so much faithfulness and accuracy, our excellent father, who was a severe judge of method, thought that he would exhibit the order which ought to be observed in compiling a correct system of Theology. Such a plan he had often and long revolved in his mind; and for this purpose had perused, with very great care, almost all the Synopses or large Treatises of Divinity that had been published. He was in some measure induced to give a representation of this scheme in the following Theses proposed for private disputation. Let the learned decide upon the skill with which he has sketched this outline, which it was his wish to display as an attempt at a Synopsis, for the sake of exercise. O, that it had been the will of Almighty God, to have enabled him to finish, as he had desired, this body of Theological Theses which he was forced to leave incomplete. For it is believed, that upwards of twenty Theses are still wanting to crown the undertaking. By an untimely death, which is a source of the deepest affliction to us, as well as to all good men, his design was frustrated; though the consummation of it would, beyond any thing else in this life, have been an object of the fondest gratification to us, his sorrowing offspring.

But since it has been the pleasure of our gracious God, against whom it does not become us frowardly to contend, to call our father from this miserable valley of tears to his own celestial mansion; we wish that he had obtained [among survivors] some equitable and candid judges of his labourious exertions and innocency; and that it had been possible for him, even by death, to escape from the rancorous teeth of calumny, which, in conformity to the precept and the example of Jesus Christ our only saviour, he endured, as long as his life was spared, without any attempt to render railing for railing, yet with such consummate patience, as almost excited the indignation of his friends against him. We wish also that a certain person had not expressed doubts respecting the eternal salvation of our father, whom we with many others openly beheld, (as we here do testify,) in a manner the most placid, surrendering up his soul to God, like one that was falling asleep, amidst unceasing and most ardent prayers, and confessing his own wretchedness and weakness, but at the same time extolling that only saving grace which shines forth upon those who believe in Jesus Christ, the Author of our salvation. We repeat our wishes, that there had not been a person who uttered serious doubts about the eternal salvation of our father. Far be it from any of us to condemn him whom God has absolved, and for whom Jesus Christ testifies, that he came into the world, and suffered death.

Alas! were we not already sufficiently unhappy in having lost one of our parents, while we are all of an age comparatively tender, the eldest of us not being yet quite seventeen years old! But may our God forbid, that they who deliver their souls into his merciful hands in the name of Jesus Christ alone, should not be made partakers of eternal salvation, or should be disappointed of their hopes of a life of blessedness! May he rather grant unto all of us, that, faithfully and constantly treading in the footsteps of our beloved father, and being active in the pursuit of truth and piety, with integrity and sincerity of mind, we may approve our lives and all our studies to God and to all good men, as highly as our revered parent, we humbly hope, approved himself and all his concerns to your mightinesses, as long as he lived. Of the great esteem in which you held him, you have afforded abundant proofs, in those innumerable and never sufficiently to-be- recounted benefits which he received from you while he lived. But stronger evidence of this you gave immediately after his decease, in the benefits which you have bestowed on our dearest mother, and on each of us their children, and which you most liberally continue to this day. O, that the time may at length arrive in which we may be enabled to requite you for these, your numberless acts of kindness to us. May God assist us thus to repay you.

But, in the mean time, that some token of a grateful mind towards your mightinesses may be extant on our part, at the earliest opportunity we bring forth from the library of our deceased parent, under the auspices of your honourable names, this rich and costly casket; and we will afterwards draw out of the same treasury, each in its due order and time, not a few other things of the same, or of a different kind which he has left in our possession, provided those which we now offer shall meet with a suitable reception from the students of Theology. But we are deeply conscious, that this offering of ours is contemptible, when placed in competition with your kindness towards us. Of all persons we should be the most ungrateful, if we did not make this acknowledgment; and still more so, if we did not confess that this is a present from our deceased parent, rather than from us. Should it hereafter be seen, that our revered father has bequeathed to us, as his heirs, his industry, piety and virtue, (which may God of his infinite mercy grant,) as he has already made us the inheritors of this production and of the other fruits of his studies; we will use our utmost endeavours never to be found deficient in our duty, but to propose to ourselves throughout the whole of our future lives, by all the means in our power, to gain the approbation of your mightinesses, and to prove ourselves always grateful to you.

May Almighty God long preserve you in safety, and render you still propitious to us. May he in the most bountiful manner crown your government with every blessing from above! So pray Your mightinesses' most devoted servants, the seven sons of James Arminius, a native of Oudewater, in our own names, and in the names of our two sisters, HERMAN, PETER, JOHN, LAURENCE, ARMINUS, JAMES, WILLIAM, DANIEL.

DISPUTATION 1 - ON THE AUTHORITY AND CERTAINTY OF THE SACRED SCRIPTURES

RESPONDENT: BERNARD VESUKIUS

I. The authority of Scripture is nothing else but the worthiness according to which it merits (1.) CREDENCE, as being true in words and true in significations, whether it simply declares anything; or also promises and threatens; and (2.) as a superior, it merits OBEDIENCE through the credence given to it, when it either commands or prohibits anything. Concerning this authority two questions arise, (i.) Whence does it belong to Scripture? (ii.) Whence is it evident, or can be rendered evident to men, that this authority appertains to Scripture? These two questions shall be discussed in their proper order. (1 Tim. i. 15; 2 Pet. i. 19; John v. 39; Heb. vi. 18. Rom. i. 5; 2 Cor. x. 5, 6; xiii, 3; xii, 12; Gal. i. 1, 12, 13, &c.)

II. The authority of any word or writing whatsoever depends upon its author, as the word "authority" indicates; and it is just as great as the veracity and the power, that is, the auqenti<a of the author. But God is of infallible veracity, and is neither capable of deceiving nor of being deceived; and of irrefragable power, that is, supreme over the creatures. If, therefore, He is the Author of Scripture, its authority is totally dependent on Him alone. (i.) Totally, because He is the all sufficient Author, all-true and all-powerful. (ii.) On Him alone, because He has no associate either in the truth of what he says, or in the power of his right. For all veracity and power in the creature proceed from him; and into his veracity and power are resolved all faith and obedience, as into the First Cause and the Ultimate Boundary. (Gal.. iii, 8, 9; 1 John v. 9; Rom. iii. 4; Tit. i. 2; Psalm i. 1-23; Gal. i. 1, 7, 8; John v. 34, 36; Rom. xi. 34-36; xiii, 1.)

III. This is proved by many arguments dispersed throughout the Scripture. (1.) From the inscriptions of most of the prophetical books and of the apostolical epistles, which run thus, "The word of the Lord that came to Hosea, to Joe], to Amos," &c. "Paul, Peter, James, &c., a servant of God and an apostle of Jesus Christ." (Hosea, Joel, Amos; Rom. i. 1; James i. 1; 1 Pet. i. 1.) (2.) From the introductions to many of the prophecies: "Thus saith the Lord," "That which I have received of the Lord, I have also delivered unto you." (Exod. v. 1; 1 Cor. xi. 23.) (3.) From the petitions, on the part of the ambassadors of God and of Christ, for Divine assistance, and from the promise of it which is given by God and Christ, such aid being necessary and sufficient to obtain authority for what was to be spoken. (Exod. iv. 1; Acts iv. 29, 30; Mark xvi. 17, 20.) (4.) From the method used by God himself, who, when about to deliver his law, introduced it thus: "I am the Lord thy God!" And who, when in the act of establishing the authority of his Son, said, "This is my beloved Son, hear ye Him." (Exod. xx. 1;

Matt. xvii. 5.) This is acknowledged by the general consent of mankind. Minos, Numa, Lycurgus and Solon, were fully aware of it; for, to give some validity to their laws, they referred them to Gods or Goddesses, as the real authors.

IV. When this authority is once known, it binds the consciences of all those to whom the discourse or the writing is addressed or directed, to accept of it in a becoming manner. But whoever they be that receive it as if delivered by God, that approve of it, publish, preach, interpret and expound it, that also distinguish and discriminate it from words or writings which are supposititious and adulterated; these persons add not a tittle of authority to the sayings or writings, because their entire authority, whether contemplated separately or conjointly, is only that of mortal men; and things Divine neither need confirmation, nor indeed can receive it, from those which are human. But this whole employment of approving, preaching, explaining and discriminating, even when it is discharged by the Church Universal, is only an attestation by which she declares, that she holds and acknowledges these words or writings, and these alone, as Divine. (John xv. 22, 24; viii, 24; Gal. i. 8, 9; Ephes. ii. 20; Rev. xxi. 14; John i. 6, 7; v, 33-36; 1 Thess. ii. 13.)

V. Therefore, not only false, but likewise implying a contradiction, foolish and blasphemous, are such expressions as the following, employed by Popish writers: "The Church is of greater antiquity than the Scriptures; and they are not authentic except by the authority of the Church." (ECCL Enchir. de Ecclesiastes) "All the authority which is now given to the Scriptures, is necessarily dependent on that of the Church." (PIGHIUS de Hierar. Eecles. lib. 2, c. 2.) "The Scriptures would possess no more validity than the Fables of Aesop, or any other kind of writing whatever, unless we believed the testimony of the Church." (HOSIUS de Author. Script. lib. 3.) But that "the Church is of greater antiquity than the Scriptures," is an argument which labours under a falsity in the antecedent and under a defective inference. For the Scriptures, both with regard to their significations and their expressions, are more ancient than the Church; and this former Church is bound to receive the latter sayings and writings of Isaiah, Jeremiah, &c., of Paul, Peter, &c., as soon as their Divine verity has been demonstrated by sufficient arguments according to the judgment of God. (Matt. xvi. 18; 1 Cor. iii. 9, 10.)

VI. But by the very arguments by which the Scriptures are Divine, they are also [proved to be] Canonical, from the method and end of their composition, as containing the rule of our faith, charity, hope, and of the whole of our living. For they are given for doctrine, for reproof, for instruction, for correction, and for consolation; that is, that they may be the rule of truth and falsehood to our understanding, of good and evil to our affections, either to do and to omit, or to have and to want. (Deut. xxvii. 26; Psalm cxix. 105,106; Rom. x. 8, 17; Matt. xxii. 37-40; 2 Tim. iii. 16; Rom. xv. 4.) For as they are Divine because given by God, not because they are "received from men;" so they are canonical, and are so called in an active sense, because they prescribe a Canon or rule, and not passively, because they are reckoned for a Canon, or because they are taken into the Canon. So far indeed is the Church from rendering them authentic or canonical, that no assemblage or congregation of men can come under the name of a Church, unless they account the Scriptures authentic and canonical with regard to the sum or substance of the Law and Gospel. (Gal. vi. 16; 1 Tim. vi. 3, 4; Rom. xvi. 17; x, 8-10, 14-17.)

VII. The Second Question is, How can a persuasion be wrought in men, that these Scriptures are Divine? For the application of this question some things must be premised, which may free the discussion from equivocations, and may render it more easy. (1.) A distinction must be drawn between Scripture, (which, as a sign, consists of a word and of the writing of that word,) and the sense or meaning of Scripture; because it is not equally important which of the two is necessary to be known and believed, since it is Scripture on account of its meanings, and because there is a difference in the method of proof by which Divinity is ascribed to the writing itself and to its significations. (2.) A distinction must likewise be drawn between the primary cause of Scripture, and the instrumental causes; lest it be thought, that the same necessity exists for believing some book of Scripture to have been written by this or that particular amanuensis, as there is for believing it to have proceeded from God. (3.) The ratio of those meanings is dissimilar, since some of them are simply necessary to salvation, as containing the foundation and sum of religion; while others are connected with the former in no other way, than by a certain relation of explanation, proof, and amplification. (John viii. 24; v, 39, 46, 36; 1 Cor. xii. 3. 2 Corinthians ii. 4, 5; iii, 7-9; Matt. x. 20; 2 Cor. iii. 11, 12; Phil. iii. 15, 16; Col. ii. 16, 19.)

VIII. (4.) The persuasion of faith must be distinguished from the certainty of vision, lest a man, instead of seeking here for faith which is sufficiently powerful to prevail against temptations, should require certainty which is obnoxious to no temptation. (5.) A difference must be made between implicit faith by which this Scripture without any understanding of its significations is believed to be Divine, and explicit faith which consists of some knowledge of the meanings, particularly of those which are necessary. And this historical knowledge, which has only asfaleian mental security, [or human certainty, Luke i. 4,] comes to be distinguished from saving knowledge, which also contains wlhroforian full assurance and wepoiqhsin confidence, on which the conscience reposes. This distinction must be made, that a correct judgment may be formed of those arguments which are necessary and sufficient for producing each of these kinds of faith. (6.) A difference must also be made between those arguments which are worthy of God, and those which human vanity may require. And such arguments must not here be demanded as cannot fail to persuade every one; since many persons denied all credence to Christ himself, though he bore testimony to his own doctrine by so many signs and wonders, virtues and distributions of the Holy Ghost. (7.) The external light, derived from arguments which are employed to effect suasion, must be distinguished from the internal light of the Holy Spirit bearing his own testimony; lest that which properly belongs to the latter, as the seal and the earnest or pledge of our faith, should be ascribed to the strength of arguments and to the veracity of external testimonies. (1 Cor. xiii. 9, 12; Gen. xv. 6, 8, with Rom. iv. 19-21; Judges vi. 36- 39; Heb. xi. 32, 33; John iii. 2, 10; James ii. 19; John v. 32-36; Matt. xiii. 2; Heb. vi. 11; x, 22; Ephes. iii. 12; Matt. xii. 38, 39; xvi, 1; Luke xvi. 30, 31; Matt. xxvii. 42; John xii. 37; Luke xxiv. 27, 44, 45; 2 Cor. i. 22; Ephes. i. 13, 14; John iv. 42.)

IX. (8.) A distinction must be drawn between (i.) those who heard God or Christ speaking to them Himself, or addressing them through angels, prophets, or apostles, and who first received the sacred books; and (ii.) those who, as their successors, have the Scriptures through their delivery. (Judges ii. 7, 10; Heb. ii. 3; John xx. 29.) For the former of these classes, miracles and the actual fulfillment of predictions, which occurred under their own observations, were capable of imparting credibility to the words and writing. But to the latter class, the narration, both of the doctrine, and of the arguments employed for its confirmation, is proposed in the Scriptures, and must be strengthened by its own arguments. (Isa. xliv. 7, 8; 1 Cor. xiv, XXII.) (9.)

A distinction may indeed be made between the truth of Scripture and its Divinity, that progress may be gradually made through a belief of the former to a belief in the latter. But these two can never be disparted; because, if the Scriptures be true, they are of necessity Divine. (John iv. 39- 42; 1 Pet. i. 21.) (10.) Lastly. We must here reflect, that the secret things of God, and the doctrine of Christ in reference to its being from God, are revealed to little children, to the humble, to those who fear God, and to those who are desirous to do the will of the Father; (Matt. xi. 25; James iv. 6; Psalm xxv. 14; John vii. 17; 1 Cor. i. 20, 27;) and that, on the contrary, to the wise men of the world, to the proud, to those who reject the counsel of God against themselves and judge themselves unworthy of everlasting life, to foolish and perverse men, and to those who resist the Holy Ghost, the mystery of God and the Gospel of Christ are hidden and continue unrevealed; nay, to such persons they are a stumbling-block and foolishness, while they are in themselves the power and the wisdom of God. (Luke vii. 30; Acts xiii. 46; vii, 51; 2 Cor. iv. 3, 4; 1 Cor. i. 23, 24.)

X. These remarks being premised, let us see how we are or can be persuaded into a belief that the Scriptures of the Old and of the New Testament are Divine, at least with regard to their essentials, that is, the sum or substance of the Law and Gospel, without faith in which, salvation can have no existence. Three things principally serve to produce this persuasion. (i.) The external testimony of men. (ii.) The arguments contained in the Scriptures themselves. (iii.) And the internal witness of God. The first of these, by procuring, after the manner of men, esteem and reverence to the Scriptures, prepares [or makes a way for] faith which is resolved into the two latter that are truly Divine, and, through them, is fully completed.

XI. 1. In adverting to human testimony, we shall omit all enemies, also the Mahometans who have embraced the dregs of a religion which is compounded of a corruption of Judaism, Christianity and Paganism. But the testimony of those who acknowledge the Scriptures is twofold. That of the Jews, who testify concerning the doctrine and the books of the Old Testament; and that of Christians who bear witness to those of the whole body of Scripture. (1.) Two circumstances add strength to the testimony of the Jews. (i.) The constancy of their profession in the very depths of misery, when, by the mere denial of it, they might be made partakers of liberty and of worldly possessions. (ii.) Their hatred of the Christian religion, which transcribes its own origin, increase, and establishment from a good part of the Scriptures of the Old Testament, and with so much confidence as to be prepared to stand and fall by their evidence and judgment alone. (Acts xxvi. 22; 9, 2 Pet. i. 19, 20; Acts xvii. 11.) (2.) The testimony of Christians. distinguished by the same mark of constancy, (Rev. vi. 9; xii, 11,) we will consider in three particulars: (i.) That of the Church Universal, which, from her own foundation to the present age, having professed the Christian as a Divine religion, testifies that her religion is contained in these books, and that they have proceeded from God. (ii.) That of each of the primitive Churches, which, being founded by the apostles, first received not only the whole of the Old Testament, but likewise the Epistles which were addressed either to them, to their pastors, or at least to men who were well known, and who delivered them by the same title to their successors and to other Churches. (Col. iv. 16.) (iii.) That of the Representative Church, as it is called, consisting of pastors and teachers, who, possessing skill in languages and in Divine things, pronounce their judgment after having instituted an examination, and confirm it [by arguments] to the flocks that are severally committed to their care. (Ephes. iv. 27.) On reviewing these diviunes, we place the Roman Pontiff below the lowest parochial priest in the Romish Church who may be more learned than his holiness.

XII. 2. The arguments contained in the Scripture are four, and those of the utmost importance. The quality of its doctrines, the majesty of its style, the agreement of its parts, and the efficacy of its doctrine. Each of these, separately considered, possesses much influence; but, when viewed conjointly, they are capable of inducing every one to give credit to them, if he is not blinded by a spirit of obstinacy, and by an opinion preconceived through inveterate habits. The Quality of the Doctrine is proved to be Divine. (1.) By the precepts delivered in these books, which exhibit three marks of Divinity. (i.) The high excellence of the actions prescribed, in self-denial, and in the regulation of the whole life according to godliness. (Matt. xvi. 24, 25; Rom. viii. 12, 13.) (ii.) The wonderful uncommonness of some actions, which amount to folly in the estimation of the natural man; and yet they are prescribed with a fearless confidence. Such as, "Unless thou believest on Jesus, who is crucified and dead, thou shalt be condemned; if thou wilt believe on him, thou shalt be saved." (1 Cor. i. 18, 24; ii, 2, 14; John viii. 24; Rom. x. 9.) (iii.) The manner in which they are required to be performed, that they be done from conscience and charity; if otherwise, they will be adjudged as hypocritical. (Deut. vi. 5; 1 Cor. xiii. 1; James iv. 12; Rom. viii. 5; 1 Pet. ii. 19.) In the first of these three is perceived a sanctity, in the second an omnipotence, and in the third an omniscience, each of which is purely Divine. (2.) By the promises and threatenings, which afford two tokens of Divine worth or validity. (i.) The manifest evidence, that they could have been delivered by no one except by God. (ii.) Their excellent accommodation, which is such that these promises and threatenings cannot possibly prove influential upon the conscience of any man, except upon his who considers the precepts, to which they are subjoined, to be Divine. (3.) The admirable attempering of the justice of God by which he loves righteousness and hates iniquity, and of his equity by which he administers all things, with his mercy in Christ our propitiation. In this, the glory of God shines forth with transcendent luster. (Rom. v. 15.) Three particulars in it are worthy of notice. (i.) That, except through the intervention of a reconciler and mediator, God would not receive into favour the sinner, through love for whom as his own creature he is touched with mercy. (ii.) That his own dearly beloved Son, begotten by Himself and discharging an office of perfect righteousness, God would not admit as a deprecator and intercessor, except when sprinkled with his own blood. (2 Cor. v. 19; Ephes. ii. 12, 16; Heb. viii. 5, 6; ix, 7, 11, 12.) (iii.) That he constituted Christ as a saviour only to those who repent and believe, having excluded the impenitent from all hope of pardon and salvation. (Heb. iii. 8, 19; v, 8, 9; Luke xxiv. 26; Rom. viii. 29.) (4.) A most signal and decisive proof, which serves to demonstrate the necessity and sufficiency of this doctrine, exists in this fact, that Jesus himself did not enter into his glory except through obedience and sufferings, that this was done for believers alone who were to be conformed to him, (Heb. x. 21, 22; iv, 14-16; John xvii. 2, 8,) and that, on being received into Heaven, He was constituted Governor over the house of God, the King of his people, and the dispenser of life eternal.

XIII. The Majesty of Their Style is proved. (1.) By the attributes which the Author of the Scriptures claims for himself; the transcendent elevation of his nature, in his omniscience and omnipotence; (Isa. xliv. 7, 8; xli, 12, 25, 26; Psalm i. 1,) the excellence of his operations, which they claim for Him as the Creator and Governor of all things; the preeminence of power, which they claim for Him as the King of kings and Lord of lords. (2.) By the absence of all "respect of persons" which is not under the influence of favour and hatred, of hope and fear, and by which God declares himself to be the same towards all men, whatever station they may occupy, uttering his commands and prohibitions, his promises and threatenings, to monarchs, (Deut. xviii. 15, 16; 1 Sam. xii. 25,) as well as to the meanest among the people, to whole nations and to single individuals, and even to the rulers of darkness, the princes of this world, Satan and his angels, and thus to the whole universe of his creatures. (3.) By the method which he employs in making a law and in giving it his sanction. It has no other introduction than, "I Jehovah am thy God;" no other conclusion than, "I Jehovah have spoken." "Be strong, for I am with thee; fear not, for I will deliver thee." Either He who speaks, truly claims these attributes for himself, and so his discourse is Divine, (Exod. xx. 2; Josh. i. 9; Isa. xliii. 5; Jer. i. 8; Deut. iv. 5,) or (let no blasphemy adhere to the expression,) it is of all foolish speeches the most foolish. Between these two extremes no medium exists. But in the whole of the Scriptures not a single tittle occurs, which will not remove from them by an invincible argument the charge of folly.

XIV. The Agreement Between Each And Every Part of The Scriptures, prove with sufficient evidence, their Divinity, because such an agreement of its several parts can be ascribed to nothing less than the Divine Spirit. It will be useful for the confirmation of this matter to consider (1.) The immense space of time which was occupied in the inditing of it, from the age of Moses, down to that of St. John, to whom was vouchsafed the last authentic revelation. (Mal. iv. 4; Jer. xxviii. 8; John v. 46.) (2.) The multitude of writers or amanuenses, and of books. (3.) The great distance of the places in which the books were severally written, that tendered it impossible for the authors to confer together. (4.) Lastly and principally, the institution of a comparison between the doctrine of Moses and that of the latter Prophets, as well as between that of the Old and that of the New Testament. The predictions of Moses alone concerning the Messiah, the calling of the Gentiles, and the rejection of the Jews, when compared with the interpretations and with the addition of particular circumstances which are found in the Prophets and the Psalms, will prove that the perfect agreement which exists between the various writers is Divine. (Gen. xlix. 10; Deut. xxxii. 21; Dan. ix. 25, 26; Mal. i. 10, 11; Psalm 2, 22, 110 132; Matt. 1,

2, 24, 27; Luke i. 55, 70; xxiv, 27, 44.) To the Divinity of the agreement between the writings of the Old Testament and those of the New, abundant testimony will be afforded even solely by that sudden, unexpected and miraculously consentaneous accommodation and befitting aptitude of all the predictions respecting the Messiah, the gathering of the Gentiles to Him, the unbelief and rejection of the Jews, and lastly concerning the abrogation which was to be made of the ceremonial law, first by its being fulfilled, and afterwards by its forcible removal. Whether these predictions were foretold in words, or foreshown by types of things, persons, facts and events; their accommodation to the person, the advent, the state, the offices, and the times of Jesus of Nazareth, was consentaneous even to a miracle. (Psalm cxviii. 22, 23; Matt. xxi. 42; Isa. lxv. 1; Acts xi. 18; Psalm xl. 7, 8; Dan. ix. 25, 26.) If the Old Testament alone, or only the New, were now extant, some doubts might be indulged concerning the Divinity of each. But their agreement together excludes all doubt respecting their Divinity, when both of them are thus completely in accordance, since it is impossible for such a perfect agreement to have been the fabrication of an angelic or of a human mind.

XV. Lastly, the Divinity of Scripture is powerfully demonstrated by The Efficacy of Its Doctrine, which we place in two particulars. In the credit or belief which it has obtained in the world, and in the destruction of remaining religions and of the entire kingdom of Satan. Of this destruction two most signal tokens were afforded, in the silencing of the Heathen Oracles, and in the removal of Idols. (1 Tim. iii. 15; Zech. xiii. 2; Zeph. ii. 11; Acts xvi. 16, 17.) This efficacy is recommended, (1.) By the peculiar genius of the doctrine, which, independently of the Divine power which accompanies and assists it, is calculated to repel every one from giving his assent to it, on account of the apparent absurdity in it, and the concupiscence of human passions which is abhorrent to it. For this is the manner in which it speaks: "Unless thou dost believe in Jesus the Crucified, and art prepared to pour out thy life for him, thou shalt lose thy soul." (Isa. liii. 1; 2 Cor. i. 2; 2 Tim. iii. 12.) (2.) By the persons through whom the doctrine was administered, and who, in the estimation of men, were few in number, mean in condition, and full of infirmities; while in God's sight, they were possessed of invincible patience and mildness, which were so conspicuous in Him who was the Prince of all, that He asked some of his familiar disciples who were offended at his doctrine, "Will ye also go away?" (Luke vi. 13; Matt. iv. 18, 19; 2 Cor. 4, xii, 12; 2 Tim. iv, 2; John 6, 67.) (3.) By the multitude, the wisdom, the authority, and the power of the enemies who placed themselves in opposition to this doctrine. Also by their love for the religion of their own country, and their consequent hatred of this novel doctrine, and by the result of both these, in their infuriated and outrageous eagerness to extirpate the Christians and their doctrine. It was opposed by the Roman empire itself nearly three hundred years, during which the rest of the world lent their assistance. This continued opposition was excited by the Jews, nay by Satan himself, who had fixed his throne in that empire. (1 Cor. ii. 8; Acts iv. 27; ix, 2; Matt. x, 1 8-22; John xvi. 2; Ephes. vi. 12; Rev. ii. 10, 13.) (4.) By the infinite multitude of men of every description, nation, age, sex and condition, who have believed this doctrine, and confirmed their belief by enduring intolerable torments even unto death. This cannot be ascribed, except through an ambitious insanity, either to ambition or to fury in such a multitude of persons of various descriptions. (Rev. vi. 9-11.) (5.) By the short time in which, like lightning, it pervaded a great part of the habitable world; so that Paul alone filled all the places between Jerusalem and Illyricum with the Gospel of Christ. (Col. i. 6; Rom. xv. 19.)

XVI. 3. These suasions are of themselves alone sufficient to produce an historical faith, but not that which is saving. To them, therefore, must be added the internal suasion of God by his Holy Spirit, which has its scope of operations, (1.) In the illumination of the mind, that we may prove what is that good, and acceptable, and perfect will of God; that we may knew the things which are freely given to us of God, and that Jesus Christ is the wisdom and the power of God. (1 Cor. iii. 7; Ephes. i. 17, 18; Rom. xii. 9; 1 Cor. ii. 12; i, 24; xii, 3.) (2.) In inscribing the laws of God upon our hearts, which consists of the infusion of a desire and of strength for their performance. (Heb. viii. 10.) (3.) In sealing the promises of God on our hearts; under which term, that by which we are sealed to the day of redemption is called a seal, and an earnest. (2 Cor. i. 22; Ephes. i. 13,14.) In this manner he who inspired the sacred Scriptures into holy men of God, who constituted in the Church, Bishops, Apostles, Prophets, Evangelists, Pastors and Teachers, who put the word of reconciliation into their mouths, is the Author of that faith by which this doctrine is apprehended unto righteousness and eternal salvation. (Acts xx. 28; Ephes. iv. 11; 2 Cor. v. 19; Rom. viii. 16.) Since his testimony is distinct from that of a man's own spirit, and since it is said to be concerning those things which are necessary to salvation, and not concerning words, letters, or writing, the Papists act most perversely in confounding these testimonies, and in requiring through the witness of the Spirit [of God] the distinction between an apocryphal verse, and one that is canonical, though the former may in reality agree with the canonical Scriptures.

XVII. But, that we may comprise in few words the force of these three proofs, we declare, 1. concerning the force of human testimony which ascribes our Scriptures to God, that the author of no composition which ever was published or is now extant can be proved with such lucid evidence as the author of these Scriptures; and that the importance of all other compositions sinks far beneath the dignity of this, not only with regard to the multitude, the wisdom and the integrity of the witnesses, but likewise with regard to the uninterrupted evenness, the constancy and the duration of the testimony. The reason this is, that the religion contained in these Scriptures has been preached to immense numbers and varieties of people, and for a very long period; which circumstance, in itself, contains no small argument of Divinity. For it is most equitable, that religion, which alone is truly Divine, and which, without any respect of nations, it is God's will that men should receive, ought also to be preached generally to all mankind. (Matt. xxviii. 19, 20; Mark xvi. 15; Rom. x. 12-18.)

XVIII. 2. We assert, that the arguments which, contained in the Scriptures, prove the Divinity of the religion prescribed in them, are so full and perfect, that no arguments can be derived for the defense of any religion which are not comprehended in these, and in a more excellent degree. (2 Cor. iv. 2- 6.) They are indeed of such high value that the truth of the Christian religion is established by them as strongly, as it is possible by any other arguments to prove that there is any true religion at all, or that a true one is possible. So that to a man who is desirous of proving, that there is any religion which is true, or that such a religion is possible, no way is more compendious and easy than to do so by these arguments, in preference to any other which can be deduced from general notions. But the most wonderful of all is, that the very thing in the Christian religion which seems to be one of the greatest absurdity, affords the most certain proof of its Divinity, it being allowed to be a very great truth--that this religion has been introduced into the consciences of men by a mild suasion, and not by the power of the sword. (1 Cor. i. 29-xxiv, ; 2 Cor. v. 11; Luke ix. 54, 55.) Of a similar tendency is the argument formerly used by St. Augustine: "If the Christian religion was established by the miracles which are related in the Scriptures, it is true; but if it was not, the greatest of all miracles is, that it has been able to obtain credit without miracles." For the internal suasion of Him who alone can work miracles, ought to stand in the place of miracles outwardly performed, and to be equally potent. (Rev. ii. 17.) And thus the very narration, contained in these books, of the miracles which were performed in the early ages in proof of the doctrine, is now, through a most beautiful vicissitude of circumstances, proved to be true by the Divinity of the doctrine when subjected to examination.

XIX. Although the inward witness of the Holy Spirit is known to him alone to whom it is communicated, yet, since there is a mutual relation between the veracity of the Testifier, and the truth of the thing which is proved, an examination may be instituted respecting the testimony itself. This is so far from being injurious or displeasing to the Holy Ghost, that by this method His veracity is rendered in all possible directions more eminently conspicuous, as being the Author not only of the internal testimony and the external word, but likewise of the significations concerning which he bears witness to both; on this account also, he has commanded us to "try the spirits whether they be of God," and has added a specimen of such a "trying." (1 John iv. 1, 2.) It will therefore be as easy to confute the man who falsely boasts of having the internal testimony of the Holy Spirit, as to be able to destroy that religion to which he professes himself to be devoted. From this it is apparent, that the inward witness of the Spirit is calculated to impart assurance to him to whom it is communicated, but not to convince any other person. Wherefore those who reckon this among the causes why they account the Scriptures Divine, are foolishly said by the Papists to beg the question, since they never employ it themselves in convincing others.

DISPUTATION 2 - ON THE SUFFICIENCY AND PERFECTION OF THE HOLY SCRIPTURES IN

OPPOSITION TO TRADITIONS RESPONDENT: ABRAHAM VLIET

I. When we ascribe Perfection to the Scriptures of the Old and New Testament, we do not mean by that word, the perfection described by the Apostle in 1 Corinthians xiii. 10; for the latter is peculiar to the life to come, in which "God will be all in all." (1 Cor. xv. 28.) Neither do we understand by it a certain absolute quality which is equally dispersed through the whole body of Scripture and each of its parts, and which cannot be withdrawn from the Scriptures by any man who confesses that they have proceeded from God, their most perfect Author. (Psalm xix. 7-9; Rom. vii. 12.) Nor do we mean such a perfection as may embrace all things generally and severally, of what description soever they are, which have at any time been inspired into "holy men," and published by them to the Church. (2 Tim. iii. 16, 17.) But by this expression we understand a relative Perfection, which, for the sake of a particular purpose, agrees with the Scriptures as with an instrument, and according to which they perfectly comprehend all things that have been, are now, or ever will be necessary for the salvation of the Church.

II. We are compelled, both by the truth of the thing itself, of which we shall hereafter treat, and by a kind of necessity, to establish this perfection of Scripture: because, without this, we shall be forced, for the sake of obtaining entire salvation, to have recourse to other revelations of God, already made, or afterwards to be communicated; but our attempt will prove abortive, unless the Divinity of these additional revelations be established by indubitable arguments. Those [new] revelations which are said to have been already made, have never yet been demonstrated in this manner; and it will be impossible to produce any such demonstrative evidence in support of those which, it is asserted, will afterwards occur.

III. But, that we may be able to establish this perfection of Scripture in a solid manner, and as if from the very foundation, we will take a brief view of the perfection of Divine revelations in general. For, by this means, we shall not only remove the error of those who entertain a different opinion, but shall also expose and shut up the source from which it is derived. We now use the expression, "Divine revelation," for the act of reveling, not for what is revealed; and we say, Divine revelation is internal, which, with the Scriptures themselves, we distinguish by the general term, "inspiration;" and that it is external by means of the enunciation or the inditing of the words spoken or revealed. Perfection, therefore, is withdrawn from the Scriptures, either in these revelations, or in those which preceded them, in the subjoined order and method.

IV. (1.) The perfect inspiration given to the prophets and apostles, who are the administrators of the Scriptures, is denied; and the necessity and frequent occurrence of new revelations after those holy men, are openly asserted. (2.) Even when this perfection is conceded, the possibility is denied of making a perfect enunciation of the inspired signification or sense by means of the outward word. The reason assigned is, that the ratio of those Divine meanings which are necessary to be known for the perfect consummation of our salvation, is diverse. For while some of them serve for the instruction of the ignorant and of babes in Christ, and for preparing their minds; others are useful for perfecting adults, and for imbuing and filling their minds with the plenary wisdom of the Spirit; and while the former class of Divine meanings [for the ignorant, &c.] may be made manifest and taught by the external word, the latter class can be offered to the minds [of adults,] and impressed upon them, only by the internal address of the Spirit. (3.) When the perfect inspiration and enunciation of all the divine meanings have been granted, it is denied that the Scriptures perfectly contain whatever has been inspired and declared that is necessary to salvation; because, as it is alleged, it was not the intention of the Spirit who inspired them, or of his amanuensis, to consign all those necessary things in writing to posterity.

V. Since these three negatives hold the following order and relation among themselves, when the first two, or when either of them is established, the third may likewise be granted, and when the third is destroyed, its predecessors may be removed, having effected the destruction of the third, we might seem to have given complete satisfaction, if we had not thought proper, according to our promise, to remove the causes of the error, and thus to cut off from the adversaries all occasion for complaining, that we had treated the controversy not according to its nature, but for the convenience of our own design and for the sake of Victoria. Wherefore to these three negatives we oppose affirmatively the following three most veritable enunciations: (1.) All things which have been, are now, or till the consummation of all things, will be necessary to be known for the salvation of the Church, have been perfectly inspired and revealed to the prophets and apostles. (2.) All things thus necessary have been administered and declared by the prophets and apostles, according to this inspiration, by the outward word, to the people who have been committed to them. (3.) All things thus necessary are fully and perfectly comprehended in their books.

VI. From this deduction it is apparent, that the acts of revelation are distinguished from the significations revealed, and yet that the matters or subjects and the significations agree with the different acts of revelation. This distinction meets the objection of the Mystics, who insist that the internal illumination of the Holy Spirit is always necessary. This we concede with respect to the act of revelation, but not with respect to the subjects and new significations. The agreement between the subjects and meanings, and the acts of revelation, refutes the Papists, who affirm, that the Church was before the Scripture, because the inditing of the word which had been previously pronounced, was posterior to the Church." This, however, is not a necessary consequence, if the same meanings be comprehended in the written word and in that which was pronounced.

VII. (1.) Commencing therefore with the proof of the first of our three affirmative propositions, (§ 5,) and, for the sake of brevity, laying aside the perfection of the revelation made under the Old Testament, we will proceed to shew, that all things necessary in the manner which we have described have been inspired into the apostles, and that no new inspiration has since their times been communicated, and that it will not be in the future. We prove this in the following manner: (1.) By express passages of Scripture; (2.) by arguments deduced from them. The first passage is, "The Holy Ghost shall teach you all things, whatsoever I have said unto you." (John xiv. 26.) From the former part of this passage we obtain the whole of our proposition: for he who "teaches all things" omits nothing that ought to be taught. The same proof is derived from the latter part of it, if it be evident that Christ told "all things" to his disciples, which is demonstrated by these his own words: "All things which I have heard of my Father, I have made known unto you." (John xv. 15.) But he "who is in the bosom of the Father," has heard of all things which ought to be revealed. "For I have given unto them the words which thou gavest me." (John xvii. 8.)

VIII. The second passage is, "The spirit of truth will guide you into all truth." (John xvi. 13.) The efficacy of this teaching will shine forth with more splendid evidence, if we suffer ourselves to be instructed by Christ in that truth through which, according to his prayer, not only the apostles, but likewise the whole Church to the end of the world, will be sanctified. (John xvii. 17-20.)

IX. The third is, "But God will reveal it unto us by his Spirit," (1 Cor. ii. 10,) that is, the wisdom which is there specified. But that no one may suppose this wisdom to be partial and serving the Church only for a certain time, let him examine the attributes which are there assigned to it. It is the wisdom which God pre-determined from all eternity, and foreordained "unto the glory" of the Church Universal, for this is meant by the word "our" in the phraseology of the apostles. (v. 7.) It is the wisdom which contains "the things that God hath prepared for ALL them who love him," and not for them only who lived in the apostolic age: (v. 9.) The wisdom which contains "the deep things of God," (v. 10,) all those "things that are freely given to us of God," as his Church, (v. 12,) and that are called, in another passage, (Ephes. iii. 8,) "The unsearchable riches of Christ." It is that wisdom which is called "the mind of the Lord, and the knowledge of which is said to be the knowledge of the mind of Christ." (1 Cor. ii. 16.) It is the wisdom of which "those alone who are perfect and spiritual" are said to be capable, (v, 6, 14, 15,) that it might not seem to be serviceable only for the preparatory instruction of the more ignorant sort, and of babes in Christ." [See § 4.] The passages already cited may suffice.

X. From among many others, let the following be received as the reasons: The First is taken from the joint consideration of the glorification of Christ, and the promise of the Holy Spirit, who was bestowed after the glorification of Christ, and who was poured forth by Him. (John vii. 38, 39.) The most copious effusion of the Holy Spirit was deferred to the time when Christ should be glorified. After his glorification, it was necessary, that it should not be any longer delayed; for Christ, "being by the right hand of God exalted, and having received the promised Holy Spirit," (Acts ii. 33,) and that "not by measure," (John iii. 34, 35,) "he shed him forth" in such copious abundance, as it was possible for him to be poured out, and to be received by mankind. So that the event which had been predicted by the prophet Joel (ii, 28,) is said then to have come to pass. (Acts ii. 16, 17.) This Spirit is the Spirit of the Father and of Christ alone; and he will plead the cause of no one except that of Christ, through the entire duration of the present life, as his Advocate against the world. (John xvi. 7, 8.) "he will not speak of himself" but from Christ; and he will "shew us those things which are Christ's, and which He will receive from him. He will therefore glorify Christ." (13-15.) From these premises it follows, that no new inspiration, after that to the apostles, will be necessary to salvation; and that what is said about the distinct periods of the Father, of the Son, and of the Holy Spirit, with regard to a revelation, is a pure invention of the human brain. By this argument, all new inspirations are refuted, with such soundness and so agreeably to the nature of the thing itself, that the doctrine which maintains the contrary cannot possibly defend itself without inventing another Christ and another Spirit; (which is a notable trait in the conduct of the great masters among the Mystics;) or it must at least substitute for Christ His vicar on earth, who, invested with plenary power, may administer the affairs of the church, as is the practice of the Papists.

XI. The Second reason is taken from the office of the Apostles, for the discharge of which, because they were immediately called by Christ himself, they were undoubtedly furnished with sufficient gifts, and therefore with sufficient knowledge. But they were constituted "able ministers of the "New Testament;" (2 Cor. iii. 6,) to which as a Testament, nothing can be added; (Gal. iii. 15;) and, as New, it will neither "wax old" nor be abrogated; (Heb. viii. 13;) after the apostles, therefore, no new inspiration will be given. They were also made ministers of the Spirit;" they were therefore instructed by inspiration in those meanings which agree with the most perfect Christians, and not with those only who are placed under the law and "the oldness of the letter." To them was also committed "the ministration of righteousness;" but this was the last of all, on account of being that which is immediately connected with life eternal, and which is likewise administered by righteousness. The apostles are also called "reapers," with regard to the prophets who were the sowers;" (John iv. 38;) but this last service was to be performed in the field of the Lord. After the apostles, therefore, no new ministration has been given; and, on this account, no new inspiration.

XII. The Third reason is drawn from the circumstance of the period at which this inspiration was communicated to the apostles, and which may be considered in two respects. (1.) It was in the time of the Messiah, which is called the last," being truly the last time with regard to a revelation. "And it shall come to pass in the last days, I will pour out of my Spirit upon all flesh." (Acts ii. 17.) "When the Messiah is come, he will tell us all things." (John iv. 25.) "God hath in these last days spoken unto us by his Son." (Heb. i. 2.) To the same effect Christ is said to have been made, "manifest in these last times." (1 Pet. i. 20.) (2.) That was "the time appointed of the Father," in which "the heir" should be no longer "as a child, under a tutor;" (Gal. iv. 1-5;) but, having arrived at full age, he might pass his life under the grace and guidance of the Holy Spirit; by whom, as "the Spirit of liberty," being illuminated, he might "with open face behold as in a glass the glory of the Lord, and be transformed into the same image from glory to glory." (2 Cor. iii. 17, 18.) After the apostles, therefore, no new inspiration, no greater perfection has been granted.

XIII. The Fourth reason will exhibit to us the glory and duration of the doctrine inspired and committed to the apostles. For it greatly excels in glory, as being "the gospel of the glory of Christ" (2 Cor. iv. 4,) who is the image of God, "the brightness of the glory, and the express character of the person, of the Father," (Heb. i. 3.) and "in whom it pleased the Father that all fullness should dwell."(Col. i. 19) indeed "all the fullness of the Godhead bodily." (ii, 9.) The law was not at all glorious, "by reason of this glory which excelled it." (2 Cor. iii. 10.) From these premises it will follow, by parity of reason, that, if the more excellent doctrine shall continue forever, no future doctrine "will have any glory by reason of this which excelleth in glory." Its duration also excludes all others: for it remains without being abolished, (2 Cor. iii. 11,)and will be preached in all the world till the end shall come," (Matt. xxiv. 14;) and Christ promises to those who administer this doctrine, that he "will be with them always, even unto the end of the world." (xxviii, 20.)

XIV. We will distinctly prove the second proposition [§ 5,] thus separated into two members. First. Those things which serve for perfection, as well as those which serve for preparation, can be and really have been declared by Christ and the apostles. Second. The apostles perfectly taught all things which are and will be necessary for the Church.

XV. Let the subjoined arguments stand in proof of the First member of the proposition. (1.) "The Son who is in the bosom of the Father," that is, who is admitted to the intimate knowledge of his secrets, "hath declared," by the outward word, "what He hath seen and heard" with the Father. (John i. 18; iii, 32.) But it is impious to suppose, that these things relate only to preparation. Nay, "the things which the apostles saw and heard they have declared," that the Church "might have communion with the Father and the Son." But perfection is placed in this communion. (1 John i. 3.) The wisdom which the apostles received through revelation of the Spirit, who "searcheth the deep things of God," has been declared by them "in words which the same Holy Spirit teacheth." (1 Cor. ii. 18.) But this wisdom belongs to perfect and spiritual men, (1 Cor. ii. 6-15,) as we have already. seen. [§ 9.]

XVI. (3.) The word, through faith in which righteousness and eternal life are obtained, is not only preparative but likewise perfective. Of this kind is "the word of faith which the apostles preached;" and for this reason the gospel is called "the ministration of righteousness," "the word of salvation," and "the power of God unto salvation to every one that believeth." (Rom. x. 8-10; 1 Cor. i. 21; 2 Cor. iii. 9; Acts xiii. 26; Rom. i. 16.) (4.) The ministration of the Spirit and of the New Testament is opposed to that of Moses, which acted the part of a school master, yet "made nothing perfect" (Heb. vii. 19,) and to "the letter" of death and of the Old Testament. This ministration of the Spirit does not serve for preparation, but contains perfection; and this is the ministration which the apostles executed, and from which they are called ministers of the New Testament and of the Spirit, (2 Cor. vi. 7,) and are said to present every man perfect in Christ Jesus. (Col. i. 8.) (5.) That word which is called "the incorruptible seed, of which we are born again, and which endureth forever," (1 Pet. i. 23-25,) is not merely preparatory. And such is the word which through the gospel the apostles have declared.

XVII. Let the following arguments establish the Second member. (1.) The whole counsel of God, which is to be "declared unto men," (Luke vii. 30,) contains all things necessary to salvation. But Paul declared to the Ephesians "all the counsel of God." (Acts xx. 27.) Therefore all things necessary to salvation were declared, &c. (2.) The Corinthians are saved by the gospel which Paul preached, provided they retain it as they received it. (1 Cor. xv. 1, 2.) Therefore, all things necessary to salvation were preached to the Corinthians. (3.) "Salvation at the first began to be spoken by Christ," and, after having been perfectly preached by him, "it was confirmed unto us by the apostles that heard him." (Heb. ii. 3.) Therefore the doctrine of the apostles perfectly contained all things which the necessary confirmation of the Church demanded.

XVIII. And lest any one should utter this cavil, "The Apostles, we allow, taught all the things which were necessary at that time, but not all those which are sufficient for the edification of the body of Christ to the end of the world," let the following arguments likewise be added. (4.) Whoever he be that "preaches any other gospel" than that which the apostles preached, and which the apostolic churches received, "he is accursed." (Gal. i. 7-9.) Therefore it is not lawful to add anything to the gospel preached by the apostles, to the end of the world. Indeed, he who makes an addition, "has perverted the gospel of Christ." (5.) In Christ Jesus, or "in the mystery of God, and of the Father, and of Christ, are hidden all the treasures of wisdom and knowledge." (Col. ii. 2 3.) But Jesus Christ and this mystery were completely preached by the apostles. (i, 25-28.) "Jesus Christ has been made unto us of God, wisdom, righteousness, sanctification and redemption;" (1 Cor. i. 30, 31;) from which the apostle concludes, that true glorying consists in the knowledge of Christ alone. (Jer. ix. 24.) Therefore the doctrine taught by the apostles contains whatever will, at any time to the end of the world, be necessary, useful and glorious to the church. (6.) The Church Universal is "built upon the foundation of the apostles and prophets," (Ephes. ii. 20, 21;) and the apostles are called "the foundations of the celestial Jerusalem," (Rev. xxi. 14,) which is the mother of us all." (Gal. iv. 26.) Therefore, the apostles have declared all things which will be necessary for the whole church to the final consummation. (7.) "There is one body of Christ, the fullness of Him that filleth all in all; one Spirit, one hope of our calling, one Lord, one faith, one baptism, one bread, one God and Father of all, and Jesus Christ the same yesterday, to-day, and forever." (Ephes. iv. 4-6; i, 23; 1 Cor. x. 17; Heb. xiii. 8.) But the apostles perfectly preached this God, this Lord, this Spirit, this faith, hope, baptism and bread, and by their doctrine animate and vivify this whole body to the end of the world. (Col. i. 24, 25.) Therefore the church ought "not to be carried about with divers and strange doctrines." (Heb. xiii. 9.)

XIX. The last proposition remains to be discussed. It commends to us the perfection of the prophetical and apostolical Scriptures; and for establishing it we produce the following arguments. (1.) This perfection is taught in the express testimonies of Scripture, which prohibit any addition to be made to those things which the Lord has commanded; and the same scriptures teach, in a manner the most convincing, that these testimonies must be understood concerning the written word. (Deut. iv. 2; 12, 28; xxx, 10-14; xxviii, 58; Josh. i. 7, 8.) The apostle therefore requires, that "no one be wise above what is written," (1 Cor. iv. 6;) and he who tells the Ephesians, "I have not shunned to declare unto you all the counsel of God," (Acts xx. 27,) confesses, that "he said none other things than those which the prophets and Moses did say should come." (Acts xxvi. 22.)

XX. (2.) This perfection is also established by the very object and matter of the saving doctrine. This is done by various methods. (i.) The entire matter of the saving doctrine consists of "the truth which is after godliness;" (Tit. i. 1.) But the Scripture perfectly delivers this truth, for it is concerning God and Christ, and the manner in which He is to be known, acknowledged and worshipped. (1 Chron. xxviii. 9; John xvii. 3; v, 23.) (ii.) The Scripture perfectly delivers the doctrine of faith, hope, and charity. But in those acts is contained whatsoever God requires of us. (1 John v. 13;1 Timothy iii. 16; Rom. xv. 4; 1 Thess. i. 3; Tit. ii. 12, 13.) (3.) They are called "the Scriptures of the Old and New Testament," because in them both these parts are completely comprehended. But nothing can be added to a Testament: nay, the testament of a prudent testator fully contains his last will, according to which he wishes the distribution of his property to be made, and his heirs to regulate their conduct. (2 Cor. iii. 6; Gal. iii. 15; Jer. xxxi. 31-34; xxxii, 38-40; Gal. iv. 1, 2.) But the whole of the saving doctrine consists of a description of the beneficence of God towards us, and of our duty towards God. (4.) The division of all this saving doctrine into the LAW and the GOSPEL, as into parts which draw forth the amplitude of the whole, proves the same thing, since both of them are perfectly contained in the Scriptures. (Luke xvi. 16; Josh i. 8; Luke i. 1-4; Rom. i. 2-6; Acts xxvi. 22, 23.)

XXI. (3.) The same perfection is proved from the end and efficacy of the whole of the saving doctrine. If the Scriptures propose this entire end and perfectly accomplish it, there is no reason why we should call a doctrine, in what manner soever it may be proposed, more perfect than the Scriptures. But they entirely intend this end and efficaciously produce it. (Rom. x. 4-10.) "This is his commandment, that we should believe on the name of his Son Jesus Christ, and love one other." (1 John iii. 23.) "These things are written, that ye might believe that Jesus is the Christ," &c. (John xx. 31.) "These things have I written unto you, that ye may know that ye have eternal life, and that ye may believe on the name of the Son of God." (1 John v. 9-13.) "On these two commandments hang all the law and the prophets." (Matt. xxii. 37-40.) "Search the Scriptures; for in them ye think ye have eternal life." (John v. 39.) The Scriptures prevent men from going down into the place of the damned; (Luke xvi. 27-30) and they prevent this sad consequence without the addition of any other doctrine whatsoever. For they render a man "wise unto salvation through faith, and perfectly furnished unto all good works." (2 Tim. iii. 15-17.)

XXII. (4.) This is also confirmed by the mode of speaking usually employed by holy men of God, and by the Scriptures themselves; according to which they indiscriminately use the term "Prophets" for the writings of the prophets, "the word of prophecy" for the prophetic Scriptures, and, on the contrary, "the Scriptures" for the prophets and for God himself; by which is signified that the word of God and of the prophets is completely one with the Scriptures; and that this word in its amplitude does not exceed the Scriptures with regard to those things which are necessary. Thus it is said, "King Agrippa, believest thou the prophets?." (Acts xxvi. 27,) that is, the writings of the prophets. (Luke xvi. 29.) "We have a more sure word of prophecy," that is, the word which is comprehended in the writings of the prophets: for it is soon afterwards called "prophecy of Scripture." (2 Pet. i. 19, 20.) "Beginning at Moses and all the prophets, he interpreted to them in all the Scriptures what they say concerning Himself." (Luke xxiv. 27.) And, on the contrary, "The Scripture saith unto Pharaoh," (Rom. ix. 17,) that is, God said it by Moses. (Exod. ix. 16.) "The Scripture hath concluded all under sin." (Gal. iii. 22.) "For God hath concluded them all in unbelief." (Rom. xi. 32.) "The Scripture, foreseeing that God, &c., preached before the Gospel unto Abraham." (Gal. iii. 8; Gen. xii. 2, 3.)

XXIII. (5.) In the last place we add the following: No subject can be mentioned, by the sole knowledge or the worship of which the church ought to bedeck herself with increased honour and dignity, and which subject is not comprehended in the Holy Scriptures. Neither can any attribute be produced agreeing with any subject of this kind, which it is necessary for the church to know about that subject, or for her to perform to it, and which the Scriptures do not attribute to that subject: (John v. 39; Rom. i. 3; Luke xxiv. 27.) Whence it follows, that the Scripture contains all things necessary to be known for the salvation of the Church, and for the glory of God. The Papists indeed speak and write many things about Mary, the rest of the saints, and about the Roman Pontiff; but we affirm, that these are not objects either of any knowledge or worship which the church ought to bestow on them. And those things which the Papists attribute to them, are such as, according to the sure judgment of the scriptures, cannot be attributed to them without sacrilege and a perversion of the gospel of Christ.

XXIV. We conclude, then, that all things which have been, are now, or to the final consummation will be necessary for the salvation of the church, have been of old perfectly inspired, declared and written; and that no other revelation or tradition, than those which have been inspired, declared and contained in the scriptures, is necessary to the salvation of the church. (2 Tim. iii. 16; Matt. iv. 3, 4; xxii, 29 Acts xviii. 28.) Indeed we assert, that whatsoever relates to the doctrine of truth is so perfectly comprehended in the scriptures, that all those things which are brought either directly or indirectly against this truth are capable of being refuted, in a manner the clearest and most satisfactory, from the Scriptures themselves alone. This asseveration we take with such solemnity and yet assurance of mind, that as soon as anything has been proved not to be contained in the scriptures, from this very circumstance we infer that thing not to be necessary to salvation; and whenever it is evident, that any sentiment cannot be refuted by the Scriptures, we judge from this that it is not heretical. When, therefore, the Papists sedulously attempt to destroy the whole perfection of Scripture by specimens of articles, which they call necessary, but which are not proved from Scripture, and by those which they consider heretical but which are not confuted from Scripture the sole result of their endeavours is, that we cannot conclude with any certainty the former to be necessary and the latter heretical.

XXV. In the mean time we do not deny, that the apostles delivered to the churches some things which related to the external discipline, order and rites to be observed in them, and which have not been written, or at least are not comprehended in those of their books which we call "Canonical." (1 Cor. xi. 34) But those things do not concern the substance of saving doctrine; and are neither necessary to salvation, perpetual, immutable, nor universal, but accommodated to the existing state and circumstances of the church.

XXVI. We likewise confess, that individual churches, or great numbers, or even all of them, if they can agree together in unity, may frame certain ritual Canons relative to their mutual order and decorum, (1 Cor. xiv. 40,) and to the discharge of those functions which minister to edification; provided those rites be neither contrary to the written word, superstitious, nor difficult of observance in consequence of being numerous and burdensome. (Col. ii. 8; Acts xv. 10, 28.) This proviso is needful to prevent those rites from being considered as a part of Divine worship, or from becoming prejudicial to the liberty of the church, whose equitable "power" in abrogating, changing, or amplifying them, is always subservient to "edification and not to destruction." (1 Cor. xiv. 5, 26; 2 Cor. xiii. 10.) In this sense we admit the distinction of Traditions into Written and Unwritten, Apostolical and Ecclesiastical; and we call those men "violators of order," (2 Thess. iii, 6; 1 Cor. xiv. 32, 33,) who oppose ecclesiastical canons that are constituted in this manner, or exclaim against them by their own private authority.

DISPUTATION 3 - ON THE SUFFICIENCY AND PERFECTION OF THE HOLY SCRIPTURES IN OPPOSITION TO HUMAN TRADITIONS

RESPONDENT: DE COIGNEE

Because the Papists contend for unwritten traditions, against the entire perfection of Scripture, as if it were for every thing sacred and dear to them. that they may be able to obtrude, on mankind, many dogmas, which, even by their own confession, are not comprised in the Scriptures, and to assume to themselves an irrefragable authority in the church; it seems, that we shall not spend our time unprofitably, if, in a few Theses, we discuss in the fear of God what ought to be maintained on the subject of Divine traditions and on the opinion of the Papists.

I. The word "Tradition," according to its derivation, signifies the act of delivering; but having been enlarged through usage to denote the object about which the act is occupied, it also signifies the doctrine itself that is delivered. We ascribe this epithet, in either or both of its senses, to a Divine acceptation, on account of its cause which is God, to distinguish it from that which is human. (1 Cor. ii. 12, 13.) And we say, "That is excellently Divine which is such at the same time in its act and in its object." We define it, Divine doctrine, manifested by a Divine act, with less excellence, by men; because, however Divine it is in its object, still it is human in the act of tradition. (2 Pet. i. 21.) The apostle Paul had regard to this when he said, "As a wise master-builder, I have laid the foundation, and another buildeth thereon. But let every man take heed how he buildeth thereupon." (1 Cor. iii. 10.) And St. Peter, when he said, "if any man speak, let him speak as the oracles of God." (1 Pet. iv. 11.)

II. Divine tradition, both with respect to its object and to its act, is variously distributed. In regard to its object. (1.) According to the actions which it requires to be performed to itself by men, we distinguish it into that which is of Faith, (1 John v. 13,) and to which we add hope, and into that which relates to morals. In the first, it is offered as an object to be believed, in the other as one to be performed. (Luke xxiv. 27; Mark i. 15; Matt. xxi. 22, 23; ix, 13.) (2.) From the adjuncts of the act required, we call one act necessary to righteousness and salvation, while another is supplementary to that which is necessary. (Heb. ix. 10.) (3.) From the duration of time, we call one perpetual and immutable, another temporary and subject to change according to the appointment of its author. (John iv. 21-23.) (4.) According to its extent, we call one universal, which binds all believers either those of all ages of the world, or those who exist at the same time; and another particular, which has reference to certain persons whether they be many or few, such as that which respects the legal ceremonies and the Levitical priesthood. (Rom. 2,:26, 27.)

III. Tradition is distinguished, in regard to the act. (1.) From its subject, into internal and external. An internal one is that which is made to the mind by the illumination and inspiration of the Holy Spirit. (Isa. lix. 21; with Ephes. i. 17-21.) To this we likewise refer that which is made to the internal senses, by sensible images formed in the inward receptacle of images. (1 Cor. ii. 10.) An external tradition is that which is made by means of signs presented to the external senses; among these the principal place is occupied by the word, in the delivery of which, two methods are employed, an enunciation made by oral speech and writing. (Rom. x. 17; 1 Cor. i. 28; 2 Thess. ii. 13-14; Gen. iii. 9-19; xii, 1-3; Ezek. ii. 5; v, 1-3. (2.) From its causes, into immediate and mediate. An immediate one is that which proceeds from God, without the intervention of man. Let permission also be granted, to us, for the sake of greater convenience of doctrine, to reckon under immediate tradition that which is made by angels, lest we be compelled to introduce many mediate traditions subordinate to each other. A mediate act of tradition is that which is performed by God, as the chief author, through the hands of a man peculiarly sanctified for its execution. (3.) According to its dignity and authority, it may be distributed into primary and secondary; so that the primary may be one, transacted indeed by man, but by a man so instructed and governed by the inspiration and direction of the Holy Spirit, (2 Sam. xxiii. 2, 3,) that "it may not be he himself that speaks, but the Spirit of the Father that is in him;" (Matt. x. 20;) that he may not himself be the crier, but the voice of God crying;" not himself the Scribe, but the amanuensis of the Holy Spirit. (2 Tim. iii. 16; 2 Pet. i. 21.) The secondary is that which is indeed according to the appointment of God, but by the will of man who administers the act of tradition at his own option. (1 Pet. iv, 11.)

IV. Internal tradition is always and absolutely necessary to the salvation of men. For in no way, except by a revelation and an inward sealing of the Holy Spirit, (2 Cor. i. 20-22) can any man perceive, and by an assured faith apprehend the mind of God, however it may be manifested and confirmed by external signs. (1 Cor. ii. 10-16.) External tradition is necessary through the pleasure of the Divine will, whether we consider that will universally; for without it he can abundantly instruct the mind of man. (1 Cor. 3,:7-10; 2 Cor. iv. 6.) Or whether we consider it according to special modes; for it is sometimes delivered by the pronunciation of lively sounds, and at other times by writing, and at times by both methods, according to his own good pleasure, and which of them soever he has seen proper to employ. (1 Cor. v. 9; Exod. 24,:7; 2 Thess. ii. 13, 14; Luke xvi. 27-31.) It is, from this very circumstance, necessary to men; and from it the inconclusiveness of this argument is apparent, "Because God formerly instructed his own church without the Scriptures by the words which he spoke himself, therefore, the Scriptures are now unnecessary."

V. Though all the doctrines delivered by God, either from his own lips or in writing, possess Divine authority; yet we may distinguish between them, and may, according to certain respects, claim a greater authority for one than for another. (1.) The efficient cause makes the principal difference. For whatever doctrine it wills more, [than any other,] it makes that doctrine be of greater authority. Thus it is said, "I will have mercy, and not sacrifice." (Matt. ix. 13.) (2.) The condition of him who administers the doctrine, obtains for it a greater or a less degree of authority. "For if the word spoken by angels, was steadfast," etc, how much more is the doctrine which is announced to us by the Son? (Heb. ii. 2-5.) (3.) The object of the doctrine produces the same effect. For, according to it, some precepts are called "the weightier matters of the law," (Matt. xxiii. 23,) while others are called "the least commandments" (Matt. v. 19;) and thus the precepts of the second table yield to those of the first. (Luke xiv. 26.) In this view the Apostle said, "This is a faithful saying, and worthy of all acceptation," in which expression let the emphatic word be observed, "that Christ Jesus came into the world to save sinners; of whom I am chief." (1 Tim. i. 15.) (4.) The nearer and more leading tendency which any doctrine has to the end proposed by the whole, the greater prevalence and authority does it possess. "If the ministration of death and of condemnation is glorious, how much more doth the ministration of life and righteousness exceed in glory!" (2 Cor. iii. 9.) (5.) The very mode of delivery adds weight to the authority. For, lest that should escape which had before been delivered only in words, the author himself commits it to writing, and thus, when by a double act, it is entrusted to the memory of others, he points it out in a manner far more excellent, than if he had been content to recommend it solely by pronouncing it in words. (2 Pet.

iii. 1, 2.) And here let the hypothesis be observed, in which it is presupposed that the matter had been delivered partly by speaking and by writing, and partly by speaking alone. The more frequent and solicitous recommendation of the written doctrine serves to strengthen this argument. (Deut. xvii. 19; 1 Tim. iv. 13; 2 Pet. i. 19.)

VI. Having given this exposition of the subject, let us proceed with the controversy which we have with the Papists, and pass upon it a few brief animadversions. It seems to be comprehended in these three questions. (1.) Is every doctrine already delivered, which has been, is now, or ever will be necessary to the salvation of the church? Does any thing of this kind yet remain to be delivered? And if it has been really delivered, when was that done? (2.) In what are those doctrines contained which it is necessary for the church to believe and practice in order to be saved? Are they in the Scriptures alone; or partly in the Scriptures, and partly in unwritten traditions from their first author? (3.) How can it be made evident with certainty to the consciences of believers, that any particular doctrine is Divine?

VII. With regard to the First question, our opinion is, that all the doctrines necessary for the salvation of the Church Universal, have been already delivered, above fifteen hundred years ago; and that no tradition has been made of any new doctrine that is necessary for the salvation of believers, since the days of the apostles. We establish our opinion by the following arguments: (1.) Because in Christ, and in his Gospel, "are hidden all the treasures of wisdom and knowledge." (Col. ii. 3.) But the apostles have perfectly announced Christ and his Gospel; (Acts xx. 26, 27;) so that an anathema is pronounced on him who preaches any other gospel than that which the apostles have preached and the churches have received. (Gal. i. 8, 9.) But that man preaches another gospel, who adds any thing to it as being necessary to the salvation of believers. (2.) Because the whole "church has been built upon the foundation of the apostles and prophets." (Ephes. ii. 20; Rev. xxi. 14.) This is not true, if there be a doctrine necessary to the salvation of any church, which has not been revealed through the prophets and apostles. (3.) Because the whole Catholic Church is one body, consisting of particular churches that possess the same nature and principles as the whole; and this Church is animated by one spirit, and led into all truth, and being called into one hope of the same inheritance, it has "one Lord, one faith, one baptism, one God and Father of all" (Ephes. iv. 4, 6,) and sealed into "the communion of the same body and blood of the Lord," by a participation of one cup and bread. (1 Cor. x. 16, 17.) (4.) Because "Jesus Christ is the same yesterday, and to-day, and forever." Whence the apostle infers, that it is wrong for the Church to be "carried about with divers and strange doctrines." (Heb. xiii. 8-9.)

VIII. Though some of the Popish divines profess to assent to this truth, yet indications sufficiently manifest their dissent from it are extant in their writings, especially in those of the Canonists. In the first place, the epithets of Universal Bishop, Supreme Pastor, Prime Head, Bridegroom, the Perfecter and Illuminator of the Catholic Church his Bride, which are ascribed to the Roman Pontiff, do not admit of this limitation of tradition. Then, the authority of governing, commanding and forbidding, of establishing and abrogating laws, of judging and condemning, and of loosing and binding, an immense and infinite authority, which is not merely attributed to him, but is actually assumed and exercised by him, excludes the same kind of circumscription. To which may be added the Decree, by which it is decided to be necessary for salvation, that every human creature be placed in subjection to the Roman Pontiff; and that, by which authentic authority is ascribed to the ancient Latin translation of the Scriptures. But, not to multiply instances, we hold it for a general argument of this dissension, that they dare not enter into an exact enumeration of unwritten traditions, and fix the number of them; they avoid this, that they may reserve to themselves the power of producing tradition in any controversy. Some of them, therefore, assert, that other doctrines are necessary according to the different states of the Church.

IX. But we most willingly confess, that the tradition which we call secondary will continue in the Church to the end of the world; for by it the doctrines which have, through the prophets and apostles, been committed to her, are by her, further dispensed to her children. For this reason, the Church is called "the pillar and ground of the truth," (1 Tim. iii. 15,) but only secondarily after the apostles, who, on account of the primary tradition, are distinguished by the title of "pillars," (Gal. ii. 9,) and "foundations," (Rev. xxi. 14,) before those epithets were bestowed on the church.

X. With regard to the Second question, [§ 6,] we say that the canonical Scriptures of the Old and New Testament perfectly contain all doctrines which are necessary to the salvation of believers and the glory of God. This is manifest, (1.) From express testimonies of Scripture, [see Disputation 2, Thesis 19,] forbidding any addition to be made to those things which have been commanded, and commanding that "no man be wise above what is written," (1 Cor. iv. 6,) though in the former of these, it is evident from the text that Moses is speaking about those precepts which were comprised in writing. (2.) From the very substance of the doctrines; and this in various ways. The scriptures contain in a complete form the doctrine of the Law and of the Gospel; they also perfectly embrace the doctrine of faith, hope and charity. They deliver the full knowledge of God and of Christ, in which is placed life eternal. They are called, and truly so, "the Scriptures of the Old and New Testament;" but to a testament nothing ought to be added. (3.) From the end at which they aim and which they attain. "These things are written, that ye may believe; and that, believing, ye may have life." (John xx. 31.) "Search the Scriptures; for in them ye think ye have eternal life." (v, 39.) (4.) From their efficacy; because, without [the aid of] any other doctrine, they sufficiently hinder any man from going into the place of torment, (Luke xvi. 28, 29;) and they render "the man of God wise unto salvation through faith, and thoroughly furnished unto all good works." (2 Tim. iii. 15-17.) (5.) From the manner of speech usually employed in the Scriptures, by which "the prophets" are understood to mean the writings of the prophets, "the prophets" and "the word of prophecy" signify the prophecies of Scripture. (2 Pet. i. 19-21.) What God said and did is ascribed to the Scriptures: thus, For the Scriptures saith unto Pharaoh;" (Rom. ix. 17;) "the Scripture, foreseeing, &c., preached before the gospel unto Abraham;' (Gal. iii. 8;) "the Scripture hath concluded all under sin." (iii, 22.)

XI. The Papists assert, on the contrary, that all things necessary to salvation are not contained in the Scriptures; but partly in the Scriptures, and partly in unwritten traditions. This their opinion they endeavour to establish, not only by the Scriptures themselves, but by the testimonies of Popes, Councils, and Fathers, nay, by certain examples which they produce of necessary doctrines which are not comprehended within the limits of Scripture. As we shall examine the strength of each of these arguments separately in the discussion which we have now commenced, we may remark by way of anticipation, that the passages of Scripture which they usually quote for this purpose, are either forcibly wrested from their correct signification, or do not determine the proposition; that the testimonies of Popes, Councils, and Fathers, being those of mere men, do not operate to our prejudice; that the instances which they adduce are either confirmed from the Scriptures, or are not necessary to salvation. This separation we consider of such necessity, that when it is once granted that they are necessary to salvation, it follows that they can and that they must be confirmed by the Scriptures; and when it is granted that they cannot be confirmed by the Scriptures, it follows that they are not necessary to salvation. So immovable and certain is this truth to our minds, that all doctrines necessary to salvation are contained in the Scriptures.

XII. To the Third question, [§ 5,] we reply: As one Delivery of Divine doctrine is primary, and another secondary; so likewise one Attestation [witnessing] respecting the divinity of the doctrine is primary, while another is secondary. (John v. 36, 37; 1 John v. 7.) The Primary attestation is that of God himself, to whom it appertains properly, originally, and per se to bear witness to his own doctrine. But he employs a two-fold mode of bearing witness: one external, which is presented to the senses of those to whom the doctrine is proposed, (John iii. 2; Heb. ii. 4; 1 Cor. i. 6-8,) and is a preparative for creating faith in the doctrine, even when this doctrine is not understood. Another internal, which impresses on the mind a true understanding of the doctrine, and an undoubted approval of it, which is the necessary, proper and immediate cause of that faith which God requires to be given to his word, and which alone is saving. The Secondary attestation is that of the Church. For having been herself certified, by means of the primary attestation, (which is that of God,) of the divinity of this doctrine, she both gives her hand and seal as a witness that God is true, (John iii. 33,) and she bears her testimony to the doctrine received from the God of truth. This testimony is pleasing to God, due to the doctrine, honourable to the church, and useful to men. (1 John v. 9; John v. 34-36.) But it is to be observed, that this testimony of the church is human and not Divine, and is less than the preceding, which is potent only in preparing the hearts, by a sort of reverence that it obtains for the doctrine, that the hearts so prepared may with sincerity, by the internal witnessing of God, yield their assent to it. (John xv. 26, 27.) Under that part of the Primary testimony which is external, we comprise the testimony of prophets, apostles, evangelists, pastors, and teachers, who are "workers together with God," provided they have been immediately called [by God himself.] But we refer it to the Secondary testimony, if they have been called mediately by the church. The Papists, who ascribe less to the internal attestation, and more to that which is secondary, than what we have explained, are deservedly rejected by us.

XIII. Having explained these matters, we grant, that the apostles delivered to the churches some things relating to order, decency, and the rights to be observed in them, which they did not commit to writing, (1 Cor. xi. 34;) but those things do not concern the substance either of the Law or the Gospel, are not necessary to salvation, are neither immutable, perpetual, nor universal, but are accommodated to the existing condition of the church, and the circumstances in which she is placed. We further grant, that either single churches, or many by mutual consent, or that all churches provided they could so agree, may frame certain ritual canons for their good order and decency, and for such direction in those duties which must of necessity be performed in them, as may contribute to their present edification. (1 Cor. xiv. 40.) But these conditions must be observed respecting them:

(1.) That these rites be not repugnant to the Written Word. (Col. ii. 18-23.) (2.) That they neither have superstition intermixed with them, nor encourage it. (3.) That they neither be accounted as divine worship, nor cast a snare upon consciences. (4.) That they be neither more numerous, nor more burdensome in practice, than may render them easy of observance. (Acts xv. 10, 28.) (5.) That the church do not deprive herself of the liberty of changing, adding, or taking away, as she shall consider her present edification to require. Such rites as these being usefully established in a church, it is unlawful for any one, of his own private authority, to gainsay or attack them, unless he be ambitious of having his name emblazoned in the list of disorderly persons, and among the disturbers of the peace of church. (1 Cor. xiv. 32, 33; 2 Thess. iii. 6.)

DISPUTATION 4 - ON THE NATURE OF GOD

RESPONDENT: JAMES ARMINIUS--WHEN HE STOOD FOR HIS DEGREE OF D. D.

I. The very nature of things and the Scriptures of God, as well as the general consent of all wise men and nations, testify that a nature is correctly ascribed to God. (Gal. iv. 8; 2 Pet. i. 4; Aristot. De Repub. 1. 7, c. 1; Cicero De Nat. Deor.)

II. This nature cannot be known a priori: for it is the first of all things, and was alone, for infinite ages, before all things. It is adequately known only by God, and God by it; because God is the same as it is. It is in some slight measure known by us, but in a degree infinitely below what it is [in] itself; because we are from it by an external emanation. (Isa. xliv. 6; Rev. i. 8; 1 Cor. ii. 11; 1 Tim. vi. 16; 1 Cor. xiii. 9.)

III. But this nature is known by us, either immediately through the unclouded vision of it as it is. This is called "face to face," (1 Cor. xiii. 12,) and is peculiar to the blessed in heaven: (1 John iii. 2.) Or mediately through analogical images and signs, which are not only the external acts of God and his works through them, (Psalm xix. 1-8; Rom. i. 20,) but likewise his word, (Rom. x. 14-17,) which, in that part in which it proposes Christ, "who is the Image of the Invisible God," (Col. i. 15,) as "the brightness of his glory, and the express image of his person," (Heb. i. 3,) gives such a further increase to our knowledge, that "we all, with open face beholding as in a glass the glory of the Lord, are changed into the same image from glory to glory." (2 Cor. iii. 18.) This is called "through a glass in an enigma," or "darkly," and applies exclusively to travelers and pilgrims who "are absent from the Lord." (2 Cor. v. 6; Exod. xxxiii. 20.)

IV. But there are two modes of this second perception from the works and the word of God. The First is that of Affirmation, (which is also styled by Thomas Aquinas, "the mode of Causality and by the habitude of the principle,") according to which the simple perfections which are in the creatures, as being the productions of God, are attributed analogically to God according to some similitude. (Psalm xciv. 9, 10; Matt. vii. 11; Isa. xlix. 15.) The Second is that of Negation or Removal, according to which the relative perfections and all the imperfections which appertain to the creatures, as having been produced out of nothing, are removed from God. (Isa. iv. 8, 9; 1 Cor. i. 25.) To the mode of Affirmation, (because it is through the habitude of the cause and principle, to the excellence of which no effect ever rises,) that of Pre-eminence must be added, according to which the perfections that are predicated of the creatures are understood [to be] infinitely more perfect in God. (Isa. xl. 15, 17, 22, 25.) Though this mode be affirmative and positive in itself, (for as the nature of God necessarily exists, so it is necessarily known,) in positively and not in negation; yet it cannot be enunciated or expressed by us, except through a Negation of those modes according to which the creatures are partakers of their own perfections, or the perfections in creatures are circumscribed. Those modes, being added to the perfections of the creatures, produce this effect, that those which, considered without them, were simple perfections, are relative perfections, and by that very circumstance are to be removed from God. Hence it appears, that the mode of Pre-eminence does not differ in species from the mode of Affirmation and Negation.

V. Besides, in the entire nature of things and in the Scriptures themselves, only two substances are found, in which is contained every perfection of things. They are Essence and Life, the former of them constituting the perfection of all existing creatures; the latter, that of only some them, and those the most perfect. (Gen. 1; Psalm civ. 29, 148; Acts xvii. 28.) Beyond these two the human mind cannot possibly comprehend any substance, indeed, it cannot raise its conceptions to any other: for it is itself circumscribed within the limits of created nature, of which it forms a part; it is therefore incapable of passing beyond the circle which encloses the whole. (Rev. i. 8; iv, 8; Dan. vi. 46.) Wherefore in the nature of God himself, only these two causes of motion, Essence and Life, can become objects of our consideration.

LET THE FOLLOWING BE OUR PROBLEMS

Have a corporeal Essence, and a vegetative and sensitive Life, any analogy to the Essence and Life of God, though such analogy be less than a spiritual Essence and an intellectual Life?

If they have this analogy, how are body and senses removed simply from God?

If they have not this analogy, how has God been able to produce this kind of Essence and Life?

VI. But in God both these are to be considered in the mode of Pre-eminence, that is, in excellence far surpassing the Essence and Life of all the creatures. (Psalm cii. 27; 1 Tim. vi. 16.)

VII. The Essence of God is that by which God exists; or it is the first cause of motion of the Divine Nature by which God is understood to exist.

VIII. Because every Essence, which is either in the superior or in the inferior nature of things, is distributed into spiritual and corporeal, (Col. i. 16;) of which, the former notes simply perfection, the latter a defection or defect from this perfection. On this account we separate corporeal Essence from God according to the mode of removal, and at the same time all those things which belong to a corporeal Essence as such, whether it be simple or compound--such as magnitude, figure, place, or parts, whether sensible or imaginable. Whence also He cannot be perceived by the corporeal senses, either by those which are external or by the internal, since he is invisible, intactable, and incapable of being represented. (Deut. iv. 14; 1 Kings viii. 1 Luke xxiv. 39; John iv. 24; 1 Tim. i. 17.) But we ascribe to Him a spiritual Essence, and that in the mode of preeminence, as "the Father of Spirits." (Heb. xii. 9.)

Therefore,

(1.) We reject the dogma of the Anthropo-morphites, [those who maintained that "the uncorruptable God" had a form or body "like to corruptible man,"] and the intolerable custom of the Papists, which they constantly practice, in fashioning a [supposed] likeness of God's Essence. (Deut. iv. 15, 16; Rom. i. 23; Isa. xl. 18; Acts xvii. 29.)

(2.) When bodily members are attributed in the Scriptures to God, that is done on account of the simplicity of those effects, which the creatures themselves usually produce only by the aid and operation of those members.

IX. As we ought to enunciate negatively the mode by which the Essence of God pre-eminetly both is and is spiritual, above the excellence of all Essences, even of those which are spiritual; so this may be done first and immediately in a single phrase, "he is, anarcov kai anaitiov without beginning and without cause either external or internal." (Isa. xliii. 10; xliv, 8, xxiv, ; xlvi, 9; Rev. i. 8; Rom. xi. 35, 36; 1 Cor. viii. 4-6; Rom. ix. 5.) For since there cannot be any advancement in infinitum, (for if there could, there would be no Essence, no Knowledge,) there must be one Essence, above and before which no other can exist: but such an Essence must that of God be; for, to whatsoever this Essence may be attributed, it will by that very act of ascription be God himself.

X. Because the Essence of God is devoid of all cause, from this circumstance arise, in the first place, Simplicity and Infinity of Being in the Essence of God.

Simplicity is a preeminent mode of the Essence of God, by which he is void of all composition, and of component parts whether they belong to the senses or to the understanding. He is without composition, because without external cause; and He is without component parts, because without internal cause. (Rom. xi. 35, 36; Heb. 2,:10; Isa. xl. 12, 22.) The Essence of God, therefore, neither consists of material, integral and quantitive parts, of matter and form, of kind and difference, of subject and accident, nor of form and the thing formed, (for it is to itself a form, existing by itself and its own individuality,) neither hypothetically and through nature, through capability and actuality, nor through essence and being. Hence God is his own Essence and his own Being, and is the same in that which is, and that by which it is. He is all eye, ear, hand and foot, because he entirely sees, hears, works, and is in every place. (Psalm cxxxix. 8- 12.)

THEREFORE,

Whatever is absolutely predicated about God, it is understood essentially and not accidentally; and those things, (whether many or diverse,) which are predicated concerning God, are, in God, not many but one: (James i. 17.) It is only in our mode of considering them, which is a compound mode, that they are distinguished as being many and diverse; though this may, not inappropriately, be said, because they are likewise distinguished by a formal reason.

XII. Infinity of Being is a preeminent mode of the Essence of God, by which it is devoid of all limitation and boundary, (Psalm cxlv. 3; Isa. xliii. 10,) whether from something above it or below it, from something before it or after it. It is not bounded by anything above it, because it has received its being from no one. Nor by anything below it, because the form, which is itself, is not limited to the capacity of any matter whatsoever that may be its recipient. Neither by any thing before it, because it is from nothing efficient: nor after it, because it does not exist for the sake of another end. But, His Essence is terminated inwardly by its own property, according to which it is what it is and nothing else. Yet by this no limits are prescribed to its Infinity; for by the very circumstance, that it is its own being, subsisting through itself, neither received from another nor in another, it is distinguished, from all others, and others are removed from it. (Isa. xliv. 9; Rom. xi. 36; Prov. xvi,

4.) THEREFORE,

Whatsoever is predicated absolutely about God, is predicated concerning Him immediately, primarily, and without [respect to] cause.

XIII. From the Simplicity and Infinity of the Divine sense, arise Infinity with regard to time, which is called "Eternity;" and with regard to place, which is called "Immensity;" Impassability, Immutability, and Incorruptibility.

XIV. Eternity is a pre-eminent mode of the Essence of God, by which it is devoid of time with regard to the term or limits of beginning and end, because it is of infinite being; it is also devoid of time with regard to the succession of former and latter, of past and future, because it is of simple being, which is never in capability, but always in act, (Gen. xxi. 33; Psalm xc. 9; Isa. xliv. 6; 2 Tim. i. 9.) According to this mode, therefore, the Being of God is always the universal, the whole, the plentitude of his essence, closely, fixedly, and at every instant present with it, resembling a moment which is also devoid of intelligible parts, and never flows onward progressively, but always continues within itself. It will be lawful, therefore, for us, with Boetius, to define Eternity in the following manner, after changing, by his good leave, the word Life into that of Essence: "It is an interminable, entire and at the same time, a perfect possession of Essence. But it seems that I may by some sort of right require this change to be made, because Essence comes to be considered in the first moving cause of the Divine Nature, before Life; and because Eternity does not belong to Essence through Life, but to Life through Essence.

THEREFORE,

Whatsoever things are predicated absolutely concerning God, they belong to Him from all eternity and all together. It is certain that those things which do not from all eternity belong to Him, are predicated about Him not absolutely, but in reference to the creatures, such as, "He is the Creator, the Lord, the Judge of all men."

XV. Immensity is a pre-eminent mode of the Essence of God, by which it is void of place according to space and limits: being co-extended space, because it belongs to simple entity, not having part and part, therefore not having part beyond part. Being also its own encircling limits, or beyond which it has no existence, because it is of infinite entity: and, before all things, God alone was both the world, and place, and all things to himself; but He was alone, because there was nothing outwardly beyond, except himself. (1 Kings viii. 27; Job xi. 8, 9.)

XVI. After creatures, and places in which creatures are contained, have been granted to have an existence, from this Immensity follows the Omnipresence or Ubiquity of the Essence of God, according to which it is entirely wheresoever any creature or any place is, and this in exact similarity to a [mathematical] point, which is totally present to the entire circumference, and to each of its parts, and yet without circumscription. If there be any difference, it arises, from the Will, the Ability and the Act of God. (Psalm cxxxix. 8-12; Isa. lxvi. 1; Jer. xxiii. 24; Acts xvii. 27, 28.)

XVII. Impassability is a pre-eminent mode of the Essence of God, according to which it is devoid of all suffering or feeling; not only because nothing can act against this Essence, for it is of infinite Being and devoid of an external cause; but likewise because it cannot receive the act of anything, for it is of simple Entity. THEREFORE, Christ has not suffered according to the Essence of his Deity.

XVIII. Immutability is a pre-eminent mode of the Essence of God, by which it is void of all change; of being transferred from place to place, because it is itself its own end and good, and because it is immense; of generation and corruption; of alteration; of increase and decrease; for the same reason as that by which it is incapable of suffering. (Psalm cii. 27; Mal. iii. 6; James i. 17.) Whence likewise, in the Scriptures, Incorruptibility is attributed to God. Nay, even motion cannot happen to Him through operation; for it appertains to God, and to Him alone, to be at rest in operation. (Rom. i. 23; Isa. xl. 28.)

XIX. These modes of the Essence of God belong so peculiarly to Him, as to render them incapable of being communicated to any other thing; and of whatever kind these modes may be, they are, according to themselves, as proper to God as His Essence itself, without which they cannot be communicated, unless we wish to destroy it after despoiling it of its peculiar modes of being; and according to analogy, they are more peculiar to Him than his Essence, because they are pre-eminent, for nothing can be analogous to them. THEREFORE, Christ, according to his humanity, is not in every place.

XX. Since Unity and Good are the general affections of Being, the same are also to be attributed to God, but with the mode of pre-eminence, according to the measure of the Simplicity and Infinity of his Essence. (Gen. i. 31; Matt. xix. 17.)

XXI. The Unity of the Essence of God is that according to which it is in every possible way so at one in itself, as to be altogether indivisible with regard to number, species, genus, parts, modes, &c. (Deut. iv. 35; 1 Cor. viii)

XXII. It appertains also to the Essence of God, to be divided from every other thing: and to be incapable of entering into the composition of any other thing: while some persons ascribe this property to the Simplicity and others to the Unity of God's Essence, several attribute it to both. But on reading the Scriptures, we find that Holiness is frequently ascribed to God, which usually designates a separation or setting apart; on this account, perhaps, that very thing by which God is thus divided from others, may, without any impropriety, be called by the name of Holiness. (Josh. xxiv. 19; Isa. vi. 3; Gen. ii. 3; Exod. xiii. 2; 1 Pet. ii. 2-9; 1 Thess. v. 23.) THEREFORE,

God is neither the soul of the world, nor the form of the universe; He is neither an inherent form, nor a bodily one.

XXIII. The Goodness of the Essence of God is that according to which it is, essentially in itself, the Supreme and very Good; from a participation in which all other things have an existence and are good; and to which all other things are to be referred as to their supreme end: for this reason it is called communicable. (Matt. xix. 17; Jas. i. 17; 1 Cor. x. 31.)

XXIV. These modes and affections are so primarily attributed to the Essence of God, that they ought to be deduced through all the rest of those things which come under our consideration in the latter momentum of the Divine Nature. If this deduction be made, especially through those things which appertain to the operation of God, then the most abundant utility will redound to us from them and from our knowledge of them. This benefit, however, they will not perform for us, if they be made subjects of consideration only in this momentum in the Divine Nature. (Mal. iii. 6; Num. xxiii. 19; Lament. iii. 22; Hosea xi. 9.)

ON THE LIFE OF GOD

XXV. The Life of God, which comes to be considered under the second [momentum] cause of motion in the Divine Nature, is an act flowing from the Essence of God, by which his Essence is signified to be in action within itself. (Psalm xlii. 2; Heb. iii. 12; Num. xiv. 21.)

XXVI. We call it "an act flowing from his essence;" because, as our understanding forms a conception of essence and life in the nature of God under distinct forms, and of the essence as having precedence of the life; we must beware lest the life be conceived as an act approaching to the essence similar to unity, which, when added to unity, makes it binary or two-fold. But it must be conceived as an act flowing from the essence, which advances itself to its own perfection, in the same manner as a [mathematical] point by its flowing moves itself forward in length, [§ 14.] It is our wish, that these things be understood only by the confined capacity of our consideration, who are compelled to use the words of our darkness, in order in any degree to adumbrate or represent that light to which no mortal can approach.

XXVII. We say "that the Divine Essence is in action by means of the life;" because the acts of God, the internal as well as the external, those which are directed inwards and those directed outwards, must all be ascribed to His life as to their proximate and immediate principle. (Heb. iv. 12.) For it is in reference to his life, that God the Father produces out of his own essence his Word and his Spirit; and in reference to his life, God understands, wills, is able to do, and does, all those things which He understands, wills, is able to do, and actually does. Hence, since blessedness consists in action, it is with propriety ascribed to life. (1 Tim. i. 11; Rom. vi. 23.) This also seems to be the cause why it was the will of God, that his oath should be expressed in these words, "THE LORD LIVETH." (Jer. iv. 2.)

XXVIII. The life of God is his essence itself, and his very being; because the Divine Essence is in every respect simple, as well as infinite, and therefore, eternal and immutable. On this account, to it, and indeed to it alone, is attributed immortality, which, therefore, cannot be communicated to any creature. (1 Tim. i. 17; vi, 16.) It is immense, without increase and decrease; it is one and undivided, holy and set apart from all things; it is good, and therefore communicable, and actually communicative of itself, both by creation and preservation, and by habitation commenced in this life, to be consummated in the life to come. (Gen. ii. 7; Acts xvii. 28; Rom. viii. 10, 11; 1 Cor. xv. 28.)

XXIX. But the life of God is active in three faculties, in the understanding, the will, and the power or capability properly so called. In the Understanding, inwardly considering its object of what kind soever, whether it be one [with it] or united to it in the act of understanding. In the Will, inwardly willing its first, chief, and proper object; and extrinsically willing the rest. In the Power, or capability operating only extrinsically, which may be the cause of its being called by the particular name of capability, as being that which is capable of operating on all its objects, before it actually operates.

ON THE UNDERSTANDING OF GOD

XXX. The understanding of God is a faculty of his life, which is the first in nature as well as in order, and by which He distinctly understands all things and every thing which now have, will have, have had, can have, or might hypothetically have, any kind of being; by which He likewise distinctly understands the order which all and each of them hold among themselves, the connections and the various relations which they have or can have; not excluding even that entity which belongs to reason, and which exists, or can exist, only in the mind, imagination, and enunciation. (Rom. xi. 33.)

XXXI. God, therefore, understands himself. He knows all things possible, whether they be in the capability of God or of the creature; in active or passive capability; in the capability of operation, imagination, or enunciation. He knows all things that could have an existence, on laying down any hypothesis. He knows other things than himself, those which are necessary and contingent, good and bad, universal and particular, future, present and past, excellent and vile. He knows things substantial and accidental of every kind; the actions and passions, the modes and circumstances of all things; external words and deeds, internal thoughts, deliberations, counsels, and determinations, and the entities of reason, whether complex or simple. All these things, being jointly attributed to the understanding of God, seem to conduce to the conclusion, that God may deservedly be said to know things infinite. (Acts xv. 18; Heb. iv. 13; Matt. xi. 27; Psalm cxlvii. 4; Isa. li, 32, 33; liv, 7; Matt. x. 30; Psalm cxxxv. 1 John iii. 20; 1 Sam. xvi. 7; 1 Kings viii. 39; Psalm xciv. 11; Isa. xl. 28; Psalm cxlvii. 5; 139; xciv, 9, 10; x, 13, 14.)

XXXII. All the things which God knows, he knows neither by intelligible images, nor by similitude, (for it is not necessary for Him to use abstraction and application for the purpose of understanding;) but He knows them by his own essence, and by this alone, with the exception of evil things which he knows indirectly by the opposite good things; as, through means of the habitude, privation is discovered.

Therefore,

(1.) God knows himself entirely and adequately. For He is all being, light and eye. He also knows other things entirely; but excellently, as they are in Himself and in his understanding; adequately, as they are in their proper natures. (1 Cor. ii. 11; Psalm xciv. 9, 10.)

(2.) He knows himself primarily; and it is impossible for that which God understands first and by itself, to be any other thing than his own essence.

(3.) The act of understanding in God is his own being and essence.

XXXIII. The mode by which God understands, is not that which is successive, and which is either through composition and division, or through deductive argumentation; but it is simple, and through infinite intuition. (Heb. iv. 13.)

THEREFORE,

(1.) God knows all things from eternity; nothing recently. For this new perfection would add something to His essence by which He understands all things; or his understanding would exceed His essence, if he now understood what he did not formerly understand. But this cannot happen, since he understands all things through his essence. (Acts xv. 18; Ephes. i. 4.)

(2.) He knows all things immeasurably, without the augmentation and decrease of the things known and of the knowledge itself. (Psalm cxlvii. 5.)

(3.) He knows all things immutably, his knowledge not being varied to the infinite changes of the things known. (James i. 17)

(4.) By a single and undivided act, not being diverted towards many things but collected into himself, He knows all things. Yet he does not know them confusedly, or only universally and in general; but also in a distinct and most special manner He knows himself in himself, things in their causes, in themselves, in his own essence, in themselves as being present, in their causes antecedently, and in himself most pre-eminently. (Heb. iv. 13; 1 Kings viii. 39; Psalm cxxxix, 16, 17.)

(5.) And therefore when sleep, drowsiness and oblivion are attributed to God, by these expressions is meant only a deferring of the punishment to be inflicted on his enemies, and a delay in affording solace and aid to his friends. (Psalm xiii. 1, 2.)

XXXIV. Although by one, and that a simple act, God understands all things, yet a certain order in the objects of his knowledge may be assigned to Him without impropriety, indeed, it ought to be for the sake of ourselves. (1.) He knows himself. (2.) He knows all things possible, which may be referred to three general classes. (i.) Let the first be of those things to which the capability of God can immediately extend itself, or which may exist by his mere and sole act. (ii.) Let the second consist of those things which, by God's preservation, motion, aid, concurrence and permission, may have an existence from the creatures, whether these creatures will themselves exist or not, and whether they might be placed in this or in that order, or in infinite orders of things; let it even consist of those things which might have an existence from the creatures, if this or that hypothesis were admitted. (1 Sam. xxiii. 11, 12; Matt. xi. 21.) (iii.) Let the third class be of those things which God can do from the acts of the creatures, in accordance either with himself or with his acts. (3.) He knows all beings, whether they be considered as future, as past, or as present; (Jer. xviii. 6; Isa. xliv. 7;) and of these there is also a threefold order. The first order is of those beings which by his own mere act shall exist, do exist, or have existed. (Acts xv. 18.) The second is of those which will exist, do exist, or have existed, by the intervention of the Creatures, either by themselves, or through them by God's preservation, motion, aid, concurrence and permission. (Psalm cxxxix. 4) The third order consists of those which God will himself do or make, does make, or hath made, from the acts of the creatures, in accordance either with himself or with his acts. (Deut. 28). This consideration is of infinite utility in various heads of theological doctrine.

XXXV. God understands all things in a holy manner, regarding things as they are, without any admixture. (Psalm ix. 8; 1 Thess. ii. 4.) On this account He is said to judge, not according to the person or appearance and the face, but according to truth. (Rom. ii. 2.)

XXXVI. The understanding of God is certain, and never can be deceived, so that He certainly and infallibly sees even future contingencies, whether He sees them in their causes or in themselves. (1 Sam. xxiii. 11, 12; Matt. xi. 21.) But, this certainty rests upon the infinity of the essence of God, by which in a manner the most present He understands all things.

XXXVII. The understanding of God is derived from no external cause, not even from an object; though if there should not afterwards be an object, there would not likewise be the understanding of God about it. (Isa. xl. 13, 14; Rom. xi. 33, 34.)

XXXVIII. Though the understanding of God be certain and infallible, yet it does not impose any necessity on things, nay, it rather establishes in them a contingency. For since it is an understanding not only of the thing itself, but likewise of its mode, it must know the thing and its mode such as they both are; and therefore if the mode of the thing be contingent, it will know it to be contingent; which cannot be done, if this mode of the thing be changed into a necessary one, even solely by reason of the Divine understanding. (Acts xxvii. 22-25, 31; xxiii, 11, in connection with verses 17, 18, &c., with xxv, 10, 12; and with xxvi, 32; Rom. xi. 33; Psalm cxlvii. 5.)

XXXIX. Since God distinctly understands such a variety of things by one infinite intuition, Omniscience or All-Wisdom is by a most deserved right attributed to Him. Yet this omniscience is not to be considered in God according to the mode of the habitude, but according to that of a most pure act.

XL. But the single and most simple knowledge of God may be distinguished by some modes, according to various objects and the relations to those objects, into theoretical and practical knowledge, into that of vision and of simple intelligence.

XLI. Theoretical knowledge is that by which things are understood under the relation of being and of truth. Practical knowledge is that by which things are considered under the relation of good, and as objects of the will and of the power of God. (Isa. xlviii. 8; xxxvii, 28, xvi, 5.)

XLII. The knowledge of vision is that by which God knows himself and all other beings, which are, will be, or have been. The knowledge of simple intelligence is that by which He knows things possible. Some persons call the former "definite" or "determinate," and the latter "indefinite" or "indeterminate" knowledge.

XLIII. The schoolmen say besides, that one kind of God's knowledge is natural and necessary, another free, and a third kind middle. (1.) Natural or necessary knowledge is that by which God understands himself and all things possible. (2.) Free knowledge is that by which he knows, all other beings. (3.) Middle knowledge is that by which he knows that "if This thing happens, That will take place." The first precedes every free act of the Divine will; the second follows the free act of God's will; and the last precedes indeed the free act of the Divine will, but hypothetically from this act it sees that some particular thing will occur. But, in strictness of speech, every kind of God's knowledge is necessary. For the free understanding of God does not arise from this circumstance, that a free act of His will exhibits or offers an object to the understanding; but when any object whatsoever is laid down, the Divine understanding knows it necessarily on account of the infinity of its own essence. In like manner, any object whatsoever being laid down hypothetically, God understands necessarily what will arise from that object.

XLIV. Free knowledge is also called "foreknowledge," as is likewise that of vision by which other beings are known; and since it follows a free act of the will, it is not the cause of things; it is, therefore, affirmed with truth concerning it, that things do not exist because God knows them as about to come into existence, but that He knows future things because they are future.

XLV. That kind of God's knowledge which is called "practical," "of simple intelligence," and "natural or necessary," is the cause of all things through the mode of prescribing and directing, to which is added the action of the will and power; (Psalm civ. 24;) although that "middle" kind of knowledge must intervene in things which depend on the liberty of a created will.

XLVI. God's knowledge is so peculiarly his own, as to be impossible to be communicated to any thing created, not even to the soul of Christ; though we gladly confess, that Christ knows all those things which are required for the discharge of his office and for his perfect blessedness. (1 Kings viii. 39; Matt. xxiv. 36.)

ON THE WILL OF GOD

XLVII. By the expression "will of God" is signified properly "the faculty itself of willing," but figuratively sometimes "the act of willing," and at other times "the object willed." (John vi. 39; Psalm cxv. 3.)

XLVIII. Not only a consideration of the essence and of the understanding of God, but also the Scriptures and the universal agreement of mankind, testify that a will is correctly attributed to God.

XLIX. This is the second faculty in the life of God, [§ 29,] which follows the Divine understanding and is produced from it, and by which God is borne towards a known good. Towards a good, because it is an adequate object of his will. And towards a known good, because the Divine understanding is previously borne towards it as a being, not only by knowing it as it is a being, but likewise by judging it to be good. Hence the act of the understanding is to offer it as a good, to the will which is of the same nature as the understanding, or rather, which is its own offspring, that it may also discharge its office and act concerning this known good. But God does not will the evil which is called that of "culpability;" because He does not more will any good connected with this evil than He wills the good to which the malignity of sin is opposed, and which is the Divine good itself. All the precepts of God demonstrate this in the most convincing manner. (Psalm v, 4, 5.)

L. But Good is of two kinds--the Chief Good itself, and that which is different from it. (Matt. xix. 17; Gen. i. 31.) The order which subsists between them is this: the latter does not exist with the Chief Good, but has its existence from it by the Understanding and the Will of God. (Rom. xi. 36.) Wherefore the Supreme Good is the primary, the choicest, and the direct object of the Divine Will; that is, its own infinite Essence, which was alone from all eternity, infinite ages prior to the existence of another good; and therefore it is the only good. (Prov. viii. 22-24.) On this account it may also be denominated, without impropriety, the peculiar and adequate object of the Divine Will. Since the Understanding and the Will of God were, each by its own act, borne towards this [Essence] they found such a plenitude of Being and Goodness in it, that the Understanding gave its judgment for commencing the communication of it outwards: and the Will approved of this kind of communication, after that method; whence the existence of a good, of what kind soever it was, which was different from the Chief Good. It cannot, therefore, be called an object of the Divine Will, except an indirect one, which God wills on account of that Chief Good, or rather He wills it to be on account of the Chief Good. (Prov. xvi. 4,.) Therefore, The Will of God is the very Essence of God, yet distinguished from it according to the formal reason.

LI. The act by which the Will of God advances towards its objects, is (1.) most simple: for as the Understanding of God by a most simple act understands its own Essence, and, through it, all other things; so the Will of God, by a single and simple act, wills its own goodness, and all things in its goodness. (Prov. xvi. 4.) Therefore, the multitude of things willed is not repugnant to the simplicity of the Divine Will. (Isa. xliii. 7; Ephes. i. 5-9.) (2.) This act is Infinite: for it is moved to will, neither by an external cause, by any other efficient, nor by an end, which is out of itself; it is not moved even by any object which is not itself. (Deut. vii. 7; Matt. xi. 26.) Nay, the willing of the end is not the cause of willing those things which are for the end; though it wills those things which are for the end to be put in order to that end. (Acts xvii. 25, 26; Psalm xvi. 9.) It is no valid objection to this truth, that God would not will or do some things unless some act of the creature intervened. (1 Sam. ii. 30.) (3.) It is Eternal; because nothing can de novo either be or appear good to God. (4.) It is Immutable; because that which has once either been or seemed good to Him, both is and appears such to Him perpetually; and that by which God is known to will any thing, is nothing else but this, his immutable entity. (Mal. iii. 6; Rom. xi. 1.) (5.) This act is likewise Holy: because God advances towards his object only on account of its being good, not on account of any other thing which is added to it; and only because his Understanding accounts it good, not because feeling inclines [him] towards it without right reason. (2 Tim. ii. 19; Rom. ix. 11; 12, 4; Psalm cxix. 137.)

LII. As the simple and external act by which the Divine Understanding knows all its objects, has not excluded order from them; so likewise may we be allowed to assign a certain order, according to which the simple and sole act of the will of God is borne towards its objects: (1.) God wills his own Essence and Goodness, that is, himself. (2.) He wills all those things which, by the extreme judgment of his wisdom, He hath determined to be made out of infinite beings possible to himself. (Prov. xvi. 4.) And, First, He wills to make them. Then, when they are made, He is affected towards them by his Will, as they have some similitude to his nature. (Gen. i. 31; John xiv. 23.) (3.) The third object of the Divine Will are those things which God judges it to be right that they should be done by creatures endowed with understanding and free-will: and his act of willing concerning these things is signified by a precept, in which we likewise include the prohibition of that which He wills not to be done by the same creature. (Exod. xx. 1, 2, &c.; Micah vi. 8.) We allow it to remain a matter of discussion, whether counsels can have a place here, provided those things about which the consultations are held be not considered as [things] of supererogation. (4.) The fourth object of the Divine Will is the Divine permission, by which God permits a rational creature to do what He forbade, and to omit what he commanded; and which consists of the suspension of an efficacious impediment, not of one that is due and sufficient. (Acts xiv. 16, 17; Psalm lxxxi. 13; Isa. v. 4) (5.) The fifth object of the Divine Will are those things which, according to his own infinite wisdom, God judges to be done from the acts of rational creatures. (Isa. v. 5; 1 Sam. ii. 30; Gen. xxii. 16, 17.)

LIII. But though nothing from without be the cause of God's volition, yet, since he wills that there should be order in things, (which order is placed principally in this, that some things be the causes of others,) just so far as God's volition is borne towards those objects, it is as if it were the cause of itself as it is borne towards others: (Hosea ii. 21, 22.) Thus the cause why He wills the condemnation of any one, this, because he wills the order of his justice to be observed throughout the universe. (John vi. 40; Deut. vii. 8.) Neither do we therefore deny, but that an act of a creature, or the omission of an act, may be thus far the occasion or primary cause of a certain Divine volition, that, without any consideration of that act or its omission, God might set it aside by such a volition. (1 Sam. ii. 30; Jer. xviii. 7, 8.)

LIV. Through his own Will, and by means of his Power, God is the cause of all other things; (Lam. iii. 37, 38;) yet so that when he acts through second causes, either with them or in them, he does not take away their own peculiar mode of acting with which they have been divinely endued but he suffers them according to their own mode to produce their own effects, necessary things necessarily, contingent things contingently, free things freely: and this contingency and freedom of second causes does not prevent that from being certainly done, or coming to pass, which God in this manner works by them; and therefore, the certain futurition of an event does not include its necessity. (Isa. x. 5, 6, 7; Gen. xlv. 5, 28; Acts xxvii. 29, 31.)

LV. Though God by a single and undivided act wills all the things which he wills; yet his Will, or rather his Volition, may be distinguished from the objects, by a consideration of the mode and order according to which it is borne towards its objects.

LVI. The Divine Will is borne towards its object, either according to the mode of Nature, or according to the mode of Liberty. According to the mode of Nature, it tends towards a primary and proper object, one that is suitable and adequate to its nature. According to the mode of Liberty, it tends towards all other things. Thus, God by a natural necessity wills himself; but He wills freely all other things; (2 Tim. ii. 13; Rev. iv. 11;) though the act which is posterior in order may be bound by a free act which is prior in order. This may be called "hypothetical necessity," having its origin partly from the free volition and act of God, partly from the immutability of his nature. "For God is not unrighteous," says the Apostle, "to forget the work and labour of love" of the pious; because he hath promised them a remuneration, and the immutability of his nature does not suffer him to rescind his promises. (Heb. vi. 10, 18.)

LVII. To this must be subjoined another distinction, according to which God wills something as an end, and other things as the means to that end. His Will tends towards the end by a natural affection or desire; and towards the means by a free choice. (Prov. xvi. 4)

LVIII. The will of God is also distinguished into that by which he wills to do or to prevent something, and which is called "the will of his good pleasure," or rather "of his pleasure;" (Psalm cxv. 3;) and into that by which he wills something to be done, or to be omitted, by creatures endued with understanding, and which is called "the will which is signified." The latter is revealed; the former is partly revealed, and partly hidden. (Mark iii. 35; 1 Thess. iv. 3; Deut. xxix, 29; 1 Cor. ii. 11, 12.) The former is efficacious, for it uses power, either so much as cannot be resisted, or such a kind as He certainly knows nothing will withstand: (Psalm xxxiii. 9; Rom. ix. 19.) The latter is called "inefficacious," and resistance is frequently made to it; yet so that, when the creature transgresses the order of this revealed Will, the creature by it may be reduced to order, and that the Will of God may be done on those by whom his Will has not been performed. (2 Sam. xvii. 14; Isa. v. 4, 5; Matt. xxi. 39-41; Acts v. 4; 1 Cor. vii. 28.) To this two-fold Will is opposed the Remission of the Will, which is called "Permission," and which is also two-fold. The one, which permits something to the power of a rational creature, by not circumscribing its act with a law; and this is opposed to "the revealed Will." The other is that by which God permits something to the capability and will of the creature, by not interposing an efficacious hindrance; and this is opposed to "the Will of God's pleasure" that is efficacious. (Acts xiv. 16; Psalm lxxxi. 13.)

LIX. The things which God wills to do he wills (1.) either from himself, not on account of any cause placed out of himself, whether this be without the consideration of any act which proceeds from the creature, or solely on occasion of the act of the creature: (Deut. vii. 7, 8; Rom. xi. 35; John iii. 16.) Or (2.) He does it on account of some other previous cause laid down on the part of the creature. (Exod. xxxii. 32, 33; 1 Sam. xv. 17, 23.) In regard to this distinction, some work is said to be proper to God, and some foreign to Him and his "strange work." (Lam. iii. 33; Isa. xxviii. 21.) This is also signified by the church in the following words: "O God! whose property is, ever to have mercy and to forgive," &c.

LX. Some persons also distinguish the will of God into that which is antecedent, and that which is consequent. This distinction has reference to one and the same volition or act of the rational creature, which if the act of the Divine will precedes, it is called the "antecedent will of God;" (1 Tim. ii. 4;) but if it follows, it is called his "consequent will:" (Acts i. 25; Matt. xxiii. 37, 38.) But the antecedent will, it appears, ought to be called velleity, rather than will.

LXI. There is not much distance between this distinction, and another, according to which God is said to will some things "so far as they are good when absolutely considered according to their nature;" but to will other things "so far as, after an inspection, of all the circumstances, they are understood to be desirable."

LXII. God also wills some things in their antecedent causes; that is He wills their causes as relatively, and places those causes in such order, that effects may follow from them; and, if they do follow, that they may of themselves be pleasing to him. (Ezek. xxxiii. 11; Gen. iv. 7.) He wills other things not only in their causes, but also in themselves. (John vi. 40; Matt. xi. 25, 26.) incident with this, is the distinction of the Divine Will into Conditional and Absolute.

LXIII. Lastly. God wills some things per se or accidentally.

He wills per se, those things which are simply and relatively good; (2 Pet. iii. 9; accidentally, those which are in some respect evil, but which have such good things united with them as He wills in preference to the respective good things which are opposed to those evil ones: thus, He wills the evils of punishment, because he would rather have the order of justice preserved in punishment, than suffer an offending creature to go unpunished. (Jer. ix. 9 Psalm i. 21; Jer. xv, 6.)

LET THE FOLLOWING BE PROBLEMS TO US

(1.) Is it possible for two affirmatively contrary volitions of God to tend towards one and the same uniform object?

(2.) Is it possible for one volition of God to tend towards contrary objects? lxiv. In this momentum of the Divine Nature, come under consideration those attributes which are ascribed to him in the Scriptures, either properly or figuratively, according to a certain analogy of affections and moral virtues in us; such as are love, hatred, goodness, mercy, desire, anger, justice, &c.

LXV. Those things which have the analogy of affections may be commodiously referred to two principal kinds. So the first can embrace those which we may call primary or principal; the second, those which are derived from the primary.

LXVI. 1The first or principal are Love, (whose opposition is Hatred,) and Goodness; and with these are connected Grace, Benignity and Mercy.

LXVII. Love is an affection of union in God, the objects of which are God himself and the good of justice or righteousness, the creature and its felicity. (Prov. xvi. 4; Psalm. xi. 7; John iii. 16; Wisdom xi. 24-26.) HATRED is an affection of separation in God, the object of which are the unrighteousness and misery of the creature. (Psalm v. 5; Ezek. xxv. 11; Deut. xxv. 15, 16, &c.; Isa. i. 24) But since God primarily loves himself and the good of justice, and at the same moment hates iniquity; and since He loves the creature and its happiness only secondarily, and at the same moment dislikes the misery of the creature; (Psalm xi. 5; Deut. xxviii. 63;) hence it comes to pass, that he hates a creature that pertinaciously perseveres in unrighteousness, and He loves its misery. (Isa. lxvi. 4.)

LXVIII. Goodness in God is an affection of communicating his own good. (Rev. iv. 11; Gen. i. 31.) Its first object outwards is nothing; and thus necessarily the first, that, on its removal, there can be no outward communication. The First advance of this goodness is towards the creature as it is a creature; the Second is towards the creature as it performs its duty, to communicate good to it beyond the remuneration promised. Both these procedures of the Divine goodness may appropriately receive the appellation of "Benignity." The Third advance is towards a creature that has sinned, and that has by such transgression rendered itself liable to misery. This advance is called Mercy, that is, an affection for affording succour to a person in misery, sin itself presenting no obstacle to its exercise. (Rom. v. 8; Ezek. xvi. 6.) We attribute these advances to the Divine Goodness in such a manner, that in the mean time we concede to the love of God towards his creatures its portion in these advances.

LXIX. Grace seems to stand as a proper adjunct to Goodness, and to Love towards the creatures. According to it, God is disposed to communicate his own good, and to love the creatures, not of merit or of debt, nor that it may add anything to God himself; (Psalm xvi. 2;) but that it may be well with him on whom the good is bestowed, and who is beloved. (Exod. xxxiv. 6; Rom. v. 8; 1 John iv. 7.)

LXX. The affections which arise from the primary ones, [§ 65,] are special, as being those which are not occupied about Good and Evil in common, but specially about Good as it is present or absent. We distinguish these affections according to the confined capacity of our consideration, as they have some analogy either in Concupiscibility or in Irascibility.

LXXI. In the Concupiscible we consider, first, Desire and that which is opposed to it; and, afterwards, Joy and Grief. We describe Desire, in God, as an affection for obtaining the works of righteousness which have been prescribed to creatures endued with understanding, and for bestowing on them "the recompense of reward:" (Psalm lxxxi. 13-16; v, 3-5; Isa. xlviii. 18, 19.) To this is opposed that affection according to which God abhors the works of unrighteousness, and the omission of a remuneration. (Jer. v. 7, 9.) Joy is an affection arising from the presence of a thing that is suitable: such as the fruition of himself, the obedience of the creature, the communication of his own goodness, and the destruction of his rebels and enemies. (Isa. lxii. 5; Psalm lxxxi. 13; Prov. i. 24-26.) Grief, which is its opposite, has its origin in the disobedience and the misery of the creature, and in the occasion given by his people for blaspheming the name of God among the Gentiles. Nearly allied to this is Repentance, which, in God, is nothing more than a change of the thing willed or done, on account of the act of a rational creature. (Gen. xv. 6; Jer. xviii. 8-10.)

LXXII. In the Irascible we place Hope, and its opposite, Despair, Confidence and Anger, and we do not exclude even Fear, which, by an Anthropo-pathy, we read, as attributed to God. (Deut. xxxii. 27.) Hope is an attentive expectation of a good work due from the creature, and by the grace of God capable of being performed. It may easily be reconciled with the certain fore-knowledge of God. (Isa. v. 4; Luke xiii. 6, 7.) Despair arises from the pertinacious wickedness of the creature, who is "alienated from the life of God," and hardened in evil, and who, after "he is past feeling," his conscience having been "seared with a hot iron," has "given himself over unto lasciviousness, to work all uncleanness with greediness." (Jer. xiii. 23; Ephes. iv. 18, 19.) What in God we call Confidence or Courage, is that by which He with great animation prosecutes a good that is beloved and desired, and puts away and repulses an evil that is hated. Anger is an affection of depulsion in God, through the punishment of the creature who has transgressed his law; by which He brings upon the creature the evil of misery for his unrighteousness, and takes the vengeance which is due to Himself, as an indication of his love of righteousness and his hatred of sin. When this is vehement, it is called "Fury." (Isa. lxiii. 3-5; Ezek. xiii. 13, 14; Isa. xxvii. 4; Jer. ix. 9; Deut. xxxii. 35; Jer. x. 24; 12, 13; Isa. lxiii. 6.)

LXXIII. We attribute these affections to God, on account of some of his own which are analogous to them, without any passion, as He is simple and immutable; and without any inordinateness, disorder and repugnance to right reason; for He exercises himself in a holy manner about all things which are the objects of his will. But we subject the use and exercise of them to the infinite wisdom of God, whose office it is previously to affix to each its object, mode, end, and circumstances, and to determine to which of them, in preference to the rest, is to be conceded the province of acting. (Exod. xxxii. 10-14; Deut. xxxii. 26, 27.)

LXXIV. Those things in God which have an analogy to moral virtues, as moderators of these affections, are partly general to all the affections, as Righteousness; and partly concern some of them in a special manner, as Patience, and those which are moderators of Anger and of the punishments which proceed from Anger.

LXXV. Righteousness or Justice in God, is an eternal and constant will to render to every one his own: (Psalm xi. 7) To God himself that which is his, and to the creature what belongs to it. We consider this righteousness in its Words and in its Acts. In all its Words are found veracity and constancy; and in its Promises, fidelity. (2 Tim. ii. 13; Num. xxiii. 19; Rom. iii. 4; 1 Thess. v. 24) With regard to its Acts, it is two-fold, Disposing and Remunerative. The former is that according to which God disposes all the things in his actions through his own wisdom, according to the rule of equity which has either been prescribed or pointed out by his wisdom. The latter, [remunerative righteousness,] is that by which God renders to his creatures that which belongs to it, according to his work through an agreement into which He has entered with it. (Heb. vi. 10, 17, 18; Psalm cxlv. 17; 2 Thess. i. 6; Rev. ii. 23.)

LXXVI. Patience is that by which God patiently endures the absence of a good that is loved, desired, and hoped for, and the presence of an evil that is hated; and which spares sinners, not only that He may through them execute the judicial acts of his mercy and justice, but that he may likewise lead them to repentance; or may punish with the greater equity and more grievously, the contumacious. (Isa. v. 4; Ezek. xviii. 23; Matt. xxi. 33- 41; Luke xiii. 6-9; Rom. ii. 4, 5; 2 Pet. iii. 9.)

LXXVII. Long-suffering, gentleness, readiness to pardon, and clemency, are the moderators of Anger and Punishments. Long-Suffering suspends anger, lest it should hasten to drive away the evil as soon as ever such an act was required by the demerits of the creature. (Exod. xxxiv. 6; Isa. xlviii. 8, 9; Psalm ciii. 9.) We call that Gentleness, or Lenity, which attempers Anger, lest it should be of too great a magnitude; nay, lest its severity should correspond with the magnitude of the wickedness committed. (Psalm ciii. 10.) We call that Readiness To Pardon, which moderates Anger, so that it may not continue forever, agreeably to the deserts of sinners. (Psalm xxx. 5; Jer. iii. 5; Joel ii. 13.) Clemency is that by which God attempers the deserved punishments, that by their severity and continuance they may be far inferior to the demerits of sin, and may not exceed the strength of the creature. (2 Sam. vii. 14; Psalm ciii. 13, 14.)

ON THE POWER OF GOD

LXXVIII. By the term "The Power Of God," is meant not a passive power, which cannot happen to God who is a pure act; nor the act, by which God is always acting in himself through necessity of nature; but it signifies an active power, by which He can operate extrinsically, and by which he does so operate when it seems good to himself.

LXXIX. We describe it thus: "It is a faculty of the Life of God, posterior in order to the Understanding and the Will, by which God can, from the liberty of his own Will, operate extrinsically all things whatsoever that He can freely will, and by which he does whatsoever He freely wills." Hence it appears, that Power resembles a principle which executes what the will commands under the direction of knowledge. But we wish Impeding or Obstruction to be comprehended under the operation. (Psalm cxv. 3; Lament. iii. 37, 38; Psalm xxxiii. 9; Jer. xviii. 6.) Therefore, From this we exclude the power or capability of generating and breathing forth, because it acts in a natural manner and intrinsically.

LXXX. The measure of the Divine Capability is the Free Will of God, and indeed this is an adequate measure. (Psalm cxv. 3; Matt. xi. 25-27) For whatsoever God can will freely, He can likewise do it; and whatsoever it is possible for Him to do, He can freely will it; and whatever it is impossible for Him to will, He cannot do it; and that which He cannot do, He also cannot will. But He does, because He wills; and He does not do, because He does not will. Therefore, He does the things which He does, because He wills so to do. He does them not, because He wills them not; not, on the contrary. Hence the objects of the Divine Capability may be most commodiously, and indeed ought to be, circumscribed through the object of the Free Will of God.

LXXXI. The following is the manner: Since the Free Will [of God] rests upon a Will conducting itself according to the mode of [his] nature, and both of them have an Understanding which precedes them, and which, in conjunction with the Will, has the very Essence of God for its foundation; and since God can freely will those things alone which are not contrary to his Essence and Natural Will, and which can be comprehended in his Understanding as entities and true things: it follows, that He can do these things alone; nay, that He can likewise do all things, since the Free Will of God, and therefore, his Power also, are bound by those alone. And since things of this kind are the only things which are simply and absolutely possible, all other things being impossible, God is deservedly said to be capable of doing all things that are possible. (Luke i. 37; xviii, 27; Mark xiv. 36.) For how can there be an entity, a truth, or a good, which is contrary to His Essence and Natural Will, and incomprehensible to his Understanding?

LXXXII. The things thus laid down [as described in the last clause of the preceding Thesis] are indeed confessed by all men; and they are generally described in the schools as things impossible, which imply a contradiction. But it is asked in species, "What are those things?" We will here recount some of them. God cannot make another God; is incapable of being changed; (James i. 17;) he cannot sin; (Psalm v. 5;) cannot lie; (Num. xxiii. 19; 2 Tim. ii. 13;) cannot cause a thing at the same time to be and not to be, to have been and not to have been, to be hereafter and not hereafter to be, to be this and not to be this, to be this and its contrary. He cannot cause an accident to be without its subject, a substance to be changed into a pre-existing substance, bread into the body of Christ, and He cannot cause a body to be in every place. When we make such assertions as these, we do not inflict an injury on the power of God; but we must beware that things unworthy of Him be not attributed to his Essence, his Understanding, and his Will.

LXXXIII. The Power of God is infinite; because it can do not only all things possible; (which are innumerable, so that they cannot be reckoned to be such a number, without a possibility of their being still more;) but likewise because nothing can resist it. For all created things depend upon the Divine Power, as upon their efficient principle, as the. phrase is, both in their being and in their preservation; whence Omnipotence is deservedly attributed to Him. (Rev. i. 8; Ephes. iii. 20; Matt. iii. 9; xxvi, 53; Rom. ix. 19; Phil. iii. 21.)

Since the measure of God's Power is his own Free Will, and since therefore God does anything because he wills to do it; it cannot be concluded from the Omnipotence of God that anything will come to pass, [or will afterwards be,] unless it be evident from the Divine Will. (Dan. iii. 17, 18; Rom. iv. 20, 21; Matt. viii. 2.) But if this be evident from the will of God, what He hath willed to do is certain to be done, although, to the mind of the creature, it may not seem possible. (Luke i. 19, 20, 34-37.) And that the mind must be "brought into captivity to the obedience of faith," is a truth which here finds abundant scope for exercise.

LXXXV. The distinction of Power into absolute, and ordinary or actual, has not reference to God's Power so much as to his Will, which uses his Power to do some things when it wills to use it, and which does not use it when it does not will; though it would be possible for it to use the Power if it would; and if it did use it, the Divine Will would, through it, do far more things than it does. (Matt. iii. 9.)

LXXXVI. The Omnipotence of God cannot be communicated to any creature. (1 Tim. vi. 15; Jude. 4.)

ON THE PERFECTION OF GOD

LXXXVII. From the simple and infinite combination of all these things, when they are considered with the mode of pre-eminence, the Perfection of God has its existence. Not that by which He has every single thing in a manner the most perfect; for this is effected by Simplicity and Infinity: but it is that by which, in the most perfect manner, he has all things which denote any perfection. And it may fitly be described thus: "It is the interminable, the entire, and, at the same time, the perfect possession of Essence and Life." (Matt. v. 48; Gen. xvii. 1; Exod. vi. 3; Psalm l:10; Acts xvii. 25; James i. 17.)

LXXXVIII. This Perfection of God infinitely exceeds the perfection of all the creatures, on a three-fold account. For it possesses all things in a mode the most perfect, and does not derive them from another. But the perfection which the creatures possess, they derive from God, and it is faintly shadowed forth after its archetype. Some creatures have a larger portion [of this derived perfection] than others; and the more of it they possess, the nearer they are to God and have the greater likeness to Him. (Rom. xi. 35, 36; 1 Cor. iv. 7; Acts xvii. 28, 29; 2 Cor. iii. 18; 2 Pet. i. 4; Matt. v. 48.)

LXXXIX. From this Perfection, by means of some internal act of God, his Blessedness has its existence; and his Glory exists, by means of some relation of it extrinsically. (1 Tim. i. 11; vi, 15; Exod. xxxiii. 18.)

ON THE BLESSEDNESS OF GOD

XC. Blessedness is through an act of the understanding: is it not also through an act of the will? Such is our opinion; and we delineate it thus. It is an act of the life of God, by which he enjoys his own perfection, that is fully known by his Understanding and supremely loved by his Will; and by which He complacently reposes in this Perfection with satisfaction. (Gen. xvii. 1; Psalm xvi. 11; 1 Cor. ii. 9, 10.)

XCI. The Blessedness of God is so peculiar to himself, that it cannot be communicated to a creature. (1 Cor. xv. 28.) Yet, in relation to the object, he is the beautifying good of all creatures endued with understanding, and is the Effector of the act which tends to this object, and which reposes with satisfaction in it. In these consists the blessedness of the creature.

THE GLORY OF GOD

XCII. The Glory of God is from his Perfection, regarded extrinsically, and may in some degree be described thus: It is the excellence of God above all things. God makes this glory manifest by external acts in various ways. (Rom. i. 23; ix, 4; Psalm viii. 1.)

XCIII. But the modes of manifestation, which are declared to us in the scriptures, are chiefly two: the one, by an effulgence of light and of unusual splendour, or by its opposite, a dense darkness or obscurity. (Matt. xvii. 2-5; Luke ii. 9; Exod. xvi. 10; 1 Kings viii. 11.) The other, by the production of works which agree with his Perfection and Excellence. (Psalm xix. 1; John ii. 11.) But ceasing from any more prolix discussion of this subject, let us with ardent prayers suppliantly beseech the God of Glory, that, since He has formed us for his Glory, He would vouchsafe to make us yet more and more the instruments of illustrating his Glory among men, through Jesus Christ our Lord, the brightness of his Glory, and the express image of his Person.

DISPUTATION 5 - ON THE PERSON OF THE FATHER AND THE SON

RESPONDENT: PETER DE LA FITE

I. WE do not here receive the name of "Father," as it is sometimes taken in the Scriptures in regard to the adoption, according to which God hath adopted believers to himself as sons: (Gal. iv. 6) Nor with respect to the creation of things, according to which even the Gentiles themselves knew God the Father, and gave Him that appellation: (Acts xvii. 28.) But by this name we signify God according to the relation which He has to his only-begotten and proper Son, who is our Lord Jesus Christ: (Ephes. i. 3) And we thus describe Him: "He is the First Person in the Sacred Trinity, who from all eternity of himself begat his Word, which is his Son, by communicating to Him his own Divinity."

II. We call Him "a Person," not in reference to the use of that word in personating, [appearing in a mask,] which denotes the representation of another; but in reference to its being defined an undivided and communicable subsistence, of a nature that is living, intelligent, willing, powerful, and active. Each of these properties is attributed, in the Holy Scriptures, to the Father of our Lord Jesus Christ. Substitence: "Him which is, and which was, and which is to come." (Rev. i. 4) Life: "As the living Father hath sent me," &c. (John vi. 53, 57.) Intelligence: "O the depth of the riches both of the wisdom and knowledge of God (Rom. xi. 33.) Will: "And this is the Father's will," &c. (John vi. 39.) Power: "Thine, O Fath er, is the Power." (Matt. vi. 13.) Action: "My Father worketh hitherto." (John v. 17.) We do not contend about words. Under the term "Person," we comprehend such things as we have now described; and since they agree with the Father, the title of "Person" cannot be justly denied to him.

III. We call Him "a Person in the Holy Trinity," that is, a Divine Person, which with us possesses just as much force as if we were to call Him God. For though the Deity of the Father has been acknowledged by most of those persons who have called in question that of the Son; yet it is denied by those who have declared, that the God of the Old Testament is different from that of the New, and who have affirmed that the Father of Jesus Christ is a different Being from the Creator of heaven and earth. To the former class we oppose the word of Christ: "I thank thee, O Father, Lord of heaven and earth," &c. (Matt. xi. 25.) To the latter we oppose another saying of the same Christ: "It is my Father that honoureth me; of whom ye say, that He is your God." (John viii. 54.) To both of these classes together we oppose that joint declaration of the whole church at Jerusalem: "Thou art God, which hast made heaven, and earth, and the sea, and all that in them is: Who by the mouth of thy servant David hast said," &c. And in a subsequent verse, "For of a truth against thy holy Son Jesus, whom thou hast anointed, both Herod and Pontius Pilate, etc, were gathered together." (Acts iv. 24-27.)

IV. We place Him "first" in the Holy Trinity: for so hath Christ taught us, by commanding us to "baptize in the name of the Father, and of the Son, and of the Holy Ghost." (Matt. xxviii. 19.) "The First" not in relation of time but of order; which order has its foundation in this: The Father is the fountain and origin of the whole Divinity, and the principle and the cause of the Son himself, which the word the" implies. (John v. 26, 27.) Pious Antiquity attempted to illustrate this [mystery] by the similitude of a fountain and its stream, of the sun and its beam, of the mind and its reason, of a root and its stalk, and by similar comparisons. On this account the Father is called "unbegotten" and the Christian Fathers ascribe to Him supreme and pre-eminent authority. It is on this account also that the name of God is often attributed in the Scriptures peculiarly and by way of eminence to the Father.

V. We attribute to Him "active generation," which likewise comprised under the word "Father;" but of its mode and ratio, we willingly confess ourselves to be ignorant. But yet, since all generation, properly so called, is made by the communication of the same nature which He possesses who begets, we say with correctness that "the Father of himself begat the Son," by communicating to him his Deity, which is his own nature. The principle, therefore, which begets, is the Father; but the principle by which generation is effected is his nature. Whence the Person is said to beget and to be begotten. But the nature is said neither to beget nor to be begotten, but to be communicated. This communication, when rightly understood, renders vain the objection of the Anti-Trinitarians, who accuse the members of the church universal of holding a quaternity (of Divine Persons in the Godhead.)

VI. We say "that from all eternity He begat," because neither was he the God of Jesus Christ, before he was his father, nor was he simply God before he was his Father. For as we cannot imagine a mind that is devoid of reason, so we say that it is impious to form a conception in our minds of a God who is without his word. (John i. 1, 2.) Besides, according to the sentiments of sacred antiquity, and of the church universal, since this generation is an internal operation and it is likewise from all eternity. For all such operations are eternal, unless we wish to maintain that God is liable to change.

VII. We have hitherto treated of the Father. The Son is the second person in the Holy Trinity, the Word of the Father, begotten of the Father from all eternity, and proceeding from Him by the communication of the same Deity which the Father possesses without origination. (Matt. xxviii. 19; John i. 1; Micah v. 2.) We say, "that he is not the Son by creation." For what things soever they were that have been created, they were all created by him. (John i. 3.) And "that he was not made the Son by adoption:" for we are all adopted in him. (John i. 12; Ephes. i. 5, 6.) But "that he proceeded from the Father by generation." He is the Son, not by creation out of nonentities, or from uncreated elements--not by adoption, as though he had previously been some other thing than the Son; for this is his primitive name, and significant of his inmost nature; but He is by generation, and, as the Son, he is by nature a partaker of the whole divinity of his Father.

VIII. We call the Son "a person," with the same meaning attached to the word as that by which we have already (§ 2) predicated the Father. For he is an undivided and incommunicable subsistence. John says, (i, 1,) "In the beginning was the Word, and the Word was with God." Of a living nature: "As I live by the Father." (John vi. 57.) Intelligent: "The Son, who is in the bosom of the Father, has declared him." (John i. 18.) Willing: "To whomsoever the Son will reveal him." (Matt. xi. 27.) "Even so the Son quickeneth whom he will." (John v. 21.) Powerful: "According to the efficacy whereby He is able even to subdue all things unto him." (Phil. iii. 21.) Active: "And I work." (John v. 17.)

IX. We call the Son "a person in the Sacred Trinity," that is, a Divine person and God. And, with orthodox antiquity, we prove our affirmation by four distinct classes or arguments. (1.) From the names by which he is called in the Scriptures. (2.) From the divine attributes which the Scriptures ascribe to him. (3.) From the works which the Scriptures relate to have been produced by him. (4.) From a collation of those passages of Scripture, which, having been uttered in the Old Testament concerning the Father, are in the New appropriated to the Son.

X. The divinity of the person of the Son is evident, from the names which are attributed to him in the scriptures. (1.) Because he is called God, and this not only attributively, as "the Word was God," (John i. 1.) "Who is over all, God blessed forever;" (Rom. ix. 5;) but likewise subjectively: "God manifested in the flesh." (1 Tim. iii. 16.) "O God, thy God hath anointed Thee with the oil of gladness." (Heb. i. 9.) Nay, he is likewise called "the great God." (Tit. ii, 13.) (2.) The word "Son" stands in proof of the same truth, especially so far as this name belongs to him properly and solely, according to which he is called "God's own Son," (Rom. viii. 32,) and "his only begotten Son," (John i. 18,) which expressions, we affirm, are tantamount to his being called by nature, the Son of God. (3.) Because he is called "King of kings and Lord of lords;" (Rev. xvii. 14; xix, 16;) and "the Lord of glory." (1 Cor. ii. 8.) These appellations prove much more strongly what we wish to establish, if they be compared with the scriptures of the Old Testament, in which the same names are ascribed to him who is called Jehovah. (Psalm xcv. 3; xxiv, 8-10.) (4.) Pious antiquity established the same truth from the name, of Logov, "the Word;" which cannot signify the outward word that is devoid of a proper subsistence, on account of those things which are attributed to it in the Scriptures. For it is said to have been "in the beginning, to have been with God, and to be God," and to have "created all things," &c.

XI. The essential attributes of the Deity which are in the Scriptures ascribed to the Son of God, likewise declare this in the plainest manner. (1.) Immensity: "My Father and I will come unto him, and make our abode with him." (John xiv. 23.) "That Christ may dwell in your hearts by faith." (Ephes. iii. 17.) "I am with you alway, even unto the end of the world." (Matt. xxviii. 20.) (2.) Eternity: "In the beginning was the Word." (John i. 1.) "I am Alpha and Omega, the first and the last." (Rev. i. 11; ii, 8.) (3.) Immutability: "But thou, O Lord, remainest; thou art the same, and thy years shall not fail." (Heb. i. 11, 12.) (4.) Omniscience is also attributed to him: For he searches the reins and hearts;" (Rev. ii. 93.) He "knows all things." (John xxi. 17.) And he perceived the thoughts of the Pharisees. (Matt. xii. 25.) (5.) Omnipotence:

"According to the efficacy whereby the Lord Jesus Christ is able even to subdue all things unto himself" (Phil. iii. 21.) But the Divine nature cannot, without a contradiction, be taken away from him to whom the proper essentials of God are ascribed. (6.) Lastly. Majesty and glory belong to Him equally with the Father: "That all men should honour the Son, even as they honour the Father." (John v. 23.) "Blessing, and honour, and glory, and power, be unto Him that sitteth upon the throne, and unto the Lamb, forever and ever." (Rev. v. 13.)

XII. The divine works which are attributed to Him, establish the same truth. (1.) The creation of all things: "A2 things were made by Him." (John i. 3.) "By whom also, he made the worlds," or the ages. (Heb. i. 2.) "One Lord Jesus Christ, by whom are all things." (1 Cor. viii. 6.) But what are these "all things?" Exactly the same as those which are said, in the same verse, to be "of the Father." (2.) The preservation of all things: all things by the word of his power." (Heb. i. 3.) "My Father worketh hitherto, and I work." (John v. 17.) (3.) The performing of miracles: "Which He works by the Holy Spirit, who is said to "have received of the things of Christ, by which he will glorify Christ." (John xvi. 14.) "By which, also, he went and preached unto the spirits in prison." (1 Pet. iii. 19.) This Spirit is so peculiar to Christ, that the Apostles are said to perform miracles in the name and power of Christ. (4.) To these let the works which relate to the salvation of the church be added; which cannot be performed by one who is a mere man.

XIII. A comparison of those passages which in the Old Testament, are ascribed to God, who claims for himself the appellation of Jehovah, with the same passages which in the New, are attributed to the Son of God, our Lord Jesus Christ supplies to us the fourth class of arguments. But because the number of them is immense, we will refrain from a prolix recital of the whole, and produce only a few out of the many. In Numbers. xxi. 5-7, it is said, "The people spoke against God, and the Load sent fiery serpents among them, and they bit the people," many of whom "died." In 1 Corinthians x. 9, the apostle says, "Neither let us tempt Christ, as some of them also tempted, and were destroyed of serpents." The passage in the 68th Psalm, (18,) which describes God as "ascending on high and leading captivity captive," is interpreted by the apostle, (Ephes. iv. 8,) and applied to Christ. What is spoken in Psalm cii. 25, 26, about the true God, ["Of old hast thou laid the foundation of the earth," &c.] is, in Heb. i. 10-12, expressly applied to Christ. St. John, in his gospel, (xii, 40, 41,) interprets the vision described by Isaiah, (vi, 9, 10,) and declares that "Esaias said these things when he saw the glory of Christ." In Isai. viii. 14, Jehovah, it is said, "shall be a rock of offense, and a snare to the houses of Israel," &c. Yet Simeon, (in Luke ii. 34,) St. Paul, (in Romans ix. 33,) and St. Peter, (1 Epis. ii. 8,) severally declare that Christ was "set for the rising and falling of many," for "a stumbling block, and rock of offense" to unbelievers, and to "the disobedient."

XIV. We call Christ "the second person," according to the order which has been pointed out to us by Himself in Matt. xxviii. 19. For the Son is of the Father, as from one from whom he is said to have come forth. The Son lives by the Father, (John vi. 57,) and the Father hath given to the Son to have life in himself." (v, 26.) The Son understands by the Father, because "the Father sheweth the Son all things that himself doeth," (v, 20,) and what things the Son saw while "He was in the bosom of the Father, he testifies and declares to us." (i, 18; iii, 32.) The son works from the Father, because "the Son can do nothing of himself: But what he seeth the Father do." (v, 19.) Thus "the Son does not speak of himself, but the Father, that dwelleth in him, doeth the works." (xiv, 10.) This is the reason why the Son, by a just right, refers all things to the Father, as to Him from whom he received all that he had. (xix, 11; xvii, 7.) "When he was in the form of God, he thought it not robbery to be equal with God; but made himself of no reputation, and took upon him the form of a servant, &c. and became obedient" to the Father, "even unto the death of the cross." (Phil. ii. 6-8.)

XV. We say "that the Son was begotten of the Father from all eternity." (1.) Because "his goings-forth have been from of old, from everlasting," and "these goings-forth" are from the Father. (Micah v. 2, 3.) If any one be desirous to give them any other interpretation than "the goings-forth" of generation, he must make them subsequent to the "goings-forth" of generation; and thus likewise he establishes the eternity of generation. (2.) Because, since the Son is eternal, as we have previously shewn, [§ 7,] and since he had no existence at all before he existed as the Son, (but it is proper to a son to be begotten,) we correctly assert on these grounds, that "he was eternally begotten." (3.) Since Logov, "the Word," was "in the beginning with the Father," (John i. 1, 9,) he must of necessity have been in the beginning from the Father; (unless we wish to maintain that the Word is collateral with the Father;) in truth, according to the order of nature he must have been from the Father, before he was with the Father. But he is not from the Father, except according to the mode of generation; for if it be otherwise, "the Word" will be from the Father in one mode, and "the Son" in another, which contradicts the eternity of the Son that we have already established. Therefore, "the Word" is eternally begotten.

XVI. From these positions we perceive, that an agreement and a distinction subsists between the Father and the Son. (l.) An Agreement in reference to One and the same nature and essence, according to which the Son is said to be "in the form of God," and "equal with the Father;" (Phil. ii. 6,) and according to the decree of the Nicene Council to be omoousiov ["of the same substance,"] "consubstantial with the Father," not omoiousiov "of like substance;" because the comparison of things in essence must be referred not to similitude or dissimilitude, but to Equality or Inequality, according to the very nature of things and to truth itself: (2.) A Distinction according to the mode of existence or subsistence, by which both of them have their divinity: for the Father has it from no one, the Son has it communicated to him by the Father. According to the former, the Son is said to be one with the Father; (John x. 30;) according to the latter, He is said to be "another" than the Father; (v, 32;) but according to both of them, the Son and the Father are said to "come to those whom they love, and to make their abode with them," (xiv, 23,) by the Spirit of both Father and Son "who dwelleth in believers," (Rom. viii. 9-11,) and "whom the Son sends to them from the Father." (John xv. 26.) May the God of our Lord Jesus Christ, the Father of all consolation, deign to bestow upon us the communion of this Spirit, through the Son of his love. Amen!

DISPUTATION 6 - ON THE HOLY SPIRIT

RESPONDENT: JAMES MAHOT

As the preceding Disputation treated of God the Father and God the Son, order requires us now to enter on the subject of the Holy Ghost.

I. The word Spirit signifies primarily, properly, and adequately, a thing which in its first act and essence is most subtle and simple, but which in its second act and efficacy is exceedingly active, that is, powerful and energetic. Hence it has come to pass, that this word is received, by way of distinction and opposition, sometimes for a personal and self-existing energy and power, and sometimes for an energy inhering to some other thing according to the mode of quality or property: but this word belongs primarily and properly to a self-existing power; and to an inhering power or energy, only secondarily and by a metaphorical communication. (John iii. 8; Psalm civ. 4; Luke i. 35;1 Kings ii. 9.)

II. But it is, in the first place, and with the greatest truth, ascribed to God, (John iv. 24,) both because He according to Essence is a pure and most simple act; and because according to Efficacy he is most active, and most prompt and powerful to perform, that is, because He is the first and Supreme Being, as well as the first and Supreme Agent. But it is with singular propriety attributed to the hypostatical energy which exists in God, and which is frequently marked with an addition, thus, "The Spirit of Elohim," (Gen. i. 9,) "The Spirit of Jehovah," (Isa. xi. 2,) and "His Holy Spirit." (lxiii, 10.) By these expressions is signified, that He is the person by whom God the Father and the Son perform all things in heaven and earth, (Matt. xii. 28; Luke xi. 20,) and that He is not only Holy in himself, but likewise the Sanctifier of all things which are in any way holy and so called. Our present discourse is concerning the Holy Spirit understood according to this last signification.

III. We may not attempt to define the Holy Spirit, (for such an attempt is unlawful,) but we may be allowed in some degree to describe Him according to the Scriptures, after the following manner: He is the person subsisting in the Sacred and undivided Trinity, who is the Third in order, emanates from the Father and is sent by the Son; and therefore He is the Spirit proceeding from both, and, according to his Person, distinct from both; an infinite, eternal illimitable Spirit, and of the same Divinity with God the Father and the Son. This description we will now consider in order, according to its several parts. (Matt. xxviii. 19; John i. 26; and Luke iii. 16; John xiv. 16; 1 Cor. ii. 10, 11; Gen. i. 2; Psalm cxxxix. 7-12.)

IV. On this subject four things come under our consideration and must be established by valid arguments. (1.) That the Holy Spirit ufisamenon is subsistent and a Person; not something after the manner of a quality and property, (suppose that of goodness, mercy, or patience,) which exists within the Deity. (2.) That He is a Person proceeding from the Father and the Son, and therefore is in order the Third in the Trinity. (3.) That according to his Person He is distinct from the Father and the Son. (4.) That He is infinite, eternal, immeasurable, and of the same Divinity with the Father and the Son, that is, not a creature, but God.

V. The first is proved by those attributes which the whole of mankind are accustomed to ascribe to a thing that has an existence, and which they conceive under the notion of "a Person:" for we assert, that all those things belong to the Holy Spirit, whether they agree with a person in the first Act or in the second. (1.) From those things which agree in the first Act with a thing that has an existence and is a

Person, we draw the following conclusion: That to which belongs Essence or Existence, Life, Understanding, Will and Power, is justly called "a Person," or nothing whatever in the nature of things can receive that appellation. But to the Holy Spirit belong: (i.) Essence or Existence: for He is in God, (1 Cor. ii. 11,) emanates from God and is sent by the Son. (John xv. 26.) (ii.) Life: for He "brooded over the waters," (Gen. i. 2,) as a hen covers her chickens with her wings; and He is the Author of animal and of spiritual life to all things living. (Job xxxiii. 4; John iii. 5; Rom. viii. 2, 11.) (iii.) Understanding: "The Spirit searcheth all things, yea, the deep things of God." (1 Cor. ii. 10.) (iv.) Will: for He "distributes his gifts to every man severally as He will." (1 Cor. xii. 11.) (v.) Lastly, Power: with which, the prophets, and other holy persons, and in particular the Messiah himself, were furnished and strengthened. (Micah iii. 8; Ephes. iii. 16; Isa. xi. 2.)

VI. The same thing is proved (2.) from those things which are usually attributed to a Person in the second Act. For of this description are the actions which are ascribed to the Holy Spirit, and which usually belong to nothing except a subsistence and a person. Such are to create, (Job xxxiii. 4; Psalm civ. 30,) to preserve, to vivify or quicken, to instruct or furnish them with knowledge, faith, charity, hope, the fear of the Lord, fortitude, patience, and other virtues; to "rush mightily upon Sampson;" (Judges xiv. 6;) to "depart from Saul;" (1 Sam. xvi. 14;) to "rest upon the Messiah;" (Isa. xi. 2;) to "come upon and overshadow Mary;" (Luke i. 35;) to send the prophets; (Isa. lxi. 1;) to appoint bishops; (Acts xx. 28;) to descend in a bodily appearance like a dove upon Christ, (Luke iii. 22,) and similar operations. To these may also be added those metaphorical expressions which attributes such passions to Him as agree with no other thing than a subsistence and a person, and as are signified in the following passages: "I will pour out my Spirit upon all flesh." (Joel ii. 28.) "Jesus breathed on them, and said, receive ye the Holy Ghost." (John xx. 22.) "They vexed his Holy Spirit. (Isa. lxiii. 10.) "Grieve not the Holy Spirit of God." Ephes. iv. 30.) To blaspheme and speak a word against the Holy Ghost. (Matt. xii. 31, 32.) "He hath done despite to the Spirit of Grace," (Heb. x. 29.)

VII. A similar bearing have those passages of Scripture which reckon the Holy Spirit in the same series with the Father and the Son. Of which class is that commanding men "to be baptized in the name of the Father, of the Son, and of the Holy Ghost;" (Matt. xxviii. 19;) that which says, "There are three that bear record in Heaven, the Father, the Word, and the Holy Ghost." (1 John v. 7;) that which declares, "The same Spirit, the same Lord, and the same God, effect the diversities of operations, institute the differences of administrations, and pour out the diversities of gifts; (1 Cor. xii. 4 -- 6;) and that which beseeches, "that the grace of the Lord Jesus Christ, and the love of God, and the communion of the Holy Ghost may be with all believers." (2 Cor. xiii. 13.) For it would be absurd to number an inly-existent quality, or property, in the same series with two subsistences or persons.

VIII. The second topic of consideration [§ 15,] contains three members: (i.) of which the first, that is, the procession of the Holy Spirit from the Father, is proved by those passages of Scripture in which he receives the appellation of "the Spirit of God and of the Father," and of "the Spirit who is of God;" and by those in which the Spirit is said to proceed and go forth from, to be given, poured out, and sent forth by the Father, and by whom the Father acts and operates. (John xiv. 16, 26; xv, 26; Joel ii. 28; Gal. iv. 6.) (ii.) The second member, that is, the procession from the Son, is proved by similar passages, which style Him "the Spirit of the Son," (Gal. iv. 6,) and which declare, that He is given and sent by the Son, (John xv. 26,) and that He therefore receives from the Son and glorifies Him. (xvi, 14.) To which must likewise be added, from another passage, (xx, 22,) a mode of giving, which is called "breathing," or inspiration. (iii.) The third member, that is, His being the third person in the Holy Trinity in order, but not in time and degree, appears principally from the fact, that the Spirit of the Father and the Son is said to be sent and given by the Father and the Son, and that the Father and the Son are said to work by Him. It is also manifest from the order which was observed in the institution of Baptism, "Baptizing them in the name of the Father, and of the Son, and of the Holy Ghost." (Matt. xxviii. 19.)

IX. All those passages of Scripture which have been produced in the preceding Theses for another purpose, prove "that the Holy Spirit is distinguished from the Father and the Son, not only according to name, but likewise according to person," which is the third part of the description which we have given. [§ 4.] Among other passages, the following expressly affirm this distinction: "I will pray the Father, and He shall give you another Comforter." (John xiv. 16.) "That Comforter, the Holy Ghost, whom the Father will send in my name." (xiv, 26.) "When that Comforter is come, whom I will send unto you from the Father." (xv, 26.) "The Spirit of the Lord Jehovah is upon me; because Jehovah hath annointed me," &c. (Isa. lxi. 1.) There are numerous other passages in confirmation of this distinction: so that the blindness of Sabellius was most wonderful, who could possibly be in darkness amidst such a splendour of daylight.

X. Lastly. The fourth part comes now to be considered. (1.)

The Infinity of the Holy Spirit is proved, both by his Omniscience, by which he is said to "search all things, yea, the deep things of God," and to know all the things which are in God; (1 Cor. ii. 10, 11; John xvi. 13;) and by his Omnipotence, by which He hath created and still preserves all things, (Job. xxxiii. 4) and according to both of which He is styled "the Spirit of wisdom and of knowledge," and "the power of the Highest." (Luke i. 35.) (2.) His Eternity is established, (Isa. xi. 2) both by the creation of all things; for whatsoever is before all things which have been made, that is eternal; and by the titles with which He is signalized, for he is called "the power of the Highest," and the finger of God." (Luke xi. 20.) These titles cannot apply to a thing that has its beginning in time. (3.) A most luminous argument for His Immensity lies in this. It is said, that "no one can flee from the Spirit of God; (Psalm cxxxix. 7;) and that the Spirit of the Lord dwells in all his saints, as in a temple. (1 Cor. vi. 19.)

XI. From all these particulars it clearly appears, that the Holy Ghost is of the same Divinity with the Father and the Son, and is truly distinguished by the name of God. For He who is not a creature, and yet has a real subsistence, must be God; and He who is from God, and who proceeds from the Father, not by an external emanation, nor by a creation performed through the intervention of any other Divine power, but by an internal emanation, He, being the power of God, by what right shall He be despoiled of the name of "God?" For when He is said to be given, poured out, and sent; this does not betoken any diminution of his Divinity, but is an intimation of his origin from God, of his procession from the Father and the Son, and of his mission to his office. A clear indication of his Deity is also apparent from its being said, that He also with plenary power distributes Divine gifts according to his own will, (1 Cor. xii. 11,) and he bestows his gifts with an authority equal to that with which "God" the Father is said to "work his operations," (4.) and to that with which the Son, who is called "the Lord," is said to "institute administrations."

XII. This doctrine of the sacred and undivided Trinity contains a mystery which far surpasses every human and angelical understanding, if it be considered according to the internal union which subsists between the Father, the Son, and the Holy Ghost, and according to the relation among them of origin and procession. But if regard be had to that economy and dispensation by which the Father and the Son, and both of them through the Holy Spirit, accomplish our salvation; the contemplation is one of admirable sweetness, and produces in the hearts of believers the most exhuberant fruits of faith, hope, charity, confidence, fear, and obedience, to the praise of God the Creator, the Son the Redeemer, and of the Holy Ghost the Sanctifier. May "the Love of God the Father, the Grace of the Lord Jesus Christ, and the Communion of the Holy Ghost, be with us," and with all saints. Amen! (2 Cor. xiii. 14.)

"If the Spirit be third in dignity and order, what necessity is there for his being also the third in nature? Indeed the doctrine of piety has perhaps taught that He is third in dignity. But to employ the expression the third in nature,' we have neither learned out of the Holy Scriptures, nor is it possible to collect it as a consequence from what precedes. For as the Son is in truth Second in order, because He is from the Father, and Second in dignity, because the Father exists that He may be himself the principle and the cause, and because through the Son there is a procession and an access to God the Father; (but He is no mere second in nature, because the Deity is one in both of them.) So, undoubtedly, is likewise the Holy Spirit, though He follows the Son both in order and dignity, as we completely grant, yet He is not at all resembling one who exists in the nature of another. Basilius Eversor 3.

"In brief, in things to be distinguished, the Deity is incapable of being divided; and resembles one vast attempered mass of effulgence proceeding from three suns which mutually embrace each other. Wherefore when we have had regard to the Deity itself, or to the first cause, or to the monarchy, we have formed in our minds a conception of some one thing. Again, when I apply my mind to these things in which Deity consists, and which exist from the first cause itself, flowing from it with equal glory and without any relation to time, I discover three things as the objects of my adoration." Gregory Nazianzen, Orat. 3 De Theolog.

DISPUTATION 7 - ON THE FIRST SIN OF THE FIRST MAN

RESPONDENT: ABRAHAM APPART

THE USE OF THE DOCTRINE

I. When an inquiry is instituted concerning this first evil, we do not agitate the question for the purpose of unworthily exposing to disgrace the nakedness of the first formed pair, which had been closely covered up, as impious Ham did in reference to his father. (Gen. ix. 22.) But we enter on this subject, that, after it is accurately known, as when the cause of a mortal disease is discovered, we may with the greater earnestness implore the hand which heals and cures. (Gal. ii. 16.) In this discussion four things seem to be principally entitled to a consideration. (1.) The sin itself. (2.) Its causes. (3.) Its heinousness. (4.) Its effects.

THE SIN ITSELF

II. This sin is most appropriately called by the Apostle, "disobedience," and "offense" or fall. (Rom. v. 18, 19. (1.). Disobedience; for, since the law against which the sin was committed, was symbolical, having been given to testify that man was under a law to God, and to prove his obedience, and since the subsequent performance of it was to be a confession of devoted submission and due obedience; the transgression of it cannot, in fact, be denoted by a more commodious name than that of "disobedience," which contains within itself the denial of subjection and the renunciation of obedience. (2.) Offense, or fall. Because as man, having been previously placed in a state of integrity, walked with unstumbling feet in the way of God's commandments; by this foul deed he impinged or offended against the law itself, and fell from his state of innocence. (Rom. v. 15-18.)

III. This sin, therefore, is a transgression of the law which was delivered by God, to the first human beings, about not eating the fruit of the tree of the knowledge of good and evil; perpetrated by the free will of man, from a desire to be like God, and through the persuasion of Satan that assumed the shape of a serpent. On account of this transgression, man fell under the displeasure and the wrath of God, rendered himself subject to a double death, and deserving to be deprived of the primeval righteousness and holiness, in which a great part of the image of God consisted. (Gen. ii. 17; Rom. v. 19; Gen. iii. 3-6, 23, 24; Rom. v. 12, 16; Luke xix. 26.)

THE CAUSE OF THIS SIN

IV. The efficient cause of this sin is two fold. The one immediate and near. The other remote and mediate. (1.) The former is Man himself, who, of his own free will and without any necessity either internal or external, (Gen. iii. 6,) transgressed the law which had been proposed to him, (Rom. v. 19,) which had been sanctioned by a threatening and a promise, (Gen. ii. 16, 17,) and which it was possible for him to have observed (ii, 9; iii, 23, 24.) (2.) The remote and mediate efficient cause is the Devil, who, envying the Divine glory and the salvation of mankind, solicited man to a transgression of that law. (John viii. 44.) The instrumental cause is the Serpent, whose tongue Satan abused, for proposing to man these arguments which he considered suitable to persuade him. (Gen. iii. 1; 2 Cor. xi. 3.) It is not improbable, that the grand deceiver made a conjecture from his own case; as he might himself have been enticed to the commission of sin by the same arguments. (Gen. iii. 4, 5.)

V. Those arguments which may be called "both the inwardly moving" and "the outwardly-working causes," were two. (1.) The one, directly persuading, was deduced from a view of the advantage which man would obtain from it, that is, a likeness to God. (Gen. iii. 5, 6.) (2.) The other was a removing argument, one of dissuasion, taken from God's threatening; lest the fear of punishment, prevailing over the desire of a similitude to God, should hinder man from eating. (iii, 4.) Though the first of these two arguments occupies the first station, with regard to order, in the proposition; yet, we think, it obtained the last place with regard to efficiency. To these arguments may be added two qualities imparted by the Creator to the fruit of the tree, calculated blandly to affect and allure the senses of a human being; these qualities are intimated in the words, "that the tree was good for food, and that it was pleasant to the eyes." (iii. 6.) But there is this difference between the two principal arguments and these qualities. The former were proposed by the Devil to persuade to the commission of sin, as such; while the two qualities implanted by God were proposed only for the purpose of persuading [the woman] to eat, if that could have been done without sinning.

VI. The inwardly-moving causes, but which became such by accident, were two. (1.) Such an affection, or desire, for a likeness to God, as had been implanted in man by God himself; but it was to be exercised in a certain order and method. For the gracious image and likeness of God, according to which man was created, tended towards his glorious image and likeness. (2 Cor. iii. 18.) (2.) A natural affection for the fruit which was good in its taste, pleasant in its aspect, and well adapted for preserving and recruiting animal life.

VII. But as it was the duty of man to resist the efficacy of all and each of these several causes, so was it likewise in power; for he had been "created after the image of God," and therefore, in "the knowledge of God," (Gen. i. 27; Col. iii. 10,) and endued with righteousness and true holiness. (Ephes. iv. 24.) This resistance might have been effected by his repelling and rejecting the causes which operated outwardly, and by reducing into order and subjecting to the Law and to the Spirit of God those which, impelled inwardly. If he had acted thus, the temptation, out of which he would have departed victorious, would not have been imputed to him as an offense against the violated law. (Gen. iii. 7-12.)

VIII. But the guilt of this sin can by no means be transferred to God, either as an efficient or as a deficient cause. (1.) Not as an efficient cause. For He neither perpetrated this crime through man, nor employed against man any action, either internal or external, by which he might incite him to sin. (Psalm v. 5; James i. 13.) (2.) Not as a deficient cause. For He neither denied nor withdrew any thing that was necessary for avoiding this sin and fulfilling the law; but He had endowed Him sufficiently with all things requisite for that purpose, and preserved him after he was thus endued.

IX. But the Divine permission intervened; not as having permitted that act to man's legitimate right and power, that he might commit it without sin, for such a permission as this is contrary to legislation; (Gen. ii. 17;) but as having permitted it to the free will and capability of man. This Divine permission is not the denial or the withdrawing of the grace necessary and sufficient for fulfilling the law; (Isa. v. 4;) for if a permission of this kind were joined to legislation, it would ascribe the efficiency of sin to God. But it is the suspension of some efficiency, which is possible to God both according to right and to capability, and which, if exerted, would prevent sin in its actual commission. This is commonly called "an efficacious hindrance." But God was not bound to employ this impediment, when He had already laid down those hindrances to sin which might and ought to have withheld and deterred man from sinning, and which consisted in the communication of his own image, in the appointment of his law, in the threat of punishments, and in the promise of rewards.

X. Though the cause of this permission may be reckoned in the number of those things which, such is the will of God, are hidden from us, (Deut. xxix. 29) yet, while with modesty and reverence we inspect the acts of God, it appears to us that a two-fold cause may be maintained, the one a priori, the other a posteriori. (1.) We will enunciate the former in the words of Tertullian. "If God had once allowed to man the free exercise of his own will and had duly granted this permission, He undoubtedly had permitted the enjoyment of these things through the very authority of the institution. But they were to be enjoyed as in Him, and according to Him; that is, according to God, that is, for good. For who will permit any thing against himself? But as in man [they were to be enjoyed] according to the motions of his liberty." (2.) The cause a posteriori shall be given in the words of St. Augustine. "A good being would not suffer evil to be done, unless He was likewise Omnipotent, and capable of bringing good out of that evil."

XI. The material cause of this sin is the tasting of the fruit of the tree of the knowledge of good and evil, which is an act in its own nature indifferent, and easily avoidable by man in the midst of such abundant plenty of good and various fruits. From this shine forth the admirable benignity and kindness of God; whose will it was to have experience of the obedience of his creature, in an act which that creature could with the utmost facility omit, without injury to his nature, and even without any detriment to his pleasure. This seems to have been intimated by God himself when he propounded the precept in this manner. "Of every tree of the garden thou shalt freely eat; but of the tree of the knowledge of good and evil, thou shalt not eat." (Gen. ii. 16, 17.)

XII. But the form of this sin is anomia "the transgression of the law," (1 John iii. 4,) which belongs to this act in reference to its having been forbidden by the law. And because this relation adhered to the act from the time when God circumscribed it by a law, the effect of it was that the act ought to be omitted. (Dan. iii. 18.) For the moral evil, which adhered to it through the prohibition of God, was greater, than the natural good which was in the act by nature. There was also in man the image of God, according to which he ought to have been more abhorrent of that act because sin adhered to it, than to be inclined by a natural affection to the act itself, because some good was joined with it.

XIII. No end can be assigned to this sin. For evil, of itself, has not an end, since an end has always reference to a good. But the acts of the end were, that man might obtain a likeness to God in the knowledge of good and evil, and that he might satisfy his senses of taste and seeing. (Gen. iii. 5, 6.) But he did not suppose, that he would gain this similitude by sin as such, but by an act as it was a natural one. It had the boundary which the Divine determination placed round about it, and which was two-fold. The one, agreeing with the nature of sin, according to the severity of God. The other, transcending sin, nay, contravening it, according to the grace and mercy of God. (Rom. ix. 22, 23.)

THE HEINOUSNESS OF THIS SIN

XIV. From the particulars already discussed, some judgment may be formed of the heinousness of this sin, which seems principally to consist of these four things. (1) That it is the transgression of a law that is not peculiar [to one person, or only to a few,] but of a law which universally bears witness to the obligation of man towards God, and which is a test of his obedience. A contempt of this law has in it a renunciation of the covenant into which God has entered with man, and of the obedience which from that covenant is due to God. (Gen. xvii. 14.) (2.) That man perpetrated this crime, after he had been placed in a state of innocence and adorned by God with such excellent endowments as those of "the knowledge of God," and "righteousness and true holiness." (Gen. i. 26, 27; Col. iii. 10; Ephes. iv. 24.) (3.) That when so many facilities existed for not sinning, especially in the act itself, yet man did not abstain from this sin. (Gen. ii. 16, 17,) (4.) That he committed this sin in a place that was sanctified as a type of the celestial Paradise. (ii, 15, 16; iii, 6, 23; Rev. ii. 7.) There are some other things which may aggravate this sin; but since it has them in common with most other offenses, we shall not at present enter into a discussion of them.

XV. The proper and immediate effect of this sin was the offending of the Deity. For since the form of sin is "the transgression of the law," (1 John iii. 4,) it primarily and immediately strikes against the legislator himself, (Gen. iii. 11,) and this with the offending of one whose express will it was that his law should not be offended. From this violation of his law, God conceives just displeasure, which is the second effect of sin. (iii, 16-19, 23, 24.) But to anger succeeds infliction of punishment, which was in this instance two-fold. (1.) A liability to two deaths. (ii, 17; Rom. vi. 23.) (2.) The withdrawing of that primitive righteousness and holiness, which, because they are the effects of the Holy Spirit dwelling in man, ought not to have remained in him after he had fallen from the favour of God, and had incurred the Divine displeasure. (Luke xix. 26.) For this Spirit is a seal of God's favour and good will. (Rom. viii. 14, 15; 1 Cor. ii. 12.)

XVI. The whole of this sin, however, is not peculiar to our first parents, but is common to the entire race and to all their posterity, who, at the time when this sin was committed, were in their loins, and who have since descended from them by the natural mode of propagation, according to the primitive benediction. For in Adam "all have sinned." (Rom. v. 12.) Wherefore, whatever punishment was brought down upon our first parents, has likewise pervaded and yet pursues all their posterity. So that all men "are by nature the children of wrath," (Ephes. ii. 3,) obnoxious to condemnation, and to temporal as well as to eternal death; they are also devoid of that original righteousness and holiness. (Rom. v. 12, 18, 19.) With these evils they would remain oppressed forever, unless they were liberated by Christ Jesus; to whom be glory forever.

DISPUTATION 8 - ON ACTUAL SINS

RESPONDENT, CASPER WILTENS

I. As divines and philosophers are often compelled, on account of a penury of words, to distinguish those which are synonymous, and to receive others in a stricter or more ample signification than their nature and etymology will allow; so in this matter of actual sin, although the term applies also to the first sin of Adam, yet, for the sake of a more accurate distinction, they commonly take it for that sin which man commits, through the corruption of his nature, from the time where he knows how to use reason; and they define it thus: "Something thought, spoken or done against the law of God; or the omission of something which has been commanded by that law to be thought, spoken or done." Or, with more brevity, "Sin is the transgression of the law;" which St. John has explained in this compound word anomia "anomy." (1 John iii. 4.)

II. For as the law is perceptive of good and prohibitory of evil, it is necessary not only that an action, but that the neglect of an action, be accounted a sin. Hence arises the first distinction of sin into that of commission, when a prohibited act is perpetrated, as theft, murder, adultery, &c. And into that of omission, when a man abstains from [the performance of] an act that has been commanded; as if any one does not render due honour to a magistrate, or bestows on the poor nothing in proportion to the amplitude of his means. And since the Law is two-fold, one "the Law of works," properly called, "the Law," the other "the Law of faith," (Rom. iii. 27,) which is the gospel of the grace of God; therefore sin is either that which is committed against the Law, or against the gospel of Christ. (Heb. ii. 2, 3.) That which is committed against the Law, provokes the wrath of God against sinners; that against the gospel, causes the wrath of God to abide upon us; the former, by deserving punishment; the latter, by preventing the remission of punishment.

III. One is a sin per se, "of itself;" another, per accidens, "accidentally." (1.) A sin per se is every external or internal action which is prohibited by the law, or every neglect of an action commanded by the law. (2.) A sin is per accidens either in things necessary and restricted by law, or in things indifferent. In things necessary, either when an act prescribed by law is performed without its due circumstances, such as to bestow alms that you obtain praise from men; (Matt. vi. 2;) or when an act prohibited by law is omitted, not from a due cause and for a just end; as when any one represses his anger at the moment, that he may afterwards exact more cruel vengeance. In things indifferent, when any one uses them to the offense of the weak. (Rom. xiv. 15, 21.)

IV. Sin is likewise divided in reference to the personal object against whom the offense is committed; and it is either against God, against our neighbour, or against ourselves, according to what the Apostle says: "The grace of God that bringeth salvation, hath appeared to all men, teaching us, that denying ungodliness and worldly lusts, we should live soberly, righteously and godly, in this present world." (Tit. ii. 11.) Where soberness is appropriately referred to the man himself; righteousness to our neighbour; and godliness to God: These, we affirm, are likewise contained in the two grand precepts, "Love God above all things," and "Love thy neighbour as thyself." For howsoever it may seem, that the ten commandments prescribe only what is due to God and to our neighbour; yet this very requirement is of such a nature that it cannot be performed by a man without fulfilling at the same time his duty to himself.

V. It is further distinguished, from its cause, into sins of ignorance, infirmity, malignity and negligence. (1.) A sin of ignorance is, when a man does any thing which he does not know to be a sin; thus, Paul persecuted Christ in his Church. (1 Tim. i. 13.) (2.) A sin of infirmity is, when, through fear, which may befall even a brave man, or through any other more vehement passion and perturbation of mind, he commits any offense; thus, Peter denied Christ, (Matt. xxvi, 70,) and thus David, being offended by Nabal, was proceeding to destroy him and his domestics. (1 Sam. xxv. 13, 21.) (3.) A sin of dignity or malice, when any thing is committed with a determined purpose of mind, and with deliberate counsel; thus Judas denied Christ, (Matt. xxvi. 14, 15.) and thus David caused Uriah to be killed. (2 Sam. xi. 15.) (4.) A sin of negligence is, when a man is overtaken by a sin, (Gal. vi, l.) which encircles and besets him before he can reflect within himself about the deed. (Heb. xii. 1.) In this description will be classed that of St. Paul against Ananias the High Priest, if indeed he may be said to have sinned in that matter. (Acts xxiii. 3.)

VI. Nearly allied to this is the distribution of sin into that which is contrary to conscience, and that which is not contrary to conscience. (1.) A sin against conscience is one that is perpetrated through malice and deliberate purpose, laying waste the conscience, and (if committed by holy persons) grieving the Holy Spirit so much as to cause Him to desist from his usual functions of leading them into the right way, and of making them glad in their consciences by his inward testimony. (Psalm li. 10, 13.) This is called, by way of eminence, "a sin against conscience;" though, when this phrase is taken in a wide acceptation, a sin which is committed through infirmity, but which has a previous sure knowledge that is applied to the deed, might also be said to be against conscience. (2.) A sin not against conscience is either that which is by no means such, and which is not committed through a willful and wished-for ignorance of the law, as the man who neglects to know what he is capable of knowing: or it is that which at least is not such in a primary degree, but is precipitated through precipitancy, the cause of which is a vehement and unforeseen temptation. Of this kind, was the too hasty judgment of David against Mephibosheth, produced by the grievous accusation of Ziba, which happened at the very time when David fled. This bore a strong resemblance to a falsehood. (2 Sam. xvi. 3, 4.) Yet that which, when once committed, is not contrary to conscience, becomes contrary to it when more frequently repeated, and when the man neglects self-correction.

VII. To this may be added, the division of sin from its causes, with regard to the real object about which the sin is perpetrated. This object is either "the lust of the flesh, the lust of the eyes, or the pride of life," that is, either pleasure specially so called, or avarice, or arrogant haughtiness; all of which, proceeding from the single fountain of self love or inordinate affection, tend distinctly towards the good things of the present life, haughtiness towards its honours, avarice towards its riches, and pleasure towards those things by which the external senses may experience self-gratification. From these arise those works of the flesh which are enumerated by the apostle in Gal. v. 19-21, perhaps with the exception of idolatry. Yet it may be made a legitimate subject of discussion, whether idolatry may not be referred to one of these three causes.

VIII. Sin is also divided into venial and mortal: but this distribution is not deduced from the nature of sin itself, but accidentally from the gracious estimation of God. For every sin is in its own nature mortal, that is, it is that which merits death; because it is declared universally concerning sin, that "its wages is death," (Rom. vi. 23,) which might in truth be brought instantly down upon the offenders, were God wishful to enter into judgment with his servants. But that which denominates sin venial, or capable of being forgiven, is this circumstance, God is not willing to impute sin to believers, or to place sin against them, but is desirous to pardon it; although with this difference, that it requires express penitence from some, while concerning others it is content with this expression: "Who can understand his errors? Cleanse thou me, O Lord, from secret faults." (Psalm xix. 12.) In this case, the ground of fear is not so much, lest, from the aggravation of sin, men should fall into despair, as, lest, from its extenuation, they should relapse into negligence and security; not only because man has a greater propensity to the latter than to the former, but likewise because that declaration is always at hand: have no pleasure in the death of him that dieth," that is, of the sinner who has merited death by his transgressions, "but that he be converted and live." (Ezek. xviii. 32.)

IX. Because we say that the wages of every sin is death," we do not, on this account, with the Stoics, make them all equal. For, beside the refutation of such an opinion by many passages of Scripture, it is likewise opposed to the diversity of objects against which sin is perpetrated, to the causes from which it arises, and to the law against which the offense is committed. Besides, the disparity of punishments in the death that is eternal, proves the falsehood of this sentiment: For a crime against God is more grievous than one against man; (1 Sam. ii. 25;) one that is perpetrated with a high hand, than one through error; one against a prohibitory law, than one against a mandatory law. And far more severe will be the punishment inflicted on the inhabitants of Chorazin and Bethsaida, than on those of Tyre and Sidon. (Matt. xi. 23.) By means of this dogma, the Stoics have endeavoured to turn men aside from the commission of crimes; but their attempt has not only been fruitless, but also injurious, as will be seen when we institute a serious deliberation about bringing man back from sin into the way of righteousness.

X. Mention is likewise made, in the Scriptures, of "a sin unto death;" (1 John v. 16;) which is specially so called, because it in fact, brings certain death on all by whom it has been committed. Mention is made in the same passage of "a sin which is not unto death," and which is opposed to the former. In a parallel column with these, marches the division of sin into pardonable and unpardonable. (1.) A sin which is "not unto death" and pardonable, is so called, because it is capable of having subsequent repentance, and thus of being pardoned, and because to many persons it is actually pardoned through succeeding penitence-such as that which is said to be committed against "the Son of Man." (2.) The "sin unto death" or unpardonable, is that which never has subsequent repentance, or the author of which cannot be recalled to penitence--such as that which is called "the sin" or "blasphemy against the Holy Ghost," (Matt. xii. 32; Luke xii. 10,) of which it is said, "it shall not be forgiven, either in this world, or in the world to come." For this reason, St. John says, we must not pray for that sin.

XI. But, though the proper meaning and nature of the sin against the Holy Ghost are with the utmost difficulty to be ascertained, yet we prefer to follow those who have furnished the most weighty and grievous definition of it, rather than those who, in maintaining six species of it, have been compelled to explain "unpardonable" in some of those species, for that which is with difficulty or is rarely remitted, or which of itself deserves not to be pardoned. With the former class of persons, therefore, we say that the sin against the Holy Ghost is committed when any man, with determined malice, resists divine, and in fact, evangelical truth, for the sake of resistance, though he is so overpowered with the refulgence of it, as to be rendered incapable of pleading ignorance in excuse. This is therefore called "the sin against the Holy Ghost, not because it is not perpetrated against the Father and the Son; (for how can it be that he does not sin against the Father and the Son, who sins against the Spirit of both?) but because it is committed against the operation of the Holy Spirit, that is, against the conviction of the truth through miracles, and against the illumination of the mind.

XII. But the cause why this sin is called "irremissible," and why he who has committed it, cannot be renewed to repentance, is not the impotency of God, as though by his most absolute omnipotence, he cannot grant to this man repentance unto life, and thus cannot pardon this blasphemy; but since it is necessary, that the mercy of God should stop at some point, being circumscribed by the limits of his justice and equity according to the prescript of his wisdom, this sin is said to be "unpardonable," because God accounts the man who has perpetrated so horrid a crime, and has done despite to the Spirit of grace, to be altogether unworthy of having the divine benignity and the operation of the Holy Spirit occupied in his conversion, lest he should himself appear to esteem this sacred operation and kindness at a low rate, and to stand in need of a sinful man, especially of one who is such a monstrous sinner!

XIII. The efficient cause of actual sins is, man through his own free will. The inwardly working cause is the original propensity of our nature towards that which is contrary to the divine law, which propensity we have contracted from our first parents, through carnal generation. The outwardly working causes are the objects and occasions which solicit men to sin. The substance or material cause, is an act which, according to its nature, has reference to good. The form or formal cause of it is a transgression of the law, or an anomy. It is destitute of an end; because sin is amartia a transgression which wanders from its aim. The object of it is a variable good; to which, when man is inclined, after having deserted the unchangeable good, he commits an offense.

XIV. The effect of actual sins are all the calamities and miseries of the present life, then death temporal, and afterwards death eternal. But in those who are hardened and blinded, even the effects of preceding sins become cousequent sins themselves.

DISPUTATION 9 - ON THE RIGHTEOUSNESS AND EFFICACY OF THE PROVIDENCE OF GOD CONCERNING EVIL

RESPONDENT: RALPH DE ZYLL

I. Among the causes and pretenses by which human ignorance has been induced, and which human perverseness has abused, to deny the providence of God, the entrance of evil (that is, of sin) into the world, and its most wonderful and fertile exuberance, do not by any means occupy the lowest stations. For since, with Scripture as our guide and Nature as our witness, we must maintain that God is good, omniscient, and of unbounded power; (Mark x. 18; Psalm cxlvii. 5; Rev. iv, 8; Rom. i. 20;) and since this is a truth of which every one is fully persuaded who has formed in his mind any notion of the Deity; men have concluded from this that evil could not have occurred under the three preceding conditions of the divine Majesty, if God managed all things by his providence, and if it was his will to make provision respecting evil, according to these properties of his own nature. And therefore, since, after all, evil has occurred, they have concluded that the providence of God must be entirely denied. For they thought it better to set up a God that was at repose, and negligent of mundane affairs, especially of those in which a rational creature's freedom of will intervened, than to deprive Him of the honour of his goodness, wisdom and power. But it is not necessary to adopt either of these methods; and that it is possible to preserve to God, without disparagement, these three ornaments of Supreme Majesty, as well as His providence, will be shewn by a temperate explanation of the efficacy of God concerning evil.

II. A few things must be premised about this evil itself, as a basis for our explanation. (1.) What is properly sin? (2.) Was it possible for it to be perpetrated by a rational creature, and how? (3.) That a chief evil cannot be granted, which may contend on an equality with the chief Good, as the Manichees asserted; otherwise, of all the evils which can be devised, sin, of which we are now treating, is, in reality, the chief; and, if we may speak with strictness, sin is the only and sole evil; for all other things are not evils, in themselves, but are injurious to some one.

III. 1. Sin is properly an aberration from a rule. This rule is the equity which is preconceived in the mind of God, which is expressed to the mind of a rational creature by legislation, and, according to which it is proper for such a creature to regulate his life. It is therefore defined by St. John in one compound word, anomia "the transgression of the law;" (1 John iii. 4;) whether such a law be preceptive of Good, or prohibitory of evil, (Psalm xxxiv. 14,) hence the evil of commission is perpetrated against the prohibitory part, and that of omission against the preceptive. But in sin, two things come under consideration: (1.) The act itself, which has reference to natural good; but under the act, we comprehend likewise the cessation from action. (2.) Anomy, or "the transgression of the law," which obtains the place of a moral evil. The act may be called the substance or material cause of sin; and the transgression of the law, its form or formal cause.

IV. II. But it was possible for sin to be perpetrated by a rational creature; for, as a creature, he was capable of declining or revolting from the chief Good, and of being inclined towards an inferior good, and towards the acts by which he might possess this minor good. As rational, he was capable of understanding that he was required to live in a godly manner, and what that equity was according to which his life and actions were to be specially regulated. As a rational creature, a law could be imposed on him by God, nay, according to equity and justice, it ought to be imposed, by which he might be forbidden to forsake the chief good, and to commit that act, though it was naturally good. The mode is placed in the freedom of the will, bestowed by God on a rational creature, according to which he was capable of performing the obedience which is due to the law, or could by his own strength exceed or transgress its limits.

V. III. But since a chief evil cannot be allowed, it follows from this, that, though evil be contrary to good, yet it cannot pass beyond the universal order of that good which is chief, but can be reduced to order by this chief good, and evil can thus be directed to good, on account of the infinite wisdom of this chief good, by which he knows what is possible to be made from evil; and on account of this power, by which he can make from this evil what he knows may be made from it. Granting, therefore, that sin has exceeded the order of every thing created, yet it is circumscribed within the order of the Creator himself and of the chief good. Since it is apparent from all these premises, that the providence of God ought not to intervene, or come between, to prevent the perpetration of evil by a free creature; it also follows, from the entrance of evil into the world, and it has entered so far "that the whole world lieth in wickedness," (1 John v. 19,) -- that the Providence of God cannot be destroyed. This truth we will demonstrate at greater length, when we treat upon the efficacy of the providence of God concerning evil.

VI. We have already said, that, in sin, the act or the cessation from action, and "the transgression of the law," come under consideration: But the efficiency of God about evil, concerns both the act itself and its viciousness, and it does this, whether we have regard to the beginning of sin, to its progress, or to its end and consummation. The consideration of the efficiency which is concerned about the Beginning of sin, embraces either a hindrance or a permission; to which we add, the administration of arguments and occasions inciting to sin; that which regards its Progress, has direction and determination; and that concerning The End and Termination, punishment and remission. We will refrain from treating upon the concurrence of God, since it is only in reference to the act, considered, also, as naturally good.

VII. The First efficiency of God concerning evil, is a hindrance or the placing of an impediment, whether such hindrance be sufficient or efficacious. (Jer. xxxi. 32, 33.) For it belongs to a good, to hinder an evil as far as the good knows it to be lawful to do so. But a hindrance is placed either on the power, on the capability, or on the will, of a rational creature. These three things must also be considered in that which hinders. (1.) On the power an impediment is placed, by which some act is taken away from the power of a rational creature, to the performance of which it has an inclination and sufficient powers. By being thus circumscribed, it comes to pass, that the creature cannot perform that act without sin, and this circumscription is made by legislation. The tasting of the tree of the knowledge of good and evil was thus circumscribed, when leave was granted to eat of all others: (Gen. ii. 17) and this is the hindrance of sin as such; and it is placed by God before a rational creature as he has the right and power over that creature.

VIII. (2.) On the capability also an impediment is placed.

The effect of this is, that the rational creature cannot perform the act, for the performance of which he has an inclination, and powers that, without this impediment, would be sufficient. But this hindrance is placed before a rational creature by four methods: (1.) By depriving the creature of essence and life, which are the foundation of capability. Thus was the attack upon Jerusalem hindered, (2 Kings 19,) as was also the forcible abduction of Elijah to Ahaziah, (2 Kings 1,) when, in the former instance, "an hundred fourscore and five thousand men were slain by the angel of the Lord," and, in the latter, two different companies, each containing fifty men, were consumed by fire. (2.) The second method is by the taking away or the diminution of capability. Thus Jeroboam was prevented from apprehending the prophet of the Lord, by "the drying up of his own hand." (1 Kings 13, 4.) Thus, sin is hindered, so as not to exercise dominion over a man, when the body of sin is weakened and destroyed. (Rom. vi. 6.) (3.) The third is by the opposition of a greater capability, or at least of one that is equal. Thus was Uzziah prevented from burning incense unto Jehovah, when the priests resisted his attempt. (2 Chron. xxvi. 18, 21.) Thus also is "the flesh" hindered from "doing what it would," "because the Spirit lusteth against the flesh," (Gal. v. 17,) and because "greater is He that is in us, than he that is in the world." (1 John iv. 4.) (4.) The fourth method is by the withdrawing of the object. Thus the Jews were frequently hindered from hurting Christ, because He withdrew himself from the midst of them. (John viii. 59.) Thus was Paul taken away, by the Chief Captain, from the Jews, who had conspired together for his destruction. (Acts xxiii. 10.)

IX. (3.) An impediment is placed on the will, when by some argument it is persuaded not to will to commit a sin. But we refer the arguments by which the will is moved, to the following three classes. For they are taken, (i.) either from the impossibility or the difficulty of the thing, (ii.) from its unpleasantness or inconvenience, its usefulness or injuriousness, (iii.) or from its being dishonourable, unjust and indecorous. (i.) By the first of these, the Pharisees and Scribes were frequently prevented from laying violent hands on Christ: (Matt. xxi. 46) for they were of opinion, that he would be defended by the people, "who took him for a prophet." In the same manner were the Israelites hindered from departing to their lovers, to false gods; for God "hedged up their way with thorns, and made a wall, so that they could not find their customary paths." (Hosea ii. 6, 7.) Thus the saints are deterred from sinning, when they see wicked men "wearied in the ways of iniquity and perdition." (Wisdom v. 7.) (ii.) By the second argument, the brethren of Joseph were hindered from killing him, since they could obtain their end by selling him. (Gen. xxxvii. 26, 27.) Thus Job was prevented from sinning "with his eyes" because he knew what was "the portion of God from above, and what the inheritance of the Almighty from on high," for those who have their eyes full of adultery. (Job xxxi. 1, 2.) (iii.) By the third, Joseph was hindered from defiling himself by shameful adultery, (Gen. xxxix. 8, 9,) and David was prevented from "stretching forth his hand against the Lord's anointed." (1 Sam. xxiv. 7.)

X. The permission of sin succeeds, which is opposed to hindering. Yet it is not opposed to hindering, as the latter is an act which is taken away from the power of a rational creature by legislation; for, in that case, the same act would be a sin, and not a sin. It would be a sin in reference to its being a forbidden act; and it would be no sin in reference to its being permitted in this manner, that is, not forbidden. But permission is opposed to hindrance, in reference to the latter being an impediment placed on the capability and will of an intelligent creature. But permission is the suspension, not of one impediment or two, which may be presented to the capability or the will, but of all impediments at once, which, God knows, if they were all employed, would effectually hinder sin. Such necessarily would be the result, because sin might be hindered by a single impediment of that kind. (1.) Sin therefore is permitted to the capability of the creature, when God employs none of those hindrances of which we have already made mention in the 8th Thesis: for this reason, this permission consists of the following acts of God who permits, the continuation of life and essence to the creature, the conservation of his capability, a cautiousness against its being opposed by a greater capability, or at least by one that is equal, and the exhibition of an object on which sin is committed. (2.) Sin is also permitted to the will; not because no such impediments are presented by God to the will, as are calculated to deter the will from sinning; but because God, seeing that these hindrances which are propounded will produce no effect, does not employ others which He possesses in the treasures of his wisdom and power. (John xviii. 6;

Mark xiv. 56.) This appears most evidently in the passion of Christ, with regard not only to the power but also to the will of those who demanded his death. (John xix. 6.) Nor does it follow from these premises, that those impediments are employed in vain: for though such results do not follow as are in accordance with these hindrances, yet God in a manner the most powerful gains his own purposes, because the results are not such as ought to have followed. (Rom. x. 20, 21.)

XI. The foundation of this permission is (1.) The liberty of choosing, with which God formed his rational creature, and which his constancy does not suffer to be abolished, lest he should be accused of mutability. (2.) The infinite wisdom and power of God, by which he knows and is able out of darkness to bring light, and to produce good out of evil. (Gen. i. 2, 3; 2 Cor. iv. 6.) God therefore permits that which He does permit, not in ignorance of the powers and the inclination of rational creatures, for he knows them all, not with reluctance, for he could have refrained from producing a creature that might possess freedom of choice, not as being incapable of hindering, for we have already seen by how many methods he is able to hinder both the capability and the will of a rational creature; not as if at ease, indifferent, or negligent of that which is transacted, because before anything is done he already ["has gone through"] has looked over the various actions which concern it, and, as we shall subsequently see, [§ 15-22,] he presents arguments and occasions, determines, directs, punishes and pardons sin. But whatever God permits, He permits it designedly and willingly, His will being immediately occupied about its permission, but His permission itself is occupied about sin; and this order cannot be inverted without great peril.

XII. Let us now explain a little more distinctly, by some of the differences of sin, those things which we have in this place spoken in a general manner concerning hindering and permission. (i.) From its causes, sin is distinguished into that of ignorance, infirmity, malignity and negligence. (1.) An impediment is placed on a sin of ignorance, by the revelation of the divine will. (Psalm cxix. 105.) (ii.) On a sin of infirmity, by the strengthening influence of the Holy Spirit against the machinations or the world and Satan, and also against the weakness of our flesh. (Ephes. iii. 16; vi, 11-13.) (iii.) On a sin of malignity, by "taking away the stony heart, and bestowing a heart of flesh," (Ezek. xi. 19,) and inscribing upon it the law of God: (Jer. xxxi. 33.) (iv.) And on a sin of negligence, by exciting in the hearts of believers a holy solicitude and a godly fear. (Mark xiv. 38; Jer. xxxii. 40.) From these remarks those acts will easily be manifest, in the suspension of which consists the permission of sins of every kind. God permitted Saul of Tarsus, a preposterous zealot for the law, to persecute Christ through ignorance, until "he revealed his Son in him," by which act out of a persecutor was formed a pastor. (Gal. i. 13-15.) Thus, he permitted Peter, who loved Christ, though he was somewhat too self-confident, to deny Him through infirmity; but, when afterwards endued with a greater energy of the Holy Spirit, he confessed him with intrepidity even unto death. (Matt. xxvi. 70; Acts v. 41; John xxi. 19.) God permitted Saul, whom "in his anger he had given to the Israelites as their king" (Hosea xiii. 11; 1 Sam. ix. 1,) through malignity to persecute David, of whose integrity he had been convinced, (1 Sam. xxiv. 17-19,) while his own son Jonathan resisted [his father's attempts against David] in vain. And God permitted David, after having enjoyed many victories and obtained leisure and retirement, to defile himself with the foul crime of adultery at a moment when he was acting with negligence. (2 Sam. 11.)

XIII. (2.) Sin, in the next place, is distinguished with respect to the two parts of the law--that which is perceptive of good, and that which is prohibitory of evil. [§ 3.] Against the latter of these an offense may be committed, either by performing an act, or by omitting its performance from an undue cause and end. Against the former, either by omitting an act, or by performing it in an undue manner, and from an undue cause and end. To these distinctions the hindering and the permission of God may likewise be adapted. God hindered Joseph's brethren from killing him; while he permitted them to spare his life, from an undue cause and end; for since it was in their power to sell him, the opportunity for which was divinely offered to them, they considered it unprofitable or useless to kill him. (Gen. xxxvii. 26, 27.) Thus Absalom was hindered from following the counsel of Ahithophel, though it was useful to himself and injurious to David; not because he considered it to be unjust, but because of its supposed injury to David; for he persisted in the purpose of persecuting his father, which he also completed in fact. (2 Sam. 17.) God hindered Balaam from cursing the children of Israel, and caused him to bless them; but so that he abstained from the former act, and performed the latter, with a perverse mind. (Num. 23.) We shall in some degree understand the reasons of this hindering and permission, if, while distinctly considering in sin the act and the anomy or "transgression of the law," we apply to each of them divine hindrance and permission.

XIV. But though the act, and "the transgression of the law," are inseparably united in one sin, and therefore neither of them can be hindered or permitted without the other; yet they may be distinguished in the mind; and hindrance as well as permission may be effected by God, sometimes chiefly with regard to the act, and at other times chiefly with regard to "the transgression of the law," and, when so done, they may be considered by us in these relations not without high commendation of the wisdom of God and to our own profit. God hindered Joseph's brethren from killing him, not as it was a sin, (because He permitted them, while remaining in the same mind to sell him,) but as it was an act. For they would have deprived Joseph of life, when it was the will of God that he should be spared. God permitted his vendition, not chiefly as it was a sin, but as an act; because by the sale of Joseph as it was an act, God obtained his own end. (Gen. xxxvii. 27.) God hindered Elijah from being forcibly brought to Ahaziah to be slain, not as that was a sin, but as it was an act. This is apparent from the end, and from the mode of hindering. From the end; because it was His will that the life of his prophet should be spared, not lest Ahaziah should sin against God. From the mode of hindering; because he destroyed two companies, of fifty men each, who had been sent to seize him; which was a token of divine anger against Ahaziah and the men, by which sin as such is not usually hindered, but as it is an act which will prove injurious to another; yet, through grace, sin is hindered as such. (2 Kings 1.) God permitted Satan and the Chaldeans to bring many evils on Job, not as that was a sin, but as it was an act: for it was the will of God to try the patience of his servant, and to make that virtue conspicuous to the confusion of Satan. But this was done by an act, by which, as such, injuries were inflicted on Job. (Job 1, 2.) David was hindered from laying violent hands on Saul, not as it was an act, but as it was a sin: this is manifest from the argument by which being hindered he abstained [from completing the deed.] "The Lord forbid," said he, "that I should stretch forth mine hand against the Lord's anointed." This argument deterred him from the sin as such. The same is also evident from the end of the hindrance: for it was the will of God for David to come to [the possession of] the kingdom through the endurance of afflictions, as a type of Christ the true David. (1 Sam. xxiv. 7.) God permitted Ahab to kill Naboth, not as that foul deed was an act, but as it was a sin: for God could have translated Naboth, or taken him to himself, by some other method; but it was the divine will, that Ahab should fill up the measure of his iniquities, and should accelerate his own destruction and that of his family. (1 Kings 21.) Abimelech was hindered from violating the chastity of Sarah, the wife of Abraham, both as it was an act, and as it was a sin. For it was not the will of God, that Abimelech should defile himself with this crime, because "in the integrity of his heart" he would then have done it. It was also His will to spare his servant Abraham, in whom indelible sorrow would have been produced by the deflowering of his wife, as by an act. (Gen. xx. 6.) God permitted Judah to know Tamar his daughter-in-law, both as it was an act, and as it was a sin: because it was the will of God, to have his own Son as a direct descendant from Judah; and at the same time to declare, that nothing is so polluted as to be incapable of being sanctified in Christ Jesus. (Gen. xxxviii. 18.) For it is not without reason that St. Matthew says, "Judas begat Phares and Zara of Thamar;" and "David the king begat Solomon of her who had been the wife of Urias;" (i, 3, 6;) and from whom in an uninterrupted line Christ was born.

XV. But since an act, though permitted to the capability and the will of the creature, may have been taken away from its power by legislation; [§ 7;] and since, therefore, it will very often happen, that a rational creature not altogether hardened in evil is unwilling to perform an act which is connected with sin, unless when some arguments and opportunities are presented to him, which are like incentives to commit that act; the management of this presenting of arguments and opportunities, is also in the hands of the Providence of God, who presents these excitements. (1.) Both to try whether it be the will of the creature to abstain from sinning, even when it is excited by these incentives; since small praise is due to abstaining in cases in which such excitements are absent. (S. of Sirach xx. 21-23; xxxi. 8-10.) (2.) And then, if it be the will of the creature to yield to these incentives, to effect His own work by the act of the creature; not impelled by necessity, as if God was unable to produce his own work without the intervention of the act of his creature; but moved to this by the will to illustrate his own manifold wisdom. Thus the arguments by which Joseph's brethren were incited through their own malice to wish to kill him, and the opportunities by which it was in their power to send him out of their way, were offered by Divine dispensation, partly in an intervening manner by the mediate act of men, and partly by the immediate act of God himself. The arguments for this malignity were, Joseph's accusation, by which he revealed to his father the wicked actions of his brethren, the peculiar regard which Jacob entertained for Joseph, the sending of a dream, and the relation of the dream after it had occurred. By these, the minds of his brethren were inflamed with envy and hatred against him. The opportunities were, the sending of Joseph to his brethren by his father, and the presenting of the Ishmaelites journeying into Egypt, at the very moment of time in which they were in deliberation about murdering their brother. (Gen. 37.) The preceding considerations have related only to the Beginning of sin; to its Progress belong direction and determination. [§ 6.]

XVI. The Direction of sin is an act of Divine Providence, by which God in a manner the wisest and most potent directs sin wherever he wills, "reaching from one end to another mightily, and sweetly ordering all things." (Wisd. viii. 1.) We must consider in this direction the point at which it has its origin and that at which it terminates. For when God directs sin wherever he wills, it is understood that he leads it away from the point to which it is not His will that it should proceed. But this direction is two-fold, unto an Object, and unto an End. Direction unto an Object is when God allows the sin which He permits, to be borne, not at the option of the creature, towards an object which in any way whatsoever is exposed and liable to the injury of sin; but which he directs to a particular object, which on some occasions has either been no part of the sinner's aim or desire, or which at least he has not absolutely desired. The Scriptures enunciate this kind of direction, generally, in the following words: "A man's heart deviseth his way; but the Lord directeth his steps." (Prov. xvi. 9.) But, Specially, concerning the heart of a King: "As the rivers of water are in the hand of the Lord, he turneth the heart of the king whithersoever he will." (Prov. xxi. 1.) Of which we have a signal example in Nebuchadnezzar, who, after he had determined in his own mind to subjugate the nations, and hesitated whether he should move against the Ammonites, or against the Jews, God managed the king's divinations so, that he resolved to march against the Jews, and to abstain from an attack upon the Ammonites. (Ezek. xxi. 19- 22.)

XVII. Direction unto an End is, when God does not allow the sin (which he permits,) to be subservient to the end of any thing which the creature intends; but he employs it to that end which he himself wills, whether the creature intend the same end, (which if he were to do, yet he would not be excused from sin,) or whether he intend another, and one quite contrary. For God knows how to educe the light of his own glory, and the advantage of his creatures, out of the darkness and mischief of sin. Thus "the thoughts of evil," which Joseph's brethren entertained against him, were converted by God into a benefit, not only to Joseph, but also to the whole of Jacob's family, and to all the kingdom of Egypt. (Gen. i. 20, 21.) By the afflictions which were sent to Job, Satan endeavoured to drive him to blasphemy. But by them, God tried the patience of his servant, and through it triumphed over Satan. (Job i. 11, 12, 22; ii, 9, 10.) The king of Assyria had determined "in his heart to destroy and cut off all nations not a few." But God executed his own work by him, whom "he sent against an hypocritical nation and the people of his wrath." (Isa. x. 5-12.) Nor is it at all wonderful, that God employs acts, which his creatures do not perform without sin, for ends that are pleasing to himself; because he does this most justly, for three reasons: (i.) For He is the Lord of his creature, though that creature be a sinner; because he has no more power to exempt or deliver himself from the dominion of God, than he has to reduce himself into nothing. (ii.) Because, as a creature endowed by God with inclination and capability, he performs those acts, though not without sin, as they have been forbidden. (iii.) Because the creature is a saw, in the hands of the Creator; and instrumental causes do not reach to the intention of the first agent. (Isa. x. 15.)

XVIII. Determination is an act of Divine Providence, by which God places a limit on his permission, and a boundary on sin that it may not wander and stray in infinitum at the option of the creature. The limit and boundary are placed by the prescribing of the time, and the determination of the magnitude. The prescribing of the time, is the prescribing of the very point or moment when it may be done, or the length of its duration. (i.) God determines the moment of time, when he permits a sin, to the commission of which his creature is inclined, to be perpetrated, not indeed at the time when it was the will of the creature to commit it; but He wisely and powerfully contrives for it to be done at another time. "The Jews sought to take Jesus: but no man laid hands on him, because his hour was not yet come." (John vii. 30.) "Yet when the time before appointed of the Father" approached, Christ said to them, "This is your hour, and the power of darkness." (Luke xxii, 53.) (2.) A limit is placed on the duration, when the space of time in which the permitted sin could endure, is diminished and circumscribed so as to stop itself. Thus Christ says, "Except those days should be shortened, there should no flesh be saved," &c. (Matt. xxiv. 22.) But in this part of the discussion also, regard must be had to the act as such, and to the sin as such. (i.) A limit is placed on the duration of the act, in the following passages: "The rod of the wicked shall not rest upon the lot of the righteous, lest the righteous put forth their hands unto iniquity." (Psalm cxxv. 3.) "The Lord knoweth how to deliver the godly out of temptations," &c. (2 Pet. ii. 9.) (ii.) A limit is placed on the duration of the sin, in these passages: "Therefore I will hedge up thy way with thorns, &c. And she shall not find her lovers: then shall she say, I will go and return to my first husband." (Hosea ii. 6.) "In times past God suffered all nations to walk in their own ways: but now he commandeth all men every where to repent." (Acts xiv. 16; xvii, 30.)

XIX. A limit is placed on the magnitude of sin, when God does not permit sin to increase beyond bounds and to assume greater strength. But this also is done, with regard to it both as an act, and as a sin. (i.) With respect to it as an act, in the following passages of Scripture: God permitted "the wrath of their enemies to be kindled against" the Israelites, but "he did not suffer them to swallow them up." (Psalm cxxiv. 2, 3.) "There hath no temptation taken you, but such as is common to man." (1 Cor. x. 13.) "We are perplexed, but not in despair; persecuted, but not forsaken; cast down, but not destroyed." (2 Cor. iv. 8, 9.) God permitted Satan, first, "To put forth his hand upon all that Job had," but not to touch him; (Job i. 12;) and, secondly, "To touch his bone and his flesh, but to save his life." (ii, 6.) "I will not destroy them by the hand of Shishak; nevertheless, they shall be his servants." (2 Chron. xii. 7, 8.) (ii.) With respect to it as a sin, God permitted David to resolve in his mind to destroy with the sword, Nabal and all his domestics, and to go instantly to him; but he did not permit him to shed innocent blood, and to save himself by his own hand. (1 Sam. xxv. 22, 26, 31.) God permitted David to flee to Achish, and to "feign himself mad;" (1 Sam. xxi. 13;) but he did not permit him to fight, in company with the army of Achish, against the Israelites, or by the exercise of fraud to prove injurious to the army of Achish. (xxvii, 2; xxix, 6, 7.) For he could have done neither of these deeds without committing a most flagrant wickedness: though both of them might have been determined [by David] as acts, by which great injury could be inflicted on those against whom it was the will of God that no mischief should be done.

XX. On account of this Presenting of incitements and opportunities, and this Direction and Determination of God, added to the Permission of sin, God is said himself to do those evils which are perpetrated by bad men and by Satan. For instance, Joseph says to his brethren, "It was not you that sent me hither, but God:" (Gen. xlv. 8;) because, after having completed the sale of their brother, they were unconcerned about the place to which he was to be conducted, and about his future lot in life: but God caused him to be led down into Egypt and there to be sold, and he raised him to an eminent station in that country by the interpretation of some dreams. (xxxvii, 25, 28; xl, 12, 13; xli, 28-42.) Job says, "The Lord hath taken away" what was taken away at the instigation and by the aid of Satan; (Job 1 & 2;) both because that evil spirit was of his own malice instigated against Job by God's commendation of him; and because, after having obtained power to do him harm, he produced no further effect than that which God had determined. Thus God is also said to have done what Absalom did; (2 Sam. xii. 11, 12; 15, 16;) because the principal parts, in the various actions employed for producing this consummation, belonged to God. To these we must add the remark, that since the wisdom of God knows that if he administers the whole affair by such a presenting, direction, and determination, that will certainly and infallibly come to pass which cannot be done by the creature without criminality; and since His will decrees this administration, it will more clearly appear why a deed of this kind may be attributed to God.

XXI. Last in the discussion follow the punishment and the pardon of sin, by which acts Divine Providence is occupied about sin already perpetrated, as it is such, not as it is an act: for sin is punished and pardoned as it is an evil, and because it is an evil. (1.) The Punishment of sin is an act of the Providence of God, by which sin is recompensed with the chastisement that is due to it according to the righteousness of God. This punishment either concerns the life to come, or takes place in the ages of the present life: the former is an eternal separation of the whole man from God; the other, which is usually inflicted in this life, is two-fold: corporal and spiritual. The punishments which relate to the body, are various; but it is not necessary for our purpose to enumerate them at present. But spiritual punishment deserves to be diligently considered: for it is such a chastisement of sin, as to be also a cause of other [sins] which follow on account of the wickedness of him on whom it is inflicted. It is a privation of grace, and a delivering up to the power of evil [or the evil one]. (i.) Privation of Grace is two-fold according to the two kinds of grace, that which is Habitual and that which is Assisting. The former is the taking away of grace, by blinding the mind and hardening the heart. (Isa. vi. 9, 10.) The other, is the withdrawing of the assistance of the Holy Spirit, who is wont inwardly "to help our infirmities," (Rom. viii. 26,) and outwardly to restrain the furious rage of Satan and the world, by employing also the ministration and care of good angels. (Heb. i. 14; Psalm xci. 11.) (ii.) A delivering up to the power of evil is, either "giving sinners over to a reprobate mind," and to the efficacy of error, (Rom. i. 28; 2 Thess. ii. 9-11,) or to the desires of the flesh and to sinful lusts, (Rom. i. 24,) or to the power of Satan, "the god of this world," (2 Cor. 4,) "who worketh powerfully in the children of disobedience." (Ephes. ii. 2.) But because from this punishment arise many other sins, and this not only according to the certain knowledge of God, by which he knows that if he thus punishes they will thence arise, but likewise according to his purpose, by which he resolves so to punish as, on account of more heinous sins thence committed, to punish with still greater severity; therefore these expressions occur in the scriptures: "But I will harden the heart of Pharaoh, that he shall not let the people go; he shall not hearken unto you, that I may lay my hand upon Egypt." (Exod. iv. 21; vii, 4.) "Notwithstanding, the sons of Eli hearkened not unto the voice of their father, because the Lord would slay them." (1 Sam. ii. 25.) "But Amaziah would not hearken to the answer of Joash king of Israel; for it came of God, that he might deliver them into the hand of their enemies, because they sought after the gods of Edom." (2 Chron. xxv. 20.) This consideration distinguishes the governance of God concerning sins, so far as it is concerned about those sinners who are hardened, or those who are not hardened.

XXII. The Pardon or remission of sin is an act of the Providence of God, by which the guilt of sin is forgiven, and the chastisement due to sin according to its guilt is taken away. As this remission restores, to the favour of God, the man who had before been an enemy; so it likewise causes the Divine administration concerning him to be afterwards entirely gracious so far as equity and justice require: that is, through this pardon, he is free from those spiritual punishments which have been enumerated in the preceding paragraph; (Psalm ii. 10-12;) and though not exempt from corporal chastisements, yet he is not visited with them through the anger of God as the punisher of sin, but only through the desire of God thus to declare that he hates sin, and besides so to chastise as to deter him from falling again into it. (2 Sam. xii. 11-13.) For which reason, the government of Providence with regard to this man is entirely different from that under which he remained before he obtained remission. (Psalm cxix. 67; 1 Cor. xi. 32; Psalm xxxii. 1-6.)

XXIII. From those topics on which we have already treated, it is clearly evident, we think, that, because evils have entered into the world, neither Providence itself, nor its government respecting evil, ought to be denied. Neither can God be accused as being guilty of injustice on account of this his governance; not only because he hath administered all things to the best ends; that is, to the chastisement, trial, and manifestation of the godly--to the punishment and exposure of the wicked, and to the illustration of his own glory; (for ends, alone, do not justify an action;) but, much more, because he has employed that form of administration which allows intelligent creatures not only of their own choice or spontaneously. but likewise freely, to perform and accomplish their own motions and actions.

DISPUTATION 10 - ON THE RIGHTEOUSNESS AND EFFICACY OF THE PROVIDENCE OF GOD CONCERNING EVIL

RESPONDENT: GERARD ADRIANS

I. The consideration of evil, which is called "the evil of culpability" or "of delinquency," has induced many persons to deny the providence of God concerning creatures endowed with understanding and freedom of will, and concerning their actions. These persons have denied it for two reasons: (1.) They have thought that, because God is good and just, omniscient and omnipotent, he would have entirely prevented sin from being committed, if in reality he cared by his providence for his rational creatures and there actions. (Mark x. 18; Psalm cxlvii. 5; Rev. iv. 8; Mal. ii. 17; iii, 14.) (2.) Because they can conceive in their minds no other administration of Divine Providence concerning evil, than such as would involve God himself in the culpability, and would exempt from all criminality the creature, as if he had been impelled to sin by an irresistible act of God's efficiency. For this reason, then, since a belief in the Providence of God is absolutely necessary, (Luke xii. 28,) from whom a considerable part of his government is taken away if it be denied that he exercises any care over rational creatures and their actions; we will endeavour briefly to explain the Efficiency of Divine Providence concerning evil; and at the same time to demonstrate from this efficiency, that God cannot possibly be aspersed with the charge of injustice, and that no stain of sin can attach to him, on the contrary, that this efficiency is highly conducive to the commendation of God's righteousness.

II. But in sin are to be considered not only the act, (under which we likewise comprise the omission of the act,) but also "the transgression of the law." The act has regard to a natural good, and is called the material cause of sin; the transgression is a moral evil, and is called the formal cause of sin. An investigation into both of them is necessary, when we treat upon the efficiency of God concerning sin: for it is occupied about the act as it is an act, and as it is done against the law which prohibits its commission; about the omission of the act as such, and as it is against the law which commands its performance. But this efficiency is to be considered: (1.) With regard to the beginning of sin, and its first conception in the heart of a rational creature; (2.) its attempt, and, through this attempt, its perpetration; and, (3.) with regard to sin when finished. The efficiency of God concerning the beginning of sin is either its hindrance or permission; and, added to permission, the administration both of arguments and occasions inciting to sin; as well as an immediate concurrence to produce the act. The Divine efficiency concerning the progress of sin comprises its direction and determination; and concerning the completion of sin, it is occupied in punishing or pardoning.

III. The First efficiency of God concerning sin, is Hindrance or the placing of a hindrance, which, both with regard of the efficiency and of the object, is three-fold. With respect to efficiency: For (i.) the impediment is either of sufficient efficacy, but such as does not hinder sin in the act. (Matt. xi. 21, 23; John xviii. 6.) (ii.) Or it is of such great efficacy as to render it impossible to be resisted. (iii.) Or it is of an efficacy administered in such a way by the wisdom of God, as in reality to hinder sin with regard to the event, and with certainty according to the foreknowledge of God, although not necessarily and inevitably. (Gen. xx. 6.) With respect to the object, it is likewise three-fold: for a hindrance is placed either on the power, the capability, or the will of a rational creature. (i.) The impediment placed on the power, is that by which some act is taken away from the power of a rational creature, for the performance of which it has an inclination and sufficient powers. This is done by legislation, through which it comes to pass that the creature cannot perform that act without sin. (Gen. ii. 16, 17.) (ii.) The impediment placed on the capability, is that by which this effect is produced, that the creature cannot commit the deed, for the performance of which it possesses an inclination, and powers which, without this hindrance, would be sufficient. But this hindrance is placed on the capability in four ways: First. By depriving the creature of the essence and life, which are the foundation of capability. (1 Kings 19; 2 Kings 1.) Secondly. By the ablation or diminution of capability. (1 Kings xiii. 4; Rom. vi. 6.) Thirdly. By the opposition of a greater capability, or at least of one that is equal. (2 Chron. xxvi. 18-21; Gal. v. 17.) Fourthly. By the withdrawing of the object towards which the act tends. (John viii. 59.) (iii.) An impediment is placed on the will when, by some argument, it is persuaded not to will the perpetration of a sin, whether this argument be taken from the impossibility or the difficulty of the thing; (Matt. xxi. 46; Hosea ii. 6, 7;) from its unpleasantness or inconvenience, its uselessness or injuriousness; (Gen. xxxvii. 26, 27;) and, lastly, from its injustice, dishonour, and indecency. (Gen. xxxix. 8, 9.)

IV. The Permission of sin is contrary to the hindering of it.

Yet it is not opposed to hindrance as the latter is an act which is taken away from the power of a creature by legislation; for, in this case, the same act would be a sin, and not a sin--a sin as it was an act forbidden to the power of the creature, and not a sin as being permitted, that is not forbidden. But permission is opposed to this hindrance, by which an impediment is placed on the power and the will of the creature. This permission is a suspension of all impediments, that, God knows, if they were employed, would in fact, hinder the sin; and it is a necessary result, because sin might be hindered by a single impediment of this description. (1.) Sin, therefore, is permitted to the power of the creature, when God employs none of those impediments which have been mentioned in the third thesis of this disputation: on which account, this permission has the following, either as conjoint or preceding acts of God. The continuance of essence and life to the creature, the preservation of his power, a care that it be not opposed by a greater power, or at least by one equal to it, and, lastly, the exhibition of the object on which sin is committed. (Exod. ix. 16; John xviii. 6; 1 Sam. xx. 31, 32; Matt. xxvi. 2, 53.) (2.) Sin is permitted also to the will, not by the suspension of every impediment suitable to deter the will from sinning, but by not employing those which in reality would hinder, of which kind God must have an immense number in the treasures of his wisdom and power.

V. The foundation of this permission is, (1.) The liberty of choice, which God, the Creator, has implanted in his rational creature, and the use of which the constancy of the Donor does not suffer to be taken away from this creature. (2.) The infinite wisdom and power of God, by which He knows and is able to produce good out of evil. (Gen. i. 2, 3; 2 Cor. iv. 6.) And therefore, God permits that which he does permit, not in ignorance of the powers and the inclination of rational creatures, for he knows all things; (1 Sam. xxiii. 11, 12;) -not with reluctance, for it was in his power, not to have produced a creature who possessed freedom of will, and to have destroyed him after he was produced; (Rev. iv. 11;) -- not as being incapable of hindering, for how can this be attributed to Him who is both omniscient and omnipotent? (Jer. xviii. 6; Psalm xciv. 9, 10;) not as an unconcerned spectator, or negligent of that which is transacted, because even before any thing is done, he has already gone through the various actions concerning it, and has, besides, an attentive eye upon it to direct and determine to punish or to pardon it. (Psalm lxxxi. 12, 13.) But whatever God permits, he permits it designedly and voluntarily, His will being immediately concerned about its permission, which permission itself is immediately occupied about sin, which order cannot be inverted without injury to divine justice and truth. (Psalm v. 4, 5.)

VI. We must now, with more distinctness, explain, by some of the differences of sin, those things which we have spoken thus generally about hindering and permitting. (1.) The distinction of sin, from its causes, into those of ignorance, infirmity, malignity, and negligence, will serve our purpose. For an impediment is placed on a sin of ignorance, by the revelation of the divine will; (Psalm cxix. 105;) on a sin of infirmity, by the strengthening of the Holy Spirit; (Ephes. iii. 16;) on a sin of malignity, by "taking away the stony heart, and by bestowing a heart of flesh," (Ezek. xi. 19,) and inscribing on it the law of God; (Jer. xxxi. 33;) and on a sin of negligence, by a holy solicitude excited in the hearts of believers. (Jer. xxxii. 40.) From these, it will be easily evident, in the suspension of which of these acts consists the permission of sins under each of the preceding classes. (2.) The distinction of sin according to the relation of the law which commands the performance of good, and of that which prohibits the commission of evil, has also a place in this explanation. For, against the prohibitory part, an offense is committed, either by performing an act, or from an undue cause and end, omitting its performance-- against the perceptive part, either by omitting an act, or by performing it in an undue manner, and from an undue cause and end. To these distinctions also, God's hindering and permitting may be adapted. For Joseph's brethren were hindered from killing him; but they were induced to omit that act from an undue cause and end. (Gen. xxxvii. 26, 27.) Absalom was hindered from following the counsel of Ahithophel, which was useful to himself, and hurtful to David; but he did not abstain from it through a just cause, and from a good end. (2 Sam. 17.) God hindered Balaam from cursing the children of Israel, and caused him to bless them; but it was in such a manner that he abstained from the former act, and performed the latter with an insincere and knavish mind. (Num. 23.)

VII. We shall more correctly understand the reasons and causes both of hindering and permitting, if, while distinctly considering in sin the act, and the transgression of the law, we apply to each of them the divine hindrance and permission. But though, in sin, the act and the transgression of the law are inseparably connected, and therefore neither can be hindered or permitted without the other; yet they may be distinguished in the mind, and God may hinder and permit sometimes with regard to the act or to the transgression alone; at other times, principally with regard to the one of them or to both, and these his acts may become objects of consideration to us. God hindered Elijah from being forcibly brought to Ahaziah to be killed, not as that was a sin, but as it was an act. This is apparent from the end and the mode of hindering. From the end, because it was His will that the life of His prophet should be spared, not lest Ahaziah should sin against God. From the mode of hindering, because he destroyed two companies, of fifty men each, who had been sent to seize him, which was a token of divine anger against Ahaziah and the men, by which sin is not usually hindered as such, but as it is an act which will prove injurious to another: but through Grace, sin is hindered as such. (2 Kings 1.) God permitted Joseph to be sold, when he hindered his murder. He permitted his vendition, not more as it was a sin than as it was an act; for by the sale of Joseph, as it was an act, God obtained his end. (Gen. xxxvii. 1,

20; Psalm cv. 17.) But God hindered David from laying violent hands on Saul, not so much as it was an act, as in reference to its being a sin. This appears from the argument by which David was induced to refrain. "The Lord forbid," said he, "that I should stretch forth mine hand against the Lord's anointed." (1 Sam. xxiv. 7.) God permitted Ahab to kill Naboth, rather as it was a sin than as it was an act; for thus Ahab filled up the measure of his iniquities, and accelerated the infliction of punishment on himself; for, by some other way than this, God could have taken Naboth to himself. (1 Kings 21.) But Abimelech was hindered from violating the chastity of Sarah--both as it was an act by which indelible grief would have been brought down upon Abraham, whom He greatly loved, and as it was a sin; for God was unwilling that Abimelech should defile himself with this crime, because "in the integrity of his heart," he would have done it. (Gen. xx. 6.) On the contrary, God permitted Judah to know Tamar, his daughter-in-law--both as an act because God willed to have Christ born in direct descent from Judah, and as it was a sin, for it was the will of God thus to declare: Nothing is so polluted that it cannot be sanctified in Christ Jesus. (Gen. xxxviii. 18.) For it is not in vain that Matthew has informed us, that Christ was the Son of Judah by Tamar, as he was also the Son of David by the wife of Uriah. (Matt. 1.) This matter when diligently considered by us, conduces both to illustrate the wisdom of God, and to promote our own profit, if in our consciences, we solicitously observe from what acts and in what respect we are hindered, and what acts are permitted to us.

VIII. Beside this permission, there is another efficiency of the providence of God concerning the Beginning of Sin, that is, the Administration or management of arguments and occasions, which incite to an act that cannot be committed by the creature without sin, if not through the intention of God, at least according to the inclination of the creature, and not seldom according to the events which thence arise. (2 Sam. xii. 11, 12; xvi, 21-23.) But these arguments are presented either to the mind, (2 Sam. xxiv. 1; 1 Chron. xxi. 1; Psalm cv. 25,) or to the senses, both external and internal; (Job 1 & 2; Isa. x. 5-7;) and this indeed, either by means of the service or intervention of creatures, or by the immediate act of God himself. The end of God in this administration is--to try whether it be the will of the creature to abstain from sinning, even when it is excited by these incentives; (for small praise is due to the act of abstaining, in those cases in which such excitements are absent,) and, if it be the will of the creature to yield to these alluring attractions, to effect his own work by the act of the creature; not impelled by necessity, as if He was unable to complete his own work without the aid of the creature; but through a desire to demonstrate his manifold wisdom. Consider the Arguments by which the brethren of Joseph, through their own malice, were incited to will his murder: these were--Joseph's accusation, by which he disclosed to his father the deeds of his brethren, the peculiar affection which Jacob cherished for Joseph, the sending of a dream, and the relation of it. Consider also the Occasions or opportunities, the mission of Joseph to his brethren at his father's request, and the opportune appearance of the Ishmaelites who were traveling into Egypt, (Gen. 37.)

IX. The last efficiency of God concerning the Beginnings of sin, is the divine concurrence, which is necessary to produce every act; because nothing whatever can have an entity except from the first and chief Being, who immediately produces that entity. The concurrence of God is not his in, mediate influx into a second or inferior cause, but it is an action of God immediately flowing into the effect of the creature, so that the same effect in one and the same entire action may be produced simultaneously by God and the creature. Though this concurrence is placed in the mere pleasure or will of God, and in his free dispensation, yet he never denies it to a rational and free creature, when he has permitted an act to his power and will. For these two phrases are contradictory, "to grant permission to the power and the will of a creature to commit an act," and "to deny the divine concurrence without which the act cannot be done." But this concurrence is to the act as such, not as it is a sin: And therefore God is at once the effector and the permittor of the same act, and the permittor before he is the effector. For if it had not been the will of the creature to perform such an act, the influx of God would not have been upon that act by concurrence. And because the creature cannot perform that act without sin, God ought not, on that account, to deny the divine concurrence to the creature who is inclined to its performance. For it is right and proper that the obedience of the creature should be tried, and that he should abstain from an unlawful act and from the desire of obeying his own inclinations, not through a deficiency of the requisite divine concurrence; because, in this respect, he abstains from an act as it is a natural good, but it is the will of God that he should refrain from it as it is a moral evil.

X. The preceding considerations relate to the Beginnings of sin. In reference to the Progress of sin, a two-fold efficiency of divine providence occurs, direction and determination. The direction of sin is an act of divine providence, by which God wisely, justly, and powerfully directs sin wherever he wills, "reaching from one end to another mightily, and sweetly ordering all things." (Wisdom viii. 1.) In the divine direction is likewise contained a leading away from that point whither it is not the will of God to direct it. This direction is two-fold, unto an object, and unto an end. Direction unto an object is when God allows the sin, which he permits, to be borne, not at the option of the creature, towards an object which, in any way whatsoever, is exposed and liable to the injury of sin; but which he directs to a particular object that sometimes has been no part of the sinner's aim or intention, or that he has at least not absolutely intended. (Prov. xvi, 9; xxi, 1.) Of this we have a signal example in Nebuchadnezzar, who, when he had prepared himself to subjugate nations, preferred to march against the Jews rather than the Ammonites, through the divine administration of his divinations. (Ezek. xxi. 19-22.) Direction unto an end is, when God does not allow the sin, which he permits, to be conducive to any end which the creature intends; but he uses it for that end which he himself wills, whether the creature intend the same end, (by which he would not still be excused from sin,) or whether he has another purpose which is directly contrary. The vendition of Joseph into Egypt, the temptation of Job, and the expedition of the king of Assyria against the Jews, afford illustrations of these remarks. (Gen. i. 20, 21; Job 1 & 2; Isa. x. 5-12.)

XI. The determination of sin is an act of divine providence by which God places a measure or check on his permission, and a boundary on sin, that it may not, at the option and will of the creature, wander in infinitum. This mode and boundary are placed by the circumscription of the time, and the determination of the magnitude. The circumscription of the time is, when the space of time, in which the permitted sin could continue, is diminished and circumscribed so as to stop itself. (Matt. xxiv. 22.) In this part also, regard must be had to the act as such, and to the sin as such. (i.) God places a boundary to the duration of the act, when he takes the rod of iniquity from the righteous, lest they commit any act unworthy of themselves; (Psalm cxxv. 3;) and when "he delivers the godly out of temptation." (2 Pet. ii. 9.) (ii.) God places a boundary to the duration of the sin when he "hedges up the way of the Israelites with thorns," that they may no longer commit idolatry; (Hosea ii. 6, 7;) when "He commands all men every where to repent," among "all nations, whom he suffered, in times past, to walk in their own ways." (Acts xiv. 16; xvii, 30.) A boundary is fixed to the magnitude of sin, when God does not permit sin to increase to excess and assume greater strength. This also is done with respect to it as an act, or as a sin. (i.) In the former respect, as an act, God hindered "the wrath of their enemies from swallowing up" the children of Israel, though he had permitted it to rise up against them; (Psalm cxxiv. 2, 3;) He permitted "no temptation to seize upon" the Corinthians "but such as is common to man;" (1 Cor. x. 13;) He hindered the devil from putting forth his hand against the life of Job; (1 & 2;) He prevented Shishadk, the king of Egypt, from "destroying" the Jews, and permitted him only to subject them to servitude. (2 Chron. xii. 7-9.) (ii.) In respect to it as a sin, God hindered David from contaminating himself with the blood of Nabal and his domestics. which he had sworn to shed, and with whom he was then in a state of contention. (1 Sam. xxv. 22, 26.) He also prevented David from going forth to battle in company with the army of Achish, (xxvii, 2; xxix, 6, 7,) to whom he had fled, and "before whom he had reigned himself mad," (xxi, 13,) thus, at the same time he hindered him from destroying his own countrymen, the Israelites, and from bringing disasters on the army of Achish. For he could have done neither of these things without the most flagrant wickedness; though the sin, also, as an act, seems thus to have been hindered.

XII. On account of this divine permission, the offering of arguments and opportunities in addition to permission, also on account of this direction, determination, and divine concurrence, God is said himself to do those evils which are perpetrated by men and by Satan: To have sent Joseph down into Egypt, (Gen. xlv. 8,) -- to have taken the property of Job, (1 & 2,) -- to have done openly "and before the sun" what David had perpetrated "secretly" against Uriah. (2 Sam. xii. 11, 12; 16.) This mode of speech is adopted for the following reasons: (i.) Because the principal parts, in the actions which are employed to produce such effects, belong to God himself. (ii.) Because the effects and issues, which result from all these, even from actions performed by the creature, are not so much in accordance with the intention of the creatures themselves, as with the purpose of God. (Isa. x. 5-7.) (iii.) Because the wisdom of God knows, if an administration of this kind be employed by him, that will certainly arise, or ensue, which cannot be perpetuated by the creature without wickedness; and because His will decrees to employ this administration. (1 Sam. xxiii. 11-13.) (iv.) A fourth reason may be added--Because God, who is the universal cause, moves into the effect with a stronger influence than the creature does, whose entire efficacy depends upon God.

XIII. Lastly, follows the efficiency of divine providence concerning sin already perpetrated; which consists in its punishment and remission. This efficiency is occupied about sin as it is such: For sin is punished and pardoned as it is an evil, and because it is an evil. (1.) The Punishment of sin is an act of the providence of God, by which sin is repaid with the punishment that is due to it according to the justice of God. This punishment either belongs to the present life, or to that which is to come. (i.) The latter is the eternal separation of the whole man from God, and his anguish and torture in the lake of fire. (Matt. xxv. 41; Rev. xx. 15.) (ii.) The punishment inflicted in this life, is either corporal or spiritual. Those chastisements which relate to the body, and to the state of the animal life, are various; but the enumeration of them is not necessary for our purpose. But spiritual punishment must be diligently considered; which is such a punishment of a previous sin, as to be also the cause of other subsequent sins, through the malice of him on whom it is inflicted. It is a privation of grace, and a delivering up to the power of evil. But Privation is either that of habitual grace, or that of assisting grace. The former is through the blinding of the mind, and the hardening of the heart. (Isa. vi. 9, 10.) The latter is the withdrawing of the assistance of the Holy Spirit, who is wont, inwardly "to help our infirmities," (Rom. viii, 26,) and outwardly to repress the temptations of Satan and the world both on the right hand and on the left; in this holy service, he also engages the ministry and the care of good angels. (Heb. i. 14; Psalm xci. 11.) A Delivering Up to the power of evil is, either "giving sinners over to a reprobate mind" and to the efficacy of error, (Rom. i. 28; 2 Thess. ii. 9-11,) or to the desires of the flesh and to the lusts of sin, (Rom. i. 24,) or lastly to the power of Satan, "the god of this world," (2 Cor. iv. 4,) "who worketh powerfully in the children of disobedience." (Ephes. ii. 2.) But because from this punishment arise many other sins, and this not only according to the certain knowledge of God, by which He knows that if He thus punishes, they will thence arise, but likewise according to his purpose by which He resolves thus to punish--hence occur the following expressions: "I will harden the heart of Pharaoh," &c. (Exod. iv. 21; vii, 4.) "Notwithstanding, the sons of Eli harkened not unto the voice of their father, because it was the will of the Lord to slay them." (1 Sam. ii. 25.) "But Amaziah would not hearken to the answer of Joash, king of Israel; for it came of God, that he might deliver them into the hand of their enemies, because they sought after the gods of Edom." (2 Chron. xxv. 20.) This consideration distinguishes the governance of God concerning sins, so far as it is occupied concerning either those sinners who are hardened, or those who are not hardened.

XIV. (2.) The Pardon or remission of sin is an act of the Providence of God, by which the guilt of sin is forgiven, and the punishment due to sin on account of its guilt is taken away. As this remission restores, to the favour of God, the man who had previously been an enemy; so it also causes the Divine administration respecting him to be afterwards entirely gracious, so far as equity and justice require. That is, through this pardon, he is free from those spiritual punishments which have been enumerated in the preceding Thesis; (Psalm ii. 10-12;) and though not exempt from corporal chastisements, yet he is not visited with them through the anger of God as the punisher of sin, but only through the desire of God thus to declare that He hates sin, and besides so to chastise as to deter the sinner from again falling into it. (2 Sam. xii. 11-13.) For which reason, the government of Providence with regard to this man is entirely different from that under which he remained before he obtained remission. (Psalm cxix. 67; 1 Cor. xi. 32; Psalm xxxii. 1, 6.) This consideration is exceedingly useful for producing in man a solicitous care and a diligent endeavour to obtain grace from God, which may not only be sufficient to preserve him in future from sinning but which may likewise be so administered by the gracious Providence of God, as God knows to be best fitted to keep him in the very act from sin.

XV. This is the efficiency of Divine Providence concerning sin, which cannot be accused of the least injustice. (1.) For with respect to the Hindering Of Sin, that which is employed by God is sufficient in its own nature to hinder, and by which it is the duty of the creature to be hindered from sin, by which also he might actually be hindered unless he offered resistance and failed of the proffered grace. But God is not bound to employ all the methods which are possible to Him for the hindrance of sin. (Rom. 1 and 2; Isa. v. 4; Matt. xi. 21-23.) (2.) But the cause of sin cannot be ascribed to the Divine Permission. Not the efficient cause; for it is a suspension of the Divine efficiency. Not the deficient cause; for it pre-supposed, that man had a capability not to commit sin, by the aid of Divine grace, which is either near and ready; or if it be wanting, it is removed to a distance by the fault of the man himself. (3.) The Presenting of Arguments and Occasions does not cause sin, unless, per accidens, accidentally. For it is administered in such a manner, as to allow the creature not only the spontaneous but also the free use of his own motions and actions. But God is perfectly at liberty in this manner to try the obedience of his creature. (3.) Neither can injustice be ascribed with any propriety to The Divine Concurrence. For there is no reason in existence why God ought to deny his concurrence to that act which, on account of the precept imposed, cannot be committed by the creature without sin; (Gen. ii. 16, 17;) which concurrence God would grant to the same act of the creature, if a law had not been made. (5.) Direction and Determination have no difficulty. (6.) Punishment and Pardon have in them manifest equity, even that punishment which contains blinding and hardening; since God is not wont to inflict it except for the deep demerit and the almost desperate contumacy of his intelligent creature. (Isa. vi. 7; Rom. 1; 2 Thess. 2, 9-12.)

DISPUTATION 11 - ON THE FREE WILL OF MAN AND ITS POWERS

RESPONDENT: PAUL LEONARDS

I. The word, arbitrium, "choice," or "free will," properly signifies both the faculty of the mind or understanding, by which the mind is enabled to judge about any thing proposed to it, and the judgment itself which the mind forms according to that faculty. But it is transferred from the Mind to the Will on account of the very close connection which subsists between them. Liberty, when attributed to the will, is properly an affection of the will, though it has its root in the understanding and reason. Generally considered, it is various. (1.) It is a Freedom from the control or jurisdiction of one who commands, and from an obligation to render obedience. (2.) From the inspection, care, and government of a superior. (3.) It is also a freedom from necessity, whether this proceeds from an external cause compelling, or from a nature inwardly determining absolutely to one thing. (4.) It is a freedom from sin and its dominion. (5.) And a freedom from misery.

II. Of these five modes of liberty, the first two appertain to God alone; to whom also on this account, autexousia perfect independence, or complete freedom of action, is attributed. But the remaining three modes may belong to man, nay in a certain respect they do pertain to him. And, indeed, the former, namely, freedom from necessity always pertains to him because it exists naturally in the will, as its proper attribute, so that there cannot be any will if it be not free. The freedom from misery, which pertains to man when recently created and not then fallen into sin, will again pertain to him when he shall be translated in body and soul into celestial blessedness. But about these two modes also, of freedom from necessity and from misery, we have here no dispute. It remains, therefore, for us, to discuss that which is a freedom from sin and its dominion, and which is the principal controversy of these times.

III. It is therefore asked, is there within man a freedom of will from sin and its dominion, and how far does it extend? Or rather, what are the powers of the whole man to understand, to will, and to do that which is good? To return an appropriate answer to this question, the distinction of a good object, and the diversity of men's conditions, must both enter into our consideration. The Good Things presented to man are three, natural, which he has in common with many other creatures; animal, which belong to him as a man; and spiritual, which are also deservedly called Celestial or Divine, and which are consentaneous to him as being a partaker of the Divine Nature. The States, or Conditions are likewise three, that of primitive innocence, in which God placed him by creation; that of subsequent corruption, into which he fell through sin when destitute of primitive innocence; and, lastly, that of renewed righteousness, to which state he is restored by the grace of Christ.

IV. But because it is of little importance to our present purpose to investigate what may be the powers of free will to understand, to will, and to do natural and animal good things; we will omit them, and enter on the consideration of spiritual good, that concerns the spiritual life of man, which he is bound to live according to godliness, inquiring from the Scriptures what powers man possesses, while he is in the way of this animal life, to understand, to will, and to do spiritual good things, which alone are truly good and pleasing to God. In this inquiry the office of a Director will be performed by a consideration of the three states, of which we have already treated, [§ 3,] varied as such consideration must be in the relation of these powers to the change of each state.

V. In the state of Primitive Innocence, man had a mind endued with a clear understanding of heavenly light and truth concerning God, and his works and will, as far as was sufficient for the salvation of man and the glory of God; he had a heart imbued with "righteousness and true holiness," and with a true and saving love of good; and powers abundantly qualified or furnished perfectly to fulfill the law which God had imposed on him. This admits easily of proof, from the description of the image of God, after which man is said to have been created, (Gen. i. 26, 27,) from the law divinely imposed on him, which had a promise and a threat appended to it, (ii, 17,) and lastly from the analogous restoration of the same image in Christ Jesus. (Ephes. iv. 24, Col. iii. 10.)

VI. But man was not so confirmed in this state of innocence, as to be incapable of being moved, by the representation presented to him of some good, (whether it was of an inferior kind and relating to this animal life, or of a superior-kind and relating to spiritual life,) inordinately and unlawfully to look upon it and to desire it, and of his own spontaneous as well as free motion, and through a preposterous desire for that good, to decline from the obedience which had been prescribed to him. Nay, having turned away from the light of his own mind and his chief good, which is God, or, at least, having turned towards that chief good not in the manner in which he ought to have done, and besides having turned in mind and heart towards an inferior good, he transgressed the command given to him for life. By this foul deed, he precipitated himself from that noble and elevated condition into a state of the deepest infelicity, which is Under The Dominion of Sin. For "to whom any one yields himself a servant to obey," (Rom. vi. 16,) and "of whom a man is overcome, of the same is he brought in bondage," and is his regularly assigned slave. (2 Pet. ii. 19.)

VII. In this state, the free will of man towards the true good is not only wounded, maimed, infirm, bent, and weakened; but it is also imprisoned, destroyed, and lost. And its powers are not only debilitated and useless unless they be assisted by grace, but it has no powers whatever except such as are excited by Divine grace. For Christ has said, "Without me ye can do nothing." St. Augustine, after having diligently meditated upon each word in this passage, speaks thus: "Christ does not say, without me ye can do but Little; neither does He say, without me ye can do any Arduous Thing, nor without me ye can do it with difficulty. But he says, without me ye can do Nothing! Nor does he say, without me ye cannot complete any thing; but without me ye can do Nothing." That this may be made more manifestly to appear, we will separately consider the mind, the affections or will, and the capability, as contra-distinguished from them, as well as the life itself of an unregenerate man.

VIII. The mind of man, in this state, is dark, destitute of the saving knowledge of God, and, according to the Apostle, incapable of those things which belong to the Spirit of God. For "the animal man has no perception of the things of the Spirit of God;" (1 Cor. ii. 14;) in which passage man is called "animal," not from the animal body, but from anima, the soul itself, which is the most noble part of man, but which is so encompassed about with the clouds of ignorance, as to be distinguished by the epithets of "vain" and "foolish;" and men themselves, thus darkened in their minds, are denominated "mad" or foolish, "fools," and even "darkness" itself. (Rom. i. 21, 22; Ephes. iv. 17, 18; Tit. iii. 3; Ephes. v. 8.) This is true, not only when, from the truth of the law which has in some measure been inscribed on the mind, it is preparing to form conclusions by the understanding; but likewise when, by simple apprehension, it would receive the truth of the gospel externally offered to it. For the human mind judges that to be "foolishness" which is the most excellent "wisdom" of God. (1 Cor. i. 18, 24.) On this account, what is here said must be understood not only of practical understanding and the judgment of particular approbation, but also of theoretical understanding and the judgment of general estimation.

IX. To the darkness of the mind succeeds the perverseness of the affections and of the heart, according to which it hates and has an aversion to that which is truly good and pleasing to God; but it loves and pursues what is evil. The Apostle was unable to afford a more luminous description of this perverseness, than he has given in the following words: "The carnal mind is enmity against God. For it is not subject to the law of God, neither indeed can be. So then, they that are in the flesh cannot please God." (Rom. viii. 7.) For this reason, the human heart itself is very often called deceitful and perverse, uncircumcised, hard and stony." (Jer. xiii. 10; xvii, 9; Ezek. xxxvi. 26.) Its imagination is said to be "only evil from his very youth;" (Gen. vi. 5; viii, 21;) and "out of the heart proceed evil thoughts, murders, adulteries," &c. (Matt. xv. 19.)

X. Exactly correspondent to this darkness of the mind, and perverseness of the heart, is the utter weakness of all the powers to perform that which is truly good, and to omit the perpetration of that which is evil, in a due mode and from a due end and cause. The subjoined sayings of Christ serve to describe this impotence. "A corrupt tree cannot bring forth good fruit." (Matt. vii. 18.) "How can ye, being evil, speak good things?" (xii, 34.) The following relates to the good which is properly prescribed in the gospel: "No man can come to me, except the Father draw him." (John vi. 44.) As do likewise the following words of the Apostle: "The carnal mind is not subject to the law of God, neither indeed can be;" (Rom. viii. 7;) therefore, that man over whom it has dominion, cannot perform what the law commands. The same Apostle says, "When we were in the flesh, the motions of sins wrought in us," or flourished energetically. (vii, 5.) To the same purpose are all those passages in which the man existing in this state is said to be under the power of sin and Satan, reduced to the condition of a slave, and "taken captive by the Devil." (Rom. vi. 20; 2 Tim. ii. 26.)

XI. To these let the consideration of the whole of the life of man who is placed under sin, be added, of which the Scriptures exhibit to us the most luminous descriptions; and it will be evident, that nothing can be spoken more truly concerning man in this state, than that he is altogether dead in sin. (Rom. iii. 10-19.) To these let the testimonies of Scripture be joined, in which are described the benefits of Christ, which are conferred by his Spirit on the human mind and will, and thus on the whole man. (1 Cor. vi. 9-11; Gal. v. 19-25; Ephes. ii. 2-7; iv, 17-20; Tit. iii. 3-7.) For, the blessings of which man has been deprived by sin, cannot be rendered more obviously apparent, than by the immense mass of benefits which accrue to believers through the Holy Spirit; when, in truth, nature is understood to be devoid of all that which, as the Scriptures testify, is performed in man and communicated by the operation of the Holy Spirit. Therefore, if "where the Spirit of the Lord is, there is liberty;" (2 Cor. iii. 17;) and if those alone be free indeed whom the Son hath made free;" (John viii. 36;) it follows, that our will is not free from the first fall; that is, it is not free to good, unless it be made free by the Son through his Spirit.

XII. But far different from this is the consideration of the free will of man, as constituted in the third state of Renewed Righteousness. For when a new light and knowledge of God and Christ, and of the Divine will, have been kindled in his mind; and when new affections, inclinations and motions agreeing with the law of God, have been excited in his heart, and new powers have been produced in him; it comes to pass, that, being liberated from the kingdom of darkness, and being now made "light in the Lord," (Ephes. v. 8,) he understands the true and saving good; that, after the hardness of his stony heart has been changed into the softness of flesh, and the law of God according to the covenant of grace has been inscribed on it, (Jer. 31, 32-35,) he loves and embraces that which is good, just, and holy; and that, being made capable in Christ, co-operating now with God, he prosecutes the good which he knows and loves, and he begins himself to perform it in deed. But this, whatever it may be of knowledge, holiness and power, is all begotten within him by the Holy Spirit; who is, on this account, called "the Spirit of wisdom and understanding, of counsel and might, of knowledge and the fear of Jehovah," (Isa. xi. 2,) "the Spirit of grace," (Zech. xii. 10,) "of faith," (2 Cor. iv. 13,) "the Spirit of adoption" into sons, (Rom. viii. 16,) and "the Spirit of holiness;" and to whom the acts of illumination, regeneration, renovation, and confirmation, are attributed in the Scriptures.

XIII. But two things must be here observed. The First that this work of regeneration and illumination is not completed in one moment; but that it is advanced and promoted, from time to time, by daily increase. For "our old man is crucified, that the body of sin might be destroyed," (Rom. vi. 6,) and "that the inward man may be renewed day by day." (2 Cor. iv. 16.) For this reason, in regenerate persons, as long as they inhabit these mortal bodies, "the flesh lusteth against the Spirit." (Gal. v. 17.) Hence it arises, that they can neither perform any good thing without great resistance and violent struggles, nor abstain from the commission of evil. Nay, it also happens, that, either through ignorance or infirmity, and sometimes through perverseness, they sin, as we may see in the cases of Moses, Aaron, Barnabas, Peter and David. Neither is such an occurrence only accidental; but, even in those who are the most perfect, the following Scriptures have their fulfillment: "In many things we all offend;" (James iii. 9;) and "There is no man that sinneth not." (1 Kings viii. 46.)

XIV. The Second thing to be observed is, that as the very first commencement of every good thing, so likewise the progress, continuance and confirmation, nay, even the perseverance in good, are not from ourselves, but from God through the Holy Spirit. For "he who hath begun a good work in you, will perform it until the day of Jesus Christ;" (Phil. i. 6;) and "we are kept by the power of God through faith." (1 Pet. i. 5.) "The God of all grace makes us perfect, stablishes, strengthens and settles us." (i, 10.) But if it happens that persons fall into sin who have been born again, they neither repent nor rise again unless they be raised up again by God through the power of his Spirit, and be renewed to repentance. This is proved in the most satisfactory manner, by the example of David and of Peter. "Every good and perfect gift, therefore, is from above, and cometh down from the Father of lights," (James i. 17,) by whose power the dead are animated that they may live, the fallen are raised up that they may recover themselves, the blind are illuminated that they may see, the unwilling are incited that they may become willing, the weak are confirmed that they may stand, the willing are assisted that they may work and may co-operate with God. "To whom be praise and glory in the church, by Christ Jesus, throughout all ages, world without end. Amen!" "Subsequent or following grace does indeed assist the good purpose of man; but this good purpose would have no existence unless through preceding or preventing grace. And though the desire of man, which is called good, be assisted by grace when it begins to be; yet it does not begin without grace, but is inspired by Him, concerning whom the Apostle writes thus, thanks be to God, who put the same earnest care into the heart of Titus for you. If God incites any one to have an earnest care' for others, He will put it into the heart' of some other person to have an earnest care' for him." Augustinus, Contra. 2 Epist. Pelag. l. 2. c. 9.

"What then, you ask, does free will do? I reply with brevity, it saves. Take away FREE WILL, and nothing will be left to be saved. Take away GRACE, and nothing will be left as the source of salvation. This work [of salvation] cannot be effected without two parties--one, from whom it may come: the other, to whom or in whom it may be wrought. God is the author of salvation. Free will is only capable of being saved. No one, except God, is able to bestow salvation; and nothing, except free will, is capable of receiving it." Bernardus, De Libero Arbit. et Gratia.

DISPUTATION 12 - THE LAW OF GOD

RESPONDENT: DIONYSIUS SPRANCKHUYSEN

I. Law in general is defined, either from its End, "an ordinance of right reason for the common and particular good of all and of each of those who are subordinate to it, enacted by Him who has the care of the whole community, and, in it, that of each individual." Or from its Form and its Efficacy, "an ordinance commanding what must be done, and what omitted; it is enacted by Him, who possesses the right of requiring obedience; and it binds to obedience a creature who abounds in the use of reason and the exercise of liberty, by the sacred promise of a reward and by the denunciation of a punishment." It is likewise distinguished into Human and Divine. A Divine law has God for its author, a Human law has man for its author; not that any law enacted by man is choice and good, which may not be referred to God, the author of every good; but because men deduce from the Divine law such precepts as are accommodated to the state of which they have the charge and oversight, according to its particular condition and circumstances. At present we will treat upon the Divine law.

II. The Divine law may be considered, either as it is impressed on the minds of men by the engrafted word; (Rom. ii. 14, 15;) as it is communicated by words audibly pronounced, (Gal. ii. 17,) or as it is comprised in writing. (Exod. xxxiv. 1.) These modes of legislation do not differ in their entire objects: but they may admit of discrimination in this way, the first seems to serve as a kind of foundation to the rest; but the two others extend themselves further, even to those things which are commanded and forbidden. We will now treat upon the law of God which is comprised in writing; and which is also called "the law of Moses;" because God used him as a mediator to deliver it to the children of Israel. (Mal. iv. 4; Gal. iii. 19.) But it is three-fold according to the variety of the object, that is, of the works to be performed. The first is called the Ethical, or Moral Law: (Exod. 20.) The second, the Sacred or Ceremonial. The third the Political, Judicial or Forensic Law.

III. The Moral Law is distributed through the whole of the Scriptures of the Old and New Testament, and is summarily contained in the Decalogue. It is an ordinance that commands those things which God accounts grateful of themselves, and which it is his will to be performed by all men at all times and in all places; and that forbids the contrary things. (1 Sam. xv. 22; Amos v. 21-24; Micah vi. 6-8.) It is therefore the perpetual and immutable rule of living, the express image of the internal Divine conception; according to which, God, the great lawgiver, judges it right and equitable that a rational creature should always and in every place order and direct the whole of his life. It is briefly contained in the love God and of our neighbour; (Matt. xxii. 36-39;) whether partly consisting of those services which relate to the love, honour, fear, and worship of God; (Mal. i. 6;) or partly consisting of those duties which we owe to our neighbours, superiors, inferiors, and equals: (Rom. 12,13, & 14;) in the wide circle of which are also comprehended those things which every man is bound to perform to himself. (Tit. ii. 11, 12.)

IV. The uses of the moral law are various, according to the different conditions of man. (1.) The primary use, and that which was of itself intended by God according to his love for righteousness and for his creatures, was, that man by it might be quickened or made alive, that is, that he might perform it, and by its performance might be justified, and might "of debt" receive the reward which was promised through it. (Rom. ii. 13; x, 5; iv, 4.) And this use was accommodated to the primitive state of man, when sin had not yet entered into the world. (2.) The first use in order of the moral law, under a state of sin, is AGAINST man as a sinner, not only that it may accuse him of transgression and guilt, and may subject him to the wrath of God and condemnation; (Rom. iii. 19, 20;) but that it may likewise convince him of his utter inability to resist sin and to subject himself to the law. (Rom. 7.) Since God has been pleased mercifully and graciously to treat with sinful man, the next use of the law TOWARDS the sinner is, that it may compel him who is thus convicted and subjected to condemnation, to desire and seek the grace of God, and that it may force him to flee to Christ either as the promised or as the imparted deliverer. (Gal. ii. 16, 17.) Besides, in this state of sin, the moral law is serviceable, not only to God, that, by the dread of punishment and the promise of temporal rewards, he may restrain men under its guidance at least from the outward work of sin and from flagrant crimes; (1 Tim. i. 9, 10;) but it is also serviceable to Sin, when dwelling and reigning in a carnal man who is under the law, that it may inflame the desire of sin, may increase sin, and may "work within him all manner of concupiscence." (Rom. vi. 12-14; vii, 5, 8, 11, 13.) In the former case, God employs the law through his goodness and his love for civil and social intercourse among mankind. In the latter case, it is employed through the malice of sin which reigns and has the dominion.

V. (3.) The third use of the moral law is towards a man, as now born again by the Spirit of God and of Christ, and is agreeable to the state of grace, that it may be a perpetual rule for directing his life in a godly and spiritual manner: (Tit. iii. 8; James ii. 8.) Not that man may be justified; because for this purpose it is rendered "weak through the flesh" and useless, even if man had committed only a single sin: (Rom. viii. 3.) But that he may render thanks to God for his gracious redemption and sanctification, (Psalm cxvi. 12, 13,) that he may preserve a good conscience, (1 Tim. i. 19,) that he may make his calling and election sure, (2 Pet. i. 10,) that he may by his example win over other persons to Christ, (1 Pet. iii. 1,) that he may confound the devil, (Job 1 & 2,) that he may condemn the ungodly world, (Heb. xi. 7,) and that through the path of good works he may march towards the heavenly inheritance and glory, (Rom. ii. 7,) and that he may not only himself glorify God, (1 Cor. vi. 20,) but may also furnish occasion and matter to others for glorifying his Father who is in Heaven. (Matt. v. 16.)

VI. From these uses it is easy to collect how far the moral law obtains among believers and those who are placed under the grace of Christ, and how far it is abrogated. (1.) It is abrogated with regard to its power and use in justifying:

"For if there had been a law given which could have given life, verily righteousness should have been by that law." (Gal. iii. 21.) The reason why "it cannot give life," is, "because it is weak through the flesh:" (Rom. viii. 3) God, therefore, willing to deal graciously with men, gave the promise and Christ himself, that the inheritance through the promise and by faith of Jesus Christ might be given to them that believe. But the law which came after the promise, could neither "make the latter of none effect," (for it was sanctioned by authority,) nor could it be joined or super-added to the promise, that out of this union righteousness and life might be given. (Gal. iii. 16-18, 22.) (2.) It is abrogated with regard to the curse and condemnation: For "Christ, being made a curse for us, hath redeemed us from the curse of the law;" (Gal. iii. 10-13;) and thus the law is taken away from sin, lest its "strength" should be to condemn. (1 Cor. xv. 55, 56.) (3.) The law is abrogated and taken away from sin, so far as "sin, having taken occasion by the law, works all manner of concupiscence" in the carnal man, over whom sin exercises dominion. (Rom. vii. 4-8.) (4.) It is abrogated, with regard to the guidance by which it urged man to do good and to refrain from evil, through a fear of punishment and a hope of temporal reward. (1 Tim. i. 9, 10; Gal. iv. 18.) For believers and regenerate persons "are become dead to the law by the body of

Christ," that they may be the property of another, even of Christ; by whose Spirit they are led and excited in newness of life, according to love and the royal law of liberty. (1 John v. 3, 4; James ii. 8.) Whence it appears, that the law is not abrogated with respect to the obedience which must be rendered to God; for though obedience be required under the grace of Christ and of the Gospel, it is required according to clemency, and not according to strict [legal] rigor. (1 John iii. 1, 2.)

VII. The Ceremonial Law is that which contains the precepts concerning the outward worship of God; which was delivered to the Jewish church, and was accommodated to the times in which the church of God was "as a child" under "the promise" and the Old Testament. (Gal. iv. 1-3.) It was instituted not only to typify, to prefigure and to bear witness by sealing; (Heb. viii. 5; x, 1;) but likewise for the discipline, or good order which was to be observed in ecclesiastical meetings and acts. (Col. ii. 14; Psalm xxvii. 4.) Subservient to the former purpose were circumcision, the Pascal Lamb, sacrifices, sabbaths, sprinklings, washings, purifications, consecrations and dedications of living creatures. (Col. ii. 11; 1 Cor. v. 7.) To the latter purpose, [that of church discipline,] were the distinct functions of the Priests, the Levites, the Singers, and the porters, or door-keepers, the courses or changes in their several duties, and the circumstances of the places and times in which these sacred acts were to be severally performed. (1 Chron. 24, 25, & 26.)

VIII. The use of this ceremonial law was, (1.) That it might retain that ancient people under the hope and expectation of the good things which had been promised. (Heb. x. 1- 3.) This use it fulfilled by various types, figures and shadows of persons, things, actions, and events; (7, 9, & 10;) by which not only were sins testified as in "a hand-writing which was against them," (Col. ii. 14,) that the necessity of the promise which had been given might be understood; but likewise the expiation and promised good things were shewn at a distance, that they might believe the promise would assuredly be fulfilled. (Heb. ix. 8-10; Col. ii. 17; Heb. x. 1.) And in this respect, since the body and express form of those types and shadows relate to Christ, the ceremonial law is deservedly called "a school-master [to bring the Jews] unto Christ." (Gal. iii. 24.) (2.) That it might distinguish from other nations the Children of Israel, as a people sanctified to God on a peculiar account, and that it might separate them as "a middle wall of partition;" (Ephes. ii. 14, 15;) yet so as that even strangers might be admitted to a participation in it by circumcision. (Exod. xii. 44; Acts ii. 10.) (3.) That while occupied in this course of operas religious services, they might not invent and fabricate other modes of worship, nor assume such as were in use among other nations; and thus they were preserved pure from idolatry and superstition, to which they had the greatest propensity, and for which occasions were offered on every side by those nations who were contiguous, as well as by those who dwelt amongst them. (Deut. 12; xxxi, 16, 27-29.)

IX. The ceremonial law was abrogated by the cross, the death and the resurrection of Christ, by his ascension into heaven and the mission of the Holy Ghost, by the sun's dispersion of the shadows, and by the entrance of "the body which is of Christ" into their place, (Col. ii. 11, 12, 14, 17,) which is the full completion of all the types. (Heb. viii. 1-6.) But the gradations to be observed in its abrogation must come under our consideration: In the first moment it was abrogated with regard to the necessity and utility of its observance, every obligatory right being at once and together taken from it: in that instant it ceased to live, and became dead. (Gal. iv. 9, 10; 1 Cor. vii. 19; ix, 19, 20; 2 Cor. iii. 13- 16.) Afterwards it was actually to be abolished. This was ejected partly, by the teaching of the Apostles among believers, who by degrees understood "Christ to be the end of the law," and of that which was then abolished; they abstained therefore voluntarily from the use of that law. Its abolition was also ejected in part, by the power of God, in the destruction of Jerusalem and of the temple, in which was the seat of religion, and the place appointed for performing those religious observances, against the contumacy of the unbelieving Jews. From this period the legal ceremonies began to be mortiferous, though in the intermediate space [which had elapsed between the death of Christ and the destruction of Jerusalem,] these rites, even in the judgment of the apostles themselves, might be tolerated, but only among the Jews, and with a proviso, that they should not be imposed on the Gentiles: (Acts xvi. 3; xv, 28; xxi, 21- 26; Gal. ii. 3, 11, 12;) which toleration must itself be considered as being tantamount to a new institution.

X. The Judicial Law is that which God prescribed by Moses to the Children of Israel, of whom He was in a peculiar manner the king. (Exod. 21, 22, 23, &c.) It contained precepts about the form of the political government to be exercised in civil society, for procuring the benefit both of natural and spiritual life, by the preservation and exaction of the outward worship and of the external discipline commanded in moral and ceremonial law, such as concerned magistrates, contracts, division of property, judgments, punishments, &c. (Deut. xvii. 15.) These laws may appropriately be referred to two kinds: (1.) Some of them, with regard to their substance are of general obligation, though with regard to some circumstances they are peculiar to the Jewish commonwealth. (2.) Others belong simply to a particular right or authority. (Deut. xv. 1, 2; vi, 19.)

XI. The uses of this judicial law also were three: (1.) That the whole community of the Children of Israel might be regulated by a certain rule of public equity and justice; that it might be "as a city that is compact together," (Psalm cxxii. 3,) [or as a body] "which is knit together" according to all and each of its parts," "by the joints and sinews" of the precepts prescribed in this law. (2.) That the Israelites might, by this law, be distinguished from other nations who had their own laws. Thus was it the will of God, that this his people should have nothing in common with other nations, wherever this was possible according to the nature of things and of man himself. These two uses related to the existing condition of the Jewish commonwealth. (3.) It had reference to future things, and was typical of them For all that state, and the whole kingdom and its administration, the chiefs of administration, the judges and kings, prefigured Christ and his kingdom, and its spiritual administration. Psalm 2; Ezek. xxxiv. 23, 24.) In this respect also the judicial law may be called "a schoolmaster [to bring the Jews] to Christ."

XII. This law, so far as it had regard to Christ, was universally abrogated. No kingdom, no nation, no administration, serves now typically to figure Christ and his kingdom or administration. For his kingdom, which is the kingdom of heaven and not of this world, has already come, and he has come into his kingdom. (Matt. iii. 2;xvi, 28; John xviii. 36; Matt. xi. 11.) But with respect to its simple observance, this Judicial Law is neither forbidden nor prescribed to any people, nor is it of absolute necessity to be either observed or omitted. Those matters are accepted which are of universal obligation, and founded in natural equity. For it is necessary, that they be strictly observed, in every place and by all persons. And those things [in the judicial law] which relate to Christ as it respects the very substance and principal end, cannot be lawfully used by any nation.

COROLLARY

The doctrine of the Papists respecting Councils and of Works of Supererogation, derogates from the perfection of the Divine commands.

DISPUTATION 13 - ON THE COMPARISON OF THE LAW AND THE GOSPEL

RESPONDENT: PETER CUNÆUS

I. Since the law ought to be considered in two respects, not only as it was originally delivered to men constituted in primitive innocence, but also as it was given to Moses and imposed on sinners, (on which account it has in the Scriptures obtained the name of "the Old Testament," or "the Old Covenant,") it may very properly, according to this two-fold respect, be compared with the Gospel, which has received the appellation of "the New Testament" as it is opposed to the Old. This may be done in reference both to their agreement and their difference; indeed, it would-be inconvenient for us to take their agreement generally into consideration without their difference, lest we should be compelled twice to repeat the same thing.

II. The law, therefore, both as it was first delivered to Adam and as it was given by Moses, agrees with the Gospel, (1.) In the general consideration of having one Author. For one and the same God is the author of both, who delivered the law as a legislator; (Gen. ii. 17; Exod. xx. 2;) but he promulgated the Gospel as the Father of mercies and the God of all grace: whence the former is frequently denominated "the law of God," and the latter "the Gospel of God." (Rom. i, 1.) (2.) In the general relation of their matter. For the doctrine of each consists of a command to obedience, and of the promise of a reward. On this account each of them has the name of hrwt "the law," which is also commonly ascribed to both in the Scriptures. (Isa. ii. 3.) (3.) In the general consideration of their end, which is the glory of the wisdom, goodness and justice of God. (4.) In their common subject, as not being distinguished by special respects. For the law was imposed on men, and to men also was the gospel manifested.

III. There is, besides, a certain proper agreement of the law, as it was delivered to Adam, with the Gospel; from which agreement the law, as given through Moses, is excluded: it is placed in the possibility of its performance. For Adam was able, with the aid of God, to fulfill the law by those powers which he had received in creation: otherwise, transgression could not have been imputed to him for a crime. The gospel also is inscribed in the hearts of those who are in covenant with God, that they may be able to fulfill the condition which it prescribes.

IV. But the difference between the law, as it was first delivered, and the gospel, consists principally in the following particulars. (1.) In the special respect of the Author. For, in the exercise of benevolence to his innocent creature, God delivered the law without regard to Christ, yet of strict justice requiring obedience, with the promise of a reward and the denunciation of a punishment. But in the exercise of grace and mercy, and having respect to Christ his anointed one, God revealed the Gospel; and, through justice attempered with mercy, promulgated his demands and his promises. (2.) In the particular relation of its matter. For the law says, "Do this, and thou shalt live." (Rom. x. 5.) But the Gospel says, "If thou wilt BELIEVE, thou shalt be saved." And this difference lies not only in the postulate, from which the former is called "the law of works," but the Gospel "the law of faith," (Rom.

iii. 27,) but also in the promise: for though in each of them eternal life was promised, yet by the Gospel it was to be conferred as from death and ignominy, but by the law as from natural felicity. (2 Tim. i. 10.) Besides, in the Gospel is announced remission of sins, as preparatory to life eternal; of which no mention is made in the [Adamic] law; because neither was this remission necessary to one who was not a sinner, nor would its announcement have [then] been useful to him, although he might afterwards have become a sinner.

V. (3.) They likewise differ in the mode of remuneration. For according to the [primeval] law, "To him that WORKED, the reward would be of debt;" (Rom. iv. 4;) and to him that transgressed, the punishment inflicted would be of the severity of strict justice. But to him that BELIEVETH, the reward is bestowed of grace; and to him that believeth not, condemnation is due according to justice tempered with clemency in Christ Jesus. (John iii. 16, 19; xi, 41.) They are discriminated in the special consideration of their subject. For the law was delivered to man while innocent, and already constituted in the favour of God. (Gen. ii. 17.) But the Gospel was bestowed upon man as a sinner, and one who was to be brought back into the favour of God, because it is "the word of reconciliation." (2 Cor. v. 19.) (5.) They differ in the peculiar respect of their end. For by the law are illustrated the wisdom, goodness, and strict justice of God: but by the Gospel is manifested a far more illustrious display of the wisdom of God, of his goodness united with gracious mercy, and of justice mildly attempered in Christ Jesus. (1 Cor. i. 20-24; Ephes. i. 8; Rom. iii. 24-26.)

THE LAW OF MOSES

VI. But the difference between the law, as it was given by Moses, and is styled "the Old Testament," and the gospel as it comes under the appellation of "the New Testament," lies according to the Scriptures in the following particulars. (1.) In the distinct property of God who instituted them. For He made the old covenant, as one who was angry at the sins which remained without expiation under the preceding [Adamic] covenant. (Heb. ix. 5, 15.) But He instituted the new, as being reconciled, or, at least as about to accomplish reconciliation by that covenant, in the Son of his love, and by the word of his grace. (2 Cor. v. 17-21; Ephes. ii. 16, 17.) (2.) In the mode of institution, which corresponds in each of them to the condition of the things to be instituted. For the law of Moses was delivered with the most obvious signs of the Divine displeasure and of God's dreadful judgment against sins and sinners. But the gospel was given with assured tokens of benevolence, good pleasure and love in Christ. Hence the Apostle says: "For ye are not come unto the mount which might be touched and that burned with fire, nor unto blackness and darkness, and tempest," &c. "But ye are come unto Mount Sion," &c. (Heb. xii. 18-24.) (3.) In the substance of the commands and promises. For the commands of the law were chiefly carnal, (Heb. vii. 16,) and contained "the handwriting of ordinances which was contrary to us:" (Col. ii. 14.) Most of the promises were likewise corporal, and stipulated engagements for an earthly inheritance, which suited "the old man." (Heb. x. 1.) But the gospel is spiritual, (John iv. 21, 23,) containing spiritual commands and the promise of a heavenly inheritance agreeing with "the new man;" (Heb. viii. 6; Ephes. i. 3,) though it promises earthly blessings, as additions, to those who "seek first the kingdom God and his righteousness." (Matt. vi. 33.)

VII. (4.) We place the fourth difference in the Mediator or Intercessor. For Moses is the mediator of the Old Testament, Jesus Christ of the, New. (Gal. iii. 19; Heb. ix. 15.) The law was given by a servant, but the gospel was given by the Lord himself revealed. (Heb. iii. 5, 6.) "The law was given by Moses; Grace and truth came by Jesus Christ" (John 1, 17.) The law was given by the hands of a mediator, (Gal. iii. 19,) agreeably to what is mentioned in other passages; (Lev. xxvi. 46; Deut. v. 26-31;) and Christ is styled "the Mediator of the New Testament." (Heb. ix. 16.) (5.) They also differ in the blood employed for the confirmation of each Testament. The old covenant was ratified by the blood of animals; (Exod. xxiv. 5, 6; Heb. ix. 18-20;) but the new one was confirmed by the precious blood of the Son of God, (Heb. ix. 14,) which is likewise on this account called "the blood of the New Testament." (Matt. xxvi. 28.) (6.) They differ in the place of their promulgation. For the Old Covenant was promulgated from Mount Sinai; (Exod. xix. 18;) But the New one "went forth out of Zion and from Jerusalem." (Isa. ii. 3; Micah iv. 2.) This difference is likewise pointed out in the plainest manner by the Apostle Paul. (Gal. iv. 24-31; Heb. xii. 18-21.)

VIII. (7.) The seventh difference shall be taken from the subject, both those to whom each was given, and on whom each was inscribed. The old law was given to the "old man." The New Testament was instituted for "the new man." From this circumstance, St. Augustine supposes that these two Testaments have obtained the appellation of "the Old" and of "the New Testament." The old law was inscribed on "tables of stone" (Exod. xxx. 1, 18.) But the gospel is "written in fleshly tables" (Jer. xxxi. 33; 2 Cor. iii. 3.) (8.) The eighth difference is in their adjuncts: and this in two ways:

(i.) The old law was "weak and beggarly," and incapable of giving life. (Gal. iv. 9; iii, 21.) But the gospel contains the unsearchable riches of Christ," (Ephes. iii. 8,) and "is the power of God unto salvation to every one that believeth." (Rom. i. 16.) (ii.) The old law was an insupportable burden, which "neither the Jews nor their fathers were able to bear." (Acts xv. 10.) But the gospel contains "the yoke" of Jesus Christ, which is "easy," and "his burden," which is "light" (Matt. xi. 29, 30.)

IX. (9.) The ninth difference shall be taken from the versity of their effects. For the Old Testament is "the letter which killeth," "the administration of death and of condemnation." But the New Testament is "the Spirit that giveth life," "the ministration of the Spirit of righteousness, and of life" (2 Cor. iii. 6-11.) The Old Covenant resembled Agar, and "gendered to bondage;" the New like Sarah, begets unto liberty. (Gal. iv. 23, 24.) "The law entered, that the offense might abound," (Rom. v. 20,) and it "worketh wrath" (iv, 15.) But "the blood of the New Testament," exhibited in the gospel, (Matt. xxvi. 28,) expiates sin, (Heb. ix. 14, 15,) and "speaketh better things than that of Abel" (12, 24.)

The Old Testament is the bond on which sins are written:

(Col. ii. 14) but the gospel is the proclamation of liberty, and the doctrine of the cross, to which was nailed the bond, or "hand-writing against us," and was by this very act, "taken out of the way." (10.) The tenth difference shall be placed in the time, both of the promulgation of each, and of their duration. The Old Testament was promulgated when God brought the children of Israel out of Egypt. (Jer. xxxi. 32.) But the New, at a later age, and in these last times. (Heb. viii. 8, 9.) It was designed that the Old Testament should endure down to the advent of Christ, and afterwards be abolished. (Gal. iii. 19; Heb. vii. 18; 2 Cor. iii. 10.) But the New Testament continueth forever, being confirmed by the blood of the great High Priest, "who was made a priest after the power of an endless life" by the word of an oath, (Heb. vii. 16-20,) and "through the eternal Spirit, offered himself to God." (ix, 14.) From this last difference, it is probable, the appellations of "the Old Testament" and "the New," derived their origin.

THE SAINTS UNDER THE OLD TESTAMENT

X. But, lest any one should suppose that the Fathers who lived under the law and the Old Testament, were entirely destitute of grace, faith and eternal life; it is to be recollected that even at that period, the promise was in existence which had been made to Adam concerning "the Seed of the woman," (Gen. iii. 15,) which also concerned the seed of Abraham, to whom "the promises were made," (Gal. iii. 16,) and in whom "all the kindreds of the earth were to be blessed;" (Acts iii. 25;) and that these promises were received in faith by the holy fathers. As this promise is comprehended by divines under the name of "the Old Testament," taken in a wide acceptation, and is called by the apostle, diaqhkh "the covenant," (Gal. iii. 17,) as well as, in the plural, "the covenants of promise;" (Ephes. ii. 12;) let us also consider how far "this covenant of promise," and the New Testament, and the gospel so called, by way of excellence, as being the completion of the promises, (Gal. iii. 16, 17,) and as being the promise," (Heb. ix. 15,) agree with and differ from each other.

XI. We place the Agreement in those things which concern the substance of each. For, (1.) With regard to the Efficient Cause, both of them were confirmed through the mere grace and mercy of God who had respect unto Christ. (2.) The matter of each was one and the same: that is, "the obedience of faith" was required in both, (Gen. xv. 6; Rom. 4; Heb. 11,) and the inheritance of eternal life was promised through the imputation of the righteousness of faith, and through gracious adoption in Christ. (Rom. ix. 4; Heb. xi. 8.) (3.) One object, that is Christ, who was promised to the fathers in the prophetical scriptures, and whom God has exhibited in the Gospel. (Acts iii. 19, 20; xiii, 32.) (4.) One end, the praise of the glorious Grace of God in Christ. (Rom. iv. 2, 3.) (5.) Both these covenants were entered into with men invested in the same formal relation, that is, with men as sinners, and to those "who work not, but who believe on Him that justifies the ungodly." (Rom. ix. 8, xi, 30-33.) (6.) Both of them have the same Spirit witnessing, or sealing the truth of each in the minds of those who are parties to the covenant. (2 Cor. iv. 13.) For since "the adoption" and "the inheritance" pertain likewise to the fathers in the Old Testament, (Rom. ix. 4; Gal. iii. 18,) "the Spirit of adoption," who is "the earnest of the inheritance," cannot be denied to them. (Rom. viii. 15; Ephes. i. 14) (7.) They agree in their effects. For both the covenants beget children to liberty: "In Isaac shall thy seed be called." (Rom. ix. 7.) "So then, brethren, we are not the children of the bondwoman, but of the free; and are, as Isaac was, the children of promise." (Gal. iv. 31, 28.) Both of them administer the righteousness of faith, and the inheritance through it. (Rom. iv. 13.) Both excite spiritual joy in the hearts of believers. (John viii. 56; Luke ii. 10.) (8.) Lastly, they agree in this particular--that both of them were confirmed by the oath of God. Neither of them, therefore, was to be abolished, but the former was to be fulfilled by the latter. (Heb. vi. 13, 14, 17; vii, 20, 21.)

XII. But there is a Difference in some accidental circumstances which derogate nothing from their substantial unity. (1.) Respecting the accident of their object: For when the advent of Christ drew near, He was offered by promise. (Mal. iii. 1.) But He is now manifested in the Gospel. (1 John i. 1, 2; iv, 14) (2.) Hence also arises the second difference, respecting the accident of the faith required on their object. For as present and past things are more clearly known than future things, so the faith in Christ to come was more obscure, than the faith which beholds a present Christ. (Heb. xi. 13; Num. xiv. 17.) (3.) To these let the third difference be added--that Christ with his benefits was formerly proposed to the Israelites under types and shadows:

(Heb. 12; Gal. iii. 16) But He is now offered in the Gospel "to be beheld with open face," and the reality of the things themselves and "the body" are exhibited. (2 Cor. iii. 18; John i. 17; Col. ii. 17; Gal. iii. 13, 25.) (4.) This diversity of administrations displays the fourth difference in the heir himself. For the apostle compares the children of Israel to the heir, who is "a child," and who required the superintendance of "tutors and governors:" but he compares believers under the New Testament to an adult heir. (Gal. iv. 1-5.) (5.) Hence is deduced a fifth difference-that the infant heir, as "differing nothing from a servant" was held in bondage under the economy of the ceremonial law; from which servitude are liberated those persons who have believed in Christ after the expiration of "the time of tutelage before appointed of the Father." (6.) To this condition the Spirit of the infant heir is also accommodated, and will afford us the sixth difference that the heir was in truth under the influence of "the Spirit of adoption," but, because he was then only an infant, this Spirit was intermixed with that of fear; but the adult heir is under the complete influence of "the Spirit of adoption," to the entire exclusion of that of fear. (Rom. viii. 15; Gal. iv. 6.) (7.) The seventh difference consists in the number of those who are called to the communion of each of these covenants. The promise was confined within the boundaries of "the commonwealth of Israel," from which the Gentiles were "aliens," being also "strangers from the covenants of promise." (Ephes. ii. 11-13, 17.) But the Gospel is announced to every creature that is under heaven, and the mound of separation is completely removed. (Matt. xxviii. 19; Mark xvi. 15; Col. i. 13.)

XIII. But these three, the Law, the Promise, and the Gospel, may become subjects of consideration in another order, either as opposed among themselves, or as subordinate to each other. The condition of the law, therefore, as it was delivered to Adam, excludes the necessity of making the promise and announcing the Gospel; and, on the other hand, the necessity of making the promise and announcing the Gospel, declares, that man has not obeyed the law which was given to him. For justification cannot be at once both "of grace" and "of debt;" nor can it, at the same time, admit and exclude "boasting." (Gal. ii. 17; Rom. iv. 4, 5; iii, 27.) It was also proper that the promise should precede the Gospel, and should in return be fulfilled by the Gospel: for, as it was not befitting that such a great blessing should be bestowed unless it were ardently desired, so it was improper that the desire of the earnest expectants should be frustrated. (1 Pet. i. 10-12; Hag. ii. 7; Mal. iii. 1.) Nor was it less equitable, that, after the promise had been made, the law should be economically repeated, by which might be rendered apparent the necessity of the grace of the promise, (Gal. iii. 19-24; Acts xiii. 38, 39,) and that, being convinced of this necessity, they might be compelled to flee to its shelter. (Gal. ii. 15, 16.) The use of the law was also serviceable to the Gospel which was to be received by faith. (Col. ii. 14, 17.) While the promise was in existence, it was also the will of God to add other precepts, and especially such as were ceremonial, by which sin might be ["sealed home,"] or testified against, and a previous intimation might be given of the completion of the promise. And when the promise was fulfilled, it was the will of God that these additional precepts should be abrogated, as having completed their functions. (Heb. x. 9, 10.) Lastly, the moral law ought to serve both to the promise and to the Gospel, which have now been received by faith, as a rule according to which believers ought to conform their lives. (Psalm cxix. 105; Tit. iii. 8.) But may God grant, that from his word we may be enabled still more clearly to understand this glorious economy of his, to his glory, and for gathering together in Christ!"

DISPUTATION 14 - ON THE OFFICES OF OUR LORD JESUS CHRIST

RESPONDENT: PETER FAVERIUS

I. Since all offices are instituted and imposed for the sake of a certain end, and on this account bear some resemblance to means for obtaining that end; the most convenient method of treating on the offices of Christ will be for us to enter into an examination of this subject according to the acceptation of the name by which He is denominated. For he is called Jesus Christ, in words which belong to a person according to the signification conveyed by them, as well as by way of excellence. In the first of those words is comprehended the relation of the end of his offices; and, in the second, that of the duties which conduce to such end.

II. The word "Jesus" signifies the saviour, who is called Swthr by the Greeks. But "to save" is to render a man secure from evils, either by taking care that they do not assail him, or, if they have attacked him, by removing them, and of consequence by conferring the opposite blessings. But among the evils, two are of the very worst description: they are sin, and its wages, eternal death. Among the blessings also, two are of the greatest importance, righteousness and eternal life. He, therefore, is a saviour in an eminent degree who liberates men from sin and death eternal, the two greatest evils with which they are now surrounded and oppressed; and who confers upon them righteousness and life. On account of this method of saving, the name Jesus agrees well with this our saviour, according to the interpretation of it, which the angel gave in Matt. i. 21. For such a method of salvation was highly befitting the excellence of this exalted person, who is the proper, natural and only-begotten Son of God; especially when other salvations were capable of being accomplished by his servants, Moses, Joshua, Othniel, Gideon, Jephtha and David.

III. The word "Christ," denotes an anointed person, who is called h y m "the Messiah," by the Hebrews. Under the Old Testament, oil was anciently used in anointing; because, according to its natural efficacy, it rendered bodies not only fragrant but agile, and was therefore well fitted for typifying two supernatural things. The First is, the sanctification and consecration of a person to undertake and discharge some divine office. The Second is, adoption, or the conferring of gifts necessary for that purpose. But each of these acts belongs properly and per se to the Holy Spirit, the author and donor of Holiness and of all endowments. (Isa. xi. 2.) Wherefore it was proper, that he who was eminently styled "the Messiah, should be anointed with the Holy Spirit, indeed "above all his fellows," (or those who were partakers of the same blessings,) (Psalm xlv. 7,) that is, that He might be made the Holy of holies, and might be endued not only with some gifts of the Holy Spirit, but with the whole of the Holy Spirit without measure. (John 3, xxxiv, ;1, 14.) But when he is called "the saviour" by anointing, it appears to us that he must for this reason be here considered as a Mediatorial saviour, who has been constituted by God the Father, and [as Mediator] is subordinate to Him. He is therefore the nearer to us, not only according to the nature of his humanity, of which we have already treated, but also according to the mode of saving, which reflection conduces greatly to confirm us in faith and hope against temptations.

IV. Two distinct and subordinate acts appertain to the salvation which is signified by the name Jesus; and they are not only necessarily required for it, but also suffciently embrace its entire power. The First is, the asking and obtaining of redemption from sin and death eternal, and of righteousness and life. The Second is, the communication or distribution of the salvation thus obtained. According to the former of these acts, Christ is called "our saviour by merit;" according to the latter he is called "our saviour by efficacy." According to the first, he is constituted the Mediator "for men, in those things which pertain to God." (Heb. v. 1.) According to the second, he is appointed the Mediator or vicegerent of God, in those things which are to be transacted with men. From this it is apparent, that two offices are necessary for effecting salvation-the priestly and the regal; the former office being designed for the acquisition of salvation, and the latter for its communication: on which account this saviour is both a royal priest and a priestly king, our Melchisedec, that is, "king of Salem, which is king of peace and priest of the Most High God." (Heb. vii. 2.) His people also are a royal priesthood and a sacerdotal kingdom or nation. (1 Pet. ii. 5, 9.)

V. But since it has seemed good to the wise and just God, to save none except believers; nor, in truth, is it right that any one should be made partaker of the salvation procured by the priesthood of Christ, and dispensed by His kingly office, except the man who acknowledges Him for his priest and king; and since the knowledge of Christ, and faith in him, are produced in the hearts of men by the power of the Holy Ghost, through the preaching of the word as the means appointed by God; for these reasons the prophetical office is likewise necessary for effecting salvation, and a perfect saviour must be a prophet, priest and king, that is, by every reason according to which this ample title can be deservedly attributed to any one. We nave Jesus therefore, that is, the saviour, by a most excellent and perfect notion called Christ, because he has been anointed by God as a prophet, priest and king. (Matt. xvii. 5; Psalm cx. 4; 2, 6; John xviii. 37.) On each of these four offices we shall treat in order, and shew, (1.) That all and each of these offices belong to our Christ. (2.) The quality of these offices. (3.) The functions pertaining to each of them. (4.) The events or consequences.

VI. The Messiah was the future prophet promised to the fathers under the Old Testament. Moses said, "The Lord thy God will raise up unto you a prophet like unto me; unto him shall ye hearken." (Deut. xviii. 15.) Isaiah also says "I will give thee for a covenant of the people, for a light of the Gentiles, to open the blind eyes," &c. (xlii, 6.) "Jehovah hath called me from the womb, and he hath made my mouth like a sharp sword," &c. (xlix, 1, 2.) The attestation, by anointing, of his call to the prophetical office, was likewise predicted: "The Spirit of the Lord God is upon me; because the Lord hath anointed me to preach good tidings," &c. (xli, 1.) So was his being furnished with the necessary gifts when he was thus called and sealed: "The Spirit of the Lord shall rest upon Him, the Spirit of wisdom and understanding," &c. (xi, 2.) Lastly, Divine assistance was promised: "In the shadow of his hand hath He hid me, and made me a polished shaft; in his quiver hath he hid me." (xlix, 2.) And this thing was publicly know, not only to the Jews, but likewise to the Samaritans, as is apparent from what the woman of Samaria said, "When Messias is come, He will tell us all things." (John iv. 25.) But our Jesus himself testifies, that these predictions were fulfilled in him, and that he was the prophet sent into the world from God. After having read a passage out of Isaiah's prophecy, he spake thus, "This day is this Scripture fulfilled in your ears." (Luke iv. 21.) "To this end was I born, and for this cause came I into the world, that I should bear witness unto the truth." (John xviii. 37.) God himself also bore his testimony from heaven, when he "opened the heavens unto Christ" immediately after he had been baptized by John, sent down upon Him the Holy Spirit, and in inaugural strains of the highest commendation seemed to consecrate him to this office. (Matt. iii. 16.)

VII. In the Quality of the prophetic office, we take into our consideration the excellence not only of the vocation, instruction and divine assistance afforded, but likewise that of the doctrine proposed by Him, according to each of which it far exceeds the entire dignity of all the prophets. (Luke 4.) For God's approval of his mission was expressed by three peculiar signs. the opening of the heavens, the descent of the Holy Ghost in a bodily shape upon Him, and the voice of his Father conveyed to him. The instruction, or furnishing, by which He learned what things he ought to teach, was not "by dreams and visions," nor by inward or outward discourse with an angel, neither was it by a communication of "mouth to mouth," which yet [in the case of Moses] was without the actual sight of the glory and the face of God; (Num. 12;) but it was by the clear vision of God and by an intimate intuition into the secrets of the Father: "For the only-begotten Son, who is in the bosom of the Father, hath declared him to us;" (John i. 18;) "He that cometh from heaven testified what he hath seen and heard." (iii, 32.) The aid of the Holy Spirit to Him, was so ready and every moment intimately near, that He, like one who was lord by possession and use, employed the Holy Spirit at pleasure, and as frequently as it seemed good to himself. But the excellence of the doctrine lies in this, that it did not announce the law, neither as being the power of God unto salvation "to him who worked and that of debt," (Rom. iv. 4,) nor as being the seal of sin and of condemnation; (Col. ii. 14;) neither did it announce the promise, by which righteousness and salvation were promised OF GRACE to him that believed; (Gal. iii. 17-19;) but it announced the Gospel, according to this expression, "He hath sent me to preach good tidings to the meek," (Isa. lxi. 1,) or, "the gospel to the poor;" (Matt. xi. 5;) because it exhibited GRACE and TRUTH, as it contained "the end of the law," and the accomplishment of the promise. (Rom. x. 4; i, 1, 2.)

VIII. The Functions which appertain to the prophetic office of Christ, are, the proposing of his doctrine, its confirmation and prayers for its felicitous success; all of which were executed by Christ in a manner which evinced the utmost power and fidelity. (1.) He proposed his doctrine, with the greatest wisdom, which his adversaries could not resist; with the most ardent zeal for the glory of God his Father, and for the salvation of men; without respect of persons; and with an authority which was never exercised by other teachers, not even by the prophets. (2.) His confirmation was added to the doctrine, not only by the Scriptures of the Old Testament, but likewise by signs of every kind by which it is possible to establish the divinity of any doctrine. (i.) By the declaration of the knowledge which is peculiar to God, such as the inspection of the heart, the revelation of the secrets of others, and the prediction of future events. (ii.) By a power which belongs to God alone, and which was demonstrated "in signs and wonders, and mighty deeds." (iii.) By the deepest patience, by which He willingly suffered the death of the cross for the truth of God, that he might confirm the promises made to the fathers, "having witnessed before Pontius Pilate a good confession." (3.) Lastly. He employed very frequent and earnest prayers, with the most devout thanksgiving; on which account he often retired into solitary places, which he spent whole nights in prayer.

IX. The Issue or consequence of the prophetic office of Christ, so far as he executed it in his own person while he remained on earth, was not only the instruction of a few persons, but likewise the rejection [of Himself and his doctrine] by great numbers, and even by their rulers. The former of these consequences occurred according to the nature and merit of the doctrine itself. The latter, accidentally and by the malice of men. Christ himself mentions both of these issues in Isaiah's prophecy, when he says, not without complaining, "Behold, I and the children whom the Lord hath given me, are for signs and for wonders in Israel from the Lord of hosts." (viii, 18.) "I have laboured in vain, I have spent my strength for naught and in vain." (xlix, 4.) But because this repulse of Christ's doctrine could not occur without proving a stumbling block to the weak, it was the good pleasure of God to obviate it in a manner at once the wisest and the most powerful, (i.) By a prophecy which foretold that this rejection would actually take place: "The stone which the builders refused, is becoming the head-stone of the corner:" (Psalm cxviii. 22.) (ii.) And by the fulfillment of that prediction, which was completed by the resurrection of Christ from the dead, and by his being placed at the right hand of God; by which Christ became the head and foundation of the angle, or corner, uniting the two walls, that of the Jews and that of the Gentiles, in accordance with these words of the prophet Isaiah, "It is a light thing that thou shouldest be my servant, to raise up the tribes of Jacob, and to restore the preserved of Israel: I have also given thee for a light to the Gentiles, that thou mayest be my salvation unto the end of the earth." (xlix, 6.) These words contain an intimation of the fruit of Christ's prophesying as administered by his ambassadors.

X. Topics, similar to the preceding, come under our consideration in the Priestly Office of Christ. (1.) The Messiah, promised of old, was to be a Priest, and Jesus of Nazareth was a Priest. This is proved (i.) by express passages from the Scriptures of the Old Testament; and which attribute to the Messiah the Name of "Priest," and the Thing signified by the name. With regard to the Name: "Thou an a Priest for ever after the order of Melchizedec." (Psalm cx. 4.) With regard to the Thing signified, "Surely He hath borne our griefs: He was wounded for our transgressions: And the Lord hath laid on Him the iniquity of us all. When thou shalt make his soul an offering for sin, He shall see his seed, &c. He bore the sins of many, and made intercession for the transgressor" (Isa. liii. 4-6, 10-12; Rom. iv. 15.) (2.) By arguments taken from a comparison of the dignity of his person and priesthood. For the Messiah is the first-begotten Son of God, the principal dignity of the priesthood, and governor over the house of his Father. (Psalm ii. 7; lxxxix, 27; Gen. xlix. 3.) Therefore, to Him appertains the excellence of administering the priesthood in the house of God, which is Heaven. (Heb. iii. 6; x, 21.) For that is properly typified by a temple, the place of the priesthood; and principally by the innermost part of it, which is called "the holy of holies." (ix, 24.) Also, by arguments deduced from the nature of the people over whom He is placed. This people is "a kingdom of priests" (Exod. xix. 6,) and "a royal priesthood" (1 Pet. ii. 9.) But the Christian Faith holds it, an indisputable axiom, that "Jesus of Nazareth is a priest," by the most explicit Scriptures of the New Testament, in which the title and all things pertaining to the sacerdotal office are attributed to him. (Heb. ii. 5.) For the Father conferred that honour upon Him, sanctified and consecrated Him; (ii, 10;) and "He was made perfect through sufferings," "that He might be a merciful and faithful High Priest, and be able to sympathize with, or to succour them that are tempted." (ii, 18.) The Father also "opened his ears," (Psalm xl. 6,) or "prepared a body for Him," (Heb. x. 5,) "that He might have somewhat also to offer," (viii, 3,) and hath placed Him, after his resurrection from the dead, at his own right hand in heaven, that He may there perpetually "make intercession for us." (Rom. viii. 34.)

XI. But the Scriptures of the Old Testament speak of the Nature and Quality peculiar to Messiah the Priest, and assert that his priesthood is not according to the order of Levi. (Psalm cx. 4; Heb. v. 5, 6.) For David speaks thus, in the person of the Messiah, "Sacrifice and offering thou didst not desire. Mine ears thou hast opened. Burnt-offering and sin-offering hast thou not required. Then said I, Lo, I come. In the volume of the book it is written of me, to do thy will, O my God! Yea, I have willed; and thy law is within my heart." (Psalm xl. 6-8.) That is, "Thou hadst no pleasure in the sacrifices which are offered by the law" according to the Levitical ritual. (Heb. x. 6-9.) They also assert, that "He is a Priest for ever after the order of Melchizedec." (Psalm cx. 4.) But the entire nature of that priesthood is more distinctly explained in the New Testament, especially in the Epistle to the Hebrews, the excellence and superiority of the Messiah's priesthood above the Levitical having been previously established. (Heb. x. 5.) This pre-eminence is shewn by the contrast between them. (1.) The Levitical priesthood was typical and shadowy; but that of the Messiah is real and true, and contains the very body and express pattern of the things. (2.) In the Levitical priesthood, the Priest and the victim differed in the subject. For the Priest after the order of Levi offered the sacrifices of other men. But the Messiah is both the Priest and the victim. For "He offered himself," (Heb. ix. 14,) and "by his own blood has entered into heaven," (ix, 12,) and all this as it is an expiatory priesthood. But as it is eucharistical, (for it embraces the entire amplitude of the priesthood,) the Messiah offers sacrifices which are distinguished by him according to the person; yet they are such as, being born again of his Spirit from above, are flesh of his flesh and bone of his bones. (x, 14; ix, 26; Ephes. v. 30; 1 Pet. ii. 5.) (3.) They differ in the mode of their institution and confirmation. The Levitical priesthood was "instituted after the law of a carnal commandment;" but that of the Messiah, after the law of a spiritual commandment, and "the power of an endless life." (Heb. vii. 16.) The Levitical was instituted "without an oath;" but Christ's "with an oath," by which it was corroborated beyond the other. (vii, 20, 21, 28.) (4.) The fourth difference is in the time of their institution. The Levitical priesthood was instituted first; that of Christ, afterwards. The first, in the times of the Old Testament: the other, in those of the New. The former, when the church was in its infancy; the latter, when it had arrived at maturity. The former, in the time of slavery; the latter, in that of liberty.

XII. (5.) The fifth distinction lies in the persons discharging the functions of the priesthood. In the former, the Priests were of the tribe of Levi, "men who had infirmities," who were mortal and sinful, and who, therefore, accounted it "needful to offer up sacrifice for their own sins and for the people's." (Heb. vii. 28; v, 3.) But the Messiah was of the tribe of Judah, (vii, 14,) weak indeed "in the days of his flesh," (5, 7,) but now when raised immortal from the dead and endued with "the power of an endless life," He is "holy, harmless, undefiled, and separate from sinners, and therefore needeth not to offer up sacrifice for himself." (7, 26, 27) (6.) We may denote a sixth difference in the end of the institution. The Levitical priesthood was instituted to ratify the old covenant; but that of the Messiah, for confirming the New. He is on this account called both "the Mediator of the New Testament," (ix, 15,) and "the surety of a better covenant, which was established upon better promises." (viii, 6.) (7.) They differ in their efficacy. For the Levitical is useless and inefficacious, "not being able to take away sins, (x, 11,) (for they remained under the old covenant,) nor could it sanctify or perfect the worshippers in their consciences, for "it sanctifieth only to the purifying of the flesh." (ix, 9, 10, 13.) But the priesthood of the Messiah is efficacious. For He hath destroyed sin and obtained eternal redemption, (ix, 12, 14.) He consecrates priests and sanctifies the worshipers in their consciences, and "saves them to the uttermost that come to God by Him." (vii, 25.) (8.) With the Apostle we place the eighth difference in the duration of each. It was necessary that the Levitical priesthood should be abrogated, and it was accordingly abrogated; (viii, 13;) but that of the Messiah endures for ever. For this difference between them we have as many reasons as for the differences which we have already enumerated.

XIII. (9.) The ninth quality by which the Messiah's priesthood is distinguished from the Levitical, is this, "Now once in the end of the world, the Messiah hath appeared to put away sin by the sacrifice of himself; (Heb. vii. 26;) and thus "by one offering hath He perfected for ever them that are sanctified." (x, 14.) But the Priests after the order of Levi "offered oftentimes the same sacrifices, "through each succeeding day, and month, and year. (x, 11; ix, 25.) (10.) The tenth property of the Messiah's priesthood is that of its nature. It does not pass from one person to another. For the Messiah has neither a predecessor nor a successor. (vii, 24, 25, 3.) But the Levitical priesthood was transmitted down from father to son. (11.) To this we add the eleventh difference, the Messiah was the only person of his order. For Melchizadeck was a type of Him, "like unto Him," but by no means equal with Him. (vii, 3.) But the Levitical Priests "truly were many, because they were not suffered to continue by reason of death;" (vii, 23;) and among them, some were of superior, some of inferior, and others of equal dignity. (12.) We deduce the twelfth and last distinction from the place in which each of them was administered. For the Levitical priesthood was administered on earth, and in fact in a certain spot peculiarly assigned to it; but though that of the Messiah commenced on earth, yet it consummated in heaven. (ix, 24.)

XIV. The Actions which appertain to the priestly office of Christ, are those of oblation and intercession, according to the following passages: "Every high priest taken from among men is ordained for men in things pertaining to God, that he may offer both gifts and sacrifices for sins: (Heb. v. 1.) And "He ever liveth to make intercession for them." (1.) Of the Messiah's Oblation two acts are described to us: the first of which is performed on earth; the delivering of his own body unto death, and the shedding of his blood. By this act He was consecrated or perfected, and opened heaven to himself: (ix, 12; x, 29, 10; ix, 24 -- xxvi,) For it was a part of his office to enter into heaven by his own blood, and "through the veil, which is his flesh," (x, 22,) flesh indeed, destitute of blood, that is, destitute of life, and delivered up to death "for the life of the world," (John vi. 51,) although it was afterwards raised up again from death to life. The second act is, the presenting of himself, thus sprinkled with his own blood, before the face of his Father in heaven; and the offering of the same blood. To which we must add, the sprinkling of this blood on the consciences of believers, that they, "being purged from dead works, might serve the living God." (ix, 14.) (2.) Intercession is the second act of the priesthood of Christ, which also contains the prayer of Christ for us, and his advocacy or defense of us against the accusation with which we are charged by the grand adversary. (vii, 25; Rom. viii. 34; 1 John ii. 1, 2.) Because the force of this intercession is partly placed in the blood by which, not only Christ himself, but also our consciences, are sprinkled; the blood of Christ is said "to speak better things than that of Abel," (Heb. xii. 24,) which cried unto God for vengeance against the fratricide.

XV. The fourth part of the priesthood of Christ lies in the Results or Consequences. That the sacerdotal office concurs to the general effect of salvation, is apparent from this--that He is called Christ by consecration, which was effected "through sufferings," through which He is said "to have been made perfect," (Heb. ii. 10,) and thus to have "become the author of eternal salvation," (v, 9, 10,) being denominated "an High Priest forever after the order of Melchisedec." "But Christ, because he continueth ever, hath an unchangeable priesthood: wherefore he is able also to save them to the uttermost that come unto God by Him." (vii, 24, 25.) But the particular results which flow from the sacerdotal functions, when considered according to the two-fold act of oblation and intercession, are chiefly these: From Oblation, accrue the reconciling of us unto God the Father, (2 Cor. v. 19,) the obtaining of the remission of sins, (Rom. iii. 24-25,) of eternal redemption, (Heb. ix. 12,) and of the Spirit of grace, (Zech. xii. 10,) the laying open of the vein for the expiation of sin, and the disclosing of the fountain for sprinkling, (Zech. xiii. 1,) the removal of the curse, (Gal. iii. 13,) and the acquisition of everlasting righteousness and of life eternal, (Dan. ix. 24,) as well as a supreme power over all things in heaven and earth, (Phil. ii. 6-10,) for his church, to whom all these blessings are communicated: (Acts xx. 28) And, to sum up all in one expression, the procuring of the entire right to eternal life, and to all things whatsoever that are necessary either for its being given, or for its reception. Intercession obtains, that we, being reconciled to God, are saved from future wrath. (Rom. v. 9.) Christ as our intercessor offers to God, perfumed with the fragrant odour of his own sacrifice, the prayers and thanksgivings, and thus the whole rational worship which justified persons perform to God; (1 Pet. i. 5;) and he receives and turns aside the darts of accusation which Satan hurls against believers. (Rom. viii. 34.) All these blessings really flow from the sacerdotal functions of Christ; because he hath offered to God the true price of redemption for us, by which He has satisfied Divine justice, and interposed himself between us and the Father, who was justly angry on account of our sins; and has rendered Him placable to us. (1 Tim. ii. 6; Matt. xx. 28.) But the results per accidens is a greater pollution and the demerits of "a much sorer punishment" from having "trodden under foot the Son of God, and counted the blood of the covenant an unholy thing." (Heb. x. 29.)

XVI. Nor is it at all repugnant to the merits and satisfaction of Christ, which belong to him as a priest and a victim, that God is himself said to have "loved the world and given his only begotten Son," (John iii. 16,) to have delivered him unto death, (Rom. iv. 25,) to have reconciled the world unto himself in Christ, (2 Cor. v. 19,) to have redeemed us, (Luke i. 68,) and to have freely forgiven us our sins. (Rom. iii. 25.) For we must consider the affection of love to be two-fold in God. The first is a love for the creature--The other, a love for justice, united to which is a hatred against sin. It was the will of God that each of these kinds of love should be satisfied. He gave satisfaction to his love for the creature who was a sinner, when he gave up his Son who might act the part of Mediator. But he rendered satisfaction to his love for justice and to his hatred against sin, when he imposed on his Son the office of Mediator by the shedding of his blood and by the suffering of death; (Heb. ii. 10; v, 8, 9;) and he was unwilling to admit him as the Intercessor for sinners except when sprinkled with his own blood, in which he might be made the propitiation for sins. (ix, 12.) Again, he satisfies his love for the creature when he pardons sins, and that freely, because he pardons them through his love for the Creature; although by inflicting stripes upon his Son, in which he was "our peace," he had already rendered satisfaction to his love for justice. For it was not the effect of those stripes that God might love his creature, but that, while love for justice presented no hindrance, through his love for the creature he could remit sins and bestow life eternal. In this respect also it may with propriety be said that God rendered satisfaction to himself, and appeased himself in the Son of his love."

XVII. It remains for us to discuss the Kingly Office of Christ. We must first consider, that the Messiah, according to the promise, was to be a King, and that Jesus of Nazareth is a King: "I will raise unto David a righteous branch, and a King shall reign and prosper." (Jer. xxiii. 5.) "David my servant, shall be king over them." (Ezek. xxxvii. 24.) But he was constituted king by unction: "Yet have I anointed my King upon my holy hill of Zion." (Psalm ii. 6.) On this account, the title of "the Messiah" belongs to him for a certain peculiar reason. Nor should He be merely a King, but the most eminent and famous among kings: "Thy God hath anointed thee with the oil of joy above thy fellows." (Psalm xlv. 7.) "I will make him my First-born, higher than the kings of the earth." (lxxxix, 27.) Nay, he is the Lord and Master of all kings: therefore, O ye kings and judges of the earth, kiss the Son." (ii, 12.) "All kings shall fall down before Him." (lxxii, 11.) He was also to be instructed in all things necessary for the administration of his kingdom: "Give the King thy judgments, O God!" (lxxii, 1.) "The Lord shall send the rod of thy strength out of Zion." (cx, 2.) "Thou shalt break them with a rod of iron" (ii, 9.) "The Spirit of Jehovah shall rest upon him." (Isa. xi. 2.) God will likewise perpetually stand near Him: "With him shall my hand be established, mine arm also shall strengthen him." (Psalm lxxxix. 21.) But God hath made Jesus of Nazareth Lord and Christ, (Matt. ii. 2, 6,) "King of kings, and Lord of lords," (Rev. xvii. 14,) "all power being given unto Him in heaven and in earth," (Matt. xxviii. 19; Acts ii. 33,) and "authority over all flesh," (John xvii. 2,) that "unto Him every knee may bow." God also furnished or supplied Him with his Word and Spirit, as necessary means for the administration of his kingdom. He hath made angels also his servants to execute his commands. (Heb. i. 6, 14.) He stands constantly nigh to Him, "being placed at his right hand till he has made his enemies his footstool." (1 Cor. xv, ,5; Psalm cx. 1.)

XVIII. We say, in one expression, concerning the Quality of the Messiah's kingdom, that it is a spiritual kingdom, not of this world, but of that which is to come, not earthly, but heavenly. For it was predicted, that such would be the kingdom of the Messiah; and such also, we assert, is the kingdom of Jesus of Nazareth. We prove the First, (1.) Because David and Solomon, and the reign of each, were types of the Messiah and his kingdom; for the Messiah is called David; (Ezek. xxxvii. 25;) and all the things spoken about Solomon which are high and excellent, belong with far more justness to the Messiah, and some of them to him alone. (2 Sam. vii. 12-16.) But earthly and carnal things are types of spiritual and heavenly things, not being homogeneous with them. (Psalm 1, 2.) (2.) It was predicted of the Messiah, that he should die and rise again, (Psalm xvi. 10,) that "he should see his seed," (Isa. liii. 10,) and that he should rise again into a spiritual life. (Psalm cx. 3.) Therefore, that he should be a spiritual King, and that his kingdom also should be spiritual. (Psalm lxxxix. 5-8; xcvi, 6-9.) (3.) It was predicted that the priesthood of the Messiah should be spiritual, a real priesthood, and not a typical one. Therefore, his kingdom also is of the same description; for there is a mutual analogy between them, according to that expression -" Ye shall be unto me a kingdom of priests," &c. (Exod. xix. 6.) (4.) Because the law of Moses was to be abrogated on account of its being carnal. But the administration of the priesthood and of the kingdom of Israel was conducted according to that law. Therefore the kingdom of the Messiah ought to be administered according to another law, which was more excellent, and therefore spiritual. (Jer. xxxi. 31-34.) But such as was the law, such were the King and his kingdom. (5.) Because the gentiles were to be called to a participation of the kingdom of the Messiah, and all of them were to be added to it with their kings, who should still continue as kings, and yet voluntarily serve the Messiah, (Psalm ii. 10, 11; cx, 3,) who should glory in him, and in him place all their blessedness. Nothing of this kind can be done, unless the kingdom of the Messiah be spiritual. (6.) Because the Jews were to be rejected by the Messiah, for their rebellion, who was unwilling to have them for his people, not to the prejudice of the Messiah himself, but to the injury of the Jews alone. (Mal. i. 10, 11; Isa. lxv, 2, 3.) This is a strong indication of a King and of a kingdom that are spiritual. (7.) The same conclusion may be drawn from the excellence, amplitude, duration, and mode of administration, of the Messiah's kingdom. But the kingdom of Jesus of Nazareth is spiritual and heavenly. For he said, "Repent, because the kingdom of heaven is at hand." (Matt. iv. 17.) "My kingdom is not of this world." (John xviii. 36.) This may also be shown in all those things which relate to that kingdom. For the King is no more known after the flesh, because he is become spiritual by his resurrection, and is "the Lord from heaven." (Rom. viii. 1 Corinthians 15.) His Subjects are those who are already born again, in their souls, of his Spirit, and who shall likewise hereafter be spiritual in their bodies, and conformed unto him. The Law of the kingdom is spiritual: for it is the gospel of God, and the prescription of a rational and spiritual worship. (Rom. xii. 8; John iv. 23, 24.) Its Blessings are likewise spiritual--remission of sins, the Spirit of grace and life eternal. The Mode of Administration, and all its Means, are spiritual; for though all temporal things are subjected to Christ, yet he administers them in such a way as he knows will be conducive to the life that is spiritual and supernatural.

XIX. The Acts which belong to the regal office of Christ are generally comprehended in vocation and judgment. If we be desirous to consider these two acts more distinctly, we may divide them into the four parts following: vocation, legislation, the communication of blessings and the removal of evils, and the final and universal judgment. (1.) Vocation is the first function by which Christ, the King, calls men out of a state of animal life and of sin, to the participation of the covenant of grace which he has confirmed by his own blood. For he did not find subjects in the nature of things; (Isa. lxiii. 10;) but as it was his office by the priesthood to acquire them for himself, so likewise as King, it is his province to call them to him by his word, and to draw them by his Spirit. (Psalm cx. 1-3; Ephes. iii. 17.) This vocation has two parts--a command to repent and believe, (Mark i. 14, 15,) and a promise, (Matt. xxviii. 19, 20,) to which is also subjoined a threatening. (Tit. iii. 8;

Mark xvi. 16.) (2.) Legislation, which we consider in a distinct form, is the second function of the regal office of Christ, by which he fully prescribes, to those who have been previously called and drawn to a participation of the covenant of grace, a rule by which they may live godly, righteously and soberly, and to which are also annexed promises and threatenings. To this must be added the act of the Holy Spirit by which believers are rendered fit to perform their duty. (3.) The third act is the communication of blessings, whether they be necessary or conducible to this animal life or to that which is spiritual, and the removal of the opposite evils, not through strict justice, but according to a certain dispensation, which is suited to the period of the present life. It is according to this that God equally "sendeth rain on the just and on the unjust," (Matt. v. 45,) and his "judgment often begins at his own house." (1 Pet. iv. 17.) (4.) The fourth and last act is the final and universal judgment, by which Christ, having been appointed by God to be the judge of all men, will pronounce a sentence of justification on his elect, and will bestow on them everlasting life; but after the sentence of condemnation has been uttered against the reprobates, they will be tormented with everlasting punishments. (Matt. 25.)

XX. To these functions it is easy to subjoin their Results or Consequences, which exist from the functions themselves, according to their nature; and, at the same time, the Events which flow from the malice of men who reject Christ as their King. Among the former are repentance, faith, and thus the church herself, and her association with Christ her head, obedience performed to Christ's commands, the participation of blessings which are bestowed on men in the course of the present life, immunity from evils, and lastly, life eternal. Among the latter, are blinding, hardening, the giving over to a reprobate mind, the delivering unto the power of Satan, the imputation of sin, the gnawings of conscience in this life, and the feeling endurance of many evils, and, lastly, eternal death itself. All these evils Christ inflicts as an omniscient, omnipotent, and inflexible judge, who loves goodness and hates sin, from whose eyes we cannot hide ourselves, whose power we cannot avoid, and whose strictness and rigor we are unable to bend. May God grant, through his Son, Jesus Christ, in the power and efficacy of the Holy Spirit, that these considerations may serve to beget within us a filial and serious fear of God and Christ our Judge.

AMEN!

DISPUTATION 15 - ON DIVINE PREDESTINATION

RESPONDENT: WILLIAM BASTINGIUS

I. We call this decree "Predestination," in Greek, Proorismon from the verb Proorizein which signifies determine, appoint, or decree any thing before you enter on its execution. According to this general notion, predestination, when attributed to God, will be his decree for the governance of all things, to which divines usually give the appellation of PROVIDENCE. (Acts ii. 28; xvii, 26.) It is customary to consider in a less general notion, so far as it has reference to rational creatures who are to be saved or damned, for instance, angels and men. It is taken in a stricter sense about the predestination of men, and then it is usually employed in two ways; for it is sometimes accommodated to both the elect and the reprobate. At other times, it is restricted to the elect alone, and then it has reprobation as its opposite. According to this last signification, in which it is almost constantly used in Scripture, (Rom.

viii. 29,) we will treat on predestination.

II. Predestination, therefore, as it regards the thing itself, is the decree of the good pleasure of God in Christ, by which he resolved within himself from all eternity, to justify, adopt and endow with everlasting life, to the praise of his own glorious grace, believers on whom he had decreed to bestow faith. (Ephes. 1; Rom. 9.)

III. The genus of predestination we lay down as a decree which is called in Scripture Proqesiv "the purpose of God," (Rom. ix. 11,) and Boulhn tou qelhmatov Qeou "the counsel of God's own will." (Ephes. i. 11.) And this decree is not legal, according to what is said, "The man who doeth those things shall live by them;" (Rom. x. 5;) but it is evangelical, and this is the language which it holds: "This is the will of God, that every one who seeth the Son, and believeth on him, may have everlasting life." (John vi. 40; Rom. x. 9.) This decree, therefore, is peremptory and irrevocable; because the final manifestation of "the whole counsel of God" concerning our salvation, is contained in the gospel. (Acts xx. 27; Heb. i. 2; ii, 2, 3.)

IV. The Cause of this decree is God, "according to the good pleasure" or the benevolent affection "of his own will." (Ephes. i. 5.) And God indeed is the cause, as possessing the right of determining as he wills both about men as his creatures, and especially as sinners, and about his blessings, (Jer. xviii. 6; Matt. xx. 14, 15,) "according to the good pleasure of his own will," by which, being moved with and in himself, he made that decree. This "good pleasure" not only excludes every cause which it could take from man, or which it could be imagined to take from him; but it likewise removes whatever was in or from man, that could justly move God not to make that gracious decree. (Rom. xi. 34, 35.)

V. As the foundation of this decree, we place Jesus Christ, the mediator between God and men, (Ephes. i. 4.) "in whom the Father is well pleased;" (Matt. iii. 17; Luke iii. 22;) "in whom God reconciled the world unto himself, not imputing their trespasses unto them" and "whom God made to be sin for us, that we might be made the righteousness of God in him." (2 Cor. v. 19, 21.) Through Him "everlasting righteousness was to be brought in," (Dan. ix. 24,) adoption to be acquired, the spirit of grace and of faith was to be obtained, (Gal. iv. 5, 19, 6,) eternal life procured, (John vi. 51,) and all the plenitude of spiritual blessings prepared, the communication of which must be decreed by predestination. He is also constituted by God the Head of all those persons who will, by divine predestination, accept of the equal enjoyment of these blessings. (Ephes. i. 22; v, 23; Heb. v. 9.)

VI. We attribute Eternity to this decree; because God does nothing in time, which He has not decreed to do from all eternity. For "known unto God are all his works from the beginning of the world:" (Acts xv. 18) and "He hath chosen us in Christ before the foundation of the world." (Ephes. i. 4.) If it were otherwise, God might be charged with mutability.

VII. We say that the object or matter of predestination is two-fold--Divine things, and Persons to whom the communication of those Divine things has been predestinated by this decree. (1.) These Divine Things receive from the Apostle the general appellation of "spiritual blessings:" (Ephes. i. 3.) Such are, in the present life, justification, adoption as sons, (Rom. viii. 29, 30,) and the spirit of grace and adoption. (Ephes. i. 5; John i. 12; Gal. iv. 6, 7.) Lastly, after this life, eternal life. (John iii. 15, 16.) The whole of these things are usually comprised and enunciated, in the Divinity schools, by the names of Grace and Glory. (2.) We circumscribe the Persons within the limits of the word "believers," which presupposes sin: for no one believes on Christ except a sinner, and the man who acknowledges himself to be that sinner. (Matt. ix. 13; xi, 28.) Therefore, the plenitude of those blessings, and the preparation of them which has been made in Christ, were necessary for none but sinners. But we give the name of "believers," not to those who would be such by their own merits or strength, but to those who by the gratuitous and peculiar kindness of God would believe in Christ. (Rom. ix. 32; Gal. ii. 20; Matt. xi. 25; xiii, 11; John vi. 44; Phil. i. 29.)

VIII. The form is the decreed communication itself of these blessings to believers, and in the mind of God the pre-existent and pre-ordained relation and ordination of believers to Christ their Head: the fruit of which they receive through a real and actual union with Christ their Head. In the present life, this fruit is gracious, through the commencement and increase of the union; and in the life to come, it is glorious, through the complete consummation of this union. (2 Tim. i. 9, 10; John i. 16, 17; xvii, 11, 12, 22-24; Ephes. iv. 13, 15.)

IX. The end of predestination is the praise of the glorious grace of God: for since grace, or the gratuitous love of God in Christ, is the cause of predestination, it is equitable that to the same grace the entire glory of this act should be ceded. (Ephes. i. 6; Rom. xi. 36.)

X. But this decree of predestination is "according to election," as the Apostle says: (Rom. ix. 6, xi,) This election necessarily infers reprobation. Reprobation therefore is opposed to predestination, as its contrary; and is likewise called "a casting away," (Rom. ix. 1,) "an ordination to condemnation," (Jude 4,) and "an appointment unto wrath." (1 Thess. v. 9.)

XI. From the law of contraries, we define reprobation to be a decree of the wrath, or of the severe will, of God; by which he resolved from all eternity to condemn to eternal death unbelievers, who, by their own fault and the just judgment of God, would not believe, for the declaration of his wrath and power. (John iii. 18; Luke vii. 30; John xii. 37 40; 2 Thess. ii. 10, 11; Rom. ix. 22.)

XII. Though by faith in Jesus Christ the remission of all sins is obtained, and sins are not imputed to them who believe; (Rom. iv. 2-11;) yet the reprobate will be compelled to endure the punishment, not only of their unbelief, (by the contrary of which they might avoid the chastisement due to the rest of their sins,) but likewise of the sins which they have committed against the law, being "everlasting destruction from the presence of the Lord, and from the glory of his power." (John viii. 24; ix, 41; 2 Thess. i. 9.)

XIII. To each of these decrees, that of predestination and that of reprobation, is subjoined its execution; the acts of which are performed in that order in which they have been appointed in and by the decree itself; and the objects both of the decree and of its execution are the same, and entirely uniform, or invested with the same formal relation. (Psalm cxv. 3; xxxiii, 9, 11.)

XIV. Great is the use of this doctrine, as thus delivered from the Scriptures. For it serves to establish the glory of the grace of God, to console afflicted consciences, to terrify the wicked and to drive away their security. (1.) But it establishes the grace of God, when it ascribes the whole praise of our vocation, justification, adoption, and glorification, to the mercy of God alone, and takes it entirely away from our own strength, works and merits. (Rom. viii. 29, 30; Ephes. 1.) (2.) It comforts afflicted consciences that are struggling with temptation, when it renders them assured of the gracious good will of God in Christ, which was from all eternity decreed to them, performed in time, and which will endure forever. (Isa. liv. 8.) It also shews, that the purpose of God according to election stands firm, not of works, but of Him that calleth. (1 Cor. i. 9; Rom. ix. 11.) (3.) It is capable of terrifying the ungodly; because it teaches, that the decree of God concerning unbelievers is irrevocable; (Heb. iii. 11, 17- 19;) and that "they who do not obey the truth, but believe a lie," are to be adjudged to eternal destruction. (2 Thess. ii. 12.)

XV. This doctrine therefore ought to resound, not only within private walls and in schools, but also in the assemblies of the saints and in the church of God. Yet one caution ought to be strictly observed, that nothing be taught concerning it beyond what the Scriptures say, that it be propounded in the manner which the Scriptures have adopted, and that it be referred to the same end as that which the Scriptures propose when they deliver it. This, by the gracious assistance of God, we think, we have done. "Unto Him be glory in the church by Christ Jesus throughout all ages, world without end. Amen!"

"The power of God is great, but it obtains glory from the humble. Do not inconsiderately seek out the things that are too hard for thee; neither foolishly search for things which surpass thy powers. But meditate with reverence upon those things which God has commanded thee: for it is not requisite for thee to see with thine eyes those things which are secret. Do not curiously handle those matters which are unprofitable and unnecessary to thy discourse: for more things are shewn unto thee, than the human understanding can comprehend. Ecclesiasticus iii. 20-23.

DISPUTATION 16 - ON THE VOCATION OF MEN TO SALVATION

RESPONDENT: JAMES BONTEBAL

I. The title contains three terms--vocation, men, salvation, (1.) The word Vocation denotes a total and entire act, consisting of all its parts, whether essential or integral, what parts soever are necessary for the purpose of men being enabled to answer the Divine Vocation. (Prov. i. 24; Matt. xi. 20, 21; xxiii, 37.) (2.) Men may be considered in a two-fold respect, either as placed in the state of animal life without sin, or as obnoxious to sin. We consider them here in this last respect. (Gen. ii. 16, 17; Matt. ix. 13.) (3.) Salvation, by a Synecdoche, in addition to vocation itself by which we are called to salvation, contains also whatsoever is necessary, through the appointment of God, for obtaining salvation or life eternal (Luke xix. 9; 2 Cor. vi. 2.)

II. We define Vocation, a gracious act of God in Christ, by which, through his word and Spirit, He calls forth sinful men, who are liable to condemnation and placed under the dominion of sin, from the condition of the animal life, and from the pollutions and corruptions of this world, (2 Tim. i. 9; Matt. xi. 28; 1 Pet. ii. 9, 10; Gal. i. 4; 2 Pet. ii. 20; Rom. x. 13-15; 1 Pet. iii. 19; Gen. vi. 3,) unto "the fellowship of Jesus Christ," and of his kingdom and its benefits; that, being united unto Him as their Head, they may derive from him life, sensation, motion, and a plenitude of every spiritual blessing, to the glory of God and their own salvation. (1 Cor. i. 9; Gal. ii. 20; Ephes. i. 3, 6; 2 Thess. ii. 13, 14.)

III. The efficient cause of this vocation is God the Father in the Son. The Son himself, as appointed by the Father to be the Mediator and the king of his church, calls men by the Holy Spirit; as He is the Spirit of God given to the Mediator; and as He is the Spirit of Christ the king and the head of his church, by whom both "the Father and the Son hitherto work" (1 Thess. ii. 12; Ephes. ii. 17; iv, 11, 12; Rev. iii. 20; John v. 17.) But this vocation is so administered by the Spirit, that the Holy Spirit is himself its effector: for He appoints bishops, sends forth teachers, endues them with gifts, grants them his assistance, and obtains authority for the word and bestows efficacy upon it. (Heb. iii. 7; Acts xiii. 2; xx, 28; 1 Cor. xii. 4, 7, 9, 11; Heb. ii. 4.)

IV. The Inly-moving cause is the grace, mercy and (philanthropy) "love of God our saviour toward man;" (Tit. iii. 4, 5;) by which He is inclined to relieve the misery of sinful man, and to impart unto him eternal felicity. (2 Tim. i. 9, 10.) But the disposing cause is the wisdom and justice of God; by which he knows how it is proper for this vocation to be administered, and wills it to be dispensed as it is lawful and befitting; and from which is formed the decree of his will concerning the administration and its mode. (1 Cor. i. 17, 18.)

V. The external cause, which outwardly moves God, is Jesus Christ by his obedience and intercession. (2 Tim. i. 9.) But the instrumental cause is the word of God, administered by means of men, either through preaching or writing, which is the ordinary method; (1 Cor. xii. 28-30; 2 Thess. ii. 14;) or without human assistance, when the word is immediately proposed by God inwardly to the mind and the will, which is extraordinary. And this is in fact both the word of the law and that of the Gospel, which are subordinate in the operations apportioned to each other.

VI. The matter or subject of vocation is mankind constituted in the animal life; men worldly, natural, animal, carnal, sinful, alienated from the life of God, and dead in sins; and therefore Unworthy to be called, and Unfit to answer to the call, unless by the gracious estimation of God they be accounted worthy, and by his powerful operation they be rendered Fit to comply with the vocation. (Matt. ix. 13; Tit. ii. 12; Ephes. ii. 11, 12; iv, 17, 18; v, 14; John v. 25; vi, 44; Matt. x. 11-13; Acts xvi. 14.)

VII. The form of vocation is placed in the very administration of the word and of the Holy Spirit. God hath instituted this administration so, as He knows to be suitable and becoming to himself, and to his justice tempered with mercy in Christ; always reserving to himself the fall and free power of not employing, for the conversion of men, all the methods which are possible to himself according to the treasures of his wisdom and power, and of bestowing unequal grace on those who are [in every respect,] equals, and equal grace on those who are unequal, nay, of employing greater grace on those who are more wicked. (Rom. ix. 21-26; x, 17-21; xi, 25, 29-33; Ezek. iii. 6; Matt. xi. 21, 23.)

VIII. But in every vocation the point of commencement, and that of termination, come to be considered. The point of commencement, whence men are called by divine vocation, is not only the state of this animal life, but likewise that of sin and of misery on account of sin, that is, out of guilt and condemnation. (1 Pet. ii. 9; 2 Pet. i. 4; Ephes. ii. 1-6; Rom. vi. 17, 18.) The point of termination is, First, the state of grace, or a participation of supernatural good and of every spiritual blessing, during the present life, in Christ, in whom resides a plenitude of grace and truth; and, Afterwards, the state of glory, and the perfect fruition of God himself. (Ephes. i. 3, 4,; John i. 14, 16; Rom. viii. 28-30.)

IX. The proximate end of vocation is, that they who have been called answer by faith to God and to Christ who give the call, and that they thus become the covenanted people of God through Christ the Mediator of the New Covenant; and, after having become believers and parties to the covenant, that they love, fear, honour, and worship God and Christ, render in all things obedience to the divine precepts "in righteousness and true holiness," and that by this means they "make their calling and election sure." (Prov. i. 24,; Heb. iii. 7; Rev. iii. 20; Ephes. ii. 11-16; Tit. iii. 8; Deut. vi. 4, 5; Jer. xxxii. 38, 39; Luke i. 74, 75; 2 Pet. i. 1, 10.)

X. The remote end is the salvation of the elect and the glory of God, in regard to which the very vocation to grace is a means ordained by God, yet through the appointment of God it is necessary to the communication of salvation. (Phil. i. 6; Ephes. i. 14.) But the answer by which obedience is yielded to this call, is the condition which, through the appointment of God, is also requisite and necessary for obtaining this end. (Prov. i. 24-26; Acts xiii. 46; Luke vii. 30.) The glory of God, who is supremely wise, good, merciful, just and powerful, is so luminously displayed in this communication both of his grace and glory, as deservedly to raise into rapturous admiration the minds of angels and men, and to employ their loosened tongues in celebrating the praises of Jehovah. (Rev. iv. 8-11; v, 8-10.)

XI. Vocation is partly external, partly internal. External vocation is by the ministry of men, who propound the word of the law and of the gospel, and who are on this account called "workers together with God, planters, waterers, builders, and ministers by whom the [members of the] church believe." (1 Cor. i. 5-9; iii, 3-6.) Internal vocation is by the operation of the Holy Spirit illuminating the mind and affecting the heart, that serious attention may be given to those things which are spoken, and that faith or credence may be given to the word. The efficacy consists in the concurrence of both the internal and external vocation. (Acts xvi. 14; 2 Cor. iii. 3; 1 Pet. i. 22.)

XII. But that distribution is not of a genus into its species, but of a whole into its parts, or of the entire vocation into partial acts which concur to produce one conclusion--which is, obedience yielded to the call. Hence an assemblage, or congregation of those who are called, and of those who answer to the call, is denominated "the Church;" (1 Cor. iii. 5, 6; Rom. i. 5;) which is itself, in the same manner, distinguished into the visible and the invisible--the visible, that "maketh confession with the mouth," and the invisible, "that believeth with the heart." (Rom. x. 10.) As man himself is likewise distinguished into "the outward" and "the inward." (2 Cor. iv. 16.)

XIII. But we must be cautious, lest with the mystics and the enthusiasts, we consider the word which is propounded by the ministry of men as only preparatory; and believe that another word is inwardly employed, which is perfective, or, (which is the same thing,) lest we suppose, that the Spirit by his internal act illuminates the mind into another knowledge of God and Christ, than that which is contained in the word outwardly propounded, or that he affects the heart and the soul with other meanings, than those which are proposed from the very same word. (1 Pet. i. 23, 25; Rom. x. 14-17; 2 Cor. iii. 3-6; 1 Cor. xv. 1-4.)

XIV. The accidental result of vocation, and that which is not of itself intended by God, is the rejection of the word of grace, the contemning of the divine counsel, the resistance offered to the Holy Spirit. The proper and per se cause of this result is, the malice and hardness of the human heart. But this result is, not seldom, succeeded by another, the just judgment of God, avenging the contempt shewn to his word and call, and the injury done to his Holy Spirit; and from this judgment arise the blinding of the mind, the hardening of the heart, "the giving over to a reprobate mind," and "the delivering unto the power of Satan." (Acts xiii. 46; Luke vii. 30; Acts vii. 51; 2 Thess. iii. 2; 2 Cor. iv. 4; Psalm lxxxi. 11-14; Isa. lxiii. 10; vi, 9, 10; John xii. 37-40.)

XV. But, because "known unto our God are all his works from the beginning of the world," (Acts xv. 18,) and as God does nothing in time which He has not decreed from all eternity to do, this vocation is likewise instituted and administered according to God's eternal decree. So that what man soever is called in time, was from all eternity predestinated to be called, and to be called in that state, time, place, mode, and with that efficacy, in and with which he was predestinated. Otherwise, the execution will vary from the decree; which charge of mutability and change cannot be preferred against God without producing mischievous effects. (Ephes. iii. 5, 6, 9-11; James i. 17, 18; 2 Tim. i. 9.)

DISPUTATION 17 - ON REPENTANCE

RESPONDENT: HENRY NIELLUIS

As in succeeding Disputations are discussed Faith, and Justification through Faith, the order which has hitherto been observed requires us now to treat on Repentance without which we can neither have fellowship with Christ, nor be made partakers of his righteousness.

I. The matter on which we are at present treating, is usually enunciated in the three Latin words, resipiscentia, pænitentia, and conversio, repentance, penitence and conversion. The Greek word, Metanoia "change of mind after reflection," answers to the first of these, terms;

Metameleia, "regret on account of misdeeds," to the second; and Ewisrofh "a turning about, a return," to the third. On this subject the Hebrews frequently employ the word h b w t "a returning," as corresponding with the third of the preceding terms; and the word μ j n or h m j n which expresses the sense of the second. But though these words are, according to the essence and nature of the thing, synonymous, yet each of them signifies a particular formal conception. The First, repentance, is a conception of the understanding; the Second, penitence, a conception of the affections or passions; and the Third, conversion, is a conception of an action resulting from both the others. The general term, therefore, comprises the understanding, the affections, and an ulterior act resulting from both the preceding. The First signifies a change of mind after any thing has been done; and, after the commission of evil, a change of mind to a better state. The Second expresses grief or sorrow of mind after a deed; and, after an evil deed, "sorrow after a godly sort," and not "the sorrow of the world," although the word is sometimes thus used even in the Scriptures. The Third denotes conversion to some thing, from which aversion had been previously formed. And, in this discussion, it is that conversion which is from evil to good; from sin, Satan and the world, to God. The First comprehends a disapproval of evil and an approval of the opposite good. The Second comprises grief for a past evil, and an affection of desire towards a contrary good. The Third shews an aversion from the evil to which it adhered, and a conversion to the good from which it had been alienated. But these three conceptions, according to the nature of things and the command of God, are so intimately connected with each other, that there cannot be either true and right repentance, penitence, or conversion, unless each of these has the other two united with it, either as preceding it, or as succeeding.

II. According to this distinction of the various conceptions, have been invented different definitions of one and the same thing as to its essence. For instance, "repentance is a change of mind and heart from evil to good, proceeding from godly sorrow." It is also "sorrow after the commission of sin on account of God being offended, and through this sorrow a change of the whole heart from evil to good." And "It is a true conversion of our life to God, proceeding from a sincere and serious fear of God, which consists in the mortification of our flesh and of the old man, and in the quickening of the Spirit." We disapprove of none of these three definitions, because in substance and essence they agree among themselves, and, sufficiently for [the purposes of] true piety, declare the nature of the thing. But a more copious definition may be given, such as the following: "Repentance, penitence, or conversion is an act of the entire man, by which in his understanding he disapproves of sin universally considered, in his affections he hates it, and as perpetrated by himself is sorry for it and in the whole of his life avoids it. By which he also in his understanding approves of righteousness, in affections loves it, and in the whole of his life follows after it. And thus he turns himself away from Satan and the world, and returns unto God and adheres to Him, that God may abide in him, and that he may abide in God."

III. We call repentance "the act of man," that we may distinguish it from Regeneration which is "the act of God." These two have some things in common, are on certain points in affinity; yet, in reality, according to the peculiar nature which each of them possesses, they are distinct; though, according to their subjects, they are not separated. We add that it is "the act of the entire man:" for it is his act with regard to the entire mind or soul, and all its faculties; and with regard to the body as it is united to the soul, and is an organ or instrument subjected to the pleasure and command of the soul. (1 Kings xviii. 37; Rom. xii. 1, 2.) It is an act which concerns the whole life of man as it is rational, and as it was born with an aptitude to tend towards sin and towards God, and to turn aside from either of them. It consists of the understanding, the affections, the senses, and motion, and concurs with all these conjointly, though subordinately, to [the production of] repentance, penitence or conversion. (1.) In this act, the Understanding performs its office both by a general appreciation of its value and by its particular approbation and disapprobation. (2.) The Affections or passions perform theirs, as they are ewiqumhtikov concupiscible, by loving, hating, mourning and rejoicing; and as they are qumoeidhv, irascible, by being angry, zealous, indignant, fearful, and hopeful. (Ephes. 3 & 4.) (3.) The Senses, both internal and external, perform their office by their aversion from unbecoming objects, and by their conversion to those which are suitable and proper. (Rom. vi. 13, 19.) (4.) Lastly, the Motions of the tongue, hands, feet, and of the other members of the body, perform their office by removal from things unlawful and inexpedient, and by their application to those which are lawful and expedient.

IV. The object of repentance is the evil of unrighteousness or sin, (considered both universally, and as committed by the penitent himself,) and the good of righteousness. (Psalm xxxiv. 15; Ezek. xviii. 28.) The evil of unrighteousness is first in order, the good of righteousness is first in dignity. From the former, repentance has its commencement; in the latter, it terminates and rests. The object may be considered in a manner somewhat different; for, since we are commanded to return to God, from whom we had turned away, God is also the object of conversion and repentance, as he is the hater of sin and of evil men, the lover of righteousness and of righteous men, good to those who repent, and their chief good, and, on the contrary, the severe avenger and the certain destruction of those who persevere in sin. (Mal. v. 7; Zech. i. 3; Deut. vi. 5.) To this object, may be directly opposed another personal object, the devil, from whom by repentance we must take our departure. (Ephes. iv. 27; James iv. 7.) To the devil may be added an object which is an accessory to him, and that is, the world, of which he is called "the prince," (John xii. 31; xiv, 30,) both as it contains within it arguments suitable for Satan to employ in seduction, such as riches, honours and pleasures, (Luke iv. 5, 6; 1 John ii. 15, 16,) and as it renders to the devil something that resembles personal service. (Rom. vi. 9, 7.) In both these methods, the world attracts men to itself, and detains them after they are united to it. From it, also, we are commanded to turn away. Nay, man himself may obtain the province of an object opposed to God; and he is commanded to separate himself from himself, that he may live not according to man, but according to God. (Ephes. iv. 22; Col. iii. 9- 17; Rom. vi. 10-23.)

V. The primary efficient cause of repentance is God, and Christ as he is through the Spirit mediator between God and man. (Jer. xxxi. 18; Ezek. xxxvi. 25, 26; Acts v. 31; xvii, 30.) The inly moving cause is the goodness, grace, and philanthropy of God our creator and redeemer, who loves the salvation of his creature, and desires to manifest the riches of his mercy in the salvation of his miserable creature. (Rom. xi. 5.) The outwardly moving cause, through the mode of merit, is the obedience, the death and the intercession of Christ; (Isa. liii. 5; 1 Cor. i. 30, 31; 2 Cor. v. 21;) and, through the mode of moving to mercy, it is the unhappy condition of sinners, whom the devil holds captive in the snares of iniquity, and who will perish by their own demerits according to the condition of the law, and necessarily according to the will of God manifested in the gospel, unless they repent (John iii. 16; Ezek. xvi. 3-63; Luke xiii. 3, 5; Isa. xxxi. 6; Jer. iii, 14; Psalm cxix. 71; in the prophets passim; Rom. vii. 6, 7.)

VI. The proximate, yet less principal cause, is man himself, converted and converting himself by the power and efficacy of the grace of God and the Spirit of Christ. The external cause inciting to repent is the miserable state of the sinners who do not repent, and the felicitous and blessed state of those who repent--whether such state be known from the law of Moses or from that of nature, from the gospel or from personal experience, or from the examples of other persons who have been visited with the most grievous plagues through impenitence, or who, through repentance, have been made partakers of many blessings. (Rom. ii. 5; Acts ii. 37.) The internal and inly moving cause is, not only a consciousness of sin and a sense of misery through fear of the Deity, who has been offended, with a desire to be delivered from both, but it is likewise [an incipient] faith and hope of the gracious mercy and pardon of God.

VII. The instrumental causes which God ordinarily uses for our conversion, and by which we are solicited and led to repentance, are the law and the gospel. Yet the office of each in this matter is quite distinct, so that the more excellent province in it is assigned to the gospel, and the law acts the part of its servant or attendant. For, in the first place, the very command to repent is evangelical; and the promise of pardon, and the peremptory threat of eternal destruction, unless the man repents, which are added to it, belong peculiarly to the gospel. (Matt. iii. 1; Mark i. 4; Luke xxiv. 47.) But the law proves the necessity of repentance, by convincing man of sin and of the anger of the offended Deity, from which conviction arise a certain sorrow and a fear of punishment, which, in its commencement is servile or slavish solely through a regard to the law, but which, in its progress, becomes a filial fear through a view of the gospel. (Rom. iii. 13, 20; vii, 7.) From these, also, proceed, by the direction of an inducement to remove, or repent, a certain external abstinence from evil works, and such a performance of some righteousness as is not hypocritical. (Matt. iii. 8; vii, 17; James ii. 14-26.) But as the law does not proceed beyond "the ministration of death and of the letter," the services of the gospel here again become necessary, which administers the Spirit, by whose illumination, inspiration and gracious and efficacious strengthening, repentance itself, in its essential and integral parts is completed and perfected. Nay the very conviction of sin belongs in some measure to the gospel, since sin itself has been committed against the command both concerning faith and repentance. (Mark xvi. 16; John xvi. 8-15.)

VIII. There are likewise other causes aiding or auxiliary to repentance, some of which are usually employed by God himself, and others of them by those who are penitent. (1.) For God sometimes sends the cross and afflictions, by which, as with goads, he excites and invites to repentance. At other times, he visits them with the contrary blessings, that he may lead them, after having been invited, by goodness and lenity to repentance. (1 Cor. xi. 32; Jer. xxxi. 18; Psalm 80 & 85.) (2.) The causes employed by penitents themselves are watching, fasting, and other corporeal chastisements, as well as prayers, which are of the greatest efficacy in obtaining and performing repentance. The other causes employed by men are likewise serviceable in exciting the ardour of these prayers. (Psalm 119; Rom. ii. 4; v, 3, 4; xii, 11, 12.) It is possible for this relation to exist between these auxiliary and the preceding instrumental causes, (§ 7,) that the auxiliary causes are subservient to the instrumental, since they excite men to a serious and assiduous meditation on the law and the gospel, and by the grace of God obtain yet more and more a right understanding of both.

IX. The form of repentance is the uprightness of the turning away from evil, and of the return to God and to righteousness. It is conformed to the rule of the divine command, and is produced by an assured faith and hope of the divine mercy, and by a sincere intention to turn away and to return. As the penitence of Saul, Ahab and Judas was destitute of this uprightness, it is unworthy to be reckoned under this title. (1 Sam. xv. 24, 25; 1 Kings xxi. 27; Matt. xxvii. 3.) But since the mind of the penitent is conscious to itself of this rectitude, or uprightness, no necessity exists for such a man anxiously and solicitously to examine whether it be so great, either intensively, extensively, or appreciatively, as the rigor of justice might demand.

X. The fruits of repentance, which may also have the relation of ends, are, (1.) On the part of God, the remission of sin according to the condition of the covenant of grace in Christ, and on account of his obedience, and through faith in him. (Luke xxiv. 47; Acts v. 31; Rom. iii. 24) (2.) On our part, the fruits are good works, which are "meet for repentance," (Matt. iii. 8; Luke iii. 8,) and "which God foreordained," that believers and penitents, who are "created in Christ Jesus unto good works, should walk in them." (Ephes. ii. 10.) The ultimate end is the glory of God the Redeemer, who is at once just and merciful in Jesus Christ our Lord. (Rev. xvi. 9.) It results not only from the gracious and efficacious act of God, who bestows repentance, and converts us to himself; but likewise from the act of the penitents themselves, by which turning themselves away from sins, and returning to God, they "walk in newness of living" all the days of their life. It also results from the very intention of repentance itself.

XI. The parts of repentance, as is abundantly evident from the preceding Theses, according to its two boundaries, (both that from which it commences, and that towards which it proceeds and in which it terminates,) are two, an aversion, or turning away from the Devil and sin, and a conversion or returning to God and righteousness. (Psalm xxxiv. 14; Jer. iv. 1.) They are united together by an indissoluble connection; but the former is preparatory to the latter, while the latter is perfective of the former. The Papists, however, make penitence to consist of three parts; and seem to derive greater pleasure from employing the word penitence about this matter, than in the use of the terms repentance and conversion. Their three parts are, the contrition of the heart, the confession of the mouth, and the satisfaction of the work; about which we make two brief affirmations. (1.) If these be received as parts of the penitence which is necessary before God, then no contrition can be so great, either intensively or appreciatively, as to be in any wise either meritorious or capable of obtaining remission of sins. No confession of the mouth, not even that which is made to God, (provided the confession of the heart only be present,) is necessary to receive remission; much less is the confession which is made to any man, even though he be a priest. And there is no satisfaction, except the obedience of the passion of our Lord Jesus Christ, by which the justice of God can be satisfied either for sin or for its punishment, even for the very least of either. (Acts iv. 12; Heb. x. 10, 14; 1 Cor. i. 30.) (2.) If these be received as part of the penitence to which, before the church, that man submits who has injured her by scandal, that he may render her satisfaction and may contribute to her edification; then indeed those words, [contrition, confession and satisfaction,] may bear an accommodated sense, and such a distribution of them may be useful to the church.

XII. The contrary to repentance is impenitence, and a pertinacious perseverance in sinning: of which there are two degrees, one the delay of penitence, the other final impenitence unto death. The latter of them has a certain expectation of eternal destruction, even according to the most merciful will of God revealed in Christ and in the Gospel; lest any one should persuade himself, that the devils themselves, and men who have passed their lives in impiety, will at length experience the mercy of God. The former of them, the delay of penitence, is marvelously dangerous, for three reasons: (1.) Because it is in the power and hand of God to make even the delay of a single hour to be a final impenitence, since to Him belongs the dominion and lordship over our life and death. (2.) Because after a habit of sinning has been introduced by daily exercise, a man is rendered anaisqhtov, incapable of feeling, and his conscience becomes "seared with a hot iron." (1 Tim. iv, 2.) (3.) Because, after the gate of grace has by the just judgment of God been closed on account of a malicious continuance in sins, no passage is open for the Spirit, who is necessarily the author of repentance. Therefore let these words always resound in our ears, "Today if ye will hear his voice, harden not your hearts." (Heb. iii. 7, 8; Psalm xcv. 7, 8.) And this exhortation of the Apostle, "Workout your own salvation with fear and trembling: for it is God who worketh in you both to will and to do of his good pleasure," (Phil. ii. 12, 13.) May this be graciously granted to us by God the Father of mercies, in the Son of his love, by the Holy Spirit of both of them. To whom be praise and glory forever. Amen.

COROLLARIES

It is not a correct saying, that "to those who relapse after having been baptized, penitence is a second plank [for their escape] after shipwreck."

Those persons act harshly who, from the example of God not pardoning sins except to him that is penitent, refuse to forgive their brother unless he confesses his fault, and earnestly begs pardon.

DISPUTATION 18 - ON THE CHURCH AND ITS HEAD

RESPONDENT: GERARD, THE SON OF HELMICHIUS

As it is of the greatest utility to hold a right belief about the church of God and its Head, and as there is at present a great controversy between the Orthodox and the Papists respecting this matter, it appears to us that we shall not be profitably occupied , if we treat of the Church and of its Head in a few Theses.

I. The Church, ecclesia, is a word of Greek origin, used in the Greek version of the Old Testament for the Hebrew word l h q , "the assembly;" (Deut. xxiii. 2; Judges xx. 2) and properly signifies a "congregation of persons called out," from the very etymology of the word and from the most frequent usage of the Sacred writings, without any distinction of the small or the great number of those who belong to such an assemblage. For sometimes it signifies the universal assembly of all those who have been called out; (Acts xx. 28; Ephes. i. 22;) at other times, an extraordinary multitude; (Acts ii. 41, 47;) and at other times, only a few persons, comprised in a single family. (Rom. xvi. 5.) This diversity in its application is made on account of one essential reason in all of them; and as this reason belongs equally to an assembly of few persons, of many, and of all, these several assemblages equally partake of the name of "the church," with this difference alone, that a congregation consisting of numerous members is called a greater church, but not more a church, according to the axiom of the Logicians, "A substance does not receive more and less."

II. According to this very general notion the church of God is defined, "A congregation of men called forth by God, out of their own nature, into the supernatural dignity of adoption as sons of God to his glory, and of those who answer this call of God." For the act of vocation, as proceeding from God who calls, and as properly received by those who are called, completes his church. Under this definition are likewise comprehended those angels who are called in Scripture "the elect;" (1 Tim. v. 21;) whether they be considered as an assembly separated from men, or as belonging to one church with men. (Psalm lxviii. 17; Jude. 14; Rev. v. 11; Heb. xii. 22.) According to this notion, the church, embracing all, is especially called "Catholic." But omitting any further mention of angels, about whose vocation the Scriptures speak sparingly, we will contemplate the church as consisting of human beings. We must here consider men in two respects--according to the primeval state in which they were created after the image of God, and in reference to their fall from that state into corruption and misery.

III. Because, when men are considered in their primitive state, they were created to be not only what they actually were, but likewise to be elevated to a state of higher felicity, agreeing with the image of God; bearing the impress of which, as children they resembled their Heavenly Father; (Gen. i. 27; Luke iii. 38;) therefore, in this state, theirs was the calling forth, by which they were called out from nature and natural felicity to partake of the fruit of Divine adoption, by the observance of the law which had been imposed on them, and which had been sanctioned by the promise of a life of blessedness assured to them through the sacrament of the tree of life, (Gen. ii. 9, 10,) and by a threat of death. They were therefore the church of God, neither redeemed by the blood of Christ, nor formed anew by regeneration of the Spirit, nor by a new creation, but they were instituted as a church by the primitive creation of God, and formed by a vocation according to the legal covenant.

IV. Before the fall, this church in reality consisted only of our first parents, Adam and Eve; but in capacity it embraced the whole of the human race that were included in their loins, and that were afterwards to proceed from them by natural propagation. This was done by God's constant and perpetual ordinance, according to which he included all their posterity in the covenant into which He had entered with the parents, provided the parents continued in this covenant. (Gen. xvii. 7; Rom. v. 12, 14.) And in this respect, the church before the fall may take to itself the epithet of "Catholic." But, as a promise of the remission of sins was not annexed to this covenant, when our first parents transgressed this law, which had been imposed as a trial of obedience, they fell from the covenant and ceased to be the church of God, (Jer. xi. 3,) they were expelled from the tree of life and out of Paradise, the symbols of life eternal and of the place in which it was to be enjoyed, and were thus by nature rendered "children of wrath." (Gen. 3.)

V. Wherefore, if a church was to be again collected from among men, it was to be called out from that state of sin and misery; but it was to be collected through the decree of the gracious mercy of God. He therefore employed such a mode of calling the members forth as was agreeable to that state, that is, the institution of a new and gracious covenant, as the word is used in the writings of the evangelism. (Jer. xxxi. 33; Matt. xxvi. 28.) This covenant exhibits remission of sins ratified by the blood of the Mediator, Christ the only begotten Son of God, and the Spirit of grace through faith in Him. (Heb. ix. 15; Gal. iii. 2, 5; iv, 19.) To a participation in this covenant men have been called "in divers manners," according to the economy of time most wisely arranged by God. First, by the declaration or solemn promise of the blessed seed, (Gen. iii. 15; Rom. i. 2,) when the heir was by appointment constituted an infant: wherefore He was also to be detained for a time under the preparatory discipline of the law economically repeated. Afterwards, by that full manifestation in the Gospel, when, according to "the time appointed of God the Father," the heir had arrived at maturity. (Gal. iv. 1-4; Matt. xi. 11-13.)

VI. But this economic distinction, and this diversity in the method of calling forth, do not make a double and in substance a different church. For it is one and the same person that is an infant and afterwards a full-grown man, not distinguished except with regard to age and advancement according to increased age. But the whole church, both before and after Christ, is called one heir. (Gal. 4.) The whole church, collected together from among the Jews and the Gentiles, is also called "one new man;" and not from those Jews only who lived after the advent of Christ, but likewise from those who lived prior to his coming, when the Gentiles were without Christ," being then aliens from the commonwealth of Israel, and strangers from the covenants of promise." (Ephes. ii. 12-15.) The church is one city, the heavenly Jerusalem, "the mother of all" those who are blessed with faithful Abraham, and who, "as Isaac was, are the children of promise." (Gal. iv. 26-28.) It is also one house of God founded upon Christ the chief corner-stone, which has been laid in a foundation the most firm and stable, through the preaching not only of the apostles, but likewise of the prophets, (Ephes. ii. 20-22,) to the latter of whom also belong Abraham, Isaac and Jacob, as well as Moses himself, who according to the authority of the promise was a son, (Heb. xi. 24-26,) although a servant in the house with regard to the economical legislation which was administered by his hands. (iii, 4.)

VII. This assembly being distinguished in the manner already described, by the names of "the one heir" and "the one new man," of "the one city" and "the one house of God," is in the most ample signification and in the widest latitude called "the Catholic Church," collected together from among men of every period and age from the first promise of the seed of the woman to the end of the world, and of all places; men who have been called forth to the participation of the grace of God, and to the service of his glory; and who are obedient to this Divine calling. (Heb. 11; xii, 22- 24.) It is distributed into two integral members, each of which is homogeneous and similar to the whole; that is, into the church before Christ, and that after Him: (Gal. iv. 1-4; Heb. xi. 40.) But as a discussion upon their agreement and difference will be a labour rather too prolix, we will not enter into it on this occasion: omitting therefore the peculiar consideration of that which was before Christ, our further attention shall be directed to that which is specially called "Christian," yet not to the entire exclusion of the other.

VIII. We may be permitted, therefore, to define the Christian church, "A congregation of believers, who have been called by the saving vocation of God from the state of corruption to the dignity of the sons of God through the gospel, and are by a true faith engrafted into Christ, as living members are to the Head, to the praise of the glorious grace of God. (Matt. v. 15, 16; Acts iv. 31; 1 Pet.

ii. 9; v, 10; Rom. viii. 28-30; vi, 5; Ephes. iii. 17; v, 30.) This, as a general definition, belongs to every congregation of believers, whether it be small or large; it also appertains to the Catholic church, which contains the entire number of believers from the time when Christ came into his kingdom unto the consummation of all things: which universal company we properly describe, if we add these few words to the previous description, "Of all the believers who have been called out from every tongue, tribe, people, nation and vocation," &c. From this it is apparent, that the Catholic or universal church differs from particular churches in nothing which relates to the substance of the church, but solely in its amplitude: an argument which ought to be diligently observed in our controversy with the Papists.

IX. The efficient cause of the church, that both produces her by regeneration and preserves her by daily education, and that perfects her by an immediate union of her to himself, is God the Father, in his well beloved Son Jesus Christ, by the Spirit of Christ who is the Redeemer and the Head of the church. (2 Tim. i. 9; 1 Pet. i. 12.) We view the gospel as the instrument, that is, "the incorruptible seed by which the church is born again." (1 Pet. i. 23, 25.) Hence those persons also whom God appointed to be ministers of the Gospel, were the instrumental causes, and are called "co-operators," or "workers together with God," of whom some are employed in laying the foundation, others in raising the superstructure. (1 Cor. iii. 5, 10; Rev. xv. 18-21; Ephes. ii. 20.) They are indeed the founders of many particular churches, by their oral preaching; but by their writings which have been delivered down to us, they are the founders of all churches and of the whole Catholic church; on this account the entire church of Christ is called Apostolical.

X. We call the act of this cause that produces the church, and preserves her, "a calling forth." This word includes, First, the point from which a commencement is made to that in which it terminates, and, then, the means by which men proceed from the one to the other. (1.) The point of commencement is the state of sin and misery, in which state, a sinner without the law is at ease and flatters himself; but to which a sinner is averse who is under the law through the vocation previously administered by the legal spirit, that is, the spirit of bondage, and from which he desires to be delivered. (Matt. ix. 13; xi, 28; Rom. 7.) The point of termination is the dignity of being adopted as the sons of God, which, also, with respect to the desire of those who have been called forth, may be fitly denominated their end. (2.) The means by which men proceed from the one point to the other, is faith in Christ, by which we obtain this dignity, and are "translated from the kingdom of darkness into the kingdom of light" and of the Son of God, through the decree of divine predestination. (Jer. i. 12; Col. i. 13; Acts xvi. 17.)

XI. Hence it will easily appear what it is that we have laid down as the matter or substance of this calling forth, about which it is conversant, and in which it exercises its operation. Sinners are the remote matter; for to them alone is an entrance into this way necessary. The still nearer matter are sinners through the law acknowledging their sins, deploring their state, and expecting redemption. (Gal. ii. 15, 16, 21; Matt. ix. 13; xi, 28; Rom. viii. 28-30.) Believers are the proximate matter, who, alone, are called to the fellowship of Jesus Christ, and to a participation of the inheritance which he has purchased for his children with his own blood, and of which he is constituted the dispenser to those who obey him. (Heb. v. 9.) For however perfect in the act, vocation is, when it has proceeded from Him who calls us, yet a relative effect is required for this purpose, that they who are called may be numbered in the name of the church. (Acts ii. 41.) Wherefore we exclude from the church, unbelievers, apostates, hypocrites, and those heretics who do not hold Christ as the head. (Ephes. i. 22.) We make a distinction between those who have not been baptized with the external baptism of water, those who have been excommunicated by the sentence of the church, and schismatics; and according to the varying distinction in each case, we affirm either that they belong to the church, or that they do not belong to her.

XII. As the form of the church is of the genus of relatives, we place it as relatively necessary, and in reality in the relation of disquiparancy, as we are enjoined to do by the relative names by which the church is called. For she is called "the body," (Ephes. i. 23,) "the bride" (John iii. 29,) "the city of the kingdom," (Heb. i. 8,) and "the house" (1 Tim. iii. 15,) in relation to "the Head," (Ephes. i. 22; Col. i. 18,) to "the Bridegroom" to "the King," and "the Master," or the Father of the family. But the relation between these things which are thus relatively placed, consists of three points or degrees, union, appointment and communication. (1.) The form therefore of the church in union is with her Head, Husband, King and Master of the house or family; which is formed by his Spirit, and by the faith of the church. (Gal. ii. 30; Rom. viii. 9-11.) (2.) In her subordination under her Head, Husband and King, which is required by the perfection and virtue of her Head, and by the necessity and usefulness of the church herself. (Ephes. v. 23.) (3.) In the influence of life, sensation and motion, which influence benevolently proceeds from the Head, and is happily apprehended by the church.

XIII. The chief end of the church is the glory of Him by whose gracious evocation the church is what she is; the glory which He completes in His gracious acts towards the church, by creating, preserving, increasing and perfecting her. (Ephes. i. 12.) To this glory is justly subordinate, that which the church is commanded to ascribe to Him, and which she will ascribe as the perfecting of her "throughout all ages, world without end." (Rom. xi. 36; 1 Pet.. ii, 9; Ephes. iii, 21; v, 20.) As the salvation of the church is the gift of her Head and King, it cannot be the end of his church, though it may be the end which she intends by her faith, and which she strives to obtain, that she may be blessed before God.

XIV. But the church is herself now distinguished according to the acts of God towards her, so far as she perceives all or some of them. (1.) She that has a perception only of the act of creation and preservation, is said to be in the way or course, and is called militant, because she must still contend with sin, the flesh, the world and Satan. (Ephes. vi. 11, 12; Heb. xii. 1-4. (2.) But she that is made partaker besides, of the consummation, is said to be in her own land, and is called triumphant. After conquering her enemies, she rests from her labours, and reigns with Christ in heaven. (Rev. iii. 21; xiv, 13.) To that part of the church which is militant on earth, the title of Catholic or universal is likewise ascribed, as embracing within her pale every particular combatant or soldier. We place neither any church, nor anything belonging to her, in purgatory, for that is a real utopia, and of great notoriety among all men.

XV. Hence, since the calling forth of the church is made inwardly by the spirit, and outwardly by the word preached (Acts xvi. 14,) and since those who are called answer inwardly by faith, and outwardly by the profession of their faith, as they who are called have an inward man and an outward; (2 Cor. iv. 16;) therefore, in reference to those who are called, the church is distinguished into the visible and the invisible from an external adjunct and accident. She is invisible, as "believing with the heart unto righteousness;" and she is visible, as "making confession with the mouth unto salvation." (Rom. x. 9, 10.) This visibility and invisibility belong neither less nor more to the whole catholic church than to each particular church. For that which is called "the catholic invisible church" does not appertain to this subject, because it can not come together into one place, and thus be exposed to view. But as more persons "are called" than "are chosen" or elected. (Matt. xx. 16.) And as many of the called profess with their mouths "that they know God, while in works they deny him;" (Tit. i. 16;) and since of the hearts of these men, God is the sole judge, who alone "knoweth them that are his;" (2 Tim. ii. 19;) therefore such persons are judged, on account of the promise, to belong to the visible church, although equivocally, since they do not belong to the invisible church, and have none of that inward communion with the Head, which is the Form of the church.

XVI. Then, since the church is collected out of "the world that lieth wholly in wickedness," (John xv. 19; Matt. xv. 9,) and as this office is frequently performed by ministers who preach another doctrine than that which the word of God contains; (2 Cor. xi. 15; Gal. iii. 1-3;) and since the church is composed of men who are exposed to deception and to falling--nay, of such as are actually deceived and fallen; on this account, the church is distinguished, with respect to the doctrine of faith, into "the orthodox" and "the heretical;" with respect to divine worship, into "the idolatrous," and that which retains the "right worship of God and of Christ;" and with respect to the moral virtues prescribed in the second table of the law into "a purer church, or into "one that is more impure." In all these respects, degrees are also to be observed, according to which one church is more heretical, idolatrous and impure, than another. But concerning all these things, a right judgment must be formed according to the Scriptures. In this relation, too, the word "catholic" is used respecting those churches which are neither oppressed with destructive heresy nor are idolatrous.

XVII. Wherefore, that question is confused and preposterous which asks, "Can the Catholic church err?" when the inquiry ought rather to be, "Can the assembly that errs be the church?" For as faith is prior to the church, and as the church obtains this appellation on account of her believing, so the name of "the church" is taken away from any church so far as she errs from the faith. Yet if this question be pressed by any one, we say that by it nothing more is asked than this, "Can it happen that at any one time there can be no assemblage or congregation of men in the whole world who have not a right faith in Christ and God," To which an answer is readily made by a negation; because the church on earth will never totally fail, but must continue to be collected together without interruption to the end of the world, although not always from the same places and nations. (Matt. xxviii. 20; Rev. ii. 5.) Otherwise, Christ will not have any kingdom on earth, and will not rule in the midst of his enemies until they be made his footstool. (Psalm cx. 1, 2.)

We have hitherto treated of the church herself, let us now briefly consider her head.

XVIII. The conditions of the Head of the church are, that it should contain within itself, in a manner the most perfect, all things necessary to the life and salvation of the church, that it should have a due proportion to the church, should be fitly united to her and placed in order with her, and that by its own virtue it may supply to her life, sensation and motion. But these conditions agree with Christ alone. For "in Him all fullness dwells;" (Col. i. 19;) "and of his fullness have all we received." (John i. 16.) Him hath the Father constituted "the Head over all things to the church;" and he bestows salvation on his body, which is the church. (Ephes. i. 22; v, 25.) By his spirit, the church is animated, perceives and moves. (Rom. viii. 9-12.) Nor is this to be understood only about internal communication, but likewise concerning external administration; for it is He who sends forth his word and his Spirit, (Matt. xxviii. 19; Acts ii. 33,) who institutes a ministry in the church, who appoints, as presidents over this ministry, apostles, evangelists, pastors and teachers. (Ephes. iv. 11, 12.) On this account, He is called "the chief

Pastor or Shepherd," (1 Pet. v. 4,) who assists and "works with" his ministers, "both with signs and wonders, and with divers miracles and gifts of the Holy Ghost;" (Mark xvi. 20; Acts iv. 30;) and who defends his church against her enemies, and procures likewise her temporal good, so far as He considers it to be requisite for her inward and eternal benefit.

XIX. This name therefore, "the Head of the Church," cannot be adapted, according to any consideration, either to the apostle Peter or to the Roman pontiff. The papists, themselves, grant that it cannot be according to internal communication; and we prove that it cannot be according to external administration, in the following manner: (1.) St. Peter was himself constituted an apostle by Christ, after the same constitution as that by which Christ is said to have appointed apostles. (Ephes. iv. 7, 11; 1 Pet. i. 1.) Therefore, the rest of the apostles were not constituted by St. Peter, which appointment St. Paul expressly denies respecting himself, when he says that he obtained his apostleship "neither of men nor by man;" (Gal. i. 1.) (2.) St. Peter is a fellow-elder. Therefore, he is not the chief of the elders. (1 Pet. v. 1.) (3.) To St. Peter "was committed the gospel of the circumcision," as that of the uncircumcision was by equal right and authority committed to St. Paul. Therefore "they gave to each other the right hand of fellowship." (Gal. ii. 7-9.) (4.) St. Peter was reprehended by St. Paul, "because he did not walk uprightly, according to the truth of the gospel;" Therefore, he was not a suitable person to receive in charge the administration of the whole church. (5.) St. James, Cephas and John, are all placed by the apostle Paul as equal in degree; nay, as being accounted columns by the churches, with no difference among them. (6.) On the twelve foundations of the new Jerusalem are inscribed "the names of the twelve apostles of the Lamb," each name on each foundation without the pre-eminence of any single one apart. (7.) St. Paul says that "in nothing was he behind the very chief apostles." (2 Cor. xii. 11.) Therefore, he was not inferior to St. Peter, who was one of them. (8.) St. Paul says that he "laboured more abundantly than all the rest." (1 Cor. xv. 10.) But he could not have spoken this with truth, if the care of managing the whole church lay upon St. Peter, and if he administered its concerns through St. Paul and other persons. The objections which the papists urge in favour of the primacy or pre-eminence of St. Peter, will be examined in the disputation itself.

XX. Hence it follows that neither does this title of "the Head of the church" belong to the Roman pontiff. For whatever portion of right and dignity belongs to him, the papists say, it is derived from St. Peter, because he has succeeded to the chair and to the functions of that apostle. But let it be allowed for the sake of argument, though by no means conceded, that the primacy of administration over the whole church was granted to Peter; yet it does not follow from this that the same right has devolved on the Roman pontiff; for, before this inference can be deduced from such a supposition, the following propositions must be previously proved: (1.) That this right was not personal but successive. (2.) That this succession was inseparably connected with a certain chair; that he who succeeded to it enjoyed this right; and that he had in fact, by some means or other, irrefragibly gained possession of this chair. (3.) That St. Peter was bishop of Rome, and that he died in Rome while discharging the duties of that bishopric. (4.) That, from the period of St. Peter's death in the discharge of his episcopal functions at Rome, this primacy has been inseparably connected with the papal chair. All these things, therefore, they must prove by undoubted arguments, since they teach it to be of the necessity of salvation that every man be subject to the Roman pontiff.

To that God in whom, by whom, and for whom all things subsist, be praise and glory forever and ever!

DISPUTATION 19 - ON THE JUSTIFICATION OF MAN BEFORE GOD

RESPONDENT: ALARD DE VRIES

As frequent mention is made in Scripture of Justification, and since this doctrine is of great importance to salvation, and is in these days, not a little controverted, it seems that we shall not be acting unprofitably if we institute a disquisition on this subject from the Scriptures.

I. Since the word "justification" is deduced from justice, from this notion its signification will be appropriately derived. justice or righteousness, when properly considered, signifies rectitude or an agreement with right reason. (Psalm xi. 7; Ephes. vi. 14; Phil. i. 11; 1 John iii. 7.) And it is contemplated either as a quality or as an act--a quality inhering in a subject, an act produced by an efficient cause. The word "justification" denotes an act that is occupied either in infusing the quality of righteousness into some person or in acquiring it for him, or in forming a judgment on a person and his acts, and in pronouncing sentence on them.

II. If, therefore, according to its quality, justification be the acquisition of righteousness, it is the act of one who by repeated acts acquires a habit of righteousness, that is, the act of a rational creature. (Ephes. iv. 24.) If it be the infusion of righteousness, it is the act of Him who infuses the habit of righteousness into a rational creature, that is, the act of God either as creator or regenerator. (Isa. v. 23.) The justification which is occupied about a person and his acts, is the act of a Judge making an estimate in his own mind of the deed, and of the author of it, and according to that estimate, forming a judgment and pronouncing sentence, that is, the act of a man justifying the wisdom and the justice of God. (Matt. xi. 19; Psalm 81,) of a Prince justifying the cause of his subject, of a Pharisee justifying himself, (Luke xvi. 15,) of God justifying the deed of Phinehas, (Psalm cvi. 31,) and our Lord's justification of the conduct of the publican. (Luke xviii. 14.)

III. From this necessary distinction of the words it appears that Bellarmine both admits an equivocation, and feigns an adversary for himself that is not adverse to him, when he proposes the state of the controversy which exists between him and us on this doctrine in these words: "Is the righteousness by which we are formally justified, inherent or imputative?" (1.) The equivocation lies in this--that the word "justification," when it is occupied about inherent righteousness, signifies the infusion of righteousness; but when it is employed respecting imputative righteousness, it signifies the estimate of the mind, the judgment, and the pronouncing of the sentence. (3.) He invents an adversary; because no one denies that the form by which any man is intrinsically righteous, and is declared to be so, is the habit or inherent quality of righteousness. But we deny that the word "justification" is received in this sense in St. Paul's disputation against the gentiles and the Jews, (Rom. 2, 3, 4, 5,) and against the false brethren, (Gal. 2, 3, 5,) or even by St. James in his epistle. Wherefore, we must maintain, either that the controversy between the papists and us, is respecting justification when received as the act of a judge, or that our controversy has nothing in common with that of St. Paul. (James 2.)

IV. The justification, therefore, of a man before God is that by which, when he is placed before the tribunal of God, he is considered and pronounced, by God as a judge, righteous and worthy of the reward of righteousness; whence also the recompense of reward itself follows by necessity of consequence. (Rom. 2, 3; Luke xviii. 14.) But since three things come under consideration in this place--man who is to be judged, God the judge, and the law according to which judgment must be passed. Each of them may be variously considered, and it is also necessary, according to these three to vary justification itself. (1.) For man may be considered either as having discharged the works of righteousness without sin, (Rom. ii. 16,) or as a sinner. (iii, 23.) (2.) God may be viewed as seated on a throne of rigid and severe justice, (Psalm cxliii. 2,) or on a throne of grace and mercy. (Heb. iv. 16.) (3.) The law is either that of works, or that of faith; (Rom. iii. 27;) and since each of these has a natural correspondence together and mutually agree with each other, justification may be reduced to two opposite species or forms; of which the one is called that "of the law, in the law, or through the law, of the works of the law, of him that worketh and performs the law, of debt and not of grace." (Rom. 2, 3, 4, 9, 11,) But the other is styled that "of faith, from faith, through faith, of a sinner who believes, freely bestowed, of grace and not of debt, and without the works of the law." (Gal. 2, 3, 5.)

V. But since the law is two-fold, of which mention is made in the question of justification, that is, the moral and the ceremonial, (for the judicial part of the law does not in this place come under discussion,) we must see how and in what sense justification is either attributed to each of them or taken away from it. (1.) Justification is ascribed to the MORAL LAW because the works prescribed are of and in themselves pleasing to God, and are righteousness itself strictly and rigidly taken, so that he who does them is on that very account righteous, without absolution or gratuitous imputation. For this reason justification cannot be taken away from it, unless for its non-performance. (1 Sam. xv. 21, 22; Amos v. 21-,3; Rom. x. 5.) Hence justification by the moral law may be defined: "It is that by which a man, having performed the duties of the moral law without transgression, and being placed before the tribunal of the severe justice of God, is accounted and declared by God to be righteous and worthy of the reward of eternal life, in himself, of debt, according to the law, and without grace, to his own salvation, and to the glory both of divine and human righteousness." (Rom. iv. 4; iii, 27; Ephes. ii. 8, 9.)

VI. (2.) But the rule of the Ceremonial law is widely different. For its works are neither of themselves pleasing to God, to enable them to come under the name of righteousness; nor have they such a consideration that absolution from sins committed against the moral law can be obtained through them, or that they can be graciously imputed for righteousness. (Micah vi. 6-8; Col. ii. 16, 20, 21.) For this reason, in the Scriptures, justification is taken away from it, not because it was not performed, but simply on account of the weakness of itself, and not of the flesh which sinned. (Acts xiii. 39; Heb. ix. 10.) Yet its use for justification is two-fold according to its double reference to the moral law and the offenses committed against it, and to Christ and faith in Him. According to the former, it is the hand-writing recording debts and sins. (Col. ii. 14 -- 17.) According to the latter, it contains a shadow and type of Christ, and of "good things to come," that is, of righteousness and life. (Heb. x. 1.) According to the latter, it shewed Christ typically; (Gal. ii. 16;) according to the former, it compelled men to flee to Him, through faith in him. (Gal. iii. 21-24.)

VII. And this is the cause why the Apostle Paul takes away justification together and at once from the whole law, though for different causes which it is not always necessary to enumerate. (Rom. iii. 20, 28; Gal. ii. 16; John v. 24; Psalm cxliii. 2; Rom. 3, 4.) But justification is attributed to faith, not because it is that very righteousness which can be opposed to the rigid and severe judgment of God, though it is pleasing to God; but because, through the judgment of mercy triumphing over justice, it obtains absolution from sins, and is graciously imputed for righteousness. (Acts xiii. 39.) The cause of this is, not only God who is both just and merciful, but also Christ by his obedience, offering, and intercession according to God through his good pleasure and command. But it may be thus defined, "it is a justification by which a man, who is a sinner, yet a believer, being placed before the throne of grace which is erected in Christ Jesus the Propitiation, is accounted and pronounced by God, the just and merciful Judge, righteous and worthy of the reward of righteousness, not in himself but in Christ, of grace, according to the gospel, to the praise of the righteousness and grace of God, and to the salvation of the justified person himself." (Rom. iii. 24-26; 3, 4, 5, 10, 11.)

VIII. It belongs to these two forms of justification, when considered in union and in opposition. First. To be so adverse as to render it impossible for both of them at once to meet together in one subject. For he who is justified by the law, neither is capable nor requires to be justified by faith; (Rom. iv. 14, 15;) and it is evident that the man who is justified by faith could not have been justified by the law. (xi, 6.) Thus the law previously excludes faith by the cause, and faith excludes the law by the consequence of conclusion. Secondly. They cannot be reconciled with each other, either by an unconfused union, or by admixture. For they are perfect simple forms, and separated in an individual point, so that by the addition of a single atom, a transition is made from the one to the other. (Rom. iv. 4, 5; ix, 30-32.) Thirdly. Because a man must be justified by the one or the other of them, otherwise he will fall from righteousness and therefore from life. (Rom. x. 3-6, Gal. iii. 10; James ii. 10.) Because the gospel is the last revelation; "for therein is the righteousness of God revealed from faith to faith;" and, after this, no other revelation must be expected. (Heb. i. 1.)

IX. From the premises thus laid down according to the Scriptures, we conclude, that justification, when used for the act of a Judge, is either purely the imputation of righteousness through mercy from the throne of grace in Christ the propitiation made to a sinner, but who is a believer; (Rom. i. 16, 17; Gal. iii. 6, 7;) or that man is justified before God, of debt, according to the rigor of justice without any forgiveness. (Rom. 3, 4.) Because the Papists deny the latter, they ought to concede the former. And this is such a truth, that, how high soever may be the endowments of any one of the Saints in faith, hope and charity, and however numerous and excellent the works of faith, hope and charity may be which he has performed, he will receive no sentence of justification from God the Judge, unless He quit the tribunal of his severe justice and ascend the throne of grace, and from it pronounce a sentence of absolution in his favour, and unless the Lord of his mercy and pity graciously account for righteousness the whole of that good with which the saint appears before Him. For, woe to a life of the utmost innocency, if it be judged without mercy. (Psalm xxxii. 1, 2, 5, 6; cxliii, 2; 1 John i. 7-10; 1 Cor. iv. 4.) This is a confession which even the Papists seem to make when they assert, that the works of the Saints cannot stand before the judgment of God unless they be sprinkled with the blood of Christ.

X. Hence we likewise deduce: That if the righteousness by which we are justified before God, the Judge, can be called formal, or that by which we are formally justified, (for the latter is Bellarmine's phraseology,) then the formal righteousness, and that by which we are formally justified, can on no account be called "inherent;" but that, according to the phrase of the Apostle, it may in an accommodated sense be denominated "imputed," as either being that which is righteousness in God's gracious account, since it does not merit this name according to the rigor of justice or of the law, or as being the righteousness of another, that is, of Christ, which is made ours by God's gracious imputation. Nor is there any reason why they should be so abhorrent from the use of this word, "imputed," since the apostle employs the same word eleven times in the fourth chapter of his Epistle to the Romans, where the seat of this point or argument lies, and since the efficacy to salvation of God's gracious estimation is the same, as that of His severe and rigid estimation would be if man had perfectly fulfilled the law without any transgression. (2 Cor. v. 19, 21.)

XI. And though Bellarmine, by confounding the word "justification," by distinguishing faith into that which is formed and unformed, by making a difference between the works of the law, and those performed by renewed persons through the virtue of the Holy Spirit, and by not ascribing a reward even to these works, unless because it has been promised gratuitously, and promised to those who are already placed in a state of grace and of the adoption of sons, by which he confesses they have likewise a right to the heavenly inheritance, by granting besides, that the reward itself exceeds the worthiness of the work, and by bringing down to a rigid examination the whole life of the man who is to be judged, though by these methods Bellarmine endeavours to explain the sentiments of the Romish Church so as to make them appear in unison with those of the apostle; (or, at least that they may not openly clash with those of St. Paul;) yet, since the Church of Rome asserts, that the good works of the Saints fully satisfy the law of God according to the state of this life, and really merit eternal life; that when we suffer for sins by rendering satisfaction, we are made conformable to Christ Jesus who gave satisfaction for sins; and that the works of the Saints, prayer, fasting, alms-giving, and others, are satisfactory [to divine justice] for temporal punishment, indeed for every punishment, and, what is more, for guilt itself, and are thus expiatory for sins; since she declares that the sacrifice of the mass is a propitiation for the sins and punishments both of the living and the dead; and since she says that the works of some men are super-erogatory, and extols them so much as to affirm that they are useful to others for salvation; since these are the assertions of the Church of Rome, we declare that her doctrine stands directly opposed to that of the apostle.

DISPUTATION 20 - ON CHRISTIAN LIBERTY

RESPONDENT: ENGELBERT SIBELIUS

I. Liberty, generally, is a state according to which every one is at his own disposal, and not bound to another person. Bondage or slavery is opposed to it, according to which a man is not his own master, but is subject to another, either to do what he commands, to omit what he forbids, or to endure what he inflicts. Christian Liberty is so called chiefly from Christ the Author, who procured it; it has received this appellation also from its subjects, because it belongs to Christians, that is, to believers in Christ. But it pre-supposes servitude; because Christ was not necessary for any, except for "those who, through fear of death, were all their life-time subject to bondage." (Heb. ii. 15.)

II. Christian Liberty is that state of the fullness of grace and truth in which believers are placed by God through Christ, and are sealed by the Holy Spirit. It consists partly of a deliverance from both the real and the economic bondage of sin and the law, and partly of adoption into the right of the sons of God, and of the mission of the Spirit of the Son into their hearts. Its end is the praise of the glorious grace of God in Christ, and the eternal salvation of believers.

III. The efficient cause of Christian Liberty is God the Father, who offers it; (Col. i. 12, 13;) the Son, who, as Mediator, confers it; (John viii. 36; Gal. v. 1;) and the Holy Spirit, who inwardly seals it. (2 Cor. iii. 17, 18.) The internal cause is the grace of God, and his love for man in Christ Jesus. (Luke i. 78.) The external cause is the ransom, or the price of redemption, and the satisfaction, which Christ has paid. (Rom. v. 6-21; vii, 2, 3.) The sealing and preserving cause is the Holy Spirit, who is both the earnest and the witness in the hearts of believers. (Rom. viii. 15, 16; Ephes. i. 13, 14.) The instrument is two-fold. One on the part of God, who exhibits this liberty; the other on the part of man, who receives it. (1.) On the part of God, the instrument is the saving doctrine concerning the mercy of God in Christ, which is therefore called "the ministry of reconciliation." (2 Cor. v. 19.) (2.) On the part of man, it is faith in Christ. (John i. 12; Rom. v. 2; Gal. iii. 26.) The matter about which it is exercised is not only sin, and the law "which is the strength of sin;" but also the power or privilege of the sons of God, and the Spirit of Christ.

IV. The form consists in deliverance from the spiritual bondage of sin and the law, both real and economical, in the donation of the right to be the sons of God, (Col. i. 13,) and in the sending forth of the Holy Spirit into the hearts of believers. (Gal. iv. 6.) Its subjects are all believers, who are freed from the tyranny of sin and of the law, and received by God on account of Christ as sons, through the grace of adoption. (Gal. iii. 26.) The chief end is the praise of the glorious grace of God; (Ephes. i. 14;) the subordinate end is the salvation of believers. (Rom. vi. 22.) The effects or fruits are two: The first serves for consolation. (Heb. vi. 18- 20.) The other, for admonition, that "being made free from sin, we may become the servants of righteousness." (Rom. vi. 18-22; 1 Pet. ii. 16.)

V. But because this liberty is opposed to the bondage which preceded it, we must on this account treat in the first place about that bondage, that the design of this liberty may be the more easily rendered evident. We must know, that the first man was created free by God; but that, having abused his liberty, he lost it, and was made the slave of him to whom he yielded obedience, that is, to sin, both as it respects the guilt of condemnation and its dominion; which is real bondage and consummate misery. To this succeeded the economical bondage, [or that of the dispensation of Moses,] which God introduced by the repetition of the Moral Law, and by the imposition of the Ceremonial. The bondage under the Moral Law was its rigid demands, by which man, being reduced to despair of fulfilling it, might acknowledge the tyranny of sin which reigned or held dominion over him. The bondage under the Ceremonial Law was its testifying to condemnation; by which man might be convinced of guilt, and thus through both these kinds of bondage might flee to Christ, who could deliver him from the guilt of sin and from its dominion.

VI. Let us now see how believers are delivered from this bondage by Christian liberty. We will restrict this consideration to the church of the New Testament, to which the whole of this liberty belongs, omitting the believers under the Old Testament. Though to these likewise belonged, through the promise of the blessed seed and through faith in Him, (Gen. iii. 15; xv, 6,) a deliverance from real bondage, the privilege of the sons of God, and the Spirit of adoption, which was intermixed with the spirit of economical bondage. (Gal. iv. 1-3.)

VII. We circumscribe Christian liberty within four ranks or degrees. The First degree consists in a freedom from the guilt and condemnation of sin, which has been expiated by the blood of Christ, by faith in which we obtain remission of sins, and justification from those things from which we could not be absolved by the law of Moses. The Second degree consists in the deliverance from the dominion and tyranny of indwelling sin; because its power is mortified and weakened by the Spirit of Christ dwelling in us, that it may no longer have dominion over those who are under grace. (Rom. vi. 14.) But both these degrees of Christian Liberty have their origin in this--that sin was condemned in the flesh of Christ, and it therefore does not possess the power either to condemn or to command. (Rom. viii. 3.)

VIII. We place the Third degree in the attempering of that rigor by which God demanded the observance of the Moral Law in the primeval state, and could afterwards have demanded it, if it had been his pleasure still to act towards men in the same manner. Indeed, God did actually demand it, but in an economical way, from the people of the Old Testament; of which he gave manifest indications in that terrific legislation on Mount Sinai. (Exod. xx. 18; Gal. iv. 24, 25.) "But we are come unto Mount Sion, and to Jesus the Mediator of the new covenant," whose "yoke is easy and his burden light;" (Isa. ii. 3; Micah iv. 2; Heb. xii. 18-24; Matt. xi. 30;) because Christ has broken the yoke of exaction, and it has been the good pleasure of God to treat with man according to clemency in the compact of the New Testament.

IX. We place the Fourth degree in a freedom from the economical bondage of the ceremonial law, which had a fourfold respect under the Old Testament. (1.) For it was the seal of condemnation, and the hand-writing, or bond of our debt. (Gal. iii. 21; Heb. x. 3, 4.) (2.) It was a symbol and token, by which the Jews might be distinguished from all other nations till the advent of Christ. (Gen. xvii. 13. 14.) (3.) It was a typical shadowing forth of Christ, and a prefiguration of his benefits. (Heb. ix. 9, 10; x, 1.) (4.) Lastly, it resembled a sentinel or guard, a schoolmaster and tutor, by whom the church might be safely kept, in its state of infancy, under the elements of the world, in hopes of the promised and approaching Messiah, and might be led to faith in Him, and be conducted to Him, as St. Paul teaches at the conclusion of the third chapter of his Epistle to the Galatians, and at the commencement of the fourth.

X. The First of these respects of the Ceremonial Law must have been removed, after the condemnation of sin was taken away, of which it was the seal. But we have already shewn in the seventh Thesis, that this condemnation has been abolished by Christ. The consequence, therefore is, that it has also obtained its end or purpose; as St. Paul teaches us in Col. ii. 14, where he says, Christ has blotted out the hand-writing of ordinances that was against us, which was contrary to us, and took it out of the way, nailing it to his cross." He sprinkled it over with his own blood and obliterated it. For the Second also of these respects, a place can no longer be found, since the Gentiles, "who were formerly far off, have been made nigh by the blood of Christ. For he is our peace, who hath made both one, and hath broken down the middle wall of partition between us. Having abolished in his flesh the enmity, even the law of commandments contained in ordinances; for to make in himself, of twain, One New Man, so making peace," &c. (Ephes. ii. 13-15.) The Third respect consisted of types and shadows which prefigured Christ with his benefits. This can on no account continue after the body or substance itself has been already displayed. (Col. ii. 17.) And, lastly, the Fourth respect, since the advent of Christ, is useless. For when the heir has arrived at the age of maturity, he no longer requires a governor, tutor and schoolmaster, but is himself capable of managing his inheritance, of being his own adviser, and of consulting his own judgment in the things to be possessed. Thus, after the church has passed through the years of infancy, and has entered on the age of maturity in Christ, it is no longer held under the Mosaic worship, under the beggarly elements of this world," but is subject to the guidance of the Spirit of Christ. (Rom. viii. 15; Gal. iv. 4-7.) Grievous, therefore, is the error of the Pharisees and the Ebionites, in which they maintained, that the observance of the ceremonial law must be joined to the gospel, even by those Christians who had previously been Gentiles.

XI. To this Fourth degree of Christian Liberty we add, the free use and exercise of things indifferent. Yet it has been the will of God, that this liberty should be circumscribed by two laws, that of charity and that of faith, (Rom. xiv. 5, 14; 13,) thus consulting his own glory and the salvation of his church. The law of faith prescribes that you be rightly instructed concerning the legitimate use of things indifferent; and sufficiently confirmed [or "fully persuaded in your own mind."] The law of charity commands you to procure the edification of your neighbour, whether he be a weak brother or one who is confirmed. You have examples in Romans 14; 1 Cor. 8; 9; x, 27-33; Acts xvi. 3. It is a part of the same law, that you should abide by the ceremonies which are received in the church, lest by an outrageous and unseasonable change you produce a schism in the church, or be the cause of much trouble.

I. Those persons, therefore, err greatly who, in abstaining from this liberty, prefer their own private advantage and happiness to the edification of their neighbour.

II. They err still more grievously who abuse this liberty to satiate the lusts of the flesh, (Gal. v. 13,) or by an unseasonable zeal to despise and offend their weak brethren. (Rom. xiv. 3, 10.)

III. But those err the most grievously of all who either affix the observance of necessity to things indifferent, or suppose those things to be indifferent which are by no means such.

XII. To these, perhaps not without profit, we shall add a Fifth degree of liberty, that is, an immunity from the judicial laws of the Jewish courts. On this subject we must hold, that the political laws of Moses contain, (1.) The political common law of nature. (2.) A particular law suited to the Jewish nation. The common law of nature embraces the universal notions of justice, equity and honesty. The particular law, as it was peculiar to the Jewish nation, was so far defined by certain determinations, according to the persons for whose benefit it was confirmed, according to the affairs and transactions concerning which it was confirmed, and the circumstances with which it was confirmed. Hence a judgment ought to be formed of the immutability and mutability of these laws. Whatever has been appointed for the general good, according to the universal principles of nature and the common design of the moral law, either by commanding or forbidding, by rewarding or punishing, it is immutable. Therefore, to such a thing Christian Liberty does not extend itself. What portion soever of the particular law has a particular respect, it is changeable. Christians, therefore, are not bound by these laws, so far as they are determined by a particular law after the manner of the Jewish Commonwealth, that is, of particular persons, actions, and of a particular end or good. But with regard to those portions of these laws which are of a mixed kind, we must distinguish in them that which is moral from that which is political. Whatever is moral, is binding, and remains either by common reason or by analogy. Whatever is political, is not binding with regard to particular determinations.

Therefore, we disapprove of the ridiculous imitation adopted by Monetarius and Carolastadius, who obliged Christian magistrates to the necessity of observing the peculiar forensic laws of Moses in their administration of justice.

XIII. The privilege or right of the sons of God, and the sending of the spirit of adoption into the hearts of believers follow this liberty from the bondage of sin and the law, to which is annexed peace of conscience. (Rom. viii. 15; Gal. iv. 5, 6.) That right consists in their being constituted heirs of God and joint heirs with Christ; and to this privilege belongs not only the blessed immortality of their souls, but likewise the deliverance of their bodies from vanity, and from the bondage of corruption into the glorious liberty of the children of God; which also comes under the name of adoption, and is called "the redemption of our bodies." (Rom. viii. 15-23.) Hence, likewise those who shall be "the children of the resurrection," are called "the children of God." (Luke xx. 36.) But the Spirit of adoption is sent into the hearts of the sons of God, as being the Spirit of the Son, that He may be the earnest, the seal, and the first-fruits of this inheritance; (Gal. iv. 6; 2 Cor. i. 22; Ephes. i. 14;) by which we are assured, that, as "our life is hidden with Christ in God, when Christ shall gloriously appear we shall also be manifested with him in glory." (Col. iii. 4.) And thus the liberty of glory, that will endure forever, will succeed to this liberty of grace, which we obtain in this world by Christ Jesus our Lord, through faith in his blood: To whom be praise forever!

In the place of a conclusion it is inquired,

I. Whether freedom from the bondage of sin, and from economical bondage, be effected by one and the same act, or by two acts? We affirm the former.

II. Whether it is lawful to eat those things which are offered in sacrifice to idols? We make a distinction.

DISPUTATION 21 - ON THE ROMAN PONTIFF, AND THE PRINCIPAL TITLES WHICH ARE ATTRIBUTED TO HIM

RESPONDENT: JOHN MARTINIUS

I. For many ages past, all who have had any knowledge of the Pope of Rome, have held no low or moderate sentiments about him, but have entertained exaggerated notions about him and uttered the most lofty and excessive eulogies. This was required by that sublime degree of dignity to which he has been elevated. Yet the things which have been spoken concerning him are so diverse, as well as adverse, as to render it matter of wonder that such various and contrary judgments and eulogies about one and the same person, can be found among men who are Christians, at least so far as their own profession is concerned. For some persons not only adorn, but literally load him with titles the most honourable, when they give him the appellation of the spouse, the head, the foundation of the Catholic Church, the vicar of God and Christ on earth, the absolute lord of the whole Christian world with regard to spiritual things, in temporal things likewise, so far as they are ordained for spiritual things, and the Prince of Pastors and of Bishops. Others disparage him with titles quite contrary, such as, the adulterer and pimp of the Church, the false prophet, the destroyer and subverter of the Church, the enemy of God and the Antichrist, the wicked and perverse servant, who neither discharges the duties of a Bishop, nor is worthy to bear the name. Uniting ourselves with the band of those who bestow on the Roman Pontiff the epithets last cited, we assert that he is unworthy of the honourable titles which precede them, and that the latter disparaging epithets are attributed to Him through his just deserts, which we now proceed to prove in a few Theses.

II. The Spouse and Husband of the church universal is one by a most particular unity, otherwise the church would be an adulteress. His properties are these: He has loved the church, has exposed or given himself for her, has purchased her for himself, with his own blood, has formed her of his own flesh and bones by the Spirit of regeneration, hath sanctified and cleansed her by his own blood and by his Spirit, that he might present her holy, unblamable and glorious. (Ephes. v. 25-27; Acts xx. 28.) He has sealed her for an espoused wife to himself by the earnest of his Spirit, as with a nuptial ring, (2 Cor. i. 21, 22; Rom. viii. 9, 15, 16,) and imparts to her his own blessings necessary and sufficient for life and salvation. (Ephes. v. 23.) To Him the church has respect, and asks, expects and receives all good things from Him alone. (Acts iv. 12; Rev. xxii. 17.) And to Him the apostles [and their successors] are preparing to present her as a chaste virgin to one husband." (2 Cor. xi. 2.) These properties belong to Christ alone: But the Roman Pontiff is not Christ. Therefore, he is neither the spouse nor the husband of the church universal. Nor can any greater affinity be framed between Christ and the Roman Pontiff, even when conducting himself in the best manner, than that which is signified by the word "the friend of the bridegroom," and "the brideman." (John iii. 29.)

III. The Head of the church is but one; otherwise the church would be a monster. His properties are these: He is united to the church by the internal bond of the Spirit and of faith (John xvii. 15-17; 1 Cor. vi. 17, 19; Ephes. iii. 17.) The church is subject and subordinate to Him. (Ephes. v. 24, 25.) He perfectly contains within himself all things necessary for the life and salvation of the church. He inspires life, sensation and motion into the church by the efficacy of the Spirit. (Gal. ii. 20.) He is affected with the evils which afflict the whole church and the members in general and in particular. (Heb. iv. 15.) He suffers the persecutions and afflictions which are endured by the church, feeling them as much as if they were inflicted on his own body, and He relieves them. (Acts ix. 4, 5.) In his person the church is raised up together, and seated together in heavenly places in Him. (Ephes. ii. 6.) And therefore, she has her woliteuma "the administration of her public affairs," in heaven. (Phil. iii. 20.) All these properties agree with Christ only. But the Roman Pontiff is not Christ; and therefore, he is neither the head of the church, nor can any affinity be established between Christ, and the Roman Pontiff, which is not signified in the name of some particular member of the body, or of a duty belonging to some member. (Rom. xii. 4-8.) And no greater dignity can belong to the Pope of Rome, under Christ the head, than that which is comprehended under the words, an apostle, prophet, evangelist, teacher, pastor, bishop, [one who can exercise] the power [of working mirades,] the gift of healing, help and government. (1 Cor. xii. 4, 6-31.) All these dignities are ascribed to the members of the body of the church. Therefore, on account of none of them does the title of "head" appertain to this Pontiff.

IV. The Foundation of the church universal is only one, because there is but one house of God and Christ. Its properties are these: It stands by its own power, and does not rest on any extrinsic foundation. (1 Tim. iii. 15.) The whole house, consisting of two people, the Jews and the Gentiles, is built upon this foundation, as upon a chief corner-stone, and is sustained, by the power implanted in it, against all things which can assail it from without, whether from above or from below, on its sides, on the right hand and on the left; it continues immovable, does not totter, is not sunk or overwhelmed, and does not fall. (Heb. iii. 6; Ephes. ii. 20-22; Matt. xvi. 18.) This foundation is the immediate fulcrum or prop and firm support to all the lively stones that are built upon it; "they who believe on Him shall not be ashamed;" but it is also a stone of stumbling and a rock of offense to those who do not believe and are disobedient; it dashes them in pieces, and they perish. (Isa. xxviii. 16; 1 Pet. ii. 4-6.) All these properties, both generally and severally, belong to Christ alone. But the Roman Pontiff is not Christ. Therefore, neither is he the foundation of the church. But the metonymy, by which the Prophets and Apostles are called "the foundations of the church," (Rev. xxi. 14,) and by which the saints are said to be "built upon the foundation of the Apostles and Prophets," (Ephes. ii. 20,) attributes nothing more to them, than their being "labourers together with God" in laying down Christ as this foundation, and in building up the whole house on Him. (1 Cor. iii. 5-12.) But St. Peter was also among these; yet he excelled none of the other Apostles in any prerogative, but was inferior to St. Paul, not indeed in power, but in "the more abundant labour" of the latter in building up the church. (1 Cor. xv. 10.)

V. God's Vicar-General, or Universal, is one who administers all things in heaven and on earth in the name, at the command, and by the authority of God. To this individual must necessarily appertain, (1.) A Power, inferior indeed, by reason of the dispensation, to his who appointed him, yet most closely approaching to it, and dependent on no other power than that of God. (John v. 22, 26, 27.) So that this power may, not undeservedly, be called autocratorical, possessing within itself absolute sovereignty, and pantocratorical, omnipotent or having power over all things. (John xvii. 2, 24.) (2.) The Knowledge, as well as the Power necessary to administer all things. It cannot be less than divine; for it must be extended to all things generally, and to every thing in particular, and this in an immediate manner if we consider the internal efficacy of government. (1 Cor. xv. 27; Rev. 2 and 3; Phil. iii. 21; Gal. ii. 20.) And this Vicar of God is only Christ, to whom alone these properties belong. But the Roman Pontiff is not Christ. Therefore, he is not God's Universal Vicar, not even in the church, because the same considerations, apply to her as to the whole universe. In the same way, the Universal Vicar of Christ will be one who pleads the cause of Christ, and who, with a power and wisdom purely divine administers all things in His name and by his authority. (John i. 6-8, 13-15.) And this is the Spirit of Christ, his advocate, the Spirit of wisdom and of the power of God, who, in the name of Christ, appoints apostles, prophets, teachers, and bishops; who leads and governs believers, but who convinces and condemns unbelievers. (Acts xx. 28; xiii, 2; Rom. viii. 14.) The Roman Pontiff is not that Spirit, nor hath he received the Spirit without measure. (Rom. xii. 3.) Neither can the Roman Pontiff, even when his conduct is most exemplary, have any other delegated power under Christ, than that which is particular; because he is not endued with the Spirit, except "according to the measure of the gift of Christ." (Ephes. iv. 7.) And this is bestowed [on the pontiff] not with regard to Christ as a priest, (for that office does not admit of a vicar, or substitute,) but as he is king and prophet supreme, and only so far as concerns the external administration of some part of Christ's kingdom and people, either by doctrine or by government, the internal administration in the mean time remaining entirely vested in Christ, as does also his Spirit. (1 Cor. iii. 5-23.)

VI. The Dominion Over Heaven And Earth, or over the whole church, (for these cannot be separated,) appertains by divine gift to Him alone who has said, "All things are delivered unto me of my Father." (Matt. xi. 27.) "All things which the Father hath, are mine." (John xvii. 10.) "All power is given unto me in heaven and in earth: Go ye therefore, and teach all nations." (Matt. xxviii. 18.) "As thou hast given Him power over all flesh, that He should give eternal life to as many as thou hast given Him." (John xvii. 2.) "Whom God hath set at his own right hand in the heavens, far above all principality, and power, and might, and dominion, and every name that is named, not only in this world, but also in that which is to come." (Ephes. i. 21.) Who is called the beginning," or the principle, "the first-born from the dead; that in all things He might have the preeminence." (Col. i. 18.) In whom the church is "complete; who is the head of all principality and power." (Col. ii. 10.) "On whose vesture and thigh a name is written KING of Kings, and LORD of Lords." (Rev. xix. 16.) Christ alone is thus described. But the Roman Pontiff is not Christ. The distinction of plenary power, with regard to spiritual, and temporals, is contrary both to plenitude of power and to the subordination of things spiritual and temporal; and has been fabricated on account of the defect of the capability of which the pontiff is destitute, to subject temporal things to himself, even among those nations over whom he has obtained the power in spiritual matters.

VII. The Prince of bishops, apostles, prophets, evangelists, pastors, and teachers, is one. (1 Cor. xii. 4, 5, &c.) If it were otherwise, there would be more than a single monarch and dictator in the church, when only one is requisite in a monarchical state and government; but then Duumviri, two governors, would hold the pre-eminence. His properties are these: To institute, sanctify, and set apart to the work of the ministry, apostles, prophets, evangelists, pastors, teachers, and all bishops in the church. (Ephes. iv. 5, 6, 11-13.) To prescribe to them what they must say and do. (Matt. xxviii. 18-20.) To furnish them with necessary and sufficient gifts. (Rom. xii. 3; 2 Cor. iii. 5, 6.) To be present with them, in the power of his Spirit and grace, while engaged in the discharge of their functions. (Matt. xxviii. 20.) To give efficacy to their ministrations. (Mark xvi. 20; 1 Cor. iii. 6.) To compel them to render an account. To make a distinction between the acts and omissions of each; and, according to the different mode of their administrations, to adjudge rewards or punishments. (1 Pet. v. 4; Matt. xxv. 19-30.) And these properties belong to Christ alone. But the Roman Pontiff is not Christ. Therefore, he is not the Prince of bishops; but if he have any claim to this office, even when he behaves himself in his best manner, he cannot be called by any other name than that of a bishop, pastor, or teacher, who ought to acknowledge all bishops as his fellow elders, without any disparity of the power which belongs to the essence of the office. (1 Pet. v. 1.)

VIII. Since, therefore, the Roman Pontiff either attributes these most honourable titles of Christ to himself, or willingly suffers them to be ascribed to him; and since he evinces no horror at the blasphemy contained in these titles, and gives no tokens of his displeasure at this ascription of them; it follows, that he puts himself in the place of Christ, and is supremely opposed to Him. There is no excuse in the explanation which is given, that "the head and foundation is ministerial, and that he attributes all these things to himself under Christ, as having been elevated by the grace or favour of God and Christ to that dignity." For the protestation is directly contrary to the fact; and he is so much the more the bitter enemy of God and Christ, as he the more confidently boasts of being defended by the authority of God and Christ. Such conduct is, in fact, under the semblance of friendship to exercise the deepest enmity, and, under the disguised pretext of a minister of light and of righteousness, to promote the interests of the kingdom of darkness and of unrighteousness. On this very account, therefore, we assert that the disparaging epithets which we laid down in our first Thesis, most justly belong to him; and this we now proceed to show by descending to particulars.

IX. First. The name of the Adulterer and The Pimp of the Church is his. (1.) He is the Adulterer of the church, both by the public and mutual profession of each other; because he calls the [Roman Catholic] church his and she neither disowns the arrogance of this title nor is afraid of the odium [attached to such assumption,] and he is the adulterer in reality. For he practices spiritual adultery with the church, and she in return with him. He commands the apocryphal writings to be accounted divine and canonical; the ancient Latin version of the Scriptures, [commonly called] the vulgate, to be every where received as the true original, and under no pretense whatever to be rejected; his own interpretations of the Scriptures to be embraced with the most undoubting faith; and unwritten traditions to be honoured with an affection and reverence equal to that evinced for the written word of God. He enacts and rescinds laws that pertain to faith and morals, and binds them as fetters on consciences. He promises and offers plenary indulgences, and the remission of all sins, through the plenitude of his power. "He exalteth himself above all that is worshipped," and offers himself as some god to be adored with religious worship. In all these acts the church, deceived by his artifices, complies with his wishes. He is, therefore, the Adulterer of the church. (2.) But he is also the Pimp or Pander of the church, because he acts towards her as the author, persuader, impelling exciter and procurer of various spiritual adulteries committed, or to be hereafter committed, with different husbands, with angels, Mary and other deceased saints, with images of God, of Christ, of the Holy Ghost, of the cross, of angels, of Mary, and of saints; with the bread in the sacrament of the Lord's Supper; and with other inanimate objects.

X. To him likewise belongs the name of The False Prophet, whom the Scripture calls "the tail," in opposition to "the head;" (Isa. ix. 15;) and this, whether it be received in a general acceptation, or in a particular sense and restricted to a certain and determinate person. (1.) In its general meaning, whether it signifies him who teaches falsehood without arrogating to himself the name of a prophet, or him who falsely boasts of being a prophet, the latter of which seems to be the proper signification of the word. (2 Pet. ii. 1; Acts xiii. 6.) For, first, he partly introduced into the church many false dogmas; and partly those which were introduced when such a great mystery of iniquity was finished, he defends, maintains and propagates. Of this kind, the dogmas concerning the insufficiency of the scriptures without traditions, to prove and confirm ever necessary truth, and to confute all errors; that it is of the last necessity unto salvation for every human creature to be under subjection to the Roman pontiff; that the bread in the Lord's supper is transubstantiated, or changed in substance, into the body of Christ; that in the mass Christ is daily offered by the priest as a propitiatory sacrifice for the sins of the living and of the dead; that man is justified before God, partly by faith, and partly by works; that there is a purgatory, into which the souls of those enter who are not yet sufficiently purified, and that they are released from it by prayers, intercessions, watchings, alms-deeds, indulgences, &c. In the Second sense, this epithet is due to him, because he says that he is a prophet, who, on account of the perpetual assistance of the Holy Spirit, which is attached to that chair, cannot possibly err in things which pertain to faith and morals. (2.) But it also belongs to him in the restricted meaning of the word; because the Roman pontiff is "the false prophet who works miracles before the beast, (Rev. xix. 20,) "out of whose mouth comes out three unclean spirits like frogs," (xvi, 13,) and who is not improperly understood to be "the tail of the great red dragon, that drew the third part of the stars of heaven." (xii, 4.)

XI. He is also deservedly called The Destroyer And Subverter Of The Church. For since the superstructure of the church "is built by the faith of the doctrine of the apostles and prophets, which rests on Jesus Christ himself, the chief Corner-stone," since it likewise increases more and more through the obedience of faith in the right worship of the Deity and in the pursuit after holiness; and since it is built up in the Lord, being fitly framed together into one body through the bond of peace and concord; (Ephes. ii. 20, 21; iv, 3; 2 Pet. ii. 5, 6;) the Roman pontiff demonstrates himself to be, in a four-fold manner, the subverter of this edifice: First, by perverting the faith. This he effects, (1.) By adding the books of the apocrypha and unwritten traditions to the prophetical and apostolical scriptures. (2.) By joining himself, as another foundation, with Christ who is the only foundation. (3.) By mixing numerous false dogmas with those which are true. (4.) By taking away some things that are true, or corrupting them by false interpretations. Secondly, by adulterating the integrity of divine worship. This he does, (1.) By an addition to the persons who alone, according to God and his command, are to be objects of worship. (2.) By the introduction of a method which is expressly forbidden by God. (3.) By introducing vain, ridiculous and old wives' superstitions. (4.) By the institution of various peculiar societies of devotees, separate fraternities, and newly fabricated religious orders of Francis, Dominic, &c. Thirdly, by vitiating the purity or soundness of holiness and morals. This he accomplishes chiefly by the following acts: (1.) By inventing easy methods of obtaining remission of sins and plenary indulgences. (2.) By declaring certain precepts in the name of councils. (3.) By absolving many persons from the obligation of their duties. (4.) By binding men to [the performance of] those things, which no one whatever is capable of understanding or accomplishing. (5.) By bringing into the Christian world the worst examples of all wickedness. Fourthly, by breaking the bond of concord and unity. This he effects chiefly by these acts and artifices, (1.) When he arrogates to himself a power over others, which by no right belongs to him. (2.) When he obtrudes many false dogmas to be believed as true, and unnecessary things as absolutely necessary. (3.) By excommunications and senseless fulminations, by which he madly rages against those who have not deserved such treatment, and who are not subject to his diocese. (4.) When he excites dissensions between princes, republics and magistrates and their subjects; or when he foments, increases and perpetuates such dissensions, after they have been raised in other quarters.

XII. It is demonstrable by the most evident arguments that the name of Antichrist and of The Adversary of God belongs to him. For the apostle ascribes the second of these epithets to him when he calls him "the man of sin, the son of perdition, who opposeth and exalteth himself above all that is called God, or that is worshipped; so that he, as God, sitteth in the temple of God, shewing himself that he is God." (2 Thess. ii. 3-8.) It was he who should arise out of the ruins of the Roman empire, and should occupy its vacant dignity. These expressions, we assert, must be understood, and can be understood, solely respecting the Roman pontiff. But the name of "The Antichrist" belongs to him pre-eminently, whether the particle anti signifies opposition, or the substitution of one thing for another; not indeed such a substitution as is lawfully and legitimately made by Him who has the power of placing things in subordination, but it signifies one by which any man is substituted, either by himself or by another person through force and fraud. For he is both a rival to Christ, and his adversary, when he boasts of himself as the spouse, the head, and the foundation of the church, endowed with plenitude of power; and yet he professes himself to be the vicegerent of Christ, and to perform his functions on earth, for the sake of his own private advantage, but to the manifest injury of the church of Christ. He has, however, considered it necessary to employ the name of Christ as a pretext, that under this sacred name he may obtain that reverence for himself among Christians, which he would be unable to procure if he were openly to profess himself to be either the Christ, or the adversary of Christ.

XIII. Although the Roman pontiff calls himself "the servant of the servants of God," yet we further assert that he is by way of eminence, That Wicked And Perverse Servant, who, when he saw that his Lord delayed his coming, "began to smite his fellow-servants." (Matt. 24, 48.) For the Roman pontiff has usurped domination and tyranny, not only over his fellow-servants, the bishops of the church of God, but likewise over emperors and kings themselves, whose authority and dignity he had himself previously acknowledged. To acquire this domination for himself, and still further to augment and establish it, he has employed all kinds of satanic instruments--sophistical hypocrisy, lies, equivocations, perfidy, perjury, violence, poison, and armed forces--so that he may most justly be said to have succeeded that formidable beast which "was like unto a leopard, a bear and a lion," and by which the Roman empire was prefigured--and to have "had power to give life unto the image of the beast, and to cause that as many as would not worship the image of the beast, should be killed."

XIV. Lastly, though from all these remarks it will readily appear that the Roman pontiff is unworthy of the name of apostle, prophet, evangelist, pastor, teacher, and of universal bishop; (1 Cor. iii. 5; xii, 28; Ephes. iv. 11;) yet, by this single argument, which is deduced from their peculiar attributes and duties, the very same satisfactory conclusions may be rendered evident to all who search the scriptures of the Old and the New Testament, and especially the epistles of St. Paul to Timothy and Titus. (1 Tim. 3;

Tit. 1.) Nor will this evasion avail any thing, "that whatever a man does through another who is his vicar or substitute, he seems to do it himself;" for it is Christ alone who makes use of the vicarious aid of these persons as ministers; and the duties which they perform, are such as ought to be discharged by those who are distinguished by those titles. (Gal. i. 7-9.) Therefore, that rightly appertains to the Roman pontiff which God threatens through the prophet Zechariah, that he will raise up a foolish shepherd, and an idol shepherd, who shall devote no attention to the sheep, but who "shall eat the flesh of the fat, and tear their claws in pieces." (Zech. xi. 15-17.) God grant that the church, being delivered from the frauds and tyranny of Antichrist, may obtain shepherds that may feed her in truth, charity and prudence, to the salvation of the sheep themselves, and to the glory of the chief Shepherd. Amen.

COROLLARIES

I. It is a part of religious wisdom to separate the Court of Rome from the church, in which the pontiff sits.

II. The Roman pontiff, even when conducting himself with the greatest propriety, must not be acknowledged by any human or positive right as the head of the church, or the universal bishop; and such acknowledgment of him has hitherto contributed, and does in its very nature contribute, not so much to preserve unity in the church, and to restrain the license of thinking, speaking and teaching differently on the chief articles of religion, as to take away necessary liberty, and that which is agreeable to the word of God, and to introduce a real tyranny.

DISPUTATION 22 - THE CASE OF ALL THE PROTESTANT OR REFORMED CHURCHES, WITH RESPECT TO THEIR ALLEGED SECESSION

RESPONDENT: JAMES CUSINE

We assert that the Reformed Churches have not seceded from the church of Rome; and that they have acted properly in refusing to hold and profess a communion of faith and of divine worship with her.

I. I feel disposed to prove, in few words, for the glory of God, for the tranquillity of weak consciences, and for the direction of erring minds--that those congregations who take upon themselves the title of "Reformed or Protestant Churches," have not made a secession from the church of Rome, and that they have acted aright, that is, wisely, piously, justly, and moderately, in refusing to hold and profess communion of faith and worship with the Romish church.

II. By the term, "the Church of Rome," we understand, not that congregation of men, who, confined within the walls of the city of Rome, profess the Christian faith, (although this is the only proper interpretation of that term;) not the court of Rome, which consists of the pope and of the cardinals united with him--not the representative church, assembled together in council, and having the Roman pontiff as president, nor the pope of Rome himself, who, under the cover of that title, extols and makes merchandise of his power. But by "the church of Rome" we understand a congregation of Christian, which was formerly dispersed through nearly the whole of Europe, but which is now become more contracted, and in which the Roman pontiff sits, either as the head of the church under Christ, but placed above a general council, or as the principal bishop inferior to a general council, the inspector and guardian of the whole church. This congregation professes, according to the canons contained in the council of Trent, that it believes in God and Christ, and performs acts of worship to them; and it approves of those canons, either because they were composed by the council of Trent, which could not err--or because it thinks that they are agreeable to the holy Scriptures and to the doctrine of the ancient fathers, without any regard to that council.

III. We call "Reformed churches" those congregations professing the Christian faith which disavow every species of presidency whatever, assumed by the Roman pontiff, and profess to believe in and to perform acts of worship to God and Christ, according to the canons which each of them has comprised in its own confession or catechism; and they approve of such canons, therefore, only because they consider them to be agreeable to the Holy Scriptures, though they yield to the primitive church and the ancient fathers severally their proper places, but always in subordination to the Scriptures.

IV. It cannot be said, that every church makes a secession, which separates from another, neither does the church that is in any manner whatever severed from another, to which it had been united; but a church is said to make a secession from another church to which it was formerly united, when it first and willingly makes a separation in that matter about which they were previously at unity. On this account it is necessary, that these four conditions concur together in the church which can justly be said to have made a secession. One of them is a prerequisite, as if necessarily precedent; the other three are requisites, as if natural to the secession and grounded upon it. The First is that it was formerly in union with the other; to which must be added, an explanation of the matter in which this union consists. The Second is, that a separation has been effected, and indeed in that thing about which it was formerly at unity with the other. The Third is, that it was the first to make the secession. And the Fourth is, that it voluntarily seceded. The whole of these conditions will come under our diligent consideration in the disputation on the present controversy about the dissension between the church of Rome and Reformed churches.

V. But the explanation of another matter must be given, prior to the discussion of this question according to the circumstances now premised; and this is, "In what generally, do the union and the separation of churches consist?" So far as they are the churches of God and of Christ, their Union consists in the following particulars: they have one God and Father, one Lord Jesus Christ, one faith, (or one doctrine of faith,) one hope of their calling, (that is, an inheritance which has been promised and for which they hope,) one baptism, (Ephes. iv. 3-6,) one bread and wine, (1 Cor. x. 16, 17,) and have been joined together in one Spirit with God and Christ, by the bond of faith and charity. (Ephes. iv. 15; Phil. ii. 2.) That is, that by agreement of faith according to truth, and by concord of the will according to charity, they may be one among themselves. This is in no other manner, than as many members of the same body are one among themselves, because all of them have been united with their head, from which, by the bond of the Spirit, life, sensation and motion are derived to each; (Rom. xii. 4; 1 Cor. xii. 12, 13; Ephes. i. 22;) and as many children in the same family are one among themselves, because all of them are connected with their parents by the bond of consanguinity and love. (1 Cor. xiv. 33; Rev. ii.

23.) For all particular churches, whether in amplitude they be greater or less, are large or small members of that great body which is called "the Catholic church;" and in this great family, which is called "the house of God," they are all sisters, according to that passage in Solomon's Song, "We have a little sister." (viii, 8.) No church on earth is the mother of any other church, (Gal. iv. 26,) not even that church from which proceeded the teachers who founded other churches. (Acts viii. 1, 4; xiii, 1, 2.) For no church on earth is the whole body, that is united to Christ the Head. (Heb. xii. 22, 23.)

VI. From this description of union among churches, and by an explanation made through similar things according to the Scriptures, it is evident, that, for the purpose of binding churches together, the intervention of two means is necessary. The First is, the bond itself by which they are united. The Second is, God and Christ, with whom being immediately united, they are mediately further united with each other. For the first and immediate relation is between each particular church and Christ. The second and mediate is between a particular church and another of its own kindred. (1 Cor. xii. 12, 13; Ephes. iv. 3; Rom. xii. 5; John xvii. 21; Ephes. ii. 11 13; iv, 16.) From these a two-fold order may be laid down, according to which this conjunction may be considered. (1.) One is, if it take its commencement from Christ, and if that bond intervene, which, issuing from Him, proceeds to every church and [adunat, makes it one,] unites it with Him. Where (i.) Christ must be constituted the Head and the very center of union. (ii.) The Spirit, which, issuing from Christ, proceeds hither and thither. (Ephes. ii. 18; v, 23; Rom. viii. 9.) (iii.) The church of Corinth, at Rome, at Philippi, &c., each of which is united to Christ, by the Spirit that goes forth from Him and proceeds towards the churches, and that abides in them. (1 John iii. 24; iv, 13.) (2.) The other order is, if it take its commencement from the churches, and if that bond intervene which, issuing from them, proceeds to Christ, and binds them to Him. Where (i.) must be placed the churches of Corinth, of Rome, of Philippi, &c. (ii.) Then may be laid down the faith proceeding from each of them. (iii.) Christ, to whom the faith of all these churches tends and connects each of them with Him. (1 John ii. 24; Ephes. iii. 17.) Because the bond of charity is mutual, it proceeds from Christ to each church, and from every church to Christ. (Ephes. v. 25.) It does not, however, remain there, but goes on to each kindred church; yet so that every church loves her sister church in Christ and for his sake, otherwise it is a confederacy without Christ, or rather against Christ. (1 Cor. xvi. 1, 2, 19.)

VII. From the relation of this union, must be estimated the Separation which is opposed to it, and which cannot be made or explained except by an analysis and resolution of their uniting together. Every particular church therefore must be separated from God and Christ before it can be separated from the church which is allied to it and of the same body; (Ephes. ii. 10, 19-22;) and the bond of faith and charity must be broken before any church can be separated from God and Christ, and thus from any other church. (Rom. xi. 17-24.) But since the Spirit of Christ, the faith by which we believe, and charity, are invisible things which belong to the very inward union and communion of Christ and the churches, it is impossible for men to form any estimate or judgment from them, respecting the union or separation of churches. On this account it is necessary, that certain external things, which are objects of the senses, and which by a certain analogy answer to those inward things, should be placed before men, that we may be able to form a judgment concerning the union of the churches with Christ and among each other, and about their opposite separation. Those external things are the word, and the visible signs annexed to the word, by which Christ has communication with his church; the profession of faith and of worship, and the exercise of charity by outward works, by which each church testifies its individual union and communion with Christ and with any other church. (Isa. xxx. 21; Rom. x. 15, 17, 10, 13; John xiii. 35.) To this is opposed its separation, consisting in this, that Christ "removes its candlestick out of his place," and the churches vary among themselves in the profession of the faith, omit the requisite duties of charity, and evince and practice hatred towards each other. (Rev.s ii, 5; 2 Chron. xiii. 8, 2, 10.)

VIII. But the churches of God and Christ, even those which were instituted by prophets and apostles, may decline by degrees, and sometimes do decline, from the truth of the faith, from the integrity of divine worship, and from their first love, (2 Cor. xi. 3; Gal. i. 6; Rev. ii. 4,) either by adding to the doctrines of faith, to that which is the object of worship, and to the modes and rites with which it is worshipped; or by taking away or by perverting the right meaning of faith, by not considering in a lawful manner that which is worshipped, and by changing the legitimate mode of worship into another form; and yet they are still acknowledged, by God and Christ, as God's churches and people, even at the very time when they worship Jehovah in calves, when they pay divine honours both to Jehovah and to Baal, when they offer to Moloch through the fire the children whom they had borne and reared for Jehovah, (Jer. ii. 11-13; 2 Kings xvi. 3; 1 Kings xviii, 21; Ezek. xvi. 20,) and when they suffer legal ceremonies to be appended to the faith of Christ, and the resurrection to be called in question: (Gal. iii. 1-3; 6; 1 Cor. xv,) even under these circumstances they are acknowledged as the churches and the people of God, according to external communion by the word and the sacramental signs or tokens, because God does not yet remove the candlestick out of its place, or send them a bill of divorcement. (Rev. ii. 5; Isa. i. 1.) Hence it arises that the Union between such churches, as have something still left of God and Christ and something of the spirit of lies and idolatry, is two-fold: the One, in regard to those things which they have yet remaining from the first institution which was made by the prophets and apostles: the Other, with respect to those things which have been afterwards introduced by false teachers and false prophets, and especially by that notorious false prophet, "the man of sin, the son of perdition." For though "their word eats as doth a canker," (2 Tim. ii. 17,) yet the goodness and grace of God have prevented it from consuming the whole pure doctrine of the Christian faith. On the other side, its corresponding Separation is as fully opposed to this last mentioned union, as the former union is opposed to its separation. When therefore the discourse turns on the separation of churches, we ought diligently to consider what thing it is about which the separation has been made.

IX. These things having been thus affirmatively premised, let us now come to the hypothesis of our question, according to the conditions which we said must necessarily be ascribed to the church that may justly be said to have made a secession from another. With regard to the First, which we have said was required as necessarily precedent, we own, that the churches which are now distinguished by the title of "there formed," were, prior to that reformation, one with the church of Rome, and had with her communion of faith and of worship, and of the offices of charity; nay, that they constituted a part of that church, as she has been defined in the second thesis of this disputation. But we distinctly and expressly add two particulars. (1.) That this union and communion is as that between equals, collaterals, sisters and members; (Sol. Song viii. 8; 1 Cor. xii. 12, 13, 17;) and not as the union which subsists between inferiors and a superior, between sons and their mother, between members and their head: that is, as they speak in the schools of philosophy, the relation between them was that of equiparancy, in which one of the things related is not more the foundation than the other, and therefore the obligation on both sides is equal; yet the Roman pontiff, seated in the chair which he calls apostolical, and which he says is at Rome, affirms the church of Rome to be the mother and head of the rest of the churches. (2.) That this union and communion is partly according to those things which belong to God and Christ, and partly according to those things which appertain to the defection or "falling away" predicted by the apostle as about to come: for "the son of perdition" is said to be "sitting in the temple of God." (2 Thess. ii. 2-4.) As far therefore as the doctrine of the true faith sounded in these churches, and as far as God and Christ were worshipped, and the offices of charity were legitimately exercised, so far were they One Church of Christ, who patiently bore with them and invited them to repentance. (Rev. ii. 20, 21.) But as far as the faith has been interpolated with various additions and distorted interpretations, and as far as the divine worship has been depraved by different idolatries and superstitions, and the tokens of benevolence have been exhibited in partaking of the parts offered to idols, so far has the union been according to the spirit of defection and the communion of iniquity. (Rev. ii. 14, 20.)

X. With regard to what belongs to the separation of the reformed churches from that of Rome, we must discuss it in two ways; because, as we have already seen, (Thesis 8,) the separation of churches is usually made both with respect to faith and worship, and with respect to charity. These separations are considered to be thus far distinguished, by the churches themselves; so that the church which is separated in reference to faith and worship, is called heretical and idolatrous; and that which is separated in reference to charity, is called schismatical. The first part of the question therefore will be this: "Have the churches which are now called the reformed, made a secession with regard to faith and worship?" Respect being had to the Second condition, (Thesis 4,) we reply, we confess that a secession has been made with regard to faith and worship. For the fact itself testifies, that they differ [from the church of Rome] in many doctrines relating to faith, and that they differ in divine worship. But the reformed deny, that they differ from the Romish church according to those articles of faith which she yet holds through apostolical tradition, or according to [that part of] worship which, being divinely prescribed, the church of Rome yet uses. Of this, proof is afforded in the following brief manner. (1.) For in addition to her laying down the word of God as the only rule of the truth, she professes to approve, in the true and correct sense, of the articles of belief contained in the apostles' creed, as those articles have been explained by the first four general councils; she likewise professes to esteem as certain and ratified those things which the ancient church decreed against Pelagius. (2.) Because she worships God and Christ in spirit and truth, by that method, and with those rites, which have been prescribed in the word of God. She, therefore, confesses that the separation has been made in those things which the church of Rome holds, not as she is the church of Christ, but as she is the Romish and popish church; but that the union remains in those things of Christ which she still retains.

XI. With regard to the Third condition, (Thesis 4,) the reformed churches deny, that they were the first to make the secession. That this may be properly understood, since a separation consists in a variation of faith and worship, they say that the commencement of such variation may be dated from two periods. (1.) Either from the time nearest to the apostles, nay at a period which came within the age of the apostles, when the mystery anomiav, that is. of iniquity, or rather, (if leave may be granted to invent a word still more significant,) when "the mystery of lawlessness began to work," which mystery was subsequently revealed, and which lawlessness was afterwards openly produced by "that man of sin, the son of perdition," who is on this very account called "that wicked," or "that lawless one," and is said to be "revealed." (2 Thess. ii. 3-8.) The reformed say, that the personage thus described is the Roman pontiff. (2.) Or the commencement of this variation may be dated from the days of Wickliffe, Huss, Luther, Melancthon, Zuinglius, OEcolampadius, Bucer and Calvin, when many congregations of men in various parts of Europe began, at first secretly, but afterwards openly, to recede from the Roman pontiff. The reformed say, that the commencement of the detection and secession must be dated from the former of these two periods; and they confess and lament, that they were themselves, in conjunction with the modern church of Rome, guilty of a defection from the purity of the apostolic and the Roman faith, which the apostle Paul commended in the ancient church of Rome that existed in his days. The papists say that the commencement of the defection and secession must be dated from the latter period, [the days of Huss, Luther, etc,] and affirm that they are not to be accounted guilty of any defection.

XII. This is the hinge of the entire controversy. Here, therefore, we must make our stand. If the reformed churches place the beginning of the defection at the true point, then their separation from the modern church of Rome is not a secession from the church of Christ, but it is the termination and completion of a separation formerly made, and merely a return and conversion to the true and pure faith, and to the sincere worship of God--that is, a return to God and Christ, and to the primitive and truly apostolical church, nay to the ancient church of Rome itself: But, on the other hand, if the beginning of the defection be correctly placed by the papists, then the reformed churches have really made a secession from the Romish church, and indeed from that church which still continues in the purity of the Christian religion. But the difference consists principally in this, that the Romish church is said to have added falsehoods to the truth, and the reformed churches are said, by the opposite party, to have detracted from the truth: this controversy, therefore, is of such a nature, that the burden of proof lies with the church of Rome as affirming, that those things of her own which she has added are true. Yet the reformed churches will not decline the province of proof, if the Romish church will permit the matter to be discussed and decided from the pure Scriptures alone. Because the church of Rome does not consent to this, but produces another unwritten word of God, she thus again imposes on herself the necessity of proving, not only that there is some unwritten word of God, but also that what she produces is the real word of God.

XIII. Lastly, the reformed churches say, what is contained in the fourth condition, (Thesis 4,) that they did not secede voluntarily, that is, they did not secede at their own instigation, motion, or choice, but with lingering sorrow and regret; and they ascribe the cause [of this secession] to God, and throw the blame of it upon the church of Rome herself, or first on the court of Rome and the pontiff, and then on the Romish church so far as she listens to the pontiff and the court of Rome, and is ready to perform any services for them. 1. They attribute the cause of this secession to God; because he has commanded his people to depart out of Babylon, the mother of fornications, and to keep themselves from idols. (Rev. xviii. 4; 1 John v. 21.) 2. They throw the blame of it on the Court or Church of Rome, which in three ways drove away the protestant churches from her communion. (1.) By her mixture of deadly poison in the cup of religion, (Rev. xvii. 4,) from which she administered those dogmas that relate to faith and to the worship of God. This mixture was accompanied by a double command. The first, a prohibitive command, that no person should draw any of the waters of the saviour from the pure fountains of Israel; the second, a preceptive, that all men should drink out of this her cup of abominations. (Rev. xiii. 15-17.) (2.) By excommunication and anathemas; by the former she excluded from her communion as many persons as refused to drink the deadly poison out of the cup which she had filled with this mixture. By the latter, she devoted them to all kinds of curses and execrations, and exposed them for plunder and destruction to the madening fury of her own satellites. (3.) Not only by instituting tyranny and various persecutions, but also by exercising them against those who were unwilling to defile their consciences by that shameful abomination. (Rev. xvii. 6.) But with what lingering sorrow and regret they have departed, or, rather, have suffered themselves to be driven away, they say, they have declared by three most manifest tokens: (1.) By serious admonitions proposed both verbally and in writing, in which they have shewn the necessity of the reformation, and the method and means of it to be a free ecclesiastical council. (2.) By prayers and supplications, which they have employed in earnest intreaties for such an assembly, for this purpose at least--that a serious and general inquiry should be made, whether some kind of abuses and of corruption had not crept into the church, and whether they might not be corrected wherever they were discovered. (3.) By the continued patience with which they have endured every description of tyranny, that has been exercised against them. After all this, the only result has been that the existing corruptions and abuses are confirmed and fully established by the plenary authority of the pope and of the court of Rome.

XIV. We have hitherto discussed this separation in reference to faith and worship. (Thesis 10.) But the reformed churches say, that they have by no means made a separation from the church of Rome in reference to charity. They invoke Christ as a witness in their consciences to the truth of this their declaration, and they think they have hitherto given sufficient proofs of it. (1.) By the exposition of their doctrine to the whole world, both verbally and by their writings, which disclose from the word of God the errors of the Romish church, and solicitously invite to conversion, the people who remain in error. (2.) By the prayers and groans with which they do not cease to importune the divine Majesty to deliver his miserable people from the deception and tyranny of Antichrist, and firmly to subject them to his Son, Jesus Christ. (3.) By the friendly and mild behaviour which they use towards the adherents of the popish religion, even in many of those places in which they have, themselves, the supremacy, while they neither employ force against their consciences, nor drive them by menaces to the profession of another faith or to the exercise of a different worship, but permit them, privately, at least, to offer that fealty and worship to God of which they mentally approve. Protestants use only the spiritual sword, that, after all heresy and idolatry have been destroyed, men, being saved, even in this life, with regard to their bodies, may be eternally saved to the day of the Lord. The prevention of the public assemblies of the Roman Catholics, and the compelling of them by pecuniary mulct or fines to hear the sermons of the reformed, may be managed in such a manner as will enable the latter to prove these to be offices of true charity. The reformed also say, that those things of which the papists complain, as being perpetrated with too much severity, and even with cruelty, against themselves and their children, were brought upon them either through the tumultuous and licentious conduct of the military, of which deeds they have themselves most commonly been the authors, partly by their demerits, and partly by their previous example; or they were brought upon them on account of crimes which they committed against the state or commonwealth, and not on account of religion. We conclude, therefore, that neither with respect to faith and worship, nor with respect to charity, have the reformed churches made a secession from that of Rome, so far as the Romish church retains any thing which is Christ's; but they rejoice and glory in the separation, so far as she is averse from Christ.

XV. The second part of our proposition remains now to be considered, which stands thus: "The reformed churches have acted properly in refusing to hold and profess a communion of faith and of divine worship with the church of Rome." This may indeed be generally collected from the preceding arguments; but it must be here more specially deduced, that it may evidently appear in what things the corruption of faith and of divine worship principally consists in the church of Rome, according to the judgment of the reformed churches. The causes of this their refusal are three. (1.) The various heresies. (2.) The multifarious idolatry, and (3.) The immense tyranny, which has been approved and exercised by the church of Rome.

First. We will treat of heresies, but with much brevity; because it would be a work of too much prolixity to enumerate all. The first, and one which does not dash with any single article, but which is directly opposed to the very principle of faith, is this, in which it is maintained, "That there is another word of God beside that which is recorded in the canonical books of the Old and New Testaments, and is of the same force and necessity with it, for the establishment of truth and the refutation of error." To this is added "that the word of God must be understood according to the sense of our holy mother, the church," that is, of the church of Rome. But this sense is that which the Romish church has explained, and will hereafter explain, by her old Vulgate Latin translation, by her confessions, catechisms and canons, in a way the best accommodated, for the time being, to the existing necessity or prevailing opinion. This is the first foundation of the kingdom of Antichrist, directly opposed to the first foundation of the kingdom of Christ, which is the immovable truth and perfection of the doctrine comprised, first, in the prophetical writings, and then, in those of the apostles.

XVI. To this we next add another heresy, which is also adverse to the principle of faith. By it the Roman pontiff is constituted the prince, the head, the husband, the universal bishop and shepherd of the whole church on earth--a personage who possesses, in the cabinet of his breast, all the knowledge of truth; and who has the perpetual assistance of the Holy Spirit, so that he cannot err in prescribing those things which concern faith and divine worship--that "spiritual man who judgeth all men and all things, yet he himself is judged of no man," (1 Cor. ii. 15,) to whom all the faithful in Christ must, from the necessity of salvation, be subject, and to whose decrees and commands, no less than to those of God and Christ himself, every Christian must assent and yield obedience, with simple faith and blind submission. This is the second foundation of the kingdom of Antichrist, directly opposed to the second foundation of the kingdom of Christ, which God laid down when he constituted Christ his Son, the King, the Husband, the Head, the Chief Shepherd, and the sole Master of his church.

XVII. Particular heresies, and such as contravene some article of faith, have reference either to the grace of God which has been bestowed upon us in Christ, or to our duty to God and Christ. Those which relate to Grace are opposed either to Christ himself and his offices, to the benefits, or to the sealing tokens of grace. (1.) To Christ himself are opposed the transubstantiation of bread and wine into his body and blood, with which is connected the presence of the same person in many places. (2.) To the Priestly office of Christ with respect to his Oblation, is opposed, in the first place, the sacrifice of the mass, which is erected on the same dogma of transubstantiation, and in which lies an accumulation of heresies, (i.) That the body and blood of our Lord are said to be there offered for a sacrifice, (ii.) To be truly and properly propitiatory, (iii.) And yet to be bloodless, for the sins, punishments, and satisfactions not only of the living, but likewise of the dead. United with this, or standing as a foundation to it, are a purgatory, and whatever is dependent upon it, (iv.) In the sacrifice of the mass, the body and blood of our Lord are also said to be daily offered, ten, or a hundred, or a thousand times, (v.) By a priest, himself a sinful man, (vi.) Who by his prayers procures for it, from God, the grace of acceptance. Heresies are likewise opposed to the priestly office of Christ with respect to his Intercession, when Mary, angels, and deceased saints are constituted mediators and intercessors, who can obtain something important, not only by their prayers, but also by their merits. The Roman Catholics sin against the kingly office of Christ, when they believe these intercessors of theirs to be the dispensers and donors of blessings. (3.) Those heresies relating to Grace oppose themselves to the benefits of justification and sanctification. (i.) To justification, when it is attributed at once to both faith and works. The following have the same tendency: "The good works of saints fully satisfy the law of God for the circumstances of the present life, truly merit life eternal, are a real satisfaction for temporal punishment, for every penalty, for guilt itself, and are an expiation for sins and offenses. Nay, the good works of some saints are so far supererogatory, as, when they perform more than they are bound to do, those [extra] good works are meritorious for the salvation of others. Lastly, when men by suffering render satisfaction for sins, they are made conformable to Christ Jesus, who satisfied for sins." (ii.) They are opposed to sanctification, when they attribute to the natural man without the grace of God, preparatory works, which are grateful to God, and through congruity are meritorious of greater gifts. (4.) They are opposed to the signs or tokens of grace in several ways: by multiplying them, by contaminating baptism with various additions, by mutilating the Lord's supper of its second part, [the cup,] and by changing it into a private mass. Those heresies which infringe upon our Duty to God and Christ as they principally relate to divine worship, and have idolatry united with them, may be appropriately referred to the second cause of the refusal of the reformed churches. (Thesis. 15.)

XVIII. The Second Cause, we have said, is the multifarious idolatry which flourishes in the church of Rome--both that of the first kind against the first command, when that which ought not to be worshipped is made the object of worship, adoration, and invocation; and that of the second kind against the second command, when the object of worship is worshipped in an image, whether that object ought or ought not to be worshipped. (1.) The church of Rome commits idolatry of The First, with things animate and inanimate. (i.) With animate things--with angels, the virgin Mary, and departed saints; by founding churches to them; by erecting altars; by instituting certain religious services and rites of worship, and appointing societies of men and women by whom they may be performed, and the festival days on which they may be observed; by invoking them in their necessities; by offering to them gifts and sacrifices; by making them preside [as tutelary beings] over provinces, cities, villages, streets, and houses, also over the dispensing of certain gifts, the healing of diseases, and the removal as well as the infliction of evils; and, lastly, by swearing by their name. She also commits idolatry with the Roman pontiff himself; by ascribing to him those titles, powers, and acts which belong to Christ alone; and by asking of him those things which belong to Christ and his Spirit. (ii.) With inanimate things--with the cross and the bread of our Lord, and with the relics of saints, whether such relics be real, or false and fictitious. (2.) Idolatry of The Second Kind is when the papists worship God, Christ, angels, the virgin Mary and the rest of the saints in an image; and when they pay to such images honour and worship by adorning them with fine garments, gold, silver and jewels; by assigning them more elevated situations in churches and placing them upon the altars; by parading them on their shoulders through the streets; by uncovering their heads to them; by kissing them; by kneeling to them, and lastly, by invoking them, or at least by addressing invocations to them, as the power or deity who is there more immediately present. We assert that the distinction of worship into latria, supreme religious adoration, and douleia inferior worship, and uperdouleia an intermediate adoration between LATRIA and DULIA--of power, into that which is superior, and that which is subordinate, or ministerial--of the representation of any thing, into that by which any thing is performed to some kind of an image and a carved shape as unto God and Christ, and that by which it is performed to an image but not as unto God and Christ. These distinctions, and the dogma of transubstantiation, we assert to be mere figments, which are either not understood by the greatest portion of the worshipers, or about which they do not think when they are in the act of worship; and to contain protestations which are directly contrary to facts. This second cause is, of itself, quite sufficient to prove our thesis.

XIX. The Third Cause is the tyranny which the church of Rome has usurped and exercised against those who could not conscientiously assent to these heresies and approve these idolatries; and which that church will continue to exercise so long as she listens to the Roman pontiff and his court. The reformed churches very properly refuse to profess communion of faith and worship with that of Rome, because they are afraid to involve or entangle themselves in the guilt of such great wickedness, lest they should bring down upon their heads the blood of so many thousands of the saints and of the faithful martyrs of Christ, who have borne testimony to the word of the Lord, "and have washed their robes in the blood of the Lamb." (Rev. vii. 14.) For, beside the fact that such a profession would convey a sufficiently open approbation of that persecution, (especially if they did not previously deliver a protestation against it, which, however, the Roman pontiff would never admit,) even the papistical doctrine itself, with the assent of the people, establishes the punishment, by the secular arm, of those whom the church of Rome accounts as heretics; so that those who, on other points, are adherents to the doctrine of popery, if they are not zealous in their conduct against heretics, are slandered as men governed by policy, lukewarm creatures, and even receive the infamous name of atheists. I wish all kings, princes, and commonwealths, seriously to consider this, that, on this point at least, they may protest that they have seceded from the communion of the pontiff and of the court of Rome. Besides, this exercise of tyranny is, in itself, equal to an evident token, that the Roman pontiff is that wicked servant who says in his heart, "My Lord delayeth his coming," and begins to eat and drink, and to be drunken, and to beat his fellow-servants. (Luke xii. 45.)

DISPUTATION 23 - ON IDOLATRY

RESPONDENT: JAPHET VIGERIUS

I. It always has been, and is now, the chief design of diabolical perverseness, -- that even the devil himself, should be considered and worshipped as a deity--than which nothing can be more reproachful and insulting to the true God; or that all thought and mention of a Deity being removed, pure atheism might obtain, and, after conscience was taken away, men might be hurried along into every kind of flagitious wickedness. But since he could not effect this, on account of the notion of a Deity, and indeed of a good one, which is deeply impressed on the minds of men; and since he knew it to be the will of the true God that he should himself alone be considered and worshipped as God, without any image; (Exod. xx. 3-5; Deut. xxxii. 17; 1 Cor. x. 20;) the devil has been trying to persuade men to consider and worship as God some figment of their own brain or some kind of creature, or, at least, to worship the true God in an image. In former days he had great success in these, his attempts; and would to God that in our times they were utterly fruitless! We might then be emboldened to enter on this discussion, merely for the purpose of knowing what idolatry is, and the description of it which anciently prevailed among Jews and gentiles, without being solicitous to deliver any admonition or caution respecting it. But since, alas, this evil holds domination far and wide in Christendom itself, we will, by divine aid, briefly treat upon it in these theses, both for the purpose of knowing what it is, and of giving some cautions and dehortations against it.

II. Commencing, therefore, with the etymology of the word, we say, Eidwlon an idol, generally, signifies some representation and image, whether it be conceived only in the mind or framed by the hands, and whether it be that of a thing which never had an existence, or of something which does exist. But, according to Scripture usage, and that of the sacred writers, it signifies, (1.) An image fashioned for the purpose of representing and honouring a deity, whether true or false. (2.) Every false divinity, whether it be the pure figment of the human brain, or any thing existing among the creatures of God, and thus real, according to its absolute essence, because it is something; but false with regard to its relative essence, because it is not a Divinity, which yet it is feigned to be, and for which it is accounted. (Exod. xx. 4; Acts vii. 41; Psalm cxv. 4-8; 1 John v. 21; 1 Cor. viii. 4; 1 Thess. i. 9; Col. iii. 5; Deut. vi. 13; [xiii, 6;] Matt. iv. 10; Deut. v, 6-9.) Latreuein (idolatry) signifies, in its general acceptation "to render service, or worship," "to wait upon;" in Hebrew, db[: But in the Scriptures, and among ecclesiastical writers, it is peculiarly employed about [acts of] religious worship and service; such as these--to render love, honour, and fear to God--to repose hope and confidence in him--to invoke him -- to give him thanks for benefits received--to obey his commands without exception--and to swear by his name. (Mal. i. 6; Psalm xxxvii, 3; 1, 15; Deut. vi. 13.)

III. Idolatry, therefore, according to the etymology of the word, is "service rendered to an idol;" but, with regard to fact, it is when divine worship is paid to any other than the true God, whether that be done by an erroneous judgment of the mind, by which that is esteemed as a God which is no God, or it be done solely by the performance of such worship, though he who renders it be aware that the idol is not God, and though he protest that he does not esteem it as a God, since his protestation is contrary to fact. (Isa. xlii. 8; Gal. iv. 8; Exod. xxxii. 4, 5.) In proof of this, the belly, covetousness, and idolatry, are severally said to be the god of some people, and covetous men are called "idolaters." (Phil. iii. 19; Col. iii. 5; Ephes. v. 5.) But so far is that opinion or knowledge (by which he does not esteem the idol as a god) from acquitting him of idolatry, who adores, invokes, and kneels to it, that from the very circumstance of his thus invoking, adoring, and kneeling to an idol, he may rather be said to esteem that as a god, which, according to his own opinion, he does not consider to be a god. (1 Cor. x. 19, 20.) This is to say to the wood, with one portion of which he has kindled the fire of his hearth and of his oven, and from another has fashioned to himself a god, "Deliver me; for thou art my god," (Isa. xliv. 15, 17,) and to a stone, "Thou hast begotten me." (Jer. ii. 27.)

IV. Idolatry is also of two kinds. The First is, when that which is not God is accounted and worshipped as God. (Exod. xx. 3-5.) The Second is, when that which is either truly or falsely accounted for God is fashioned into a corporeal image, and is worshipped in an image, or according to an image. The former of these is prohibited in the first commandment: "Thou shalt not have other gods," or "another god, before me," or "beside me." The latter, in the second command, "Thou shalt not make unto thyself any likeness; thou shalt not bow down thyself to them, nor serve them." (Exod. xx. 3-5; 1 Cor. x. 7.) From this, it appears, that idolatry may also be considered in another view, and in three different ways. The First mode is, when the true God is worshipped in an image. The Second is, when a false god is worshipped. The Third, which partakes of both, is when a false god is worshipped in an image. The first mode is of a more venial description than the second, according to that passage, "And it came to pass, as if it had been a light thing, for Ahab to walk in the sins of Jeroboam," who had worshipped Jehovah in calves, and had taught others to do the same, "that he went and served Baal, and bowed himself down before him." (1 Kings xvi. 31.) The third mode is the worst of all; for it consists of a double falsehood, of a feigned divinity, to whom such worship does not belong, and of an assimilated divinity, when of The One to whom it is an assimilation, it is not a likeness. (Isa. xl. 19, 20; Jer. x. 14) Varro has observed that, by the last of these modes, all fear of God has been taken away, and error has been added to mortals.

V. In the prohibition, that the children of Israel should have no God except Jehovah, the Scriptures employ three words to express "another God." The first is r j a (Exod. xx. 3) The second, d z and the third, r k r (Psalm lxxxi. 9.) The first signifies, generally, "any other god;" the second, "a strange god;, and the third, "a strange and foreign god." But though these words are not so opposed to each other, as not occasionally to coincide, and to be indiscriminately used about a god that is not the TRUE ONE; yet, from a collation of them as they are used in the Scriptures, it is easy to collect that "another god" may be conceived under a three-fold difference; for they were either invented by their first worshipers; or they were received from their ancestors, or they were taken from other nations. (Deut. xxxi. 16, 17.) The last of these occurs, (1.) Either by some necessity, of which David complains, when he says, "They have driven me out this day from abiding in the inheritance of Jehovah, saying, Go, serve other gods.(1 Sam. xxvi. 19.) (2.) Or by persuasion; as the heart of Solomon was inclined by his wives to worship other gods. (1 Kings xi. 4, 5.) (3.) Or by the mere choice of the will; as Amaziah took the gods of the children of Seir, after he had come from the slaughter of the Edomites. (2 Chron. xxv. 14.) In these degrees the Scriptures present to us a difference between a greater and a less offense. For since Jeroboam is frequently accused of having made Israel to sin and of increasing the crime of idolatry; (1 Kings xii. 30; xiv, 16;) and since the children of Israel are often said to have "provoked God to jealousy with strange gods, whom they knew not and whom their fathers did not fear," (Deut. xxxii. 16,) it appears that the invention or fabrication of a new god is a more grievous crime, than the adoration of "another god" whom they received from their ancestry. And since it greatly contributes to the dishonour and reproach of Jehovah, to take the gods of foreign nations as objects of worship, by which, those gods plainly seem to be preferred to Jehovah, and the religion of those nations, to the law of Jehovah, this crime, therefore, is, of all others, by far the most grievous. (Jer. ii. 11, 13.)

VI. In the prescription of the second command, that nothing which is esteemed as a god be worshipped in an image, the Scriptures most solicitously guard against the possibility of the human mind finding out any evasion or lurking place. For, with regard to the matter, they forbade images to be made of gold and silver, the most precious of the metals, and therefore, of any metal whatever, or of wood or stone. (Exod. xx. 23; Isa. xliv. 12 13; Jer. ii. 27.) It prohibits every form, whether the image represent a living creature, any thing in the heavens, the sun, the moon, or the stars; any thing on the earth or under the earth, a man, a quadruped, a flying creature, a fish or a serpent, or a thing that has no existence, but by the madness and vanity of the human brain is compounded of different shapes, such as a monster, the upper parts of which are human, and the lower parts those of an ox; or one whose upper parts are those of an ox, and the lower, those of a man; or one, the higher parts of which are those of a beautiful woman, and the lower those of a fish, terminating in a tail. It prohibits every mode of making them, whether they be formed by fusion, by sculpture, or by painting; (Jer. x. 3, 9, 14; Ezek. viii. 10, 11;) because it says uinversally, "Thou shalt not make unto thee any likeness." And it adds a reason which excludes generally every kind of material and every method of fabrication: "For ye saw no manner of similitude, on the day that the Lord spake unto you in Horeb out of the midst of the fire. Take ye, therefore, good heed unto your souls, lest ye corrupt yourselves, and make you a graven image, the similitude of any figure," &c. (Deut. iv. 15-19.)

VII. But with regard to the mode of worship, and to the actions pertaining to it, scarcely any thing can be devised or invented, and can be performed to idols, (that is, both to false deities themselves and to the images of false divinities, and to those of the true God,) which is not expressly said in the Scriptures to be hateful to God, that no one may have the least pretext for his ignorance. For the Scriptures take away all honour and service from them, whatever may be the manner in which they are performed, whether by building temples, high places or groves by erecting altars, and by placing images upon altars; or by offering sacrifices, burning incense, by eating that which is offered in sacrifice to idols, by bending the knees to them, by bestowing kisses on them, and by carrying them on their shoulders. (Exod. xx. 5; 1 Kings xi. 7; xii, 31-33; 2 Kings xvii. 35; Ezek. viii. 11; Num. xxv. 2; 1 Kings xix. 18; Isa. xlv. 20; Jer. x. 5.) The Scriptures also prohibit men from placing hope and trust in idols, forbid invocation, prayers and thanksgivings to be directed to them, and will not suffer men to fear them and to swear by them; because idols are as unable to save as to inflict injury. (Psalm cxv. 8; Jer. v. 7.) The Scriptures do not permit men to yield obedience to idols, because a graven image is a teacher of lies and vanity; (Jer. ii. 5-8, 20; xi, 8-13;) and false gods often require of their worshipers those things from which all nature, created and uncreated, that of God and of man, is most abhorrent. (Lev. xviii. 21.)

VIII. But, because the human mind is both inclined and fitted to excogitate and invent excuses, nay even justifications, for sins, particularly for the sin of idolatry, and because the pretext of a good intention to honour the Deity serves the more readily as a plea for it, [this propensity of mind,] on account of conscience not equally accusing a man either for the worship which he offers to a false divinity, or for that which he presents to the true God in an image, as it does for the total omission of worship, and for a sin committed against the rules of equity and goodness which prevail among mankind; our attention will be profitably called to the consideration of what is the judgment of God concerning this matter, by whose judgment we must stand or fall. Let us take our commencement at that species by which the true Deity is worshipped in an image, as Jehovah was in the calf which Aaron fashioned, and in those which were made by Jeroboam. (Exod. xxxii. 4; 1 Kings xii. 28.) God has manifested this, his judgment, by his word and by his acts. (1.) First, by his word of declaration, God has shewn what are his sentiments both concerning the fabrication of an image and the worship offered to it. The Fabrication, he says, is "a changing of the glory of the incorruptible God into the similitude of an ox that eateth grass, into an image made like to corruptible man, and to birds, and to four-footed beasts, and creeping things." (Psalm civ. 20; Rom. i, 23.) But the Worship, he says, is offered, not to God, whom they wished to represent by an image, but to the calf itself, and to the image which they had fabricated. (1 Kings xii. 32.) For these are his words: "They have made them a molten calf, and have worshipped it, and have sacrificed thereunto." (Exod. xxxii. 8.) And St. Stephen says, "They made a calf in those days, and offered sacrifice unto the idol." (Acts vii. 41.) On this account also he calls them, "gods of gold and silver," "other gods and molten images." (Exod. xxxii. 31; 1 Kings xiv. 9.) Secondly, by His word of threatening, by which he denounces destruction to those who worshipped the calf that Aaron formed, and to Jeroboam and his posterity. (Exod. xxxii. 9, 10; 1 Kings xiv. 10, 11.) (2.) God has also displayed his judgment about idolatry by his acts. He not only fulfilled this, his word of threatening, by cutting off Jeroboam and his posterity, (2 Chron. xiii. 15-20,) and by destroying many thousands of the Israelites; (Exod. xxxii. 28;) but likewise by chastising similar sinners by another horrible punishment, that of blindness, and of being delivered over to a reprobate mind." (Rom. i. 24-28.)

IX. Such, then, is the judgment of God concerning that species of idolatry which is committed with the intention of worshipping that God who is truly God. Let us now see how severe this judgment is against that species in which the intention is to offer worship to that which is not the true God, to another god, to Moloch, Baal, Chemosh, Baal-peor, and to similar false gods, though they were esteemed as gods by their worshipers. (Deut. xxix. 17; xxxii, 14-17.) Of this, his judgment, God has afforded most convincing indications, both by his word and his acts. In this word of declaration two things occur, which are most signal indications of this. First is, that he interprets this act as a desertion of God, a defection from the true God, a perfidious dissolution of the conjugal bond by spiritual adultery with another, and a provoking of God himself to jealousy. The Second is, that he says this adultery is committed with demons and devils. For these are some of the strains of Moses in his very celebrated song: "They sacrificed unto devils, not to God; to gods whom they knew not," &c. (Deut. xxxii. 17.) And the royal psalmist sings thus: "They sacrificed their sons and their daughters unto devils, unto the idols of Canaan," (Psalm civ. 37, 38,) which they did when they compelled any of their offspring to pass through the fire to Moloch. (Lev. xviii. 21.) The apostle Paul agrees with this when he says, "The things which the gentiles sacrifice, they sacrifice to devils and not to God;" (1 Cor. x. 20;) whether this signifies, that some demon lay concealed in those images; or that those sacred rites were performed according to the will and prescription of demons, either openly, by oracles, responses, and the verses of prophesying poets, or secretly by the institutes or maxims of the world, (Arnob. lib. 6; Aug. de Civ. Del. lib. 8, 23,) that is, of wicked people, of whom Satan is called "the prince," and among whom he is said to have his throne. (1 Pet. iv. 3; 2 Cor. iv. 4; Rev. ii. 13.) The denunciations of punishments for this crime, and the execution of these threats, are described generally throughout the whole of the sacred Scriptures.

X. If the things, thus explained from the Scriptures, be applied to Latriav, the divine adorations, and to Qrhskeiav, the religious ceremonies or superstitions which are employed in the popish church; it will clearly appear, that she is guilty of the crime of the two-fold idolatry which has now been described. (Thesis 4.) Of the First Kind she renders herself guilty, because she presents divine worship to the bread in the Lord's supper, to the virgin Mary, to angels and departed saints, to the relics of Christ's cross and of the saints, and to things consecrated. Of the Second Kind she renders herself guilty, because her members worship, in an image, God, Christ, the cross of Christ, the virgin Mary, angels and saints. Each of these charges shall be demonstrated; and, we will confirm them in as brief a manner as possible, after having closed up all the evasions, through which the worshipers of idols try to creep out when they are held fast bound.

XI. 1. First. Concerning the sacrament of the Lord's supper, to which "all the faithful in Christ, according to the method always received in the [Roman] Catholic church, present in veneration the worship of latria, or supreme adoration, [which is due to the true God.] Nor is this most holy sacrament to be the less adored because it was instituted by Christ our Lord, that it might be received, as the Council of Trent says, (Session 13, 5,) when it frees us from one part of the sacrament. To this we subjoin, in the discharge of another part of the duty we have undertaken: But the worship of latria or supreme adoration, cannot be paid to the sacrament of the eucharist without idolatry. (1.) It cannot be paid even in the use of the eucharist, because bread continues to be bread still, with regard to its substance, and it is not transubstantiated or changed into the body of Christ by consecration. For the eucharist would thus cease to be a sacrament, of whose essence it is to consist of an external thing; and the body of Christ would thus begin to exist anew; for nothing can be changed into that which had no previous existence. (2.) Much less can this worship be paid to the sacrament in its abuse. Because, though a legitimate consecration might [be supposed to] have the power of transubstantiating, yet an illegitimate consecration cannot effect a transubstantiation. For all right of consecration depends on the divine institution: but a consecration to adore, and not to receive, is foreign to the design of the institution, and therefore inefficacious. (Matt. xxvi. 26;1 Corinthians x. 16; xi, 25.) Therefore, the Roman Catholic church commits idolatry, as she presents to the sacrament of the eucharist the service of latria, or supreme adoration, which is due to the true God alone.

XII. Secondly. In the worship which the papists perform to the virgin Mary, angels and departed saints, we say they commit idolatry in two ways--in reference to the act of adoring them, and to that of invoking them. (1 Kings xix. 18; 2 Kings xvii. 11,16, 35.) (1.) In adoring them, when they do reverence to all and to each of them by altars, masses, festivals or holy days, vigils, fasts, images, candles, offerings, by burning incense, by vows, pilgrimages, and genuflections. All these acts relate to latria or supreme adoration, and to divine worship, when presented to the true God according to his will, or to false gods through the superstition of men. (2.) In invoking them, when the papists "betake themselves to the prayers, and to the help and assistance, afforded by the saints," as the Council of Trent says, (Session 25,) and when they return thanks to them for the benefits which they receive. (Lombard. lib. 4, dist. 25.) But they have this recourse to the Prayers of angels and saints, as their intercessors, mediators, patrons and advocates, who intercede. (1.) With a pious affection, by which they desire the wishes of those who pray to them, to be fulfilled. (2.) With their glorious and most holy merits, which are presented in favour of those who, with suppliant intreaties, require their prayers. They have this recourse, also, to the Help and Assistance of angels and saints, as to auxiliaries or helpers, preservers and the guardians of grace and glory; that is, the liberal dispensers of all blessings, their deliverers in necessities, whom they also denominate their life, salvation, safety, hope, defense, refuse, solace, yea, their only hope, and their safe fortress. But these are titles which belong to God and Christ alone, as the decorations of the highest excellence, wisdom, benevolence and power; than which nothing can be conceived more illustrious, as is manifest from the Scriptures, in which these titles are read as attributed to God and Christ; (Psalm xlvi. 1, 2; xviii, 1, 2; xxxvi, 7, 10; lxii, 2, 3, 6; Isa. xlv. 20; Acts iv. 12;) when the supreme honour of invocation and adoration is offered to them by holy men. And though the turpitude of this idolatry be exceedingly foul and disgusting, yet how immensely is it aggravated by rendering the reason which serves as a pretext to them for that deed; than which reason nothing can be imagined to be more injurious to God and Christ. (1.) To God, when the papists say that our heavenly Father has given half of his kingdom to the blessed virgin, the queen of heaven, whom they also denominate "the mistress of the world," "the star of the sea," "the haven or port of salvation," and "God;" (Gul. Biel. in Can. Miss. Lect. 80;) and when they say that since God has both justice and mercy, he retains the former of these himself, but has granted the exercise of mercy to his virgin mother, and therefore, that we must appeal from the court of the justice of God to the court of the mercy of his mother. (2.) To Christ, nothing can be more injurious than this; because the papists say that Christ is not only an advocate, but that he is a judge, and as such, will discuss all things, so that nothing will remain unpunished; and therefore, that God has provided for us a female advocate, who is full of mildness and suavity, and in whom is found nothing that is harsh or unpleasant, who is, also, on this account, called "the throne of Christ," on which he reposed. (Anton. page 4, tit. 15, cap. 14.)

XIII. Thirdly. That the papists defile themselves with idolatry in paying reverence to the relics of the cross of Christ and of the saints, by performing unto them acts both of adoration and of invocation, is proved, partly from their own confession, and partly from the very exercise of those religious acts which they offer to them. (1.) The Council of Trent publishes the confession, when it says, (Session 25,) "Those persons are to be wholly condemned, who affirm that honour and veneration are not due to the relics of saints; or that those relics, and other sacred monuments, are unprofitably honoured by the faithful; and that resort is vainly made to the sepulchers of saints, for the purpose of obtaining their assistance." The next confessor on this subject is "the angelical doctor," who is believed to have written all things well concerning Christ. For he says, (Sum. p. 3, Qu, 25,) that the adoration of latria, or supreme worship, must be given to the cross of Christ on account of the contract [into which it came] with the members of the body of Christ. This is a reason quite sufficient to Antoninus to affirm (Anton. p. 3, tit. 12, c. 5) that not only is the cross of Christ to be adored, but likewise all things belonging to it-- the nails, the spear, the vestments, and even the sacred tabernacles. In accordance with these confessions, the Roman Catholic church sings, "Behold the wood of the Cross! We adore thy cross, O Lord." (2.) Another method the papists have of declaring their idolatry by various acts--when they adorn the relics of the cross of Christ and of the saints, with gold, silver, and jewels; when they wrap them in fine lawn napkins and in pieces of silk or velvet; when they carry them about with great pomp, in processions instituted for the purpose of returning thanks and making requests; when they place them on altars; when they suspend before these relics gifts and curses; when they present them to be viewed, kissed, and adored by kneeling, and thus themselves adore them; when they light wax candles before them, burn incense to them; when they consecrate churches and altars by their presence, and consider them as rendered holy; when they institute festivals to them; when they celebrate masses to their honour, under this idea, that masses celebrated upon an altar on which relics are placed, become more holy and efficacious; when they undertake pilgrimages to them; when they carry them about as amulets and preservatives; when they put them upon sick people; when they sanctify their own napkins or handkerchiefs, their garlands, and other things of the same kind, by touching them with these relics, that they may serve for the same purposes; because they think that grace and a divine virtue exist in them, which they seek to obtain from them by invocations, and other services performed before them; they use them for driving away and expelling devils and bad spirits; and they do all these things which the heathen did to the relics of their idolatry. To all these particulars, must be added that most shameful illusion--the multiplication of relics, and the substitution of such as belong to other persons than to those whose names they bear. Hence, the origin of that witty saying, "The bodies of many persons are honoured on earth, whose souls are burning in everlasting torments." (Cal. de relig.)

XIV. The Fourth specimen, partly of the same idolatry, and partly of a superstition much worse than that of the heathens, the papists afford not only in the dedications and consecrations of churches, alters, vases, and ornaments which belong to them, such as the cross, the chalice and its covers, linen clothes, the vestments of priests, and of censers; also in the consecration of easter wax candles, holy water, salt, oil for extreme unction, bells, small waxen figures like dolls, each of which they call "Agnus Dei," and of cemeteries or burial grounds, and things of a similar kind, but likewise in the use of things thus consecrated, for the papists pray in these consecrations, that God would furnish or inspire the things now enumerated, with grace, virtue and power to drive away and expel bodily and spiritual evils, and to bestow the contrary blessings; they use them as actually possessed of such grace and virtue; and perform to them religious worship. We will here produce the following few instances of this matter: They have ascribed remission of Sins to visitations of churches thus consecrated. They use the following words, among others, in their formularies of consecrations, on the cross to be consecrated: "Deign, O Lord, to bless this wood of the cross, that it may be a saving remedy to mankind, that it may be the solidity of faith, the advancement of good works, the redemption of souls, and a safeguard against the fierce darts of enemies." In the formularies on holy water, these words occur: "I exorcise or adjure thee, O creature of water, that thou become exorcised water to put to flight all the power of the enemy, to root him out, and to displant friendly greetings with his apostate angels," &c. This is part of the formulary in the consecration of salt: "I exorcise or adjure thee, O creature of salt, that thou be made exorcised salt for the salvation of believers, that thou mayest be healthful soundness of soul and body to those who receive thee," &c. Also, the following words: "Deign, O Lord, to bless and sanctity this creature of salt, that it may be, to all who take it, health of mind and body; and that what thing soever shall be sprinkled with it, may be devoid of all filth or uncleanliness, and of every attack of spiritual wickedness." But they attribute to the consecrated small wax figures, which they call "Agni Dei," the virtue of breaking and removing every sin, as the blood of Christ does; and, according to this opinion, they use the same things, reposing their hope and confidence in them, as if they were actually endued with any such power.

XV. But that the papists commit the second species of idolatry in the worshipping of images, (Theses 4, 6, & 10,) is abundantly proved from their own confession, the forms of consecration, and their daily practice. (1.) Their own confession may be found in the canons and decrees of the Council of Trent, in which it is affirmed, (Session 25,) "The images of Christ, of the blessed virgin, and of other saints, are to be held and retained, especially in churches; and due honour and veneration are to be exhibited to them; so that by the images which we kiss, and before which we uncover our heads, and prostrate ourselves, we adore Christ, and venerate the saints whose likenesses those images bear; this is what was sanctioned by the second Nicene Council." Let the acts of that Council be inspected, and it will appear that the adoration and invocation which were established by it, are mere idolatry. To these, let Thomas, and the multitude of their divines, be added, who are of opinion that images must receive the same services of adoration, as those with which the prototypes which they represent are worshipped. (2.) The formularies of their consecrations make a similar declaration; for the image of the virgin Mary is consecrated in the following form: "O God, sanctify this image of the blessed virgin, that it may bring the help of saving aid to thy faithful people, if thunder and lightning prevail; that hurtful things may be the more speedily expelled; that inundations caused by rains, the commotions of civil wars, or the devastations committed by pagans, may be repressed and appeased at its presence. (1 Kings 8.) In the consecration of the image of John the Baptist, the following words occur:

"Let this sacred image be the expeller of devils, the invoker of angels, the protector of the faithful, and let its intercession powerfully flourish in this place." (3.) In the daily practice of the papist, most of those acts, both of adoration and invocation, are performed to images, which we have already mentioned as having been exhibited to the saints themselves; and they usually perform those acts [which they think due] to the saints, to their images, or in their images, but seldom indeed do they by a pure [mental] glance look up to the saints themselves, being under the influence of this opinion--that the honours [which they thus pay to images] belong to the prototypes themselves, and therefore that the prayers which they address to them will by this means be the more readily and speedily heard and answered.

XVI. The papists do not indeed deny, that they present this worship, these services, and acts both of adoration and invocation, to the sacrament of the eucharist, to the virgin Mary, to angels and departed saints, to relics and things consecrated, and to these images: at least they are unable to deny this, except by an evident untruth. Yet they excuse themselves under the pretense of certain exceptions and distinctions, which they consider to be of such value and power, as to exempt from idolatry those acts which are performed by themselves with such an intention of mind, but which, when performed by others, are really idolatrous. These exceptions are, First. According to the three-fold excellence of divine, human and intermediate, there is a three-fold honour. And here the distinction is produced of Latreia "latria" or divine worship, douleia "dulia" or human worship, and uperdouleia "hyperdulia" or intermediate, or between both. To this may be added what they say, that most of the acts which relate to this worship are analogous. The Second exception is from the intention of those who offer those religious services. The Third is in the difference between intercession and bestowing, that is, between the office of mediator as discharged by the [popish] saints, and as discharged by Christ Jesus. The Fourth is in the distinction between an image and an idol.

XVII. The First subterfuge has three members. To the first of these we reply, (1.) The Scriptures do not acknowledge any excellence that is called "hyperdulia or intermediate," or that is different from divine excellence except what is according to the functions, graces and dignities through which some rational creatures, by divine command, preside over others and minister to them--men as long as they remain in this mortal life--and angels to the end of the world. Therefore, no homage paid to a creature is pure from idolatry, except that which is offered to superiors who live in this world, and which is approved by the Scriptures. (Psalm lxxxii. 1, 6; John x. 35.) (2.) That intermediate excellence, and the worship which is accommodated to it, are rejected by the Scriptures, since they condemn the "worship paid to angels" (Col. ii. 18,) and commend Hezekiah for having "broken in pieces the brazen serpent that Moses had made; for unto those days the children of Israel did burn incense to it." (2 Kings xviii. 4) To the second monster of this subterfuge we reply, the distinction of worship into latria and dulia is vain in this case; for the apostle claims the worship of dulia [which the papists call an inferior or human adoration] for the true God alone, when he blames the gentiles for having "done service to those which by nature are no gods." (Gal. iv. 8.) And this word, in its general acceptation, signifies the service which ought to be performed, or which lawfully can be, to those only with whom we have to do according to godliness, and this according to the law which is either common to mutual charity, (Gal. v. 13,) or that which has a more particular reference to such persons as have constant transactions with each other. (Ephes. vi. 5, 6.) But with those persons to whom the present discussion relates, (placing the angels as an exception,) we have according to godliness no transactions, neither are we bound, by any law, to them for service. To the third member our answer is, (1.) To offer sacrifice, to burn incense, to erect churches and altars, to make vows, to institute festivals, fasts and pilgrimages, [to angels or saints,] and to swear by their names, and not analogical or relative services, but univocal or having one purpose, and such as are due only to the true God. (2.) Though prostration itself is law fitly given to men on account of their analogical similitude to God, yet, when it is an act of religion, it is considered as so peculiarly due to God, that the whole of divine worship is designated by it alone. (1 Kings xix. 18; Matt. ix. 18.) Christ likewise denies prostration to the devil, (Matt. iv. 8,) and the angel in the Apocalypse refuses it when offered to himself. (Rev. xix. 10.)

XVIII. The distinct intention of the worshipers, is the Second subterfuge that they use to remove from themselves the idolatries of every kind of which they have been accused. In the first of these intentions they say, concerning the adoration of the sacrament of the Lord's supper, that their intention is to honour, not the bread, but the true body of Christ. In the second, that the adoration, even divine adoration itself, which they perform to a creature, is not offered to it as to God; that is, they perform the acts of worship with the design of procuring for the creature such esteem and veneration as in reality belongs only to the divine Majesty. In the third, that by giving honour to a creature, they do not stop there, but that God may be glorified in and through the creature. (Greg. de Val. lib. 2, c. 1 & 3.) In the fourth, that they do not honour the image itself, but its prototype. To all these distinctions we reply, (1.) The deed is in every case contrary to the intention; and they in reality do the very thing which, in their intention, they profess themselves desirous to avoid. (2.) The judgment of God is adverse to their intention; for he does not interpret the deed from the intention, but forms his judgment of the intention from the deed. God himself has exposed an intention that is in accordance with such a deed, although the man who does it puts in his protestation about his contrary intention. This intention is evident from the following passages: "They have made them a molten calf and have worshipped it, and have sacrificed thereunto, and said, these be thy gods, O Israel, which have brought thee up out of the land of Egypt." (Exod. xxxii. 8.) "He falleth down unto it and worshippeth it, and prayeth unto it, and saith, Deliver me, for thou art my god." (Isa. xliv. 17.) "They sacrificed unto devils, not to God," &c. (Deut. xxxii. 17.) (3.) We add, if these distinctions possess any validity, neither Jews nor heathens could at any time have been accused of having committed idolatry; for, by the same distinctions as these, they would be able to justify all their acts of worship, whether offered to a true or to a false deity, to the supreme God, to inferior divinities, or to an image. For [on these principles] their intention never feared the works of their own fingers, but those persons after whose image such works were formed, and to whose names they were consecrated. Their intention never honoured angels, demons, or the minor gods, except that such services should redound to the honour of the supreme Deity; (Lactan. Inst. 1. ii c. 2;) it never wished to procure such esteem and veneration for them as belongs solely to the majesty of God supreme; and it never worshipped a false deity.

XIX. The Third exception has a special tendency to justify the invocation of the virgin Mary and the saints; (Thesis 16;) for the papists say that they invoke them, not as the prime authors and donors of blessings; nor as Christ, whom God the Father hath constituted the high priest, and to whom he has given all power in heaven and on earth; but that they invoke them, in truth, as friends, intercessors and donors, yet in subordination to Christ. To this we reply, First, from the premises which they grant, they may themselves be convicted of idolo-dulia, or inferior worship offered to idols; for they confess that the invocation which they practice to the virgin Mary and to saints is the adoration of dulia. But they fabricate idols of the virgin Mary and of saints before they invoke them by heresy, both by falsely attributing to them the faculty of understanding their prayers, of interceding for sinners, not only feelingly, but also meritoriously, and of granting the things requested, and by presenting to them, as possessed of these qualifications, the worship of invocation; for this is the mode by which an idol is fabricated of a thing that has had a real existence. To this argument strength is added from the circumstance that, although these saints might know the things for which the papists pray, might intercede for them with a pious feeling, and, as spirits," might bestow what they have requested; yet as they could not bestow them, "with power" they ought not to be invoked. Secondly. By the words, "insubordination to Christ," they in reality destroy such a subordination and introduce a collaterally. If this be true, then on that very account they are likewise idolaters; because the worship, which God the Father wishes to be given to his Son, is that of latria, or divine adoration. For it is the will of the Father, "that all men should honour the Son, even as they honour the Father." (John v. 23.) But subordination is removed, and collaterally is introduced, (1.) Universally, when all these saints are said, by their own merits, to intercede for and to obtain blessings, and to dispense the blessings thus obtained, which are two tokens of the eversion of subordination and of the introduction of collaterally. (2.) Specially, this collaterally exists [from their own showing] between Christ and the virgin Mary; as is evident, (1.) the names under which they invoke her, when they denominate her "the queen of heaven," "the mistress of the world," "our salvation, harbor, defense, refuge and solace," who is able to command our Redeemer in virtue of her authority as his mother. These expressions place Christ in subordination to her. (2.) But this is likewise evident, from the cause on account of which they say she ought to be invoked. As a Female Advocate, because, since Christ is not only a man and an advocate, but likewise God and a Judge, "who will suffer nothing to pass unpunished; the virgin Mary, as having in her nothing that is harsh and unpleasant, but being all mildness and suavity," (Thesis 12,) ought to act as intercessor between him and sinners. And as a Female Dispenser of Blessings; because "God the Father has given half of his kingdom to her, (that is, to administer his mercy while he reserves the exercise of justice to himself,") and has conferred upon her a plenitude of all grace, that out of her fullness all men may receive. This is nothing less than to hurl Christ from his throne, and to exalt the virgin Mary in his place.

XX. The Fourth subterfuge is the distinction between an image and an idol. The papists say, an image is the likeness of something real; an idol, that of something false. When Bellarmine explains this definition, he commits a fallacy; for, in interpreting "something false," he says, since it is a being, it is not that which it is feigned to be, that is, God. But that the difference which he here makes is a false one, many passages of Scripture prove. The image which Rachael purloined from her father, is called "anidol;" but it was the image of a man. (Gen. xxxi. 34.) Stephen calls the molten calf "anidol," and it was made to represent the true God. (Acts. vii. 41.) The calves of Jeroboam were representations or images of Jehovah, yet they are called "idols" by the Greek and Latin translators. (1 Kings xii. 28.) Micah's image is also called "an idol" and yet it was "set up" to Jehovah. (Judges xvii. 4; xviii, 31.) Among the "dumb idols" unto which, the apostle says, the Corinthians "were carried away," were statues of men, and probably images of "four-footed beasts, of creeping things, and of birds." (Rom. i. 23.) Yet Bellarmine would with difficulty prove that these are things, which have no existence. Wherefore if an idol be that which is nothing, that is, a sound without reality and meaning, this very distinction, which is purely an invention of the human brain, is itself the vainest idol, nay one of the veriest of idols. Such likewise are those distinctions and intentions which have been invented, for the establishment of idols and of the impious and unlawful adoration of idols, by the church of the malignants, by the mother of fornications, who resembles the "adulterous woman" mentioned in Prov. xxx. 20: "She eateth and wipeth her mouth, and saith, I have done no harm," or "I have not wrought iniquity."

COROLLARY

It can be proved by strong arguments from the Scriptures, that the Roman pontiff is himself an idol; and that they who esteem him as the personage that he and his followers boastingly depict him to be, and who present to him the honour which he demands, by those very acts shew themselves to be idolaters.

DISPUTATION 24 - ON THE INVOCATION OF SAINTS

RESPONDENT: JAMES A. PORT

I. From the hypothesis of the papists, we denominate those persons "saints," whom the Roman pontiff has by his canonization transferred into the book of saints. (Bellarm. de Beat. Sanct. lib. 1, c. 8.) From the truth of the matter, we also call those persons "saints," who being sprinkled with the blood of Jesus Christ, (1 Pet. i. 2,) and sealed with the characters of the Holy Spirit, the sacred fountain of all holiness, have been illustrious in this world by the sanctity of their lives, which flows from their spiritual union with Christ; but who, as it regards the body, being now dead, still live in heaven with Christ as it regards the soul. (Rev. xiv. 13.) Of this description were the patriarchs of old, the prophets, the apostles, the martyrs, and others like them. The invocation of saints is that by which men have recourse to their intercessions, interest, patronage and assistance, for the sake of imploring, intreating, and obtaining their aid.

II. But the papists assert, that the saints are invoked for three reasons: (1.) That they may vouchsafe to intercede by their prayers and their suffrages. (2.) That, through their merits, and on account of them, they may obtain by their petitions the things which are asked of them. (3.) That they may themselves bestow the benefits which are required. For the papists have invested departed saints with these three qualities; that, being nearer to God, they have greater freedom of access to him and to Christ, than the faithful who are yet their survivors in the present life; that, by works of supererogation performed in this life, they have obtained by their merits [the privilege] that God shall hear and grant their prayers; and that they have been constituted by God the administrators of those blessings which are asked of them:

And thus are they appointed mediators, both by merit and efficacy, between God, nay between Christ and living believers.

III. Yet upon all these things the papists have not had the hardihood to erect, as a superstructure, the necessity of invoking the saints: They only say that "It is good and useful suppliantly to invoke them;" and that "those persons hold an impious opinion who deny that the saints ought to be invoked." (Can. and Dec. Coun. of Trent, Sess. 25, c. 2.) But perhaps by these last words, which have an ambiguous meaning, they wished to intimate the existence of this necessity. For not only does he deny that saints ought to be invoked, who says that it is not necessary to invoke them, but likewise he who says that it is not lawful: The words, when strictly taken, bear the former signification, that invocation is not necessary; but the latter meaning of its unlawfulness, when they are understood as opposed to the words which preceded. Even Bellarmine, when he had affixed this title, "The saints ought to be invoked," immediately subjoined the following thesis: "The saints are piously and usefully invoked by the living." (De Beat. Sanct. lib. 1, c. 19.) But that most subtle and evasive council often trifled with ambiguous expressions, being either compelled into such a course on account of the dissensions among its chief members, or else being perversely ingenious on account of its adversaries, whose blows it would not otherwise have been able, with any degree of speciousness, to avoid. We will, therefore, inquire concerning the invocation of saints, Is it necessary? Is it lawful and useful?

IV. With regard to the First of these questions, we say, (whether the papists assent to our affirmation or dissent from it,) that it is not necessary for believers in the present state of existence to invoke the saints who are engaged with Christ in heaven. And since this necessity is--either according to the duty which surviving believers are bound to perform to the saints who have departed out of this life, and who are living with Christ; or according to the end for the sake of obtaining which, invocation is laid down as a necessary means; we affirm that, by neither of these methods is the invocation of saints necessary.

V. (1.) It is not necessary in reference to duty; because the invocation of saints has neither been commanded by God, nor is it sanctioned with any promise or threatening, which it would of necessity have been if it had to be performed as a duty by the faithful during their continuance in the world. (2.) It is not necessary in reference to the means; because neither the merits nor the intervening administration of the saints is necessary to solicit and to obtain the blessings which the faithful in the present life make the subject of their prayers; for otherwise, the mediation and administration of Christ either are not sufficient, or they cannot be obtained except through the intercession of departed saints, both of which are false; and that man who was the first of the saints to enter heaven, neither required nor employed any saint as a previous intercessor.

VI. Since, therefore, it is not necessary, that believers now living upon earth should invoke the saints who reign with Christ, if the papists take any pleasure in the approval of a good conscience, they ought to employ the utmost circumspection in ascertaining, whether it is not the better course to omit this invocation than to perform it, even though it might be made a subject of disputation whether or not it be lawful, about which we shall afterwards inquire. We affirm that it is preferable to omit all such invocation, and we support this assertion by two arguments, (1.) Since "whatever is not of faith," that is, whatsoever does not proceed from a conscience which is fully persuaded that the thing performed is pleasing to God, "is sin;" and since that may, therefore, be omitted without sin, about which even the smallest doubt may be entertained respecting its lawfulness, since it is found that it is not necessary; it follows from these premises, that it is better to omit than to perform invocation. (2.) Since the papists themselves confess, "that the difference between the worship of latria and that of dulia, or between divine and human adoration, is so great, that the man who presents that of latria to any object to which no more than dulia is due, is guilty of idolatry;" and since it is a matter of the greatest difficulty for the common people, who are ignorant and illiterate yet full of devotion to the saints, to observe this difference at all times and without any error; there is much danger lest those who invoke saints should fall into idolatry. This is a reason which also militates against the invocation of saints, even though it were proved that such invocation is lawful.

VII. The next inquiry is, "Is the invocation of saints lawful and useful?" Or, as the Council of Trent has expressed it, "Is it good and useful to invoke the saints?" Or, according to Bellarmine's phraseology, "Are the saints piously and usefully invoked?" (De Beat. Sanct. lib. 1, cap, 19.) We who hold the negative, say, that it is neither pious nor useful to invoke the saints. We prove this assertion, first, generally; secondly, specially, according to the particular respects in which the papists invoke the saints, and maintain that they may be invoked.

VIII. First. We prove generally, that it is not pious, thus:

Since no action can, of itself and properly, come under the appellation of piety or godliness, except that which has been prescribed by God, by whose word and institution alone every action is sanctified, otherwise it will be common; and since it is certain, that the invocation of saints has not been commanded by God, it follows that such an action cannot be called "pious." Some action may, however, be called "pious" by a metalepsis, because it has been undertaken for the sake of performing a pious action. But such a case as this does not here occur. By the same argument, we demonstrate that it is not useful; because all religious worship, not prescribed by God, is useless, (Lev. x. 1,) according to the express declaration of God, (Isa. xxix. 13,) and of Christ: "But in vain do they worship me, teaching for doctrines the commandments of men." (Matt. xv. 9.) But the papists say, that the invocation of saints is religious worship.

IX. Secondly. We prove the same thing, specially, according to the relations in which the papists invest the saints when they invoke them. (1.) We say, the saints cannot be piously and usefully invoked as the donors of benefits; because God has not constituted the saints dispensers of blessings either celestial or terrestrial; for this is the office bestowed on Christ, to whom the angels are under subjection as his servants in this ministration. Besides, if even, in imitation of angels, the saints did, in this world, perform their subordinate service to Christ at the command of God; yet they ought not on this account to be invoked; for, before this can be done, a full power of dispensing is required, which may distribute blessings as it pleases; but the angels render in this world only a ministerial and instrumental service to Christ, for which reason neither is it lawful to invoke them as the donors of blessings. But the saints cannot, in imitation of the angels, perform a service to Christ ministerially and instrumentally, unless we assert that they all ascend and descend after the manner of angels. Since, therefore, they possess neither the power nor the capability of bestowing blessings, it follows that they cannot be either piously or usefully invoked as the donors of benefits. 10. (2.) The saints cannot be piously and usefully invoked as those who by their own merits have obtained the privilege of being heard and answered by God; because the saints have not been able to merit any thing for themselves or for others. For they have accounted it needful to exclaim, with David, "Our goodness extendeth not to thee." (Psalm xvi. 2.) And "when they had done all those things which were commanded them," they felt the necessity of confessing, not only with humility but with the greatest truth, "We are unprofitable servants;" (Luke xvii. 10;) and truly to intreat God "to forgive the iniquity of their sins," and "not to enter into judgment with his servants." (Psalm xxxii. 5; cxliii, 2.) Therefore, we cannot piously plead, in our own behalf, that which is falsely attributed to the saints; and that cannot be usefully bestowed upon others, of which the saints themselves had not a sufficiency.

XI. (3.) Lastly, they cannot be piously and usefully invoked in the capacity of those who, as our friends, unite their prayers with ours, or who intercede before God by their prayers in our behalf; because the saints in heaven are ignorant of our particular necessities, and of the prayers of the faithful who are dwellers upon earth. (Isa. lxii. 16; 1 Kings viii. 36; 2 Kings xxii. 20.) For the assertions about the mirror or glass of the trinity, is a very vain fable, and receives its refutation from this very circumstance, that those angels who always behold the face of God the Father, (Matt. xviii. 20,) are said to be ignorant of the day of judgment. (Mark xiii. 32.) Those assertions about a divine revelation [to the saints and angels] have a foolish and ridiculous circle; and those about the explanation which may be given by means of angels, or of the spirits of persons recently deceased, are equally vain; because the Scriptures make no mention of those tokens or indications, even in a single word: without such mention, we feel scrupulous, in matters of such vast importance, about receiving any thing as true, or about undertaking to do any thing as pious and useful.

XII. We add, finally, that by the invocation of saints, the papists are injurious towards Christ, and, therefore, cannot engage in such invocation without sacrilege. They are unjust to Christ in two ways: (1.) Because they communicate to the saints the office of our Mediator and Advocate, which has been committed by the Father to Christ alone; and the power conferred [on that office]. (1 Tim. ii. 5; Rom. viii. 34; 1 John ii. 1.) Neither are they excused by what they say about the saints being subordinate to Christ; for by the circumstance of their alleging the merits of saints, and of their invoking them as the dispensers of blessings, they destroy this subordination and establish a collaterally. (2.) Because they detract greatly from that benevolent affection of Christ towards his people, from his most merciful inclination, and from that most prompt and ready desire to commiserate, which he manifests. These properties are proposed to us in the Scriptures in a manner the most lucid and plain, that, not being terrified with the consideration of our own unworthiness, we may approach, with confidence and freedom, to the throne of grace, "that we may obtain mercy, and find grace to help in time of need." (Heb. iv. 16.)

XIII. When we say that the saints must not be invoked, we do not take away all veneration from them, as the papists calumniously assert. For we confess that their memory is to be venerated with a grateful celebration. But we circumscribe our veneration within these bounds: First. We commemorate with thanksgiving the eminent gifts which have been conferred on them, and commend them for having faithfully used those gifts in the exercises of faith, hope and charity. Secondly. As much as in us lies, we imitate their examples, and endeavour to demonstrate, by our works, that the holy conversation which they had in this world is grateful to us who aspire to be like them. Lastly. We congratulate them on the felicity which they enjoy with Christ in the presence of God; and with devotion of soul we earnestly pray for the same felicity for ourselves, while we hope and trust that we shall enjoy it through the all-sufficient intercession of Christ, through which, alone, they also themselves have been made partakers of eternal happiness.

COROLLARY

In the invocation of saints, do the papists commit idolatry?
We decide in the affirmative.

DISPUTATION 25 - ON MAGISTRACY

RESPONDENT: JOHN LE CHANTRE

I. Not feeling much anxiety about the origin and etymology of the word, we say that from the manner in which it is used, it has two meanings: for it either signifies in the abstract, the power and the function itself; or, in the concrete, the person who is constituted the administrator of this function with power. But, because the abstract consideration is more simple, and lays down the law to the concrete, therefore we will occupy ourselves first and chiefly in the description of it. (John xix. 10, 11; Ephes. i. 21; Rom. xiii. 1.)

II. We therefore define magistracy, in the abstract, a power pre-eminent and administrative, or a function with a preeminent power, instituted and preserved by God for this purpose, that men may, in the society of their fellow-men, "lead a quiet and peaceable life, in all godliness and honesty," in true piety and righteousness, for their own salvation and to the glory of God. (Rom. xiii. 1-3; 1 Tim. ii. 2; 1 Pet. ii. 13; Prov. xxix. 4; Psalm 62; Isa. xlv. 22, 23.) For the more extensive explanation of this definition, we will consider the object--the efficient and the end, which are the external causes of this function, and the matter and the form, which are the internal causes, from which we will derive all the rest.

III. The object of this function is the multitude of man kind, who are sociable animals, and bound to each other by many ties of indigence and communication according both to nature and grace, and who live together in common society. This object, likewise, comprehends the end for which, that is, those for whose benefit magistracy has been instituted. Hence, likewise, this power deservedly obtains the name of public authority," as it is, first, immediately and principally occupied concerning the condition and conduct of all the people and the whole society; but, secondarily, concerning the state and benefit of each member, though it intends, of itself, both the good of the whole, and that of each individual in the entire society. (Num. xi. 12; 2 Chron. i. 9, 10; Rom. xii. 4, 5; 1 Cor. xii. 12-27; Ezek. xxxiv. 2.)

IV. The efficient cause which not only institutes magistracy, but also maintains it, is God himself. In him must be considered power purely free and independent, the best will, and the greatest capability, as the principles of its institution and preservation. (1.) Power rests on creation, and through that, upon the right of the dominion which God has over all created things, but especially over men. (Rom. xiii. 1, 2; John xix. 10, 11; Psalm xxiv. 1 Jeremiah xxvii. 2, 6.) (2.) The will of God, in its institution, is through four kinds of his love: (i.) His love of order among all created things; (1 Cor. xiv. 33;) (ii.) His love towards men themselves, both towards those who are placed in authority, above others, and especially towards those who are put in subjection; (2 Cor. ix. 8; 2 Kings xi. 17;) (iii.) His love of obedience to his own law; (Judges ii. 16, 17; 2 Chron. xxxiv. 31 32;) (iv.) His love of that submission which those who are equals by nature, render to others who are their superiors, merely through the will or good pleasure of God. (Psalm ii. 9, 12.) (3.) But Capability, and that of the highest kind, was likewise necessary for this purpose, both on account of that ambition of being eminent with which men are infected, and on account of the power or capability of an infinite multitude; and it is employed by God through an internal impression upon the hearts of men, of the necessity of this order, (1 Sam. x. 26; xi, 7,) and through the external defense of it. (Josh. i. 5-9.)

V. The end of the institution of magistracy, is the good of the whole, and of each individual of which it is composed, both an animal [or natural] good, "that they may lead quiet and peaceable lives;" (1 Tim. ii. 2;) and a spiritual good, that they may live in this world, to God, and may in heaven enjoy that good, to the glory of God who is its author. (Rom. xiii. 4.) For since man, according to his two-fold life, (that is, the animal and the spiritual,) stands in need of each kind of good, (Num. xi. 12, 13,) and is, by nature the image of God, capable of both kinds; (Gen. i. 26; Col. iii. 10;) since two collateral powers cannot stand, (Matt. vi. 24; 1 Cor. xiv. 33,) and since animal good is directed to that which is spiritual, (Matt. vi. 33,) and animal life is subordinate to that which is spiritual, (Gal. ii. 20; 1 Cor. xv. 32,) it is unlawful to divide those two benefits, and to separate their joint superintendence, either in reality or by the administration of the supreme authority; for, if the animal life and its good become the only objects of solicitude, such an administration is that of cattle. But if human society be brought to such a condition that the spiritual life, only, prevails, then this power [of magistracy] is no longer necessary. (1 Cor. xv. 24.)

VI. The matter, of which this administration consists, are the acts necessary to produce that end. These actions, we comprehend in the three following classes: (1.) The first is Legislation, under which we also comprise the care of the moral law, according to both tables, and the enacting of subordinate laws with respect to places, times and persons, by which laws, provision may be the better made for the observance of that immovable law, and the various societies, being restricted to certain relations, may be the more correctly governed; that is, ecclesiastical, civil, scholastic and domestic associations. (Exod. xviii. 18-20; 2 Chron. xix. 6-8; 2 Kings xiii. 4, 5.) (2.) The second contains the vocation to delegated offices or duties, and the oversight of all actions and things which are necessary to the whole society. (Deut. i. 13, 15, 16; Exod. xviii. 21, 22; 1 Pet. ii. 14; 2 Chron. xix. 2, 8-11, Num. xi. 13-17.) (3.) The third is either the eradication of all evils out of the society, if they be internal, or the warding of them off, if they be external, even with war, if that be necessary, and the safety of society should require it. (Prov. xx. 26, 28; Psalm ci. 8; 1 Tim. ii. 2.)

VII. The form is the power itself, according to which these functions themselves are discharged, with an authority that is subject to God alone, and pre-eminently above whatever is human; (Rom. xiii. 1; Psalm lxxxii. 1, 6; Lament. iv. 20;) for this inspires spirit and life, and gives efficacy to these functions. It is enunciated "power by right of the sword," by which the good may be defended, and the bad terrified, restrained and punished, and all men compelled to perform their prescribed duties. (Rom. xiii. 4, 5.) To this power, as supreme, belongs the authority of demanding, from those under subjection, tribute, custom, and other burdens. These resemble the sinews, by which the authority and power necessary for these functions, are held together and established. (Rom. xiii. 6.)

VIII. But though there was no employment for this power before the introduction of sin into the world, because there were then only two human beings, both of whom were comprised in one family; yet we are of opinion, that it would also have had a place in the primitive integrity of mankind, and that it had not its origin from the entrance of sin; for we think this can be proved from the nature of man, who is a social animal, and was capable of deviating from his duty--from the limits of this power--from the causes which induced God to institute it--from the natural and moral law itself, and from the impression of this power on the hearts of men, provided any great number of men had been propagated prior to the commission of the first sin. (Gen. iii. 6; 1 Tim. ii. 1-iv, ; 1 Kings x. 9; Exod. xx. 12-17.)

IX. But this power is always the same according to the nature of its function and the prerogative of its authority; and it suffers no variation, either from the difference in number of those to whom this power is confided in a monarchy, an aristocracy, or a democracy, or from the difference of the manner in which this power is given, whether it be derived immediately from God, or it be obtained by human right and custom through succession, inheritance and election. Under all these circumstances, it remains the same, unless a limitation, restricted to certain conditions, be added by God, or by those who possess the right of conferring such a power. (Josh. xxii. 12; 1 Tim. ii. 2; 1 Pet. ii. 13; Judges 20; 1 Sam. xvi. 12; 2 Sam. 1; 1 Kings xi. 11, 12; xiv, 8-10.) And this limitation is equally binding on both parties; nor is it lawful for him who has accepted of this authority, by rescinding the conditions, to assume a greater power to himself, under the pretext that those conditions are opposed to his conscience or to his condition, and that they are even injurious to the society itself.

X. Since the end of this power is the good of the whole, or of the entire association of men, who belong to the same country or state, it follows that the prince of this state is less than the state itself, and that its benefit is not only to be preferred to his own, but that it is also to be purchased with his detriment, nay, at the expense of life itself. (Ezek. xxxiv. 2-4; 1 Sam. xii. 2, 3; viii, 20.) Though, in return, every member of the state is bound to defend, with all his powers, yet in a lawful manner, the life, safety and dignity of the prince, as the father of his country. (2 Sam. xvi. 3.)

XI. From the circumstance, also, of this power having been instituted by God and restricted within certain laws, we conclude that it is not lawful for him who possesses it, to lift up himself against God, to enact laws contrary to the divine laws, and either to compel the people who are committed to his care to the perpetration of acts which are forbidden by God, or to prevent them from performing such acts as he has commanded. If he acts thus, let him assuredly know, that he must render an account to God, and that the people are bound to obey the Almighty in preference to him. (Deut. xvii. 18, 19; 1 Kings xii. 28-30; xiii, 2; 1 Kings xxii. 5.) Yet, on this point, the people ought to observe two cautions: (1.) To distinguish actions which are to be performed, from burdens which are to be borne. (2.) To be perfectly sure that the orders of the prince are in opposition to the divine commands. Without a due observance of these cautions, they will, by a precipitate judgment, commit an act of disobedience against the prince, to whom, in that matter, they are able, in an orderly manner, under God, to be obedient.

XII. The functions which we have described as essential to this power, are not subject to the arbitrary will of the prince, whether he may neglect either the whole of them, or one of the three. If he act thus, he renders himself unworthy of the name of "prince;" and it would be a better course for him to resign the dignity of his office, than to be a trifling loiterer in the discharge of its functions. (Psalm lxxxii. 1-8; Ezek. xi. 1-13.) But here, also, a two-fold distinction must be used: (1.) Between a degree of idleness accruing from the function, and vice coming into it. (2.) Between loitering, and hindering these duties from being performed in the commonwealth; for the latter of these faults (hindrance) would bring speedy destruction to the society, while the commonwealth can consist with the former, (laziness,) provided other persons be permitted to perform those duties.

XIII. We conclude further, from the author of the institution from the end and the use of the office--from the functions which pertain to it, and from the pre-eminent power itself, when they are all compared with the nature of Christianity, that a Christian man can, with a good conscience, accept of the office and perform the duties of magistracy; nay, that no one is more suitable than he for discharging the duties of this office, and, which is still more, that no person can legitimately and perfectly fulfill all its duties except a Christian. Yet, by this affirmation, we do not mean to deny that a legitimate magistracy exists among other nations than those which are Christian. (Acts x. 31, 48; Exod. xviii. 20-23.)

XIV. Lastly. Because this power is pre eminent, we assert that every soul is subject to it by divine right, whether he be a layman or a clergyman, a deacon, priest, or bishop, an archbishop, cardinal, or patriarch, or even the Roman pontiff himself; so that it is the duty of every one to obey the commands of the magistrate, to acknowledge his tribunal, to await the sentence, and to submit to the punishment which he may award. From such obedience and subjection the prince himself cannot grant any man immunity and exemption; although in apportioning those burdens which are to be borne, he can yield his prerogative to some persons. (Rom. xiii. 1; 1 Pet. ii. 13; v, 1; John xix. 10, 11; Acts xxv. 1, 10; 1 Kings i. 26, 27; Rom. xiii. 5.)

END OF THE PUBLIC DISPUTATIONS